Every Step a Struggle

Other Books by Frank Manchel

Film Study: An Analytical Bibliography. 4 Vols.
An Album of Modern Horror Films
Great Science Fiction Films: Revised Edition
Great Sports Movies
The Box Office Clowns: From Bob Hope to Woody Allen
Gangsters on the Screen
Women on the Hollywood Screen
An Album of Great Science Fiction Films
The Talking Clowns: From Laurel and Hardy to the Marx Brothers
Yesterday's Clowns: The Rise of Film Comedy
Film Study: A Resource Guide
Cameras West
Terrors of the Screen
When Movies Began to Speak
When Pictures Began to Move
Movies and How They are Made

Published and Forthcoming by New Academia Publishing

Cinema and Visual Culture

SUPER HEROES, edited by Wendy Haslem, Angela Ndalianis, and Chris Mackie.

VISUAL CULTURE IN SHANGHAI, 1850s-1930s, edited by Jason Kuo.

SHOPPING FOR JESUS: *Visual Culture and the Marketing of Christianity,* edited by Dominic Janes.

HERETICAL EMPIRICISM, by Pier Paolo Pasolini
Ben Lawton and Louise K. Barnett, trs., eds. With Ben Lawton's new Introduction and the first approved English-language translation of Pasolini's essay, "The Repudiation of the 'Trilogy of Life'."

IMAGING RUSSIA 2000: *Film and Facts,* by Anna Lawton

BEFORE THE FALL: *Soviet Cinema in the Gorbachev Years*
by Anna Lawton

Every Step a Struggle

Interviews with Seven Who Shaped the African-American Image in Movies

Frank Manchel

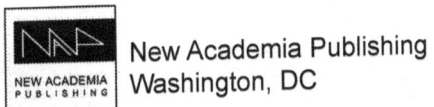

New Academia Publishing
Washington, DC

Copyright © 2007 by Frank Manchel

New Academia Publishing, 2007

All rights reserved. No part of this book may be reproduced or transmitted in any form or by any means, electronic or mechanical, including photocopying, recording, or by any information storage and retrieval system.

Printed in the United States of America

Library of Congress Control Number: 2006935711
ISBN 978-0-9787713-6-2 hardcover (alk. paper)
ISBN 978-0-9787713-0-0 paperback (alk. paper)

New Academia Publishing, LLC
P.O. Box 27420
Washington, DC 20038-7420
www.newacademia.com - info@newacademia.com

Three people proved indispensable to this book: the person who encouraged me to never give up, the individual who changed her life to make this project possible, and the friend who loved me blindly throughout my journey. Her name is Sheila Manchel. As I have dedicated my life to her, so I dedicate this book.

Contents

List of Illustrations — viii
Acknowledgments — xi

Introduction — 1
1. Heroes and Villains: Lorenzo Tucker — 45
2. The Movies, Mr. Griffith, and Miss Gish: Lillian Gish — 169
3. Scarred By History: Clarence Muse — 205
4. The Well-Intentioned Poet: King Vidor — 309
5. The Man Who Made the Stars Shine Brighter: Woody Strode — 355
6. Somebody Who Refused to Be Nobody: Charles Edward Gordone — 413
7. From Actor to Activist: Frederick Douglass O'Neal — 439

Works Cited — 464
Index — 476

Illustrations

1. Lorenzo Tucker, romantic leading man of race films between 1928 and 1934 — 29
2. Al "Slick" Chester, leading character actor in race films of the 1930s — 30
3. Lillian Gish, one of the cinema's greatest stars — 31
4. King Vidor and Daniel L. Haynes, *Hallelujah* — 32
5. The author with Clarence Muse, 1972 — 33
6. Woody Strode, *Spartacus* — 34
7. Frederick Douglass O'Neal, great champion of actors' rights, in *Pinky* — 35
8. Arthur John Jack Johnson, heavyweight boxing champion (1908-1915) — 36
9. Spike Lee, *Do the Right Thing* — 37
10. Ivan Dixon and Leonard Parker, *Nothing But a Man* — 38
11. Pearl Bowser, ground-breaking scholar on independent race productions — 39
12. Emory Richardson and Mel Ferrer, *Lost Boundaries* — 40
13. Jim Brown in *Slaughter*, a blaxploitation film of the 1970s — 41
14. Lorenzo Tucker — 44
15. Al "Slick" Chester — 142
16. Jack Johnson and Stanley Ketchel, 1909, Looking for the Great White Hope — 143
17. Harry Belafonte — 144
18. Bill "Bojangles" Robinson, *One More Spring* — 145

19.	William Greaves, leading independent filmmaker	146
20.	Oscar Micheaux, "The Father of Race Productions"	147
21.	Leroy Bowser	148
22.	Pearl Bowser	149
23.	Program from *Springtime for Henry*, Universal Theatre Inc.	150
24.	Lorenzo Tucker and Ethel Moses, *Wages of Sin*	151
25.	Oscar Micheaux's money problems shown in his 1929 film, *The Wages of Sin*	152
26.	*The Black King*	153
27.	Laura Bowman and Lorenzo Tucker, *Veiled Aristocrats*	154
28.	*Harlem after Midnight*	155
29.	Ethel Moses, *Temptation*	156
30.	*Temptation*	157
31.	Oscar Polk and Bee Freeman, *Underworld*	158
32.	Stepin Fetchit, Lorenzo Tucker, *Miracle in Harlem*	159
33.	*Miracle in Harlem*	160
34.	The author with Lillian Gish	168
35.	Lillian and Dorothy Gish	200
36.	Clarence Muse	204
37.	Leigh Whipper	293
38.	Dooley Wilson, Humphrey Bogart, Ingrid Bergman, *Casablanca*	294
39.	Jack Johnson losing his crown in one of the most crooked fights in history	295
40.	*So Red the Rose*	296
41.	Janet Beecher, Daniel L. Haynes, Harry Ellerbe, Margaret Sullavan, *So Red the Rose*	297
42.	Clarence Muse, Dickie Moore, *So Red the Rose*	298
43.	Clarence Muse, *So Red the Rose*	299
44.	Clarence Muse, Margaret Sullavan, *So Red the Rose*	300
45.	Hattie McDaniel and Jeanne Crain, *Margie*	301
46.	King Vidor	308
47.	King Vidor preparing scene	336

48. Fanny Belle DeKnight, Harry Gray, Nina Mae McKinney, Daniel L. Haynes, and Vidor, *Hallelujah* — 337
49. Daniel L. Haynes, William Fountaine, Nina Mae McKinney, *Hallelujah* — 338
50. Daniel L. Haynes, William Fountaine, *Hallelujah* — 339
51-61. Scenes from *Hallelujah* — 340-350
62. Woody Strode — 354
63. Johnny Sheffield and Woody Strode — 398
64. *The Buccaneer* — 399
65-66. *The Last Voyage* — 400-401
67. Woody Strode and Gordon Scott, *Tarzan's Fight for Life* — 402
68. *Spartacus* — 403
69. *Sergeant Rutledge* — 404
70. John Ford — 405
71. Woody Strode and Jock Mahoney, *Tarzan's Three Challenges* — 406
72. *Genghis Khan* — 407
73. *The Professionals* — 408
74. *Black Jesus* — 409
75. Joe Namath and Woody Strode, *The Last Rebel* — 410
76. Charles Edward Gordone, the first African-American Pulitzer-Prize dramatist — 412
77. Abbey Lincoln, Jazz Legend, in *Nothing But a Man* — 434
78. Leonard Parker, Helene Andindell and Ivan Dixon, *Nothing But a Man* — 435
79. Frederick Douglass O'Neal, the first African-American to head the Actors Equity Association — 438
80-81. Ethel Waters and Jeanne Crain, *Pinky* — 460-461

Acknowledgments

Thirty-eight years ago I started out on a pilgrimage to learn about the history of African-American film images. The quest has been long and challenging, and is far from over. But with this book a debt has been paid to seven people whose encouragement, generosity and artistry contributed to an historical document that may shed light not only on the past, but also on the present and the future. A debt is still owed to nine other individuals who also merit a place in the history of American films and African-American Studies. Strength and time permitting, I will take up that task shortly.

For now, let me make clear how this work came to be. First and foremost, I had the privilege and honor to work at the University of Vermont. Unless one understands that this institution, through its faculty, students, staff, and administration maintained unwavering support and encouragement for this project, you cannot appreciate the enormity of the obligation I feel to UVM. Three times they funded my efforts, two times they gave me sabbaticals to pursue my research, and countless times they provided released teaching schedules to painstakingly finish the task at hand. No one proved more timely or more thoughtful during the process than did Professor Willi Coleman.

I would like to thank Dr. Paul S. Unger, Patty "Painless" Nunnink, and Michelle Paschall for the gift of life.

Undoubtedly, many personalities have been overlooked or forgotten because of age and time. But among those scholar-colleagues who gave freely, consistently, and fruitfully of their knowledge; the following individuals come to the forefront: Pearl Bowser, Robert Chrisman, Virginia Clark, Mary Jane Dickerson, Kate A. Hoffman, James Loewen, Mbuelo Mzamane, Joseph Won, and Kari Winter. These professionals found time in their busy schedules to review specific chapters and offer constructive criticisms. And, of course, there were the many, many scholars whose pioneering scholarship made my efforts possible. I am especially grateful to *The Black Scholar* for letting me reprint my essay "The Man Who Made the Stars Shine Brighter: An Interview with Woody Strode." In addition, all quotations in the interviews are included by permission of the applicable interviewee.

Yet without the help of a gifted support team, the research would not have been accessible to a larger community. I wish to single out for their sensitivity, good-nature, and technological skills Hope Greenberg and Salli Griggs. Their invaluable contributions deserve more thanks than I can put into words.

But if not for Anna Lawton, my sensitive and visionary publisher, who put everything together, the journey would still be in process. Her patience and judgment proved indispensable in the last stages of this undertaking.

There are, however, invaluable companions whom I have respected and valued for many years. They realize that my gratitude goes far beyond this simple recognition for having read this entire manuscript and given me unstinting encouragement during the life of this project. Here I refer to Martha Day, Littleton Long, and Hilary Neroni. Still further, of all the people who encouraged me to go on and on when the going seemed fruitless, none of my scholarly colleagues has proved more supportive and wiser than Denise Youngblood. She has been extraordinary.

How does one properly pay tribute to the artists who gave the interviews: Lillian Gish, Charles Edward Gordone, Clarence Muse, Frederick Douglass O'Neal, Woody Strode, Lorenzo Tucker, and King Vidor? In fulfilling a promise to let your words help tell the story, I offer my eternal thanks for your many kindnesses and your friendship in those very early, lonely days.

I would like to pay special thanks to my sister Rose Manchel, who has performed more tasks for this book than can be remembered and received less appreciation than she deserves. She has been terrific. So too have my brother and sister Louis and Barbara Wachtel. Their love, hospitality, and support are deeply appreciated.

Finally, despite the countless contributions by others, no one lived through *Every Step a Struggle* longer or felt the intensity with which it evolved more than my beloved family. My sons, Steven and Gary, did much of the early research with me, and together we became better people because of our exposure to the hopes and frustrations of African-Americans. I take great pride in what they have done with their knowledge and how they are living it everyday with my irreplaceable daughter Sharon and my two precious grandchildren, Harrison and Benjamin. As for Sheila, my wife of forty-eight years, to whom this book and its author are dedicated, I offer not so much undying thanks, but rather a plea for forgiveness for all the time and discomfort I caused her throughout this period in our lives. She is the most remarkable person I know and love.

Introduction

"People are greedy, selfish, lonely; they love; they hate; it's all universal."

Robert Townsend[1]

I

If cultural historians are right, no civilization has been more influenced by its image-makers than have those of us who grew up in the twentieth century. The visual values of the popular movie stars, the solutions to our problems provided in the oft-repeated screen stories, and the sterile stereotyping of various groups proved so believable, so indelible on our collective psyches, that emotion dominated reason. Consequently, many pundits believe that modern society is shaped more by perception than by reality.

The evolution of this psychological phenomenon is instructive. For the first half of the century, the evolving screen formulas became a major educational force. Mainstream moviemakers grew powerful and wealthy by realistically and simplistically presenting messages that unconsciously shaped the spectators' dreams, desires, fears, and personal relations. Many gratified viewers mistook the illusions for certainty. Effortlessly, the seemingly undemanding forms of entertainment passionately encouraged us to be ruled by our senses rather than our brains. Then came the explosive sixties and the controversial cultural revolutions that destabilized our confidence in popular art. As scholars sought to explain the basis of the chaos and confusion, the revisionist media reflected the genuine struggles taking place daily in our streets and in our homes.

What is still unclear to many observers is the nature of the struggles themselves. Traditionalists take the position that it was a "we versus them" battle. What was going on in the sixties, for conservatives, amounted to a counterculture trying to upend the dominant hegemony. Consequently, the issues are framed in binary terms: right versus wrong, high culture versus low culture, and good versus bad. More recent cultural historians, like Stuart Hall, insist on viewing the times as the start of an anti-colonial era, where global cultures revolted against colonization worldwide. Instead of positing the battle in positive/negative terms, he argues for a cultural system that allows people to be inclusive of their diversity.

Either way, film, in particular, proved disorienting to society. Following the breakup of the studio system in the late 1950s, the movie moguls lost control of film content and audience dependability. Every movie made in America competed fiercely with every other movie released to gain widespread popular acceptance. Experimentation by independent artists unsettled viewers who once found the film narratives reassuring. Where for over fifty years spectators could confidently predict the character types and values produced in traditional film formulas, sixties movies challenged us to consider the consequences of letting entertainment shape our behavior and judgments.

What especially fascinated me in those perplexing films during the 1960s were the startling changes in the representation of African-Americans. The once accommodating marginalized black performers not only rebelled against white society, but also their rebellious actions became the focus of the narratives rather than just the subplots. At first, the stories centered on racial and sexual injustices in white society: e.g., *A Raisin in the Sun* (1961), *Gone are the Days/Purlie Victorious* (1963), *Nothing But a Man* (1964), *One Potato, Two Potato* (1964), *In the Heat of the Night* (1967), *Guess Who's Coming to Dinner* (1967), *Up Tight* (1968), and *The Learning Tree* (1969). However, when audience tastes changed, the industry lost a first amendment battle in the courts.[2] Hollywood understandably abandoned its Motion Picture Production Code for a Ratings System in the late sixties, and filmmakers sought to capitalize on their newfound artistic freedom. Following on the commercial success of such action-packed films as *Bonnie and Clyde* (1967), *Butch Cassidy and the Sundance Kid* (1969), and *The Wild Bunch* (1969), business interests wisely explored the commercial value of marketing a "New Negro" screen image to reflect the black power struggle in America. If audiences wanted something new, the filmmakers now were willing to make changes.

Thanks to the work of cultural historians, we no longer trust such a simplistic dichotomy of good versus bad. Not only do we appreciate how there is no one-to-one link between a screen representation and a spectator's identity, but also we recognize the value of analyzing how we see ourselves and how others see us. Thus the value of studying screen representations is in understanding how those icons came to be, and what forces shaped their creation and perpetuated their role in film history. Imagine how valuable film study could be if we had the ability to appreciate the contributions of those artists whose work contributes to cultural history, but is now dismissed because it is out of step with the times.

Back then, movies about civil disobedience, racial vengeance, and black pride paralleled what was taking place in society, and many young people identified fervently with counterculture values. The "Melting Pot" theory got replaced by racial pride. Now it was acceptable to be both an American and hold allegiance to one's ethnicity. Anti-establishment narratives gave us clear-cut ideas about what was wrong in a postwar colonial world. Many whites even began to be self-conscious of the advantages that their color and status brought them. These very same stories also terrorized conservatives, who found the revisionist messages excessive and dangerous. Diversity be damned; protect the status quo.

Over the next six years, defiant and determined black performers like Bernie Casey, James Earl Jones, Jim Brown, Paul Winfield, Richard Roundtree, Moses Gunn, Yaphet Kotto, Richard Pryor, Ron O'Neal, Billy Dee Williams, and Fred Williamson, along with Cicely Tyson, Diahann Carroll, Diana Ross, Diana Sands, Pam Grier, and Tamara Dobson vigorously rebelled against conventional wisdom. In America's movie houses, a new generation found validation for its values. The problem was that the battle became not one of equality of roles and images, but also one of positive black representation and achievements. Only later did we understand we could build on the past, not merely reinvent the present.

Conservatives reacted just as strongly to what they perceived as narratives that irresponsibly inflamed passions in our culture. Heated debates over basic human rights exploded on college campuses and in public arenas. Passion bred neither tolerance nor understanding.

In the midst of this struggle for the hearts and minds of an enflamed generation rebelling against the ruling power structure, a number of individuals who had played critical roles in constructing the old and then discredited African-American screen imagery became alienated not just from their professions, but from younger generations. The Black Nationalist movement's attack on these celebrities helped define the progressives' new image of African-Americans. It did not suggest what was owed them for breaking the barriers that empowered the present. How the scorned performers reacted to the shock waves of unchained black pride teaches us about the problematic nature of representation.

What follows is not a statistical summary of how everyone felt at this moment in history, nor is it meant as a substitute for other approaches to film study. These are personal feelings that build on individual experience and reflection. I am not interested in positing one point of view against another. If anything, the stories of these older celebrities recounted here call out for multiple analyses; they resonate with ideas that should benefit anyone interested in the relevance of the past to the present. I hope that the material aids its reader in discovering the complexity of responsible film criticism. The self-conscious elderly storytellers reveal their motives for their actions and thereby allow us to differentiate between generalizations and particulars about black film history. More than anything else, these pioneering entertainers reveal how much race, gender, class, age, and timing shaped their art and life.

Let me be very clear on one central theme. I have no desire to be an apologist for a colonial and imperialist ideology. This book is not interested in finger pointing or in pigeonholing. My purpose is to recall the pioneering contributions by important personalities currently ignored or disparaged by conventional wisdom. Their stories, then, can enrich our history.

This book contains annotated transcriptions of seven interviews with seasoned film celebrities taped thirty-five years ago. The term "interview" is somewhat misleading. More like encounters between strangers unable to communicate clearly, these conversations provide a sampling of unstated assumptions about race and gender. More to the point, they illustrate how little we understand ourselves. They add to the growing literature on how we see and define each other. Because pursuing the complexity of such representational issues goes beyond the scope of this project, I use the term "interview" for convenience rather than precision.

The tapings took place between November 1971 and August 1972. Initially, my discussions began as research on the representation of black themes and images in American film history. You will not be surprised by the fact that the emblematic questions I raised never got answered, or that misunderstandings were commonplace. Few people agreed on what anything meant. We had neither the time nor the inclination to explore fully the complexity of W.E. DuBois' dilemma in defining what being a Negro meant to America. In the end, the conversations provided an archive on not only the thoughts and values of the personalities themselves, but also on racial differences both in 1972 and three decades later.

The persons selected for my research may seem unrelated, but I will explore how they represent a particular moment in history. Except for the fact that all the individuals were entertainers, little uniformity appeared in their make-up and their cultural backgrounds. Lillian Gish and King Vidor were both white; the former was born in Springfield, Ohio; the latter, in Galveston, Texas. At the time of the interviews, Gish lived in New York; Vidor, California. The other personalities in this book were

African-American. Lorenzo Tucker, born in Philadelphia, was living in Harlem; Frederick Douglass O'Neal, born in Brooksville, Mississippi, also resided in New York. On the West Coast were other black pioneering artists: Clarence Muse, born in Baltimore; Woody Strode, Los Angeles; and Charles Edward Gordone, Cleveland. The contributions these seven artists made to American culture range from acting and directing to writing and producing, not just with film, but also in theatrical and musical history.

Casual readers might be surprised that white entertainers are included in this anthology. Why not include them? Film representation has never been the result of either a specific group or a single collaboration. Anyone aware of film history from *The Birth of a Nation* (1915) to *Bamboozled* (2000) realizes the process by which the screen standardizes conventions. These particular personalities—Gish and Vidor—were two of the primary molders of public opinion concerning African-American film representation. Their stories shed light on how misunderstood and misguided movies distorted history.

Do not be misled into thinking this idea was part of my initial approach. Chance more than design brought us together. My student projectionist at the University of Vermont in the early 1970s was Jason Robards, Jr., who contacted his famous father about helping me get interviews for my study. Lillian Gish I met during her 1971 visit to the UVM campus. These contacts led to other links, and by the end of my labors I had interviewed more than seventeen celebrities, including the people in this book.

The stories that come first are because the individuals are dead and no longer can tell their own tales. To sophisticated readers of African-American times gone by, the facts, on the surface, appear familiar. The personal narratives recall the influences that literature, music, art, radio, movies, economics, culture, and politics had on both the personalities and our national racial character. You will find in their words a sense of the passion of the political and cultural battles waged throughout America. As expected in such African-American show business recollections, the storytellers focus on their experiences mainly in the five major entertainment centers in the twentieth century: New Orleans, New York, Chicago, Kansas City, and "Hollywood."

However, here familiarity and fact take separate roads. Personal histories produce counter-narratives, reasons why this and not that, rationalizations for actions questioned by new generations about the choices of the past. Such Rashomon accounts appear especially apt for today because of our current interest in the anxious, confused, and chaotic years of the sixties and early seventies. These were the days of notorious assassinations, civil unrest, and revolutionary movements. It was an era in which countless African-Americans concluded that whites had betrayed them and demanded not only more control of their lives, but also questioned the behavior of controversial icons. Aesthetics seemed to flip-flop. The issue was no longer breakthroughs in art. Now the concern was how one applied art to racial representation. Great stars like Louis Armstrong and Sidney Poitier, long embraced by world audiences, were maligned as Uncle Toms and throwbacks to minstrelsy. Even the remarkable artist and political activist Harry Belafonte found himself adrift in a recently politicized black world because he didn't fit the image of the "New Negro." Particularly problematic for black progressives was Belafonte's light skin color, an issue for many African-Americans throughout race history. As evident throughout this book, the screen image of African-Americans during the twentieth century depended more often than not with how dark-skinned the actor appeared to the audience. "I never underestimate," explains analyst Stanley Crouch, "the skin-tone factor."[3] The memorable people you meet in this collection fit perfectly into the complexities of those revisionist years. They, too, found themselves accused of "selling out." One moment, they were lauded for their contributions to popular culture; the next moment, they were denigrated for their roles in perpetuating racist and sexist imagery. One moment in time, they are artists; another moment their artistry appears embarrassing to black history and culture.

My secondary interest, at the time, was in finding out what these film personalities thought about the so-called "blaxploitation" boom (films by and about African-Americans made between the late 1960s and the early 1970s), and where it would take black images. Not surprisingly, our encounters took us far beyond those limited goals. As the reader will discover, these until-now-private conversations disclose intriguing attitudes about not only where we were, but also how far we have come. They are thus historical documents about our past.[4]

No claim is made that these highly personal revelations remain all inclusive of the times. However, the thoughts and actions of these seven people and my presentation of them chart how such beliefs and behavior resulted from the culture of our society and heritage. They illustrate how artists use their art to respond to the challenges of their age. Their responses remind us how quickly taste changes, and the penalties imposed on breakthrough performers who fall out of favor with popular audiences. As you will discover, the heated debate over what it means to be "black" pervades this book.

Nevertheless, as James Baldwin made clear, "... the question of color, especially in this country, operates to hide the graver questions of the self."[5] My presentations remind each of us how much race and perception play in shaping human relationships. Such reminders should prove useful to students of history and culture. Especially intriguing is how well the stories validate the old chestnut, "The road to hell is paved with good intentions."

II

But why are these interviews being published for the first time now? It is not an idle question. The answer provides an essential key to understanding how and why this book evolved, as well as learning how my experiences may benefit you.

It helps for the reader to appreciate how problematic this journey was for me. On the one hand, being white, growing up in a Jewish section of Brooklyn, and knowing only about other ethnicities and races outside the white mainstream from public schools, movies, radio, and sports hardly prepared me for the revolutionary world of the postwar decades. On the other hand, my background reminds us of the choices I made and how cultural icons molded me (and, I assume, many in my generation).

I realize, of course, that not everyone shares my passions. Even more to the point, I appreciate the fact that passion is no substitute for substance. My encounters with the personalities in this book highlight the limits of my understanding the agendas that chance meetings produced. I do not delude myself by assuming I knew then and now what took place between the interviewees and me. I realize that my perspective is tied to the questions that I pursued and the people that I met. While what I report to you is as I remember it, my account has more than its share of unintentional, but inescapable biases and omissions. I take some relief in listening to Melvin Van Peebles' recollections about the making of his 1971 film, *Sweet Sweetback's Baadasssss Song*. Early in his narration on the Criterion laser disc, he justifies talking about his life and experiences by modifying Tennyson's famous line, "We're part of all that we met." My experiences may be valuable to others.

In 1969, the year that the idea for this book took hold, I was in my second year as an associate professor in the College of Arts and Sciences at the University of Vermont (UVM), teaching courses in English Education for secondary school teachers. Perhaps only those of us who lived through the sixties can grasp what it was like to train new teachers of English in that turbulent period. While society struggled to reconstruct itself, much of public education fought to keep its conservative biases. Teaching teenagers how to write, for example, remained the primary responsibility of English instructors, who relied almost exclusively on literary analyses for instruction. Black literature was rarely mentioned, let alone read in the classroom because of the authors' presumably objectionable language and imagery, not to mention the low regard in which black writers themselves were held by the Establishment. The mass media were even farther down on the educational scale. True, you could use "suitable" screen adaptations of classic novels to spark bored students, and now and then complement your lessons with audiovisual material. Nevertheless, few superintendents, principals, department heads, or parent-teacher organizations encouraged higher education to graduate prospective teachers with an expertise in writing across the curriculum, black literature, or mass media. Further, colleges did not recruit film scholars, mainly because few graduate programs produced film scholars. What there was of film teaching occurred mainly in departments of English or Communication. Moreover, those who taught such novel subjects were highly suspect by their colleagues, who frowned on popular culture in the classrooms.

My being brought to the University of Vermont epitomized Emerson's observation that, "The business of education is mischief." Absurd as it sounds, I literally was hired to revamp English Education in Vermont. We are the State University, and the professors back then had a unique vision. UVM's English Department had read my doctoral dissertation (*Film Literature*); they knew my commitment to film as a new form of literature and the importance of minority issues in the curriculum.[6] In addition, my youthful zeal in revolutionizing the English curriculum was evident in my earliest publications; each calling for an end to what I considered an outmoded system. A favorite saying of mine from those early days remains, "We are living in the twentieth century, preparing teachers for the twenty-first century, using nineteenth century methods."

Reading this, the word "revolutionizing" seems pretentious. I do not mean to be. It is just a clue to how naive and romantic I was. Having spent most of my childhood in Brooklyn (1941-1953), I came to dislike my public education intensely. Because of staid classroom drills and inflexible reading lists, my teachers unwittingly persuaded me that they knew nothing worth remembering. (Of course, to paraphrase Mark Twain, "It's amazing, in hindsight, how much those teachers have learned in the last forty years.") Although I did not realize it, by the time I was ten I had made it a point to follow George Bernard Shaw's advice to never let school interfere with my education. My most rewarding moments came in movie theaters, at baseball games, listening to the radio, and randomly reading library books.

I did not live in an interracial neighborhood. My only friends were Jews. While my heritage directed me to a desire to help fight racism, I could only do that if my personal contacts and surroundings reinforced those liberal leanings. Not knowing or associating with anyone but lanzman might have kept me culturally illiterate if not for the movies, sports, and books.

African-Americans grew to have a special place in my unconscious thinking, I suspect, because of my growing up during the Second World War. As the plight of German Jews became better known to Americans, young people like myself realized the affinity that we had with blacks. Those connections become apparent to later generations when they see a recent documentary *From Swastika to Jim Crow*. The story of the 1200 German refugees who fled to America beginning in 1933 discusses many similarities between Jews and African-Americans: "Jewish refugees and blacks understood mutual racial terror and oppression albeit from very different historical perspectives and histories. We still had racial terror in the south; we still had a segregated country. We still had lynching, so there was a common understanding...." These ties took a turn in the late sixties, when the Black Power struggle affected my thinking about this book.

I cannot stress this point strongly enough. As alluded to earlier, I have read extensively over the past sixty years about the negative influences of the media on our society. The overwhelming conclusion of many cultural critics is that we became, we are, and we remain a global population seduced by the misrepresentations of the media. Some of this criticism is valid, including some allegations about the harmful effects of film and television on our mental health. The questions, however, are just which ones, just how widespread such effects are, and just how long these negative effects remain with us. However, what has rarely been recorded or understood is the fact that any medium with the power to do harm also has the power to do good. Ironically, the naysayers who condemn the media's weaknesses ignore the gifts by which the media can help redress social injustice.

Ten years of formal education in New York and Brooklyn public schools taught me little about the role of African-Americans in our nation's complex history. What I knew about being an other, I learned from the anti-Semitism around me. These were the days, remember, when Hebrew was not considered a respectable foreign language; when we called a Chinese restaurant by the common racist epithet, the "Chinks"; and when our major textbooks on American history almost universally referred to African-Americans during the nineteenth century as "Sambo." What historian Leon Metz lamented later about the history of Native-American scouts on the Western frontier was true for the knowledge provided on all minorities: "… a word here, an expression there, a paragraph now and then … [but] there's nothing ever said about these remarkable men who did so much for their own people and the government of the United States."[7]

There were two exceptions to Brooklyn's cultural wasteland: Ebbets Field and the local movie houses. (TV was not yet a factor; we did not own our first television set until 1952.) During the period I went to Midwood High School, classrooms were so overcrowded that the school was on triple session. That meant I could get off early enough (depending on my schedule or my proclivity to cut school) to work at the New York baseball parks. Working as a vendor for the George Stevens concessions at Ebbets Field, for example, in the period between 1949 and 1953 (my high school years) gave me the rare opportunity to meet and watch regularly ballplayers like Jackie Robinson, Roy Campanella, Don Newcombe, Jim Gilliam, Willie Mays, and Monte Irvin. (My lifelong-friend, Arnold S. Gunar, reminds me that we, the "candy-butchers" at Ebbets Field, even got interviewed several times by Jackie Robinson for his local radio show.) To watch Frank Robinson and Larry Doby play, I sold peanuts at Yankee Stadium. (Although several of these ballplayers were not on New York teams, I could see them when they played at our ballparks.) They revolutionized major league baseball. On radio, I not only followed the New York baseball teams, but also the New York Knicks basketball team (they had broken the color line with Sweetwater Clifton, an ex-member of the Harlem Globetrotters); and the championship prize fights of Joe Louis, Sugar Ray Robinson, Ezzard Charles, Floyd Patterson, Jersey Joe Walcott, and Archie Moore.

These were also the days when one went to the movies the way one turns on the television today. We never asked, "Do you want to see a movie?" For us, it was always, "What film do you want to see?" Going routinely to the Elm, the Midwood, the Avalon, and the Kingsway movie theaters exposed me to films like *Lost Boundaries*, *Pinky*, *Intruder in the Dust*, and *Home of the Brave* (all in 1949), *No Way Out* and *The Jackie Robinson Story* (both in 1950), *Cry, the Beloved Country* and *The Harlem Globetrotters* (both in 1951).

The film scholar reads repeatedly about the negative criticism directed at these well-intentioned, white-produced films about African-Americans, and how they gave the nation a false impression of black life. There is much value in knowing this, and the fact that the black performers and their fictional experiences provided considerable wealth and influence for a white Hollywood, but not for the African-American players. However, for people like me, these unique white films about black problems stirred in me a social consciousness rare in my immediate surroundings. They raised questions about racial differences, self-identity, and what America was about.

Again, I blush at how overstated all this sounds. It implies that all I did was follow the lives and problems of African-Americans. Clearly, that is not true. However, what is true is that for a kid growing up in the forties and fifties, the exposure to these icons and issues was extraordinary. I was getting an education through the media entirely alien to what I was being taught in school. Later, Marxist scholars published theories about popular culture providing alternatives to the dominant hegemony, while feminist film theorists and psychoanalytical critics explored the relationships between entertainment and ideology. Dr. bell hooks, for example, asked the important question, "If we, black people, have learned to cherish hateful images of ourselves, then what process of looking allows us to consider the seduction of images that threatens to dehumanize and colonize?"[8] Her solution was to find a "way of seeing which makes possible an integrity of being that can subvert the power of the colonizing image. It is only as we collectively change the way we look at ourselves and the world that we can change how we are seen."[9] I never needed any convincing that we could manage the media the way it manipulated us, because I consciously experienced it early in my youth.

What's more, I saw it operate in my children's lives. During the seventies, when black films could not be shown in Vermont, I took my two sons to New York in 1972 to share my research with them. I remember watching *Slaughter* in a Broadway theater filled with more than a thousand black people, and the only two whites were my ten-year old son, Steven, and myself. All during the film the audience was screaming, "Kill the honkies!" Finally, near the end, Steven started yelling with them. On another occasion, I took my nine-year old son, Gary, to see *The Legend of Nigger Charley*. He rooted enthusiastically for the black cowboy rebel shooting the white villains. Neither son made a racial distinction in watching movies about good guys and bad guys.

Television was to have an equally important effect on me. My earliest memory is of watching a Brooklyn Dodger game on television with a female cousin visiting us from Birmingham, Alabama. She was so distraught by the appearance of Robinson and Campanella that she left the room and refused to see the end of the ball game. More vivid, to me and the rest of the nation, were the six o'clock TV news reports and specials about the murder of Emmett Till, a fourteen-year old black boy; the bus boycott in Birmingham; the school integration fights in Arkansas and Mississippi; the non-violent boycotts and sit-ins in North Carolina and Tennessee; the Freedom Rides throughout the South; Governor George Wallace literally barring black students from entering the University of Alabama; the murder of Medgar Evers on June 11, 1963; and the August 28, 1963 March on Washington, where Dr. Martin Luther King delivered his famous "I Have a Dream" speech.

Ever since these television experiences, it has been difficult for me to take all this negativism about the media very seriously, when the predictable critics usually omit or ignore the positive and responsible use of the media. Again, let me be clear. I am not in favor of a blind acceptance of the media, nor do I wish to be its apologist. Of course, the media must be responsible. So must the public and the critics when making judgments about the media.

What was not clear during those years and would take decades to grasp was the notion of "structured absences." As Richard Dyer explains, "A structuring absence ... refers to an issue, or even a set of facts or an argument, that a text cannot ignore, but which it deliberately skirts round or otherwise avoids, thus creating the biggest 'holes' in the text, fatally, revealingly misshaping the organic whole assembled with such craft."[10] Dyer is certainly right in arguing that the concept often is misunderstood, because many people believe simplistically that the term refers to acts of omission in the text, or to what we wish the filmmakers had included in their narratives.

It is true that my vicarious experiences had left me unaware and unprepared to understand the complexities of the issues to which I was being drawn. Whether because of acts of commission or omission, the movies forced me to respond intuitively instead of intellectually to its messages. Moreover, since there was no one I knew who took the time to discuss the racial problems, I was, as you will soon discover, bewildered and confused by my experiences doing the interviews in this book. The people I met bore little resemblance to their images in print or on screen. Nevertheless, these films and sporting events got me involved and questioning. Without them, my life would have taken a different course. Try asking yourself how different your life might be if not for your exposure to the mass media and athletics.

By the time I had left high school, the American film industry had started to move away from what Thomas Cripps called its "universalizing apparatus ... [that] diluted cultural density and muted political debate."[11] My childhood experiences with films, however, had raised my consciousness about racism and sexism. And, not just with African-Americans. Even guileless adolescents like me realized that no one person could replace collective action in mediating the deep-rooted problems in our society. What we did not appreciate was the way in which the films co-opted us into thinking that the solutions were both obvious and acceptable to the American public. Moreover, I actually believed that society embraced heroes and worthy causes, and that they rewarded those who spoke out against injustice.

Over the next decade, my exposure to African-American issues and how they shaped us remained exclusively in the public sector. Actually, that is not quite accurate. When I graduated from Ohio State University in March 1957, I decided to enlist in the Army's six-month program (rather than do the standard two-year stint): six months on active duty and five-and-a-half years in the Army Reserves. The result was that I did my six-month stint at Fort Jackson, South Carolina. By sheer chance, I had a weekend pass the Saturday after President Dwight David Eisenhower had announced the previous evening that he was sending a thousand federal troops into Little Rock, Arkansas, to enforce high school integration. That Saturday in September 1957, I saw first-hand the dread of trying to reform segregation, because at noon the Ku Klux Klan came into Columbia. I will never forget the image of the Klan members in their uniforms, minus the masks, standing on every downtown street corner, with nothing but a liquor bottle in a brown bag, for about an hour. No one moved outside the store he or she was in. While local residents carried on as if nothing were going on outside, the rest of us stared in sheer terror and apprehension at the proceedings.

What relevance does all this have to this book? A lot. It helps explain my motives, my methods, and my failures.

Only when I entered Teachers College, Columbia University in 1963, did my formal education begin to merge with my life experiences. By now, I had switched from being an English teacher at New Rochelle High School to being a college professor at Southern Connecticut State College (now University). Several incidents during that period are worth noting.

First, there was my teaching schedule at New Rochelle High School. Most members of the English Department divided their time between classes for "slow learners" (Non-Regents students) and those for the college-bound student. Since there was no curriculum for the former, we were told to keep these "unwanted and unmotivated" students busy and out-of-trouble. What books they read were edited versions of the classics, like *Silas Marner* and *Tale of Two Cities*. One's teaching status was linked to the ability to teach honors classes.

However, there was a group of "Young Turks" who wanted to change New Rochelle High School. Many of them later moved on to careers in college teaching at very prestigious schools. Membership in the group depended on doing something "relevant" (the big buzzword of my time; similar in importance to "political correctness" today). I came up with an alternative to the watered-down reading exercises for the Non-Regents students: studying books and plays that had been made into films. The relevance to this story is the fact that the students found print meaningless, but the films powerful and persuasive. For example, in reading Laura Hobson's *Gentleman's Agreement*, the predominantly Irish and Italian students felt nothing for the problems of Jews fighting anti-Semitism. The class never saw it as their concern. Equally disturbing, they blamed the Jews for working up the blacks in the present civil rights disturbances. In seeing a 16mm print of Elia Kazan's 1947 screen adaptation, however, they reacted strongly against anti-Semitic acts because the people being hurt were Gregory Peck and Dean Stockwell. Here was Cripps' "universalizing apparatus" theory, but from another perspective.

Second, the film-book method served as the basis for my presentation at a special New York State Institute offered at Teachers College. The seminar's reactions to my approach to teaching slow-learners encouraged me to enter Teachers College's doctoral program, and I decided to write my thesis on film as a new form of literature. Ironically, my thesis proposal on a film topic took over a year-and-a-half to be accepted by the governing committee, but by then I had already written the dissertation and was prepared to defend it.

Third, it was the unique makeup of the English Department at Teachers College that opened the possibility of using film as an art form and as a social force in school programs. Scholars like Louis Forsdale pushed for film study; Robert Bone, author of the seminal work, *The Negro Novel in America*, helped change the educational community's thinking about books suitable for the classroom; and Robert Allen's linguistic theories made us question everything we had assumed about the role of language in society.

The fourth and fifth reasons I list only to show how once more my life brushed against historical developments: New Rochelle High School became the first Northern school to be desegregated (the community had been practicing de facto segregation); and Ann Schwerner, the mother of the civil rights martyr, Michael "Mickey" H. Schwerner, who was murdered in Mississippi (along with James E. Chaney and Andrew Goodman) on June 21, 1964, taught biology at the high school.

From September 1963 to June 1967, while teaching English Education at Southern Connecticut State College and finishing my degree at Teachers College, I had many opportunities to test my theories about the role of movies in changing people's attitudes, values, and behavior. One of my primary interests became the image of African-Americans in film, inspired directly by my experiences in Brooklyn and my contacts with Professor Bone. Moreover, by the time I departed for Vermont, I had published an article on the impact of white children watching Michael Roemer's *Nothing But a Man* (1964).[12] Reading those youthful essays quickly reveals the idealism and gullibility of an author shaped by both filmdom's' structured absences and an emerging social awareness.

Thus, by the time I arrived at the University of Vermont in 1967, my background in film, my commitments to changing the status quo in

English Education, and my publishing goals were clearly formed, if only half-baked. Significantly, the University promised that if it moved into mass communications, I could switch from training teachers to teaching film courses.

It was while I was giving my by-now standard anti-establishment lecture at an English conference in 1969, that I met an individual (best unnamed) who asked me to do a book with him on the image of blacks in film. What probably drew him to me were my academic credentials and my overzealous publications. What drew me to him were his commercial publications and show business contacts. Moreover, he had one of the best agents in the business. A deal was struck, a contract signed with a major publisher, and the research begun.

Almost immediately things went sour. After protracted telephone calls and frustrating correspondence, the partnership was dissolved. Not the book contract! I was committed to doing the book, and the publisher agreed with my plans.

To strengthen the research (and being star-struck from all my years in the movie theaters), I decided to interview people in the film business. Contacts were made, and arrangements were completed.

By October, 1971, I finally began making contacts for the interviewing process in New York City. Among the people who talked to me about their experiences in film were Lillian Gish, Lorenzo Tucker, and Alfred "Slick" Chester. In late December, I flew to Los Angeles. (The stories about each experience in New York and California are told before presenting the individual interviews.)

What is useful to recall is that the interviews took place during the explosive debate over what to call African-Americans. Elderly people like Tucker and Chester insisted on being addressed as "Negroes." African-Americans under the age of forty insisted on being called "Black." In addition, people on the West Coast had a different orientation to the role of blacks in Hollywood films than did the independent film artists on the East Coast. The more I tried to adapt to the different personalities' language and cultural battles, the more insecure I became. It rarely occurred to any of us that there were larger issues than what's in a name. Only now does it seem obvious to me that it is not your color, but your actions and attitudes that determine your worth to yourself and to others.

My identity crisis reflected why the problems of one group could not be isolated from the problems of other groups. We do not live in a vacuum. Our behavior and our actions are intertwined with the acts and behavior of others. In addition, blacks under forty used a Jive language, which was completely unfamiliar to me. (Melvin van Peebles claims that he used the problems that whites had with Jive to make *Sweet Sweetback's Baadasssss*

Song away from the eyes of censors.) I'm certain that one reason I later temporarily abandoned the project was the feeling, reinforced as you will read, that being white, Jewish, and a romantic academic made it almost impossible for me to get through to the people I was interviewing. For their part, they often wanted to know why they should talk to me. How could I help "the cause"?

In late December, 1971, I flew to California expressly to meet with James Earl Jones and Jason Robards, neither of whom did I meet during the trip. The former was undergoing personal problems (discussed elsewhere), and the latter turned me over to Sylvia Silvano, an assistant, who graciously set up appointments with Charles Edward Gordone, Woody Strode, Roscoe Lee Browne, Cecily Tyson, Mae Mercer, Brock Peters, and Ivan Dixon. Strode got me an interview with Jim Brown and John Ford. I had previously arranged appointments with Clarence Muse and King Vidor. Over the next two years, through the contacts I had made, I got additional interviews with James Earl Jones, William Marshall, Ruby Dee, and Frederick Douglass O'Neal. While I never did get to talk with James Whitmore, he sent me a reel-to-reel tape, answering the questions I had asked him in a letter about his performance in Carl Lerner's film version of *Black Like Me* (1964).

Over the next three years, academic issues and publication of *Film Study: A Resource Guide* (1973) occupied all my professional time. The one bright spot was that I got to teach several courses on black images in film. By 1977, in what I foolishly thought was an escape from the academic wars, I agreed to become the Associate Dean of the College of Arts and Sciences. Does that tell you anything about how naïve I was?

During my tenure as dean, I revised and expanded *Film Study: A Resource Guide* into the four-volume work *Film Study: An Annotated Bibliography*. It was while writing Chapter Three on "stereotyping" that I began to reflect on the interviews held in the early 1970s. The material in the revised work summarized the significant publications in African-American film history from the turn of the century to the late 1980s.[13] Again ironically, the work on African-Americans in my book dovetailed with the new boom in black films in Hollywood. By the mid-1990s, writers like Kevin Young were proclaiming the return of the blaxploitation era. "Everybody," he wrote, "even the guys at the *Beverly Hills 90210* Keg House fraternity knows the '70s are back."[14]

I left the Dean's Office in 1989, returned to the English Department, took two years to complete *Film Study: An Analytical Bibliography*, and worked on my classes in film.

Nevertheless, the unpublished interviews continued to intrigue me. At the urging of colleagues, I submitted a grant to the College of Arts and

Sciences to transcribe the tapes in 1990. A year and a half later, the rough transcriptions were done. What I needed to do then was to go through them carefully for accuracy. That is, I needed not only to verify that the written and spoken words jelled, but also to examine the narratives for their structured absences, their conscious acts of omission and commission.

III

I laugh quietly when I presume to judge the accuracy of what these individuals said about themselves and the times they lived. What arrogance! It won't take much effort on the part of the reader to discover that the interviewees have a very selective memory, that they shape their answers to make themselves look good and to justify the decisions they made during their careers.

Let me be clear here. Knowing that we had different agendas did not prove fatal to my objectives. I was not meeting these personalities to debate issues. These encounters were about sharing experiences, not about reaching a consensus. The same should be true for the reader. We do not have to agree with any conclusions. We just need to be cognizant that truth is not a top priority in these meetings. "The tragedy of film history," Louise Brooks wrote, "is that it is fabricated, falsified by the very people who make film history."[15] She understood why the early years of Hollywood history are littered with fictional information. Not many people took "Tinsel Town" seriously, and even fewer thought it an art form. However, while Hollywood matured and gained artistic stature, many of its creative people did not. "... Film celebrities," Brooks reminds us, "continue to cast themselves as stock types–nice or naughty girls, good or bad boys–whom their chroniclers spray with a shower of anecdotes."[16] I hope that I am not too guilty of that charge.

Much more difficult for the reader may be an ability to place oneself back in those times, to understand where these people came from, their intellectual segregation from gender and racial politics, and why the aforementioned personalities did what they did. Clearly, we are under no obligation to accept what they say as fact. At the same time, it is difficult to judge fairly what one does not comprehend fully.

Let me be clear. I recognize that my task as a researcher is to evaluate the worth of what I found. It is equally important to appreciate that these people educated me on many unexplored issues dealing with life and racial politics. The recounted experiences, more than the details, may prove your most valuable encounter with the past. That was definitely true for me. I hope that you can empathize and understand why these people say what they say and did what they did. Understanding, however, is not the same as approving the choices made.

As I reflected on the issues related to representation, identity, and memory, it seemed that the strategies of conventional anthologies using interviews did not fit my needs. While their stylistic manuals insisted that a properly proofread transcript be free of errors in standard grammar, punctuation, and spelling, the paradoxical nature of this project suggested another method. To show my difficulty in communicating with the personalities and the language problems they presented, I needed to approximate what the actual experiences were like, how the words and the ideas unsettled me personally and professionally. At the same time, the reader needs to be conscious that the stories, being spontaneous and improvised, raised many issues that remained unresolved. On the one hand, I wanted accuracy; on the other hand, I needed poetic license.

Consequently, I have purposely used misspellings, grammatical errors, and incorrect punctuation to capture the flavor of the encounters I present to the reader. They represent no disrespect to the personalities. Just the reverse is true. My experiences were so memorable to me that I want to try to replicate them for the reader. The annotations, meanwhile, force you to remember that these are counter narratives, while also revealing how my mind reacted to the information I was processing. Thus, the reader gets the chance to make language and stylistic adjustments in somewhat the same manner that the author did thirty years ago.

Let me restate what I said at the outset. The interviews presented in this book represent what I believe large numbers of people thought and felt in the early seventies. In addition, because the individuals interviewed represent those times in a way not found anywhere else in the literature of black film history, the interviews provide useful contacts with the past. With my forty-eight years of hindsight evaluating the snail-like evolution of African-American screen images, I retain very mixed reactions to the glacial progress that black screen images and African-American filmmakers have made against the deeply-seated, powerful forces in world cinema. Once upon a time, I believed that the Jim Crow conditions of the screen stayed in place because of the power of the Southern box-office. Then I believed it was really due to the racism of white America itself.

I no longer think that. I believe the ugly forces that support a rear-guard action against African-American films–and other alternative images–are worldwide. Jon Kilik, a successful Independent producer, has taught me that artists like Spike Lee have trouble getting funded not because their projects are poor (in some instances, they may be), but because they may do poorly abroad. In other words, foreign distributors determine what films they send around the world based on the appeal they think the films will have for global audiences. And since there is the flawed perception that blacks films don't make money (based on too many obviously unreliable variables to list sensibly), those who control the funding of films refuse to spend much money on their being made. If you do not believe me, ask Melvin Van Peebles. To this day, *Sweet Sweetback's Baadasssss Song* has not been distributed abroad.

A major value of these interviews is that they tell the sad story of a struggle against prejudice and cruelty that has persisted throughout the twentieth century in the world of film. The battles fought by individuals like Lorenzo Tucker, Clarence Muse, Woody Strode, Charles Edward Gordone, and Frederick Douglass O'Neal are in many respects still being fought by Bill Duke, Mario Van Peebles, Spike Lee, John Singleton, Robert Townsend, Charles Burnett, Julie Dash, and others. I hope that this new generation will not end their careers with the bitterness and frustration of those who paved the way for them in film.

One way to link these interviews to modern black film history is to confront the issues of identity and race. For example, there is the construct of the "mulatto." Seen today as a colonial/slave term, it is rarely used by sensitive people. Back in the seventies, the term was used routinely in discussing skin color. How thoughtfully one applies it to analyzing film history may determine how the actors' memories are received. We should consider, therefore, some of the problems the construct presents. For example, Donald Bogle's summary of the five major stereotypes of African-Americans in movie history defines the "mulatto" as the tragic figure trying to pass for white: "Usually the mulatto is made likable–even sympathetic (because of her white blood, no doubt)–and the audience believes that the girl's life could have been productive and happy had she not been a 'victim of divided racial inheritance.'"[17] Bogle's analysis rarely sees "the tragic mulatto" construct as describing light-skinned men. Misunderstood, his study can, however unintentionally, reinforce the negative image that the lighter the prettier and that white is better than black.

Let me be clear on this point. On the one hand, I realize this topic of racial tone is far too large to encapsulate in such a limited space. Moreover, I believe that Bogle's representations do not necessarily privilege lighter skin performers. He is mainly commenting on society's representations. On the other hand, one cannot meaningfully link the interviews in this book to modern black film history unless one acknowledge the prevailing issues of race and identity in the first seventy years of the twentieth century.[18]

This proved particularly problematic for Lorenzo Tucker, whose screen roles were preoccupied with the effects of "passing" on both men and women. That is, if "getting-over" appeared foregrounded at the opening of his screen narratives, it was undercut by an awareness of one's black heritage at the end. Moreover, as Pearl Bowser points out, "... there are many instances in ... films [featuring Tucker] in which the community embraces the so-called mulatto not as different but as one of many. And the whole idea of getting over, or passing, is the response to whether you can manage to work in the system that will only allow you if you have this particular look."[19]

Still further, there is the issue of what causes this race construct. Documentary filmmaker Louis Massiah argues that ever since the sixties, the dilemma has become more acute. Before that time, your race construct depended on your ancestry–i.e., European versus African. Since then, we no longer think in such simplistic terms. Now we see the race construct resulting from "history and necessity."[20] A second way to receive the interviews is to appreciate the quagmire over what constitutes a "black" or "race" film. For example, Bowser believes that, "Between 1912 and 1948, 350 race movies were produced by 150 companies, many of which were owned by whites, particularly after the 1920s."[21] Her research, like that of most of her predecessors, makes clear that films made by whites, but dealing with black-oriented themes, were once routinely considered to be "race films." Recently, however, artists like Jesse Rhines define "a film [as] black that comes out of the African-American culture and presents a point of view that is a product of that culture." He delineates black films by saying their "director, writer, and producer should be black, but definitely the director."[22]

That was certainly not the case in 1971. If we took that position back then, many of the independent African-American films starring black actors, including Paul Robeson in *The Emperor Jones* (1933), would have been discounted because they were directed and produced by whites. If we had taken Rhines' position, it would have also ruled out some of the most discussed movies featuring African-Americans in film history: e.g., *Hallelujah* and *Hearts in Dixie* (both in 1929), *Imitation of Life* (1934 and 1959), *The Green Pastures* (1936), *Cabin in the Sky* and *Stormy Weather* (both in 1943), *Pinky*, *Lost Boundaries*, *Intruder in the Dust*, and *Home of the Brave* (all in 1949), *Carmen Jones* (1954), *Island in the Sun* (1957), *Porgy and Bess* (1959), and *Nothing But a Man* (1964). To put it another way, James Baldwin wrote, "The most important thing about this movie [*Carmen Jones*]–and the reason that, despite itself, it is one of the most important all-Negro movies Hollywood has yet produced–is that the questions it leaves in the mind relate less to Negroes than to the interior life of America."[23] It is also a point that Eric Lott makes repeatedly about antebellum blackface minstrelsy, "an established nineteenth-century theatrical practice, principally of the urban North, in which white men caricatured blacks for sport and profit...."[24] For him, "The minstrel show was less the incarnation of an age-old racism than an emergent social semantic figure responsive to the emotional demands and troubled fantasies of its audiences."[25] That is, analysis sometimes reveals more about the audience than about the show. In short, as Professor Hilary Neroni points out, "Studying these films today would fall under studying representations of race in film, not studying black cinema, which today is understood as black filmmakers."[26]

By the end of the sixties, debates about black aesthetics and representation were everyday issues to many people. These polemics took their toll on film attendance. For example, in the summer of 1970, the *Christian Science Monitor* reported arguments taking place between white and black film professionals over the dilemma of Hollywood's new "black films." On the one hand, a white screenwriter argued that "black audiences are staying away from Hollywood movies in droves." On the other hand, a black actress explained, "I haven't taken a consensus, but I know how I feel and how my friends feel. We stay away from films we don't associate with."[27] However, by 1972, *Movie Digest* was exclaiming that many in the nation's 22 million African-American population were "wolfing down the movies available. And Saturday night at the movies is again returning to black communities everywhere across the country."[28]

African-Americans may have been buying tickets, but organizations like the National Association for the Advancement of Colored People considered Hollywood's black films like *Shaft* (1971), *Superfly,* and *Come Back Charleston Blue* (both in 1972), "cultural genocide."[29] Why? If you read *Variety*, its answer was that, "Among recent 'black' films the preoccupation has been overwhelmingly with the underworld—guns, beatings, trick babies, pimps—so that a single film, Fox's *Sounder* (1972), by concentrating on normal reality in a Negro farm film of the Depression times has been as different among current black product as Walt Disney releases are different from Andy Warhol eavesdropping on white delinquents."[30] According to Pauline Kael, "When a popular culture is as saturated in violent cynicism as ours, and any values held up to oppressed people are treated with derision as the white man's con, or an Uncle Tom's con, the cynicism can't fail to have its effect on all of us." Thus, she concluded, "What M-G-M and Warner Brothers and all the rest are now selling is nothing less than soul murder, and body murder, too."[31] Thomas Cripps, writing from the vantage point of history, offered another answer: "In the recent heady days of Hollywood—the misnamed blaxploitation era—many black filmmakers responded to the opportunity, *de novo*, as though Hollywood had no black history and only a thriving present and glowing future. The epoch ended in disaster."[32]

In 1972, the *New York Times* responded to the outcries and did a spread on how prominent artists like Gordon Parks, Lena Horne, Jim Brown, Martin Ritt, Maya Angelou, Imamu Amiri Baraka, and Lonne Elder III felt about the new films.[33] Elsewhere, Alvin F. Poussaint attacked the white filmmakers who, he argued, by exploiting black culture were harming black unity;[34] while Barbara Morrow Williams pondered the choices black communities had and what censoring the new black films would do to black film employment.[35] Ellen Holly summed up the chaos by writing two years later, "More than a hundred 'black' films have come and gone in recent years. In the avalanche of buffoons and super studs that can't be taken any more seriously than Batman and Captain Marvel, plain honest-to-goodness black men of human stature who can be taken seriously are scarce as hen's teeth. I suspect it's because the white-controlled film industry still has terrible difficulty dealing with black men as peers."[36] Worth remembering is that these black-action films competed with Oscar-winning films like *The French Connection* (1971) and *The Godfather* (1972).

In my interview with King Vidor, he made clear that one of the difficulties that he had in the late twenties had to do with the fear of theaters across the country having blacks and whites intermingle on a large scale. Interestingly, this is the same problem that occurred with the exhibition of black films in the 1990s, and the alleged causes of the riots that broke out during the initial screenings of movies like *New Jack City*, *Juice*, and *Boyz 'N the Hood* (all in 1991). In an attempt to resolve some of the problems associated with the release and exhibition of black-themed movies, the National Association of Theatre Owners (NATO), at its NATO/SHOWEST '92 Annual Convention, convened a panel on, "The Importance of Black Films in America and in the World."

At the outset, it was obvious that recent black-oriented movies made money both for producers and exhibitors: "*House Party* grossed $27 million; *New Jack City*, $48 million; *Eddie Murphy Raw*, $51 million; *Boyz 'N the Hood*, $58 million." The grosses were especially impressive because of the small production costs. Nevertheless, the panel wanted to address the mainly white exhibitors' fears about the alleged violence associated with showing black-theme movies and the concerns that it raised for theater staff and patrons. It was clear that unless these problems were resolved, not only would the exhibitors avoid showing the films, but also it would strangle the production process itself. After all, why make films that cannot be shown in theaters?

Doug McHenry, producer of *New Jack City*, insisted that the problem was bogus. He then gave specific reasons why. First, people had to realize how America's racist history had resulted in today's massive unemployment of black youth and those in poverty-stricken ghettoes. That fact has also made the plight of black youth a popular subject for African-American movies and for attracting young blacks to see these films. Second, it is not the films that cause the violence. Sometimes, it results from a problem that existed before the showing of the films. Thus, when the young people show up, there are already bad feelings between certain individuals. Another cause may be the public events occurring during the run of the film. A case in point is the Rodney King beating which aired on the news repeatedly during the week that *New Jack City* opened. Nothing in the film was as provocative as what was being seen on the evening news. It is wrong, therefore, to ignore that aspect in any analysis of black-theme movies and related violence. Third, the violence that did occur at the openings of these few black-theme films occurred only during the initial screenings. There was none after the first weekend. Fourth, McHenry pointed out, the violence had occurred, in large part, because exhibitors mishandled security, oversold the shows, and incited the crowds by being disrespectful to them. Fifth, distributors shared some blame, because they had misjudged the demand for such movies and booked them in small, rather than large, theaters.

The panel ended, as *Variety* reported, with "Filmmakers, distributors, and exhibitors ... [saying] that they will attempt to curb consumer trepidation in 1992, as 14 black-themed films head for release."[37] While NATO/SHOWEST '92's panel did not get much attention either at the Las Vegas convention or in the media, it serves as an illustration of how the problems Vidor experienced in 1929 were still evolving in 1992.

Of course, the problem is far more complex than this smattering of articles represents. My purpose is not to debate the issue, but only to alert the reader that the issue of a black aesthetic that pervades this series of interviews done over thirty years ago is relevant to the present. One can also speculate that the debate provides an opportunity to elevate the status and stature of race films, while at the same time reevaluating the nature of film aesthetics in general.

Moreover, how are we to determine the reception to these "black" or "race films" if we cannot even agree on where they were shown from 1900 on, or even what constitutes a segregated theater? For example, scholars wrestle with the difficulty of categorizing the white-owned movie houses that segregated blacks in the balcony, and the vaudeville houses and saloons that doubled, at times, for movie theaters. In 1909, according to one black weekly newspaper, the *Indianapolis Freedman*, America had one hundred twelve "colored" movie houses, "with those outside major cities being mostly five and ten cent theaters, vaudeville and moving pictures ... [with] many of these venues ... owned by whites." A year later, the same paper estimated that at least fifty three of these "colored theaters" were owned and operated by African-Americans.[38] Later, Norman Kagan found that distributors of black films in the thirties counted on "13,000,000 American blacks in about 500 theatres, plus midnight performances in southern white theatres."[39] Tino Balio interpreted the figures differently, stating that there was about one Southern movie house "for every thirty thousand blacks, [and most Southern movie theaters].... did not admit them at all."[40] Currently, Bowser and her colleagues have determined, there was a point in film history when nearly twenty-five percent (four hundred theaters) of American movies houses "catered to African American audiences."[41]

Just as exhibition dominated the direction taken by the mainstream American film industry throughout most of this century, it also affected independent filmmakers, black and white. To appreciate many of their economic and social disadvantages, it is essential to grasp how legalized movie segregation operated starting in the silent era. According to Douglas Gomery, the sanctioned discrimination took three forms. One way was by neighborhoods. Blacks congregated at their movie houses (owned mostly by whites); whites attended white theaters. Second, time allocations enforced segregation. That is, blacks could only attend movies at certain hours or on certain days. Third, race prejudice in theaters existed by designated areas, usually by segregating blacks to special entrances and the balcony.[42] During the 1930s, Margaret Thorpe commented, "The twelve million American Negroes [sic] seem to be the only considerable section of the population who cannot go to a movie whenever they have the price."[43] The fallout from this humiliating practice was that not only did many African-Americans shy away from movie-going, but also that independent filmmakers got smaller bookings and therefore a more limited income for producing movies than did white filmmakers. Bowser points out, "Many of the black producers who surfaced after *The Birth of A Nation* (1915) were so pressed for funds that they made only one or two films."[44] It was not until the thirties that segregated black movie-going began to change in the North; the South began changing a decade later. The reason, not surprisingly, was first because of economic pressures; and, finally, because of the decision of the U.S. Supreme Court in 1954.[45]

What about the African-American actors themselves? Black entertainers, as Alex Albright surmises, followed a familiar pattern throughout most of the early twentieth century. A successful African-American performer posed a threat to a white actor's livelihood. Consequently, the latter shifted his or her routines and made it nearly impossible for the former to follow. Thus, the rise of black minstrelsy may well have created white vaudeville and, for decades after, the exclusion of black entertainers. When African-Americans made breakthroughs in vaudeville, whites sought refuge on the Broadway stage.[46] There were always exceptions, of course, and Albright's notion may oversimplify a more complex history. For example, Renee A. Simons believes that, "Despite the difficulties, obstacles, limitations, exploitation and personal disappointments, black minstrels were significant in American theatre history because they again established a place for black performers in American show business."[47] Nevertheless, it seems reasonable that whatever the pattern, it made race and caste critical issues in an African-American performer's career.

What contributions can the discussions in this book make to the ongoing debate? To answer that, we need to address the question of film scholarship at the start of this project. Black films did not attract the attention of the first major film historians. For those interested in "pioneering" black film study in the late sixties, the only two "scholarly" sources were Peter Noble's *The Negro in Film* (1948) and V.J. Jerome's pamphlet, *The Negro in Hollywood* (1950). Edward Mapp's *Blacks in American Film: Today and Yesterday* did not appear until 1972; Donald Bogle's first edition of *Toms, Coons, Mulattoes, Mammies, & Bucks: An Interpretive History of Blacks in American Films* and James P. Murray's *To Find an Image: Black Films from Uncle Tom to Super Fly* until 1973; Daniel J. Leab's From *Sambo to Superspade: The Black Experience in Motion Pictures* and Gary Null's *Black Hollywood: The Negro in Motion Pictures* until 1975; and Thomas Cripps' *Slow Fade to Black: The Negro in American Film, 1900-1942,* until 1977. Scholarly publications were not all that was lacking.

Another major source of information on African-American show business is the black press. We should bear in mind what you would discover in 1971, searching through the pages of the black newspapers, assuming you were near a major library or could afford to travel to one. Throughout the first fifty years of this century, many of the nearly forty African-American newspapers—e.g., the New York *Amsterdam News*, the *Pittsburgh Courier*, the *New York Age*, the Baltimore *Afro-American*, and the *Chicago Defender* —faced a dilemma. If they attacked stage and screen productions that marginalized blacks, they ran the risk of decreasing black employment in the arts. Whites, who have always controlled American entertainment, were not going to employ African-Americans in unpopular and unsuccessful commercial ventures. However, if the black press acted as cheerleaders for the black-oriented productions, they encouraged derogatory myths and practices about black life and history. In hindsight, it seems that many researchers of my generation—e.g., Bogle, Cripps, Leab, Maap, Murray, and Null—were influenced by the dilemma faced by black journalists of the past: at what cost to the future do I criticize the present? Some modern readings of earlier works have a tendency to forget the context in which these groundbreaking studies were written.

Having highlighted some of the reasons why this publication took the path it did, we can now turn our attention to its purpose. A lot has changed in the past thirty-eight years since this research has unfolded, and not just in film. However, a considerable amount has not. In part, that is what this book is about.

IV

The notion of preparing an anthology of annotated interviews dating back to the early 1970s advanced in various forms over the last decade, and the labor before you is quite different from its early organization. Including all the interviews in one volume proved too unwieldy. Consequently, I decided to study one self-contained section of the collection: those interviews by people who had pioneered in their fields and have since died. The format is to proceed chronologically—starting with my first interview with Lorenzo Tucker and ending with Frederick Douglass O'Neal's comments—thereby giving the reader an opportunity to explore the nature of film study as well as the history of African-American screen images. Each interview begins with an introductory essay and then offers brief comments, when appropriate, during the interview. The interviews are not equal in length. Some people gave me more time, others less. Some discussions are more complex and provocative than others are. However, each gave me a better understanding of the struggle and the price people paid for trailblazing in their profession and life. To make the passage easier still, let me summarize the study chapter by chapter.

Chapter 1 examines the career and views of Lorenzo Tucker, the actor who played the leading man in many of the films made by Oscar Micheaux, the dean of race movies. Known to many as the "Black Valentino," Tucker provides a look at the skin-tone problems faced by a certain portion of African-Americans not only in their careers, but also what happened to them once the black pride movement took hold in the late 1960s. We met twice, once in November and again in December, 1971, which accounts for the length of the chapter. Tucker invited other actors in race movies to these meetings: e.g., Alfred "Slick" Chester, Bee Freeman, Kenn Freeman, and Walter Richardson. Also present at the second interview are Leroy and Pearl Bowser. The interaction between those people on the issues facing the black community during the early seventies not only prepares us for the interviews that follow, but also reveals many of the difficulties between the different generations.

Chapter 2 is concerned with the thoughts of Lillian Gish, arguably the greatest actress in silent film history. In sharing her thoughts about *The Birth of A Nation* (1915) and the treatment of African-Americans in film, she reveals a considerable amount of information on what her mentor, D. W. Griffith, must have felt about the film and antebellum history.

Chapter 3 provides the first contact with performers on the West Coast. Clarence Muse, the black actor with the most screen credits up to 1972, pioneered many firsts in the history of African-Americans in theater and film. Among other things, he starred in the first talking film featuring an all-black cast, *Hearts in Dixie* (1929). At the same time, he was, next to Stepin Fetchit, one of the most controversial black performers to outsiders who wanted to reform Hollywood. Thus for many he came to epitomize the then negative epithet, "Uncle Tom." Listening to his side of the story allows us to flesh out the difficulty blacks faced as they tried to find employment in the world of entertainment in the twentieth century.

Chapter 4 gives another look at the issues Hollywood dealt with during the coming of the sound revolution in the late twenties. The interview with King Vidor, one of the directorial giants in movie history, reviews the conditions surrounding the making of *Hallelujah* (1929), the first commercially and critically acclaimed all-black talking film. Like the Gish interview, this discussion has the advantage of showing how major white celebrities dealt with the very issues and films discussed by African-American artists in the early 1970s.

Chapter 5 explores the world of Woody Strode, the athlete, who along with Kenny Washington, broke the color line in professional football. Strode's close, personal relationship with the legendary John Ford gave him rare opportunities not only to revise the screen history of black troopers in a film like *Sergeant Rutledge* (1960), but also to see first hand the difficulties involved in revising film procedures. Although portions of this chapter originally appeared in *Black Scholar*,[48] they focused only on the films Strode made. Here, for the first time, is the complete text of the successes and failures of the formidable actor's career, as well as the problems that he encountered with a new generation of black activists.

Chapter 6 contributes the most outspoken comments not only on the times, but also on a number of people interviewed in this study. Charles Edward Gordone, the first African-American playwright to win a Pulitzer Prize, met me at a time when the frustration of the project had begun to wear me down. Since he was also frustrated by events both in the theater and in film, we shared our problems in a surprisingly candid moment. Particularly revealing are the difficulties he was having with other black personalities about the nature and direction of the African-American theater.

The final chapter takes us back to New York and an interview with Frederick Douglass O'Neal, the first black to be elected president of Actors

Equity Association (AEA). His observations about the role of African-Americans in stage and film history complement the interviews that preceded them. The reader gets the chance not only to see how much has been learned in a year of research, but how many of the problems still persist to the present time.

For those readers who did not live during these volatile years, this ambitious anthology allows you to go beneath the surface of traditional accounts analyzing the explosive events occurring during the early 1970s, when the entertainment industry underwent a revolution in the representation of blacks on the screen. It deals with seven prominent personalities who did not always understand why they did what they did in representing the images of African-Americans in the movies. Two of these personalities, Gish and Vidor, did what they did because they believed that they knew the truth about the Old South. Each struggled to create a cinematic language that would make it possible for others to understand their point of view. They epitomize what Martin Luther King explained, "There is little hope for us until we become tough-minded enough to break loose from the shackles of prejudice, half-truths, and downright ignorance."[49] The other five personalities made many compromises to a Jim Crow mentality in order to change the manner in which blacks were represented on the stage and screen. In the process, they touched our lives. Until you have walked in their shoes, you will not know what you would have done in their place. As one tribute to the past puts it, "They went in the back door so we could go through the front."[50]

Frank Manchel
University of Vermont
June 30, 2006

1. Lorenzo Tucker. From the 1931-32 Independent Race production *The Black King*. Courtesy of the Manchel Collection, Burlington College.

2. Al "Slick" Chester. From the 1948 Independent Race production *Miracle in Harlem*. Courtesy of The Manchel Collection, Burlington College.

3. Lillian Gish. From D.W. Griffith's 1920 film *Way Down East*. Courtesy of The Manchel Collection, University of Vermont.

32 Introduction

4. King Vidor (left) and Daniel L. Haynes. Publicity shot for *Hallelujah* (1929). Courtesy of The Manchel Collection, Burlington College.

Introduction 33

5. The author with Clarence Muse. January 6, 1972. Courtesy of The Manchel Collection, Burlington College.

6. Woody Strode. Publicity shot from Stanley Kubrick's *Spartacus* (1960). Courtesy of The Manchel Collection, University of Vermont.

7. Frederick Douglass O'Neal in John Ford/Elia Kazan's *Pinky* (1949). Left, Nina Mae McKinney. Right, Jeanne Crain. Courtesy of The Manchel Collection, University of Vermont.

8. Arthur John Jack Johnson, Heavyweight Boxing Champion 1908-1915. Courtesy of The Manchel Collection, Burlington College.

9. Spike Lee. From *Do the Right Thing* (1989). Courtesy of The Manchel Collection, Burlington College.

38 Introduction

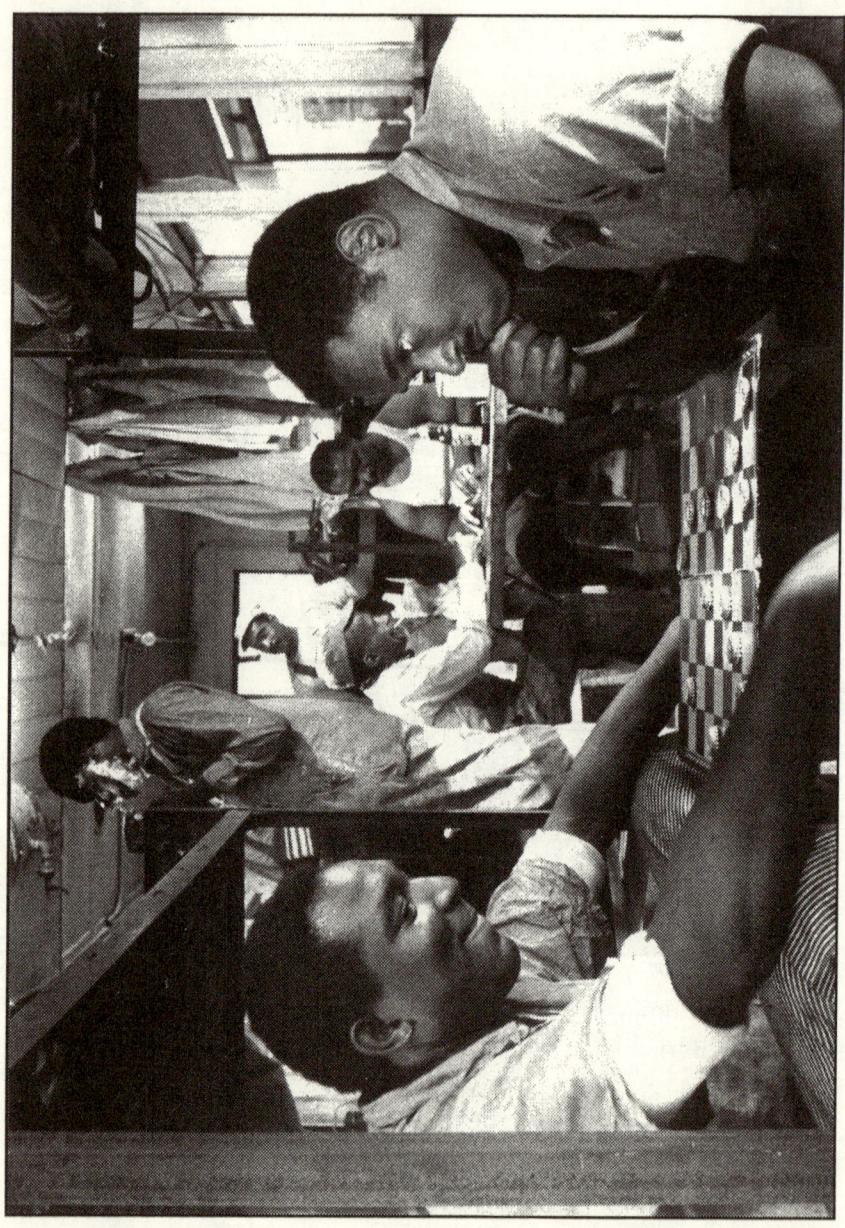

10. Ivan Dixon [touching chin] and Leonard Parker. From Michael Roemer's *Nothing But a Man* (1964). Courtesy of The Manchel Collection, University of Vermont.

11. Pearl Bowser. The independent scholar who spearheaded research into Race Movies. Courtesy of The African Diaspora Images Collection.

12. Louis de Rochemont's 1949 *Lost Boundaries*. From left to right, Emory Richardson and Mel Ferrer. Courtesy of The Manchel Collection, Burlington College.

13. Lobby Card for Jack Starette's *Slaughter* (1972). Courtesy of The Manchel Collection. University of Vermont.

Notes

[1] Thulani Davis, "Local Hero: Workin' 40 Acres and a Mule in Brooklyn," *American Film* 14.9 July/August (1989), 26.

[2] For more information on Joseph Burstyn, Inc. v Wilson case, see "The Miracle Case."

[3] Henry Lewis Gates, Jr., *Loose Canons: Notes on the Culture Wars* (New York: Oxford University Press, 1992), 159.

[4] I wish to acknowledge a debt for the strategy in this book to two works: Henry Lewis Gates, Jr.'s *Thirteen Ways of Looking at a Black Man*; and Orson Welles and Peter Bogdanovich's *This is Orson Welles*. Although we took strikingly different approaches to our subjects, my introduction and the bold-face annotations in this book were influenced by their methodology.

[5] Gates, *Loose Canons: Notes on the Culture Wars*, 131.

[6] For the reasons why I have modified my position on film as a new form of literature, see Manchel, *Film Study: An Analytical Bibliography*, Vol. 1, 135-136.

[7] Donna E. Lusitana, "Indians and the Army," in *The Real West* (Arts & Entertainment Network, 1993).

[8] bell hooks, *Black Looks: Race and Representation* (Boston: South End, 1992), 6.

[9] Ibid.

[10] Richard Dyer, *The Matter of Images: Essays on Representation* (New York: Routledge, 1993), 105.

[11] Thomas Cripps, *Making Movies Black: The Hollywood Message Movies from World War II to the Civil Rights Era* (New York: Oxford University Press, 1993), 4.

[12] Frank Manchel, "Teaching Nothing but a Man," *Media and Methods*, October (1967), 10-13.

[13] Frank Manchel, *Film Study: An Analytical Bibliography*, Vol. 4 (Rutherford, NJ: Fairleigh Dickinson, 1990), 851-953.

[14] Kevin Young, "Blame It on the Boogie," *SF Weekly* 18 May (1994), 11.

[15] Louise Brooks, *Lulu in Hollywood* (New York: Knopf, 1982), 74.

[16] Ibid., 74.

[17] Donald Bogle, *Toms, Coons, Mulattoes, Mammies, & Bucks: An Interpretive History of Blacks in American Films*, 2nd ed. (New York: Continuum, 1989), 9.

[18] I wish to thank Prof. Hilary Neroni for her help on this section.

[19] Pearl Bowser, "The Micheaux Legacy," *Black Film Review* 7, 4 (1993), 14.

[20] Ibid., 14.

[21] Eleanor Blau, "With Dignity: Films by Blacks for Blacks," *New York Times*, 22 Oct. 1990, 13.

[22] Geraldine Fabrikant, "The Harder Struggle to Make and Market Black Films," *New York Times*, 11 Nov. 1996, D1.

[23] James Baldwin, *Notes of a Native Son* (New York: Dial, 1963), 49.

[24] Eric Lott, *Love and Theft: Blackface Minstrelsy and the American Working Class* (New York: Oxford University Press, 1995), 3.

[25] Ibid., 6.

[26] E-mail, May 27, 2006.

[27] Kimmis Hendrick, "Seeking What Black Film Audiences Want," *Christian*

Science Monitor, no. 4 (1970), 4.

[28] "Black Movies: New Dynamite at the Box Office," *Movie Digest* (1972), 61.

[29] Gordon Parks, "Black Movie Boom--Good or Bad?," *New York Times*, 17 Dec. 1972, D3.

[30] Robert J. Landry, "U.S. Films: Black, Red & Blue," *Variety* (1973), 45.

[31] Pauline Kael, "The Current Cinema: Notes on Black Movies," *New Yorker* 43.41 (1972), 165.

[32] Thomas Cripps, "New Black Cinema and Uses of the Past," in *Black Cinema Aesthetics: Issues in Independent Black Filmmaking*, Ed. L. Gladstone (Athens: Ohio University, 1982), 20.

[33] Parks, "Black Movie Boom--Good or Bad?" D3, 19.

[34] Alvin F. Pouissant, "Stimulus/Response: Blaxploitation Movies--Cheap Thrills That Degrade Blacks," *Psychology Today* 7.9 (1974), 22.

[35] Barbara M. Williams, "Filth Vs. Lucre: The Black Community's Tough Choice," *Psychology Today* 7.9 (1974), 102.

[36] Ellen Holly, "Where Are the Films About Real Black Men and Women?," *New York Times*, 2 June 1974, B11.

[37] John Evan Frook, "Bff Unwraps Plan to Boost Black Pix," *Variety* (1992), 39.

[38] Gregory Waller, "Another Audience: Black Moviegoing, 1907-16," *Cinema Journal* 31.2 (1992), 4.

[39] Norman Kagan, "Black American Cinema: A Primer," *Cinema* 6.2 (1970), 6.

[40] Tino Balio, *Grand Design: Hollywood as a Modern Business Enterprise, 1930-1939* (Berkeley: U of California Press, 1995), 2.

[41] Pearl Bowser and Jane Gaines, "New Finds/Old Films: Black Gold," *Black Film Review* 7.4 (1993), 4.

[42] Douglas Gomery, *Shared Treasures: A History of Movie Presentation in the United States* (Madison: University of Wisconsin Press, 1992), 156-158.

[43] Margaret F. Thorpe, *America at the Movies* (New Haven: Yale University Press, 1939), 9.

[44] Blau, "With Dignity: Films by Blacks for Blacks." C13.

[45] Gomery, *Shared Treasures: A History of Movie Presentation in the United States*. 163-164, 168.

[46] Alex Albright, "Micheaux, Vaudeville & Black Cast Film," *Black Film Review* 7.4 (1993), 7.

[47] Renee A. Simmons, *Frederick Douglass O' Neal: Pioneer of the Actor's Equity Association* (New York: Garland, 1996), 9-10.

[48] Frank Manchel, "The Man Who Made the Stars Shine Brighter: An Interview with Woody Strode," *Black Scholar* 25.2 (1995).

[49] Martin Luther King and Coretta Scott King, *The Words of Martin Luther King, Jr* (New York: Newmarket Press, 1987), 17.

[50] Reuben Cannon et al., *Dancing in September* (United States: HBO Home Video, 2001), videorecording.

14. Lorenzo Tucker, often referred to as "The Black Valentino." Courtesy of The Manchel Collection, Burlington College.

1
Heroes and Villains: Lorenzo Tucker

> "It is one of the bitter ironies of American history, ... that motion picture technology, with its singular potential for good or evil, grew during the same time period (1890-1915) that saw the systematic, determined, and almost hysterical persecution and defamation of blacks and other minority groups."[1]
>
> James Snead

Lorenzo Tucker prided himself on being a light-skinned Negro who refused to remain quiet about the black power movement. At the time, the ex-stage and screen actor was in his mid-sixties; I was a very impressionable thirty-six. His story jump-started my odyssey into black film history, showing me the complexity of the subject and teaching just how superficial judging the past by the values of the present can be. Tucker and I were separated by more than profession, race, and age. Yet those differences demonstrate not only the sticky situations that a researcher faces doing oral history, but also the dramatic changes taking place in American society during the early seventies. My background did not prepare me adequately for what was to come. You may face the same dilemma. Therefore, before we consider Tucker's narrative, a few caveats might help.

At the outset, the reader needs to know something about Tucker's "agenda," as well as our struggle defining terms and concepts. For example, when these interviews occurred (November 6 and December 4, 1971), the actor was enraged by the use of terms like "black" and "African-American" in place of the then more traditional labels "Negro" and "Colored." A major reason for his agitation was that the language shift further marginalized light-skin blacks like Tucker. He also viewed those African-Americans who represented this cultural shift as opportunists who misled the uninformed white community about the complexity of black life. Thus, modern sensibilities may be jarred encountering the performer's resentful outbursts about the changes taking place in American race relations during this period from the late sixties to the early seventies. How the black power movement defined African-Americans and viewed black film history directly challenged Tucker's outlook of himself and his professional life.

I had another perspective. Having studied with Robert A. Bone, I believed it was important to understand what made African-Americans a distinctive group in our culture. To quote Bone directly, the differences between blacks and others "stem from a group past, with its bitter heritage of slavery, and from the group present [1965], with its bitter knowledge of caste. They stem from contact, either immediate or historical, with the folk culture of the Southern Negro, which has left its clear stamp on Negro life in the North. They stem from long experience with separate institutions: with a Negro press, Negro church, Negro hospitals, and Negro colleges. They stem from the fact that most Negroes still spend most of their lives within the geographical and cultural confines of a Negro community."[2] After nearly a quarter of a century exploring this phenomenon, I find it useful to balance Bone's perspective with Valarie Smith's observation, "More recently, this conception of the authentic black subject has undergone dramatic transformation in response to the changing demographics of African American communities. While early in the twentieth century the majority of African Americans were located in the rural South, waves of migration to the North and West led to concentrations of blacks in urban communities in these other regions. The subsequent industrialization and underdevelopment of urban centers, and the decline in steady, decent-paying jobs for semi- and unskilled laborers, thus erected black communities disproportionately. As a result, the idea of the urban has become virtually synonymous with notions of blackness blight in public discourse; markers of drug and gang culture, rather than those of indigenous vernacular black culture, have circulated and been read increasingly as signs of racial (and geographical) authenticity."[3] Equipped with these two insights, we can better grasp what troubled the individuals not only here, but throughout the book.

Understandably, no topic was more central to the Tucker interviews than the construct of the "mulatto." How well one recalls the observations on that issue made earlier may determine how the actor's tale is received.

Tucker, the embodiment of the light-skinned performer during the first half of this century, was like many African-American bourgeois entertainers in this book – a hardworking individualist who participated in almost every significant phase of black, or "race," films and theater up to the 1960s. He was proud of his independence and his ability to overcome racial and personal handicaps. What he says later in the interviews stems from the assumption that his professional life offered a paradigm for anyone interested in a career in show business, an assumption often ignored by even the best of the modern commentators.

One should also bear in mind Alex Albright's reflections on the patterns that black entertainers followed throughout most of the early twentieth century and the perceived threat it posed to white artists, as well as Renee A. Simons' counter-arguments concerning the valuable role African-Americans played in the entertainment world. In Tucker's case, he had a choice. He could have "passed," but decided not to. Accordingly, his recollections disclose a compelling facet about the complex history of black show business.

Even so, sections in the Tucker interviews may offend the reader's modern receptivity. For example, the middle-class performer makes provocative assertions about the manner in which a skin-color caste system operated in black vaudeville and the changes that people like Tucker achieved. Those declarations about race, representation, and black progressives remain as debatable today as they were then. Yet, Tucker's reflections on the period under discussion – the late 1920s – are central to our apprehension of black film history. According to Richard Grupenhoff, "The late 1920s were the high point of black vaudeville. Numerous touring companies criss-crossed the country in automobiles, busses and trains, through the often hostile country of the white society, in order to play to the isolated communities of blacks outside New York."[4] William Dillard, a black trumpet player who did the criss-crossing, observes that the reason black vaudeville theaters were so important was that "we only had church and ballrooms and the vaudeville theaters. You wouldn't be allowed in the opera house. But you could go to see vaudeville."[5] Imagine how satisfying it must have been to local black audiences to see representatives of their own race performing on stage and bringing to the isolated communities a sense of black culture. But the pressures these entertainers faced from segregationists, municipal Jim Crow regulations, and exploitive business executives, made such touring hazardous. Yet, Tucker never calls attention to the dangers of performing for hostile audiences. Instead, he takes a very positive view of race relations during those years. His comments, therefore, offer an attitude that can broaden and enhance the revisionist conclusions of modern film scholarship.

James Snead also cautions us on the term, "independent film." His feeling is that the concept is used frequently to contrast shoestring budget movies with lavish Hollywood productions. That superficial contrast could ignore the benefits derived from being outside the restraints found in carefully supervised formula filmmaking and industry dependence on major profits.[6] As we will discover, Tucker's stock is tied to how working as an "independent" made use of the freedoms such as free-lance productions provided. A major question that I pursue here is: Are the films he appears in concerned with developing a positive black aesthetic, or do they seek to provide a black clone of mainstream movies?

Tucker's livelihood in show business depended in large measure on how his work was received by black and white audiences; and his recollections of the theaters, segregation practices, and the personalities often conflict with current assessments of independent black films and their aesthetic merits. His attitudes, therefore, add another dimension to the historical discussions about race relations in show business. In 1971, for example, Tucker professed astonishment at the interpretations given his films; as well as outrage at the direction contemporary "black" films had taken. As far as he was concerned, the policy back then was to play the film, not to analyze its subject matter.

Thus, the black films Tucker discusses provide unexpected information about the cultural wars evolving during the early 1900s. Since these alternative movies were culturally constructed and targeted for a specific audience, they reveal not only the filmmakers' perceptions about race, gender, and American society, but also the social and political attitudes about black choices and desires at the time. Since these movies were usually shot on locations inescapably linked to the story, the films offer snapshots of the marginalized material and physical world in which the personalities lived. For example, Tucker's attitudes about the civil rights movement, as well as his recollections of the "race" movies he made, grow out of the ideological battles taking place among black intellectuals since the turn of the century, when Booker T. Washington's philosophy about manual labor was challenged by black dissidents like W.E.B. DuBois and William Monroe Trotter. By the time Tucker was entering high school, the cultural wars had shifted to Harlem, where it was, as Thulani Davis observes, "a world marked by a light-skinned educated elite and a brown-skinned majority of thousands of working people."[7] On the one hand, as film historians recall, the black cultural elite saw it as their self-appointed duty to elevate many less fortunate African-Americans migrating from rural to urban areas, so that these sojourners could more successfully integrate into American society. On the other hand, people like Marcus Garvey opposed integration and fought for a "Back to Africa" movement. While many educated observers followed the debates about integration versus self-determination in books and newspapers, the public followed the battles in the "race films" of the twenties and thirties.

In 1971, Tucker's reactions to these movies and to revisionist interpretations of them recalled some of the social pressures that affected the production policies of independent black filmmakers. Mainstream companies had the assurance that every film they made would be shown. Not so for the independents. They had to choose their subject matter carefully, because their movies got booked on a film-by-film basis. Thus race movies, more than Hollywood films, required a shrewd assessment of what would sell at subsequent-run theaters. Unlike the major studios, these minor producers did not benefit from flagship theaters. Tucker's comments, because *they may* echo what the "average moviegoer" wanted, contribute to an understanding of what the black filmmaker was hearing as he made his rounds distributing his products.

The melodramatic "race films" did more than gratify an African-American audience's desires for an alternative to Hollywood racial representations. They proved to be topical, speaking directly to the ongoing debates over black identity and its relationship to skin color. Cripps points out in his survey of these 1920s black independent productions that the films "retailed a black bourgeois success myth, a manual for those on the make, and a caution to the weak-willed who might be diverted from success by urban temptations."[8]

How did black spectators receive these up-lifting messages? Conventional wisdom, sometimes described as the "embourgeoisment thesis," often gives the impression that movies generally set "the cultural norms to which all groups aspire."[9] Nevertheless, scholars like Mary Carbine argue that during the first thirty years of this century, black movie houses produced different results in Chicago. There, "the movie theater provided the inhabitants of Black Metropolis with the opportunity to construct a specifically African-American, urban, popular culture."[10] Since Tucker often made personal appearances at theaters showing his films, he had direct knowledge on how the films were received. Consequently, his comments attacking revisionist judgments about these cinematic "messages" dealing with race and gender should not be summarily ignored.

Still further, Tucker and I engaged in the perennial debates about why Hollywood stereotyped blacks the way they did, and why many early "race" films were constructed as they were. Were blacks disparaged merely to satisfy white perceptions? Did independent black films exist primarily as a reaction against Hollywood productions? And what about Walter Burrell's observation, published at the time these interviews were conducted: "How black people think of themselves is undisputedly influenced by standards set and held by whites"?[11]

The end result, as scholars from W.E.B. DuBois to Cornell West have theorized, was to make too many black people conscious of serving two standards – those set by whites and those set by blacks. It produced, as Jane Gaines notes, a black self-contempt which "is the product of internal conflict set in motion by the dual motors of dominant and subordinated cultures."[12] More to the point, as Ronald J. Green insists, "The issue of twoness is important for an understanding of Oscar Micheaux [Tucker's film mentor], of race movies, and of [Thomas] Cripps' thesis about them."[13]

This "double-consciousness" clearly operates during the interviews transcribed in this book. It is not unique to Tucker. No one I interviewed ever felt he or she could think of themselves as a performer. First, it had to be, "What kind of black actor am I?" and "What have I done to enhance or to harm the representation of black people?" Only after those questions were addressed could we focus on the history and aesthetics of the films themselves.

In an attempt to deal with many of these issues, as well as to understand the journeys of show business personalities like Tucker, I have inserted annotations throughout the interviews to try to balance what was known in 1971 with what we know today. In such instances, my intention is to give the reader the benefit of hindsight rather than to maintain the rhythm of the interviews.

Given these caveats about black entertainment and film scholarship, we turn to our primary subject. No substantive information is available on Tucker, the man or his career. The best evidence can be found in Richard Grupenhoff's *The Black Valentino*. Consequently, there are times when the subsequent interviews overlap with his research. Rather than being repetitive, however, they allow us the opportunity to see the anecdotes and recollections in the context of the early seventies. Thus, the brief biography that follows provides an entree into what Tucker says later and its relevance to modern readers.

Born on June 28, 1907, in Philadelphia, Lorenzo Tucker was the first of two children of John and Virginia (Lee) Tucker. From the beginning, he entered a subordinate middle-class society that sought to uplift itself by integrating into a dominant white world. This "double consciousness" would express itself throughout the future actor's life and career. After his father died in 1913, the family separated because of economic hardship. Mrs. Tucker was forced to send her children to a family farm in Virginia. A promising student, Lorenzo eventually disappointed his mother by deciding to become an entertainer rather than a doctor. The nineteen-year-old's apprenticeship followed a pattern similar to most black entertainers during the first twenty years of this century. Tucker entered show business as a dancer in a nightclub sketch. Soon he was trying his luck in vaudeville as a hoofer and straight man, before finding a niche in a minstrel show as the interlocutor or master of ceremonies.

Tucker's career goals changed dramatically when he met the unconventional and independent author, filmmaker, and entrepreneur Oscar Micheaux in 1926. Their unappreciated collaboration, discussed shortly, remains a necessary part of African-American film history. From 1927 to

1936, Tucker starred in eleven of Micheaux's pictures. He got his name, "The Black Valentino," because a movie exhibitor not only wanted an inexpensive film to screen with Rudolph Valentino's *Son of the Sheik* (1926), but also one that would attract a black audience. Therefore, the savvy Micheaux quickly displayed a photograph of Tucker, bragging that this was "The Black Valentino."

Tucker continued to alternate his stage career with making all-black films throughout the 1930s and 1940s, but increasingly the race movies were directed and distributed by white producers who now began dominating the inexpensive, but fashionable, race market. Among them were *The Emperor Jones* (1933), *Straight to Heaven* (1937), *Boy! What a Girl* (1946), and *Reet-Petite and Gone* (1947). Except for the Robeson film, almost no evidence exists that describes conclusively the situations Tucker found himself in, the production practices of the filmmakers, and the reception of the films themselves. Readers, therefore, need to be cautious about what they read in Grupenhoff and in the following interviews.

After serving in the Army Air Force during the first two years of World War II, where he both produced shows and fought as a tail gunner in Europe, Tucker survived a plane crash and soon was transferred to the infantry, where he saw combat in France and Germany. Honorably discharged after the war ended in 1945, the ex-dog soldier discovered that post-WWII integration made the traditional race films obsolete. Consequently, he returned to the stage, where his longest-running credit was in an all-black production of *Anna Lucasta* in England in 1953. Working with other black stars such as Butterfly McQueen and Dooley Wilson, Tucker next joined the short-lived Negro Drama Players (1957), a group which rekindled the approach taken by Harlem's famous Lafayette Players and brought Broadway shows with black casts to the South.

Realizing that his type of acting no longer was marketable, Tucker abandoned show business in 1962, and supported himself as an autopsy assistant in New York City. By the mid-seventies, he had enough of Manhattan and moved to Hollywood, where he made one last attempt at reviving his acting career. He complained, however, that his light skin proved too great an obstacle in the reverse racism of the contemporary era. Eventually, Tucker took a job as a nighttime security guard so his days would be free for interviews. In 1981, he was honored with the Audelco Recognition Award, given to stimulate interest in the arts in black communities. On August 19, 1986, the Black Valentino died of lung cancer. "To the very end," wrote his biographer, "he insisted he still had something to prove."[14]

No understanding of Tucker or his views can exclude his influential relationship with the legendary and complicated Micheaux, the dean of

African-American filmmakers, who was, as Bowser states, "perhaps the most important single figure in the history of race movies."[15] Thankfully, in the last decade, considerable evidence has surfaced to document the details of Micheaux's life and career. Among the best works are Joseph A. Young's book-length study on the artist as a novelist, *Black Novelist as White Racist: The Myth of Black Inferiority in the Novels of Oscar Micheaux*; Pearl Bowser and Louise Spence's *Writing Himself into History: Oscar Micheaux, His Silent Films, and His Audiences*; and a book by Bowser and her colleagues on the same subject and era, *Oscar Micheaux and His Circle: African-American Filmmaking and Race Cinema of the Silent Era*. In addition, a useful video documentary, *Midnight Ramble: Oscar Micheaux and the Story of Race Movies* exists. This increasing wealth of validating material has encouraged many commentators to write theoretically about Micheaux's life, his production values, and the aesthetics of "poor cinema." Here, it seems useful to provide an overview of Micheaux's life and work to contextualize both Tucker's career and the interviews that follow.[16]

The fifth of thirteen children born to former slaves in Metropolis, Illinois in 1884, Oscar Micheaux, like Tucker, reflected an ambiguous attitude about black bourgeois values. It is difficult to determine why many of the lessons he apparently learned during the first seventeen years of his life resulted in a strong dislike for black clergymen, a passion for learning, and an unwavering belief in Booker T. Washington's self-help philosophy.[17] We do know that after Micheaux left home in 1901, he tried a number of jobs, most notably as a Pullman porter, before he decided to return to the life of a farmer and purchased a homestead in South Dakota.

As Micheaux approached his thirtieth birthday, "the hardworking, bookish, somewhat priggish young man" decided to circulate his ideas on the virtues of the West, Washington's doctrines, and the difficulties of interracial marriages.[18] His first book, *The Conquest: The Story of a Negro Pioneer* (1913), featured a protagonist, Oscar Devereaux, who failed to marry his true love because of racial barriers, and wed instead the black daughter of a no-account African-American preacher. Those who knew the author surmised that Micheaux was merely recycling his life (e.g., he had a number of problematic relationships with white women) into prose fiction. Skin-color and caste confrontations became his thematic trademarks in subsequent books and films. However, there was a problem. "Micheaux, like other black writers of the assimilationist school," argues Joseph A. Young, "idealistically assumed that the assimilation of black and white cultures would occur only if Blacks could pass for white; or, if passing for white was a cosmetic impossibility, Blacks could become fit for American culture by adopting Anglo-Saxon myths, Anglo-Saxon values, and Anglo-Saxon philosophy."[19] The end result, according to Young, was that

Micheaux's novels reflected the author's obsession with becoming white and his willingness "to exaggerate the worst side of black character."[20] Gaines argues that Micheaux's formulaic treatment of race relations in his novels and films involved "asking questions that still cause white, as well as black, Americans incredible discomfort." She then goes on to discuss the strengths and limitations on using his autobiographical references in his work to understand the man and his values.[21]

In turning to writing, Micheaux had also turned his attention to salesmanship and self-promotion. The reasons are unclear. Nevertheless, by his third book, *The Homesteader* (1917), the unorthodox writer had established a familiar pattern. The plots of his seven novels, almost all were autobiographical, relied heavily on melodramatic stories emphasizing the perennial issues of light-skinned blacks "passing" as whites, caste, and mulattoism.[22] For Micheaux's heroes and heroines, the color-issue appears to have been a matter of choice; and that choice determined one's sense of personal worth, as well as making a commentary on black identity. Michelle Wallace amplifies this concept, by offering a reason why the "mulatto" concept died. She asserts, "The concept may have died precisely under the weight of the subtle polemics of Micheaux and other artists in the theatre and in film who felt as he did but who are not so well remembered today."[23] By reminding us, that the pioneering director was not a mulatto, she points out that he still "employed the palette of African-American skin colors with skill and imagination."[24]

Thus, when the black-owned Lincoln Motion Picture Company, the first such enterprise in American film history, tried to get the rights to film *The Homesteader*, it came as no surprise that Micheaux rejected their offer to buy the rights to the novel and decided to do the screen adaptation himself. His film debut proved prophetic about his future subject matter and its intended audience. As Mark A. Reid suggests, the pioneering filmmaker "created characters that were either in the process of migrating from the South to the North or were northern inhabitants of an urban ghetto."[25] More importantly, Bogle comments that Micheaux's feel for the perceived desires of the black community not only gave [him] the means to succeed for so many years, but also "to teach them.... And teach he did."[26] Mainly social melodramas highlighting racial identity, Reid observes, Micheaux's films "were imaginative reflections of a proud, aggressive New Negro whose new morality condoned retaliatory action against white racist aggression."[27] True, but the question is why.

Serious scholars have yet to provide evidence that can demonstrate that Micheaux acted as a missionary rather than as a clever entrepreneur. At the very least, bell hooks contends, Micheaux's movies "work to transgress boundaries to offer perspectives, different 'takes,' on black experience that can be found/seen in no other cinematic practice during his day."[28] Gaines sees him as a contrast to Griffith, "… the most prolific and the most daring of the early film pioneers."[29]

To further his new career, Micheaux moved first to Chicago and then to New York City, where the real economic power existed. In the process of forming The Micheaux Film and Book Company in 1918, he learned the basics about financing, production, and distribution. Between the appearance of *The Homesteader* (1919) and *The Betrayal* (1948), Micheaux, almost single-handedly, made and distributed over forty films, many of them full-length features (scholars have yet to agree on the actual number). How he succeeded where others failed, what were the major influences on his work, and what were his goals remain unclear. We do know, however, that following the release of *Body and Soul* (1924), the film that introduced Paul Robeson to the movies, Micheaux attempted with mixed results to distribute his race-conscious films in Europe.[30]

Domestically, the aggressive entrepreneur appeared to target his melodramatic films at the limited number of segregated theaters across the country. It was a daring move, considering his willingness to tackle issues that not only had historically separated blacks and whites, but also were deliberately avoided by Hollywood. Why he chose to do so has been the subject of much speculation. Nevertheless, he seemed to benefit from one of the ironies faced by early independent filmmakers in American movie history. "*Because of*, rather than *in spite of*, limited budget and screening opportunities," discerns James Snead, "the adept filmmaker can exploit his or her marginal position to make the kinds of statements and images which go against the prevailing rules and codes."[31] Modern scholars often assume that Micheaux was such a filmmaker, using his writings and movies to shape and articulate a revolutionary black message. Yet Tucker's comments in the following interviews unintentionally reinforce Young's controversial view of Micheaux as a hack writer and opportunist who was "a bit too sentimental for a hard-boiled materialist and too spiritual for an earnest logical positivist...."[32]

It is clear that rather than accept the segregated distribution and exhibition system, the maverick entrepreneur developed a unique door-to-door approach. Micheaux visited nearly every community that housed a race theater or had a movie house that catered to blacks on special nights.

Unlike mainstream filmmakers, the crafty producer always had to fight for the screening of each new production. Exhibitors would be shown still photographs of Micheaux's latest film, doing "socko" business. The glossy stills, as Gary Null notes, "might depict Lorenzo Tucker, his leading black male, embracing a nude woman, or perhaps they would show a Harlem dance review. Micheaux asked the managers to advance him twenty dollars, and he would send them the film. Most of the cinema mangers apparently fell for this technique and advanced him the money. In about a month, Micheaux would have enough money to finance the film."³³

The Oscar Micheaux Book and Film Company employed techniques that reflected its shoestring budgets. It also epitomized the early days of filmmaking, before Hollywood became a major industry and industrialized its production process by a strict division of labor. Micheaux was the ultimate independent artist, the "one-man show." After authoring the script, locating suitable lighting and camera equipment, and casting the picture, he proceeded to his directing chores. Lacking studio facilities, the all-inclusive filmmaker relied heavily on improvisation, using a single cinematographer, shooting his scenes on the streets and areas related to the story or in his New York apartment. Rarely did he rehearse or reshoot a scene.

No one seems to have viewed Micheaux's production process the same way. Why should they? No hard evidence exists that explains his attitudes about narrative construction or technical preferences. For instance, Norman Kagan recalls one way Micheaux operated: "'We're making movies here!' he'd insist when some of his stage professionals argued over his techniques."³⁴ Other critics provide harsher commentaries. "The slap-in-the-face irrationality of many Micheaux fade-outs," J. Hoberman observes, "seems to me indicative of his profound pessimism and understandable mistrust of American justice."³⁵ Grupenhoff sees it differently: "Always working under the limitations of low budgets and time constraints, Micheaux was apparently willing to sacrifice quality for quantity."³⁶ The validity of these declarations about Micheaux's artistic and social intentions is vital to Tucker's posthumous fight with revisionist film historians. At issue is whether Micheaux's concern for socially uplifting messages took precedence over his commercial pursuits, or were they a clever way of drawing audiences to the box office.

Over his thirty-year career, the resourceful Micheaux often surmounted many of the budgetary and social obstacles faced by other independent black filmmakers. However, the economic effects of the Great Depression and Hollywood's switch to all-talking films almost destroyed Micheaux's modus operandi. Again, scant documentation exists to verify just how he survived. Tucker claims that Micheaux always lived well; it was just the films that exhibited economic constraints. But we do know that three years after *Wages of Sin* (1928), he was advertising his latest production, *The Exile* (1931), as a further commitment to making all-black productions, but now, thanks to a 1929 re-financing of his company, the films would be all-talking movies.³⁷ This switch to sound, apparently, had occurred a year earlier with *A Daughter of the Congo* (1930). Whatever the truth, as the thirties wore on, Micheaux allegedly became increasingly "a marginal, if controversial ghetto figure."[38]

Adding to Micheaux's production problems were the attitudes of state and municipal censorship boards, as well as various pressure groups. Even though current research indicates that African-American films rarely encountered "censorship problems because white censorship boards simply never took the time to look at them,"[39] Micheaux's films like *Within Our Gates* (1920), *Body and Soul* (1924), *The Exile* (1931), and *God's Stepchildren* (1938) proved the exception. For example, *Within Our Gates'* depiction of a lynching was so graphic that "a racially-mixed censorship board fought against its Chicago opening."[40] *The Exile* was pulled from release on its opening day in Pittsburgh because "the idea of a Negro beating up a white man and making love to a girl ... was 'too much'... [and] shocked the finer sensibilities of some of the white [censors]," reported the *Pittsburgh Courier*. After "some minor talking parts were deleted," the ban was lifted.[41] And then there were the attacks on *God's Stepchildren*. The film was so controversial, notes Abiola Sinclair, "that fights broke out between light and dark complexioned Blacks."[42] Furthermore, in 1938, the Young Communist League asked that the picture be banned "because it slandered Negroes, holding them up to ridicule, playing light-skinned Negroes against their darker brothers."[43]

As always, there is a difference of opinion about the reasons for the filmmaker's strategy for depicting "color fetishism." Critic J. Hoberman speculates that Micheaux's censorship battles may have arisen from his characteristically brusque social messages.[44] Filmmaker Ken Jacobs, on the other hand, feels that Micheaux's fights with censors resulted from his "own political naiveté" that made his perspective on race problems appear "embarrassing mind-boggling bluntness."[45] And what is one to do with the fact that many of the films were reworkings of the filmmaker's novels, which Young fiercely declares were "unwitting illustrations of how oppressive myths have been forced on Blacks, especially black novelists..."?[46] The possibility also exists that Micheaux was so frustrated by his economic and cultural circumstances that he just enjoyed making a living by venting his anger at unjust social taboos.

Yet, opposition to Micheaux's films was not limited to whites alone. Regardless, he persisted. In doing so, he helped forge a split between the black community and its leaders. As Reid describes, Micheaux's approach did well with the public, but poorly with "black and white critics who wanted to define aesthetic standards."[47] The dichotomy, points out Michael Eric Dyson, has yet to be resolved, with many African-Americans still arguing over how black spokespersons get "anointed."[48] It is an explosive issue in the interviews that follow.

In his last film, *The Betrayal* (1948), Micheaux was still breaking down barriers. As Thomas M. Pryor commented: "Just for the record, and that alone, *The Betrayal*, [is the] first all-Negro motion picture to have a Broadway premiere...."[49] However, by then, no one seemed interested in the tireless filmmaker's work. He may not have been totally ignored by intellectuals, but it is apparent from the evidence available that Oscar Micheaux was not the darling of film societies, scholarly journals, and fan retrospectives. Nowhere does one read that during his life he ever had financial security as a filmmaker, or critical acclaim as an artist. According to Raymond Rohauer, the "majority of his [Micheaux's] films were unpopular with black audiences ... rarely revived, and he died in relative obscurity...."[50] No doubt, he would be both shocked and delighted by the current interest in his work. Certainly, Micheaux was still trying to reverse his fortunes when he died in Charlotte, North Carolina, on April 1, 1951.

While the quality and messages of Micheaux's pioneering works remain problematic, his contribution to film history now appears non-debatable. From Hoberman's perspective, Micheaux's work exhibited "a tenacity unparalleled in American independent cinema."[51] Robert J. Sye insists, "Although some of his films left much to be desired, Micheaux is to be credited for his courage, his sincerity and his success in opening doors for black thespians."[52] hooks considers Micheaux much more than a black man trying to better his race, " ... [because] he refused to accept the notion that black cultural production should simply be a response to white representations of blackness, and thereby only portray blackness in a positive light."[53] Bowser, however, is willing to concede nothing regarding Micheaux's talent. "For years," the archivist and scholar argues, "poor and cheaply produced 16mm reductions added to the perception of Micheaux ... as an inept filmmaker, an evaluation based solely on shoddy prints of his sound films, an evaluation that doesn't hold up when one looks at an exceptionally well-preserved sound title such as *Swing* (1936), or Micheaux's more recently discovered silent films."[54]

But what about the overlooked links between Micheaux and his favorite leading man? Surely, if the films are important, then so are the people who made them. Their memories can add to our understanding of the pictures' worth. Again, only scant documentation exists to help us in that quest. We can begin, however, with the notion that Micheaux hired Tucker as a handsome star to woo beautiful black women in such film melodramas as *Wages of Sin* (1928), *Daughter of the Congo* (1930), *The Exile* (1931), *Veiled Aristocrats* (1932), and *Temptation* (1936).[55] The operative words are "melodramas," "handsome "and "beautiful black women." They highlight the controversial and artificial standards of race and gender representation that contemporary film theorists deconstruct as the basis for their revisionist interpretations of Micheaux's films. Each term helps clarify how the star saw his boss and the process whereby black vaudeville became the nurturing grounds for African-American film history.

Consider why. In simplified terms, Micheaux's contemporaries, as discussed earlier, saw his movies as reveling in melodramatic narratives that offended the sensibilities of spectators tutored by classical Hollywood cinema. The screen stories frequently followed an African-American mistaken for white, or a black person interracially marrying to gain freedoms generally denied to black people. Like the major studios, however, Micheaux knew his audiences favored melodramas that had an upbeat ending. As a consequence, his episodic and sensational plots, relying heavily on far-fetched coincidences, appeared to many Hollywood-conditioned moviegoers before this generation to be silly, far-fetched, sentimental, and sloppy filmmaking. Did Micheaux know that? Did he care? His travels certainly kept him in close contact with exhibitors and spectators, the best source of information on what movies to make next and what needed changing. Tucker's perceptions offer an insider's look at these films and what they meant to the performer. Young's criticisms about Micheaux's seven novels assert that he was and remained a "pulp novelist" throughout his career.

The debate over Micheaux's thematic insistence on racial uplift remains unresolved. The messages were straightforward enough. But the frequency and manner with which Micheaux returned to issues of "passing" and "miscegenation" caused many segments of the black community to accuse him of deplorable stereotyping and racial caricature. That is, Micheaux's perceived preference for light-skinned actors as paradigms for beauty appeared to denigrate racial pride throughout his well-intentioned melodramas, unintentionally giving some spectators the distinct feeling that the lighter the better, the darker the poorer. Certainly that was Young's view of the sources of many of those films. Does Tucker agree? Is that how he perceived his part in the process? What are his reactions to Micheaux's alleged color fetishism?

Then there is the "cultural baggage" that the reader and viewer bring to the debate. Green and Neal, Jr., for example, take issue with this popular misperception of "a color scheme" that pervades the filmmaker's world: "The good characters are portrayed by actors who are light-skinned and have Caucasian features, while the bad characters are played by darker actors with sub-Saharan features." The critics caution Micheaux's detractors that his racial polarization is only a "tendency," not a consistent pattern in the films.[56] Green and Neal, Jr. also observe that those who disapproved of Booker T. Washington (like W.E.B. DuBois) and considered him an "'Uncle Tom' ... are likely to see toms in all of Micheaux's male leads, since they are

Micheaux's embodiments of Booker T. Washington's ideals,"[57] the point being that good intentions do not prevent images and ideas from being misunderstood and interpreted negatively. Moreover, Green and Neal, Jr. raise the question of how much Micheaux's conscious racial stereotypes resulted from his unconscious acceptance of racist values, what Young claims permeates Micheaux's writings. Such distorted representations could also have resulted from a conscious marketing ploy.

Not so, argue the filmmaker's defenders. "Rarely, if ever, did Micheaux," asserts Richard Grupenhoff, "depict members of his race in a negative light. That is not to say that his films lacked negative behavior. Micheaux's films were often melodramatic, and as such presented a world of good versus evil, with its obvious heroes and villains.... Still, while there are negative characters in Micheaux's films, there are no negative stereotypes held up to ridicule."[58] If so, then is there a way to separate the films from the novels; or, if that fails, to explain why Young's judgment is wrong and the defenders' point of view is valid?

The filmmaker was not a naive bystander in these disputes. He even defended himself in an article in 1925, saying that he "always tried to make my photoplays present the truth, to lay before the race a cross section of its own life, to view the colored heart from close range."[59] But how much can we trust the self-promotion of the producer? According to Rhines, "There is no indication that the creation of 'art' was Micheaux's objective.... [His] objective was 'to make a difference.' In fact, Oscar Micheaux was a race man – the title given by *Blacks* to those men who worked to uplift African America as a race."[60]

Such debates exacerbated a black underclass with its "double-consciousness" challenged by escapist films that assured them racial barriers were no obstacle to success if one rejected self-pity and instead worked at solving one's problems. "Though he did not conceive of his work as documentaries, making the camera mirror life," as bell hooks charges, "he did want black folks to see images on the screen that were not stereotypes or caricatures."[61] Did they see them that way? If so, why did he lose his audience so often? In addition, how does one discredit Young's belief that "double-consciousness" dehumanized Micheaux's writings?

Because Micheaux's problematic techniques were not understood or appreciated by everyone, his cinematic solutions to race hatred produced predictable results. Those who bought his ideology saw Micheaux as a far-thinking black activist. Tucker flirts with that position, wanting to have it both ways. But are Tucker's views self-serving? Throughout the interviews that follow, he defends the filmmaker's poor production values and limited budgets as secondary to the ideological and political stands Micheaux made on racial identity. However, Tucker is not always an objective witness. In defending Micheaux, he is also defending *his* black middle-class heritage as played out in the screen melodramas.

From a critical perspective, Pearl Bowser and Louise Spence offer the most generous interpretation of Micheaux's methods and motives. They begin by arguing that his collected works (i.e., personal papers, public pronouncements, novels, and films) "illuminate the degree to which Micheaux used his self-constructed social identity, political point of view, and status as African-American entrepreneur to create, promote, and shape the reception of his works."[62] Their position relies heavily on seeing him as a self-made man who believed strongly in Booker T. Washington's position of self-help. That explains why they believe that Micheaux almost always infused his works, especially those about "passing" and "miscegenation," with messages about blacks taking responsibility for their own lives. They view these efforts at "racial uplift" as serving two additional functions: they helped justify what he did, and they assisted audience identification. This was particularly true, as the interviews reveal, when it came to the thorny issue of color fetishism.

According to Bowser and Spence, critics who attack Micheaux's methods and techniques fail to see the complexity in his approach. Such misguided judges overlook the fact that Micheaux's reliance on race betrayal plots grew out of his shrewdness in reworking the conventions and stories of nineteenth-century sentimental melodrama. Instead of simply using clichéd situations where characters' mistaken identities of characters are predictably resolved, the resourceful self-promoter exploited the narrative revelations to highlight challenges to "social taboos and legal prohibitions against miscegenation."[63] Rather than simplifying individual black aspirations and deceptions, Micheaux sought to illustrate the effects of racism on black people through the depiction of light-skinned African-Americans trying to pass as white and entering into interracial marriages. Often his characters, by internalizing their negative feelings about being black, unconsciously revealed the complexity of self-hatred by not only isolating themselves but by also betraying their race.[64] In other words, the narrative focus is not on passing, but on betrayal. For Micheaux, argue Bowser and Spence, the story did not merely reflect the existence of social taboos, but served instead as an attack on them. His characters become personifications of social and moral ideals instead of psychologically motivated individuals.[65] That is, "by centering the African American experience, he offered a bold critique of American society." Bowser and Spence then add, "To understand the scope and complexity of this critique, we must see it as a political enterprise that both codified the values of the time and attempted to mold them."[66]

Although Tucker lacks the intellectual sophistication of a Bowser or

Spence, his arguments take a similar tack. Moreover, the interviews that follow represent one aspect of a black middle-class defense not only of Micheaux's works, but also of the contributions made by many neo-conservative, African-American show business personalities during the first half of this century. That defense, however, comes at a time in Tucker's life when he was suffering from critical, cultural, and economic isolation.

On the other hand, those who found Micheaux's movies insufferable picture him as an "Uncle Tom." They ridicule the performers, dismiss the filmmaker's techniques, and scoff at his messages. He is seen as no different from other commercial filmmakers, a person interested in making a living off popular films. Thus, Snead charges that Micheaux's ideological and political problems dimmed when compared to his production practices: "The always insufficient financial backing for his projects led to a sloppy, 'single-take' aesthetic, compounded by the often insufficient attention to heavy-handed scripts, badly directed actors, and primitive handling of lighting and camera movement."[67] Null sees him as "a wheeler-dealer" who "used every exploitationary gimmick he could muster to grab the audience."[68] One of the director's contemporaries complains, "Micheaux, in his direction, shows a tendency to drag out scenes as well as pad speeches. Where speed is to be expected, the picture dives into slow tempo, which is ruinous."[69] Green and Neal, Jr. quote numerous sources that disparage Micheaux's penchant for overstating black vices while minimizing black virtues, for his slandering of African-Americans by polarizing them into dark and light categories, and for his mean-spirited stereotyping of black characters. "Micheaux's ridicule," the authors contend, "is often directed at what he perceives to be a lack of business sense and intelligence in black people, shortcomings he presents as racial types."[70]

Although this academic debate occurs long after the interviews in this book, it is essential to understanding how Tucker not only sees himself, but also the history of black show business. Tucker, the light-skinned black actor, is the star of many Micheaux films that feature themes about "passing" and "miscegenation." To the performer, an attack on Micheaux's casting techniques is an attack on his light-skinned stature and values. In one way or another, he links skin color and ideology to the merits of Micheaux's output. To attribute aesthetic purposes to Micheaux's problematic production skills is to go against what the actor experienced making the movies.

Just how valuable is Tucker's personal experience in assessing an artist's motivations? In addition, there is, of course, the old saw about letting the works speak for themselves. Who cares what Tucker says about the films? To appropriate Micheaux's mission in his books and films as a discourse on contemporary black pride that insists on cultural diversity is to assault Tucker's memory of the artist and the times. Tucker was, after all, the leading man in most of Micheaux's feature films. What did he understand about his roles and what they represented? What confidences, if any, did he share with Micheaux? Finally, at the time of these interviews, conventional wisdom looked disdainfully on Micheaux's overall interpretation of African-American society during the first half of the twentieth century. Consequently, Tucker offered his own revisionist analysis of the filmmaker's work, but with an unexpected result. While more observers that are detached had discounted naive links between form, function, and ethnicity, Tucker strongly defended them and the man he believed epitomized an integrated America.

Lorenzo Tucker Interview with Mrs. Julia Garnett Tucker, and Alfred "Slick" Chester
November 6, 1971

Tucker: In browsing through [the *New York Times Book Reviews*], I saw a small article. [It] reads: "Black Performers, I am looking for information, anecdotes, and materials dealing with black performers during the history of American films. Would it be possible to publish this brief letter in your magazine? Thank you for your courtesy, Frank Manchel, Associate Professor, University of Vermont, Burlington, Vermont."

Therefore, I dropped him a postcard stating that I might be of some help to him, because I was the first Negro leading man in Negro films. I say "Negro films" because in those days they were not called "black films." However, we will get to that later.

So, today, the sixth of November, 1971 – two days back – Mr. Manchel called me long distance and asked if he could come and be granted an interview. So I've invited one of my old side-kicks, the "heavy" in most of the films I played in, and also [a member of] the very famous Ida Anderson Players from way back, Albert "Slick" Chester.

Ida Anderson, a talented dramatic actress during the teens and twenties, got her first big break with Anita Bush and the Lafayette Players in 1915. Two years later, she formed her own touring company of Lafayette Players and appeared in many cities along the East Coast and in the Midwest. "Slick" Chester was among the company's regular performers.[71]

Tucker: Now we are waiting for our guest, Mr. Manchel.
[Pause]
And now, ladies and gentlemen, our guest has arrived, Mr. Manchel, and we're going to go on with the interview. Mr. Manchel, it's a pleasure

to meet you.

Manchel: Good thing it's not on videotape!

Tucker: [Laughter] Well, it's on this tape, so it's all right. So carry right on and feel free to ask any questions you feel like.

Manchel: Well, let me start off by mentioning something to you about what I'm trying to do. Then we can go from there and see what we can get from each other. I'm trying to write a book about the history of the black man in American films, starting from the early films with [Thomas] Edison up to the present – 1971, 1972. The book is due at the publisher July, 1972. Most of the information I have is second-hand. Primarily taken from newspaper reports....

Tucker: Just a moment. Could I cut something in?

Manchel: Sure.

Tucker: I hated to stop you on this, but it's all information. Speaking of going back to, say, from the days of Edison. You know, actually the first talking picture should be brought into – which is a later date – with Sissle and Blake.

While Tucker is clearly wrong on what was the first talking picture, he is right about the famous musical team. Noble Sissle and Eubie Blake were two of the most prominent African-American entertainers during the first half of the twentieth century. Their 1921 hit musical, Shuffle Along, *is often credited with starting a black musical renaissance on Broadway. In addition, the team starred in one of the first important sound shorts,* Snappy Tunes, *in 1923. Although they did other musicals and films together, the men also made many important contributions independent of the other. For example, Sampson considers Blake "the dean of ragtime piano players" and the one person over a seventy-year period to most popularize the black musical genre.[72] Sissle is noted not only for appearing with his band in a number of movies during the late thirties and early forties, but also for helping found the Negro Actor's Guild.[73]*

Tucker: We don't want to forget this as we're going up the ladder because they weren't – back in those days – they were old enough as performers, but they weren't in movies.

Tucker is referring here to theatrical feature films. Sissle and Blake did appear in a number of musical shorts.

Tucker: So, I'm sorry, but let's not forget that as we go along.

Manchel: Let's pick up that point.

Tucker: Well, we have a spot that we can use that in later. But I just didn't want it to be forgotten. So carry on.

Manchel: In going over the newspapers and the magazines, and all the people that I meet.... Everyone says that there was no racism; there was no problem with black performers. On the other hand, as a film historian, I've gone through thousands of materials dealing with the history of motion pictures that go back to around 1840 or 1850, but almost nothing exists on black films.

I'm referring here to the pre-history of movies, the time of the inventors and the patents.

Manchel: Nothing exists by way of performers. Nothing exists by way of stills. The only film prints that I've seen of any consequence are in the Library of Congress.

Since 1971, there have been enormous breakthroughs in recovering missing African-American movies, thanks to the efforts of people like Pearl Bowser, executive director and founder of African Diaspora Images/C.E.F.S., an archive documenting the history of black films; Eileen Bowser, Head of Acquisitions at the Museum of Modern Art (MOMA); and the staff at the Library of Congress.[74]

Manchel: Almost all the sound tracks are bad; parts of the prints are destroyed. There's been no money put in. All the information that's been published is inaccurate. By and large – you could write a book that would be garbage – but nothing seems to exist.

Tucker: I'll tell you why some of that is. The Negro – you would almost have to go back and start speaking of the Negro in show business and bring that up to date with the Negro in motion pictures. They didn't feel that he was capable of doing motion pictures until later years. It took a person like Oscar Micheaux to say, "Well, white people are doing this. Why can't Negroes do this?" Yet today, we contradict ourselves on something. We have a certain amount of blacklists going around and they're saying, "Why do we imitate whites?" Well, our advancement in America has been to imitate whites!

Here Tucker is reacting to the negative criticism of his long-since-defunct stock company, Negro Drama Players.

Tucker: I'm sorry I got on to that, but we'll go back. It started out with the Negro in vaudeville; then primarily he was just a dancer and a comedian. I think this talk [gets] ... a little mixed up, but maybe you can sort it out in your writing. [In the telling], we should hear from the performers – like Sissle and Blake and Leigh Whipper – and some of those that were in the beginning of show business.

Leigh Whipper, the great character actor in films like Of Mice and Men *(1937),* Mission to Moscow, *and* The Ox-Bow Incident *(both in 1943), was also the first black artist in Actors Equity and one of the founding members of the Negro Actors Guild.*

Tucker: To start in motion pictures was a great thing for them. They never achieved anything until later years, until – actually a lot of the white companies patterned from Oscar Micheaux's pattern. Micheaux had nothing to deal with in story form, what some of the Negroes are calling today the "caste system."

Although the skin color issue is covered in the introduction, it's worth mentioning Jane Gaines' point, "Before the black pride movement, blacks in the United States might have seen color as a stigma either carried on by and projected onto themselves, or tied up in some way with interracial conflicts.... Class difference within black society was then [1927] analogous to caste difference between races in the United States...."[75]

Tucker: He couldn't have a butler and a rich family among the Negro families unless he used the fair-complexioned Negro as the millionaire and the other indigent-type Negro as the butler and the porter. They rebel against that today, but this was the beginning of them in motion pictures. Today, if you use them all together, it still isn't believable. If you have an all-black film, and you had a black millionaire and a black porter, it just doesn't seem possible. Yet things like that are happening in Haiti. All over. I've traveled all over the various islands and this is happening. In America, it hasn't been accepted yet. There has to be some sort of a difference.

If you recall, in something you were looking at a few minutes ago, I don't refer to pictures back in those days as "black films." I disagree with most of the leaders, the American leaders, on this. About five years ago, every Negro, whether he was a performer, politician, banker, or what have you, was insulted to be called "black." He would fight you. A Negro couldn't call another Negro "black;" he would be insulted. All of a sudden, through politics and a few dollars being circulated around, the Negro leaders have instilled into the Negro population that everything that isn't white is black.

Well, there are more colors than black and white! The spectrum is set up with more than two colors. So why isn't it that our race is acknowledged as having more than one color? You have black Negroes, and you have mulattoes, and whites, and you have all colors.

These films in those days were called "Negro films." We were all Negroes. American Negroes. Until I die, I shall refer to them as "Negro films."

I grant any interview under these circumstances, because I think that in another seven or eight years, the black people, when they find out that they have put themselves into a little niche with nobody to help them, not even Puerto Ricans, light people, or any other color, that they don't have enough people to help them become a predominant race in anything, in business or anything else. Then they're going to be very sorry. Then they're going to want to sue you for writing a book about "black films." I think we ought to stay with "Negro." I'm sorry that I cut in and took up so much time. Carry on.

Manchel: May I call you "Slick"?

Worth noting is the fact that many of Oscar Micheaux's performers often were typecast as black versions of white stars. Chester's image was labeled, "the colored Cagney."[76]

Chester: Yeah, sure!

Tucker: Yes, he doesn't mind.

Chester: What Mr. Tucker is saying is very true. This has got to be a problem now where the light Negro, like ourselves ... having a light Negro ... where are they going in show business? Everything today is black. We have a lot of talented light Negroes, too. What is going to become of the light Negro performer?

None of us in that first meeting ever imagined one of the great ironies of the period: Ron O'Neal lost the role of the no-nonsense private detective in Shaft *(1971) because he was not black black, but somehow got the starring role of the Harlem drug dealer in* Superfly *(1972). The latter film proved to be the most popular and controversial blaxploitation film of them all.*

Manchel: You were always more discriminated against than any other of the black performers – or the Negro performers – over the years because when they wanted to have a Negro, they had to have a real "black" person.

Fredi Washington, one of the stars of Imitation of Life *(1934) – the largest grossing film in black theaters during the 1930s*[77] *– tells of the "mulatto" problem from an African-American woman's perspective. In responding to what Peter Noble meant when he said she had a difficult time getting "straight-forward American roles,"*[78] *the actress in 1972 answered, "Well. That you just didn't get roles unless something very special came along. You know, like a role in* Imitation of Life.

Ok. It's made to order, you see. Unless it was something like this, you didn't get it. I spoke to, who was it – the Hungarian director [Zoltan Korda]. He directed Cry the Beloved Country (1951) – the Broadway musical by Maxwell Anderson and Kurt Weil Lost in the Stars appeared in 1949 and the film version by Daniel Mann in 1974 – it was on the stage. Well, anyway, he sent for me for a role. And when I walked in, he said, "Hmm. I thought I was going to see a Colored girl." "Well," I said, "I am Colored." So he said, "You look like Joan Crawford!" I said, "Well, I don't consider that as any compliment." [Laughter] He said, "Well, you're too intelligent-looking for the role." I said, "Do you really mean what you said?" I said, "Do you think that there are no intelligent-looking or intelligent Colored people?" I said, "There's no point in me talking to you." I said, "You just don't understand anything."[79]

In the video production, Lena Horne: The Lady and Her Music (1982), the legendary star described how MGM executives had Max Factor create a special make-up to put on Ms. Horne's skin to be certain that audiences saw her as "colored." The lotion was called "Light Egyptian."

Manchel: And when there was a part for passing or mulatto, then they gave it to a white person because –
Tucker: That's right! That's right!
Manchel: So you never got a break either way.
Tucker: We had our problems. We had to suffer those problems then, and today I don't see why we have to suffer them today. May I insert this? One of the greatest musical shows that was ever on Broadway – Negro – *Shuffle Along* [1921] and now I'll go back to say *Runnin' Wild* [1923] – they all had a mulatto type of chorus girl. They were beautiful.[80]
Chester: That's right!
Tucker: Today, nothing has exceeded that yet.
Manchel: Does that still exist today, the problem of the mulatto going into show business?
Tucker: Yes!
Chester: Definitely. Definitely.
Tucker: Yes. Well, you notice the commercials on television.
Chester: Every day.
Manchel: The mulatto is still discriminated against?
Tucker: Yes. He's discriminated against now in the profession, more so than the black person was to get started in it.

Tucker's constant use of "He" brings up the issue, raised by scholars like Bowser, about the screen image of black women. In her words, "The unformed or underdeveloped image of black women in film persists, it seems, because we are still preoccupied with getting on with the revolution; and male bias does not rate as high as racism or colonialism at this time."[81] *Walter Burrell describes the problem this way: "It's almost paradoxical, but I've always imagined that if people throughout the world were to judge the sexuality of Black people in the U.S. by the films this country has produced, then from the 20's up to the '60s, they must have thought that Black women were never won; that they were simply* had, *and usually by white men."*[82]

Manchel: In other words, the people who are breaking down the racial barriers are only "black" black performers.

Tucker: Yes, they're only breaking it down to say, "This is the black race." And it is not entirely a black race. It's not a black race!

Manchel: Slick, did you want to say something else?

Chester: Only to that point there. Mr. Tucker said.... As far as Negro performers were concerned, we were on the ground floor, in a way of speaking. I mean, Tucker and myself, he was the first really Negro leading man we had. I came along, and I was typed as I am as a roughneck or a gangster – that type of performer. But today, we have nowhere to go. Mr. Tucker and myself, we're trying to elevate the light Negro. Where are the young light Negroes that have talent? Where are they going today? And the background of these films – you say you don't get a good sound, you don't get a good print from them – so I don't know what your answers would be if you don't dig and get some of these. There must be some around somewhere.

Tucker: Let me get back to this. I know that this part about what we've gone through. Saying, "Where are we going?" That isn't as much the question as saying, "You must have variety."

Chester: Right.

Tucker: And having the thing all black.... I'll tell you the truth, personally, I'm an American Negro. I don't care to look at an all-black show. And I mean that. Why? Because I was a great person for Martin Luther King. I thought that he started a great thing. Integration in the world. All peoples were equal. I was, oh gee, one hundred percent for that. But I got lost in the shuffle. The shuffle is, when Martin Luther King died [1968], everyone started their little black thing. Black hates white. Now white hates black. Now within the same Negro race, black hates light. And light couldn't give a damn about them, because they hate them. So you see, you have – you're heading actually for nowhere.

This debate still rages today. For example, the playwright August Wilson, reports Paul Goldberger, "Denounces society's failure to support all-black theaters, and argues that the values of the black community are compromised if black actors, directors and playwrights can only work within the structure of the mainstream, white-dominated theater." Opposing him in this on-going debate is critic Robert Brunstein, who sees Wilson's position as reminiscent "of the arguments for black separatism that were heard in the 1960s, and that it goes against the American tradition of integration."[83]

Tucker: I do think, and I'm a firm believer in this, that if this sort of thing is written to show [the split] that it will sort of help some [African-Americans]. This is what actually happened back in those days, back when we made those pictures. We did not have that type of hate. We mixed it up. We used it as story form.

Now, the networks have been complaining, well we don't have types of stories for Negroes. Well, they [modern black performers] want to play the same types as the millionaires, as the white guys. If it's believable in a thing, then I'm for it.

Manchel: Right! What difference does it make?

Interestingly, Vincent Canby, the influential film critic of the New York Times, was writing by 1976 that, "By next week, I may be eating my hat, but right now it seems as if more and more films that once would have been categorized as black films are really films for the general market. They are black films that you don't have to be black to respond to favorably, or to find dreary and pretentious, or foolish and inept."[84]

Tucker: It doesn't make any difference. But sometimes, you've got to even things up to make it seem that it is believable. Oscar Micheaux used a lot of things that I, being of a light complexion, my brother was an outcast. This became great story material throughout the country. Well, why? Will he accept his brother? He's passing and so on and so on.

Bowser and Spence make the point that contrary to popular perception, "passing," was neither rare nor routinely rejected by African-Americans during the early 1900s. They offer evidence that nearly a half-million blacks in 1921 America carried on the deception. Moreover, many people, including the press, took the position that "passing as white" was the result of despicable Jim Crow laws; and that those who felt the need to deceive should be more pitied than despised.[85]

Tucker: This has to be faced again because this is happening more today than it ever happened before. The Negro people of my complexion, we are not bothering about this one that is called a "brother." He wants to be called a "brother" when he wants something. We're going on and working. I'm associating myself with white people and working with white people because I understand them better. They don't have the kind of hate that my American Negroes have.

Again, there's a split in the race. When the final thing comes down, who are they going to have to help them? Because I ain't black and neither is the Puerto Rican. They're going to be standing out there saying, "Please help me. I'm black."

I'm sorry. Every now and then I cut in and get on a subject.

Julia Tucker: You get on your soapbox, and no one else can say a word.

Manchel: I'm a little worried about Slick, because his wife isn't feeling well. I don't want to –

Chester: That's all right.

Manchel: Let me ask you some questions about how you started, what your background was – so I can put you in the book as a kind of developed character.

Chester: The way I started into show business, you mean?

Manchel: Where you were born and how you grew up....

Chester: I was born in New York City. I was born in downtown New York City. I was raised in Harlem.

Manchel: Do you remember what year?

Chester: I was born ... 1900.

Manchel: The date?

Chester: February 26th. I was born downtown, and I moved to Harlem in 1911. I went to show business in 1920 as a dancer. I was in vaudeville as a dancer in a show called "The Five Cubanollahs [?]". Then I went into dramatics. With the Ida Anderson Stock Company – I mean the Lafayette Stock Company.

Manchel: Tell me about the Lafayette Stock Company, because Mr. Tucker mentioned that as well.

Chester: Well, I didn't do too many shows with the Lafayette Stock Company. I was quite young. I didn't really get into the depths of it. Just a couple of shows. Then Ida Anderson branched away from it and formed her own group.

Manchel: Now, let me ask you a couple of questions about what it was like when you were young. You were about twenty years of age in 1920.

Chester: That's right.

Manchel: All the material that I've read indicates that black people could not get the same kind of Equity card or union card. There was a special union for blacks. If you joined Equity, you had to pay more money. Is that true?

Tucker: No.

Chester: No. No.

Tucker: In those days, Equity hadn't begun.

Chester: That's true. They hadn't begun in those days.

Manchel: Then what was it? ASCAP [American Society of Composers, Authors & Publishers], or what were the unions? The White Rats? Whatever it was that was in vaudeville?

Tucker: Could I cut in just a moment, please? You're going back now maybe to Pantages Circuit days.

According to Abel Green and Joe Laurie, Jr., a major shift in vaudeville occurred in 1911-1912. The Keith-Albee Circuit had established a monopoly in the East, which angered many performers and producers in show business. Consequently, a number of minor circuits began to grow in importance as the actors and business people flocked to them as an alternative to the highhanded tactics of the Keith-Albee monopoly. One of these smaller, important white groups was the Pantages Circuit, whose stronghold was in the West. Vaudeville continued to flourish into the 1920s, but eventually found its audiences lured away by radio and sound films. By 1928, the Pantages' theaters were taken over by the new Radio-Keith-Orpheum Movie Company, RKO.[86]

Tucker: The Negro – there was a certain circuit that they had: T.O.B.A. And they were called "T.O.B.A. shows." They actually worked for themselves. If I was a comedian and a straight man, we'd own the show. It's like the famous [Henry] Drake and [Ethel] Walker; they had their own show. They had a circuit up and down for years. You had all-Colored theaters to play to.

Manchel: Were there Colored theaters available?

Chester: Yes.

Tucker: They were owned by whites. [John T.] Gibson in Philadelphia owned probably the only – The Gibson, the Dunbar [the old Gibson], and the Standard –

Sampson explains that white producers took an active interest in black shows in the early 1920s, and that their involvement eventually led to the elimination of black entrepreneurs. The most prominent of these white producers were A. E. Lichman and Frank Schiffman. By the end of the decade, John T. Gibson, a black producer much admired by African-American performers, sold his Philadelphia holdings to white producers and left the field.[87]

On a related note, black filmmakers also were having similar problems. For example, a major flu epidemic that spanned the nation drove out a majority of the African-American producers from the industry. Those black filmmakers that remained, reported Variety, fell by the wayside when sound took over in the late 1920s.[88]

Chester: The "81".

Tucker: The "81" in Chicago – I mean, in Atlanta.
Chester: No. That was owned by whites.
Tucker: Yeah.
Manchel: There was the T.O.B.A. And were there theaters in every large city in the country?
Chester: Yes. Philadelphia, Washington, Baltimore, Chicago. Then you went on with the whole Southern circuit. That was all through Atlanta and towns like that. Am I speaking loud enough?
Manchel: Sure.
Chester: Those were the circuits that we had to play. In other words, we had, I'd say about twenty weeks on a circuit.
Manchel: Did you have any discrimination? Could you, for example, go on the Schubert Circuit or onto the [Martin] Beck Circuit?
Chester: Well, I'll tell you. In 1925, I was with a show called "7-11." We were the first Colored show on the American scene in burlesque, if you have heard of that.

The Pittsburgh Courier claimed that this musical revue, run by white producer Jack Goldberg, was a major hit on the black Columbia Circuit.[89]

Manchel: Yes.
Chester: We went.... A man named Jack Goldberg was the manager of the show. We had Howard and Brown was the –
Manchel: Bob Howard was in it?
Chester: No, no. Garland Howard and Mae Brown were the owners of the show. They took it on a burlesque circuit.
Tucker: Could I cut in for just one more second? I want to bear some of these things out. Jack Goldberg was the manager of that show. Who produced it?
Chester: Garland Howard produced it
Tucker: Garland Howard was an adagio dancer. A Negro. And his wife, Brown, was his partner. Jack Goldberg was the manager – Jewish – and became later years, the Jack Goldberg office, and Jack Goldberg produced some pictures, which we will come to later.
Chester: With his brother Bert.
Tucker: With his brother Bert. And Lou. Don't forget Lou.
Chester: They're in California? Or where are they?
Tucker: Florida.
Manchel: They're still living?
Tucker: I don't know. We're going to get to that later.
Chester: Jack is dead. I know Jack is dead.

Jack Goldberg, an important personality in black film history, often teamed with his brothers Bert and Lou, to produce African-American films. Clearly, Jack was the major force, and dubbed by a white journalist, "the Abraham Lincoln of Harlem."[90] Throughout the 1930s and 1940s, the brothers operated a number of independent film companies, including Lincoln Productions, Goldport Productions, International Road shows, Jubilee Pictures, Hollywood Pictures, and Herald Pictures. Just as white producers had cornered black theaters in the twenties, so white producers like the Goldbergs dominated black films in the 1940s.[91] Yet, as Norman Kagan points out, the Goldbergs differed from other white producers: "... they initiated a plan which allowed talented students from Tuskegee, Hampton, and Howard Universities to work and learn at their studios." Moreover, he continues, the Goldbergs paid their employees better than did other white producers: "$100 a week for principals, $60 for supporting actors."[92]

Tucker: Jack is dead. He has done a lot for the Negro in motion pictures and in the theater. I also – well, we'll come to this later. Go ahead.

Manchel: I've got some more questions. There's been some questions about employment practices. If there was a black circuit – a Negro circuit or a Colored circuit – were you paid a different wage scale from the white performers who also traveled the vaudeville circuits?

Chester: I don't think there was too much difference in those days. Of course, I imagine – we played the Pantages Circuit with different acts and things and the money wasn't too much different.

Manchel: How about the business where they used to have contracts where if a white actor was canceled, they got two weeks cut off salary, but a black man was just cut off and stranded?

Tucker: He's speaking of the Keith-Albee Circuit. They used – do you mind if I cut in? I'm sorry. They used – back in those days, they had Buck Dodson, Bill Robinson was Bojangles....

Manchel: Bert Williams?

Tucker: No, Bert was never in vaudeville comedy like that. They – those people – they booked their seasons well in advance. They had a few Negro acts, and I want to be frank with you.... They were what we called "pleasing the Negro audience that sat in the balcony." Every now and then, they had to have a Negro –

Chester: What he's referring to is back on the Keith-Albee Circuit. You had twenty-six weeks. You were booked for twenty-six weeks.

Tucker: And they would move you around –

Chester: I think that's what you were referring to.

Manchel: Yes. About the Negro circuit and – Am I right in saying that they used to call it "Nigger Heaven" because you couldn't let black people sit –

Tucker: Yes. That's right. That was called in a lot of theaters "Buzzard Roost." "Nigger Heaven."

Charlene Regester offers valuable insights on just what segregated theaters might have meant to black audiences during the early part of the twentieth century. From her perspective, "These theatre experiences signify how class differences infiltrated the African-American community and how segregated theatres forced blacks to engage in W.E.B. DuBois' 'double-consciousness', where blacks viewed themselves from the perspective of being both black in America while at the same time adopting the white-socio-economic values and standards unique to American culture."[93]

Manchel: And no black was allowed to sit in the orchestra –
Tucker: No, no, no.
Manchel: And you had to have a separate entranceway to get into the theater?
Tucker: Well, right here, we're in New York City now. I'm at 137 Madison. This is 1971. November. Just about twelve years ago, at 116th Street, RKO, the theater there – it's a church now – RKO ... owned by the Loew's Corporation ... it hasn't been over twelve years ago that Negroes weren't allowed to sit downstairs there.
Manchel: But how can that be?
Tucker: Oh, that can be very easily –
Manchel: I mean so late...?

Douglas Gomery's extensive research indicates that it wasn't until 1965 that blacks were welcome in most "mainstream movie theatres." Prior to that, they experienced "nothing less than total humiliation," especially in the South because of the "Jim Crow" statutes.[94]

Tucker: Yes.
Manchel: Incredible.
Tucker: This has nothing to do with –
Manchel: It has everything to do with it.
Tucker: With the picture business, as I say.
Manchel: Well, it does. I'll try to bring it out later how it does.
Tucker: All right. Carry on.
Manchel: Because the backbone of the theater was very important. Because the relationship between the theater and the movies in the silent era was absolutely interwoven. It just doesn't make sense, a lot of the things that I've heard.
Tucker: Well, I was speaking of the theater owners. The policy of the

thing. The prejudice of it. This has to do with productions. I was trying to differentiate. Well, carry on.

Manchel: The work that you did, if you were successful, could you make it over to the Keith-Albee Circuit? Or did you keep pretty much to–

Chester: If you had a strong act, yes.

Tucker: Everybody was plugging for us.

Chester: Yes, that was the epitome if you could get on the Keith-Albee Circuit. And if you played the Palace, you were really the tops.

Tucker: Buck and Bubbles and a few played there.

John William (Bubbles) Sublet and Ford Washington (Buck) Lee were one of the most famous song-and-dance teams in black theater history. Their greatest success came in performing in the Ziegfeld Follies.

Manchel: Was there much concern, on the part of Buck and Bubbles and Robinson, for Colored people in general? Or did they pretty much cater to white people and turn their back on Colored people?

Chester: They had to go along with the program, I imagine that –

Tucker: That's happening today, right on television. You find that most of the – I keep cutting in – if they played the Keith-Albee Circuit or something, they catered to the people that were putting them on and the audience that they were having. Right now, we have the same thing going. If I got on, I want to be quite frank with you, that's what I would do.

For a wonderful satire on TV black stereotyping, see Robert Downy, Jr.'s Putney Swope *(1969), and Spike Lee's* Bamboozled *(2000), and Reggie Rock Bythewood's* Dancing in September *(2001).*

Manchel: Look out for yourself.

Tucker: Yes. You look out for yourself. If white people were instrumental in buying my program and seeing that I got on and they liked my work, by all means, I'd play to them.

Manchel: What about black people? Or Colored people? What were they doing by way of audience? Was there any kind of movement in a Colored press or circles?

Chester: They had Colored newspapers.

Manchel: Did they make an issue of more black performers? More Colored acts? Go against the segregation? I mean, did anyone care?

Chester: No.

Tucker: No. Nobody cared.

Chester: Nobody.

Tucker: Mr. Micheaux, which we'll get to later, never financed his picture off Negroes. There were white theater managers.... Well, there were theater managers throughout the South that were prejudiced.

Manchel: When you went for a job, or for example, suppose you wanted to work in films, there was a lot of film activity going on in New York here in the early days. Could you get jobs at the studio? They were hiring guys for five dollars a day.

Chester: White films?

Manchel: Yeah. You couldn't get in?

Chester: You could get an extra in them.

Manchel: You could get an extra? But for the most part, you could only get a kind of walk-on part.

Tucker: You wouldn't get that.

Manchel: Why not?

Tucker: Well, Twentieth Century-Fox – I went out ... no! Famous Players, that was Paramount. I went out there, this was in later years, after they made – at that same studio – *The Emperor Jones* [1933] with Paul Robeson, which I sat in the cabaret scene because I had been a leading man in motion pictures.

Tucker has this recollection a mite confused. The independent film was shot at the Astoria Studios on Long Island. DuBose Heyword, who wrote Porgy, *adopted Eugene O'Neill's play to the screen, and Dudley Murphy directed. Novice independent filmmakers John Krimsy and Gifford Cochran headed the production. In one of the first independent black film festivals (1971), the planners stated the fame and importance of the picture went beyond aesthetics, "because it showed the attitudes of both black and white producers, actors, and fans in the 1930s, with due notice of 'racial stereotyping,' which came under attack after Adolph Hitler made 'race' notorious."*[95]

Tucker's recollection relates to a prologue to the main narrative that Heyword had created for the film. In the Harlem cabaret sequence, Tucker and his friend remain in the background for the three days necessary to shoot the scene. Elsewhere, he claims that it was the casting director, not the producer, that gave the extras the work.[96]

Tucker: The producer of this picture said, "Well, we don't have a part for you, but you can work." Lionel Monagas and I worked, and they said, "Keep your back to the camera." So we worked. There were things that were done for us, but it wasn't that you could walk out as extras and sign up and play. No.

It's just what's happening, Mr. Manchel, today. Or Frank, as you prefer to be called. The Negro people are setting up now – they're saying they're black. And nobody but black can walk out. And if they just need a black person, well, they'll hire him. If they don't, then the whole race is left out of the picture....

Now Actors Equity.... I'm a member of Actors Equity, and I have been since 1931. I am a member of Screen Actors Guild, and I have been since 1931 [sic]. I'm paid up to date as of today. We say that you must have the job if you blend in the scene, or if you look like the person. Well, this holds true with the union, but the producer has his idea and the Negro people that are pushing certain people.

Manchel: Doesn't that work against you, though?

Tucker: It does work against you! Yes. Now, I'll give you a clear example. Lawrence Welk put on a Colored performer in his show. Arthur Duncan. Have you seen him? He blends in perfectly with that group of people. Blends in socially, visually, and talent-wise. This is what I'm trying to say.

Manchel: A question I wanted to ask you: "Where did you get the training to appear in films if you couldn't get jobs with movies in the twenties and you...?"

Chester: Well, I guess it just came natural. You take most performers nowadays, I mean. I don't know if you find it this way, but I do; kids go into show business nowadays have to be pushed in a lot of ways. They have no talent. A lot of them have no talent.

Manchel: Yes, they're apprentices.

Chester: That's right. Take years ago: a man went into show business, he had to have some sort of a talent. We didn't have mikes; if you were a singer, you were a singer! Let's face it. You had to throw your voice all over the theater. You didn't have these mikes to help you. If you were an actor, you were a dramatic actor. When I was in the Anderson Stock Company, we'd be doing a show this week, and reading the script for next week. We had to cram all this stuff in our heads. It came naturally to us then. We had no tutoring, no schooling.

Manchel: If you weren't good, you just didn't survive.

Chester: That's all. If you didn't fit in, you didn't survive.

Manchel: What about the life that you had on the stage in the twenties? Were you able, for example, when you went on the road, to be able to find a place to eat? Or to find a place to sleep?

Chester: According to what town you were in.

Manchel: I gather a lot of towns you couldn't stay in the hotels.

Chester: That's right.

Since Tucker is about to mention Fredi Washington, it is worth interjecting her recollections about the out-of-town tryouts for the upcoming Broadway production of Black Boy *in September of 1926. "The Davenport Hotel in*

Stamford, Connecticut," the light-skinned actress explains, "wired New York that they could accommodate the company – the entire company – it was all male at that point. So we came up, and most of the cast got there before I got there, before [Paul] Robeson got there, and they were sitting in the lobby, reading, I suppose, waiting for the rest of the company to come in. I came in, I registered, and as I was about to leave the desk, Robeson came in.... He started to register, and they told him they were sorry but they didn't have any more space.... And Robeson said, "What do you mean you don't have any more space?" [Someone nearby said to the clerk], "You wired that you could accommodate the entire company and this happens to be the star of the play.... You don't have any more, or you just don't intend to accommodate Mr. Robeson?" The situation was resolved by the actor staying at a friend's home.[97]

Tucker: May I cut in? That is true. Fredi Washington, who you saw in this picture with us, was working for Actors Equity for quite some time, a few years back, and I can't remember exactly what year this was –

When I [Tucker] toured with [the 1951-52 Negro Dramatic Guild's all-black production of] *Harvey* with Dooley Wilson [and Butterfly McQueen], we had that [show] on the road for United – Ben Zucker – United Artists. I was manager of that and played in it – Dr. Chumley, myself.

We broke down a lot of places during that time, which I think it was right after the war [WWII]. Around 1945 or something. A lot of the places [hotels we stayed in], I sent in to Actors Equity.... They catalogued it, and there was a book put out on where Negro performers could stay throughout the South and the places that would accept them. Of course, that tied right in, and it was used and helped along the way with the Urban League and with the Civil Rights Movement and with letting people get into hotels. We were some of the first pioneers that broke down – I stayed in some hotels in Texas, and they didn't know what I was. Of course, I turned it in afterwards to Equity that I had stayed there. We wrote them a letter that they had accommodated a Negro in their hotel on such and such a day, and would they please continue. We would put people of reputation and things in their hotels. It wasn't a belligerent type of thing, by any means.

Manchel: I gather that both of you feel that there was no discrimination at all in Screen Actors Guild or Equity in all the years, from 1930 to the present, that you were aware of?

A break occurs here, and when we resumed the conversation, we were talking about The Birth of a Nation *(1915).*

Manchel: What was it really like?
Julia Tucker: Now, you see, I didn't see the picture.
Manchel: No, but you know about what people thought about it.

Julia Tucker: I can only talk about my group of friends. *The Birth of a Nation* was considered racist, they didn't approve of it, and it was picketed.

Manchel: Let me ask you a question about that –

Tucker: Well, *Uncle Tom's Cabin* was about the same –

Manchel: *Uncle Tom's Cabin* was the most popular show from the 1870s or so right up to the present day. There were more stock companies with *Uncle Tom's Cabin* and more films made of *Uncle Tom's Cabin* than most films. But I just saw the Jack Johnson film.

I am talking here mainly about William Cayton's Oscar-nominated documentary, Jack Johnson (1970). *My comments also relate to Martin Ritt's 1970 screen adaptation of Howard Sackler's 1968 Broadway hit,* The Great White Hope, *starring James Earl Jones and Jane Alexander reprising their stage roles as Jack Jefferson (a thinly veiled Jack Johnson) and Ellie Bachman, his white mistress.*

Seen from today's perspective, the conversation seems even more striking, given Jane Gaines's perceptive observations about differences between the failed 1915 attempts to ban The Birth of the Nation *and the successful banning of Micheaux's* Within Our Gates (1919)*: "Whereas protest against a film in this period did not mean that it would be banned (and it might even insure that it drew crowds), the threat of a race riot meant that exhibitors and city officials would cooperate to keep a film off the screen."[98] Gaines also reminds us that Thomas Cripps reported that Oakland exhibitors financed boycotts primarily to gain Griffith's film valuable notoriety.[99]*

Manchel: At the same time that *The Birth of a Nation* was on, there was the thing about the "great white hope" [a term popularized by Jack London]; they wanted someone to kill Johnson. That's when Jess Willard beat him, about a month or two after *The Birth of a Nation* was released. Did any of you ever watch the Jack Johnson films? Did they ever mean anything in your lives? Or did you resent the fact that he was married to white women and hung around with white people? Was that ever a problem at all? Who was it that you were identifying with as you were growing up?

Tucker: He was a champion to me. You were asking me, I guess. He was a great guy. A great champion with white and Colored. As a boy – I had the pleasure, in later years, of meeting with Jack Johnson, personally, when he was at the Flea Circus on Broadway – I guess you did too, Slick.

Chester: Yes, well, you cut me off. I worked with him. I'll tell you about Jack Johnson. Lot of people say he was white-woman-crazy. He wasn't. White women were crazy about him. They're the ones that bothered him. I remember being on the road with him; I seen it many a times. He liked Colored women, if the truth be told about him.

Manchel: Nobody knows that, Slick. There was just a film –

Chester: Even when he was married to white women, why he would still have his Colored women. He liked Colored women. There's no question about it. They say that he chased white women, but that's not true.

For more discussion on Jack Johnson, see the Clarence Muse interview.

Manchel: That's what they say in the [Cayton] film that was just made that I just saw yesterday.

Tucker: A little bit of the show [*The Great White Hope*] that was on Broadway – a Colored woman was the one telling on him because he associated with her. She was trying to let this white woman know that he had been with her. And he had.

Manchel: Well, while you three were growing up – you went to the movies, all of you? Did you ever object – were you ever conscious of the fact that there weren't any Colored people on the screen? Did that make a difference to you at all?

Julia Tucker: I would like to inject this one thing where the white woman and the Colored man is concerned. I think that the white race, and especially the white men, they resent the Negro man. This is why they held them down so long....

Manchel: Absolutely!

Julia Tucker: ... because of their white women.

Manchel: That's the great white fear: that the black man is going to rape your wife or your daughter.

It's worth recalling Pauline Kael's comments made near the time this interview was conducted: "If the freedom of blacks has always involved a sexual threat to white men – who fear their wives and daughters would prefer blacks, and imagine that for blacks freedom means primarily sleeping with white women, and turning them into whores – the black-macho movies have exploited retaliatory black fantasies."[100]

Julia Tucker: That's right. And this should be brought out. It's not always the Colored man after the white woman.

Manchel: Yup, yup. No question.

Julia Tucker: The white woman has given the Colored woman more and more competition than their own.

Manchel: Absolutely!

Julia Tucker: It's always swept under the rug. Every time something comes up, even today, you hear, "He raped her," whether it was a rape case or not. That's the first thing in the white man's mind.

Manchel: The white woman always wanted the black man, and the white man always wanted the black woman too. He never wanted to marry her. He wanted to use her when she was a maid. If she had to work there, she had to "go down" for the white guy in order to keep her job.

Julia Tucker: But he did very well by the Colored woman, because that's how the Colored woman was able to help her own man was through the white man.

Tucker: He did very well by a lot of them. [Laughter] This is why I never intend to let the white race go, because as white as my complexion is, I am sure that some white person "helped" way back down the line in my family.

Chester: We're all bleached out

Tucker: Well, looking at his color, you'd figure.

Manchel: Here's an interesting point, if all of you feel this way. The white producers that made films in the first twenty years claim that the reason they never used Colored performers or made Colored films is because there wasn't any audience. Nobody really cared. They said that Colored people went to the white shows.

As early as 1921, J.A. Jackson complained in Billboard that African-Americans in show business existed in an "economic slavery" that made any hopes of their black-cast and black-produced movies competing successfully against white films hopeless.[101] The critic for Variety made a similar observation a decade later: "The only solution [to the problems of black films] seems to be for the producer of Negro films to forget the drama and go for out and out farce or light comedy."[102] Film producer Ted Toddy repeated the assertion twenty-six years after: "Negro audiences did not care for the heavy emotional dramas. Their choice in film entertainment is the picture which features light comedy, outdoor adventures, musical comedies with an abundance of singing and dancing, and comedy romances."[103]

Interestingly, Mary Boyle reported in 1997 that, "Market research shows blacks go to the movies more than whites. Fifty-two percent of all blacks go to the movies at least once a month, compared with 31 percent of whites and other minorities...."[104]

Tucker: Right.

Manchel: If you made a Colored film, nobody came to the Colored film. They were in to make money. And if you couldn't make money, why make the film?

Tucker: This is why you asked the question just now. We'll go back to it. How did you feel about going to see all-white movies? Well, it was a system. You were born to see that. You see, I'm a graduate of the New York Institute of Photography, and I studied television before that, and we had the coordinating council for the Negro performers create this code of ethics: that anything that is shown on the screen to kids or to a young family is instilled in them, and it grows in them; therefore, if the kids were taught that you should see mixed shows on television, they would believe that when they grow up. We were never taught that because all we saw was white. It was a system.

But, today, now that they're seeing mixed ones, they'll believe these things. I enjoyed seeing them, and I'll tell you the truth, I think right now I just don't feel that I could accept all-Colored dramas, myself as a Negro performer, on television. I like them mixed. I like mixed themes.

Julia Tucker: I'm for integration.

Tucker: I'm for integration. I mean it a hundred percent. I am not all black.

Manchel: Is it true – the point I'm going over and over again, because I want to be very certain of this in the research – Were the white producers justified in not making Colored films because they could not make any money off making Colored films?

Tucker and Chester: Yes.

Tucker: Yes. Because the Negro audiences would not buy them themselves. Today, Frank, they're not buying, the Negroes, Colored shows downtown on Broadway.

Manchel: Right.

Tucker: They're not buying Negro films today. It is not worth a producer's money to make an all-Negro film today.

Julia Tucker: Not all-Negro. May I just say this?

Tucker: Yes. My wife's speaking. The voice of experience.

Julia Tucker: No, I'm not in the field at all. This is just general knowledge. I do feel that some of the pictures that were made, they should have had Colored in the picture.

Manchel: They shouldn't have had people in black face?

Julia Tucker: Forget about the black face. This picture, *The Battle of the Bulge* [1965], I think it was a big scene. It was an all-white scene. I think my husband was in that [battle].

Manchel: They did the same thing in *The Longest Day* [1962].

These two films are all-star studded spectacles about World War II. Not only did Lorenzo Tucker take part in the Normandy invasion, but also he remained in combat until the Allies entered Berlin.[105]

Julia Tucker: Yes. There are several that I have in mind. I don't exactly remember the names. Now Colored [soldiers] should have been given – not all the Colored – but they should have had Colored [soldiers] because Colored [troops] were in it.

Because of the controversy surrounding PBS's broadcast of Liberators: Fighting on Two Fronts in World War II *(1992), Mrs. Tucker's charges raise the issue of evidence concerning Tucker's military service. That is not to deny he saw action in Europe. However, it is necessary to know with what army unit. From my limited information, the U.S. military was a segregated organization during World War II. Initially, both black soldiers and nurses were given special assignments and kept away from white troops. For example, John J. O'Connor writes, "Twelve months after the bombing of Pearl Harbor in 1941, some 500,000 blacks had been inducted into a rigidly segregated army. They were restricted to their own barracks, movies houses and PX's." He goes on to say that black servicemen "were restricted to the minor roles of mess attendants or cooks. Black workers weren't even allowed in the war industries." Interestingly, Sharon Robinson states that it wasn't until January 1945 that "the United States announced that black troops would be allowed to fight on German soil alongside white troops" [10]. As to Tucker's fighting on June 6, 1944, it is possible since Grupenhoff cites Lorenzo's recollections about the night before the battle.*[106] *However, with what unit did Tucker fight? The troops were segregated. African-Americans still were having trouble getting into battle. For example, the all-black 761st Tank Battalion, one of three such groups formed by the army, was stationed in the United States and did not get its combat ready orders until three days after D-Day. Moreover, they did not arrive in France until early October, 1944. There is also the question of memories being less than reliable. For example, it is undeniable that African-American soldiers helped liberate death camps like Buchenwald, Dachau, and Mauthausen. Nevertheless, there is no evidence that these camps were set free by all-black units like the 761st Tank Battalion or the 183rd Engineer Combat Battalion. At the same time, the 761st did play a valuable role in the Battle of the Bulge, yet they are nowhere to be seen in Paramount's* Patton *(1970).*[107]

Manchel: Westerns are the same way. You never saw a Colored man in the West.

Julia Tucker: I just wanted to bring that in.

Chester: So, true to life things.

Lorenzo and Julia Tucker: Yes.

Julia Tucker: You don't owe us anything; that I don't feel. But if you want to tell a story, tell it right, be fair, and give employment.

Manchel: Let me go back to employment because that's the part that we left off before. We were talking about 1920, when you went into vaudeville, and you were on the circuit and all that business. Where did young black people go for entertainment? To vaudeville? To nightclubs? To what?

Chester: What age group are you talking about?

Manchel: We're talking about your age, when you people dated. When

I was young, when we went out, we took a girl out to the movies. We took a girl out for an ice cream soda. We took a girl out to a show or something of that sort. We always tried to imagine that we were Bill Hart or John Wayne. We always identified with the hero on the screen. A Valentino.

Chester: I'll answer that. I may be wrong, but I'll say around twenty, twenty-two, twenty-three years old, we didn't have any – many theaters that we could go to. Unless you sat up in the gallery. So we took a girl on a date; if she were the type of girl who liked dancing, we took her to a nightclub. Or if she wasn't that type, we took her for an ice cream. There weren't too many theaters we could go to, that we could walk right in the front door. We had to go upstairs.

Manchel: So by and large, when you went out, you stayed away from the movies. They weren't your kind of entertainment.

Chester: We went to neighborhood theaters. I mean we went to neighborhood theaters where you go in and they have a regular show. You'd go there once a week. But movies, when I was growing up, I think it was more a middle-age group of entertainment. My mother used to go to the movies every day. I knew where to find my mother every night: it was the movie theater. But just a young person, twenty-two, twenty-three; he's not going to many movies.

According to one source, the black intelligentsia of the 1920s and 1930s dismissed black films "as a waste of good opportunities."[108]

Manchel: The movies over and over again showed Colored people either as servants or as slaves. And nobody objects to that, among Colored people?

Tucker: Because that's what they were. That was the system then. We knew that.

Manchel: You accepted it?

Tucker and Chester: We accepted it. We knew it.

It is worth repeating the point that many serious students of film believe that society has underestimated the damage done by misrepresentation. Valarie Smith points out, "Historically, black directors have considered [mainstream black images validated in The Birth of a Nation*] ... to be negative and, by extension, false representations of African-Americans that threaten the lives and conditions of "real" black people."*[109] *Interestingly, in February 1972, just a couple of months after this interview, the Black Cinema Library-Research Center in Los Angeles was running a black movie festival of the old films and explaining to the public that, "Movies since the beginning have formed stereotypes.... And oddly enough, people tend to accept and believe these stereotypes.... If the young people can be* *helped to see the historical significance of the old pix, they can lend a hand in destroying the black myths and stereotypes, thus causing black film producers, editors and actors to present more realistic movies, plays and TV shows."*[110]

>Manchel: You never got angry about the system?
>Tucker: No!
>Chester: No.
>Manchel: Because you were brainwashed?
>Tucker: You could call it that. Yes, we were brainwashed.

Tavia Nyong'o provides a fascinating perspective on the effects of black stereotypes on white and black audiences, Using examples of the 'products of white imagination' from Uncle Tom's Cabin, The Story of Little Black Sambo, *and* Bamboozled, *she discusses "racial kitsch ... [that] holds our gaze, stops our conversations, and in its demand for attention in spite of itself, is an equal embarrassment."*[111] *Nyong'o explores several oppositional strategies to such repulsive imagery, concluding that we need to find "a way out of scapegoating, and thus, out of bloodletting that accompanies with such monotonous reliability our attempts to regain our innocence."*[112]

>Chester: That sort of thing never crossed our minds.
>Manchel: Who were your favorite stars?
>Chester: In those days? I liked Bronco Billy. I liked the Westerns.
>Manchel: Bill Hart? Tom Mix? Hoot Gibson?
>Chester: Yeah, yeah.
>Manchel: Tell me, Slick, when did you decide to go into motion pictures?
>Chester: Well, I'll tell you. I didn't decide. As I told you, I left the Ida Anderson Stock Company, and Mr. Micheaux at the time was looking for talent. I don't know if I had too much talent, but anyway, that's who I started with. Micheaux. He was picking up talent, and he was looking at young guys, like Mr. Tucker and myself. That's how it happened. It's one of those things you just drift into.
>Manchel: Did you ever try to go to anyone else besides Oscar Micheaux?
>Chester: Well, I made pictures for – you remember Mr. [Clarence] White?
>Tucker: Yes, we'll get to that later.
>Chester: There was a man named Mr. White.... Mr. Goldberg, Jack Goldberg, who made pictures. I knew Jack by working with him in the theater. I worked with him for years with musical comedy shows. To tell you truth, I've been in so many pictures; I don't know what I've been in.

Manchel: Do you remember how much you got paid for making a movie? What your wages were like?

Tucker: You'd probably have that better than we do.

Manchel: I'll find it out.

From what I have discovered, none of the black performers could make a living working from independent films. Tucker, for example, always had to take extra jobs – e.g., house painter, medical assistant – to pay the rent. Moreover, there were no long-term contracts. You were hired on a picture-by-picture basis.

Chester: I will tell you, it wasn't a hell of a lot of money.

Manchel: Did you have a contract to make a number of films?

Chester: No.

Manchel: You worked from film to film?

Chester: We worked day to day.

Manchel: How long did it take to make a film?

Chester: Only a little time. Averaged about a month, didn't it? Just about a month.

Manchel: About a month. Did you get a script, or did you have to ad lib on the set?

Chester: Oh, you got a script.

Manchel: How long did it take you to work on – did you have any rehearsals?

Chester: We had run-overs or run-throughs. As I was telling before, in those days, people that went into show business, they had to have something. You just couldn't waltz into the show – I'm a performer. You had to–

Tucker: They were seasoned.

Chester: When we started show business, you didn't start saying, "I want to be a dramatic actor," or "I want to be a movie star." These kids today that make more than – they walk on and the next thing they know, they're stars. They didn't do that [in the old days]. You went into vaudeville. You had people that took you aside and said,"Can you dance?" "Yeah, I can dance." And you danced.

Manchel: Did you – when you made the films, what kind of directors did you have? Did they help you much? Or did they just roll the camera? For example, someone has said that most black productions, most Colored productions, only had one cameraman because there was just no money to make the film.

Tucker: I said that. Yes, it's true.

Manchel: Only one cameraman? Did you do many retakes?

Chester: Not too many of them.

Manchel: Because you didn't have any money?

Chester: Well, you had a certain amount to work on – budget to work on – you couldn't do too many retakes. They would print out all right. Take Micheaux, he directed most of his pictures, they turned out all right.

Manchel: How much time did they take a day? What time did you start in the morning?

Chester: Oh, we started very early in the morning. Sometimes started around six-thirty, seven o'clock. We'd work all day.

Manchel: Then what would they do for lunch? They had the box lunch. Would you go out to eat?

Chester: We ate sandwiches. You did catch as catch can.

Manchel: Did you work seven days a week? Or did you work five days?

Chester: It was according to what the picture was. How long. What type of picture it was.

Manchel: What about the people you worked with. Did they have to get other jobs when they were working in film? Or could they –

Chester: Most people just stayed with show business. You take rehearsals. We never got paid for rehearsals in those days. You never got paid for rehearsal like you do today. With Equity and these things today, you get paid for rehearsals. You didn't get paid in those days for rehearsals. Sometimes you just had to – you wouldn't be working, but you'd still have to rehearse. I'm talking about theater now.

Manchel: What about films?

Chester: Well, film. You never got paid for rehearsal, but we didn't do too much rehearsing. We read our scripts. We'd run through them. Then we'd start shooting.

Tucker: Right! I'm so glad you asked me because I wanted to insert something in. Mr. Micheaux only hired people that were in the profession.

Manchel: He never took amateurs?

Tucker: Yes. You would come in, and he would tell you then, "Be at my place tomorrow," if you were going to do a scene. He would sit up all night and get all the stuff. He was very clever; MGM and all of them knew about him on the coast. If you ever go out there and ask about him. The old heads of the studios, they wondered how he did it.

He would get every scene, we'll say that Mr. Chester was in, and have all that in one day, which would take six months for the major studios. He would shoot – get everybody in those scenes to come in tomorrow. He'd be there at seven-thirty. No union to control us at that time. This was before the Screen Actors Guild. He'd say, "Mr. Chester, here's your part." He'd read it over there in the corner. "Now we'll take a run-down." In the meantime, the cameras – the lights are being set up, the cameras and so forth. Well, even before we got into studios, the lights were set up. We'd have to have – like in this apartment here – right where we are sitting now – the sunlight transferred through reflectors up into here; and we could line this light up in the bathroom any way we wanted to. That's why the lighting was so poor that you see in some of the films.

Manchel: Yes. Colored films are very bad –

As pointed out earlier, many modern critics reject the notion that aesthetics are synonymous with art. They argue that just the reverse is true. That is, the less emphasis the independents placed on technique, the more room the shoestring producers had for experimentation.

Tucker: Yes. I'll tell you why. You couldn't use electricity and the cameras weren't motorized.

Manchel: You had to crank them.

Tucker: Yes. You're using just the dim sunlight reflected by reflectors. He'd say, "You ready?" Then if the first one was bad, we'd do one retake. Slick and I had a thing that we used to do. Slick – when we finished a scene, it would be like this [laughter]. Slick would smile and when the director would say, "Cut!" We cut. We didn't waste a smile. Not even a grin.

Chester: That's true. That's true. I remember one time – I think he was making *Harlem After Midnight* [1934] at that time. He [Micheaux] wanted to take some shots. In that particular picture, I was supposed to be a stool pigeon. I was supposed to go into this police station to stool on someone, and he [Micheaux] had his camera set up across the street from the police station in the hallway.

Harlem After Midnight, Micheaux's fifteenth picture, had Tucker playing a mobster.

Tucker: Micheaux did a lot of "stealing."

Chester: As the cops were changing shifts, I was going in and they were going out. I go in there and I stay about three or four minutes, and I come back out, and the camera's still grinding. That's how we did –

Tucker: We were chased out of bars....

Chester: We've been run out of cities.

Manchel: He didn't own his own equipment?

Chester: No. But he was a clever man. No question about it.

Tucker: He was a genius.

Manchel: Since you're interested in talking about Micheaux, let me ask you some questions from what I found out. The rumor has it that he started off by going around taking pictures of Mr. Tucker, and then he would travel starting in September. He'd rent a car, and then he'd go to every town in America, every town that he could reach, and show them the pictures of the stars, and he'd say, "This is the film I'm going to make. And if you'll give me money...."

Tucker: Yes. This is my leading man –

Manchel: "... this is what I'll do. Then he would go until about May. September to May. Then he would say he had enough money and come back to New York, and he did his filming almost always in the spring.

Tucker: Right.

Manchel: Then he'd make the film within a month and take it out on the road. Then he'd show the film he made last year and bring the pictures for next year. That's how he survived.

Tucker: That's right.

Manchel: What kind of guy was he? Was he a friendly guy?

Tucker: Oh my goodness, yes. He called me "Big Boy." I used to call him "Doc." We'd get in such heated arguments, you could hear us: "Now, Doc.... He'd say, "Yeah, Big Boy, you know you can't do a thing like that! Now how are you going to...." I'd say, "Doc, so and so...." We used to just carry on –

Manchel: Did he have a plantation dialect?

Tucker: No.

Manchel: Was he a tall man? Short?

Tucker: Tall. I'm six-foot-one. He was six foot-three.

Manchel: Slight? Heavy?

Tucker: He was pigeon-toed, and he walked like this. He wore, in the winter, a long overcoat down to there and a slouch hat.

Chester: You'd see him coming; he'd see us and say, "Hi."

Tucker: He was a great guy. On Seventh Avenue, whenever you saw him, he was just like a – let's see – like a statue, he was so big.

Manchel: And he was always broke, though, I gather.

Tucker: Well, he was broke business-wise.

Chester: Yeah, he was not broke personally.

Tucker: No. Not personally, no. A lot of people, a lot of performers, they used to say, "This guy is worth a million dollars. Why should we work for him for this?" It was always a hassle.

Chester: He'd always pay his people, though.

Tucker: Yes. I had a thing here. I can't find it to save my life. I've been looking for it, but I'm going to say it like this. This was – the picture was playing downtown – *Thousands Cheer* [1943] – with Ethel Waters. I didn't intend to go to Saratoga that year. That was – around '28, '29. Anyhow, I was sort of getting away from working with Micheaux because I was into shows, "MCING" [Master of Ceremonies] at various places....

Tucker is a bit confused here. The 1943 MGM movie, Thousands Cheer, *had a slim plot about an all-star variety show entertaining the troops. Ethel Waters and Lena Horne were among the few blacks directed by George Sidney in the production. Although Tucker had met Micheaux during the spring of 1926, he first appeared in the director's 1927 movie,* A Fool's Errand. *Over the next six years, Tucker would appear in ten more Micheaux movies. It is true, however, that at the time the actor had no idea just how successful his screen career with Micheaux would be. For example, his second film,* When Men Betray, *although completed by the end of the summer in 1927, was not released until two years later. Thus, it is misleading for the actor to say that he "was getting away from working with Micheaux." It is more precise to say Tucker made good on a contract to "MC" for a Saratoga cabaret in the spring of 1928. The gig came to an abrupt end, when Micheaux contacted him to come back for a role in a new production,* Wages of Sin *(1928).*[113]

Chester: He was getting too big for us.

Tucker: I'd gotten too big. So I was working up at Jack's Cabaret, on Congress Street, in Saratoga [Springs, New York]. MCing. At that time, the very famous jockey, Earl Sande, was in our place every night, and we were having drinks together. He never "gave me a race," or anything like that, but he was there.

Anyhow, Micheaux sent me a letter. This is how great a friend we were, and, knowing performers, how – bad luck was on us at that time. He says, "Send me the pawn tickets for your suits in pawn. I will send you a ticket to come on down. We're going to make a picture in two weeks." This is the way –

Chester: Oh, yeah. That's the way he was.

Tucker: I kept that letter, and it was raggedly. Somebody has gotten it from me. I don't know where it is. And it said, "Oscar Micheaux." So, you don't call him back with something like that. I quit the job. This is how much confidence I had. And this was the beginning of the racing season.

I came on down and walked into the office, which was 200 135th Street. So he laughs, "We're glad to see you. Everything in pawn?" I said, "As usual." He used that in those days. Whenever you went on a show – see, we didn't have the union – first thing, you'd tell a producer was, "Look, my rent is due, and all my clothes are in pawn. Tuxedo, everything." "Well, how much does this cost?" Right away, you'd get an advance. That's how you worked.

Chester: That's how you kept your pants.

Manchel: Whatever happened to Oscar Micheaux? I understand he went bankrupt in the silent period and came back in the thirties.

Bowser and Spence state that it was "voluntary bankruptcy," and that "… in late 1929, despite the collapse of the stock market, he reemerged as Micheaux Pictures, and later as Picture Corporation, with some of the films 'presented' by A. (that is, Alice) Burton Russell, his wife."[114]

Tucker: This part – I'll tell you something a little later – on an interview I had with him. I don't know the exact date, but this is before his death. We'll get to that a little later in here. Since you're asking – I don't know if I could find it that quick. You and Slick talk. I don't know if he was bankrupt at that time.

Chester: Did his wife die?

Tucker: That I don't know.

Manchel: She's supposed to be living out in New Jersey, but nobody seems to be able to find her. Slick, a lot of the films – almost all of the films that I read about and seen – always dealt for the most part with three major themes: one with rent parties, one with nightclubs, and one with gamblers. Those seem to be mostly the only kinds of black films, or Colored films, that were made. Why was that?

Chester: Well, I think because the Negro really had nothing to write about.

Julia Tucker: That's right.

Manchel: What about slavery? What about unemployment?

Chester: He was trying to get away from those things.

Tucker: And they're bringing it back now.

Chester: They were trying to get away from those things. What he was trying to do was write about everyday life, which was really going on in those days.

Stephen Fay echoed much of what was being said publicly and privately during this period in an article about the treatment of blacks in films for Commonweal. *One of his conclusions, seconded by many people I talked to in my series of interviews, was that "Who but a Negro can portray a Negro, and who should coach him but a black man, and who should mobilize him but a black screenwriter?"*[115]

Tucker: Slick, would you…? Now, this is dated October 2, 1949. I had just finished Cambridge, School of Radio Broadcasting. I had a disc jockey show for some time. So I went to Mr. Micheaux – I was to build something. I wanted to do a testimonial on him on radio. I didn't continue it – I'll get to that later. This is what he wrote to me: "To Whom It May Concern. This is to certify that I have known Lorenzo Tucker for twenty years, during which time he worked in many pictures that I produced. I've also found him agreeable, trustworthy, and willing at all times to serve, and efficiently.

Any consideration given him will be appreciated by very truly yours, Micheaux Pictures Corporation." This is his headlines: 40 Morningside Avenue, Oscar Micheaux.

Manchel: So he still had a motion picture corporation?

Tucker: Yes. His books were selling, but he was sick with arthritis. He was in a wheelchair in the house. I was so surprised to see him in that condition that his wife told me, she said, you have to wait. And he came out like that. Well, it was the same reunion we always had. He said, "This thing has got me so crippled up – arthritis."

Manchel: Did he ever have much resentment against the motion picture industry for not giving him –

Tucker: None whatsoever. None.

Manchel: None? Did he ever try to get his pictures picked up by the big studios?

Tucker: He always wanted to be Oscar Micheaux Productions. Therefore, he had nothing against them. He did want Negro people to finance and put money in, which they never would, and today they haven't.

Manchel: Well, they're starting now. [James] Baldwin's doing it, and [Sidney] Poitier and [Harry] Belafonte, and Ossie Davis.

Tucker: Well, Belafonte isn't getting it from Negroes. And Baldwin either.

Manchel: I see. Are they getting it from their own money? Or from white people?

Tucker: Their own and white people. They're not getting it all from Negroes.

Manchel: What about – Let me go back to you. When you went into films, were there many other black producing companies – or Colored companies? Could you go from one to...?

Chester: You're talking about stage or...?

Manchel: No. Films now. Were there many people that you could go to to apply for jobs?

Sampson claims that the three major periods of independent black filmmaking occurred during the post-WWI era, just prior to WWII, and following WWII.[116] *Interestingly, of the producers that Tucker and Chester cite, two are black – Oscar Micheaux and Ralph Cooper – and four are white – Ted Toddy and the Goldberg brothers (Jack, Bert, and Lou). Sampson makes no mention of a Clarence White.*

Chester: On film? At that time there was Micheaux. White came in later. I think Jack Goldberg came in in that era, too.

Manchel: Toddy Pictures was around.

As was typical of the white and black independent filmmakers, Ted Toddy constantly established different production companies, e.g., The Dixie National

Pictures (1940), and Toddy Pictures (1941).[117] *Norman Kagan observed, "The works of the Goldberg brothers, Ted Toddy, and other white filmmakers interested in the Negro market at that time were literally producer's films. Micheaux was a black filmmaker who made black films, but would have happily made his own about whites if he could have. The Goldbergs never made movies with white players, and had no urge to do so."*[118]

Manchel: How about the Lincoln Motion Picture Company? That was with Noble and Lincoln Johnson [sic].

Originating in Los Angeles in 1916, The Lincoln Motion Picture Company is the first independent black cinema organization to produce feature films in American movie history. Its major executives included Noble M. and George P. Johnson, Clarence Brooks, and J.T. Smith. Its final production, By Right of Birth, *came out in 1922.*[119]

Tucker: That was on the coast.
Manchel: That was on the coast. You had nothing to do with them?
Chester: No, I did go out to California to make a motion picture. What was the name of that concern? That Ralph Cooper paid the balance for?
Tucker: Yeah, that was a million dollar – that was Toddy – the million-dollar picture.

There is some confusion here. Toddy never released a million-dollar film in California. He did, however, establish a distribution company – Consolidated National Film Exchange – in 1941 to handle films made by Dixie National Pictures and Million Dollar Productions.[120]

Chester: That was definitely – about three –
Tucker: That was in later years. Ralph Cooper –

Ralph Cooper, a popular orchestra leader and song-and-dance man, appeared in both Hollywood movies and black independent films. In addition, he ran a number of independent movie companies including Million Dollar Productions. "Cooper's pictures," explained Clyde Taylor, "boasted slicker production values and more professional acting and casting. They were part of a new era when most 'race' movies were made on the fringes of Hollywood."[121]

Chester: That was later years. I went out there, and it wasn't so hot, and I didn't even bother.
Manchel: Did you ever meet any of the other performers you worked with? Any of the other Colored performers, did they have any stories or experiences that could be helpful in the book? People you had met who

had tried to work on a film, but had gotten the part cut out? Stories, for example, when [Bill "Bojangles"] Robinson did his films with Shirley Temple, he was always doing his solo numbers alone, so that if the Southern distributor didn't want to show it, they could just cut that part out of the film and just put it back together and there was no problem.

Here I am referring to the influence of the Southern box office on Hollywood productions. Performers like Robinson could have his musical numbers (and those he performed with others) cut out of the film and not affect the storyline. Recently, these issues are restaged in Joseph Sargent's made for-TV film Bojangles *(2001). This bland biopic dwells on the struggles between Robinson and studio head Darryl F. Zanuck to change audience perceptions about blacks. For more information on Robinson, see the Clarence Muse and King Vidor interviews.*

Tucker: No. I don't – I don't think that I would like to even mention that if it was [true], because I think it was nice enough of the white film company to have him. I didn't hear of any.

Chester: *Amos 'n' Andy* for radio, I mean, for television.

Tucker: You see, everything was fine. The *Amos 'n' Andy* program was – that was great entertainment. We know most of the performers that did that. Anyhow, we found now that this Urban League, which I'm very grateful for a lot of things that they've done, they came in and this was discarding the Negro image. They ridiculed something like that. Now, they have – they're upholding the Negro leaders in an all-black thing. So, who's mixed up?

Manchel: If you knew that answer, we'd all be wealthy.

Tucker: Well, I'm going to find it out. Believe me when I say it, because it isn't me.

Manchel: Let me ask you to talk about images. The guy who's getting hit from pillar to post now is Lincoln Perry "Stepin" Fetchit. He claims that he was a great asset to Colored people in the thirties because he always presented – even though it was the shuffling and lazy Negro on the screen – he always did it with a tongue in cheek, and Colored people always knew that he was joking. They loved him. He says that people have the wrong image of him.

Singer Alfred Buchanan pointed out that the African-American press at first considered Fetchit an acceptable screen personality, "but it was quickly realized that he was actually doing a great deal more harm than good to the Negro cause."[122] *The controversy over his "Uncle Tom" routines remains to this day. For more information on Stepin Fetchit, see the Clarence Muse interview.*

Tucker: He's right. Now – when Step came here after he had worked – did you see him yet?

Manchel: No, I'm trying to get an interview.

Tucker: I did a small tour with him. The Tidewater district. With the Goldbergs.

Tucker: Well, Step and I didn't get along too well because Step was very –

Manchel: You're on tape now. Do you want this on tape?

Tucker: That's all right. He wanted to do as he –

Chester: He was very – Step was a man –

Tucker: You cut it off?

Manchel: Yeah.

Chester: That's good.

Tucker: Because I was.... He wasn't disciplined. This is why he isn't in movies today. I'm glad you cut it off. I was going to let it go because he might have a chance of hearing it, and it would be very bad.

He – I can go back to tell you when Joe Louis first won the championship. Step was in front of the little gray shop. I'm sitting in his car. He was here. "Tucker! Who's the two greatest Negroes in the world tonight?" I said, "Joe Louis" – he [Fetchit] was doing so well – three Cadillacs and all this and that. It wasn't him in my estimation, but I turned around – "and Stepin Fetchit." You see one of those things. Well, Stepin Fetchit was a great pioneer. You've got to write about him.

Manchel: Oh, yeah. But –

Tucker: But as far as uplifting, you see there's a little difference in this sort of thing we're speaking of. He showed the indigenous Negro. Well, this is him. He exists today, right out here. I don't deny that he doesn't live. Everybody wants to cut him out of the black people, and they want to cut us out too. There's a terrific borderline in there that carries so much study.... He pioneered, he did a lot, and he was entertaining. He got in that shuffle – the *Amos 'n' Andy* bit – and then he did himself a lot of harm too.

Manchel: Why was that?

Tucker: With Gary Cooper and all.

Manchel: I don't know the story at all.

Tucker: Well –

The story that Tucker told me off the tape was that Fetchit was so arrogant that he refused to let Gary Cooper drive his cars.

At this point, we took a break to change tapes. When we resumed, we were talking about Buck and Bubbles.

Chester: Buck and Bubbles. They were not in *Darktown Follies* [1919 and 1921].

Tucker: I know they were not.

Chester: That was way before their time. Nat Nazarro, that was their manager's name. He brought them as kids here. Now, where their original home was, I can't say, but he brought both of them as kids here. He managed them for years. In fact, they had trouble even breaking their contract with him. Nat Nazarro.

Tucker: I remember him.

Chester: As far as these film companies [I am showing Slick a list of film companies] are concerned – I don't recognize but three of them.

Manchel: Which three do you remember?

Tucker: I've got a list that Norman Kagan sent me – quite a few of them were incorrect. They came from such reliable sources. A lot of things, too, are confused with full-length [features] and musical shows.

Tucker is unfair to Kagan who, in 1970-71, was an NYU graduate student working on his doctorate and helping start a re-examination of black film history. For example, in his "Black American Cinema" essay, Kagan had described Micheaux's production techniques more completely than anyone else to date had.[123] *Moreover, many of the things I was questioning Tucker and Chester about were influenced by Kagan's research.*

Chester: Famous Artists. I remember them.

Famous Artists, a black production company active in the late twenties, was one of the companies on my list, obtained from the Kagan article. Noteworthy is the fact that almost no books currently written on black films refers to Famous Artists.

Manchel: What sort of people were they?

Chester: Well, I never did any work for them. I couldn't tell you.

Manchel: Do you know anything about the quality of the films they made?

Chester: No.

Manchel: Micheaux, I gather, was the biggest....

Tucker: He was a genius.

Chester: What was the name of the white boy?

Tucker: Clarence White.

Chester: I mean what was the name of the film production –

Tucker: No. He always wanted me to work for him. He operated out of Long Island. He was a very fair Negro. In fact, he looked white. He was interested in making Negro pictures. None of them ever got beyond Micheaux's achievements. Therefore, they built their work around Micheaux because he was the one who achieved something in film. You can get a lot of these things [information about black films] that makes for good reading, but there isn't much to go on.

Manchel: His specialty [Micheaux's], I want to get this straight now, was to show the Colored man, the Negro, as he was today, and that's why he did the rent parties, the nightclub scenes, and the gamblers....

Tucker: Yes. He wasn't trying to show slavery and all this. Micheaux tried to use a topic of the day – the gambling, the "rent parties" as you say, which they no longer exist, but in those days, they were quite a thing. People had apartments, and they gave a house rent party on a Saturday, and four Saturday nights out of a month, and they had it made. I'll tell you the truth; it's good work now.

Manchel: Who were some of the leading men you worked with? You were the star. You were the heavy, Slick. Who were some of the other people that you worked with?

Tucker: Well, there wasn't any other –

Chester: To tell you the truth, there was only, outside of Tucker, leading men – we had one young fellow who came into the business, but he didn't do too much – Paul Johnson. He was a very handsome boy, but I don't think he made maybe but two pictures. Tucker did most all of the leading man work, back then. There were so few.... In those days you had to be nice-looking ... things like that.

Manchel: Did you have to be light skinned in order to work with Micheaux? Would he take people who were really black?

Chester: Oh no.

Manchel: It made no difference to him?

Chester: As long as you had talent.

Manchel: As long as you had talent. Were there many Colored people who wanted to work in films?

Chester: As I was saying before, he had to have people that were talented. They had to be picked.

Manchel: But you had a lot of people on the circuits?

Chester: Yes. You had a lot of shows, like dramatic companies, where they could pick out people they wanted. They would approach people. Like Lawrence Chenault, and A.B. Comathiere. People like Charlie Olden. These were the people from the leading dramatic companies, the type he wanted.

Lawrence E. Chenault, the leading independent black film star of the silent era, was a highly regarded singer who performed with the most famous African-

American entertainers of the 1920s,[124] *while A.B. Comathiere first gained fame with the Lafayette Players Stock Company and then as a superb character actor in Micheaux films like* The Brute *(1920) and* Deceit *(1921).*[125]

> Manchel: How about the ladies? Do you remember any of the leading ladies in the plays you worked with?
> Chester: Yes. I worked with Ethel Moses, Fredi Washington, and Bee Freeman.
> Tucker: Show him a picture of this thing. We could have had her here [Bee Freeman] for the meeting.
> Manchel: Maybe next time.

*Bee Freeman, who was known as "the Sepia Mae West," [*Underworld *1936] did appear at the second interview, later in this transcription.*

> Manchel: Tell me about each one of those girls. Any interesting stories about what happened with them on the sets?
> Chester: Bee Freeman, she always followed Mae West acts.
> Manchel: The vamp? Bee Freeman was the vamp?
> Chester: Yes. In *Runnin Wild* or *Shuffle Along*, the dark complexioned make-up was experimented with and taken from her – Bee Freeman. You should by all means speak with her. She was also the mother to me as the father in *Anna Lucasta* in Europe.
> Manchel: Who was the other one? Moses?

Ethel Moses, who starred in a number of Micheaux films in the 1930s, began her show business career as a dancer. Working at first with her two sisters, Lucia and Julia, she gained fame performing in many famous nightclubs. Some critics referred to her as "The Negro Harlow."[126] *Among her best-known films are* Temptation *and* Underworld *(both in 1936), and* God's Stepchildren *(1937).*

> Chester: Ethel Moses.
> Manchel: What about her?
> Tucker: I'd like this on here – very beautiful. You'll see her picture. I'd like to have this – just as I'm saying it – I've tried on two occasions to get her for an interview. Haven't I? I've contacted them. I don't know the problem, but she's never shown up. To me, she was one of the grandest little persons. She was, as you might say, the "Ruby Keeler" of today – that we were speaking of today – of Negro films. She was one of my leading ladies.
> Chester: Beautiful girl.
> Tucker: I would be glad to give you any information leading to her

capture. But I have been insulted by contacting her. [Julia Tucker comes back into the room] This is my wife. We've been speaking of Ethel Moses, since it came up. She insulted my home by not coming and by disappointing me in a couple of interviews.

Manchel: Is she ill maybe? Is she old?

Tucker: I don't know. I don't know what the problem is, but I refer her to you and let you know with all honesty that that person is still alive and available through some means.

Manchel: Maybe I can get the low down –

Tucker: I don't know how or why – but we'll work it out.

Manchel: Moses, Freeman, now....

Tucker: This is – you'll see –

Manchel: What are you watching?

Tucker: She's right here – all of her information. I have photographs of her right here.

Manchel: Fredi Washington. What kind of girl was she? What kind of actress?

Chester: Great.

Although Fredi Washington only made three Hollywood films – Imitation of Life *(1934),* Drums of the Jungle *(1935), and* One Mile from Heaven *(1937) – and appeared briefly in a few black independent films, she remains one of the most remembered African-American actresses of her time. Bogle calls her "Iridescent Fredi" and believes that "For black Americans ... [she] was for a time the great black hope."*[127]

The lovely and sensitive actress was born Fredericka Carolyn Washington in Savannah, Georgia, in 1903.[128] *She came to the theater, she claims, by accident. During a brief break in her convent schooling, the star-struck teenager did some singing in New York and quickly decided that "they paid more money in theater than they do in religion."*[129] *So she quit school, returned to Broadway, and applied for a job in Sissle and Blake's long-running Broadway hit* Shuffle Along. *This was about 1923, she explained, when many people who had guts and couldn't dance were having a little trouble finding work in the chorus lines of black musicals. She was right! Fredi Washington soon became one of the twenty-five other wannabes in the show. Shortly after joining the song-and-dance musical, the company went on the road. From that one experience, she eventually formed an act and started playing night clubs like New York's Club Alabam on West 44th Street [sic]. (This might also be the Club Alabam in Los Angeles.)*[130] *A bit of seasoning over the next two years landed her overseas, where she performed in many, but not all, of Europe's "high spots." Bogle claims that she went to Europe after* Black Boy.[131]

When she returned to America in the early part of 1926, she won her first dramatic role in an otherwise all-male play, Black Boy. *The Jim Tully-Frank Dazey drama used a familiar pattern for black plots: the rise and fall of an African-American boxer. But for Washington, it created two milestones: it was the first of two appearances with Paul Robeson (the other would be in* The Emperor Jones*); and it would be the first time she played a woman "passing" for white.*[132]

Contrary to what has been written about her, the light-skinned Washington claims that she never made the stage, or films, a way of life. That was because she felt the work was not steady enough or emotionally satisfying. She was, however, committed to the stage as opposed to the screen. She appeared occasionally in shows, e.g., Singin' the Blues *(1931),* Run Little Chillun' *(1933), and Mamba's Daughter (1938), but never in* Porgy *or* Macbeth*, as is often reported.*

She made even fewer films. In fact, Washington claims that Universal Pictures, the studio that made Imitation of Life*, tried to pressure her into signing a long-term contract, but she refused. They told her that they wanted to make her into a star. In addition, she responded, "Now you may teach me about movies, but the ability I brought with me from Broadway is mine. If you don't mind I had a little chip on my shoulder, too, you know, the things that they have been doing out there – taking advantage. I made up my mind that this would not happen."*[133]

However, her life was noteworthy in other ways. For example, in 1937, she helped found the Negro Actors Guild and served as its secretary. At other times, she wrote a weekly dramatic column for the newspaper, The People's Voice. *Bogle points out that she also did pieces on the problems of African-American actors.*[134]

When she was interviewed by one of my students in 1972, Fredi Washington was living a quiet life (after the recent death of her husband) in Stanford, Connecticut.[135]

Tucker: *Imitation of Light* [1934].
Chester: That was the film.
Tucker: I don't know – see a lot of things went down on file, but it wasn't doing anything, you know, Slick? A lot of these things, these names ain't worth a dime, and they really didn't do anything and nobody heard of them. But, it's nice to mention.
Manchel: Let me put it another way. What were the big films in the twenties? The big Colored films? What were the names – if I can get ahold of things to look for information? What were the big films?
Tucker: In the twenties? Let me see.
Manchel: *Scar of Shame* [1927] and *Ten Nights in a Barroom* [1926] someone said?[136]
Tucker: That's all that was done. There wasn't anything else done.
Manchel: There were no Colored films then?

Tucker: Colored? No.
Manchel: No Colored films at all?
Tucker: Did you say Colored or color?
Manchel: Colored films.
Tucker: No. Other than those, no. *Hearts in Dixie* [1929] was Stepin Fetchit.
Manchel: That was in 1928 [sic]. That was Clarence Muse's first film, I'm told. No?
Chester: Nah. Clarence, he was playing butlers and hackies and cabdrivers and things in pictures ever since he left here and went out to the coast.
Manchel: I'd like to get hold of him – I've written to someone – do you know him?
Chester: He made a few commercials out there.
Manchel: Yes, gas stations.
Tucker: Isn't he around? I heard he was sick. Yeah, he was back here. He wanted me to do a vaudeville thing with him.
Manchel: So we've got Moses, Freeman, who else, Fredi Washington. Anyone else you fellows played with?
Chester: There's others, but they're passed on. Hilda Offley and them kinds of women –

Not much is reported about Hilda Offley's career. One can see her, however, in the 1948 independent black musical Miracle in Harlem, *along with Stepin Fetchit, Sheila Guyse, and Creighton Thompson.*[137]

Tucker: Yes, that's a problem now, there's only about three or four of us left.
Manchel: But I'd like to make certain that I give as many people a place in the book as deserve a place.
Chester: Well, Hilda Offley deserves a place.
Tucker: In any book.
Manchel: Hilda Offley?
Tucker: O-F-L-A-Y [sic].
Manchel: What was her specialty? Was she a...?
Chester: Dramatic.
Manchel: Dramatic actress.
Tucker: I don't have any pictures of Hilda Offley either.
Chester: I have a picture of her at home with Stepin Fetchit and her. Didn't I give you that picture of her laying in a coffin?
Tucker: In a coffin. That was with Jack Goldberg. I've got it here, but you can't see her in the coffin. [Laughter] Are you finished with that that

you were doing? [Tucker is referring to my list of names.] Because there were some things that you were asking about, and I have the answer. I have some of them right here.

Manchel: Let me have the answers.

Tucker: This book is so messed up – I had it in order at one time.

At this point, Lorenzo is pointing to various items in his scrapbook. At other times, he is passing around programs and photographs.

Manchel: While you're looking, you once mentioned something to me –

Tucker: That was in the Amsterdam News. Carry on.

Manchel: You were saying I ought to ask you about the early companies. The black companies. Lafayette....

Thompson offers valuable information on the company that included, in addition to Bishop, actors such as Charles S. Gilpin and Arthur "Dooley" Wilson. "All of those actors went on to have significant theater careers and all but [Carlotta] Freeman played noteworthy roles in the cinema."[138]

Tucker: Oh yes. Before Slick came in, this came up. This is a good question. The Lafayette Stock Company was, in my estimation, the first and the best dramatic company and, say, a thing that exhibited talent, that has ever been in the Negro race. They have never come up to it. The Lafayette Stock Company – Andrew Bishop was one of our great leading men – also we're going back to this color situation.

Mr. Bishop was a light man and blonde, but he was a Negro. Well, parts of that company were light complected Negroes. Let's say the majority of them. And the others were darker. It was integrated within the race. This, I think, is why it was successful.

It toured. We had companies in Chicago. Philadelphia. California. And it went on and on for years and years. Their policy was to play the plays that white people had played on Broadway and bring them to a Negro public. *The Trial of Mary Dugan* – I had the pleasure, myself, of playing the attorney in that. *Madame X*. These things are very, very good. These are dramatic plays. You do not have to be a Negro to play them. You do not have to be any nationality.

The Negro people today have shunned all of these things, and they're playing problem things – where they only find one or two people that are interested in their problems. God knows, I'm not interested in some of the things that they're playing.

But, this made theater. And again you'll say that you asked us earlier, did the Negro appreciate going to the theater and seeing white plays?

Well, let's say *The Trial of Mary Dugan* or *Madame X*. Whether it's written by a white or Colored, it's not a white play or a Colored play – it's an incident. Just whites played it first. So if we can play those things, and go back to things like that, we'll have theater again among Negroes.

I'll tell you the truth. I had quite a tiff with a chap that's producing some documentaries now. I won't call his name. He told me, I'm doing quite well. "Well," I says, "I don't know for how long." He says, "I'm just projecting the Negro in things." I said, "If you just do that, you're limited."

Tucker is talking about William Greaves here. Later, he tries to disguise it, by saying on tape that he is a personable man. He gives himself away, however, by claiming that the two have never met. As for Greaves, the quickest response to the charges is that the Brooklyn Museum's 1992's tribute to him stated: "For nearly half a century, Greaves has been a force in independent filmmaking, a pivotal figure in the history of African-American film, and a tireless chronicler of the African-American experience. The Harlem-born actor-turned-filmmaker played a critical role in black filmmaking in the sixties and, with Black Journal, *pioneered African-American television network journalism."*[139]

Tucker: I think that we should integrate and do plays about people, where we don't have to be involved in all these other things, like prejudice and things like that. And there's so much material going around like that. Of course, some of our best writers are militant writers. This is where another problem is. I'll tell you, I foresee something: that the white man has to write a non-political show for Negroes to be a success. I see that coming. He's the only one that is non-political.

Manchel: Let me ask you. The shows ... or the films, you did for Micheaux, were they all original? Did he write them all himself?

Tucker: Yes. Every one. There was never a play that Mr. Micheaux had done that was written by anyone else. Don't be confused by the fact that he had three or four novels out. One or two or three or four.... He thought that these would be great novels, so he published them.

But he could write a movie. He'd have an idea, Frank, how this movie is going to be about so-and-so. He would start that thing and write three or four scenes tonight and some more the next night. Half his picture wasn't done before it was finished.

And knowing this, I would have to go by the house ... sometimes, and I worked with him a bit. Even after the pictures were out. I told you before; I had quite an interest in filmmaking. (This is why I want to do this movie myself – in 8 millimeter.) I'd edit it. I'd help him edit some of the pictures. We'd have film all over the floor, but he was actually a genius in that. He could roll that stuff so fast by hand, you hardly could keep up with him.

Chester: He was way before his time.

Tucker: He was something that was out of, we might say, out of Mars. The big companies in California, they would say, "How can a man like this do everything and we have a staff of five or six hundred people? And this man did this. And produced a picture."

Manchel: Has this series in *The Amsterdam News* been running long?

Tucker: No. This was on the black arts when they had their fair, and they just did that section on that.

Manchel: Did George Davis ever come to you for anything at all?

I tried, but never located the Davis material in the Amsterdam News.

Tucker: Yes. He was here just before I went on vacation in July, and I asked him if he would come back when I came back from vacation. I think he was from Washington. He said he had to go down there. I didn't hear a thing from him until this was put in the papers.

I also spoke to Mr. Washington. I said, "I have quite a bit of information, and I think some of this stuff should go to the public and should be known." He said to me, I have a friend [William Greaves] on Channel Thirteen or something like that. I said, "Bring your friend up and let's see if we can't get a film documentary or something like that for television. We have got to now start using what we have to get these things done." He said, "I'd be only too happy." And, Frank, that's the last I've heard of him.

Manchel: Yeah. You'd think this fellow, [William] Greaves, who is the producer for *Black Journal*, would want to meet you fellows.

Tucker: Well, Greaves is a gentleman that I don't know. I think I could do it myself. Bill Greaves, yes, but he has his own little thing that he's doing. I would much prefer, may I say, to do a documentary on this myself, since I'm in the business. Why publicize Bill Greaves?

Manchel: It seems to me that – well, we'll talk about it again. But let me just be sure that I get it because we're liable to forget. This Bishop, now, Andrew Bishop?

Tucker: Oh, you're speaking of Andrew Bishop. Well, he was a matinee idol of the Negro race in dramatics. The Lafayette Stock Company and Oscar Micheaux used him in later years. He was working for the city in Cleveland, Ohio. And he used to come in the summer, and Micheaux would always get a picture and have Andrew starring in it. He was quite a guy. Blonde hair, blue eyes, loved by all the Negro people throughout the United States. Here's a photograph of Andrew right here. This is Ethel Moses, right here.

Manchel: She's a beautiful woman.

Tucker: Yes. She was my leading lady in quite a few pictures. This is Fredi Robinson with the team of Flo and Fredi, traveling throughout the United States. Here's a photograph of Andrew Bishop there. And this is Hilda Rogers? This is Fredi Washington. This is a run down, stage and screen, that was in the *Afro-American Newspaper*, August the 21st, 1937.

Manchel: This is the one you have on the wall?

Tucker: Yes. This is when Fredi Washington had just completed *Temptation*. I don't know whether it was for Metro-Goldwyn-Mayer or Fox Studios or what.

Twentieth Century-Fox is the studio and the correct title is One Mile From Heaven *(1937). When Fredi Washington, who played the seamstress in the film, was asked in 1972, what the film was about, she replied, "That was about a widow, a seamstress, she lived alone. Bill Robinson was the policeman, and she was on his beat. I'm trying to think now how she got this job – she adopted this child.... Turned out that the child was white, and when they found this out, they wanted to take the child away from her. I don't remember how it came out" [Washington Interview]. One reason many people have not seen the film may be because the* New York Times' *Thomas Pryor put it in "the hodgepodge of Class C Celluloid."*[140]

Tucker: They were contemplating doing Negro motion pictures, or doing pictures that would be geared to the Negro public. Well, the Negro press got ahold of their ideas, and they publicized a thing like this: "Who would Fredi Washington, at that time, have as her leading man? Well, Ralph Cooper, Saul Johnson, Slick Chester, Lorenzo Tucker, and Jack Carr?"

Manchel: And Lorenzo Tucker got it?

Tucker: No, it never materialized, because they never made any pictures again. You see, the white studios were only interested in a few things that would get them over the – what we called – the "Crumb situation," giving so much to the Negro public; and well, you accept that. This is this and you accept that.

The Negro still didn't get to the point that they should produce ... some pictures of their own and distribute them among the Negro people. And they could've made some money. I have a lot of ideas, even today, how that could've been done. Of course, I didn't have the money to do it. Even after I finished in television, I wanted to work with that in Harlem.

On this interview, you'll get to some of this, too. That I tried for so many years....

Manchel: Was there much competition between you and Slick in the early days for the roles?

Tucker: Well, Slick, myself, Billy Andrews, Perceval Wayne – we were all a certain type of Negro, and if there was one job available down on Broadway, all of us would call each other up and go down, and whichever one got it, we'd come out and shake hands and that was it. We were all friends. Today – sometimes, they'd look at us and they'd say, "We'll hire two." Today, it's quite different. It's a secretive sort of thing.

Getting back to this. This is *Veiled Aristocrats* [1932]. I don't know if you have this on your list. Oscar Micheaux – all talking. We've passed the silent stage. We could go back to it. We're up in talkies now. An all-star Colored cast. This had the great Laura Bowman, which was one of the feature players with the Lafayette Stock Company. She played my mother in a lot of things. She was also the mother when *Anna Lucusta* was put on Broadway. Georgia Burke had the on-stage part, but Laura was the stand-by for the entirety of the show. If you read down the cast of these *Veiled Aristocrats*, you'll see Lawrence Chenault was one of the matinee idols of yesteryear. Walter Fleming, Lorenzo Tucker, Laura Bowman, Jacqueline Lewis. Carl Mahon, who was an Indian type of guy. Here he is here. We had all sorts of people and complexions in our pictures.

Chester: What year was that?

Veiled Aristocrats is important in Tucker's career because it concluded his first series of films with Micheaux. Following a brief stint as an extra in The Emperor Jones *(1933), he became discouraged making a living as an entertainer, married Katherine Godfrey, moved to Long Island, and spent a couple of years working as a house painter.*[141]

It is fascinating to compare Tucker's list of players in the film with those singled out by the Pittsburgh Courier. *While the announcement touts Tucker – whom it calls "the colored John Gilbert of the film" – Bowman, Guy, and Gary – "Broadway's 'charm girl'" – it ignores Lewis, Fleming, and Mahon. Instead, the* Pittsburgh Courier *cites "Katherine Noisette, former beauty contest winner; Pauline Webster, night club dancer; A. B. Comethiere, noted dramatist...."* [142]

Tucker: I will have to go back to that. Willie Lee Gilford. I'll have to go back to that, Slick. I don't know. Here's Mabel Gary, who went to London and starred in musical comedies and became very popular.

Right here on the left you'll see Barrington Guy, who was raised on the campus of Howard University, and dramatics, and Shakespearean roles. Barrington Guy, in later years, became Barry Valentina with Vincent Lopez's orchestra, and he was never known again as Barrington Guy, and he went on to greater things.

This piece that I have right here – I'm terribly sorry that we're doing this in this order – I think that maybe we should....

At this point, we ended the November 6 interview, agreeing to meet again in the near future. Over the next few weeks, I corresponded with Lillian Gish and Clarence Muse. When Lorenzo contacted me at the end of November for a second session on the night of December 4, 1971, I also arranged to meet with Ms. Gish earlier that day. Her interview follows this one.

The night I arrived at Lorenzo Tucker's Harlem apartment, I learned that he had invited a number of people who also had played significant roles in black show business. As the conversations began, the topic of the "mulatto construct" again remained high on the agenda.

Pearl Bowser, Leroy Bowser, Lorenzo Tucker, Bee Freeman, Julia Garnett Tucker, Walter Richardson, and Kenn Freeman. December 4, 1971

Tucker: *Shuffle Along* [1921], Broadway musicals, when the Colored first got on Broadway.

B. Freeman: And they didn't have "blacks" then; they had Colored people.

Manchel: I know! Lorenzo told me already.

Tucker: That's right!

Tucker: She [Bee Freeman] is the person that they patterned the "gold makeup" from.

Manchel: Now the "gold makeup." What do you mean by the "gold makeup"?

Tucker: Because they only had makeup....

B. Freeman: They didn't have any....

Tucker: She would not....

B. Freeman: I would not make up.... What I did, I'd walk on stage practically with street makeup on. Well, it was the first time that they had had Colored showgirls in a show.

Tucker: *Shuffle Along!*

B. Freeman: They had had "bouncers" and "ponies" and things, but not showgirls. I was very sharp really to be a showgirl. All the other girls were talking.... So they put me at the end of the line. And when I came on, I couldn't do anything but wear clothes and walk across the stage. On opening night of *Shuffle Along*, I had twenty-one curtain calls! They were saying.... Nobody knew what to do with me, because I couldn't do anything.... Just walk out. And just by luck, I happened on it. And I walked out with strong street makeup on. And the next day, everyone was talking about the color.

Tucker: [agreeing] Mmn, hmmn....

B. Freeman: They started making up a darker make-up. Not for blacks, because there was no such thing as blacks, this is something new.

Manchel: Right....

Tucker: They used color.

B. Freeman: They made all the Ziegfeld girls use the brown-tinted and the....

Tucker: And this was the beginning of....

Manchel: And they called that "gold make-up"? When was *Shuffle Along*?

B. Freeman: *Shuffle Along* was ...'22 [sic].

Manchel: Twenty-two...?

Tucker: And please, let me insert this in, you don't mind. And then she became from then on the Theda Bara, "the Colored Theda Bara," the vamp, and this is all she ever played until she played the mother, in England, to my father in *Anna Lucasta*.

B. Freeman: And my son made me do that.

Manchel: [laughs] When was that?

B. Freeman: I died every night.

Tucker: 1962 and 1964. Her son directed *Anna Lucasta* in London. And had his own group also. He was the first Negro admitted to a repertory group, an American Negro, in England and played it there with them.

K. Freeman: I played in a thing called *Because I am Black*.

Tucker: And to give you, just a second. I want to give you an aside why he's here. Kenn is, naturally, the son to Ms. Freeman. And Kenn played in two or three pictures. Three films. But he didn't play in the Micheaux pictures. He was with Goldberg. And Bill Greaves, the same guy that is doing documentaries, was in the last one in New York.

Tucker is referring to Miracle in Harlem *(1947), directed by Jack Kemp.*[143]

Manchel: Ms. Freeman, was there much discrimination in the theater against blacks or Coloreds or Negroes in the early days?

B. Freeman: Not really. What we found, when we came back from England [in the mid-sixties] is that the light-colored people had trouble. There was discrimination in this way. I used to go to casting directors ... [who wouldn't hire her because she was light-skinned]. We had ignorant people.... They would say, "We can't have Coloreds." We had also the thing of Negroes being supersensitive, and feeling that they should be in a family situation, which was not true, unless there was a producer that was trying to prove something. Or a producer that was doing [Bernard] Shaw, with an integrated cast.

But I think there was far more theater years ago with Colored players in it than there is today. What you do have is that groups like the NAACP are talking about casting Negroes as maids and.... I always had a feeling – I'm sure – that actresses would rather play the part of being a maid than have to be one. Actresses, if they weren't doing that part, would have to be a maid. Well, the NAACP raised the hue and cry, and then [parts] became very skimpy, because the producers didn't know whether they'd be challenged by the NAACP. And they became very conscious of the Negro in the theater. Slowly things began to bow out. And when it came back, it came back purely as a black thing. Not as a Colored thing.

Tucker: The NAACP did kill Negro show business.

B. Freeman: Oh yes, it did!

Tucker: Definitely!

B. Freeman: Because with "Buddy," they picketed. Can you imagine? The NAACP picketed *Anna Lucasta*.

Manchel: Why? Why did they object to it?

K. Freeman: They were picketing because they had to separate the audiences. The blacks couldn't sit downstairs.

B. Freeman: That was in St. Louis, wasn't it?

Tucker: Try to think, because it's important.

Manchel: You know it's an interesting story. Before I came, I was with Lillian Gish, and we spent about an hour and a half together. And her manager was telling us that there's been a story in *Newsweek* in the last two or three weeks about Eartha Kitt. Who.... Did you know the story about that? Eartha Kitt had made when ... she was at the White House ... obscene comments to Lady Bird Johnson about racial segregation in the country. Well, it seems that *Newsweek* uncovered that Eartha Kitt is now in South Africa, getting some fantastic salary, $1500 or something, and she's playing only to segregated audiences, only to whites. It was wrong in America to do it, but in Africa where no one supposedly knows about it, then she'll play to segregated audiences. So I mean they'll play both sides.[144]

Tucker: She's not a truthful performer. Because if she were, she wouldn't do it there either.

K. Freeman: I didn't approve of what she did.

B. Freeman: I didn't either. I felt that that was absolutely so wrong, but see the thing is this.... I get so tired of our people being "professional blacks," you know. Everything on being black, but then they go in another country – they go to South Africa. I'm surprised that she would even go there.

At this point, with everyone talking at once, Lorenzo tried to distract the conversation and started showing some still photographs from Anna Lucasta.

110   HEROES AND VILLAINS

K. Freeman: *Anna Lucasta* was a big success in Paris, at the Follies Bergere. Why we came back to New York, I don't know.

Kenn is talking about Lorenzo's brief revival of the play in New York's Greenwich Village in 1956. The all-black production also had a short run in the Catskills.[145]

B. Freeman: Black people started selling their color.
Tucker: I'll get you the material, Frank.
Manchel: If you could do that for all these people though, Lorenzo. If I'm going to talk about Kenn, or I'm going to talk about Mrs. Freeman, or I'm going to talk about you.... If I can suggest the kind of roles various people had so that your careers were not a shot in the pan – just one film and then disappeared, or the film didn't go and, therefore, there was no work for you.
Tucker: I'd like to add something else if you don't mind. I hate to keep cutting you off, but I forget these things. Kenn has done quite a bit of research also, and he was interested in doing a book himself on the Negro performer. Kenn probably can give you some information on that.
Manchel: Well as I said to you....
Tucker: [interrupting] Kenn is the historian for the Negro Actor's Guild.
Manchel: Oh really?
K. Freeman: Yeah. That was a thankless job.
B. Freeman: Well, he wanted to build an archive, which the Negro Actors Guild certainly needs.
Tucker: Well, what I wanted to do was to build a photographic archive.
B. Freeman: He's got a copy of something. I bet you there's not another person in the United States – I don't know who's in Britain – who has it. He has an original copy of *In Dahomey*.
Manchel: What was *In Dahomey*?
B. Freeman: *In Dahomey* was a musical comedy of [Bert] Williams and [George] Walker. They played it in Great Britain, and Buddy [Kenn Freeman] picked up this score in Great Britain.

Written in 1902, In Dahomey *is often credited with not only establishing Walker and Williams as major stars, but also being their greatest success.*[146]

Manchel: There's a man whom I'm getting very friendly with. He [Dr. Errol Hill] teaches black theater at Dartmouth. He's chairman of the drama department, and he's very interested in this [research]. And this kind of thing may be very worthwhile for you, Mrs. Freeman; and for you, Kenn. I may be able to set up with Errol, maybe a visit for you to Dartmouth ... to meet with his group. They're putting on lovely kinds of things; and that may be a break. I don't know if that would help you or not. But it certainly would give you some kind....

B. Freeman: Everything helps where we can be exposed and right, instead of somebody speaking for us ... when we can speak for ourselves.

Manchel: That's the point I'm saying.

Tucker: Let me say this, too. There are some people that you'll run across who are willing to help, and they know the need of this thing. And there are others that don't want to help, and they're selfish. I'm going to say this so everyone can hear me. I spoke to Ralph Cooper the other day. I didn't ask him to come here for this interview, but I sort of tapped him because I felt that you had planned to see him. So I said, "Ralph, a lot of things are happening and so and so. (I was surprised to see him. I had heard he was dead, number one.)

B. Freeman: I was so surprised to see him on television, Ralph Cooper.

Tucker: So I said, "Well, I'm glad to hear your voice and so on and so on." And I got his phone number, he's at the State Department, and I'm going to give it to you. He says," No, I'm all right and so on and so on. What's happening?" I said, "Well, there's a gentleman doing an interview now. He's going to do a book, and he wants to initiate black studies in his University and so forth and so on." [He said,] "Well, now, about that, you see, I'm very opposed to anything like that." See, he led right off. I say, "Well, I tell you the truth...."

B. Freeman: [interrupting] What reason did he have?

Tucker: Well he gave me.... I say, "I know just what you're going to say. And I'm with you, but let's talk about it." So he says, "Well, you see people get all this information and then they make the money, and we have nothing." I say, "Ralph, what you have is in the public domain, number one." And I say, "If the public never knows anything about it, it isn't worth a dime to you or to anyone else."

B. Freeman: [interrupting] That's right, All the things he got....

Tucker: I said, "Now, Yes." He says, "Well the thing of it, is I'm capable of doing my own book."

B. Freeman: But he hasn't done it.

Tucker: I said," I am, too!"

B. Freeman: He hasn't done it....

Manchel: Let me tell you....

Tucker: Excuse me, I want to finish. I said, "I am, too.... " It takes more than a notion to do a book. And we know this. And I said, "All the

Negroes, they have dreams of writing. C. Miller is writing a book. Now Irvin C. Miller, I talked to him last night...."

Manchel: Who?

Irvin C. Miller, entertainer, writer, and producer, is best remembered for his annual productions of Brownskin Models, *which tried to do for black women what Ziegfeld's Follies did for white women. The revues began in the twenties and remained popular up to World War II.*[147]

Tucker: Now he knows show business from A to Z. Used to have the *Brownskin Models,* and so and so on. So when I talked to him, this was last year, wasn't it, Joe? He said, "Yeah, I....

B. Freeman: I said I got so mad....

Tucker: He said, "Yeah, I'm going to mention Micheaux. You know, Micheaux was a good businessman. I'm going to mention him in my book."

B. Freeman: Big deal!

Tucker: Yeah.

B. Freeman: But what about Larry?

Tucker: But you see these people write to suit themselves. Now I feel in the information that I am giving you, Frank, and we are giving you, you are not going to write a book about me, you are not going to write a book about me, or Kenn, or Ralph Cooper. You are going to write a book. You see, but these people leave out a lot of people because they want to center themselves.

B. Freeman: But the very funny thing is, they never get anywhere. You see they have the idea, but nothing ever happens.

Tucker: They only hurt the market because it isn't a general thing. I'll give anybody to you that I can, that I think will help to come by and talk.

B. Freeman: It's just like he never existed. And I can't understand this, because Buddy has really hired so many people; and the people that he hasn't hired personally....

B. Freeman: All the mention that Larry has gotten here or in New York – they all have come from white fellas.

B. Freeman: That's right.

Tucker: And that's the side that I'm staying on.

B. Freeman: And Mrs. [Pearl] Bowser is the only Colored one....

Pearl Bowser, at the time the founder of Chambra Films, was just beginning her invaluable work in black film studies. She and her late husband, Leroy, join the discussion shortly.

Tucker: And we had to convert her, my wife and I.

B. Freeman: And I worked her over because they kept coming here, they would research, get here, see what Larry looked like....

Tucker: The minute they'd see my complexion, that was the end of it.

K. Freeman: You see ... and I knew it.

B. Freeman: You know what was a funny thing about that. Kenn did it in Great Britain. This was something; this was the first time this had ever been done. He picked an English – we had some English actors – and he picked a white girl for my understudy in *Anna Lucasta* – and she went on, and she was good, I'm sorry. And he had a Chinese girl play the sister-in-law.

B. Freeman: Well, that should have been very interesting.

Tucker: It was.

B. Freeman: It was ... it was beautiful. Because Buddy has a thing: if you're not family.... And that's the way it's supposed to be done. And if you good at it, and I'm sorry, they were both very, very good.

Tucker: I had the pleasure of him directing me.

B. Freeman: I had the pleasure of him directing me.

Tucker: He is a director, and a damn good one.

B. Freeman: And he had me crying every day.... Every day! Every day I was crying at rehearsal.

Tucker: And he didn't spare her one minute. [Laughing] She used to cry on my shoulder.

B. Freeman: Oh yes! Because I'd never done a mother before.... I'd always played the vamp, and in my mind, I was still the vamp.

Tucker: In your mind, you thought your son... [Laughing].

B. Freeman: No, no, no no! Because, baby, when I get on stage, he's not my son. He's my director, and I call him Mr. Freeman, just like I think every other actor is supposed to do.

Tucker: Well, it's the same thing with me.

B. Freeman: When I'm on stage, I call him Mr. Freeman.

Tucker: I knew him when he was just like this.

At this point, we took a short break. When we returned, we were discussing Leigh Whipper, the great character actor in films like Of Mice and Men *(1937),* Mission to Moscow, *and* The Ox-Bow Incident *(both in 1943), who also became the first black artist in Actors Equity and one of the founding members of the Negro Actors Guild.*

B. Freeman: I think that Leigh, he is very biased towards certain things. And I think it would be great for you to talk to Clarence Muse, because Leigh has done an awful lot in the business, there's no getting away from that. But his scope has never been as great as Clarence Muse's.

Manchel: Do you happen to have a copy of Clarence Muse's pamphlet? He once wrote one on the actors, or on acting, about the prejudice and discrimination...?

Tucker: But he wasn't for all black when the thing....

B. Freeman: Oh yes! Wasn't he the first one who did something in a white face?

Tucker: Yes, He played *Dr. Jekyll and Mr. Hyde* [1929].

B. Freeman: He did it in a white makeup!

Tucker: Yes, and on top of that, Clarence Muse ... Rupert Marks. Rupert Marks was blonde hair and blue eyes and was a Negro, like Marty Holly, and he always had two or three very fair complexion Negroes in all the shows that he had, and he did it right.

B. Freeman: Micheaux did the same thing.

Tucker: Micheaux did the same thing. I certainly, after all my efforts, I would certainly like this to be known and to be said, Frank.

Manchel: Wait, let me get that straight again.

Tucker: Clarence Muse, Rupert Marks, *The Trial of Mary Dugan*.

Manchel: That was based on a Micheaux novel, wasn't it?

Tucker: Yes! Well, they did all of the stock plays, Clarence Muse and the Lafayette Players. They did *Across the Border*, *The Trial of Mary Dugan*, everything that was a stock play. These stock plays have been made over and over in Hollywood – musicals, and all this under different titles....

At this point, the Bowsers arrived, and we took a short break. When we resumed, Pearl Bowser was discussing Oscar Micheaux's Scar of Shame (1927), *and the reaction of a group of students to it. Nearly three decades later, Pearl Bowser refined her thoughts on the controversial film in an important article for* Cinema Journal.[148]

P. Bowser: And there was that kind of reaction. They enjoyed it. I saw that film thirty years ago. It was fantastic. It was a memorable experience from something which they knew nothing about. I mean here, where you're right at the heart of the community, and you don't think in terms of pure entertainment, right, because these films aren't necessarily entertainment....

B. Freeman: Not really, not to the standard that you do today.

P. Bowser: Much more informative, because they were. They happened, and they were a part of history.

Tucker: That's right.

P. Bowser: And to have these young, militant.... One night, we had a group of kids who came to see *Right On* in 1971. They came to see that. Well, but the film never showed up. I mean the guy who made the film; he just did not arrive. There was no money. He didn't think of that particular area as being something he was going to make money at. But that was it. The way in which the kids reacted, once I said, "Well, I'm sorry, I know you came to see *Right On*, but we don't have it, and we've substituted the kind of program." What we did was jazz from the 1940s. I had just finished a program of an old film and a new film. I had the old film; I didn't have the new film. But I had this other, this jazz film, and the program was a huge success. By the end of it, I expected that there was going to be anger because they didn't get what they came to see. It was a film that was billed all over the community as a film to see the last poets, and that's what they came for.

B. Freeman: Well now listen, you spoke about it and this is what I had been meaning to say. Where these children don't realize that Colored people have had maids, and Colored people have lived as whites. They don't understand it, or they just reject the whole thing.

L. Bowser: Well, they understand it. It's more than that. For blacks to deal with some of these issues, a lot of them don't ... especially the course that I used to teach. The emphasis is that during the slavery period, a lot of black people owned slaves. But it goes beyond that. It goes into a sociological, historical perspective of understanding how cultural development took place from not only slavery, but into the 1920s, DuBois, into a period of its existence. So when you examine it from a historical perspective, yes there is a possibility that blacks could own slaves. Yes, there is a possibility that blacks could have mated with whites. Yes, there is a possibility that blacks could be part of an old system that may be alienated to them; but this is there, this is the reality that happened. And you know, the amazing thing about these youths today is that they are dealing with the reality and not the fantasy. See, the fantasy, there was a period in black history when there was, what you would call a fantasy.

I think that if you were to read Arna Bontempts' book; not him, the other one, in – Oh! The one who did a study on Chicago, The two, the one who died last year. Well, that study of Chicago, of the black community, the black metropolis. What was it ... St. Claire?

Leroy Bowser is referring to St. Clair Drake and Horace R. Cayton's two-volume work, Black Metropolis: A Study of Negro Life in a Northern City. *The other reference is to Arna Bontempt's and Jack Conroy's* They Seek a City.

L. Bowser: That study gave you a historical perspective to say that there are changes that took place that ran from fantasy into reality. But more than that, like my students are talking and saying in effect, "Yes, we understand that there was a whole survival question that went on in the

1920s and went on in the 1910s and likewise. Like my parents, how do I survive to make a child that will go on to school? What do I have to take to make my child get an education, and what did my grandmother have to go through, in terms of survival to make it?" These are all steps, and the kids today understand this.

B. Freeman: But I don't think they've been given the whole picture! This is what I mean. Because now, when I was coming up, I was born and brought up in Boston. Many of the Colored people there had servants, and they had white servants; and you know why? Because at that time, that was Irish. They were what you called the "Green Girls." They'd come over from Ireland, and they'd land, and they'd work for anybody. They didn't have a thing about color, because they didn't know anything about color. So, they would go down there and get these girls; and they'd work them for practically nothing, for room and board. These were Colored people. They didn't think about them being Colored people, because they just wanted to work. As they stayed longer....

L. Bowser: You should see some of the stuff that the kids are turning out in Trenton. The kids are turning out some stuff in Trenton [New Jersey], in film that is out of sight. Because they disappear in film, do it. They give them a camera, they say, "Shoot what you see!" These kids have shots and things that are out of sight. I mean twenty, fifteen, you can see them, they're out of sight.

B. Freeman: You know their lives are so open: that's what I mean, they wander, and they're like flowers. And if they were just given the right things, just given things that are not so poisonous.

Tucker: So Militant!

B. Freeman: So Militant! That's it. If they were just given the overall picture as, it honestly is.

L. Bowser: They're not militant. They're not militant.

B. Freeman: They are....

L. Bowser: They're militant in the terms.... You know, we have a press that turns out things that say "militant." But like, look at your life, when you were young, when you were eighteen. You looked at your parents, and you said, "Well, I got to do this and this." I did the same thing, because I looked at my parents, and I said, "You're not doing this... and I've got to do this."

B. Freeman: No, I got to draw the line there, because you did not do the things these kids are doing today.

Richardson: You were spiritually adjusted on that.

B. Freeman: That's right. I cannot....

Richardson: They do not have the spiritual adjustment.... I grew up right around the corner on 137th Street.

B. Freeman: I was brought up in such an entirely different background and I cannot just....

P. Bowser: You have to appreciate the fact that the environment that you grew up in was small, very small.

B. Freeman: That's right! Oh, I appreciate it!

P. Bowser: The masses of black people was very small. And when you're dealing with the greater numbers of blacks that are educated and exposed and are involved. Many more are involved now than....

B. Freeman: Oh, definitely.

P. Bowser: And when I say involved, I'm not talking primarily about politics. I'm just talking about people in the forefront of the theater, of acting, of musicals, whatever it was. And they were there, and they were sort of the middle classes.

B. Freeman: Yes, that's right.

P. Bowser: Upper middle-class.

B. Freeman: But answer me this, Mrs. Bowser. How do these kids come to feel that something is owed to them? They don't have to work for it, they don't want to go to school, they're going to steal and take it 'cause they're owed.

P. Bowser: That's the emotional reaction, and I eradicate that immediately.

B. Freeman: How can you eradicate that?

P. Bowser: My reaction to the present, younger generation is that they have not been given any sense of a history. An involvement that precedes them.

Interestingly, the same issue had surfaced with the release of John Singleton's Rosewood (1997). For example, E.R. Shipp recalled his father and others "stood as fortresses to protect their progeny from the painful, though rich African-American history."[149] Bernard Weintraub confirmed how more than blacks sought to keep secret the murders of a group of blacks in Rosewood, Florida, in 1923. Not until 1982, he pointed out, did the matter begin to emerge in the public consciousness.[150]

Tucker: That is true.

P. Bowser: The militancy that you talk about, that I reject in terms of its terminology, is that it's talking about people who have a sense of the present and no sense of the past. It's what's going on now; it's the excitement in the 1960s and 1970s.

B. Freeman: You know who I blame? I blame your leaders for that. They have opportunities that we did not have....

P. Bowser: No, no, no, it's not opportunities. I mean it's deliberate exclusion in the schools, in terms of history, in terms of involvement of another kind of self and presence, anywhere in an American city which is in the Northeast. So they have a sense of their own well being at the moment, and they are in control. And they will do and they will effectuate. They're not leaning in any other direction, because there's no other direction to lean in.

L. Bowser: Let me give you an example, because I was out in Newark, well, last week.

Tucker: You're saying it wrong.

L. Bowser: No, well 'New-ARK'. [Laughing] [Everybody joins in laughing] I was out in Newark last week. It's a fantastic place where wonderful things are going on. Because the kids have a sense of.... When she talks about a perspective of history, the kids are studying the Marcus Garvey movement of the 1920s, the Harlem Renaissance of the 1920s. Now what children do we know of within the New York City school system that are talking about the New Lafayette Theater, of Claude McKay?

B. Freeman: Well, this is good.

L. Bowser: But this gives them that perspective to say, that there were, even though, they don't know from looking at ... what parents are saying, "Well, my parents were Uncle Tom and so on...."

B. Freeman: Right.

L. Bowser: "My parents fought what they had to fight, in the manner in which they had to fight, in the time in which they had to fight."

P. Bowser: And that's the presence that we have today.

L. Bowser: You see, and that's the presence that they have to continue on because their children are going to have to fight another fight, where they'll look back on their parents; and they'll say to their parents, "Why didn't you do this, and why didn't you do that?" And the black parents will say, "I did do this, and I did do that. I did as much as I could do." So, no longer are the parents put upon. If you watch the Irish, if you watch the Jews, if you watch all the other powerful groups, they treat the older people, they give that historical perspective – that each one of the older generation that fought and tried, they give them respect; and now – this is why the film project is so important – because now children are beginning to say, "Man you're right."

P. Bowser: The thing is that they are not insensitive. I think there's been a denial....

Tucker: This is my argument, Frank. They don't know; they just don't know.

B. Freeman: I don't think my argument is with the children, or about the children. I feel sorry for them. My argument is with the so-called, and I will say "Black" in quotes, because I don't like the term. I don't like the "Black" leaders brainwashing these young people to the fact that they don't have any past. It's not against the children. I feel sorry for them. I don't care what you say, because when it's all over, they still have to go out in the world and make it. And they've got to make it with everybody – black, white, yellow, and red. And they're not being trained for this.

P. Bowser: But you also have a responsibility to this, because you represented something very concrete during the time that you had a presence on stage, and when you were in the forefront. When you talk about being in Boston and representing a tiny segment of the black society, which was just doing one kind of thing, you must appreciate the time that this was happening. You didn't live in a vacuum. You were also part of a massive superstructure of white society over you, which in many instances dictated to you. Maybe that's not the right word.

Tucker: It's alright.

P. Bowser: But it did define, in many ways, where you were going and what you were doing. In terms of the movies, in terms of the newspapers, and in terms of the magazines.

Tucker: It was cut out.

P. Bowser: So when people look back on that whole period, it may not be as you remember it, or as you envision it.

B. Freeman: Or lived it!

P. Bowser: Or lived it! But what they get is a sort of secondhand experience that comes out of the movies, out of the magazines, and out of the written word. So that your responsibility in all this is to be able to appreciate, in your presence and in the time it was happening, what the superstructure was around you, and how it was distorting, much as the superstructure is distorting now....

B. Freeman: You know, I will be quite honest with you. I have no patience with any structure that is built on hate. And this is the whole thing about this black thing that has got me absolutely disgusted. Because – wait just a minute, Lucy – I was brought up among.... I never knew Negroes, really much, until I came to New York. I was a grown woman.... I mean, I was taught to respect people. I still have that, and I resent anybody, any race whether it is Colored, black, whatever you call yourself, Jew, anything. I hate it when you build, when you try to build a structure on the thing of hating other people, because you feel that they have mistreated you. There's not a race in the world that has, at some time, has not been in slavery. So we have certainly, the Colored race, we have certainly had plenty of it. But I think it's time now to teach our young people, yes it happened, it was a bitter thing, it was a terrible thing, but now, because the world is moving too fast for this to put everything in their little pockets. The blacks are being put into little pockets that they have created themselves.

L. Bowser: You have to go beyond your understanding, because hate is not really the essence of what....

B. Freeman: Hate is the essence of life, honey. If you hate, you can only go just so far.

L. Bowser: It's not the essence of life.

B. Freeman: It's the essence of death.

L. Bowser: When you deal with the black community today. Look at the music. If you want to look at something, start to examine the music that has come from the 1920s, when you listen to a Pharoah Sanders ... or listen to a Bessie Smith.... You know, Bessie Smith sang a song. What was it? Yellow...?

Pharoah Sanders, the famous tenor saxophonist, first gained fame in the early 1960s, playing with such legendary artists as Billy Higgins, Don Cherry, and John Coltrane.[151] *According to Gerald Early, battles between new and older tenor saxophonists focused on who was more important to jazz in the sixties.*[152]

P. Bowser: "Yellow Girl"?

L. Bowser: No, no, it wasn't Bessie ... but she sang a song....

Richardson: "Yellow Belly"... 1919, 1920. I worked with her when the Lafayette Theater was first opened.

It's possible that the song is W.C. Handy's "Yellow Dog Blues."

L. Bowser: But she sang a song about ... even the whole "St. Louis Blues" in its tempo, the mood, you get into a Pharoah Sanders today.... The thing about the black community that you will recognize is that there is a dynamity that is taking place all the time. When you get into film, if you take film, you pick a film from the 1920s, what Micheaux did, and you go into, what I consider the extremes of today, of a Melvin Van Peebles' *Sweetback*. Because that I think is.... You're going to have to go a long way before you beat a *Sweetback*.

Melvin Van Peebles' Sweet Sweetback's Baadasssss Song *(1971), in its time the most violent and outspoken attack on white racism, is frequently credited with initiating the so-called "blaxploitation" era of films in the early 1970s. Today, it is considered one of the classics of African-American filmmaking, and Van Peebles has recently re-released it in the prestigious Criterion Laser Disc collection, with a special audio commentary.*

Almost as valuable as the original film is Mario Van Peebles' Baadasssss! *(2003). The director was nearly thirteen years old when he appeared in his father's film, and in this docu-drama on the original movie, he portrays what it was like during the making of* Sweet....

L. Bowser: You've got a thing that says there is a reality, the reality is born of oppression, and we are building a culture that's going to fight that oppression. The youth are recognizing that cultural.... What people give to, what actors give to, everyone gives to it in his own form ... painters. If you examine some of the painters. We have ... we bought....

Well, Nikki Giovanni. Nikki Giovanni took off; she made this record with the New York Community Choir. She made this record with the New York Community Choir, and then she decided to go to Africa.... She went to Africa, and when she came back, she suddenly found out that she had a hit on her hands. A hit to a point, that it took me three weeks to find that record. Three weeks to find that record! But when I examined that record, it was worth the money. Her poetry had changed.

Pearl Bowser confirms that the album that her late husband is referring to is The Truth Is On Its Way *(1971). It contains Giovanni's poetry from her books,* Black Feelings, Black Talk, Black Judgment *and* Recreation. *In her letter to me, Bowser comments, "It was very common during that period [early 1970s] to hear black poets with jazz backup whether it was in a club or on record" (19 Mar. 1997). In addition, Ellis B. Haizlip, producer of WNET-TV's* Soul! *commented on the record's dust jacket, "To try to throw out of the mind all those terrible myths about America, to try to look as clearly as possible, one is still confronted with a whole system of contradictions. A great many of these contradictions are due to the fact that the American people have not yet, by and large, been able to resolve their relationship to the old world (that they fled) or to the new world (that to some degree at least, one may say) they conquered."*

B. Freeman: Oh yes! I imagine that I am very narrow, and I admit that I am very prejudiced about some things – extremely prejudiced about some things, and I am honest about that.

At this point, everyone is talking at once and getting very agitated.

Tucker: I'd like to insert something. This is great!

L. Bowser: We came from here. We came here.... Everything has to be analyzed about where we came from....

B. Freeman: I mean I won't lie about that. I am a prejudiced person – I want things, but nobody has to tell me that I have black blood, but nobody has to tell me that I don't have white blood. And I have white relatives that I respect just as much as I do my black relatives, and I resent people that cannot be whole enough to say, "Yes, I have white blood, I have Colored blood, I have all kinds of bloods." And that's what the American Negro has. Many of them. And we have respect for everybody, have respect for everybody. Have as much respect ... when you look in the mirror, you cannot say that everybody in your whole background....

P. Bowser: Yeah, but that's not what I want to appreciate in terms of....

B. Freeman: I want to appreciate people ... people.

P. Bowser: I don't want to appreciate them. It's such an anomaly to talk about black people and white people because that's meaningless. Not the issue.

B. Freeman: But that's what the blacks are doing!

P. Bowser: No, no, no, no.

B. Freeman: Honey, we hear them everyday! I listen to the radio....

By now, it's hard to understand each other, and so Lorenzo tries to calm things down.

Tucker: I'd like to insert something here. There's a certain amount of them doing that, but Mrs. Bowser is above that ... and I sort of like ... [to go on]. I'm enjoying this immensely.

I beg your pardon now [Laughing]. In terms of *Sweetback* and so forth and so on, they are saying we did our thing and they are doing their thing.

B. Freeman: And I appreciate that!

Julia Tucker: I appreciate this also.

[Everyone is now speaking simultaneously]

L. Bowser: I look to my father ... he [worked] as a subway porter....

B. Freeman: We were not fools....

Richardson: The first time I got married....

B. Freeman: Things have broken down... Politically, you have to watch things. This thing that Nixon is doing ... in his Cabinet ... surrounding himself with ... everything that's happened to the Negro. It's happened just since Nixon ... and it's frightening. I think we're more involved in politics today in our thinking, even if we are not more active. Because we're specialized.

We had a chance to travel, to see things.... I say you don't know anything until you travel, until you get out of this country. You see, we're brainwashed – "America's the greatest country. In the world" – and I went to Great Britain, and found out that they had electric percolator coffee [Laughs] and we didn't have this gadget here. And I began to realize the ... to be honest ... all over the world, people are doing things and this is just a little pocket of the world.

Everyone begins to settle down and start listening to each other.

Richardson: People are prejudiced without a reason.

B. Freeman: That's right!

P. Bowser: As a performer during a certain period of American history, it's much easier to look back and talk from a sense of presence....

B. Freeman: Don't you think we all have to do that if we're honest?

P. Bowser: No, no, no, I'm not saying that. I'm saying that much of our history is written, not from its present stance, but from, in terms of looking back and being able to be more objective....

Tucker: And it must be told honestly!

P. Bowser: It's only objective inasmuch as you're here in 1970, and you're talking about what happened in 1950. You can be more objective and look at it a little bit more removed from the powers that were present and eminent then and you can see a little more. And all I'm trying to say is that the kind of congenial has to happen now with the generations that happen to be so important in terms of black presence. And I know you don't like that term but I want to use it anyway.

B. Freeman: Oh, I don't object to other people using it, don't misunderstand me....

P. Bowser: In terms of our black presence in the '70s, the fact is that here for the first time we have an interest, an audience, and a motivation about a history that has not yet been written.

Manchel: It certainly is.

P. Bowser: We're talking about a whole reinterpretation of history, literally. We're talking about being a lot more objective in 1970 about a history which dates back to 1860, or 1850s, 1700s.... For the first time, as an adult, I read a book about New York, which talked about slavery. I didn't learn anything about that as a child, and my mother certainly knew nothing about that. But what I am saying is that the atmosphere is here for a whole different kind of approach and attitude, and it demands from each of us a kind of objectivity that we're not all prepared to give. It means that we have to look back and be critical about a period that we thought we knew so much about and abstract that and also talk about and with....

Tucker: We can only explain.

B. Freeman: That's right.

P. Bowser: We're talking from the period of the '70s and for them, the important thing is that they ought to know that all this other thing took place, which is suddenly being vomited on the market ... from every area.

B. Freeman: I say this, I quite agree with you. The only thing is I say ... We must all feel as Colored people, that we have our thinking and not feel that all of us have to think the same way.

P. Bowser: No, all I'm begging from you is that we put those kinds of feelings in reserve....

B. Freeman: I can't.

P. Bowser: No, that's the kind of thing, we ask that our emotional reactions to it, we try to be more objective.

B. Freeman: But like you say – don't misunderstand me – I don't want anybody to call me "black," but I do not object to anybody using the term.

Richardson: But I would find it just as hard for me to get a job if I went to a black man in 1971, as it would have been ten years ago. Ten years ago, if I went to a Jew, I could have got the job. Down at the theater, they won't hire me now because of my color. I'm not a Colored man; I'm a black man.

L. Bowser: Let me give you some perspective on what has changed in our whole area. We went to a press conference two weeks ago. Atlantic Records gave a press conference for Max Roach. There was a question of music as to whether or not that music should be, before the introduction of that music, whether or not white musicians should be introduced playing that music. And the response was one of saying that it is our value system, we play the music the way we feel the music is. And it is not our necessity to introduce the music to the white musicians, but rather that the white musicians learn to play the music the way we played music. When we take a camera and shoot a scene, what you see on the screen is your value system. It's a thing you see, when you walk down 135th Street, you see the bars, you see the junkies, you see the people; it's a value system that you have that you're shooting upon, that you film upon. When a famous musician plays a piece of music, he's not playing it based on a white value system; he's playing it on his system, of what he's about. And in the 1920s when people wrote blues, they didn't write blues upon saying whether this is the way Park Avenue would judge the blues. This is the way I feel it! Jazz became a thing, this is the way I feel!

B. Freeman: And that's what we have to do. Whether you feel as the general public, or the general group, as we say today, you have to do it as you feel it. And I think that's the only way we can be honest.

L. Bowser: But your contribution.... See the beautiful thing about the black contribution.... We look back on the '20s and '30s, and we start hearing music, we start seeing films, and we start reading books that were written in the '20s or....

Books! If you go back to reading the books that were written in the 1810s, and you start reading books there, and you suddenly realize that there was a whole cultural system that everybody contributes to....

B. Freeman: You know what I think?

L. Bowser: Martin Delaney did one thing ... DuBois, of all the youngsters that ever existed in our world.... DuBois was a giant ... because he fought.... Marcus Garvey was a giant in the '20s. Nobody else can deny that!

Tucker: The Black King. Marcus Garvey.

B. Freeman: You know what I think was. I think that we were happier then....

At this point, we had to change the tape. When we resumed, the topic switched to current events.

L. Bowser: The Board of Education ... and they said, "You will fly the Liberation Flag." Suddenly all of Newark, the whole New Jersey State Legislature, is saying, "You got to stop this."

Look what happened when in Brooklyn, when we decided in Brooklyn, that we would control the cable TV in Brooklyn. And we entered the first black franchise for cable TV. The state legislature decided that, "Well, we'll put a moratorium on cable TV, mainly because there was a group of blacks who had the first franchise for two and a half million people in Brooklyn." Every step is a struggle.

Readers might appreciate that nearly forty years later this similar conversation took place on NPR's African-American Roundtable *on June 2, 2006. Host Ed Gordon brought up the fact that there was a generational struggle going between a "new generation" and the "Civil Rights generation." In his words, "... we shouldn't romanticize the Civil Rights generation.... We saw this kind of generational shift be contentious even back then [the sixties]. But it is hard for the old guard to sometimes not only give up the spotlight, but see the differences in tactics that the new generation will take." Prof. Nat Irvin agreed with Gordon: "Sometimes an older generation is not able to appreciate how you've got to operate in the new world you live in." He went on to remind his radio audience that "... they sometimes suffer from ... thinking that this current generation doesn't appreciate the sacrifices that others have made on their behalf." Finally, author Yvonne Bynoe put the issue bluntly: "If we [black America] are not comfortable with this new crop, then you have to question what was the struggle supposed to be about?"*[153]

B. Freeman: [interrupting] Yes, but ... this is what I mean....

L. Bowser: And we understand the struggle. The struggle comes politically. The struggle comes musically.

B. Freeman: In everything....

L. Bowser: In film, in acting, writing.... Every step is a struggle.

Tucker: Please, let me insert something in here because I....

Richardson: You're losing ground.

Tucker: I'm losing something. I followed you closely, with all the anti-situations. The Liberation Flag in Newark is incorrect. There should be one flag, and that is the American flag. There is no such thing as putting up a liberation flag in a school in America. And I wouldn't give a good goddamn who says that it's right. This is not right.

B. Freeman: Because if they do it, then....

Tucker: No! It's not right! And this, just a second, just a second, please, I haven't finished. And as far as Newark, this is great. But when you have a community or a city that is run solely as a black community, there is no integration. This is wrong. This is un-American!

L. Bowser: There is an element that you have to understand. We live in a community that is composed of blacks, Puerto Ricans, and Italians.

Richardson: Jews....

L. Bowser: Very few Jews....

Richardson: There's some....

L. Bowser: There's very few Jews. Most of it, Italians. The Italians are Mafioso, no question about it, they control it. The Mafia. The Italian flag flies predominately in this community....

B. Freeman: Over your schools?

L. Bowser: To the point, that if you don't fly it, you will be shot.

B. Freeman: Well honey, we live in Greenwich Village.

L. Bowser: No, I'm talking about.... This is, this is South Brooklyn. This is the Waterfront. If you don't fly the Italian flag, you will be shot, your window will be broken, or a bomb.... So everybody either flies it or.... No, it's not simply a question of being un-American. They're simply saying, "We will fly it."

In Newark, the thing, it's not a question of being un-American. It's a question, and what these young teenagers told me, a whole group of them, it's a value system that they were dealing with.

Richardson: Well, we have a value system, too.

L. Bowser: I'm talking about these seventeen and eighteen year olds....

Tucker: Well, they're not going to run the world....

L. Bowser: They are.... Hold on, let me finish this. They are the generation; they are the generation that we have to look to....

Tucker: We are not going to look to them as running anything yet!

L. Bowser: Twenty years from now, we won't even be looking at them.

Tucker: Well, what are you going to do?

B. Freeman: Twenty years from now, honey, there will be....

Tucker: You won't have a nation if you let them run it.

L. Bowser: Twenty years from now....

P. Bowser: What you're thinking about now is eighteen year olds....

Coincidentally, as I was working on this section of the interview, Newsweek *did a feature story on black families, and authors John Leland and Allison Samuels wrote, "Three decades after the heyday of the civil rights movement, black America is facing a generation gap, similar to the one that divided white America in the '60s."*[154]

L. Bowser: eighteen year olds, they have a value system....

B. Freeman: I'm terribly sorry that you're so wrapped up in one, about these seventeen, eighteen year olds.

L. Bowser: No, no.

Tucker: We can't have them as people that are running the world.

B. Freeman: When they come out. They understand....

L. Bowser: No, no understand....

B. Freeman: Understand what, boy?

L. Bowser: Listen, Listen! But, understand what I'm trying to say.

Richardson: We've got white men getting jobs.

Tucker: I understand. I've listened to you.

L. Bowser: No. I'm trying to point out that the value system that they are now functioning under....

Tucker: America has a value system too.

L. Bowser: No, no, no, I'm just talking about them.

K. Freeman: Integrity, but they gave....

B. Freeman: I'm going to be the mediator here....

L. Bowser: They're in the value system, and they're all turning out ... they are turning out music.

Tucker: They are turning out music, but is it acceptable to everybody?

L. Bowser: In the 1920s, were the blues and the jazz that were made out by the musicians that were doing the *avant-* work ... was that acceptable?

Tucker: Yes, but let me tell you this.

L. Bowser: Was that acceptable? Who accepted it?

Tucker: When it comes down to who's buying. Are they buying this music...?

L. Bowser: When you get into a Pharoah Sanders....

Tucker: We don't know what these people are buying these kids.

L. Bowser: When you get into even the type of music that is being projected today, or the type of film, or the visual work that is being done today by the black youth. The question is "How is that being accepted?"

B. Freeman: Well, it hasn't been to a great extent. I mean, I admit that it's different and it has been accepted, but is it just accepted in a group, or is it an overall picture, where it is being universally accepted as it was, as the composers were, the Negro composers were, say, twenty-five years ago?

L. Bowser: They're dealing with themselves today. And they will be here fifty years from now.

B. Freeman: I hope so....

L. Bowser: All right, they're going to be here fifty years from now. They think they are making the same contributions to what they think is a struggle, that anyone else could make. In their lifetime, they can say, "This is what I feel." Wait a minute, because this is important. In their own lifetime, they're saying this is what I feel. You know, when I was a teenager, and I went out in the street and got myself my first pair of peg pants, my father whipped my head because he didn't think peg pants should be worn in the street. But this was my value.

Tucker: Yeah that was....

L. Bowser: These kids, these kids....

B. Freeman: But you don't look too bad. You haven't done too bad since your father whipped you.

L. Bowser: It's not a matter of him whipping me. I had my value system.

B. Freeman: And you still have it.

L. Bowser: Just as kids today have their value systems.

B. Freeman: I'm glad you said that 'cause you still have your values.

Tucker: I wouldn't put too much on these kids. The value you are putting on isn't doing as much as you think it is doing. You're a teacher; I'm an outsider. I don't see too many results from their thinking.

P. Bowser: The important thing is you're not looking out from the proper perspective. You're taking all your years....

Tucker: All right. Well, this is very great.

P. Bowser: You're going to take all your years of experience and rub it against an eighteen year old who has his presence in this year. And you're denying yourself.

L. Bowser: That's hard to do.

Tucker: The image that you want to say ... The same girl that's married to [John] Lennon, she says that she has a painting at the museum. They say she doesn't have anything made. She says she has it there, it's in the air. Well, this is great. We can all put this just together, just like that. What's her name, Ona, [Yoko Ono] Lennon's wife, the Beatles? Did you see her interview the other night? She has a painting at the museum. In the museum today there's no painting....

[Tape cuts off momentarily]

P. Bowser: It's not displacing.... That's not really the issue. What we're all still talking about – the point I'm trying to make is we're talking about the 1970s, the same thing DuBois were talking about in the 1930s, the same thing as Frederick Douglass was talking about in the late 1800s. We're still talking about racism in America. We are defining it for our presence and ourselves.

B. Freeman: But you know, there's a very funny thing that happened. And I thought, remember when they were having that school thing over in Brooklyn? And remember how that was on TV and remember all the screaming and hollering against the school board, and so forth. Then I saw this forest tailor hassle was going on. Know what was funny to me? Those women that were out on that line, reminded me so much of the black women that were out in the same thinking, the same screaming, the same hollering, and when they turned backs they were all the same shade of.... [Laughter] And I said, "This is the funniest thing!" It brought to mind the thin line there is.

Tucker: I think we have a lovely discussion.

Richardson: I do too. I would like to say....

Tucker: What did you say?

Richardson: I would like to say while things are going like this, the youngest man in the house, eighty-two years old, let me tell you remember this: [singing]:

When you walk through the storm
Keep your head up high
And don't be afraid of the dark.
At the end of the storm, there's a golden star
And a sweet summer breeze of a lark.
Walk on through the wind,
Walk on through the rain
Though your dreams be tossed and torn.
Walk on! Walk on, with faith in your heart
And you'll never walk alone; you'll never walk alone.

[Applause]

Tucker: Still got a voice.

Richardson: Something you go home with, yeah!

Tucker: Just, my wife is fixing a little cracker, you know, with some cheese on it.

Richardson: Hmm, that's good.

Tucker: While she's doing that, Walter, will do for me "Without a Song." [*Carousel*, 1945]. Let's break the monotony.

Richardson: What you mean, monotony?

[Laughter]

L. Bowser: The thing that gets me is every night, I look, I listen, you know, I work very late. And the one song, when I was a kid, I went to Abyssinia, and Abyssinia, you know, lift up your voice and they didn't have....

Richardson: "The Negro Anthem."

L. Bowser: Everybody had to learn it.

Richardson: I was with him two hours before he [Handy] was killed. I know how to advise anybody in the sign of musical business. Mr. Handy, we went hungry all through the west. I was with Bessie Smith. We opened the Lafayette Theater. We were doing *a cappella* songs and so on. I used to black up and dress, I would always dress you know, you know that. And I, my comedian, he was an English fella, traveling the world, but I just came out of the First World War. And they put up a loud speaker. You could hear Bessie Smith from the theater on 132nd street up 'til 140th street. That's how big a voice ... And we needed that sort of thing for her. Bessie Smith....

P. Bowser: Did you see her in *St. Louis Blues*? Did you see her on film?

Richardson: That's what she was singing on these loud speakers, "St. Louis Blues." W.C. Handy. Harry Bradford was there, her agent.

Tucker: She said, "Did you see her on film?"

Richardson: Oh no, no, no, no.

L. Bowser: Oh, you missed it.

P. Bowser: Somehow or other, we've got to arrange it for you to see that film.

Tucker: But you saw her.

B. Freeman: Tell me, did you get much response?

Tucker: The night of the program you didn't see Bessie...?

Richardson: Oh yes! Yes, yes. I went to Florida that same night. I went to Florida that same night and....

Tucker: What year is it?

Richardson: Fred O'Neal. And his wife called him, and she saw it also.

P. Bowser: I'd like to screen it for you.

B. Freeman: I'd like to speak for a moment....

L. Bowser: Fred O'Neal saw it?

Tucker: Fred O'Neal's wife, he was in Washington, she called him from New York.

L. Bowser: But Fred was in Florida!

Richardson: No, Fred was in Florida with us, because we had dinner together at my brother's house.

Tucker: He was in Washington the day before and then, because he told me.

Richardson: We were there, we were there at the convention, and I left there at 8:00 in the morning.

Tucker: It hasn't gone unnoticed.

P. Bowser: Before the film is vaulted to the closet of broken movies, I want you to see on a personal level – I'd like to screen it for you to see.

Richardson: I can't, I didn't hear you....

P. Bowser: I'd like to screen the film, for you, personally, to see.

Richardson: Anytime, any place, anywhere.

P. Bowser: Before it gets deposited into a sort of obscure, only for scholarly work and so on. I'd like you to see it.

Tucker: And that's my girl.

Richardson: I'll give you my card.

P. Bowser: Next week, next week.

Richardson: Let me know at least six or eight hours before; I tune pianos, you know. I've got to make a living. I've got to work.

Tucker: He does all the Apollo theaters.

Richardson: I've got to work.

Tucker: Walter, would you.... I know Frank would be glad if you do this. Would you do "Without a Song"?

Richardson: I'll do anything you ask. I like to sing *a cappella* because Blanche Callaway was a beautiful musician for me in Miami that I really love. And I haven't heard her play for fifty some odd years.

B. Freeman: How is she? I'd really love to see her.

Richardson: Oh! She is beautiful.

B. Freeman: I think about her since....

Richardson: She talked about me three times a day....

B. Freeman: Oh no, I'd love to see her. She's some gal.

Richardson: You know, it's ... fifty years ago.

B. Freeman: Great, great kid. We had many fun times together.

Richardson: What did you say?

Tucker: "Without a Song."

Richardson: [singing]
Without a song, the day would never end.
Without a song, the road would never bend.
When things go wrong, oh! Man ain't got a friend.
Without a song, that field of corn would be deserted now.
That field of corn would see no plow, no where.
When a man is born, but he's no good, no how.
Without a song, I've got my troubling woes, and shoes.
I know the gord in the road.
I'll get along as long as the song is strumming my soul.
I'll never know what makes the rains fall
I'll never know what makes the grass grow tall
I only know there is no love at all without a song.

Tucker: Thank you, Walter.

B. Freeman: You can really hit those C's.

[Laughter]
Tucker: Thank you.
Manchel: Thank you.
Richardson: I love to sing, you know, that's my life.

Tucker: And incidentally, you know, the program that I'm working on now – this is in its infancy – "Reflections of Yesteryear," not the movie version of it, but the radio type. Richardson and Carl, the society pianist, are going to be my first two people and I want to have yesterday, today. and tomorrow. Yesterday, Walter; today, a present artist; and tomorrow, a newcomer. And I hope it will be going on the boards around the first of the year.

Richardson: This young girl used to be, when they tempted me, and I sang a song named "Davy." You see, they tempted me to bite the apple in the head of a basket of fruit and that sort of thing. And I says I'm going to sing about:

[Starts singing]
Children, Children, Wake up and save your soul,
Before old Jordan rolls....
Sinners! Sinners! This is the day,
If you're tired of the living
And you want to be forgiven
Bend your knees and pray.
[Just what we have been talking about]
Oh, your room is just beyond the river.
 Don't you roam, oh, sinner, don't you stray.
Just believe, have faith and you will be forgiven.
Until that mighty day when you reach Heaven.
 Oh! Beyond the curtain,
[I can't think of the lyrics]
And you'll know your home is there to stay.
And just believe and you will be forgiven, sinner.
Happiness will be born. Sorrow will be gone
When you reach that judgment morn.

Tucker: That was a godsend.
B. Freeman: That was a good one.
Richardson: That was a song.
L. Bowser: Who wrote that?

Richardson: I've got the song here. You want to see it? "Down here when you're dead."

L. Bowser: But it would be interesting. How many black men wrote the songs?

Tucker: This was a black man, Don Haywood. He wrote, "I'm Coming

Virginia." That theme song was for the South.

Richardson: I helped him write it, and my name was not on it. Ethel Waters make it famous in two places.

[Singing]:
Stop the traffic to Dixie hold it right on the vine.
That old home of mine, that my heart is a 'yearning
'Cause I'm longing to be where a light is always burning
In a window for me.
My lyric was:
See the shadows are falling. 'Twas an evening in June
And the nightingales are calling to the silvery moon.
Oh my heart is a 'yearning 'cause I'm longing to be
Where a light is always burning in a window for me.
I'm coming Virginia. I'm coming to stay.

Richardson: I wrote that song, and you know why my name's not on it? Cook. Will Marion Cook. I got on the boat, to go to England, and Paul [Robeson] was there with *ShowBoat*. And my show closed his show.

B. Freeman: You know.... Cook was the only director that ever slapped my face. He slapped my face because he wanted me to make a note.

Tucker: You've heard of that?

B. Freeman: Something, I don't remember, and he knew. And he said I could make it, and I didn't make it, and he walked right up to me and slapped my face.

Richardson: Excuse the expression, listen to this. Listen to what Will Marion Cook told me. There's a song that I was trying to sing for him before I went to Europe. "You black, son of a so and so, you'll never sing." That's what he said.

B. Freeman: He was a tough director.

Richardson: When I came back from Europe, he kissed me all over. But he had Neil, and I don't get no royalties from this song. And to get to Tom Neil and end this.... and ask him.

Tucker: He put his name on it, didn't he?

Richardson: He put his name to five or six songs. Now his son, the boy, what's his name? When his mother died, I sang at the funeral. He wrote me, he was ambassador to some parts of Africa, and he came to Robert's funeral, he'd gotten so thin. I used to sing in his mother's school in Washington. But anyway, Mercer Cook ... and he came, "Mr ... I know you're not going to remember Me...that's how lucky I am." I said, "Yes I do." He said, "No you don't." I said, "Well you used to send me back and forth from Washington to school and my mother was teaching you and blah, blah, blah." You know what my mother said and he said, "I'm Mercer Cook." And I was shocked. When I go to Washington, I go to see him. He comes here; he comes to see me. I'm a bachelor, he comes and we go out and.... He's gotten thin now. But he's a marvelous boy, a beautiful boy.

L. Bowser: Who did the camera work...?

B. Freeman: All white. Because at that time nobody wanted to go into the mechanics of anything. They wanted to be a star. They wanted to be in front of the camera, but they weren't interested.

Tucker: Could I just insert something? I think I became one of the first cameramen in television when I came out of the army. I took a course at NBC, and I majored in the crane camera. I had no place to go; that's why I'm not a cameraman today.

L. Bowser: Who did the camera work for very early films?

B. Freeman: Whites.

Tucker: All white. We didn't have any....

P. Bowser: It was a training ground and a proving ground for guys who wanted to make it to Hollywood.

B. Freeman: And you would go on one picture and you would see the same crew over and over again.

P. Bowser: And some of them had changed their names so they wouldn't be associated with that.

Tucker: Don Mullkins in Fort Lee, I think he made all the Colored pictures that were ever made. And I know when he had a camera that wasn't any bigger than that! And he has all the equipment in the East now that does most of the stuff for Hollywood here then it's given....

P. Bowser: Is he the guy from The Museum of Modern Art?

Tucker: No. Don Mullkins is a cameraman. And when they went into sound, Don started out with a thing, he has a trunk. I've seen him on First Avenue through shooting the stuff from the coast, everything. If I talked, they'd hang me when they see me because it's from the old days. But these guys started out, and like you say, they couldn't make it there, they made it with Colored pictures. We made them.

P. Bowser: But with the budget, most of the editing was done right with the camera.

B. Freeman: That's true. Micheaux could tell what amount of film it would take to walk to the door.

P. Bowser: Micheaux would also leave in his grossest errors.... As you examine the independent black producer, like Micheaux, who did fine films and moved on into 'talkies,' that's real easy to trace because he was there in the present when all this was happening around him. When you look at *Scar of Shame*, for instance, you can see there are [black aesthetics] involved in the silent era and [they] are also prominent in talking pictures.... The reason why the film was so important is because it was the master of all [it] preceded in terms of [black aesthetics].

Tucker: When Micheaux converted, or started, well we would say converted, it wasn't this big a deal when he started to make the first talking picture. There was a thing that he decided. He said, "To make some money, we'll go into talking pictures." And he worked out a budget and he was hassling over that budget and everything. And the first talking picture that Micheaux made was *Hastings on the House*. The studio, electricians, and that, he just didn't know how to manage this, but I want to be frank with you in saying this, they, union-wise, they had to charge him, but they played ball and they did everything in the world for this man that could have been done.

B. Freeman: It was incredible. You couldn't get the cooperation today.

Tucker: And to give him and to let him do. And the man was [incredible]. After hours, they wouldn't relinquish. And the union.... That man went hungry....

B. Freeman: They were just in pictures because they had the love of making them.

Tucker: And Mrs. Bowser said something to me and her husband oneday. This is why every now and then I like to check in with something, Frank, when you're talking because I have a reason for this. Some things that went on she said to me, and I respect her for that, and I'm going to see that it's done that way. She said, "I think it should be told as it is." And a lot of things that I might intercede in on that this is going on doesn't exactly reflect maybe my thing at this particular moment. But things have been done and this is the way that it must be told and must be recorded. Professor Manchel, for you, if you're going to write anything, it must be as it is because I don't want it any other way.

P. Bowser: How do you feel about the kind of material that Micheaux used? Granted, he wrote most of his material, how do you feel about the kinds of scripts that he wrote?

Tucker: Very bad. He wasn't a good scriptwriter.

B. Freeman: He wasn't a highly educated man.

P. Bowser: Yes. That needs to be said. But beyond that. The man had certain ideas.

Tucker: Yes. The ideas.

P. Bowser: From the period in which he was writing, he may not have been the master of having captured everything, but he was the most productive black....

L. Bowser: I'm more interested in how did Micheaux....

P. Bowser: What I want to know is how you reacted to what he was doing at the time he was doing it.

B. Freeman: I think everybody respected Micheaux.

Richardson: Everybody loved Micheaux.

B. Freeman: We used to laugh at the things he did, but you had to have a lot of respect for the man. Because you watched him work with his whole heart and soul. Sometimes he hardly moved. And he never was rude. He respected....

Richardson: He was a gentleman in every which way, in every walk of life.

B. Freeman: He didn't use dirty language on the set. He always treated you as ladies and gentlemen. And he expected you to be the same to him and you were. I have a great deal of respect for this man, because I realize that he had great limitations; and he rose above all of them. He was fantastic.

L. Bowser: Well, how were his films? Compared to like.... What I'm interested in....

Tucker: You can't compare him with today.

L. Bowser: I always think that there are, regardless of what you would like to think, there were always controversial figures, like a Melvin Van Peebles.

Tucker: You wouldn't. You can't compare his stuff....

L. Bowser: Was there any filmmaker in that period that you would look upon similar to a Melvin Van Peebles?

Tucker: No.

P. Bowser: Think of Melvin Van Peebles in silent films. Don't think of him in terms of language.

L. Bowser: Were there any individuals turning out films, not Micheaux, but films of something of a controversial nature that nobody would show?

Tucker: No. No.

L. Bowser: Understand what's happening. Look, Melvin Van Peebles today.... We went to a white movie distributor and asked him, "Why won't you distribute Melvin Van Peebles' film?" And he said, "I do not think that those films are worthy of distribution."

Tucker: I have the answer to that. They're not.

L. Bowser: That's what he said. It has nothing to do with the fact that there was a film out there. And my point is, was there a filmmaker in the 1920s and 1930s....

Manchel: That's not true. There was not a filmmaker, but there was a man in film that was more controversial than Van Peebles, Jack Johnson. The films that Johnson did were far more controversial ... not as a personality, as an image, the very same thing that you're talking about.

P. Bowser: That's because he was a political figure.

Manchel: No, he was a social figure in films. Jack Johnson's films resulted in all the legislation that prohibited not only the films from being shown in the states where there are racists. [Johnson] became someone who, in a sense, offered a kind of [aggressive] image to young black kids. He also set up the kind of machinery that eventually was to go in operation against *The Birth of a Nation* (1915) and to discourage anyone from hiring Colored people, or from, in a sense, making any films dealing with Colored themes. So Jack Johnson, in spite [of his being a boxer and not an actor then].... I wouldn't like this to get around before [the book] comes out.... The fighter Jack Johnson. It was Jack Johnson from 1908 to 1915 whose films ... [before a black film alternative appeared who made the difference].

L. Bowser: Did he turn out films?

Manchel: Well, he signed for films. In other words....

P. Bowser: As an actor.

Manchel: As an actor. Or he would contract to have his films recorded. And then of course he would go on to, as many fighters did, in vaudeville and burlesque, and do stage. But the concept, Van Peebles is small potatoes. For all you say about Van Peebles, he's a one-film man. Even though he may have made one or two other films, *Sweetback* is still one film, and *Sweetback* is still primarily a large city film. I mean outside of your large cities.... It's not a question of selling; it's....

L. Bowser: I'm not concerned about what it's done. It has caused ripples.

Larry was absolutely right about the importance of Van Peebles' influential film. In addition, the distinguished musician, screenwriter, director and author got his initial film recognition not from Sweetback ... *but from* The Story of a Three-Day Pass *(1968).*

Manchel: Yes, but you're talking about ripples with distributors; and you're really, the one thing that you have got to make a point of for a national figure is that.... The point is that Van Peebles is small potatoes.

P. Bowser: He's not small potatoes in terms of what he's made on film. He's small potatoes in terms of....

Manchel: He's small potatoes as a filmmaker. He's made one film, and that film is the first one that's come commercially. So he may be, or he's yet to be tried. But Jack Johnson offered for the first time in the history of motion pictures, because by and large black people didn't go to movies. It wasn't their medium. It wasn't their interest, it wasn't their... [Uproar].

P. Bowser: That's not true.

Manchel: Oh yes. But be very careful with *Variety*. *Variety* makes a lot of statements and a lot of....

L. Bowser: The point is that there are periods within time where there are, let's say, what is considered the normal of what you could do in films and the individual that produces films that excite the audience; causes, let's say, the polemic that may be necessary. Then we have a historical perspective to the point. You pointed out that, sure that within a given period, Jack Johnson caused certain polemics to exist.

Manchel: It's not just the polemics. You've got to talk about it in the milieu in which it was created. Movies up to 1915, before *The Birth of a Nation*, were called tapes, or the poor man's amusement. They were shown in storefronts and travel and carnival shows, and, by and large, they were a part of vaudeville acts as chasers and fill ins. So you're talking about films in a day in which anybody made films and stars weren't known; and there were fly-by-nights, hundreds and hundreds of producers. You're talking about guys who used to walk in when they couldn't get any work on Broadway, used to walk in for five dollars a day. They took any part they could. You hired your friend or your relative. Jack Johnson made fifty thousand dollars to sign to have his five films shown. Fifty thousand dollars in a day when a guy was getting five dollars! Jack Johnson had his picture shown in places where the black people didn't have a theater, let alone get in to "Nigger Heaven" in the last row.

And Jack Johnson offered black people, you talk about Marcus Garvey, nobody knew about him. The fact that he was a big name and he was a great man and all that, he was in a New York paper or he was in some paper that went around. But most people in the country, black and white, didn't read about Marcus Garvey. We find now what we missed ... but everybody read about Jack Johnson. And everybody knew about Jack Johnson. He offered a tremendous threat. When you talk about race riots, when you talk about the Ku Klux Klan rising up, when you talk about people exploiting racism, when you talk about legislation where people went berserk and tried to keep him out, you're talking about Jack Johnson. And there's no film in the history of motion pictures that's ever equaled the kind of input every time a Jack Johnson film appeared. And when he beat a white man, they'd edit it out. And when you talk about "The Great White Hope," you're talking about seven years and Jack Johnson's films are what.... Remember when you talk about "The Great White Hope," you're talking about an era without television, without radio, without motion pictures being shown, and then you talk about Jack Johnson's name being on everyone's lips and then you think," My God, what a man Jack Johnson was." You got to put it in the milieu.

P. Bowser: You're talking about one milieu of film, you're talking about news. [Inaudible]

Manchel: You're talking about hero worship, you're talking about sport.

P. Bowser: You're not talking about Hollywood....

Manchel: But the fact is that Jack Johnson's image was one of the images that precluded Colored people, or black people, or Negro people from getting jobs because no distributor, no exhibitor, wanted to show a black film. He had to face the local sheriff; he had to face the state censorship.

P. Bowser: But the same thing was true of any kind of black producer; no matter what....

Manchel: There were no black producers.

P. Bowser: There were none at that time....

Manchel: 1913 is when you have your first Colored company [Inaudible] that *Variety* reports about. But you're talking about fly by night. You're talking about a paragraph in *Variety*. You're talking about a name that may get a little ego bill, or trip....

L. Bowser: We're going into a little bit more than that. If you stick with Jack Johnson, there were, and this is what I said, I was trying to emphasize that the concepts were built upon many layers that not only were about the film or the fight.... If you were to take the 1890s, you get a whole populace movement that took place. You got the whole change in historic.... The point is that film does not exist by itself alone.

Tucker: We know that.

L. Bowser: If it does not exist by itself alone, what are some of the other elements?

Tucker: We are trying to tell you the other ones. Jack Johnson....

L. Bowser: No, No! What are the other elements that are built into what makes a film? Let me give you an example. If you look at some of the WWII films shown on television today, and you look at the literature, the music, examine them from four or five perspectives, from sculpture to art, to music, to film, to music. Then you get into the point for saying if I take all these elements and transform these elements into 1900 or 1800 – whatever you do to transform them – you say that they all exist concurrently, that society is built and this thing all moves along was so full of parallel paths. They may not be parallel, they may vary at one point or another. They may say that Jack Johnson did a film here, music did a thing here, art did another thing here, literature did another thing at another point. That says what is the history of what we're talking about.

Manchel: Your point is well taken, but I think that you've got to.... You're trying to say, "Was there a black producer who was working on the development of the art of the film?" But the point I'm trying to bring out to you....

L. Bowser: Was there a black writer?

Tucker: No.

P. Bowser: I don't think you're in a position to qualify when he's good. He's writing for another generation and another period, and there are other people to evaluate whether he's good or not. We're not present in the future....

B. Freeman: I think it's pretty sad when you have to say that because they are black....

L. Bowser: We don't support black theater.

Tucker: You don't have any to support.

B. Freeman: I don't see any reason to support somebody because he's black. I support theater that's good.

L. Bowser: No creative things take place without other creative arts....

Manchel: You say there are a number of cultural forces at work that shape and influence any art form. But I think that given that kind of perspective, you still have to understand that motion pictures didn't get projected on the screen until 1895. And they didn't become an art form until *The Birth of a Nation*, until 1915. Within that twenty-year period, motion pictures were made primarily for money. It had nothing to do with art. And the people that turned them out, turned them out on a mass-produced machinery line. If you want to take your kind of formula for anything, you still have to go back to Jack Johnson. Even if you want to exclude the idea of a personality. Because there were a number of fight films....

L. Bowser: Regardless of what you say, you're starting in 1900.

Manchel: Well, you got to start when films start. You can't talk about an art form that didn't exist until 1895. I'm trying to follow you. Your argument during the evening is the absolute, crucial importance of historical perspective on any particular action, particularly for black people.

L. Bowser: I don't think just for black people.

P. Bowser: You're valid. Stick to it, because the first film that was ever made included blacks. Blacks were used in Edison's film. It's critical, because the image and the importance, as far as your viewing audiences were concerned, the people that were making the film, the consciousness of the creative endeavor was always there. Who were the comics? Blacks! Who were the stereotypes? Blacks!

L. Bowser: That's true. If we take the minstrel concept.

Manchel: You're going along a number of streams here. Let's talk about the minstrel concept. The minstrel concept was white men in blackface until after the Civil War.

L. Bowser: No! No! No!

Manchel: Yes! Yes! Yes! In 1840, the most popular form of entertainment in the 1800s was the minstrel show. From 1840-1885. And by and large, black people were not featured in the minstrel shows predominantly till 1860s.

L. Bowser: Very early minstrels were always black.

Manchel: No sir, I don't think so. They were black face, but not blacks.

Tucker: Just one second. Mr. Richardson went to Europe with *Piccaninny Days*, the first minstrel show that left America, and went to London. Mr. Richardson, help us out on this please.
Richardson: Well, I can say.... You've got me in a bind. You can help me, because I can't think of just who it was.
Tucker: Didn't you go to Europe with *Piccaninny Days*?
Richardson: Yes.
Tucker: Well, in your early days of show business ... how old were you?
Richardson: When I went to Europe? The first time? 1919.
Manchel: The heyday of the minstrel shows was over.

Actually, the concept of the "minstrel" show was extremely important to black film history, because many of the African-American performers who appeared in movies had their training in vaudeville shows barnstorming in the South during the first twenty years of the twentieth century. These traveling vaudevillians, as Albright observes, ballyhooed themselves as "minstrels," although the traditional minstrel formula had disappeared by the turn-of-the century.[155]

Tucker: Was this the first minstrel show that had left the United States for there? Or were there others before that?
Richardson: I can't say that, but I can say this: that boys were doing the black face around the minstrel shows. They had to do it black face because of the fact that....
Tucker: Answer this. Because of the fact that what?
Richardson: That....
Tucker: Because it was the only type of work that Negroes were given at that time.
Richardson: Yes.
P. Bowser: Negroes were doing it. Whites were doing it.
Tucker: And whites were doing it to support themselves.

At this point confusion took over, and the interview ended shortly after that.

15. Al "Slick" Chester. Courtesy of The Manchel Collection, University of Vermont.

16. Heavyweight champ Jack Johnson stands over his defeated challenger, Stanley Ketchel. 1909. By 1911, White America grew so angry with Johnson's victories that Congress banned interstate screenings (newsreels) of Johnson's championship fights for the remainder of his reign. Courtesy of The Manchel Collection, Burlington College

17. Harry Belafonte. The first mainstream black film star. Courtesy of The Manchel Collection, Burlington College.

18. Bill "Bojangles" Robinson in a publicity shot from Henry King's *One More Spring* (1935). From Left to right, Walter Woolf King, Jane Darwell, Bojangles, Warner Baxter, (unknown), Henry King. Courtesy of The Manchel Collection, Burlington College.

19. William Greaves. The inscription, "Looking Forward to Fall-Winter of 1982" refers to the artist's visit to the University of Vermont.

20. Oscar Micheaux, "The Father of Independent African-American Films." Courtesy of The African Diaspora Collection.

21. Leroy Bowser, ardent champion for black film studies. Courtesy of The African Diaspora Collection.

22. Pearl Bowser in Paris at a press conference publicizing a tribute to Oscar Micheaux. The festival was titled "Independent Black American Cinema 1920-1980." It was an extension of the pioneering festivals she started in the United States. Courtesy of The African Diaspora Collection.

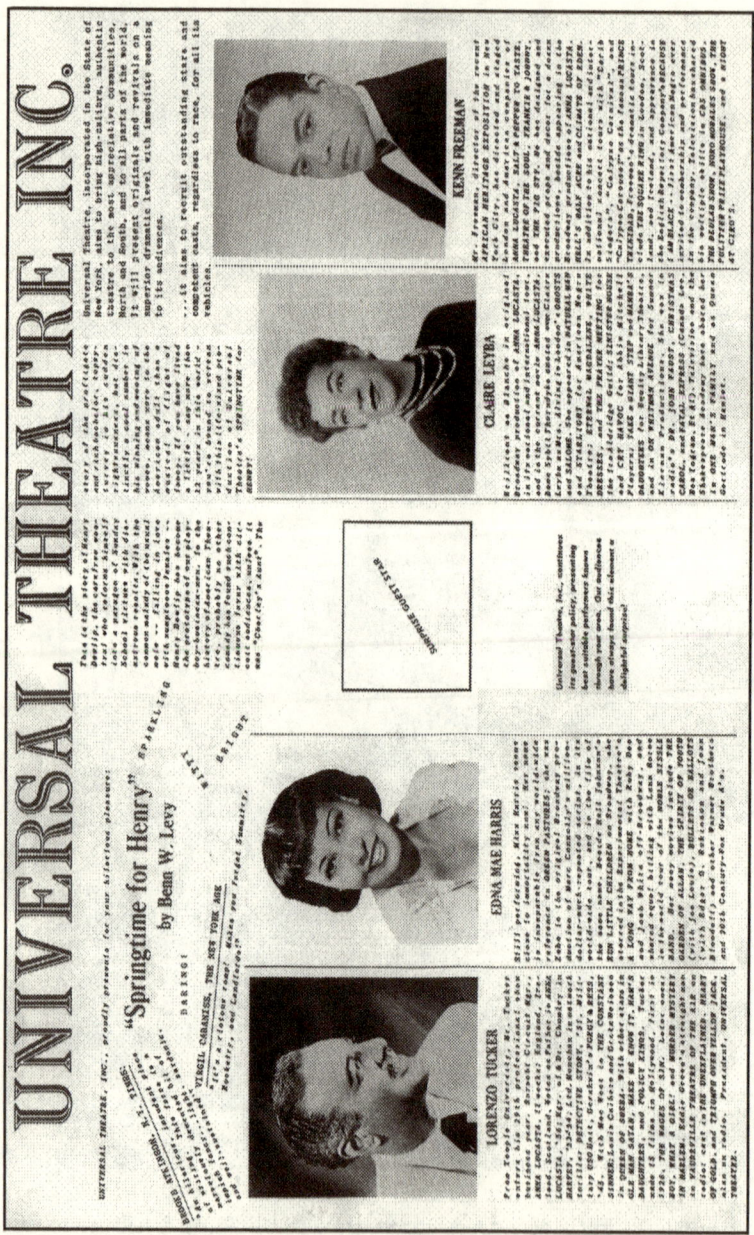

23. A copy of The Universal Theatre Inc. Program for *Springtime for Henry* with an all-black cast. Courtesy of the Manchel Collection, Burlington College."

24. Lorenzo Tucker and Ethel Moses in Oscar Micheaux's *Wages of Sin* (1928). Courtesy of The Manchel Collection, Burlington College.

25. Publicity shot for Oscar Micheaux's *The Wages of Sin* (1928). Courtesy of The Manchel Collection, Burlington College.

26. Publicity for Budd Pollard's *The Black King* (1931). Courtesy of The Manchel Collection, Burlington College.

27. Publicity for Oscar Micheaux's *Veiled Aristocrats* (1932). Laura Bowman and Lorenzo Tucker. Courtesy of The Manchel Collection, Burlington College.

28. Publicity for Oscar Micheaux's *Harlem After Midnight* (1934). Note the emphasis on skin-tone in the advertisement. Courtesy of The Manchel Collection, Burlington College.

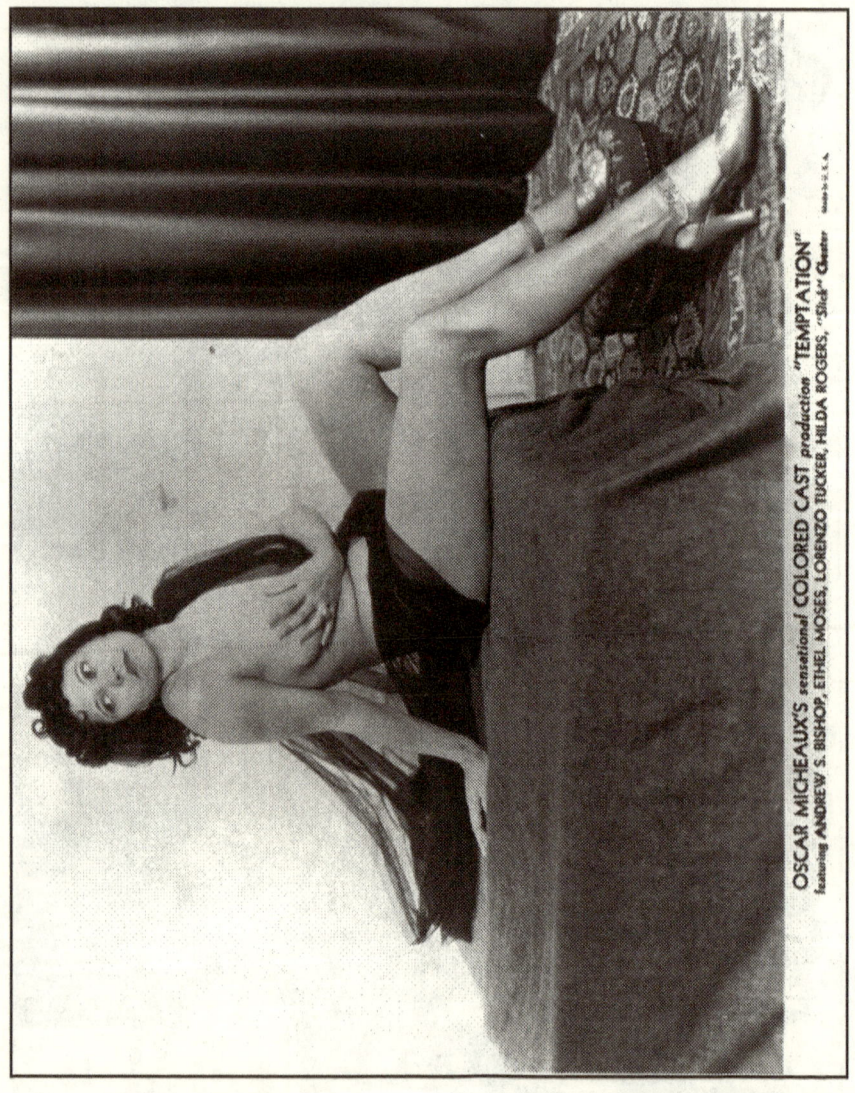

29. Ethel Moses in a publicity shot from Oscar Micheaux's *Temptation* (1936).

30. From Left to right, Andrew S. Bishop, Hilda Rodgers and Ida Forsythe in Oscar Micheaux's *Temptation* (1936). Courtesy of The Manchel Collection, Burlington College.

158 HEROES AND VILLAINS

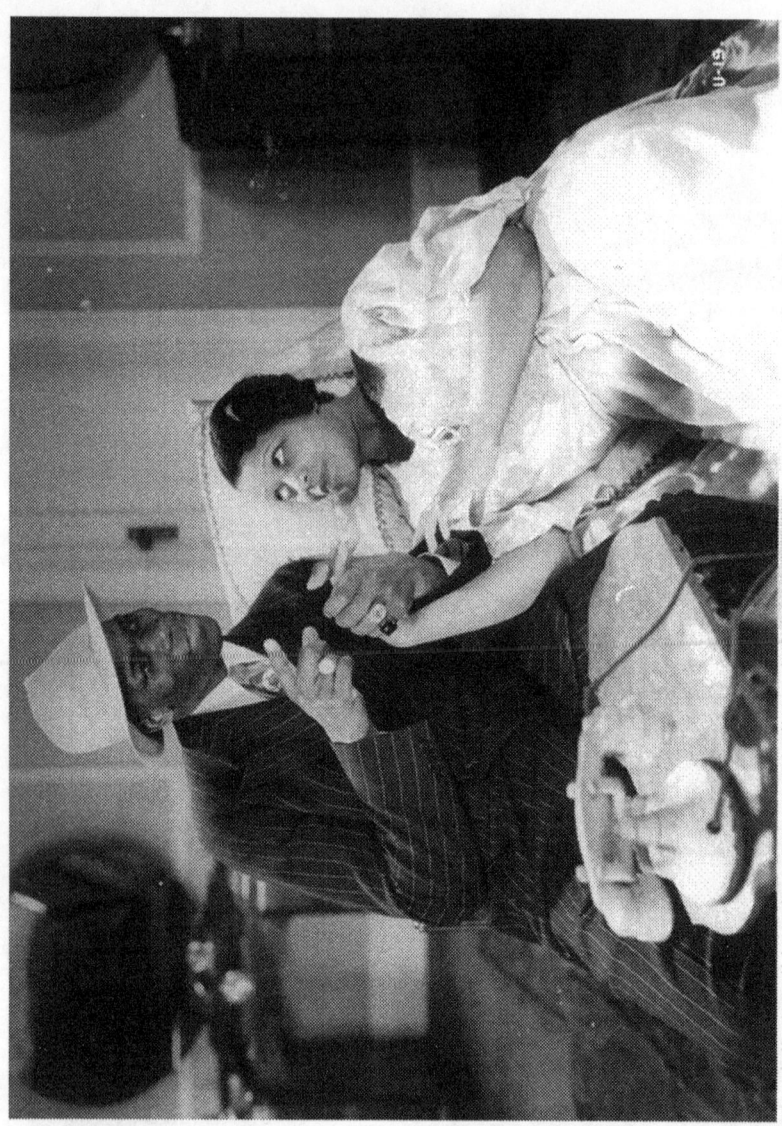

31. Oscar Polk and Bee Freeman in Oscar Micheaux's *Underworld* (1936). Courtesy of The Manchel Collection, Burlington College.

32. Publicity for Jack Kemp's *Miracle in Harlem* (1948). Stepin Fetchit, upper left-hand corner; Lorenzo Tucker, extreme right. Courtesy of The Manchel Collection, Burlington College.

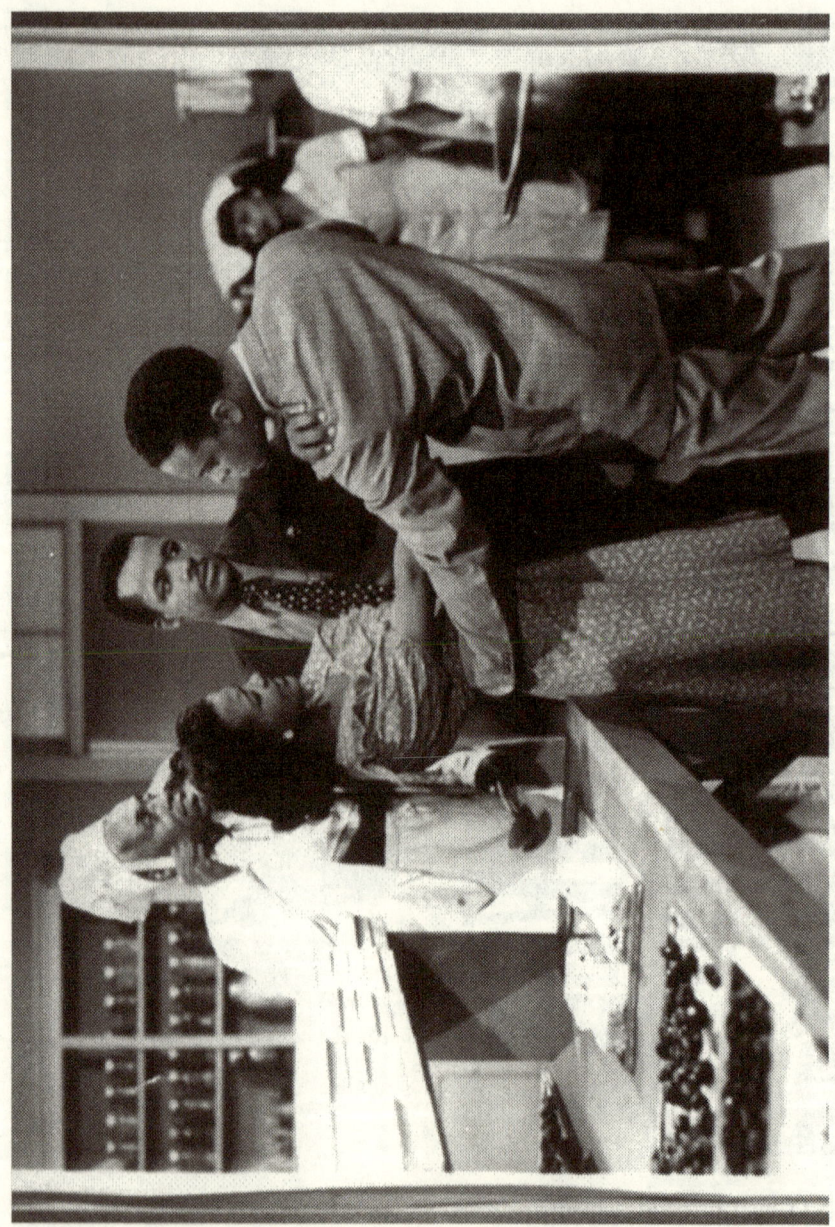

33. Jack Kemp's *Miracle in Harlem* (1948). From left to right, Stepin Fetchit, Sheila Guyse, William Greaves, and Kenneth Freeman. Courtesy of The Manchel Collection, Burlington College.

Notes

[1] James Snead, *White Screens/Black Images: Hollywood from the Dark Side* (New York: Routledge, 1994), 108.

[2] Robert A. Bone, *The Negro Novel in America*, rev. ed. (New Haven: Yale University Press, 1965), 2.

[3] Valarie Smith, ed., *Representing Blackness: Issues in Film and Video* (New Brunswick, NJ: Rutgers University Press, 1997), 2-3.

[4] Richard Grupenhoff, *The Black Valentino: The Stage and Screen Career of Lorenzo Tucker* (Metuchen, NJ: Scarecrow, 1988), 93.

[5] "Re-Creating the Era of Black Vaudeville," *New York Times*, 28 June 1990, C15.

[6] Snead, *White Screens/Black Images: Hollywood from the Dark Side*, 108-109.

[7] Wesley Brown et al., *W.E.B. DuBois: A Biography in Four Voices* (San Francisco, CA: California Newsreel, 1997), videorecording.

[8] Thomas Cripps, "'Race Movies' as Voices of the Black Bourgeoisie: The Scar of Shame (1927)," 43.

[9] Mary Carbine, "'the Finest Outside the Loop': Motion Picture Exhibition in Chicago's Black Metropolis, 1905-1928," *Camera Obscura* 23 (1990), 10.

[10] Ibid., 32.

[11] Walter Burrell, "Beulah or Bitch? The Soul Sister as a Sex Symbol," *Soul Illustrated* 1971, 24.

[12] Jane Gaines, "Fire and Desire: Race, Melodrama, and Oscar Micheaux," in *Black American Cinema*, Ed. Manthia Diaware (New York: Routledge, 1993), 66.

[13] J. Ronald. Green, " 'Twoness' in the Style of Oscar Micheaux," in *Black American Cinema*, Ed. Manthia Diaware (New York: Routledge, 1993), 29.

[14] Grupenhoff, *The Black Valentino: The Stage and Screen Career of Lorenzo Tucker*, 152.

[15] Blau, "With Dignity: Films by Blacks for Blacks," c13.

[16] The best listing of sources on Micheaux scholarship appears in Gaines, 276-277n.

[17] Kenneth W. Porter, " Micheaux, Oscar," in *Dictionary of American Negro Biography* (New York: Norton, 1982), 433.

[18] Ibid., 433.

[19] Joseph A. Young, *Black Novelist as White Racist: The Myth of Black Inferiority in the Novels of Oscar Micheaux* (Westport, CT: Greenwood, 1989), IX.

[20] Ibid., X-XI.

[21] Ibid., 154-156.

[22] Grupenhoff, *The Black Valentino: The Stage and Screen Career of Lorenzo Tucker*, 70.

[23] Michelle Wallace, "Oscar Micheaux's within Our Gates: The Possibilities for Alternative Visions," in *Oscar Micheaux and His Circle: African -American Filmmaking and Race Cinema of the Silent Era*, ed. et. al. Pearl Bowser (2001), 63.

[24] Ibid.

[25] Mark A. Reid, *Redefining Black Film* (Berkeley: University of California Press, 1993), 11.

[26] Bogle, *Toms, Coons, Mulattoes, Mammies, & Bucks: An Interpretive History of Blacks in American Films*, 110.

[27] Reid, *Redefining Black Film*, 11-12.

[28] hooks, *Black Looks: Race and Representation*, 134.

[29] Gaines, "Fire and Desire: Race, Melodrama, and Oscar Micheaux," 7.

[30] "Paul Robeson, Miss Russell Star in Micheaux's Latest Film, Body and Soul," *Pittsburgh Courier* 14 Feb. 1925, 3.

[31] Snead, *White Screens/Black Images: Hollywood from the Dark Side*, 109.

[32] Young, *Black Novelist as White Racist: The Myth of Black Inferiority in the Novels of Oscar Micheaux*, XI.

[33] Gary Null, *Black Hollywood: The Negro in Motion Pictures* (Secaucus, NJ: Citadel, 1975), 9-11.

[34] Kagan, "Black American Cinema: A Primer," 3.

[35] Jay Hoberman, "American Fairy Tales," *Village Voice*, 29 May 1984, 48.

[36] Grupenhoff, *The Black Valentino: The Stage and Screen Career of Lorenzo Tucker*, 74.

[37] "Micheaux Film Corp.: All-Talking Pictures Will Be Produced on More Expansive Scale," *Pittsburgh Courier*, 8 Jan. 1931, 8.

[38] Jay Hoberman, "Blankety-Blank," *Village Voice*, 12 June 1984, 58.

[39] Gomery, *Shared Treasures: A History of Movie Presentation in the United States*. 161.

[40] Reid, *Redefining Black Film*, 12.

[41] "Censors Lift Ban on 'the Exile'; to Play at Roosevelt Next Week," *Pittsburgh Courier*, 13 June 1931, 9.

[42] Abiola, Sinclair, "Oscar Micheaux Film Festival July 10-11," *Amsterdam News*, 5 July 1986, 27.

[43] Clyde Taylor, "Crossed Over and Can't Be Black: The Crisis of 1937-1939," *Black Film Review* 7.4 (1993), 25.

[44] Hoberman, "Blankety-Blank," 58.

[45] Kagan, "Black American Cinema: A Primer," 3, 5.

[46] Young, *Black Novelist as White Racist: The Myth of Black Inferiority in the Novels of Oscar Micheaux*, XI.

[47] Reid, *Redefining Black Film*, 13.

[48] Michael E. Dyson, *Race Rules: Navigating the Color Line* (Reading, MA: Addison-Wesley, 1996), 50.

[49] Thomas M. Pryor, "The Betrayal," *New York Times*, 26 June 1948, 1Q.

[50] Paul Robeson, Oscar Micheaux, and Facets Video, *Body and Soul* (Chicago, IL: Facets Video, 1994), videorecording. Prologue.

[51] Hoberman, "Blankety-Blank," 158.

[52] Robert J. Sye, "Black Cinema Expo '72: Black Cinema Library-Research," *Ebony*, no. May 1972 (1972), 160.

[53] hooks, *Black Looks: Race and Representation*, 136.

[54] Bowser and Gaines, "New Finds/Old Films: Black Gold," 2.

[55] Burt A. Folkart, "Lorenzo Tucker: 'Black Valentino' Dies," *Los Angeles Times*, 21 Aug 1986, 28.

[56] J. Ronald Green and Horace Neal, Jr., "Oscar Micheaux and Racial Slur." Reply To "The Rediscovery of Oscar Micheaux, Black Film Pioneer," "*Journal of Film and Video* 40.4 (1988), 69.

[57] Ibid., 69-70.
[58] Richard Grupenhoff, "The Rediscovery of Oscar Micheaux, Black Film Pioneer," *Journal of Film and Video* 40.1 (1988), 46.
[59] hooks, *Black Looks: Race and Representation*, 133.
[60] Jesse A. Rhines, *Black Film/White Money* (New Brunswick, NJ: Rutgers University Press, 1996), 24-25.
[61] hooks, *Black Looks: Race and Representation*, 134.
[62] Pearl Bowser and Louise Spence, "Identity and Betrayal: The Symbol of the Unconquered and Oscar Micheaux's 'Biographical Legend'," in *The Birth of Whiteness: Race and the Emergence of U.S. Cinema*, Ed. Daniel Bernardi (New Brunswick, NJ: Rutgers University Press, 1996), 58.
[63] Ibid., 65.
[64] Ibid., 64.
[65] Ibid., 66.
[66] Ibid., 65.
[67] Snead, *White Screens/Black Images: Hollywood from the Dark Side*, 113.
[68] Null, *Black Hollywood: The Negro in Motion Pictures*, 11.
[69] "Rev. Of the Exile (Negro Talker)," *Variety*, 27 May 1931, 57.
[70] Green and Neal, "Oscar Micheaux and Racial Slur." Reply To "The Rediscovery of Oscar Micheaux, Black Film Pioneer," 68.
[71] Henry T. Sampson, *Blacks in Blackface: A Source Book on Early Black Musical Shows* (Metuchen, NJ: Scarecrow, 1980), 332-333.
[72] Ibid., 336.
[73] Robert Kimball and William Bolcom, *Reminiscing with Sissle and Blake* (New York: Viking Press, 1973), 228.
[74] Bowser and Gaines, "New Finds/Old Films: Black Gold," 4.
[75] Jane Gaines, "The Scar of Shame: Skin Color and Caste in Black Silent Melodrama," *Cinema Journal* 6.4 (1987), 17.
[76] Roger Fristoe, "Spotlight on Speed Museum's 'Black Film Series'," *The Courier-Journal*, 2 Feb. 1992, 26.
[77] Gomery, *Shared Treasures: A History of Movie Presentation in the United States*, 161.
[78] Ibid. 183.
[79] Frank Manchel, *Interview with Fredi Washington. Conducted by Barbi Mortimer for Dr. Frank Manchel* (1972), Audiocasette.
[80] For information on *Runnin' Wild*, see Sampson's *Blacks in Blackface*, 297-298.
[81] Pearl Bowser, "Black Women in Cinema," in *Black Cinema Aesthetics: Issues in Independent Black Filmmaking*, Ed. Gladstone L. Yearwood (Athens: Ohio University, 1982), 51.
[82] Burrell, "Beulah or Bitch? The Soul Sister as a Sex Symbol," 21.
[83] Paul Goldberger, "Critic's Notebook: From Page to Stage--Race and the Theater," *New York Times*, 22 Jan. 1997, C11.
[84] Vincent Canby, "Are Black Films Losing Their Blackness?," *New York Times*, 25 April 1976, D15.
[85] Bowser and Spence, "Identity and Betrayal: The Symbol of the Unconquered and Oscar Micheaux's 'Biographical Legend,'" 69.
[86] Abel Green and Joe Laurie, Jr., *Show Biz from Vaude to Video* (New York: Henry Holt, 1951), 270-272.

[87] Sampson, *Blacks in Blackface: A Source Book on Early Black Musical Shows*, 22.
[88] "Jewish Museum's Retrospective on Black Filmmaking, Back to 1916," *Variety Weekly*, 25 Mar. 1970, 1.
[89] Sampson, *Blacks in Blackface: A Source Book on Early Black Musical Shows*, 18.
[90] Daniel J. Leab, *From Sambo to Superspade: The Black Experience in Motion Pictures* (Boston: Houghton, Mifflin, 1975), 188.
[91] Henry T. Sampson, *Blacks in Black and White: A Source Book on Black Films* (Metuchen, NJ: Scarecrow, 1977), 7.
[92] Kagan, "Black American Cinema: A Primer," 6.
[93] Charlene Regester, "From the Buzzard's Roost: Black Movie-Going in Durham and Other North Carolina Cities During the Early Period of American Cinema," *Film History* 17 (2005), 115-116.
[94] Gomery, *Shared Treasures: A History of Movie Presentation in the United States*. 155.
[95] "Festival of Black Films," *Variety*, 7 Apr. 1971, 7.
[96] Grupenhoff, *The Black Valentino: The Stage and Screen Career of Lorenzo Tucker*, 83-84.
[97] Manchel, *Interview with Fredi Washington. Conducted by Barbi Mortimer for Dr. Frank Manchel*.
[98] Gaines, "Fire and Desire: Race, Melodrama, and Oscar Micheaux," 50.
[99] *Slow Fade to Blackface: The Negro in American Film, 1900-1942*, (New York: Oxford University Press, 1977), 68.
[100] Kael, "The Current Cinema: Notes on Black Movies," 159.
[101] Albright, "Micheaux, Vaudeville & Black Cast Film," 8.
[102] "Rev. Of the Exile (Negro Talker)," 57.
[103] Ted Toddy, " *******," *Motion Picture Herald*, 12 Apr. 1947.
[104] Mary Boyle, "All Black Cinema, All the Time," *Burlington Free Press [Vermont]*, 6 Feb. 1997, 15.
[105] Grupenhoff, *The Black Valentino: The Stage and Screen Career of Lorenzo Tucker*, 124-126.
[106] Ibid., 124. See also O'Connor C24.
[107] For more information see Lou Potter, *Liberators: Fighting on Two Fronts* (New York: Harcourt Brace Jovanovich, 1992).
[108] Clyde Taylor, "Black Silence and the Politics of Representation," in *Oscar Micheaux & His Circle: African-American Filmmaking and Race Cinema of the Silent Era*, ed. Pearl Bowser et al. (Bloomington: Indiana University Press, 2001), 25.
[109] Smith, *Representing Blackness: Issues in Film and Video*, 1.
[110] "Turn Stereotypes into 'Study Course' Black Cinema Group Defuses Valuaties," *Variety*, 9 Feb. 1972, 5.
[111] Tavia Nyong'o, "Racial Kitsch and Black Performance," *The Yale Journal of Criticism* 15:2 (2002), 371-372.
[112] Ibid., 381.
[113] Grupenhoff, *The Black Valentino: The Stage and Screen Career of Lorenzo Tucker*, Grupenhoff, "The Rediscovery of Oscar Micheaux, Black Film Pioneer," 61-63.
[114] Bowser and Spence, "Identity and Betrayal: The Symbol of the Unconquered and Oscar Micheaux's 'Biographical Legend,'" 211-212.
[115] Stephen Fay, "The Era of Dummies and Darkies," *Commonweal* 92.1 (1970), 128.

[116] Sampson, *Blacks in Black and White: A Source Book on Black Films*, 2, 5.
[117] Ibid., 66.
[118] Kagan, "Black American Cinema: A Primer," 7.
[119] For more information see Donald Bogle, *Bright Boulevards, Bold Dreams: The Story of Black Hollywood* (New York: One World Ballantine books, 2005), 21-24, 165-166, 168-169, 172; Sister Francesca Thompson, "From Shadows 'N Shufflin' to Spotlights and Cinema: The Lafayette Players, 1915-1932," in *Oscar Micheaux & His Circle: African-American Filmmaking and Race Cinema of the Silent Era*, Ed. Pearl Bowser et al. (Bloomington: Indiana University Press, 2001), 37-38; Taylor, "Black Silence and the Politics of Representation," 4-6.
[120] Sampson, *Blacks in Black and White: A Source Book on Black Films*, 66.
[121] Taylor, "Black Silence and the Politics of Representation," Taylor, "Crossed over and Can't Be Black: The Crisis of 1937-1939," 24.
[122] Singer Alfred Buchanan, "A Study of the Attitudes of the Writers of the Negro Press toward the Depiction of the Negro in Plays and Films: 1930-1965" (Dissertation, University of Michigan, 1968), 230.
[123] Kagan, "Black American Cinema: A Primer," 2-3.
[124] Sampson, *Blacks in Black and White: A Source Book on Black Films*, 508.
[125] Ibid., 511.
[126] Fristoe, "Spotlight on Speed Museum's 'Black Film Series,'" 26.
[127] Bogle, *Toms, Coons, Mulattoes, Mammies, & Bucks: An Interpretive History of Blacks in American Films*, 60.
[128] For a more detailed biography, see Bogle, *Bright Boulevards, Bold Dreams: The Story of Black Hollywood*.
[129] Manchel, *Interview with Fredi Washington. Conducted by Barbi Mortimer for Dr. Frank Manchel*.
[130] For more information, see Bogle, *Bright Boulevards, Bold Dreams: The Story of Black Hollywood*, 107, 130, 139, 205, 246, 354, 364.
[131] Ibid., 130.
[132] For details on the play, see Anatol I. Schlosser, "Paul Robeson: His Career in the Theatre, in Motion Pictures, and on the Concert Stage" (Dissertation, New York University, 1970), 82, 93.
[133] Manchel, *Interview with Fredi Washington. Conducted by Barbi Mortimer for Dr. Frank Manchel*.
[134] Bogle, *Bright Boulevards, Bold Dreams: The Story of Black Hollywood*, 153.
[135] Manchel, *Interview with Fredi Washington. Conducted by Barbi Mortimer for Dr. Frank Manchel*.
[136] The best information on these films is found in the writings of Bowser, Spence, and Gaines.
[137] G. Williams Jones, *Black Cinema Treasures: Lost and Found*, Foreword by Ossie Davis ed. (Denton, TX: University of North Texas Press, 1991), 106-117.
[138] Thompson, "From Shadows 'N Shufflin' to Spotlights and Cinema: The Lafayette Players, 1915-1932," 21.
[139] "William Greaves: Chronicler of the African-American Experience," (The Brooklyn Museum, 1992).
[140] Thomas M. Pryor, " One Mile from Heaven," *New York Times*, 19 Aug. 1937, 23.

[141] Grupenhoff, *The Black Valentino: The Stage and Screen Career of Lorenzo Tucker*, 105, 110.

[142] "*Veiled Aristocrats* at Roosevelt," *Pittsburgh Courier*, 31 Jan. 1934, 6.

[143] For more information on the film, see Jones, *Black Cinema Treasures: Lost and Found*, 106-117.

[144] Readers might find it useful to read "Why Negroes don't like Eartha Kitt," *Ebony* 10 (December 1954): 29-38. For another side to Kitt's image, see Bogle, *Bright Boulevard*, 321-325.

[145] Grupenhoff, *The Black Valentino: The Stage and Screen Career of Lorenzo Tucker*, 135.

[146] Ann Charters, *Nobody: The Story of Bert Williams* (New York: Macmillan, 1970), 68-77.

[147] Sampson, *Blacks in Blackface: A Source Book on Early Black Musical Shows*, 108-111.

[148] Bowser and Spence, "Identity and Betrayal: The Symbol of the Unconquered and Oscar Micheaux's 'Biographical Legend'."

[149] E. R. Shipp, "Taking Control of Old Demons by Forcing Them into the Light," *New York Times*, 16 Mar. 1997, H13.

[150] Bernard Weintraub, "Stirring up Old Terrors Unforgotten," *New York Times*, 19 Feb. 1997, D1.

[151] Barry Kernfeld, "Sanders, Pharoah," in *New Grove Dictionary of Jazz* (New York: Macmillan, 1988), 414.

[152] Gerald Early, "White Noise and White Knights: Some Thoughts on Race, Jazz, and the White Jazz Musicians," in *Jazz: A History of America's Music*, ed. Geoffrey C. Ward and Ken Burns (New York: Alfred A. Knopf, 2000), 325.

[153] Host Ed Gordon, "NPR African-American Round Table," in *Whistleblowers* (2006).

[154] John Leland and Allison Samuels, "The New Generation Gap," *Newsweek*, 17 Mar. 1997, 53.

[155] Albright, "Micheaux, Vaudeville & Black Cast Film," 36.

34. The inscription reads "For Frank Manchel; With fond wishes for your family, you, and the book; In remembrance; Lillian Gish" Courtesy of The Manchel Collection, University of Vermont.

2
The Movies, Mr. Griffith, and Miss Gish: Lillian Gish

> "Why should a modern industrial nation, once torn apart by a war to resolve the fate of the slave-supported plantation system, not only tolerate but enthusiastically support repeated complimentary portrayals of the vanquished? What needs, desires, and assumptions did these films confirm?"
>
> *Edward D. C. Campbell, Jr.*[1]

There is the wonderful story told by Richard A. Blake about the performers in *The Whales of August* (1987) watching the dailies, and Bette Davis, who co-starred with Lillian Gish in this her last film, becoming increasingly upset over the tribute given to one of Gish's close-ups. "Exasperated, Miss Davis exclaimed, 'Of course, it's a great close-up. She invented the goddam shot.'"[2]

Bette Davis was not altogether wrong. Gish literally grew up with the movies. Over a seventy-five-year span, beginning in the teens, Gish made more than one hundred films. Moreover, Kevin Brownlow believes, "Lillian Gish is no ordinary actress; by common consent, she is one of the greatest of this century."[3] The operative word is "century."

At the same time, we cannot ignore that the great actress played a key role in the creation and defense of D.W. Griffith's *The Birth of a Nation* (1915), the single most influential movie in justifying white supremacy, defaming blacks, and distorting our memory of the American Civil War. This movie remains the encyclopedia of what white America thought about African-Americans at the start of the twentieth century. Equally important, as Jane Gaines discovered, this one film, which she labeled "a cultural and political time bomb," acted as the catalyst for a "series of black responses that have continued through the 1990s."[4]

In the pages that follow, Gish, without embarrassment or apology, explains why and what the filmmakers attempted to do in their story about race relations in American history. Neither the star nor the director invented the myths. "The irony of the (first) Great American Movie – *The Birth of a Nation* – also being a racist work of art," points out Armond White, "is not an aberration. It's a legacy, owing to the complications and tensions of America's racial life that are also apparent in Twain, Hawthorne, Melville, Faulkner."[5] Nevertheless, the cinematic power of the people who solidified those images in *The Birth of Nation* remains so powerful today that I have seen modern students bewildered and stunned by the iconography of the film. The actor's reasons for what she and Griffith did provide an unwitting legacy of American traditionalism.

Gish was born to Mary Robinson McConnell and James Leigh Gish in Springfield, Ohio, on October 14, 1893. When scholars questioned the accuracy of the date, James Frasher, her lifelong manager, noted that, "She was the same age as film. They both came into the world in 1893."[6] Five years later, her beloved sister, Dorothy, was born on March 11, 1898.

The children's father was neither an ideal provider nor husband. Eventually he moved the family to New York City, where he then abandoned them. Desperate to survive and with few opportunities open to her, Mary Gish tried her luck at acting and joined Proctor's Stage Company, where she adopted the name Mae Bernard.[7] Within months, while the troupe was playing small towns in Ohio, Lillian, at the age of five, made her stage debut in a melodrama entitled, *In Convict's Stripes*. She was billed as "Baby Lillian." Dorothy, as soon as she was able, joined the family pounding the boards.

Since children's roles were a staple in turn-of-the-century drama, the Gishes traveled extensively. Crucial to appreciating the interview that follows is an awareness of how difficult it was for the Gish sisters growing up in this environment. Outside of a tremendous dependence on their mother, the two girls, by all accounts, mastered only two things in their early childhood: a lifelong discipline in their acting skills and a healthy respect for religion. They had little time to learn anything else, and what they did learn about life and history was almost all self-taught. They had no formal education. As a result, Gish, throughout her life, occasionally exhibited, as will become evident later, a number of educational deficiencies.

It was through an accident of fate that the Gish sisters entered film in 1912. Mary Pickford, whom they had known as Gladys Smith on stage, made movies for D.W. Griffith, often called the "Father of Film." The young women decided to visit their friend, who persuaded the famous director to cast the Gishes in his melodramatic silent films. They made their screen debut the day of their visit in a potboiler entitled *An Unseen Enemy* (1912).

Lillian's chance meeting with Griffith began a remarkable friendship and professional partnership. Together they made more than forty films, including such classic movies as *The Birth of a Nation* (1915) – the controversial Civil War epic that elevated Gish into stardom – *Intolerance* (1916), *Hearts of the World* (1918), *Broken Blossoms* (1919), *Way Down East* (1920), and *Orphans of the Storm* (1921). However, Gish did more than just appear in Griffith's movies. As the *Hollywood Reporter* observed, "Gish helped write his stories and intertitles and came up with ideas for promotion."[8] Years later, when Gish wrote her autobiography, she titled it, *The Movies, Mr. Griffith, and Me*. Although she usually referred to him in public as Mr. Griffith, many historians feel that he was her great love, thus explaining why she never married.

So much has been written about Griffith's importance to film history that it is unnecessary to delve into who he was and what he accomplished. Alfred Hitchcock may have summarized it best when he said, "Every time you see a movie, you see something that originated with D.W. Griffith."[9] While Griffith did not originate many of the techniques credited to him, he certainly raised film narrative to an art form. My evaluation of the famous director and the important works about him is found elsewhere.[10] Suffice it to say, he remained devoted to his Southern roots, a love of the theater, and an unwavering belief that film was a new universal language that could alter the course of history.

The deep and passionate relationship between Gish and Griffith suggests that what follows in the interview about the history of the Civil War and her attitudes about African-Americans reflects not only her views, but also those of Griffith. Consequently, hearing her speak about those times and realizing how they represent the paternal racism of a bygone era offer a unique opportunity to view Griffith's films from the perspective of someone who knew intimately the thinking of the man who made *The Birth of a Nation*.

By the end of the teens, Griffith and Gish began to separate professionally. At first, he encouraged her to direct, giving his star the opportunity to make a five-reeler featuring Dorothy, *Remodeling Her Husband* (1920). Two years later, they parted. Gish always claimed that the break occurred because Griffith made the beau geste of telling her to take advantage of her star power and go elsewhere, but historians often point out that by 1922, the famous director not only had lost his popularity with the public, but also had begun drinking heavily. Interestingly, the years between 1922 and 1925 remain the most obscure in Gish's career, with most of the information dealing with two memorable films, *The White Sister* (1923) and *Romola* (1924).

Then in 1925, Gish made an incredible deal with MGM, giving her major artistic control of her films. In the handful of years that followed, she made three classic movies: *The Scarlet Letter* (1926), *La Boheme* (1926), and *The Wind* (1928). However, by the end of the decade, her luster with the public had begun to dim.

Here we need to consider just what her image was in the Silent Era. The *Hollywood Reporter* once described her as a "large-eyed, porcelain-skinned actress [who] often portrayed virginal, childlike young women she called 'ga-ga babies.' But even in these roles, she displayed an indomitable spirit...."[11] Richard A. Blake put it differently: "In her work for D.W. Griffith, Gish had been typecast as the child-woman, victimized by her surroundings, yet ever able to endure and triumph."[12] But as Penelope McMillan accurately observed, Gish may have been perceived "as an 'ethereal aura' that projected purity, frailty, and vulnerability"... but the actress in reality "was strong-minded, opinionated and independent."[13]

Of all the characterizations about Gish's image, none is more relevant to the following interview than Richard Dyer's speculations about the manner in which screen lighting fashioned her into the personification of "whiteness ... an ideal of purity as embodied in the white woman."[14] He arrives at this conclusion by examining the norm for Hollywood lighting in the 1920s: "North" lighting. In his words, "Three-point lighting, soft light, gauzes, and focus could all be employed to create the halos and glows of feminine portraiture."[15] Gish became the apotheosis of that screen convention. That is, "Lillian Gish could be considered the supreme instance of the confluence of the aesthetic-moral equation of light, virtue, and femininity with Hollywood's development of glamour and spectacle."[16] Thus for Dyer, what gives Gish immortality is not the fact that she was the most famous star of her times (she wasn't), but that she lasted so many decades, has always been associated with Griffith, and used such magnificent restraint in her acting. If, as he argues, it is fair to single out actors as black stars, it seems perfectly reasonable to signify her as a white star.[17] Gaines concurs and states that in the years between 1918 and 1920, the way Gish was lighted on the screen came "to standardize the 'characteristic glow of white women.' It is as though in the history of cinema, all lighting decisions were thenceforth made with Lillian Gish in mind."[18]

When the talkies came in, she refused to compromise with her style and appeared out-of-step with the new Hollywood image of the flapper or fallen woman. Although she made two early sound films, *One Romantic Night* (1930) and *His Double Life* (1933), Gish decided to devote her time to her first love, the stage. For the next sixty-three years, she spent most of her career in the theater, appearing in such classic roles as Helena in *Uncle Vanya* (1930), Camille in *Camille* (1932), Ophelia in *Hamlet* (1936), Vinnie in *Life With Father* (1939), and Miss Madrigal in *The Chalk Garden* (1956). Tennessee Williams acknowledged that he formulated the role of Blanche in *A Streetcar Named Desire* for her, but her mother's illness prevented her from trying out for the part. She also played Mrs. Carrie Watts in the 1953 production of *A Trip to Bountiful*. Gish's appearances on television were limited to distinguished productions like *The Day Lincoln Was Shot*, *The Sound and the Fury*, *Arsenic and Old Lace*, and *A Trip to Bountiful*.

The extraordinary actress did not, however, completely abandon the movies. Her first film in the 1940s was as a Norwegian wife in *The Commandos Strike at Dawn* (1942). Her consequential contemporary film roles were in *Duel in the Sun* (1946) (she played Lionel Barrymore's wife and received her only Oscar nomination), *Portrait of Jennie* (1948), *The Night of the Hunter* (1955), *The Unforgiven* (1959), *The Comedians* (1967), *A Wedding* (1978), and her last film, *The Whales of August* (1987).

Film was also a major part of her life off stage. For example, she made it a point in her later years to champion film causes like historic preservation, especially promoting a re-release of Abel Gance's *Napoleon*, as well as obtaining a special Oscar for Henri Langlois, the famed curator of the *Cinematheque Francaise*. At the same time, she received the movies' highest acclaim. In 1970, she was awarded an honorary Oscar by The Academy of Motion Picture Arts and Sciences; in 1982; she received the Kennedy Center Lifetime Achievement Award; and in 1984, Gish became the twelfth recipient of the American Film Institute's similar honor.

Her sister Dorothy died in 1969. She died at ninety-nine, on February 28, 1993.

I first met Lillian Gish on October 25, 1970. She, along with her manager, James Frasher, who faithfully handled her affairs for a quarter of a century, had come to the University of Vermont to deliver a lecture, "Lillian Gish and the Movies." I had the honor of introducing her. Thinking back to the extraordinary evening, I'm reminded of the first words Melvyn Douglas used to introduce her the night she received her Honorary Oscar: "Miss Lillian (as D.W. Griffith used to call her) is the youngest human being in the theater tonight – if youth be measured by zest, enthusiasm, and sheer physical strength." As she talked to us about films made by Griffith, Keaton, and Fairbanks, Sr., no one would have believed that this woman was seventy-seven years old! Afterwards, when she and Frasher came to our home to meet some of our film students and have a late dinner, Gish showed no signs of her age.

From what I have learned, Gish remained that sharp throughout the remainder of her life. As an example, there is a wonderful anecdote from *The Whales of August*, a movie she starred in at ninety-three years of age. Rather than directly confront her bossy co-star Bette Davis, the mischievous Gish frequently pretended she was hard-of-hearing during the shooting and missed her cues from Davis: "I just can't hear what she's saying." To Davis' outrage, Gish had no difficulty picking up her cues from the other performers. Only when director Lindsay Anderson gave Gish her co-stars' lines, did Gish perform properly.[19]

At some point on October 25, I explained to the star about the project I was working on, and how important it would be for me to interview her on Griffith, *The Birth of a Nation*, and her understanding of the treatment of African-Americans in film history. She agreed to an interview. Through the mail, I made the meeting for December 4, 1971.

I arrived at the appointed time at her New York apartment. While waiting for Gish to get ready, I heard two memorable stories from Jim. The first had to do with the recent publication of Lena Horne and Richard Schickel's book, *Lena*, which adversely affected Horne's career for a year. She encountered tremendous trouble with white and black audiences in 1971 because so much of the book had to do with her outspoken condemnation of the way white people had treated her and her disapproval of the way blacks were behaving then. The second story dealt with Gish as having been considered, at one point, for the child's role in *The Clansman* [1906], but having been turned down by the author, Thomas Dixon. When she did see the original play in New York, according to Jim, which her mother took her to see, she was extremely excited by it.

The interview began with our talking about D.W. Griffith's parents.

Lillian Gish Interview
December 4, 1971

Gish: They [Jacob and Mary Oglesby Griffith] had a farm. It wasn't a big one, not enough to be a plantation. But they did have five slaves; and the father, D.W.'s [Griffith's] father, was, as you know, a colonel in the Confederate Army. When he came back and the war was over, the slaves won their freedom. They didn't want to leave. So they stayed on; they went on working just as they were, helping apparently the women in the family plow the fields. They got used to that during the war.

Manchel: Hmmm.

Gish: And they all worked together, and they paid them a salary, and they stayed on and lived there until they moved from the farm. I think that gives the reason that Griffith always used to say, tell me and everybody around, that he loved these people, they were his children. And that he was raised with them and that he understood them better than he understood us, the white people.

Manchel: Yes. Why would.... [Seymour] Stern uses the argument [to defend Griffith] ... because a man was born a Southerner doesn't automatically make him prejudiced. [20]

Gish: Well, if you read the history of the Civil War, any number of them freed their slaves, and they wouldn't leave. They were family. And what a wonderful way to know that you were going to be taken care of from the cradle to the grave. And mostly they were used in the house with the children. They went to school with them. They worked, the children worked too, you know, and looked after the cows and the sheep, and milked. They all worked ... together.

Manchel: Except when they grew up. Was there a problem then? As far as....

Gish: Well no, they kept on working.

Manchel: They're part of the family?

Gish: And they didn't ... they weren't sent out. They weren't equipped to work on railroads and build the country. They were equipped to be part of the family and be looked after and be in the home and be told what to do. And I'm sure they were fed whatever they raised. The people in the South, particularly after the Civil War was over....

Manchel: Do you remember at all when Griffith first became aware of this attack [the charge of racism] on him?

Gish: Oh, he wasn't aware of it at all until ... It happened after it [The Birth of a Nation] opened, and he was shocked! He was shocked into making Intolerance [1916]. That's why he gave up doing The Mother and the Law [1915], which he had already photographed. It was finished that day. It was finished while he was cutting and titling and getting the score ready for The Birth of a Nation. He had finished that complete picture. Then this shock came! Well, he couldn't ... it came from every direction. He couldn't answer all his critics, so he made a film called Intolerance ... the prejudice and the injustice to man throughout the ages, beginning with Babylon and coming up to the modern period. And he said, "I can't answer them all. I can answer them with this. Think as I think or be damned."[21]

Manchel: That's an interesting point. Somebody, I don't remember who it was, somebody was doing a study of Griffith. I think it was [Seymour] Stern, or somebody, not Stern, [Thomas] Cripps. But the point he made was that critics have always defended Griffith by saying that he made Intolerance as the answer to those critics of The Birth of a Nation. And yet there's no racial remarks at all in the four stories in Intolerance. Was that deliberate?

Gish: Well, there is. It's racial and religious. The High Priests in Babylon, the High Priests of Baal, were jealous of Ishtar, the new goddess.

Manchel: That would be religious.

Gish: [The new goddess] was getting to be more popular. That was the religious theme.

Manchel: But the racial one?

Gish: Well, there were the....

Manchel: There wasn't a distinction between religion and racial?

Gish: Well, if you wanted to pick out, do a thing in history on color, what would it be?

Manchel: I don't know ... maybe the slaves in Egypt? The business of race and the Jews?

Gish: Well, but they were white people, the slaves. White people have been slaves longer than black people in the history of the world.

Manchel: That could be true. I never thought of it that way. I'm just trying to find....

Gish: Women! There are more women slaves in the world now than there are other kinds of slaves. I didn't know that until I went down through Macedonia and back in that country up above Montenegro and around through that primitive country. Why, the donkeys are treated better than the women!

Manchel: But in the modern period, there's almost no blacks used at all in *Intolerance*, if I remember correctly.

Gish: Oh, the modern! But they were not in that story. This was a story between Capital and Labor.

Manchel: Right, right.

Gish: This is when Capital got too big for its britches. And they had to be put down. And he was on the side of Labor. Now, I think if Griffith were alive today, he'd be the opposite. I'd think that he'd think Labor has gotten too big for its britches.

Manchel: You think he'd be in favor of Capital.

Gish: I think he'd be out with Labor, with labor leaders running the government. Just because they have power over these poor little taxi drivers that tell me they didn't want that last strike. They didn't vote for it.

Manchel: My sister [Rose Manchel] told me the same thing. The [New York taxi drivers] apologize when you get in [their cabs].

Gish: They are in the hands of these men. And who's important in Washington? Is it a man called Nixon, who happens to be our president at the moment, or is it Mr. [George] Meany? As I listen to Mr. Meany, he thinks he is. He's got control of the country. He's against power, I think.

The Egyptians had white people as slaves. The Colored people had been told that they are African, and they are Egyptian. Egyptians are much more Semites than they are black. They are white people.

Manchel: I was just thinking, I'm doing a book now on comedy,[22] and I'm trying to do this chapter on [Mack] Sennett. Sennett was very jealous of D.W. Griffith when Griffith was making *The Birth of a Nation*. Therefore, he made *Tillie's Punctured Romance* [1914] as a feature film to show that he was as good as the fellow who had taught him. Wasn't there any publicity at all in 1914 about what *The Clansman* was about?

Gish: Oh, we were all sworn to secrecy. Because Mr. [*Thomas*] Ince and all the people would copy every picture.... It wasn't just *The Birth of a Nation*. Anything we did, the minute Mr. Ince or any of these people found out, they'd get out [a similar picture before we did]. Ince found out about *Intolerance*, so he came out with *Civilization*. They all had spies so that they could get them into the Griffith company to find out what his next project was, and then they made theirs.

Manchel: I never knew that.

Gish: Oh yes, why we were sworn to secrecy. Not allowed to ... we didn't go about. Maybe that's why Griffith kept us working. [Laughing] I don't know. But he certainly kept us working.

Manchel: I know that.

Gish: Day and night. We never had any social life. And I know that when we were called into rehearsals ... I couldn't swear to this ... but when he started rehearsing *The Birth*, he didn't rehearse it all the way through as a complete story. He rehearsed episodes of it. But when I would see him, he would talk about *The Birth of a Nation*. He said the villain, because I always asked him who the villain was, he said that the villain, of course, was always War. But the human villain is Thaddeus Stevens, because he went down South, and he said and told these childlike people that he was going to crush the white South under the heel of the black South.

In the film, of course, Stevens was called the Hon. Austin Stoneman, Leader of the House of Representatives. Ralph Lewis played the role.[23] And he took the big Colored man.

Manchel: Siegmann?

Siegmann played the light-skinned villain, Silas Lynch, who became Piedmont's Lieutenant Governor. It was standard practice at the time for white actors to impersonate significant black characters in silent films.

Gish: Yes, George Siegmann. Silas Lynch [in the film]. And he kept telling him, "I'll build you a Kingdom." You know, "The Kingdom that will take over this South." He was the villain, and if you look at it, everyone that went wrong was led backward by that man. And the Colored people within the family, they were the ones that saved the family. Now we didn't have Colored actors. We had Madame in the studio. We were a family in that studio. Madame played I don't know how many parts. Madame Sul-te-Wan.

According to Thomas Cripps, of all the black performers who worked with Griffith, he admired and appreciated Madame Sul-te-Wan the most. The feeling was mutual. "A fellow-Kentuckian, she admired and loved Griffith, who responded by promoting her from a menial to an actress."[24]

Bogle provides an invaluable account of this woman, whom he calls "budding Black Hollywood's most important performer...."[25] She was born "Nellie Wan in Louisville, Kentucky, in 1873." Nellie eventually married and had two sons before moving with her family to Arcadia, California in 1910. In the next few years, she proved to be an extraordinary businessperson and found it advantageous to change her name to Madame Sul-Te Wan.[26] Her meeting with Griffith and their close ties are carefully described in Bright Boulevards.

Manchel: She played the fat mammy in *The Birth of a Nation*?

Jennie Lee, a white woman in black face, played the role of the faithful mammy.

Gish: No, no. She was a little woman. She played the one that danced. And all through there, I'd point out, "There's Madame, there's Madame." Everything that came up that she would play, because everyone doubled. You know Bobby Harron plays one of the Colored men. You may not know it, but you know the one that peeks under the curtain and sees the Camerons. That's Bobby Harron.
Manchel: Oh really.
Gish: He plays my brother.
Manchel: I didn't know that.
Gish: You see we had no money. If I could have doubled, I would have doubled. Everybody doubled.
Manchel: I know. I gather there was a lot of money short. But there were many black people, weren't there, in the scenes with....
Gish: That's when he went to.... You mean the cotton fields. It was down in Death Valley for one day with Wally [Walter Long] and Miriam Cooper. I've forgotten whoever worked in that scene. I didn't go. We didn't.
Manchel: How about in the Negro militia scenes when the Ku Klux Klan came to rescue the ...?
Gish: They were white men.
Manchel: They were white men?
Gish: They were the same men who played the Klansmen.
Manchel: But outside that one day in Death Valley, there were no black people at all, Colored people at all, used in the film?
Gish: We didn't have any....
Manchel: Just in Death Valley is where you got them, on that one day?
Gish: That's right.

Cripps disagrees, pointing out that numerous California black extras were housed in barracks to accommodate their appearances in both the black militia and crowd sequences. Moreover, he places the location shooting as closer to Hollywood than Death Valley.[27]

Manchel: That's incredible that he was able to create that [effect]. As you say, to use only three hundred men [to produce] that kind of story and magnetism.

Gish: Oh, and they advertised [a cast of] eighteen thousand.

Manchel: Yes.

Gish: And, you know, I always thought while I was there and working, it's much more dramatic to tell the truth, that Griffith could create two wars with three hundred people. I think that's more difficult to do than with eighteen thousand people. Anybody could do that.

Manchel: In the story of *The Birth of a Nation*, you mention that.... I'm trying to think how you just worded it. You mentioned something to the effect that the villain was supposed to be Thaddeus Stevens, and [that] one of the problems that was discussed in *The Birth of a Nation* is that, on one hand, D.W. Griffith tries to present as accurately as possible history as it was written ... Woodrow Wilson and a number of other people and in [Matthew] Brady photographs ... and yet in the story of Thaddeus Stevens, he distorts almost everything connected with Thaddeus Stevens' life. For example, Thaddeus Stevens had never been married; therefore, he didn't have any children. Thaddeus Stevens had died almost a year or two after the Civil War and had never traveled down South. He is accurate in the sense that Thaddeus Stevens was the man who controlled the Reconstruction [period]. He's accurate in the fact that he was the most powerful opponent to Lincoln, but then he....

Gish: Maybe that's what motivated all of this. That he had this.... In that little while, he expressed ideas that would have led up to this in Griffith's... [mind]. What he didn't do. I know that he was his [Griffith's] target.

Manchel: He was his target. How do you explain then the business that ... is it Siegmann, is that how you pronounce it, George Siegmann?

Gish: Siegmann.

Manchel: George Siegmann betrays Thaddeus Stevens in the film *The Birth of a Nation*. He has pretensions toward you, he wants to marry you, and he then vows to ... I think at one time he captures you at the end of the film, and there's a point where you are held prisoner and you are rescued at the last minute by the Ku Klux Klan. That wasn't Thaddeus Stevens' fault though.

Gish: Well, it was his fault insofar as he told this man he was going to be king. And a king has whatever he wants.

Manchel: I see, I see.

Gish: But my turning against him wasn't because he was black. You saw me turn against the man I loved [Henry B. Walthall, who plays Colonel Ben Cameron] when he wouldn't shake hands with him [Siegmann]. He didn't speak to him.

Manchel: That's very interesting. No one's ever mentioned that.

Gish: That's why I say [that] if you look at that film and dissect that film, you see that Griffith is on the side of the black people. And that's what shocked him.

Prof. Gaines offers an intriguing commentary on racism in and surrounding The Birth of a Nation. *In discussing the issue of the film's censors, she worried about her audience being annoyed with her for not being more virulent toward those people who supported the movie. "There is no denying," she writes, "that history will not let up on these individuals. But is it now or will it ever be possible to separate the racism of the groups who rallied around the film from what might be called the racism of the film?"*[28] *She goes on to examine DuBois' theory that the film can be "implicate[d] ... in the culture of lynching without saddling it with the entire blame."*[29]

Manchel: Let me pursue that, on the side of the black people. Anyone who's a member of the family in the film, Griffith is extremely kind to. Anyone who is loyal or faithful is treated with a great deal of respect and kindness and even tenderness, particularly when the old man is beaten and when the family is mishandled. And [when] the [loyal] family [servant is beaten by renegade black troops]....

Gish: To rescue them?

Manchel: ... the old people come to rescue him. But how about the pictures [of vicious stereotypes of African-Americans] that Griffith's always been attacked and Cripps mentions in his article ["Reaction of"]? How about the scenes with the black legislature when they put their feet on the table?

Gish: Hasn't he still got that little note? That it's history?

Griffith placed footnotes justifying his imagery and intertitles at the bottom of the frame through many sections of the film. William R. Grant IV takes another position. He sees the film as establishing for more than eight decades the negative stereotypes of African-Americans, "the archetypes Hollywood then utilizes for the portrayal of African Americans." [30]

Gish: If you look at that film, you'll see that Griffith is harmed by the black people and....

Manchel: But the argument against that being history, people have said, is that while that may have been an incident in history, what Griffith did on the screen was to make an incident appear to be an overall general truth.

Gish: It does not say that. It tells where this happened. And he had those little notes, footnotes, where they came from, the book and then the original prints; you'll find them. Everything he has of that time is authenticated.[31]

Manchel: But the impression you get is that the whole South was like that. You think that's an inaccurate impression?

Gish: I don't think that. I think this is what ... how Stevens and his ilk [thought]. I suppose it's like the Republicans and Democrats today. However, getting back to Lincoln and these people. Now he loved ... as you see all through that Lincoln visit, he was a beloved figure, North and South. He [Griffith] always maintained that the whole history of the country would have been different had Lincoln been allowed to live.

Manchel: He says that in the film, too.

Gish: He loved everything he stood for, and he loved his background and his tolerance. That war had to come. That people couldn't make a country half slave and half free. All of that. Black people today don't realize how many thousands of white men died to make them free.

Manchel: I'll tell you an interesting story that you may not have heard. I interviewed, I think I mentioned at one point, the man who was considered to be "the Black Valentino of the Silent Era," a man by the name of Lorenzo Tucker. When I was at Lorenzo's house, he was there with another fellow, a fellow by the name of Slick [Chester], who was one of the early black heavies of the silent era. Both of them are "mulattos," and both of them refused to be called blacks or Afro-Americans. They were very much opposed to the militancy that now exists. They argued that they were Colored people, and that they were Negroes, and that they had made Negro films. They were very much into integration. They were older people.

Gish: They probably had some of the best blood in the South in their veins. When ... black men took a mistress, they didn't take little cute white girls; they took fine specimens of charming black girls. If you look at the bodies of the black people today, who among our athletes do you find in the greatest number? Black people! Architecturally, their bodies. You know it takes food to make bones, and it takes generations to make handsome these people. I learned that when I went to Europe in the early twenties. I was asked to dine with royalty. I went to Spain. There was royalty. Six feet seven inches tall. No other white people were that way. Even the British ambassador, who was six feet and seemed awfully tall to me, the Duke was an Italian aristocrat, nephew of the King of Italy, the nephew was six feet seven. And the most beautiful man I've ever seen, because he was perfectly proportioned architecturally.

Manchel: I've never seen finer skin than I've seen on Princess Margaret. We had dinner with her one night when we were in England, about a year ago. She is a very short woman.

Gish: Yes, but she's a peasant.

Manchel: Yeah, but she had such lovely skin. [Princess] Margaret's a peasant?

Gish: They're peasants!

Manchel: Oh, oh, yes. I mean the skin, the color.

Gish: They're peasants compared to these long lines, say a thousand years of aristocracy. They've had good food, and they've never had to stoop over and reach and work in the soil. That's what makes peasants. They are so close to the soil all the time. And I didn't know that until I worked. And peasants in Europe, peasant doesn't mean what peasant means here. It means something low. Over there it means an aristocrat of the soil. They're not such things as....

Manchel: You know you'd be wonderful teaching linguistics, language. [Laughing]

Gish: [Laughing] Oh, I've had my education. My work. But I've learned so much because of that. But that's what peasant means. Because when I was in Germany and Austria working with Hugo von Hofmannstahl and Max Reinhardt on a film, I went, I was going to play a peasant, so they took me for a week to visit and live with the peasants. And I found out what aristocrats these people were. And waiting to be my guide was a man called Histower, [?] who was a great artist and painted most of the churches down through that part of Austria. And I didn't think he'd tell me at first that he was a peasant. And we went to one farm, and a man came out with a baby in his arms and another little one. And then in back of him were some more children, you know, stuff like that, obviously his own. And in back of that the ducks and chickens and the dogs. All the farm animals came to meet us. I thought oh, what a picture. This was the most beautiful thing. We don't have things like this. We had lunch with them. And when we left, I said to Mr. Histower [?], I said, "Oh, I should think that if ever you look for a model for the Christ use, that's your face." Then he said. "I've painted it many times. He's my brother." And then I found out that he'd disgraced the family. He'd left the land and become an artist. He couldn't do anything worse for the family than that.

Manchel: I gather that same thing happened with [Princess] Margaret's husband, Anthony Armstrong.

Anthony Charles Robert Armstrong-Jones, 1st Earl of Snowdon, is a photographer, and he divorced Princess Margaret Rose, Queen Elizabeth's sister, in 1978.

Gish: Yes, Armstrong. But [Prince] Phillip is royal.

Manchel: And a lovely man. My wife met him just accidentally. But very down-to-earth, very warm.

Gish: Oh, he is. We did a benefit here for him. We had six or seven Dollies; we were all dressed as Dollies. We had Ethel Merman, Lauren Bacall, Arlene Francis, and Lee Remick. Me.... We raised over a million dollars.... He couldn't have been more charming.

The reference here is to the main character in the hit musical, Hello Dolly.

Manchel: He's quite a guy. May I ask you some questions about the various people in *The Birth of a Nation*, just some background on what they were like as individuals? Siegmann, am I pronouncing that right?

Gish: Siegmann. He's German. George Siegmann. He was a great big fellow. He played the villain in *Hearts of the World* [1919], too.

Manchel: What sort of man was he?

Gish: He was Griffith's assistant, as well as an actor. And a good-natured fellow, did what he was told. Could look awfully menacing because he was so heavy, and big and tall.

Manchel: Did he do much in films at all? Was he much of an actor after *The Birth of a Nation*?

Gish: Oh yes, Oh yes. *Hearts of the World*, and all those pictures.

Manchel: I've never seen *Hearts of the World*, but I understand from everything that I've read there's a scene in there in which a soldier embraces a dying....

Gish: That's the greatest thing of all. That's the picture I'm looking for, because that was another answer to his critics. That story that Griffith wrote was of an American snob ... just a horrible person. Played by Bobby Harron. And he was sent to war, the First World War, so that was hard on him. He goes to France and falls in love with a little nobody French girl, which I played. He loves her, but he hates himself for loving her. "You're nothing but a little shrimp; you should just marry another shrimp and have a lot of little shrimp." Then finally, he is in the war and gets hurt.

You know in the First World War, what they did? They laid down the barrages so that the people in the trenches had to go forward and see what they did. They made sure there were barrages in the back so if you were in the trenches you were going to be killed back there if you didn't go ... [forward] as you were told. You'd be killed by the barrage in the front or the barrage in back.

Anyway, they got hit by shrapnel, this black man and this white man, and they found themselves in this shell hole.

According to Stern, Gish began using this episode, incorrectly told since Harron kisses the black man on the cheek, not the mouth, as a defense against the charges of racism leveled at D.W. Griffith in 1954.[32]

Gish: And the black man is awfully hurt, and there is only a little bit of water.... And he's delirious and calling for his mother. So the two of them, he [Harron, the white man] picks him up because there are shells all bursting around them, and he's the only one who has water.... So he gives him [the name of the actor?] the rest of his water. Then the man gets worse, and he [Harron] can see he's dying; he [the black soldier] talks to [Harron, imagining it is] his mother, and says, "It hurts, kiss it. It hurts, kiss it." And Bobby Harron leans over and kisses him full on the mouth and holds it. Now this is a dangerous scene at that time. Now, maybe now, when they do have [such things].... Think of it. But to do it then, and not to a white man, but a black man, and no one ever....

Manchel: Did Bobby have trouble after that? Making movies? Or was he too big a star?

Gish: You see the black man was their hero, and he converted the snob.

Gerald R. Butters, Jr. does not cite Hearts of the World *in his explanation on how Griffith's racial stereotyping contributed to the director's decline. But he does insist that by the mid-twenties, several of Griffith's films reinforced the filmmaker's position: "His stories were ultimately about white male masculinity – their divine and natural right to judge and punish everyone. In the filmmaker's narrative system, dominance over non-whites is required to maintain the hegemony of white men."*[33]

Manchel: Who played that part of the black man? Do you remember that?

Gish: I don't know, and I looked all over the world. I think this picture was deliberately destroyed because all the pictures before that are intact.

Manchel: You know that there are a number of articles that appeared in March of 1915, which claimed that there were parts of *The Birth of a Nation* that were censored. And have never been seen since. I don't know if I mentioned that to you or not.[34]

Gish: I haven't seen *The Birth of a Nation* lately, but I've never seen that, unless they took out those footnotes that made for authenticity.

Manchel: No. They claim that there was a scene at the beginning in which slaves were put on boats from Africa, and there was a scene at the end, Seymour Stern wrote about it, too [*Griffith*, 66, 85], at the end of the film in which the black people were herded onto boats and sent back to Africa.

Gish: I never saw it. I was there for all the cutting and the running [of the film]....

Manchel: And you never saw any of those things?

Gish: So help me I cannot remember any of that.

Manchel: Well, if he had done it, you certainly would have seen it.

Gish: Well, I didn't play in it. But I don't think that we would have had the money to build the boats. Think what it would have cost to ... [build] the boats. We didn't have money. We only took a scene once. We only had one negative.

Manchel: Did you do many rehearsals before the scene?

Gish: Certainly, we rehearsed the thing for months. They had it all written on paper – how many feet – because every scene in rehearsal in a room was fifteen feet. He didn't want it to be twelve when it got a few weeks later. When he would get excited about it and forget the tempo of it. Now last night I saw [the film] *Nicholas and Alexandra*. I was there [Soviet Union] for five years. It ran for three hours and a half. But if they had rehearsed that and timed it, they would have gotten some excitement. It's a great mother of a story, and I adored the book.

Manchel: I haven't read the book. In Stern's work and some other people's work, they mention that the actual shooting of *The Birth of a Nation* began in July, and I'm trying to think exactly when they say it started. They claim it started in July, and it took about six months to do.

Gish: Oh no! It took nine weeks, and I worked on it.

Manchel: Yeah, here it is. It says it started July 4, 1914, and lasted six months.

Gish: It's not true.

Manchel: It took nine weeks to ...?

Gish: It took nine weeks! And when it was put together, it wasn't much over that. There was only one scene that was made more than once, and that was Mae [Marsh's] scene because she forgot to wear that blouse.

Manchel: I remember that you told me that story. You were so thrilled because she had to change for the death scene twice.

Gish: Oh, yes, everybody was envious. We, in all our scenes, we had one chance at them, and that was all. It was like live television.

Manchel: I'm curious now, do you have any idea how many months [the film] went into rehearsal before the July 4 shooting?

Gish: We rehearsed for weeks and weeks, only at night, or when it was raining. We had to work all the rest of the time making other movies. He couldn't dare stop a minute because he had all these people on salary. So he had to keep turning them out, turning them out, and all the people that were there and all the directors ... because all his assistants usually turned into directors. Actors, too. And as you know, Elmer Clifton went on to become quite a famous director. Even I directed.

Stern relies heavily on Clifton's 1946 recollections for describing the production of The Birth of a Nation.[35]

Manchel: You told me.

Gish: Called *Remodeling Her Husband* [1920] for Paramount. A five-reel comedy. I'd like to find it. I'd like to see how many of Dorothy's comedies are around.[36]

Manchel: I don't see any of Dorothy's comedies around at all. Are there any around?

Gish: I saw ... I saw *Nell Gwyn* [Paramount-British National, 1926]. Directed by Herbert Wilcox. He started the English movie company. Then it became successful because *Nell Gwyn* got an American release and that began their comeback.

Manchel: Because it would be wonderful to have a retrospective showing of her films.

Gish: Oh, they're wonderful. Over at the Museum [of Modern Art], they've got a Civil War story with Dorothy, in which she's adorable. I can't remember the name of it. *The Littlest Yank* [Triangle-Fine Arts, 1917] I think is the name of it. Is it, Jim [speaking to James Frasher in the other room]?

Frasher: Yes, it is.

Gish: Have they got any more over there, do you know?

Frasher: They have none of her Paramount films.

Gish: They wouldn't have those, because Paramount is sitting on them. MGM is sitting on their films.

Frasher: They have some of her pictures, but as far as they know, through very extensive research. Eileen Bowser [the distinguished curator] says as far as she knows anywhere in the world, there are not any of her [Dorothy's] Paramount products. They are all gone. She says you can't say that for sure because sometimes they do appear.

Manchel: Private collectors.

Gish: They might be in Russia.

Frasher: They did a whole....

Gish: They sent us two from Russia.

Frasher: They [Museum of Modern Art] did a whole program on Dorothy. Everything. Extensive. Almost a year's research trying to find them. With every contact they had in the world. Not one did they uncover.

Manchel: I'd love to see one. I've never seen any at all, except for the one you showed that evening [at the University of Vermont].

Frasher: With a little Jazz music, that's marvelous.

Gish: *Nell Gwyn?*

Frasher: No, they don't have a print of *Nell Gwyn*. That was on loan.

Gish: Are you sure? I saw it there.

Frasher: That was on loan.

Manchel: On loan from whom?

Gish: From England.

Frasher: From England, or from Eastman House [in Rochester, New York]. Now Eastman House has some of the films. But they have none of the Paramount films.

Manchel: But Eastman House is very difficult to get films out. [It] may be different if it's one museum to another.

Gish: Oh! Please find out if they have any. I think they'd let me see them. I don't want to have them, but I think it's a pity to have anything as good as Dorothy was and not [available].

Manchel: Magnificent. We could not get over laughing at that scene with her as a tomboy....

Gish: That was just a little bit of her talent.

Manchel: But it was the first time I had ever seen her.

Gish: Now *Romola* [*Inspiration*-Metro Goldwyn, Henry King, 1924] is still in existence. Dorothy played ... [Tessa, a peasant woman].

Manchel: The only thing I knew about *Romola* was the picture I got for the book [*When Pictures Began to Move*].

Gish: Well, *Romola*, as Douglas Fairbanks, Sr. always said, it was the most beautiful picture ever made, because it was so authentic, fifteenth century Florentine. And that's quite a period.

Frasher: Just an interruption about Dorothy. There is a sequence in a talkie film by Otto Preminger, called *Centennial Summer* [1946].

Manchel: Jeanne Crain is in that.

Frasher: Yes. Linda Darnell plays the girl, Dorothy is the mother, Constance Bennett is the sister who is a vamp. There is a scene in there that is the most brilliant piece of ... acting of Dorothy's where Walter Brennan is the husband. And she suddenly gets it into her head that Constance Bennett is trying to steal him. And the story is that she makes him rise up in the world from job to job to the president of the railroad he is running. Dorothy's reaction to these photographs as they change, it's about four minutes, and it's the funniest sequence. It's the best thing in the whole film.

Manchel: I think that film is in circulation.

Frasher: The only thing funnier in the movie is, of course, when Constance Bennett and Dorothy Gish both sing. They both claimed that's what killed Jerome Kern.

Jerome Kern wrote the music for Centennial Summer.

Manchel: You know my wife couldn't get over your stories, Jim. You hit and run. [At this point, Frasher left the room, leaving Ms. Gish and me both laughing.]

Another question I wanted to ask you about *The Birth of a Nation*. There was great confusion about who owned the film *The Birth of a Nation*. There was a group, Stern says, there was a group called Kinemacolor Clansman Corporation that was started in 1912 by [Thomas] Dixon [Jr.], and then [Raymond A.] Cook claims that it was started in 1911 ["The Man Behind"], another one from Dixon. And then another man comes along, Stern again, says that under Griffith in 1914, Epoch Producing Corporation was started.

Actually, Stern claims that both Griffith and Aitken incorporated the company on February 8, 1915, although it had been functioning for some time earlier.[37]

Gish: Aitken. Harry and Roy Aitken.

Manchel: Harry and Roy Aitken in their book [*The Birth of a Nation Story*] claimed it started in 1913. And someone ... Cripps says 1915; it was started to distribute *The Birth of a Nation*. Do you have any knowledge about that?

Gish: I would say that I didn't know about money in those days. I wasn't interested.

Manchel: But would you know, for example, whether Griffith owned *The Birth of a Nation*, or whether the Aitkens owned *The Birth of a Nation*, or who was responsible for it?

Gish: The Aitkens. I can tell you this. Not us, but the Aitkens. We were told that rich people, rich men, were very dangerous, and that we'd just better stay away from them. You know, we were [very young] actresses in the movies....

Manchel: I remember that, yes.

Gish: This was done to protect us, because we were very young, much younger than anyone would allow us to be or actresses today. And these two would come to the studio in a Rolls Royce, or a very fancy car, and then they'd be all dressed up in hats with fur collars, and we'd hide if they came in. We'd look at them from through the crack in the scenery. We'd never meet them.

Manchel: Did you ever meet Thomas Dixon at all?

Gish: No. I had a letter from him. It's in my files someplace. If I haven't sent it to the Library of Congress. Telling about this little girl he knew ... Charming letter in longhand. Jim, did you send the Thomas Dixon letter down to Washington?

Frasher: No, and I don't think they much care.

Manchel: There's a story about Thomas Dixon's widow. He was married, I think, twice. His first wife died, and his second wife's name is Madeline. And he wrote a book called *Southern Horizons*, which is his autobiography.[38] He wrote a number of books, including *The Leopard Spots* [1903] and *The Clansman* [1905], and then made the play [1906] which became *The Birth of a Nation*. And somebody suggested that I write, perhaps I can get a copy of that and see what Dixon's version of *The Birth of a Nation* was and his relationship [to it].

Very helpful in this regard is Raymond Allen Cook's biography of Dixon.[39]

Manchel: And I wrote a letter to someone [Mrs. Joan Spencer, Reference Librarian, April 30, 1971] in South Carolina, where she [Madeline] was supposed to live. We got a letter [May 11, 1971] back saying she wasn't there; she was at a place called St. Anne's Home in Concordia, Kansas. Then we sent the letter [May 19, 1971] to Concordia, Kansas, and it came back opened a month later and a stamp on it saying, "address unknown." And then we heard from somebody in Washington saying she was mentally committed. Mrs. Dixon. And no one seems to know where she is or what's happened to her.

Gish: But I did hear this story about the money. That he [Dixon] was supposed to get $25,000. They just didn't have it to give him, and persuaded him to take a percentage, and that was awfully hard to do. He got $10,000.

Manchel: Right. $10,000 was what he was supposed to get.

Gish: A percentage. He made over; I don't know how many millions of dollars.

Manchel: He lost it all. He lost it all. The same way that D.W. Griffith....

Gish: Well, because he thought he could do the same as Griffith.

Manchel: That's right, he started to make a movie – I think it was called *The Birth of a Race*.

Paula J. Maassood refers to the project as "ill-fated ... [because it] fell victim to a shortage of funds and competing political visions."[40] *The Birth of a Race (1918), made as a reaction to* The Birth of a Nation, *had limited distribution and then disappeared from film history.*[41]

Gish: Yes, he was going to outdo Griffith. It looked so easy up there.

Manchel: He was a very egocentric man. He was supposed to have been a great orator. I think it is curious that you never met him. He was a very strange guy.

Gish: Never met him. But I know of him.

Manchel: Do you remember attending any of the previews, either at Clune's Auditorium [February 8, 1915, in Los Angeles] or at the Liberty Theater [February 20, 1915, in New York]?

Gish: Oh, yes, I, oh, yes, I remember going to Clune's. Wasn't the Philharmonic showing movies at that time?

Manchel: The Philharmonic. It's now called the Philharmonic. Originally it was called Clune's.

Gish: It held three thousand people, didn't it?

Manchel: Yes.

Gish: Well, we were just overcome by them.

Manchel: There was controversy on that. Some say that it was supposed to be shown in the afternoon; and then as the story goes, it had to be canceled because angry Negroes had gotten an injunction and it was moved up to that evening. The evening of February 8 at 8 p.m. Do you remember whether it was in the afternoon or the evening?

Gish: I think I would remember such a thing. I don't remember anything about that film, except that it was a great success out there, and [that it] was called *The Clansman*.

Manchel: Right, right.

Gish: And then he [Griffith] didn't want to bring it into New York until he showed it to [President Woodrow] Wilson, because he wanted to be sure that he had not taken liberties with history.

Manchel: Now that's an interesting point. I just want to make sure before we go on to that one. From what your memory tells you, quoting you, you remember the show in the evening, not in the afternoon.

Gish: It just opened and ran the way movies did in those days.

Manchel: No preview, no special opening performance?

Gish: No, no.

Manchel: It just opened up.

Gish: Just opened. I don't ever remember that being shown in a preview. That came in later.

Manchel: I see, I see. Now about Wilson. That's a very interesting story. In fact, I mentioned it to you last time. There are several stories on that. One ... of all of them, you are the first one who says differently, which may be of interest to you. Everyone claims that Dixon, who was a classmate of Wilson's at John Hopkins, they were both graduate students together, Dixon wrote to Wilson to ask him to see the film. Now if I understand what you are saying, Griffith wanted Wilson to see the film to make certain that he hadn't misinterpreted history.

Gish: Griffith went there with that film and saw it in the room with the President. Of course, we were all so impressed with this.

Manchel: Yes, I would think so.

Gish: But we didn't go to the White House to see the President then any more than we would today.

Manchel: And Griffith went with it, and Dixon I know was there.

Gish: I'm sure of it. Now Dixon might have been there.

Manchel: But there was no preview or show in New York that you know of, before the Wilson showing?

Gish: Honestly.... [Frasher hands us a letter.] Thank you, Jim.

Manchel: Thank you very much. It's a very lovely letter. May I read this into the tape? I want to finish this because I'm very fascinated with the point that you have here about Wilson. To your understanding, there was no showing in New York prior to Griffith's going to the White House to show Mr. Wilson the film?

Gish: Oh no. He wanted him to see it before it came into New York.

Manchel: Before it came into New York.

Gish: California, remember, was a country place in those days. It wasn't the metropolis it is today. This [New York] was the great Mecca for everything in America at that time, as it is now.... Much more than it is now. We have other great cities. And he [Griffith] wanted the okay of Wilson, who taught this history at Princeton [University] and then became our President. He thought if he puts his okay on it, then it is authentic history, as he believed it to be. And Wilson gave it to him with those words. He was quiet. He said his heart stopped. When it was over, Wilson didn't say a thing. Wilson just sat there in silence for a long time, and no one dared speak. And then he finally said those wonderful words, I thought, "It's like writing history with lighting, and it's all too true."

Manchel: Do you know that he recanted? He said he never said that.

Gish: Yes, because then it became a political issue, and his advisors said that nobody heard him say that, and he could just say he didn't.

Manchel: I would imagine Griffith not being upset with the President taking it back three months later, because he would have understood why he had to.

Gish: Yes.

Manchel: Do you remember anything at all about the New York opening?

Gish: I wasn't there for that. But I came along after. Because Mr. Griffith kind of wanted to show it off. And I was allowed to go to the box office and sit on one of those tall seats. And I still remember the smell of cigar smoke. And I sat there, and Griffith beaming as he told people, "No seats left. No seats left." [We began laughing, as Gish acted out the scene.] Everybody said, "You can't make a twelve-reel film. It hurts their eyes. They won't go to see it." Everybody ... everybody was against this.

Manchel: I've always been amazed that with people of your stature, that he never once called on any of you to help him defend the film against the critics.

Gish: We were too young.

Manchel: You were too young. But even the older people in the film.

Gish: We were busy making other films. Griffith was paying them. That was his stock company. They were out there making other pictures.... We all had to work.

Manchel: And nobody bothered you, nobody harassed you? I mean today, if somebody made a film that was unpopular, the star would have trouble getting work.

Gish: Oh, but they weren't bad. Reporters and newspaper people weren't interested in us. They didn't even know who we were. Our names weren't even used in the programs on screen. We were just workmen.

Contemporary viewers sometimes forget that the cast credits for The Birth of Nation *did not appear on screen at first. According to Stern, the only two people credited on screen were Dixon and Griffith in 1915.*[42] *There was, however, a program printed for the performances at Clune's Auditorium, which did include not only the names of the cast, but also the titles of the main musical numbers performed by a full orchestra.*

Manchel: You know, it's amazing to try to think back, and how far ago it was and people weren't stars. And the names you have now. My sister is frightened to meet you even now.

Gish: Yes, you see all the press agents have built this up. There were no such things as press agents [then].

Manchel: Another couple of questions I wanted to ask you along this line. You don't remember ... there was a film called *Hoodoo Ann* [1916].

Gish: Yes. Mae's.

Hoodoo Ann, *directed by Lloyd Ingraham, is notable for being one of Mae Marsh's best films for Triangle and for having a screenplay by Griffith using the pseudonym Granville Warwick.*[43]

Manchel: And there was a woman, a black woman in the film who played the housekeeper called Cindy.

Gish: Really?

Manchel: I don't remember her name?

Gish: I mean was she a little woman?

Manchel: Yes. She wore a bandanna around her head. She was slight woman, thin, very dark....

Gish: That was Madame Sul-te-Wan.

Manchel: And she told through voodoo what was to come.

Gish: That was Madame undoubtedly. I can't remember.

Manchel: She wore a bandanna around her head. She was a very slight woman, thin, very dark....

Gish: I'm sure that was Madame. She played all [the black parts]. She was the one we had. It is her, isn't Jim?

Frasher: It is.

Gish: Same woman?

Frasher: The same woman.

Manchel: Amazing.

Gish: She was with Griffith when he died, you know.

Manchel: You told me that. She never, she never issued any statements about the film. About Griffith.

Gish: ... [There was no need for one.] It was so obvious to all of us that what Griffith said was true.... He was used in those days as Mr. [William Harrison] Hays [head of the Motion Picture Producers of America] later on. Any censorship, any trouble that came up, poor Griffith, as head of the industry, had to go at his own expense to Washington and try to settle it for the whole industry. There were no heads, but he was recognized as the man who represented films.

Manchel: Another thing about censorship. D.W. wrote a pamphlet about the rise of free speech, right after *The Birth of a Nation* [The Rise].

Gish: Yes, yes.

Manchel: And even in that he never mentions anything about race. He never refers anything to the Colored question. He wanted, the argument it seems to me, that I am trying to sort out, the argument seems to be that Griffith defended the filmmaker's right for free speech, but made no reference to the distortion or to the attacks on him concerning race.

Gish: Well, he didn't think there should be. He had no race prejudice. He said ... this is indicative of the way Griffith felt. He felt that every story had to have a villain; it had to have a menace. Well, anytime you have a villain, it was ... it caused trouble. Finally, he did *Broken Blossoms* [1919]. And the English just had a fit because the father beat the child, and he said, "I guess we can't take anybody for a villain now except the Americans." They didn't realize that just because one man's bad, that the whole nation isn't bad.

Manchel: There's another point about D.W. in the film. I'm still not clear. On one hand, he claims to be very authentic with *The Birth of a Nation*; and yet when it suits his purposes, he was very unauthentic.

Gish: Where?

Manchel: In Thaddeus Stevens, for example.

Gish: He said it was patterned after him! He didn't say it was Thaddeus Stevens. Obviously, he knew he didn't have a family, and maybe he didn't have a Colored mistress. I don't know.

Manchel: Oh, he did. He did have a Colored mistress.

Gish: But then he had ... that was authentic.

Manchel: Yes, yes.

Gish: But it was patterned. He never said it was; he never told us it was. He said this character is patterned after....

Manchel: And the Ku Klux Klan, too, is different in the film, because the dates of the film disagree with the rise of the Ku Klux Klan. It had started right after the Civil War, had lasted for two or three years and then been disbanded. And in the film it goes up to 1871, when a new type of Klan arose, one that Griffith himself later was to make a distinction that was the old Klan he felt was a justified organization....

Gish: And the new one he was against.

Manchel: Yes, yes.

Gish: Well, that sounds like him. I don't remember that, but it sounds like him.

Manchel: Now from what I've been reading in the history, they tell me that there were a lot of race riots that started around that time. Wasn't there any concern, or was there any fear?

Gish: Oh, yes, he had to go to Boston, to all these places, Chicago. The militia was called out. But when *Orphans of the Storm* [1922] went to France, the same thing happened there. It seems that he was dynamite whatever he touched. They didn't like the way he treated the French Revolution. And have you seen that it's been running lately on television.

Manchel: Yes, yes. Channel 13, I think.

Gish: And it's wonderful. I saw it....

Manchel: Nowhere near like seeing it on a large screen. I think it....

Gish: It's true. Even so, believe me, you don't look away from that screen. If you do, you lose some of the story. You'd never go to sleep or put it down.

Manchel: No, we had ... we showed *The Birth of a Nation* a couple of weeks ago, and that woman [Vermont organist] was there. She played [the score], and it was just lovely. I wanted to ask you one or two questions about Jennie Lee. Was she black? She played the mammy.

Gish: No. Jennie Lee was in our stock company, under salary.

Manchel: Was she always a bit player? Did she ever go anyplace?

Gish: I think she's something in that hoodlum picture with Mae. I think she plays some part. She played mothers. As Josephine Crowell [played Mrs. Cameron in *The Birth of a Nation*] did.

Gish may be referring here to The Mother and the Law, *which was incorporated into* Intolerance *[1916]. Wagenknecht and Slide list Lee only in the credits of* The Birth of a Nation. *The authors of* D.W. Griffith and the Biograph Company *indicate that she played in a number of Biograph movies and that she died in 1925.*⁴⁴

Manchel: And William de Vaull, Jake. He played the old Colored man?

Gish: What was his name?

Manchel: William de Vaull. [Spelling the name] De VAULL.

Gish: I think they were all in our stock company.

Manchel: And Tom Wilson [Stoneman's black servant] was a white man.

Gish: Yes, he was. He was in our stock company.

Manchel: And Gus, Walter Long, what about him?

Gish: Oh, Walter Long played all kinds of parts. He played the bad man, one of the bad men, in the gangster [section in] *Intolerance, The Mother and the Law.*

Manchel: Hmm.

Gish: You see that picture [*The Mother and the Law*] was taken and finished, and then when he did *Intolerance* [in four parts] – he did Babylon, did France, and did Crucifixion. The first *The Mother and the Law* looked too small to him. And he did it all over. He remade that picture entirely.

And Miriam Cooper, who played the moll, the bad girl in that play, a member of a Southern family, and Miriam is living in one of the Carolinas.

Manchel: Miriam Cooper? Do you know anyone at all that I could speak to or pursue this with as far as Griffith's treatment, or the general treatment of Colored people, or black people, in films that is available now?

Gish: Jimmy Smith, if he's alive. He's a Colored. Or his wife. I don't remember if she was there at that time or if she came later, his wife. But Jimmy cut that picture.

The authors of D.W. Griffith and the Biograph Company *identify a James Edward Smith, who acted as the assistant to Biograph's Daniel Shay, film editor.*⁴⁵ *Bogle comments on a Jimmy Smith who worked with Charles Butler, both casting directors "who ran a casting office for colored people...."*⁴⁶

Manchel: You wouldn't happen to have any contacts with any black personalities over the years?

Gish: Only Madame and her sons. I told you, I was making a television out there.... They may not remember me.... She had two little boys. And Griffith looked after them ... when she needed money. [He] was awfully generous, not only to Madame, but to older people. [Adolph] Lestina [an actor who began with Griffith at Biograph], who played in all those [early] pictures. Well, Lestina when Griffith came into the theater, I think he loaned him a stick of grease paint. And Griffith didn't have the money to buy a stick of grease paint. As a result, he [Griffith] took care of him all his life until he died. If he didn't have a job, he gave him money. He had a memory for people who helped him.

Manchel: People had a short memory for him, I gather. They didn't help him very much.

Frasher: Who was the beautiful black man, I think he was Mr. Griffith's chauffeur, who came to the performance in Louisville?

Gish: Oh yes.

Frasher: He's marvelous, that man – extremely intelligent.

Gish: See if you can get in touch with him.

Frasher: Through Charles Lowe, you can get in touch with him ... Louisville. He's still alive....

Gish: He told us about the chauffeur.

Frasher: And the chauffeur came to the reception.

Gish: Came to our reception. And I met him. That's right, that's right.

Frasher: And he told you stories about Mr. Griffith....

Manchel: Do you know any people, personalities today, either one of you, who have worked in films in the last fifteen or twenty years who know [Harry] Belafonte or [Sidney] Poitier? Anyone who might be of help to me in getting to meet some of these people and talk to them about their experiences in the movies? Because I'm getting to meet a number of people, I think, on the second level, but outside of a person like yourself....

Gish: Roscoe Lee Browne, wherever he is. He played with us in *The Comedians* [Peter Glenville, 1967]. He's a poet and a charming gentleman....

I did actually get to interview Roscoe Lee Browne, when I went out to Los Angeles in January 1971. To my everlasting regret, the audiotape broke and could not be restored.

Frasher: James Earl Jones.

Gish: James Earl Jones. However, I don't know James Earl Jones. I met him once at Lucy's [Lucy Crowell, Gish's agent].

I did finally get to interview James Earl Jones in New York in 1972. More about that interview elsewhere.

Manchel: I'd love to talk to him about *The Great White Hope*, and how he did that.

Howard Sackler's 1968 Broadway play, The Great White Hope, *made Jones a star. Martin Ritt's screen adaptation was made two years later. Both Jones (as Jack Jefferson – a pseudonym for Jack Johnson) and Jane Alexander reprised their stage roles. The movie marked the latter's screen debut. Jones' debut in films came in Stanley Kubrick's masterpiece,* Dr. Strangelove or, How I Learned to Stop Worrying and Love the Bomb *(1963).*[47]

Frasher: He's handled by Lucy Crowell.
Gish: My agent.
Frasher: Miss Gish's agent.
Manchel: Do you think that I could impose on her?
Gish: Oh, I could call her. See if you can get her on the phone, and I'll ask her now.
Manchel: Oh, that would be marvelous. I tell you I won't ask you any more questions, but ... if you'd be kind enough to autograph this picture for me, because I want to hang it in my office.

The picture was taken backstage just before I introduced Gish at her University of Vermont lecture, and it hung in my office until I retired in 2000.

Gish: I want to talk to Lucy. She'll know where James Earl Jones is. I don't know if he is New York or California.

Gish did get me an interview with Jones, who was in California. Unfortunately, when I contacted him in Los Angeles, he begged off the promised interview. As I remember the reason, he said that he was going through a very difficult time in his life, trying to decide whether he was first a black actor, then an actor. He did, however, ask me to contact him later in the year in New York.

Manchel: Well, I'm going out to California for ten days the first ten days in January, to meet a man named Clarence Muse. I don't know whether you know that name or not, but he was a black actor who worked in the 30s, 40s, and 50s.
Gish: Certainly, the black actors have come a long way. It is wonderful.
Manchel: Buster Keaton, in his book, talks about the fact that there was no segregation.

Actually, Keaton says that segregation existed on stage during his youth and childhood, but then the color line was broken afterwards.[48]

Gish: None whatsoever. In the theater, I never knew who was who. They went to different churches. That was all.

Manchel: Some people say that there was a different door that black people had to go into.

Gish: Certainly not! They were no different than we were.

Manchel: A black person didn't ... [have a different door] to go through in the theater?

Gish: In fact, a little black child was more interesting to me because her color was different. She wasn't as commonplace as the others. I liked her better, and we played together. There was never any prejudice against anyone in the theater. It's the true democracy, if you've been raised in it as Dorothy and I have since we were four and five years of age. And as I say, Mother used to tell us, she was Episcopalian, all generations of the Church of England, and she'd say, "Go to your own church if you can; but if you can't, go to any church. It's better than no church." So we'd go to whatever was there. We went to church on Sunday; we didn't have to work. That's where we went.

Manchel: Do you know a lot of people are trying to make it an anti-Semitic thing. Because they claim that the [Harry] Cohns, the [Adolph] Zukors, and the [Marcus] Loews [the Jewish film moguls of Hollywood's Golden Age]....

Gish: They were smart and got into it [the movies]. Why weren't the others? They had the same chance. Why didn't they get into it?

Manchel: They said they were all Jewish though, and the blacks were kept out because the Jews kept them out.

Gish: Oh, I don't think the blacks had the foresight and the incentive. The Jewish people ... my cousin teaches school in Berkeley in California. And ninety-five percent of her children are Jewish, and she said, "I feel so sorry for the gentile children." And I said, "Why?" She said, "They can't keep up with the Jewish children." I said, "Why? Are they that dumb?" She said, "No. The parents work with the Jewish children. The others don't....There is a closer relationship with the Jewish people. They stand by each other." They stand by their families. Look how good they are as husbands, as mothers. Next to the Chinese, ... We have so few of them here, but they're a unit too. We're not a unit as the Jewish children are. We didn't know that as children.

Manchel: I'm just trying to probe and think of all the things that have been said about Griffith and *The Birth of a Nation* and blacks in films in general. I'm trying to feel your reactions to them and understand it.

Gish: As far as I can see, that man was as near to being a Christian gentleman as any man I ever knew, and that was love thy brother as thyself. And he'd say, "A smile is a smile, a tear is a tear the world over, but when you start making gestures, you must remember we have certain gestures in the Western world that might not be understood in the Eastern world, so therefore you'd better imitate animals or birds, because they can always make themselves understood if they want something." So we watched animals.

Manchel: Did he ever become bitter about the...?

Gish: He never was bitter the way he was treated. And that was one of reasons I made that remark. He, when I came out to sell his story in California, they said, "Oh, I always thought you had brains and apparently I was wrong. Now who do you think would be interested in the old man?" He always called himself, "the old man." "Who'd want to tell his story?"

Manchel: I bet you can make a fortune with that film. Telling a story about him would be prime for a great movie.

Gish: If you ever get this man on the screen as he was, he was so beloved by everybody. I sound as if I just loved this man as a human [being]....

35. From left to right: Lillian Gish and Dorothy Gish in a scene from D.W. Griffith's *Orphans of the Storm* (1922). Courtesy of The Manchel Collection, University of Vermont.

Notes

[1] Edward D.C. Campbell, Jr., *The Celluloid South: Hollywood and the Southern Myth* (Knoxville: University of Tennessee Press, 1981), 4.
[2] Richard A. Blake, "Lillian Gish Dies after 75 Years in Film," *America*, 20 Mar. 1993, 14.
[3] Kevin Brownlow, "Lillian Gish," *American Film* 9.5 (1984), 22.
[4] Gaines, "The Scar of Shame: Skin Color and Caste in Black Silent Melodrama," 6.
[5] Armond White, "Stepping Forward, Looking Back," *Film Comment* (2000), 35.
[6] David Thomson, *The New Biographical Dictionary of Film. Expanded and Updated* (New York: Alfred A. Knopf, 2004), 348.
[7] Ralph Haven Wolfe, "The Gish Film Theater and Gallery: The Ohio Roots of Dorothy and Lillian Gish," *Journal of Popular Film and Television* 22.2 (1994), 58.
[8] "Lillian Gish Dies after 75 Years in Film," *Hollywood Reporter*, 1 Mar. 1993, 29.
[9] William K. Everson, "David Wark Griffith," *Film Society Newsletter*, 1 (1963), 26.
[10] Manchel, *Film Study: An Analytical Bibliography*, 1360-1391.
[11] "Lillian Gish Dies after 75 Years in Film," 29.
[12] Blake, "Lillian Gish Dies after 75 Years in Film," 14.
[13] Penelope McMillan, "Death Takes Screen Legend Gish and Dance Star Keeler; Lillian Gish Starred in Epic Silent Movies," *Los Angeles Times*, 1993, 1A+.
[14] Dyer, *The Matter of Images: Essays on Representation*, 23-24.
[15] Ibid., 23.
[16] Ibid., 23.
[17] Ibid., 24.
[18] Gaines, "Fire and Desire: Race, Melodrama, and Oscar Micheaux," 202.
[19] McMillan, "Death Takes Screen Legend Gish and Dance Star Keeler; Lillian Gish Starred in Epic Silent Movies," 1A+.
[20] Seymour Stern remains one of Griffith's strongest defenders and most prolific commentators. For a useful listing of his most relevant essays, see Manchel, *Film Study II*, 1374ff.
[21] For a critical examination of the film's censorship problems, see Gaines, "Fire and Desire: Race, Melodrama, and Oscar Micheaux," 222-223,230, and 233-234.
[22] Frank Manchel, *Yesterday's Clowns: The Rise of Film Comedy* (New York: Franklin Watts, 1973).
[23] Gish here amplifies the arguments of Seymour Stern, "Griffith: 1—The Birth of a Nation," *Film Culture*, 36 (1965), 176-198. The best source on Stevens is Fawn M. Brodie, *Thaddeus Stevens: Scourge of the South* (New York: W.W. Norton, 1959).
[24] Thomas Cripps, *Slow Fade to Black: The Negro in American Film, 1900-1942* (London; New York: Oxford University Press, 1977), 45.
[25] Bogle, *Bright Boulevards, Bold Dreams: The Story of Black Hollywood*, 16.
[26] Ibid., 7-8.
[27] Cripps, *Slow Fade to Black: The Negro in American Film, 1900-1942*. Thomas

Cripps, "Reaction of the Negro to the Motion Picture the Birth of a Nation," *The Historian*, 25.3 (1963).

[28] Gaines, "Fire and Desire: Race, Melodrama, and Oscar Micheaux," 232.

[29] Ibid., 233.

[30] William R. Grant, *Post-Soul Black Cinema : Discontinuities, Innovations, and Breakpoints, 1970-1995, Studies in African American History and Culture* (New York: Routledge, 2004), 24.

[31] Details about Griffith's sources are provided by Stern, "Griffith: 1—The Birth of a Nation," 34-38.

[32] Ibid., 16-18.

[33] Gerald R. Butters, *Black Manhood on the Silent Screen, Culture America* (Lawrence: University Press of Kansas, 2002), 170.

[34] For a useful discussion of the censorship issues, see Gaines, "Fire and Desire: Race, Melodrama, and Oscar Micheaux," 222-223, 230, 233-234.

[35] Stern, "Griffith: 1—The Birth of a Nation," 53-56.

[36] Lillian Gish and Ann Pinchot, *The Movies, Mr. Griffith & Me* (Englewood Cliffs, NJ: Prentice-Hall, 1969), 223-226.

[37] Stern, "Griffith: 1—The Birth of a Nation," 51.

[38] Thomas Dixon, *Southern Horizons: An Autobiography* (Unfinished manuscript).

[39] Raymond A. Cook, *Fire from the Flint: The Amazing Careers of Thomas Dixon* (Winston-Salem, NC: John F. Blair, 1968).

[40] Paula J. Massood, *Black City Cinema: African American Urban Experiences in Film* (Philadelphia: Temple University Press, 2003), 46.

[41] For specific details, see Gaines, "Fire and Desire: Race, Melodrama, and Oscar Micheaux," 97-98.

[42] Stern, "Griffith: 1—The Birth of a Nation," 5.

[43] Edward Wagenknecht and Anthony Slide, *The Films of D.W. Griffith* (New York: Crown, 1975), 261.

[44] Cooper C. Graham et al., *D.W. Griffith and the Biograph Company* (Metuchen, N.J.: Scarecros, 1985), 266.

[45] Ibid., 297.

[46] Bogle, *Bright Boulevards, Bold Dreams: The Story of Black Hollywood*, 62.

[47] For details see 'James Earl Jones' in next volume.

[48] Buster Keaton and Charles Samuels, *My Wonderful World of Slapstick* (New York: Doubleday, 1960), 78.

36. Clarence Muse. Inscribed: "1972 To: Dr. Frank Manchel, A man dedicated to people in the film industry. Black people, in his new book, are the stars. We are grateful, sir. Sincerely, Clarence Muse." Courtesy of The Manchel Collection, University of Vermont.

3
Scarred By History: Clarence Muse

> "Muse's early roles were neither great nor heroic, and taken out of their historical context they might seem far from impressive.... But they appeared at a time when being black and human in the movies was neither easy nor expected."
>
> Donald Bogle[1]

Clarence Muse, the resilient African-American character actor who appeared in more films than any other black performer in history, made the successful transition from vaudeville and the theater when he starred in Hollywood's second talking film, the first all-black musical, *Hearts in Dixie* (1929). No one will ever know just how many movies Muse actually appeared in, since many of his minor roles went uncredited. The conventional wisdom places the number over two hundred films. Most often, he found himself cast as a trusted and loyal individual who could be counted on to do the right thing. On rare occasions, he could be seen as an angry slave seeking justice as in King Vidor's *So Red the Rose* (1935), or the noble musician in Bernard B. Ray's *Broken Strings* (1940).

Hearts in Dixie proved to be the turning point in Muse's film career. The movie, directed by Paul Sloane, was primarily a film featuring black entertainers performing comedy, dance, and music. The slight narrative focused on a romanticized South, where an elderly ex-slave struggles stoically to maintain a living for his family. Clarence Muse plays Nappus, the noble tenant farmer. Stepin Fetchit played his ne'er-do-well son-in-law.

While the film elevated Fetchit to stardom, as Gerald R. Butters, Jr. explains, it had a different impact on Muse. On one hand, Fetchit was forever typecast as "a shuffling, lazy... [and mindless Negro with an] uneducated drawl...."[2] On the other hand, Muse's performance established him as a dignified and noble actor with a beautiful voice. "Muse's role," Butters reports, "was more of a breakthrough than Fetchit's in the advancement of African-American masculinity in the cinema."[3] That persona remained with the actor for the rest of his career.

Yet Muse's Hollywood typecasting remains controversial. There are those who dismiss him as the traditional spineless servant, fawning on the white establishment. For example, Singer Alfred Buchanan pointed out that "Clarence Muse ... was basically a respected actor – especially for the role of Gabriel in the film of *The Green Pastures* [1936] – and was a respected columnist for the *Courier* reporting on developments in the film capital, and author and co-producer of *Way Down South* [1939]. But he was attacked both for the roles which he played and for some reports on motion picture developments in which he was thought to be overly subservient to film producers and overly optimistic."[4] Gary Null put it differently, "Unfortunately, Muse either failed to realize or refused to perceive that the derogatory way in which Hollywood depicted black people was bound to perpetuate racial bias by retaining a tradition of demeaning blacks, thus making a sort of negative political statement."[5] And C. Gerald Fraser summed up what the actor's critics had been calling him for close to fifty years: "Hollywood's perennial Uncle Tom."[6] By 1943, the label became so offensive to Muse that he sued a California paper for describing him that way.[7]

But those critics sympathetic to the paradox that black actors faced in the days of the studio system separate the roles that Muse was permitted to play from the way in which he played them. Donald Bogle, who categorizes Muse as an "Uncle Tom" specialist, nonetheless perceives him as the most "inhibited" black actor of his generation, and explains that the actor's restrained performances "appeared at a time when being black and human in the movies was neither easy nor expected."[8] The historian also reminds us that Muse took his work quite seriously, always trying "to invest his servant roles of the 1930s with a semblance of dignity and a seriousness of purpose."[9] Moreover, Peter Noble, the first critic to write in detail about African-American performers, found Muse to be "one of the outstanding character actors in Hollywood...."[10]

What is sometimes forgotten is that Clarence Muse, the man, not the actor, pioneered a number of memorable achievements in the history of African-American entertainers in the twentieth century. He was the first black stage actor to appear in white face; he helped found the famous Lafayette Players in Harlem; he was the second actor (after Frank Wilson) to play the lead in the play *Porgy* (premiered in 1927) before it became *Porgy and Bess*; he was the first black performer to star in a Hollywood movie; and he was the first black screenwriter to achieve credits on a Hollywood film – Bernard Vorhaus' *Way Down South* (1939). In addition, Muse was more than an actor; he was a producer, an author, and a composer. Among his memorable songs was the popular hit made famous by Louis "Satchmo" Armstrong, "When It's Sleepy Time Down South."

Born on October 7, 1889, in Baltimore, Maryland, the versatile Muse initially considered law as a profession after graduating from Dickson College School of Law in 1911. However, he quickly gave it up when he saw "black lawyers with patches in their pants chasing ambulances."[11] It was an experience shared by the likes of Paul Robeson in law, and Charles S. Gilpin in medicine. Within a year, Muse had moved from being an itinerant musician singing on riverboats and at circuses to becoming a member of a quartet billed as "The Royal Poinciana Four" at the Breakers Hotel, a Palm Beach, Florida resort.

Later in 1912, as a result of his good fortune in a poker game, Muse moved on to Jacksonville, Florida where he became a partner in an outdoor theater, thus beginning his life as a minstrel and vaudeville performer. Several years on the road, however, convinced him to switch to theater management, and Muse settled in Kansas City, where he ran a local theatre.[12] It's worth remembering that these were the times when many hotels and rooming houses posted signs reading, "No Negroes, Jews or Dogs Allowed."

Not content to remain behind the scenes, the ambitious artist shifted to New York, where he became one of Harlem's most popular entertainers and revolutionized black theater by helping found a number of African-American acting companies. Here, for one of the earliest times in American history, black performers got the chance to develop their talents in meaningful and challenging roles that reached beyond comedy and musicals. These performances, geared to black audiences, also provided images that are more positive for African-Americans who had become accustomed to seeing themselves represented in theatre almost exclusively as buffoons and minstrels. It was during this stage in his career that Muse performed in white face on stage. So successful were black companies like the Lafayette Players that later, when the group became known as the Elite Amusement Company, they toured in the major cities along the eastern part of the United States.

Sister Francesca Thompson, whose mother, actress Evelyn Preer, and father, actor Edward Thompson, benefitted from her parents performing in many of these pioneering companies. They provided their daughter with a number of anecdotes about what life was like in early black theatre and some of Muse's roles and behavior.[13]

After leaving Harlem in the early 1920s, Muse next turned to booking acts and producing shows like *Miss Bandanda* (1927). Eventually, he settled in Chicago and led a busy life as a performer, composer, writer, producer, and theatre manager. Occasionally, he agreed to star in prominent productions like *Porgy*. At the same time, across the country, it became fashionable to have "plantation night" in neighborhood theatres, where black performers got some extra work.[14]

Muse's move to Hollywood films occurred with *Hearts in Dixie* (1929). Although the first all-black musical catalogued many of Hollywood's stereotypes of African-Americans, it proved a good showcase for the talents of the performers, including Stepin Fetchit. Further, the Fox film demonstrated how ideal black voices were for sound movies. But despite the film's popularity, the studio did not follow up with more African-American films. Years later, *Variety* speculated it was because "producers have long steered clear of the colored angle, fearing a reaction in the south."[15] It's also worth noting that for most of the actor's screen career, reviewers referred to African-American performers as "Negro," "Colored," "Sepia," or "Dusky."

However, a curious thing happened to Muse, who, following the release of *Hearts in Dixie*, decided to remain in the film industry. Instead of getting a standard seven-year contract, he did not quickly appear in another Fox film. Rather, he shuttled back and forth among the major studios; mostly playing stereotyped servant roles, while turning himself into one of the film industry's most recognizable character actors. What distinguished Muse from other black actors of the period was the dignity and energy that he invested in his parts. Yet, he could do little to alter the white stereotypes of blacks. Not even the fact that there were more than two hundred fifty movie theatres with a combined seating capacity exceeding one hundred fifty thousand seats catering specifically to black audiences had a mediating effect on the white producers to turn out more black-theme films.[16]

Throughout the next decade, the highly trained stage actor had many chances to challenge the stereotyped interpretations of blacks on the screen. If the *Pittsburgh Courier* was accurate, he played in over fifty movies between the middle of 1933 and the end of 1934.[17] Together with colleagues like Hattie McDaniel and Louise Beavers, Muse felt it made sense to bring about reform internally. If anyone knew how demeaning acting was for African-Americans, these performers did. In their minds, it was better for black audiences to see familiar faces on the screen than to see no black performers at all. Muse addressed these issues in a pamphlet, *The Dilemma of the Negro Actor* (c. 1932). Arguing that it is commerce rather than prejudice that drives the film industry, he told black actors that they had a choice to make: focus on reaching African-Americans or be content satisfying white stereotypes.[18]

Although committed to film, Muse continued to perform on radio and on the stage throughout the 1930s. The center of his work was Los Angeles. His 1933 program dedicated to the memory of Evelyn Preer, his colleague from the Lafayette Players days who had died the year before, became an annual event on radio station KRKD. He starred in a 1936 production of

Eugene O'Neill's *The Emperor Jones* at the Wilshire-Ebell Theatre, and produced *Run, Little Chillun* for the Federal Theatre Project in 1939. The latter was revived on Broadway in 1943. Muse also wrote the music and sang in his *Harlem Heab'n*, a modern symphony performed at the Hollywood Bowl.

As the thirties ended, Muse found less and less satisfaction from his roles in mainstream films and turned his attention to screenwriting, hoping to create better parts for black actors. Earlier in his career with the Lafayette Players, he had helped adapt Paul Laurence Dunbar's *The Sport of the Gods* (1921) for Reol Productions, an independent film company developed by people close to the black acting ensemble. In 1940, he wrote and partly financed his second independent film project, *Broken Strings*. Nevertheless, no one in Hollywood seemed interested in Clarence Muse on the eve of World War II. Frustrated by having to settle for insignificant roles in studio potboilers, he turned more and more to community service and composing.

Yet when enraged African-American intellectuals like Walter White of the NAACP in 1942 renewed their attacks on the film industry's racist treatment of black artists, Muse became one of Hollywood's strongest defenders. The regrettable conflict occurred with White's visit to California. The NAACP leader insisted that black audiences "resent the fact that their billed stars are almost without exception placed in the role of servants when appearing in pictures."[19] It was an argument that White had made a decade earlier, when films like *Hearts in Dixie* were first being released, and Muse had not forgotten or forgiven the reformer's comments about the film's being nothing more than "of the minstrel show, 'Befo' de war' type."[20]

Out of either self-interest or a feeling that you do not air your dirty laundry, the character actor declared to the press, "... we belong to the only profession where there is no discrimination." He singled out the Screen Actors Guild as the nation's model of how to safeguard the rights and dignity of performers.[21] Muse justified his apologist position by claiming that calls for changes in racial representations usually resulted in more unemployment for black actors because the movie makers became scared over just what images should be shown. Hattie McDaniel concurred. She firmly believed that her career suffered "not only [from] the movie producers' stubborn reliance on formulaic stereotypes," but also from the trouble caused by "the NAACP's Walter White."[22]

The results of the NAACP's visit had mixed effects on Hollywood and Muse. On the one hand, as Cripps reports, the major studios entered into an agreement with the NAACP that promised an end to "pejorative roles, to place Negroes in positions as extras they could reasonably be expected to occupy in society, and to begin the slow task of integrating blacks into the ranks of studio technicians."[23] On the other hand, not everyone was as positive as Cripps was about the importance of the 1942 Agreement transforming Hollywood's stereotyping of blacks. Muse believed that instead of the studios changing their policies, the producers just cut back on the number of black roles. Besides, he pointed out, if there were to be new roles, the choices should be influenced by insiders rather than outsiders. It was a position that has made him a pariah to many black reformers ever since. Even the film industry itself, when it made two major all-black musicals – *Cabin in the Sky* and *Stormy Weather* (both in 1943) – failed to give Muse any visibility. Especially disconcerting was the fact that by the mid-1950s, the standard bearers for blacks in Hollywood found themselves unemployed.

After three decades of working in mainstream and independent films, Muse went into semi-retirement upon completing his role as "Honey-Man" in Otto Preminger's *Porgy and Bess* (1959). However, he never completely abandoned films, returning to make movies like Sidney Poitier's *Buck and the Preacher* (1972), Robert Scheerer's *The World's Greatest Athlete* (1973), and Michael Schultz's *Car Wash* (1976). His final film was Carroll Ballad's *The Black Stallion* (1979).

During the 1950s, when television replaced movies as America's number one form of entertainment, the misunderstood actor worked on *Playhouse 90*, the *Kraft Music Hall*, the *Hallmark Hall of Fame*, and the series *Casablanca* and *The Swamp Fox*.

In 1971, when I first started working on this project, True Boardman, the screenwriter of films like *The Last Train from Madrid* (1937), *Pardon My Sarong* (1942) and *The Painted Hills* (1951), was teaching a summer course at the University of Vermont. Over several weeks, we discussed my interest in black film history, and he agreed to help me meet some Hollywood personalities. Clarence Muse was one of them.

Throughout the fall, Muse and I corresponded about the possibility of my interviewing him. Rereading those letters now brings back just how innocent I was and how cantankerous he could be. What did I know about Muse's bitterness toward "Eastern Black [and white] film critics, who," as Lindsay Patterson says euphemistically, "hadn't treated his past participation in films very sympathetically."[24] I certainly had no idea that he was considered the "perennial Uncle Tom."

The first letters we exchanged began my education. Boardman, who was then director of the Academy of Television Arts and Sciences, had opened the negotiations for an interview, before my letter of September 29, 1971 reached the screen actor. Muse's initial reaction (October 3, 1971) was that he wanted more information about me "and on what level can we get together in presenting a true, informative treatise on a business that had black pioneers as well as white pioneers in developing talking pictures." My favorite line from Muse was, "Now, if you are not like many members of the academic society who write worthless books for prestige and in order to earn a buck, then there is good reason we should have an interview in January as you suggested." By the end of November, it was agreed that I would call him when I arrived in Los Angeles around January 3.

Somehow Robert J. Sye (then executive director of the Black Cinema Library-Research Center in Los Angeles); and I met and we agreed to visit Clarence Muse together at his home, the Muse-Awhile Ranch (after a song he wrote) in Perris, about two hours away. When we finally arrived, he gave us both a rough time with questions about our backgrounds, what we wanted to know, and how could he be sure that we truly cared about black performers. On the other hand, Ena, his Jamaica-born wife, could not have been more friendly and gracious. Finally, Muse was satisfied, and agreed to an interview, only it would have to be on another day. Talk about outrage! I had very little money, the renting of a car had been a burden for me, the driving had been time-consuming, and now he wanted to schedule the interview for another day. In hindsight, I suspect that Clarence Muse wanted to collect his thoughts and revisit his own history before he presented it to me. Whatever his reasons, I had no choice.

A couple of days later, we all met again. The interview that follows is a faithful transcription of what took place for over five hours. I had come with a list of names and topics that I wanted Muse to discuss. For that reason, we began with reactions to people and then turned to his biographical history. Muse, in his eighties, enjoyed rambling, singing, and telling stories. If I challenged him too forcefully on any one point, he threatened to cancel the interview and ask me to leave. Those places where problems occurred are indicated by the word "Cut." Muse made us stop, and we regrouped with the microphone off. More often than not, he was eating or sipping a soft drink, and I found it hard to understand what he was saying, creating problems with names and spellings.

In going over the tapes and reading the transcription, I am aware now of things that did not seem to matter then. For example, Muse never mentions his three children or his first wife. Although he had worked hard in the business end of his stage career, he makes very little mention of the casting problems of black actors and rarely focuses on many of the major roles he performed in his extensive film history. Perhaps the most poignant awareness is that almost every person he refers to is someone from the black Hollywood establishment of the studio years who were under attack by black progressives and critics in the early 1970s.

The interview, understood from today's vantage point, is as much a defense of the early film pioneers as it is Muse's perspective on his own work. Normally, I would not have given thumbnail sketches of so many performers when the essential material is available elsewhere. But Muse's hidden agenda was to make me and others aware of the contributions of those who had come first, who had done what others could not or would not do, and in the end made it possible for so many people to move beyond the stereotypes of the formative stages of film history. Listening to him thirty-four years ago, I got the impression that he was telling me what a black man felt about what white men thought about African-Americans. He was tutoring me about how fleeting fame is, and how there are no guarantees that what is acceptable at one time would be acceptable in the future. He was explaining how no training or hard work or good faith could act as a guarantee against changing tastes and changing times. He wanted to make it clear that playing janitors and servants is not the important thing. It was how you played them, not what you played. He made clear that this was a history lesson, and that my generation had overlooked, ignored, or misunderstood the price that he and others had paid to make things better.

A lot of the bluster and exaggerated claims are merely masks to cover the scars, "the slings and arrows of outrageous fortune." As I have gone through the annotation process, I have tried to call the reader's attention to the dilemma of these artists who were damned if they appeared in the stereotyped roles of their times and buffeted by fortune if they didn't.

Muse and I continued to correspond throughout the next six years. By now, he referred to me as "Brother Frank." One letter (July 3, 1972) concerned his desire that I not editorialize; he felt the story as he told it was dramatic enough for me not to intrude. He even referred to our agreement that I would show the material to him before it went into print. Regrettably, his death made that impossible. Another letter (January 16, 1972), told me what he was doing to make me "famous." Rarely did I receive word from him that did not also include some clipping about him and a speech he was giving or an award he was receiving. In fact, the last letter I got (May 28, 1978) included a copy of the letter he had received from his alma mater, Dickson School of Law, informing him that he was the unanimous choice of the faculty and trustees to receive the honorary degree of Doctor of Law at the June 3rd Commencement exercises that year.

Then in September of 1979, Clarence Muse suffered a stroke. A month later, on October 13, the "Dean of African-American character actors" died.

We can be assured that he would not like everything that follows. Certainly, he never wanted to be corrected. In this case, he is not alone.

However, as Louise Brooks once wrote, "The tragedy of film history is that it is fabricated, falsified by the very people who make film history."[25] She understood why people said what they did, given the evolution of film. I hope that Clarence Muse understands why I felt his recognition would better stand the test of time and be of greater value to people today if we told the story not quite the way he wanted it. The major parts are there.

Clarence Muse Interview with Bob Sye and Ena Muse
January 6, 1972

Muse: Two distinguished gentlemen come and disturb me in my castle this morning. Both of them very ambitious if only now into the new creative world, [to] change the thinking of people. And, of course, we got into many subjects. One of them's named Frank Manchel, and [the other is] Robert Sye. He's a gentleman of the other hue.... I thought it might be a good idea at this time to ... kind of bring him up to date – Mr. Sye – who's going to do a very interesting thing at the Negro History week. I think that's ... you might tell me what date is it?
Sye: February 7 through 13th [1972].
Muse: And where will it be?
Sye: At the Ballroom Theatre.
Muse: And where is that?
Sye: In Los Angeles, California, on the corner of Coliseum and La Brea.
Muse: Coliseum and La Brea. That's a very magnificent place.[26]
Muse: So the great subject comes up, Frank, as usual, "Why black is beautiful".... I come up with this. "I'm certainly in agreement with people of other races, who dare to ask [their] black friend or acquaintance, 'Why black is beautiful.' Then with a warm expression of gratitude, one feels willing to patiently spell out the ingredients that make black beautiful. Of course, you must take into consideration, at first, that this phrase is only applying to skin color. And we must admit in the beginning it is merely a weakness of man, that skin color should be so important to human harmony. Black is beautiful because its passport is truth. By 'truth,' I mean black people of today can stand ten feet tall having learned of their many contributions to ... the past and present day society. Black is beautiful because those with black skins are creative, they love life, and they love life in the raw. They begin a day with a beat, a tempo, which is definitely a part of the earth upon which they live, because the earth is always in action. The earth has discipline. It moves around, in its rolling way, with definite precision, and a beat of the drum is a part of that great universal tempo.

I have no intention of being caught up in a philosophy that seems rather serious, because I feel that when one loses that art of laughter, his rhythm of life is uptight. When a man says, 'I hate to see the evening sun go down,' and 'If I'm feeling tomorrow like I feel today,' he's admitting unconsciously that he's out of rhythm. And when he cries out in outrage, loudly, 'Stop the world, I want to get off,' and his little old pal comes along, with a git fiddle, singing a line or two from a protest song; then, without ceremony, he understands how happy he really is. Because black is beautiful!

We could go on, tearing apart the molecules wrapped up in the expression 'black is beautiful'; and if we are not careful, in our summation, we could become a static satellite. So, why not let a whole multitude of people grab the golden ring on the carousel? And why not let this mood and attitude create an environment of togetherness that is truly a journey into space ... a space that has enough acreage to accept all people as they are, what they are and who they are ... as James Weldon Johnson has said, the old time black preacher had the power of pulling together diverse languages of people from diverse parts of Africa with his power of oratory. His ability as an actor, and his voice was a marvelous instrument. We should be able to travel along and have some good times in this treatise, with a fascinating drum beat, with an enchanted melody, into the lives of folks, who are folks, and folks who know how to get along with folks."

This is taken from a treatise known as *Black People Is*. And it's copyrighted 1970, all rights reserved by the author, Clarence Muse; and it is known to these two gentleman for their edification. But by no means, should it ever be a commercial product. Now if you dare rub this off on me, the continuity will show itself that something has been omitted, and I think our good conscience could take you into the reality of the thing.... Thank you.

CUT

Manchel: Clarence, I would like to get some reactions from you on a number of key personalities in the history of the black man in film. First, Bert Williams.

Muse: Oh, you would pick up with that one. I note that somebody said to me – that was in the crowd one day – I showed them a book called *Black Magic* done by Langston Hughes and another man, Mezzner [sic]. They covered the black entertainment world all the way from the slave ships up to the present day [1966]. [He] remarked to me, "Well, that's just a pictorial so, so, and so a black thing."

But I think it was a very unfair statement of a tremendous job, because nobody ever before ever thought about putting any of the things done [by African-Americans] in the entertainment world into a package before. And that if you dare to just say that there was simply headlines; at least, you are really in a position to ask me a question today because you read *Black Magic*. Otherwise, you would never of heard of Bert Williams. He wouldn't have meant a thing to you.

Now we go back on the Bert Williams thing. Number one, many people don't know it, Bert Williams was a native of the Bahamas. Many people don't know he graduated from high school right here in Riverside. Many people don't know that he played "Othello" at Riverside, his high school, in his graduating class.

If Muse's memory of Bert Williams' life and career is sometimes unreliable, he was not entirely at fault. The most gifted African-American entertainer of his day often said, "Nobody in America knows my real name and, if I can prevent it, nobody ever will." The material in Black Magic *about the African-American star who had to perform in blackface is mostly anecdotal, with a heavy emphasis on pictures.*

Far more informative is Ann Charters' biography about Williams. She writes that he was born Egbert Austin Williams on November 12, 1874 in Antigua, the West Indies. Eleven years later, the Williams family settled in Riverside, California. After his graduation from Riverside High School, he enrolled at Stanford University, but left during his freshman year to make some money as a touring entertainer. By 1892, he had not only gained a reputation as a talented comedian and singer working with Martin and Seig's Mastodon Minstrels, but also learned firsthand about the racial prejudice in turn-of-the-century show business. According to Tom Fletcher, towns all over the United States had "big signs" that read, "Nigger, Read and Run," or "Nigger, Don't Let the Sun Go Down on You."[27]

In 1895, Williams was twenty-one years old when he met George Walker, a year his junior. The two men would form one of the greatest comedy teams of the era, playing on the theme that they were "real Ethiopians" with a true Southern background. While forced to adhere to burnt cork stage traditions; the two gifted comedians did everything possible to humanize the hated caricatures of African-Americans. Their partnership, which specialized in all-black musicals, ended when Walker died in 1909.

For the next thirteen years, Williams became a featured comedian in all-white shows. In addition, the Broadway artist starred in two film shorts – Darktown Jubilee *and* A Natural Born Gambler *– in 1914. At the time of his death in 1922, the forty-seven year old entertainer, who made people laugh by making them sad, was considered by many show business personalities to be the greatest comedian in America. "Bert Williams," Booker T. Washington once explained,* *"has done more to make white people appreciate the Negro Race than any man, living or dead, past or present."*[28]

Muse: Many people don't know that when he went to San Francisco, he met another tremendous artist, one of the greatest of the boards, a man named George Walker. And then they teamed up. [They] thought they had an idea, [they] went out to make some money in San Francisco, [they called their act] "Williams and Walker."

Williams, Bert Williams, was a tall, very fine-looking mulatto; and George Walker was a real honest-to-God child of the Ethiopian type. They made a team. Strange enough at the time, they thought that they had the thing all figured out. Bert Williams, being a mulatto, was the straight man; and George Walker, the dark fellow, was supposed to be the comic end of it.

Unlike Williams, Walker was an energetic singing comedian who rarely resorted to blackface. Their act, "Two Real Coons," offered an alternative to white performers in blackface. According to Black Magic, *"Coon Shows" operated in contrast to the popular minstrel and* Uncle Tom's Cabin *shows in vogue during the late 1800s and early 1900s. Their major value was in laying "the groundwork for public acceptance of Negro women and of the Negro male on the stage other than in burlesque."*[29] *Muse's pioneering work with groups like the Lafayette Players grew out of the work started by Williams and Walker.*

Muse: And they had a singing team; and at that time, Bert had a very excellent baritone voice. And his famous song was "Bedelia": "Oh, Bedelia, I love you Bedelia." He made himself very famous singing that. And they went to New York and went down to a very famous place [Koster and Bial's Music Hall on 34th Street and Broadway] in New York, in those days in vaudeville, a theatre downtown, and anyhow, it was there. They didn't go over so big.

Actually, Williams and Walker, now billed as "The Two Real Coons," first came to New York to appear in a show called The Gold Bug *(1896). It lasted less than a week. They then were booked at Koster and Bial's Music Hall. Contrary to Muse's recollections, the act proved to be a sensation.*[30]

Muse: So there was another little old-fashioned slapstick team, Ham and somebody, can't think of the names, Ham and somebody, but it's in that *Black Magic*, you can check the actual names.

No such information is available in **Black Magic**. *Muse may be thinking about S.H. Dudley, whose vaudeville act included a mule; Hamtree Harrington, a* *popular headliner; William McConnell, the team's manager; or the effect that the popular act of McIntyre and Heath (white men in blackface) had on Williams and Walker as the foursome toured together in 1897-1898.*

Muse: They got this booking, and [someone] said, "You know you got your act backwards. It ain't gonna go over cause it's all wrong." See, Bert was tall, and George Walker was short, but very nappy, well-dressed .... "The act should be changed. Bert should black up his skin, and the little fellow should be the straight man, and should wear his clothes." And George Walker turned out to be the greatest dresser that ever was known in show business. His tailor could do anything ... when he moved his arm, he didn't allow the sleeve to even wrinkle and the guy had to work, work ... until that came out, that's how sharp he was in clothes.

And immediately when they turned the act around, George Walker became the lead and Bert Williams became the comic. They were a sensational success. And some six or seven great Broadway plays came from this combination, like *The Policy Players* [1899], *In Dahomey* [1902], and *Bandana Land* [1907].

And, of course, that great piece ... that became the first black operatic thing of the day was the thing called *Abyssinia* [1906], written by a black man in New York. Done most of their works.

According to Black Magic, *most of the Williams and Walker shows were written by three African-American writers: Will Marion Cook, Will Vodery, and Alex Rogers.*[31] *Jesse A. Shipp wrote the book for* Abyssinia.

Muse: And this particular piece of work [became] the top thing on Broadway. In fact, Broadway was in a slump until the Williams-Walker shows came to Broadway [and] put new life in it.

These two men appeared before the King of England and all over the world. They were the key winners in the beginning of black show business on Broadway.

Then ... to make the story come down real tight, George Walker died. Now the very interesting thing when you say what was Bert Williams to me ... When George Walker died, their tightness, their friendship, their working together, was so well-rooted, that George ... that Bert Williams went into his little brownstone house ... in New York and said, "That's the end of me in show business." And quit completely, nobody, period.

It took the Episcopal priest, several visits, and several different rap sessions, to finally convince him to go see [Florenz] Ziegfeld [Jr.] who had sent for him, and wanted to put him in the *Ziegfeld Follies* [1910]. And he plainly said, "Nothing can happen, George is not there." Well, they finally convinced him, and on opening night of [the] *Ziegfeld Follies*, is when he came on with the poker game thing in pantomime. [He did] several other things, but the pantomime thing was the thing. And he delayed the show forty-five minutes. They would never let him off the stage.

According to Archer, the poker game skit, performed with British comedian Leon Errol, was introduced in the 1911 Ziegfeld Follies.[32] *Eddie Cantor did not join the* Ziegfeld Follies *until 1917.*

Muse: And at that time Williams did a sketch with Eddie Cantor, put [burnt] cork on him, and he was playing the sissy boy. And he says, "Oh my goodness, I didn't know I sent my boy to that kind of a school. What happened?" [It got a big] laugh.

Now that was ... a little short thumbnail sketch of a great man like Bert Williams.... Bert Williams was an institution, so was George Walker, so was Ada Overton Walker, all of that particular clan made the greatest bit of entertainment....

And then there were the choirs! There was a sensation in those days for great choirs. There was a fellow named "Bass" Foster, sang bass in Philadelphia. They'd have seventy-five people singing in the great choruses.

Ada Overton Walker, the wife of George Walker, was famous for her dancing and an important part of the musicals starring her husband and Bert Williams. "Bass" Foster was also a long time associate of the famous Williams and Walker Company in Broadway musicals.

Muse: They'd be singing "Swanee River" as a finale; and at the finale, when the last call was made – bing, bing, bing, bing – and this great human voice, which you don't hear many of them, these great basses, he would hit that bottom note, [Muse lowers his voice, imitating Foster] boom, and he'd ring all through the theatre, just like they do in the [theatre] today. Does that answer your question?

Interestingly, Muse made no mention of Williams' brief forays into film, the difficulties the comedian had in raising funds to film his routines, the reactions of white audiences to the two silent Biograph films he made, or to the attempted film biography of the performer's life. Daniel Leab observes that Williams' short films only reached black audiences because the distributors always used the same rationalization, "They would like to use the film, but 'the southern territory would resent and not exhibit the pictures of a Negro star.'"[33]

Manchel: Excellent. Charles Gilpin.

Muse and Gilpin knew each other from their early days in vaudeville at New York's old Lincoln Theatre, which was torn down in 1913. He joined Gilpin at precisely the time when the new Lafayette Players Stock Company came into being during the mid-teens.

Born late in 1878 in Richmond, Virginia, Charles S. Gilpin began his legendary stage career at the turn of the century and performed in William and Walker's Abyssinia. *He soon became an integral part of the two most famous Black stock companies of the era: The Negro Players (formed in 1912) and the Anita Bush Stock Company (formed in 1914). Later, the noted actor created the title role in Eugene O'Neill's* The Emperor Jones *in 1920. He has described by one black critic as "the first modern American Negro to establish himself as a serious actor of first quality."*[34]

The Colored Players Film Corporation, owned by both Jews and blacks, starred Gilpin in his only film, Ten Nights in a Barroom *[1926].*

According to Peter Noble, the gifted stage performer was hired to star in Universal's 1927 remake of Uncle Tom's Cabin: *"Gilpin, an intelligent, proud, and sensitive person, had many heated discussions with director [Harry] Pollard on the manner in which the novel should be filmed and the beloved Negro character should be portrayed."*[35] *Gerald R. Butters, Jr. is even more specific: "Apparently, Gilpin's overly aggressive reading of the script, his refusal to submit to the total authority of the director, and his drinking caused the studio to fire him."*[36] *Depending on which source you read, Gilpin either resigned in protest or was fired by the studio. He returned to New York, as Eileen Landay reports, where "... he took a job operating an elevator."*[37] *The crusading performer died in 1930. Cripps credits him with being "America's greatest black actor."*[38]

CUT

Muse: Well, we've just been checking out, trying to get some idea about black artists in pictures. And we're particularly interested in bringing these personalities to the fore. But unlike what has happened in the past in these types of things – [which] seem to simply say that's the guy that built the bridge and he played in so and so – we're trying to see in what ways these many personalities, in what way did they fit into the very well organized system of control between labor and artistry and money. In other words, these people are all part of the society; what part did they add to the growth of society? Not so much in the personal characterization of what they probably portrayed on the screen, but, more to my way of thinking, what did they contribute to the formation of a happier time for the people living in the society.

And it's quite a bunch of names; and I think it might be a good idea to give you the immensity of it and then just only a part of it.... I would say Bessie Smith, Bojangles, Willie Best, Paul Robeson, Stepin Fetchit, Mantan Moreland, Lena Horne, Ethel Waters, Rochester, Rex Ingram, and, above all, the Theatre Owners Booking Association. That organization carried the black soul through the South many years ago. Black people called it "the T.O.B.A.;" and they also added another very, very descriptive title by saying, "Tough on Black Actors."

The Theatre Owners and Booking Association (T.O.B.A.) originated in Chattanooga, Tennessee in 1920.[39]

Muse: Then we go look up fellows like Daniel L. Haynes, of the *Hallelujah Superiors*, Oscar Pope, *The Green Pastures*, excellent thing. *The Green Pastures* was a show that played on Broadway five years – a long time before they made it into a picture.

Marc Connelly's Pulitzer Prize-winning play premiered on February 26, 1930; it was adapted to the screen by Warner Brothers in 1936.[40]

Muse: And *Carmen Jones*. Hammerstein the Second, the great writer, saw the original play at the Hollywood Bowl; and while sitting in the theatre that night, [he] decided why shouldn't it be [rewritten] in a new way ... I can see black people becoming the whole Spanish play. And *Carmen Jones* was born in his mind, and it came out to be one of the big things in life.

The 1954 screen adaptation of the hit Broadway musical was directed by Otto Preminger and starred Harry Belafonte, Dorothy Dandridge, Pearl Bailey, Roy Glenn, Diahann Carroll, and Brock Peters. More information on the production is provided in my interview with Brock Peters.

Muse: Hattie McDaniel, *Gone With the Wind* [1939] ... [Muse laughs] ... Just to think, we're talking about the growth.... Here we are with all these years just mentioned, running back, and all these many years we've had the Academy Awards, the winners, and the only woman in the history of the show business who ever received an Academy Award, straight up, first-class, was Hattie McDaniel and the only black woman, and there's no....

In 2001, Halle Berry won the Oscar for Best Actress for her role in Marc Forster's Monster's Ball. *Berry became the first black actress to win a leading Academy Award.*

Hattie McDaniel often talked about the negative effects on her career of winning the Oscar for Best Supporting Actress in Gone With the Wind. *What was not said was shown in film assignments. For example, the two films she made in 1942 – George Keighley's* George Washington Slept Here *and Elliott Nugent's* The Male Animal *– revealed how poorly her career had progressed since her Academy Award. Her two comic maid performances, according to Jill Watts, "are consigned to demeaning eye-rolling and embarrassing gaps in their knowledge, only reinforcing major elements of traditional black stereotypes."*[41]

Born June 10, 1893 in Wichita, Kansas, Hattie McDaniel began her stage career in her early teens. By the 1920s, the talented singer had become a vaudeville headliner. In 1931, the robust actress moved to California to work in radio. A year later she made her film debut in David Howard's The Golden West *(1932). Almost every part called for her playing a kindhearted, sharp-tongued maid. Prior to* Gone With the Wind, *her best roles were as the housekeeper, Aunt Dilsey, in John Ford's* Judge Priest *(1934), Ma Beck in David Butler's* The Little Colonel *and Malena Burns in George Stevens'* Alice Adams *(both in 1935), "Mammy" in James Whale's* Show Boat *(1936), and Mrs. Walker in William Wellman's* Nothing Sacred *(1937). She died on October 27, 1952.*[42]

Indicative of modern-day finger pointing is a scene from a TV film on Bill Robinson, allegedly depicting Walter White's Hollywood meeting with Bojangles, Fetchit, and McDaniels. The Hollywood stalwarts appear as crass performers who could care less about White's calls for reform in movies.[43]

Muse: When you think of people like Lena Horne in the picture [business], and you think of Ethel Waters, you think of a lot of very fine artists. We may try to examine this later, see what happened. And the only man in later years, of course, down to the present [to have won an Oscar for Best Actor is] ... [Sidney] Poitier.

Sidney Poitier received the 1963 Academy Award for Best Actor for his performance in Ralph Nelson's Lilies of the Field. *Since then, Lou Gossett, Jr. won Best Supporting Actor in Taylor Hackford's* An Officer and a Gentleman *(1982), and Denzel Washington has won two Oscars – Best Supporting Actor in Edward Zwick's* Glory *(1989), and Best Actor in Antoine Fuqua's* Training Day *(2001). Morgan Freeman has also won an Oscar for Best Supporting Actor in Clint Eastwood's* Million Dollar Baby *(2004).*

Muse: Now it seems to me I like to go back ... we'll dig in here. I don't know why Jack Johnson's name was included in this list. I imagine it was just a case of here is a very important personality that came along during the time of the Gilpin and *The Emperor Jones* success in New York, which is another story of its kind. Jack Johnson was very effective, because he was a guy that met this black-and-white situation head-on. Jack Johnson, the fighter, didn't care any more about a guy being white than if he was green or yellow. If he got in that ring, he'd better know his stuff because he would lick him and he did. And he felt the same way in his private life. He felt like if he wanted to go out and marry a white woman, [he could] which he did all [sic] the time.... If he felt like he wanted to drive his car out on the street eighty miles an hour in a twenty-mile zone, he did. And everything that they said you couldn't do, Jack Johnson did.

John Arthur "Jack" Johnson, the first African-American fighter to become heavyweight champion of the world, was married four times. According to Finis Farr, three of Johnson's wives were white women. For more details on the controversial champion, see my interview with James Earl Jones.

Muse: Now it might have something to do with the thinking of the time when [Bill] "Bojangles" [Robinson], the great dancer in New York, came into prominence.

Born Luther Robinson on May 25, 1878, in Richmond, Virginia, the great tap dancer and actor lost his parents at a very early age and was reared by his grandmother. By the time he was seven years old, he had quit school and changed his name to Bill. He acquired the name "Bojangles," which he claimed meant "happy-go-lucky," during his early days in show business. During the early 1900s, he appeared in nightclubs, toured the various vaudeville circuits, and appeared many times in Broadway shows. His film career flourished in the 1930s, where he had contracts with RKO (1930-34) and Twentieth Century-Fox (1934-38). Robinson's most famous films featured him opposite Shirley Temple: The Little Colonel *(1935),* The Littlest Rebel *(1936),* Rebecca of Sunnybrook Farm *and* Just Around the Corner *(both in 1938). In addition to being recognized as one of the foremost entertainers of his generation, Bojangles was one of the most beloved individuals in Harlem and was named its honorary Mayor in 1933.*

Yet, Robinson, like many other successful African-American performers of the times, came under attack for playing obsequious servant roles. What I find fascinating is the manner in which current biographical sketches on the artists describe the performers. For example, in Contemporary Black Biography, *the focus of the criticism quite obviously is on Bojangles' four Fox films with Shirley Temple, for which he, like Muse, is labeled the "quintessential Uncle Tom." Then, like many of Muse's detractors, the critic goes on to say, "In the context of the time, however, Robinson's appearances with Temple were a giant step for blacks in Hollywood."[44] In the Showtime's biopic on the star, there is a scene where Robinson is told off by a militant African-American and the humiliated Bojangles [Gregory Hines] says, "You know, you try to be nice to folks your whole life; and then, all of a sudden, you're a goddamn 'Uncle Tom.'"[45]*

After a heart attack forced Bojangles into retirement at age seventy, he missed the excitement of his show business life and spent his remaining days in depression. The famous entertainer died on November 15, 1949.[46]

Muse: He was a very terrific man that could run backwards faster than a lot of people could forwards. He won a million dollars doing so. But "Bojangles" had another very tender, very definite attitude toward life. He was always helping people. He was always doing something for them. He married a girl ... [and] was married eighteen years before he learned how, through her, to write his name. [Actually, Bojangles was married three times.] And he had a manager [Marty Forkins] that was so terrifically honest, which don't happen today. They just shook hands, and he was the manager for forty years. [He] never robbed him of a penny. And when "Bojangles," died, I was at his funeral in New York.

Robinson's body lay in state for two days at Harlem's 369th Regiment Armory, and over twenty thousand devoted fans and friends paid their last respects. One writer expressed what Bojangles meant to his generation: "Schools closed and crowds lined the streets from Lennox Avenue to Duffy Square to watch the funeral procession. Cole Porter, Duke Ellington, Jackie Robinson and Irving Berlin were among the honorary pallbearers. Bill Robinson's friends and fans were a rainbow coalition long before rainbows became politicized."[47]

Muse: Everybody was worried about how much money ... [Robinson's family] would have; what happened, nobody knew. Three, four days later, his manager shows up to ... [Robinson's] wife [Elaine Plaines]; he had had a hundred thousand-dollar insurance policy on "Bojangles;" that money was turned over to her.

And [there are] many other fine things [in black history], because it seems to me the power, the influence, of the Gilpins and the Johnsons and the Bessie Smiths that preceded [today] might have been running in this new stream that we're trying to create here. We're trying to see how this water flows.

There was Willie Best, a very interesting person, [a] boy [sic] with no background, educational background, but with a lot of artistry; and, of course, he was an imitator. He tried to imitate what he saw in other great artists like Stepin Fetchit. But he never had the schooling of Stepin Fetchit.

Beginning his screen career as "Sleep 'n Eat" in Little Miss Marker (1934), *Willie Best did not use his real name until a year later. The Mississippi-born comedian specialized in controversial character roles portraying African-Americans as lazy half-wits who could barely talk and walk at the same time.*

Critics generally agree that Best's screen persona was modeled after Stepin Fetchit. For example, Variety pointed out in its review of West of the Pecos (1934) that the bit player was a "carbon copy of Stepin Fetchit."[48] Six months later, in a review of The Arizonian, the trade paper again commented on the character actor's style, saying, "Willie Best (colored) is depended on for most of the comedy, and he manages to draw a few laughs, even if having to borrow everything of Stepin Fetchit's except his agent to accomplish the fact."[49]

Of the nearly seventy feature films that he appeared in between 1934 and 1951, his most remembered roles were in pictures like The Littlest Rebel (1935), Blondie (1938), The Ghost Busters (1940), and Cabin in the Sky (1943). Donald Bogle felt that not only was Willie Best the first of Fetchit's imitators, but the one "closest in style to the comedian's comedy routines." According to the records of the Screen Actors Guild, Willie Best died on February 26, 1962.[50]

Muse: Stepin Fetchit had the most unusual schooling of any artist I've ever known in my long career.

Of all the people discussed with the interviewees in this book, Lincoln Theodore Monroe Andrew "Stepin Fetchit' Perry generated the most interest among the interviewees. Buchanan pointed out that in the African-American press, Fetchit "became the symbol of the Negro actor who willingly perpetuated the worst type of stereotype."[51] At the time these interviews were conducted, even the mention of his name or his controversial screen routines drew outrage from young black and white progressives who found his screen image deplorable. However, individuals over forty expressed compassion and respect for one of the rare African-Americans who achieved star status in Hollywood's first fifty years. As seen here, Clarence Muse, like Jim Brown and John Ford, took strong exception to the abuse directed at Fetchit, choosing instead to see him as a victim of his times. Elsewhere, Muse called him "the most admirable person I ever met"[52] and "the fastest comical dancer you ever saw."[53] Joseph McBride spoke for many whites like myself, when he wrote, "... in looking at his [Fetchit's] performances ... cooler second sight must admit that Stepin Fetchit was an artist, and that his art consisted precisely in mocking and caricaturing the white man's vision of the black: his sly contortions, his surly and exaggerated subservience, can now be seen as a secret weapon in the long racial struggle."[54]

Born in Key West, Florida, on May 30, 1892, Perry, before Al Jolson in The Jazz Singer, *moved the burnt-cork traditions of the vaudeville stage to films in 1927, with a bit part* In Old Kentucky. *"Until he came along," Fetchit argued, "the movies had used only whites mimicking Negroes."[55] After appearances in a handful of 1929 films – e.g.,* Fox Movietone Follies of 1929, Show Boat, The Ghost Talks, Innocents of Paris, *and* Hearts in Dixie *– he became a favorite of the black press, which frequently carried stories about his talent and success in* movies. For example, Lawrence F. LaMar's report of Fetchit's new role in Henry King's Carolina (1934) had the headline, "Stepin Fetchit Sets New Fox Movietone Record: Assigned to Three Major Productions, 'Step' Is As Busy As the Proverbial Bee – Comic Will Be Seen in Novel Role."[56] A year later, when the actor was criticized in a film article by New York novelist Herb Howe, Bernice Patton ran a story that began, "Stepin Fetchit, filmdom's ace comedian, is being besieged, bewailed, and bombarded with sympathetic queries, protests, and complaints from thirteen million Negro fans throughout America, because they feel he has been ridiculed in the June issue of the New Movie Magazine...."[57] Peter Noble, however, remembers the early sound days of Fetchit's career differently, observing the actor not only "demeaned" himself, but also brought "Negro dignity to its lowest common denominator."[58]

By the end of the decade, Fetchit's film career had evaporated. Variety reported in 1941 that the once wealthy comedian was broke.[59] He spent the rest of his life struggling to survive in nightclubs and by rare guest appearances on TV talk shows. Six months after my interview with Muse, a local Vermont paper ran a story about the eighty-one-year-old Fetchit "sobbing on the steps of the Federal Building in Indianapolis and [asking] the public to judge whether he was a discredit to his race in his 1930s movies."[60] Not much support for the destitute African-American entertainer appeared. One exception was a brief piece in an obscure magazine, where the author argued that "Stepin Fetchit did the best he could [during this racist era in American history], and his best was damned good."[61] Lincoln Perry died on November 19, 1985.

Muse: When he was on the Hearts in Dixie thing, I was amazed to see the writer, who was Walter Weems, change this man around completely.

Ignored by many of today's mainstream film historians, the controversial movie not only gave Muse his start in Hollywood films, but also made Stepin Fetchit a movie star. No one seemed indifferent to the film. White film critics remain polarized in their reactions to this early sound film. Mordant Hall, for example, found it "... something that is restful, a talking and singing production that is gentle in its mood and truthful in its reflection of the black men of those days yonder in the cornfields."[62] Henry Dobbs, acknowledging that the filmmakers seemed "sincere" in their efforts, nevertheless felt that the movie had done an injustice by transplanting "the lachrymose myths of 'Uncle Tom's Cabin,'" once more to the screen. The only saving grace, "despite the tinsel and the gaudiness, the pathos and the mountebankery to order of tradition were the performances of Muse and Fetchit."[63] Alexander Walker, writing nearly forty years later, found it "a musical travesty of the Deep South blacks ... which had plenty of tuneful numbers but Stepin Fetchit in his definitive eye-rolling performance."[64] African-American critics hedged their reactions, trying, on the one hand, to praise the rare appearance of a "black" film; and, on the other hand, showing concern over the caricatures blacks had to perform.[65] *A fuller discussion of the film occurs later in this interview.*

Muse: Now once Stepin Fetchit was a carnival performer. [He was the] fastest dancer I've ever known; every move he made was swift, and what have you. And I was seeing Mr. Weems sit him down; talking to Stepin Fetchit for hours. He'd say, "'Step,' I'm creating for you a characterization that's going to make you very famous, going to get you lots of dough." And they would rehearse him day after day in slow speed, what have you. In fact, most of ... what I'm saying is repetition, Frank, because you'll find it on the tape from the Hollywood Museum. This education of making Stepin Fetchit, this artist as he turned out to be is very much misunderstood by the audience ... [today].

This happened many times in this whole black struggle. The many moments of frustration mixed up. We don't know what side they're on. It's been the process, and yet it is the system that controls that sort of movement. They mix you up, they cross you up, they divide and rule, they've been doing that, and they're still doing it!

We get down to a magnificent woman like Lena Horne who stands up straight and tall for honesty in the pictures.

Muse's reference to the "black struggle," Ms. Horne's "standing up straight," and the confusion in Hollywood opens up one of the most controversial episodes for African-Americans and the film industry. Its value is in remembering that black Hollywood at one time disavowed the famous singer-actress. Five years after my interview with the eighty-two-year-old actor, he would tell another interviewer that Lena Horne's unrelenting support of Walter White's position "incurred forever the enmity of every Black bit player and character actor then in Hollywood."[66]

The story of the NAACP's struggle for better film roles began with the release of D.W. Griffith's The Birth of a Nation *(1915). This particular stage of the battle against African-American stereotypes occurs at the start of World War II and carries through the war itself. Syndicated columnist, Walter White, a prominent member of the NAACP and a leading spokesperson for black civil rights, believed that the war provided him with a unique opportunity to reform the images and treatment of blacks in and on film. Working with prominent politicians like the 1940 Republican Party standard bearer, Wendell Wilkie, and Hollywood executives at Twentieth Century-Fox, White capitalized on the desire of the newly created Office of War Information to make movies that pictured America as a united nation. His campaign to reform Hollywood appeared to be at the price of the African-Americans currently established in motion pictures; e.g., Hattie McDaniel, Clarence Muse, Willie Best, Bill "Bojangles" Robinson, and Louise*

Beavers. Thus, the Hollywood old-timers rebuffed every effort that White made to change conditions in mainstream films. "In laying his cards on the table," Muse complained of the NAACP leader's visit to Hollywood, "Mr. White didn't see fit to address the Screen Actor's Guild, the greatest organization in America that protects the rights and lives of its members under the maxim, 'All men are created equal,' which has been written into its character and so executed."[67] *Caught in the middle were screen newcomers like Lena Horne and Rex Ingram. The best account of the political confrontations and consequences can be found in Thomas Cripps, Making Movies Black: The Hollywood Message Movie from World War II to the Civil Rights Era.*[68]

The Brooklyn-born Lena Horne began her career in show business during the early 1930s. Working her way up from the chorus line to a blues-singing sensation, she made her film debut in Harry Popkin's independent black musical, The Duke Is Tops *(1938). Although few people took note of the "race" film, the sophisticated nightclub singer did catch the attention of Walter White, who soon decided that he had in this seductive entertainer the means to reform movie stereotypes. Her break came in 1942, following engagements at two well-known Hollywood nightclubs. MGM signed her to a seven-year contract. Her initial films – e.g.,* Panama Hattie *(1942) and* Thousands Cheer *(1943) – had her doing bit parts, mainly as an entertainer. However, her role as the temptress Georgia Brown in* Cabin in the Sky *(1943) made her a star.*

The tragedy was that she never had a chance to enjoy it. "I was picked at that time to be what they thought a black woman was like," she said in a 1971 interview on NET's Black Journal. *"I was picked even before my own development, and when they picked me they found that they had a tiger by the tale because they didn't really know what was outside of me, and I was made to look like someone not me." Her battles with the studio to change the images of blacks; the problems she faced being married first to a black man, divorcing him, and then remarrying a white conductor, Lennie Hayden; the confrontations with Hollywood black conservatives; and her being blacklisted during the McCarthy era reveal important information on the difficulties African-American performers faced during the 1940s and 1950s. Fortunately, the cultural revolutions of the 1960s brought her considerable fame and satisfaction.*[69]

Muse: It was a very sad thing that happened with Walter White when I first introduced him to [Darryl F.] Zanuck [at Twentieth Century-Fox]. I made the interview possible for Mr. Walter White of NAACP. And as soon as he got in there, right away he stopped defending [African-American studio performers] and [started] kicking down Hattie McDaniel because she was black and Lena Horne was light; and they [MGM] didn't use Lena Horne at the time to the extent that they had thought that they [the NAACP] should have because of her color. Well, that became a mixed up conflict and Walter White was a man who was so white, you never knew he was a black man.

While Muse's resentment toward White is understandable, it is in no way accurate. He was hardly the man who introduced the noted civil rights leader to Zanuck. In all probability, it was Wilkie, who served on the board of Twentieth Century-Fox.[70]

Muse: All of these things ... [are] all tied up in the ever-moving system controlling things. That battle became very vicious there for a while, the Lena Horne thing.

In 1942, when Lena Horne became the first African-American woman to receive a long-term contract at MGM, she ran into problems with members of the Hollywood black establishment. In her autobiography, she describes the situation: "There was talk about me for many months in Hollywood, and it finally culminated in a protest meeting. I was called 'an Eastern upstart' and a tool of the NAACP and I was forced to get up and try to explain that I was not trying to start a revolt or steal work from anyone and that the NAACP was not using me for any ulterior motive."[71] *The only black person Ms. Horne remembers giving her any support was Hattie McDaniel. She also remembers that a breach occurred between her and Ethel Waters that never healed.*

Muse: And then Lena Horne grew up and began to understand it better. She got away from that mess, because, after all, pictures were made in black and white. And when they photographed a black man on black and white [film], he was black; and when they photographed a white man on the screen, he was white; and when they photographed a mulatto on the screen, he was still white. So that was a problem that really was behind it. I couldn't make Lena Horne make them [the film audience] know that she was a Colored woman, which they [MGM] didn't want to do at the time. They wanted to put make-up on her and then didn't. So that happened.

What Muse is referring to is the dilemma MGM found itself in during Ms. Horne's early screen career. At first, the studio found itself accused of trying to pass the light-skinned singer off as white; then it was attacked because it made her use makeup to darken her skin.[72]

Muse: Ethel Waters was a tremendous force in the theater. She won everything they haven't nailed down, dramatic academy things on Broadway and what have you. The Ethel Waters tradition is one to be reckoned with. I think we ought to take time out later on and really break down some real inside facts on the great woman Ethel Waters, who came all the way from a sixteen-year-old girl down in a little cafe in Philadelphia to the top.

Ethel Waters, the legendary blues singer, Broadway star, and screen actress, "was at the head of the long line of black entertainers who achieved recognition, fame, money, and success in show business," wrote C. Gerald Fraser.[73] Yet with all her critical acclaim, she lived as troubled a life as any artist of her era. She grew up in a violent environment, had to perform in places where she feared for her life, and never had it easy finding steady employment. Throughout, as one observer pointed out, "No matter where she performed, no matter what or whether she sang, she touched people with the pain, humor, and above all, the dignity of her spirit."[74]

Born on October 31, 1896, in Chester, Pennsylvania, the no-nonsense performer always felt as if she was an outsider looking in on the rest of the world. She began life as the result of her thirteen-year-old mother having been raped at knife-point. The details of her poverty-riddled childhood, as well as a disastrous marriage at thirteen, are described in her 1950 autobiography – His Eye is on the Sparrow. *Her long and distinguished theatrical career began when she was seventeen, singing "St. Louis Blues" at a vaudeville theater in Baltimore. Over the next two decades, she gained fame as nightclub entertainer, often refusing to appear in theatrical productions like* Porgy and Bess *because "those plays never seemed quite true to life to me." She added, "The characters in them had been created either by white men or by Negro writers who had stopped thinking colored."[75] Following headline performances at famous Harlem cabarets like The Cotton Club and The Plantation Club, she started appearing in hit shows. Her three most famous stage performances were in* Mamba's Daughters *(1938),* Cabin in the Sky *(1940), and* The Member of the Wedding *(1950). "If Ethel Waters was popular in the twenties," explained William Gardner Smith, "when the nation was wild and prosperous, she was the voice of America in the decade of the thirties."[76] She gained further distinction by recreating her role of Petunia Jackson in Vincente Minnelli's film version of* Cabin in the Sky *(1943); and her memorable depiction of Bernice, the cook, in Fred Zinnemann's adaptation of* The Member of the Wedding *(1952). Although she appeared in less than a dozen movies between 1929 and 1959, she garnered two Oscar nominations for Best Supporting Actress: one for her outstanding performance as the mother of a light-skinned daughter trying to pass as white in* Pinky *(1949); the other for being the spiritual advisor to a young Julie Harris in* The Member of the Wedding. *The latter role, which she created on Broadway two years earlier, won her the Best Actress Award from the New York Drama Critics. In 1950, Miss Waters also gained recognition for the 1950-1953 television series,* Beulah, *which featured her as a maid to a wealthy lawyer and his family. What is most striking about Miss Waters' illustrious career is how little satisfaction it brought her, and the abuse she* encountered over forty years as a black entertainer. She told interviewers, "I'm the kind of woman, if I was mad at you I'd just as leave kill you as look at you. I came up hard and willful. I was a dead-end kid, playing in the gutter. An eye for an eye and a tooth for a tooth – that was what I lived by for years and if anybody did me wrong, I was a powerful adversary."[77] Her greatest pleasure in the last years of her life seemed to be the rebirth of her religious faith. Ethel Waters died on September 1, 1977.

Muse: And there's Rochester! He was famous, we all know, the world over ... became famous just because he had a husky voice and had an attitude on a trial thing.... I did one [radio show] two weeks before with the famous comedian, Jack Benny. And here he comes along and does that [routine of his and gets the job].

Eddie "Rochester" Anderson was born in Oakland, California, in 1906. Both his parents were stage performers who hoped that their son would become a popular singer. Although he entered show business singing in the chorus of Struttin' Along (1923), his big break came with his screen performance as Noah in The Green Pastures (1936). But it wasn't until he played Little Joe Jackson in the all-black musical film Cabin in the Sky (1943) that MGM offered him a seven-year contract.[78]

Today, he is better remembered as Jack Benny's valet. He first auditioned for the great comedian in 1937, and what was supposed to be a one-shot appearance lasted for over two decades on radio, television, and film. His hoarse delivery and delightful mugging made him a favorite with both black and white audiences. Earl J. Morris praised the comedian as "the patron saint to the colored domestic workers throughout the United States."[79] Once asked for his opinion on the way African-Americans had been depicted on stage and screen, he refused to enter into the controversy, saying he didn't want "to propagandize."[80] His movie career as a character actor spanned nearly thirty years, beginning in 1936. Eddie "Rochester" Anderson died on February 28, 1977.

Muse: I was up here in Omaha at the time. I heard him, and I fell out of the chair. And the very fact that a black man was named "Rochester," not "George" ... "Sam." This was what they called progress, Frank, in that time. We're not gonna call him "Sam" and "George" like everybody. We're gonna call him "Rochester," as if he was from Britain. And it was successful with the audience.

But it's all part of the same system. Rex Ingram, great, great actor.

Rex Ingram, whose career on Broadway and in film spanned more than fifty years, is best remembered for his screen roles as "De Lawd" in William Keighley and Marc Connelly's film The Green Pastures (1936), "the Genie" in Michael Powell's

The Thief of Baghdad *(1940),* and Tambul in Zoltan Korda's Sahara *(1943).*

Born aboard a Mississippi river boat in 1895, the veteran actor originally wanted to be a doctor and received a degree from Northwestern Medical School in 1919. Arriving in California that same year, he soon lost interest in medicine and switched to acting. The tall and striking performer with the rich baritone voice made his film debut in the first Tarzan movie in 1919. Over the next decade, according to The Amsterdam News, *he played "varied movie roles – all in the idiom of the times – porters, jungle natives, butlers."*[81]

Near the end of the 1920s, he also began working on the stage and made his New York debut in Ol' Man Satan *(1932). Following his success in* The Green Pastures, *he began speaking out against Hollywood stereotypes of African-Americans. As* Variety *explained, "... the fame and stature he attained ... [in the film] was no bar to two years of unemployment in the field when he would portray no role that would not put the Negro in a better light. He was far ahead of his time in that respect."*[82] *Destitute, he made a comeback playing King Christophe in the WPA-sponsored play,* Hati *(1938). Other important stage performances included roles in* Cabin in the Sky *(1940) and* Anna Lucasta *(1944).*

During the fifties, Ingram also found work on television, appearing on the Kraft Television Playhouse *and* Playhouse 90. *The gifted actor died of a heart attack on September 19, 1969.*

Muse: And he played one of the characters under me in *Porgy* [the stage play on which the musical *Porgy and Bess* was based]. I played Porgy; I was Porgy in the theater. All through the nation, I was the cripple; Rex Ingram was one of the guys [Crown] who shot craps [on Catfish Row]. I forgot just the particular character, but we can check that out.

And here we come into the T.O.B.A., which was really the only fluid thing in the black entertainment of the time that kept black actors alive. They played around forty weeks down through the South, all through the South connecting with black audiences only. That's told in your masterpiece tape you got over there, so we're not going to repeat that.

Daniel L. Haynes came on the horizon, and it looked like he was going a long way, but he got tired and couldn't stand the pressure and he backed out.

Daniel L. Haynes, born in 1894 in Atlanta, Georgia, originally thought of being a minister. In fact, he came to New York with the hope of getting further religious training, but got sidetracked by an offer to play Charles Gilpin's understudy in a hit play. When the star fell ill, Haynes went out and gained instant fame. His starring role in King Vidor's Hallelujah *(1929), the second all-talking, all singing black musical, brought him screen recognition, but not a long movie contract. After making a handful of films – e.g.,* The Last Mile *(1932), King Vidor's* So

Red the Rose *(1935), and* The Invisible Ray *(1936) – over the next six years, he returned to Harlem and the theater. He died on July 28, 1954.*

Muse: Some of the things he did were very effective, but he didn't have that stamina to remain. It took a lot of guts to stay in this damned business, you know; it wasn't a polite thing. And Haynes was one who says I had enough and he quit.

Oscar Polk ... I can't remember very much about him right now. I gotta check; I'm kind of hazy.

Despite the fact that Oscar Polk did a considerable amount of work in movie, radio, and theater in the 1930s and the early 1940s, not much is known about him. The standard biographical references report that the dancer-actor was born on Christmas Day in Marianna, Arkansas. His big break came in 1935 with the role of Gabriel in the 1935 Broadway production of The Green Pastures; *and then he went to Hollywood to repeat the part in William Keighley's screen adaptation in 1936. Like Muse, once there Polk decided to stay. His most important screen roles were in* Gone With the Wind *(1939) and* Cabin in the Sky *(1943). His appearance in Oscar Micheaux's* Underworld *(1936) presented him in a more serious role than his standard Hollywood comic servant image.*

Again, Polk, like Muse and his Hollywood stalwarts, had his share of detractors. However, what I find valuable to recall here is the controversy surrounding the productions of The Green Pastures. *From our vantage point, we tend to forget just how controversial it was to make all-black productions that showcased African-American talent and still crossover the color line. As with* Porgy and Bess, The Green Pastures *offended many people such as the Rev. F. Langton, who said, "If this film is allowed, the Divine Judgment cannot but befall on this country."*[83] *Similar problems, noted earlier in the introduction to this book, faced many of the African-American commercial films in the late 1960s and early 1970s. The pioneering actor died on January 4, 1949.*

Muse: *The Green Pastures*, of course ... [everyone knows] the history. And I told you about *Carmen Jones* a while ago, and how it happened with Hammerstein.

Manchel: Could you repeat that on tape? We didn't get that on tape.

Muse: Yes, we did. I told you then while I was going down there that Hammerstein was sitting there listening to *Carmen*, and he saw *Carmen [Jones]* from the audience. I told you that up in the early part of your tape. Look out for ... [a bad] memory. Don't get caught in ... [forgetting], you could get hurt.

And *Gone With the Wind*; of course, it speaks for itself. It was the masterpiece of that woman [Margaret Mitchell] – she was something. I met her, Margaret somebody, down in Georgia. But she stayed there; and they did scenes just like she wanted. And what happens is ... [that the film] can repeat itself [in] every generation, and it's always a successful thing, because it's real Americana from the Southern man's point of view. And he's entitled to his point of view.

Muse is referring here to Mitchell's role as consultant on the making of David O. Selznick's production of Gone With the Wind.[84]

Muse: It's a much better point of view than what was so roughly put together in *The Birth of a Nation* [1915]. But the thing that makes [David Wark] Griffith hang on ... [in film history], I think, what bothers [film historians] most.... [is that] Griffith is the man who invented the close up. He invented the whole technique of making pictures.

For most of this century, it was common to credit Griffith with inventing many film techniques. In the last decade, however, the conventional wisdom argues that his strength was in refining early techniques and presenting them in an extraordinary fashion. The controversies surrounding The Birth of a Nation *are well documented.*[85]

Muse: And in doing this [in *The*] *Birth of a Nation*, he brought all of his many ingenious avenues of expression into the stuff. But he give ... [the] poor subject matter a lot of hell. Now I don't blame [people] for raising a lot of hell [about the racism in the film]. But I don't think any of us can stop the fact that the man was a great artist ... and the same thing [occurs] when we get down here talking about *Gone With the Wind*. That was a tremendous thing. And a Southern guy directed that [film], which was unusual.

Muse is referring to King Vidor, who did some finishing touches on Gone With the Wind. *The two principal directors, however, were George Cukor and Victor Fleming.*

Muse: In my *Cabin in Cotton* [1932] ... when I replied to that thing we were talking a few minutes ago ... And I thought this was very interesting. You should know about this, too, Frank.

Cabin in the Cotton, *a Warner Bros. film directed by Michael Curtiz, tells the melodramatic story of a sharecropper's son who has to choose between his folks and his sweetheart's wealthy family. The cast includes Richard Barthlemess, Dorothy Jordan, Bette Davis, Henry B. Walthall, and Tully Marshall. As listed in* Variety's *extremely negative review of the film, Clarence Muse plays an "Old*

Blind Negro."[86] *To be more precise, he was a blind sharecropper, deeply in debt to the exploiting white family. Peter Noble appears to be the only commentator who agreed with Muse over the worthiness of the role or the film.*[87] *Most film historians who refer to the movie do so to indicate that it marked the first time that Bette Davis appeared as a femme fatale on screen. Interestingly, James Baldwin considers the star and her performance in* 20,000 Years in Sing Sing *(1933) as the initiation of his insights into caste and skin color distinctions.*[88]

Muse: *Cabin in the Cotton* was made in the thirties at Warner Bros. I was there, and I was turning out to be a great friend of the writer who was Paul Green of North Carolina.

Paul Green, the screenwriter, adapted Harry Harrison Kroll's novel of the same name. Little information is available on the dramatist turned screenwriter, who seems to have had an extremely short stay in Hollywood. Larry Langman tallies only four screen credits to him.[89]

Muse: A University man ... Ph.D., Ph.D., Ph.D. [Laughter]. Slave cropping story that was done by Paul Green of North Carolina, which was all about black farm workers.

Muse is arguing that the story's emphasis on sharecroppers (who are mostly white, not black) being exploited by wealthy landowners somehow justifies why some poor people turn to a life of crime. The film has several scenes showing how the sharecroppers resort to criminal acts in order to feed their families and to protect themselves. Moreover, the law is shown favoring the corrupt landowners.

Muse: [Green's] indictment of this segment of society ... thieves and drunkards and racketeers ... should be balanced with men like [Al] Capone. And so folks [during the Depression] who were also anti-social and ... [agreed with] Capone's attitude, [after] watching the system [on screen], [felt they] had a right to take some of the advantages he took.

Remember at this time [1930s], they, black people, were creating protest songs! In fact, [they were] the original creators of protest songs. We [need to] tell that, [black people] spoke the truth [in their] words and the music.

And I feel that this spiritual power was intensified, and ... [black people] found a formula for survival. I don't believe you can [stop] a person [from getting ahead], but you can slow him up like that. For the time comes when he discovers [himself, and] his good thinking comes out. And I believe you can find a portion of positive value in this great struggle. Positive – black is beautiful.

Now remember, *Cabin in the Cotton* was the first picture ever received by Russia and allowed to be played in the Russian theaters.

Absolutely not true. For details on Soviet films and American imports of the period, read Denise J. Youngblood, Soviet Cinema in the Silent Era: 1918-1935.⁹⁰

Muse: That was the first breakthrough, because it dealt with Russia reforming the proletariat. [The theme was to prove that] the proletariat [through a successful revolution against the landowners in the film] could make it. So I told him [Green], he's got to think of those scenes [as ones] that [proceed to show the sharecroppers rising up] in order to approach this idea [of a proletarian revolt].... He has to get up underneath ... that [ideology] and follow the system through. I think he's got to do much more investigating, to do deeper writing.... You've got to keep thinking. I don't think ... [he] went deep enough....

You got Dooley Wilson, who was a great guy. He did the song, the first song in the picture, with....

Best known for his memorable stage role in Cabin in the Sky *(1940), and his film performances in* Casablanca *(1942) and* Stormy Weather *(1943), Arthur "Dooley" Wilson was born in Tyler, Texas on April 3, 1894. He had a successful career in the theatre, movies, and television. The artist died on May 30, 1953.*⁹¹

Manchel: [Humphrey] Bogart.
Muse: Bogart ....
Manchel: *Casablanca* [1942].
Muse: *Casablanca*, but he did the number ...
Manchel: "As Time Goes By."
Muse: "As Time Goes By." I did the series based on that [movie] for thirty-nine weeks for Warner Brothers for TV. And I played the same piano, did the same part ... and I did Sam for thirty-nine weeks with great success for Warner Brothers.

The ABC television series Casablanca *appeared during the 1955-1956 season. In addition to Muse playing Sam to Charles McGraw's Rick Blaine, the cast included Anita Ekberg (Ilsa Lund Laszlo), Peter Van Eyck (Victor Laszlo), and Marcel Dalio (Captain Renaud).*

Muse: Then Butterfly McQueen ... magnificent. Now there's a characterization that stuck out in that great million-dollar production of *Gone With the Wind*. In fact, that black figure you see over there, over in the corner, the statue around there, is her body. She ... I'll have to show you that later on.

During the last years of her life, Butterfly McQueen kept trying to justify her controversial performance as Prissy, the terrified servant, who exclaimed, "Lawdy, Miss Scarlet, I don't know nothing about birthing babies" in Gone With the Wind. *She claimed on a talk show in 1971 that when she created the role of the lame brained maid, it was at a time that she didn't know much about slavery, and black militancy was not prevalent.[92] Elsewhere, she insisted that her role was "an all-too-valid picture of a particular type of Negro – one for whom she feels a certain pity."[93] Perhaps, the saddest comment she made was, "You know today [1970] they call me an old Uncle Tomisina. I don't drink and I don't talk too much about America...."[94]*

Born Thelma McQueen on January 8, 1911, in Tampa, Florida, the squeaky-voiced actress began her Broadway career in Brown Sugar *(1937), before making her screen debut in* Gone With the Wind. *Typecast in similar roles for the next decade, she withdrew from films after her performance in King Vidor's* Duel in the Sun *(1947). The remainder of her life saw her doing social work, earning a college degree from the City College of New York in 1975, tutoring aspiring performers, and doing guest stints on television and in films. She died at eighty-four-years-of-age on January 7, 1996.*

Muse: And the individuality of these people ... It may be the big thing that we're looking at, whole personalities. Maybe we're losing sight ... They were definite personalities that had to be reckoned with. [The key point is that you'd hear a name] ... Butterfly McQueen, [and then] you didn't hear no more for months, for years. And that's [the tragedy] ... the artistry of what she was doing [and how difficult it was to survive or get recognition].

Rex Ingram.... I've mentioned him a while ago.

[Canada] Lee, did the thing in the *Lifeboat* [1944].

Best remembered for his depiction of Bigger Thomas in the 1941 Broadway production of Native Son *and as the sensitive country preacher who journeys to Johannesburg to save his son in Zolton Korda's film,* Cry, The Beloved Country *(1951), Canada Lee epitomized the plight of the African-American actor whose fame masked the hardships of working in a racist world.*

Born Leonard Lionel Cornelius Canegata on March 3, 1907, in New York City, the enormously resourceful individual spent a lifetime adapting to new situations and trying different professions. "All my life," he once explained, "I've been on the verge of becoming something. I'm almost becoming a concert violinist and I run away to the races. I'm almost a good jockey and I go overweight. I'm almost a champion prize fighter and my eyes go bad."[95] It was in his boxing stage that he adapted the name "Canada Lee." When an eye injury ended his boxing career in 1933, he decided to make a living as an actor. Success in Orson Welles' all-black WPA production of Macbeth *(1936) eventually led him to Welles' 1941 stage adaptation of Richard Wright's great novel and to stardom.*

His film debut in Alfred Hitchcock's Lifeboat *(1944) made him very conscious of the problem of appearing in mainstream Hollywood films. His depiction of a servile steward was perceived by certain critics as not only reinforcing negative images of blacks, but also of providing "a performance of dignity to a role of dubious significance."*[96] *Because of his outspokenness on racial and social issues, the famous stage actor often found himself unemployed and appeared in only a few films:* Body and Soul *(1947),* Lost Boundaries *(1949), and* Cry, The Beloved Country. *Following the completion of the filming of Alan Paton's novel, Lee tragically became ill. Two years in and out of hospitals, plus being blacklisted in the United States, finally led to his death on May 8, 1952.*

Muse: And we exchanged houses. He came out here to do *Lifeboat*, with the company; and at the same time, I'm putting on *Run, Little Chillun* on Broadway. He loaned me his home up on.... What do you call them top floors?

Manchel: Penthouse?

Muse: He loaned me his penthouse. One night about two, three o'clock in the morning, he called me up long distance, and I heard him say, "Clarence, I forgot to tell you.... I didn't put it in the letter, but out on the porch ... on the north end, you'll see a pot. And I got a geranium in it. For God's sake, don't forget to water it." So the next day I go water it. And I came to find out that the geranium was three years old, and it was eighteen inches high. [Laughter] The geranium grew like trees. Boy, that geranium was something in his life.

Nina Mae McKinney. I did *Safe in Hell* [1931] with her. I did a West Indian running a hotel thing ... terrific picture. She's a terrific artist.

Branch Huston based Safe in Hell, *a First National movie directed by William A. Wellman, on a play. The plot involved a colony of international rogues who live on an exotic island, safe from the law. Clarence Muse played Newcastle. His opinion of the film was not shared by the* New York Times' *critic who wrote, "Nina Mae McKinney, the too seldom seen temptress of* Hallelujah, *as a dark-skinned barmaid, is about the only entertaining item in the film."*[97]

Muse: More ought to be done about Nina Mae McKinney, because she did a magnificent job in that first picture.

Nina Mae McKinney, born in Lancaster, Pennsylvania, in 1912, came to New York when she was twelve to find work as an actress. Five years later, the sensitive performer won the role of "Chick" in King Vidor's Hallelujah *(1929). Years* later, the Chicago Defender *wrote that the actress began what many believed was "a fairy story of the life of Cinderella."*[98] *Considered by many historians to be the first recognized African-American screen actress in mainstream movies, Ms. McKinney spent most of the thirties doing cabaret engagements in England. When asked why she spent so much time in Europe, the blunt entertainer stated that "Race stars" were treated better abroad.*[99] *Of the few movies she made during the decade, the two most noteworthy were* Sanders of the River *and* Reckless *(both in 1935). When her Hollywood career resumed during the forties, the film columnist for the* Chicago Defender *claimed that McKinney "was the greatest dramatic actress of the Negro group since the late Evelyn Preer."*[100] *Her most significant screen appearance of the decade was in Elia Kazan's* Pinky *(1949). She died in New York City in 1967. Nina Mae McKinney and Daniel L. Haynes are discussed more fully in the King Vidor interview.*

Muse: And there is Fredi Washington, who is in that thing with the.... You'll see it around here, several times ... what's the name of it? With the mulatto thing ... in motion picture....

Manchel: *Island in the Sun* [1957]?

Muse: No.

Manchel: *Imitation of Life* [1934]?

Imitation of Life, *made twice (1934, 1959), is an adaptation of Fannie Hurst's novel about Beatrice Pullman who is befriended by Aunt Delilah, a black woman. Both women have daughters, but the African-American child tries to pass for white to avoid living as a second-class citizen. In director John M. Stahl's 1934 version, Claudette Colbert stars as the successful white woman; Louise Beavers plays the "Mammy" stereotype, and Fredi Washington interprets Aunt Delilah's troubled Peola. In director Douglas Sirk's 1959 version, Lana Turner has the Colbert role; Juanita Moore, the Delilah part; and Susan Kohner, a white actress, plays a light-skinned woman trying to pass.*

Ms. Washington's other noted screen performance was as Undine in Dudley Murphy's film adaptation of Eugene O'Neill's drama, The Emperor Jones *(1933).*

Muse: *Imitation of Life* [1934], Fredi Washington. See, ... I think with all these names ... instead of being put on the spot, to go and tell you how much I think of each one ... that's a lot of hoo-hoo, hoo. But it's often nice to hear these people's names ring again.... People who have a personal interest in any one of them [can] look them up.

All of these people have well-written histories ... about [them]. If you like them, go dig in and find out about them, because I think Frank's going to run out of space trying to get them all in there. And when he gets to Bojangles, that'll be the happy moment – his civic life, his theater life, everything that's so magnificent. And think, he didn't even ... know what a Ph.D. meant. And yet he was a world success. I don't know many world successful Ph.D.s, because I guess they come along....

Manchel: Okay. Clarence, what about Ethel Waters? You said we wanted to cover more about Ethel Waters that we didn't get in the quick run through.

Muse: You know, when Ethel Waters entered the business, in Philadelphia nightclubs, she had a partner. There was a girl partner, and I've been trying to think of the girl's name all morning.

In her autobiography, Ms. Waters talked about forming an act with Maggie and Jo Hill in 1917.[101]

Muse: And she had a partner; there were two of them. And they began their career in nightclubs.

Now that I think of it ... the big kickoff in her life was when she got to New York, and she sang in a nightclub on Fifth Avenue called "The Bucket of Blood." Now it wasn't just a name. That was it; it was the bucket of blood.

Muse may be talking about Edmund (Mule) Johnson, who ran Edmond's Cellar at 132nd Street and Fifth Avenue. Ms. Waters referred to it "as the last stop on the way down in show business."[102] *The date is about 1918. At the time, "Rose of Washington Square" was a popular ballad associated with Sophie Tucker.*

Muse: And the guy – that guy running it – he always wore a great big, knitted red tie. The style like you got coming on now, that was in. Everything repeats, you know. We always wear them big knots. Now the Manhattan shirt people are selling all them ties ... on the radio and television until you get sick of the damn ties, you wish for somebody to come on for relief. But they all got into the big ties.

Now she was down in there singing her big song hit. The peculiar thing [was] the humor. In the nightclubs of that period, it was something they ... like they try to do in modern pictures, but it then ... it was all off beat. The humor was always sort of colored on the vulgar side, like the dirty jokes. Now she was singing, to a tremendous audience, packing them in every night, "I got the rose of Washington Square." The song was "I am the 'Rose of Washington Square'." And she was singing this thing, "I got the rose of Washington Square," and she puts her hand where the rose was on the table, and she turned her back and did her business across the table. Then.... pretty soon, she was a very, very famous nightclub entertainer in New York City.

Then she married a guy, a big pimp guy, in Chicago. I'm trying to think of his name. He was a black fellow.... A guy named Earl Sampson, who was really a promoter. He died up here; I had to bury him, but a tremendous guy. And he brought Ethel Waters into the focus of big show business.

Ms. Waters discusses Earl Sampson in her autobiography.[103]

Muse: And she was sensational. She had the most magnificent body you'd ever seen. This woman had a body that was perfect; I mean, all the way down. And he [Earl Sampson] knew what it was all about in handling her. Her dancing made her a big success in several shows he produced. And down the line ... suddenly, when she was in her thirties, she began to find out that she had dramatic ability.... She didn't know anything about which she had. Anyhow, she played these two great shows – *Mamba's Daughters* [1939] and *Cabin in the Sky* [1940] – and won ... dramatic leads.... [and got an Oscar nomination for her performance in *Pinky* (1949)].

CUT

At this point, Muse began teasing Bob Sye and me about our knowledge of black theater history.

Muse: You're supposed to know some black stuff. You kind of act like amateurs; you pretend you don't know nothing. Why [don't you know about *Mamba's Daughters*]? Yeah, it's in there [We're all laughing]. So you can laugh when you get home and show it to your boys, nine and eleven [my sons Gary and Steven]. Say see, this is your dad I'm talking to. Straighten him out when he ain't straight. Watch what he tells you in school. Now if he don't give it to you straight, you go to the library and look it up. And you check behind this, because your dad don't make his mouth no Bible.

Okay, so then you get down there with her and *Mamba's Daughters*, and she upset Broadway with Helen Hayes and those kinds of people. The greatest thing that ever hit Broadway at the time was *Mamba's Daughters*. Ethel Waters took it hook, line, and sinker. And all her life, everything she went into, she became the king, because she had that drive.

Mamba's Daughters, *based on the novel by DuBose Heyward, featured Ethel Waters as Hagar, the black woman adrift and alone in a racist white society. Al-*

though the Broadway production was short-lived, critics praised the actress' powerful performance.

Muse: This is the thing that I've been talking about. And all those many names we had down there, the element of the success of every one of those names we had down there before, depends entirely on how much drive they had. There wasn't nobody gonna say, "Oh come do, come up, come on, I want to help." If you don't have that drive ... white folks, black folks, whoever's in the way, and move through, you didn't move, baby. You just laid there and perished. And that's why black people today, in the multitudes, with communications being so strong.... they've always had the drive and an individuality in the way they live ... [lives] of intent. Drive!

That's evidence. You can look at athletic games, which represents the full capacity of man; his thinking, his energy and everything else goes into athletics. Bums can't make good in athletics; [you] gotta have a mind. And so you look and say, "Well, there's a baseball." Look at all the trouble to get a black man playing baseball. I mean, baseball belongs to black people when it comes to stardom. When you look at football; oh my god, who would have a team without a black star on it.

Muse is referring to Jackie Robinson's signing with the Brooklyn Dodgers organization in 1946, before moving up to the major leagues the following year. When the twenty-eight year old sensation broke the modern baseball color line in 1947, it is not a well-known fact that African-Americans had been in organized baseball from its start, and had only left because white players felt them a threat to their jobs. Moreover, many great black ballplayers demonstrated their athletic talent in the Negro League. Muse makes no mention of this, either because he knew little about baseball, or because he never considered any ball game significant unless it was played in the major leagues. [104]

Muse: You can't manufacture those black stars every night, because ... they eat soul food and [cultivated] that little garden business they had in the back. They eat the right food and that is why they had the stamina. Man, look at that a boy ... on Minnesota [Vikings]; oh my god, I've never seen a man with such legs.... He ain't no accident!

I do not know whom Muse is talking about on the Minnesota Vikings. It could be anyone of eight ballplayers, including Carl Eller and Oscar Reed. [105]

Muse: He's up there, in a fair competition, where ... [the white man] doesn't get a chance to say, "Law and order," or "This is where you supposed to be out...." There, in the middle of that football field ... he's on an even grip. And on the even grip, Mr. W. [the white man] doesn't match up. He'll knock Mr. W. out and take the ball over the goal, and come back and say, "What next?"

And then every one of the teams, every team you see on there, the black is the superior winner. And basketball. Let's laugh that off, don't say no more about the [Los Angeles] Lakers; you know the Lakers. All down the line. So, these are not accidents.

This is the one time in life when the black people of America have an equal chance, an even chance to show what's going on. And when they go on, they all come out winners. And if that [opportunity] was associated in the system [racist institutions] all the way down, we wouldn't be here knocking our brains out now, trying to write the black story and trying to beg our way [into American history]. We would be in, if we had a fair shake [the way we do in] the athletics.

I can only assume that Muse is talking about modern athletics as he saw them in contrast to the first half of the century. Even so, his comments reveal that, for him, progress was measured in small steps and seen from the perspective of how far African-Americans had come in fifty years. Anyone familiar with the power structure in contemporary sports realizes full well just how much further sports needs to go to put "others" on an equal footing in management and ownership of big league teams.

Muse: Athletics, to me, represents a whole growth of a new attitude in our society. Those guys could not be great champions if they didn't have what it takes, because some great white boys are in there. You have some great white boys, but there's always a black boy just a little bit ahead.

CUT

When the tape resumed, we were talking about Buck and the Preacher *[1972]. An independent film made by Sidney Poitier (in his directorial debut) for Columbia Pictures, it starred Poitier as a former Union soldier, who, after the Civil War, becomes wagon master to a group of ex-slaves as they look for a new life in the West. Harry Belafonte (co-producer of the film with Poitier) is the reformed hustling preacher, willing to fight for the homesteaders. Muse has a minor role as Cudjo, one of the more prominent homesteaders.*

The reviews of the movie are worth noting since they recall the mood of the times. Most critics acknowledged that the film was targeted at black audiences, but disagreed just how fresh it was. On the one hand, the westerners were mainly African-Americans, unique for Hollywood and the genre. The blatant attacks on white supremacist values also added to the movie's relevance to the 1970s. On the other hand, the reviewers often found it cliche-ridden and unconvincing. One critic went so far as accuse Poitier of making "one of the black films that 'exploit their race's dilemma for personal profit'" and goes on to say that the "fledgling director's handling of the cast amounted to presenting them as a 'mostly anonymous mass of niggers indistinguishable from the piously and paternally treated darkies of Olde Hollywood.'"[106]

Muse: The future is contingent on what was done before.... If Poitier had come in at the time we had started, the time we've been talking about.... See, I've known Poitier a long time.

I knew Belafonte when he was washing dishes, trying to sing them English ballads. That little old common guy from down in the West Indies.... He wasn't born in the West Indies; his people were. And they took him back, and he came back with a banana song that was the beginning of the [his success].

Sye: You're talking about [Harry] Belafonte now.

Harrold George Belafonte Jr. was born on March 1, 1927 in New York. Soon after, his parents, who were West Indian, returned home. Although he only spent five years in Jamaica, and then grew up in Harlem, the future artist and political activist was profoundly influenced by his West Indian heritage. After being discharged from the Navy in 1945, he attended the New School for Social Research, where he was a classmate of Marlon Brando and Tony Curtis. By 1948, he had tried his hand as a pop-music singer and within three years was a cabaret headliner.

His screen debut in Gerald Mayer's Bright Road *(1953) made little impact on moviegoers. Still, following his Broadway debut in John Murray Anderson's* Almanac, *Belafonte was signed by Otto Preminger for the lead in* Carmen Jones *(1954). Near the end of the decade, he signed a three-picture deal (the last two are with his own production company, HarBel Productions Inc.) with Twentieth Century-Fox:* Island in the Sun *(1957),* The World, The Flesh, and The Devil, *and* Odds Against Tomorrow *(both in 1959).*

Aware of the power of the movies to affect behavior and values, Belafonte's intentions were to use his films "as a weapon against stereotyped portrayals of the Negro in films and a socially constructive force in the industry."[107] But his performances of "docile cardboard characters," according to critics like Guy Flatley,[108] proved so disappointing to his fans that the idealistic producer abandoned his plans to spend "fifty per cent of his time" producing films in the sixties.[109]

Most of his time during the sixties was spent working with Martin Luther King and fighting for civil rights. Like many outspoken African-Americans of his generation, Belafonte often found himself at odds with opposing viewpoints about his contributions and motives.

The versatile artist resumed his film career in the late 1960s, first with his production of The Angel Levine *(1970) and then with a series of movies starring the singer with Sidney Poitier:* Buck and the Preacher *(1972),* Uptown Saturday Night *(1974),* Let's Do It Again *(1975), and* A Piece of the Action *(1977).*

At the time I was interviewing Muse, the socially minded, singer-actor was speaking out against the violence in so-called blaxploitation films: "I'm very much concerned because I believe there is a dangerous spiraling taking place.... Something subliminal is happening to the audience – if the film is not violent, then it is not dramatic enough for them."[110]

Belafonte's most recent films include The Player *(1992),* Pret-a-Porter *(1994),* White Man's Burden *(1995), and* Kansas City *(1996). In addition to his theatrical career, he continues to remain a champion of political causes. For more information, see G. Fogelson, Henry Louis Gates, Jr., and Arnold Shaw.*

Muse: Belafonte! He does that [Calypso].... And he still wants to try to do a ballad. He hasn't got what it takes. Well, he can't. But there ain't nobody on earth can beat him doing Calypso. Nobody. You think so?

CUT

Here the tape becomes garbled, as Muse talked about his experiences doing a WPA production of Porgy *on the West Coast during the 1930s. We pick it up at the point he is remembering about the difficulty in managing the company and a script woman, who regularly checked out the performances.*

Muse: I brought a lot of people out here [for the show]. But some of them never did get on the stage ... one hundred and eighty-six people ... just too many of them. We had a thing though, where there was a parade, and people just kept going in and around the trunk of the tree.... But boy, they were working and getting a check. Of course, they had to have discipline, because that was my first rule....

At this point, Muse began to talk in a stream of conscious about his days in repertory theater. Although he had performed in most of the top flight African-American troupes of the teens and twenties, the versatile actor also wrote, starred, and managed many acting companies himself. In the material that follows, he offers some recollections on his experiences in the South and on the West Coast before World War II. For example, during the period of the WPA in the late-1930s, actors had to be on the rolls of one Federal Theater Project or another in order to qualify for a weekly payment of ninety dollars. The production referred to is probably Hall Johnson's Run, Little Chillun! *which he produced and directed in Los Angeles in*

1935. *A drama contrasting Christian and African-American spiritual beliefs, it premiered in 1933 and had Fredi Washington in a minor role.*[111]

Muse: I had a girl, a secretary, who was terrific. She checked them lines every night, and if a guy missed three or changed three lines, I get her to get them to do rehearsal time next morning. You had to stay right with the book. And then [Ed] Sullivan wrote it up; that's when he got national stuff on his chain.

Many big stars in Hollywood, who wanted to learn their business, would go see the run of the show. Then that rebounded to the point where we'd advertise in the paper that they [the public] would see two stars [every night at the play].... as long as they [the public] turned up, they [the stars] would be there. When the intermission came, there were always a couple of stars that had to stand in the lobby. The damn thing ran for two years.

Now the seats, the first ten rows, this is common money, was forty-five cents. The scalpers bought up, every day, all of them damn seats; and the big white folks paid five dollars and fifty cents to sit in them. [Laughter] I don't ... you know ... these things happen. People forget that, and you ought to remind them of that. They [white people] paid five dollars and fifty cents for a forty-five cents seat.

The same as when we played that T.O.B.A. thing down South, in Atlanta. It got so that I knew the man who was the president of the Coca-Cola. You know how I knew? Well, Thursday night we had white folks' night in the show. The Negro can't come to theater that night. They could pay forty cents all week. Two dollars for white folks on Thursday night, and they packed them in. And this guy was always ... had the box. The president of Coca-Cola. And that's where I met him.

Now, to me, I laugh at this stuff, because.... How do you change the things that have happened? This ... is the way it happened. And ... the only guys that beat it were smart enough to stay out [of the system] and didn't let the damn thing run over them. It didn't run over me. It could crush you if you got in the way. It happened. Could you imagine paying two dollars for a forty...? And this is packed!

You know where the girl was discovered? I hear her every morning.

Ena: Dinah Shore.

Muse's assertion raises an interesting point about ethnicity. That is, if an individual's features don't reveal any racial characteristics, if the person considers himself or herself to be of a certain classification, and nothing in his or her behavior draws attention to their belonging to a particular group, what is to be gained by someone else labeling that individual as a member of a particular group? Nowhere in Bruce Cassidy's biography of the star is there any information to corroborate Muse and Sye's assertion that Dinah Shore was an African-American. It is a rumor that persists since the 1970s, but has yet to be substantiated.

Frances Rose Shore was born on March 1, 1917, in Winchester, Tennessee to Jewish parents. Because Jews were a significant minority in her hometown during her childhood, the young girl experienced many forms of racial prejudice. It is a point made clear in her stories about her youth.

In the 1930s, she hosted a fifteen-minute Nashville radio show, where her theme song was "Dinah." She officially changed her name to Dinah Shore in 1944. After leaving Tennessee near the end of the thirties, she began a remarkable career as a popular singer and gained momentum during the 1940s, when she also made her film debut in Thank Your Lucky Stars (1943). Although inconsequential as a movie actress, Ms. Shore became one of the most famous television personalities of the 1950s. Following a brief retirement to rear her family in the sixties, she returned in the 1970s to pioneer daytime television talk shows. Among her many honors was the distinction of being the most acclaimed actress by the Emmy Awards, tying with Mary Tyler Moore for winning eight statuettes. She died of cancer at seventy-six on February 24, 1994.

Muse: Dinah Shore. Dinah Shore came on one of my white night shows in Memphis. Her mother was there with her. [She was] a young gal about sixteen. And she wanted to sing to the white audience, "St Louis Blues." Now the Cat playing the piano ... you know how they have to pull all the stuff up ... they don't know nothing out there but this key. And everybody playing the F sharp C minor. You can put the music down, but that's a gag, you know. They didn't read the words. [Laughter] They got the key....

So I said, "You really want to?" And she said, "Oh, I want to sing St Louis Blues." So they ... them guys cooked behind her, and she stopped the show cold!

Next time I ran up on Dinah Shore was during World War II, when we had to go to San Diego, to a ... thing down there, up in the camp. And she was one of the artists on the train. We had Lena Horne, Hattie McDaniel; we had everybody on the bus. And all these soldiers all up in the trees and everything. And when her time come on, Dinah Shore, by request, sang twenty-two of her records [Whistles] before they let her go. She come up, she was black from the beginning.

Sye: Yeah, I heard that rumor....

Muse: That's right.... Joseph Cotton belongs to the black race.

Joseph Cotton, the distinguished stage and screen actor, was born on May 15, 1905, in Tidewater, Virginia. In his candid and freewheeling autobiography, he covered many topics, including his stage and screen associations with Orson

Welles. Yet no where in the memoir spanning more than forty years in show business does he indicate that he was an African-American. The international star died on February 6, 1994.

> Ena: They call that "Creole."
> Muse: He's a Creole.
> Manchel: I didn't know that.
> Sye: I never knew about Joseph, I knew about Dinah for some years.
> Muse: Memphis ... so you see the race thing ... something like that. Funny thing about just a little bit of black that kind of messes you up.
> Manchel: Tell them the story about *Cry, the Beloved Country*.
> Muse: That was a hell of a thing. That was here. Say they're going to produce this damn thing, and I get a wire one time in July. Never forget it. Fourth of July. So I went down past the pump house right down there on the way to go up, and the thermometer was reading one hundred sixteen. Of course, dry heat up there; you can take it. Okay. So they sent me to come to New York to see if I wanted to play this ... what's the name of it?
> Manchel: *Cry, the Beloved Country.*
> Muse: *Cry, the Beloved Country*. I go by plane. And I get up to New York; it's eighty-six, in New York, but the humidity was up to eighty-seven. And if they don't hurry up and carry me to one of those air-conditioned hotels, I'd have been a goner, man....
> Kurt Weill was this guy, F1 German son of a gun. I never cared for him. He wasn't for real either. So they went over there, and I saw the powers that be.... I wasn't sold on the damn tale, because I didn't like to have it so South African. Canada Lee finally took the damn thing. They had to ship him almost in a crate to get him in there.

Muse is mixing up the Zoltan Korda/Alan Paton production of Cry, the Beloved Country *(1952) with the Broadway musical version,* Lost in the Stars *(1949). The show had music composed by Kurt Weill, a libretto by Maxwell Anderson, and was directed by Rouben Mamoulian. Sidney Poitier, who turned down a part in the musical, co-starred in the film, and had to become an indentured servant to Korda in order to work in the racist-controlled country.[112] Muse felt that Lee had to undergo similar insults to perform his role. Also worth noting is that the stage producers allegedly wanted Paul Robeson for the lead, but had to settle for Todd Duncan.[113]*

In 1995, Darrell James Roodt remade the movie, this time starring James Earl Jones, Eric Miyeni, and Richard Harris.

> Muse: See.... I said, "No, I don't want to be in it...." They were very

nice about it. It cost them about five grand to take me there and sit me in the hotel. I ... had a good time....

So Canada took it. I've often saw him years after [sic], and Canada said to me that was the dumbest thing he'd ever done. "That was a rough deal I made."

They [South Africans] have no use whatsoever for people of color; they don't know nothing. And everybody who comes out there, who's turned out to be great artists, they can't go back. They can never go back home. Warwick comes from down there. The girl. Ain't that Warwick?

Sye: Dionne Warwick.

Muse is wrong. Dionne Warwick was born in East Orange, New Jersey, on December 12, 1941.

Muse: Can't go back down there.
Sye: You know Lee Elder just came from down there.

Lee Elder was a leading black professional golfer in the late 1960s and 1970s.

Muse: Well, he left.... The show closed forever. He can't go back.
Sye: You know that's a bad scene.
Muse: You don't go back. Period. Why do you want to hear about that? That's that negative tone....
Sye: There is a reported rumor that the Oscar [statute] for the Academy Awards of Motion Picture Arts and Sciences was done from the body of a guy, one Woody Strode. Do you know anything about that at all? Whenever I see Woody, I'm going to ask him directly. Now I don't know where it says it's Woody....

The assertion about Woody Strode being the model for the statue has often been claimed by various sources. Most sources, however, agree that the trophy was conceived by Cedric Gibbon, designed by Frederic Hope, and created by George Stanley. Margaret Herrick coined the name, "Oscar." In my discussions with Strode, we talked about the controversial German filmmaker, Leni Riefenstahl, who, during her good will tour in California, used him as a model for a painting commissioned by Hitler for the 1936 Olympics in Berlin. It was that same physical appearance and flair for action that shaped his screen image. His posing for Riefenstahl may be the source for the Oscar stories that Muse perpetuates here.

Muse: [Pointing to a bust] See how much Woody is in that. Sixteen people in that. That black head. See that over there in the corner? Yeah, how much Woody do you see?

Sye: I see Woody's head, and jaw.

Muse: No ... some people's eyes, some people's ears, some people's nose.

Sye: That's by example, right?

Muse: Go ahead and move it.

Sye: This is the head you're talking about?

Muse: Yeah. Biggest thing you got there is Woody's lips.

CUT

Sye: You mentioned to me, and I'm asking it for the sake of clarity....

Muse: Don't apologize.

Sye: No, I'm not apologizing. I'm just informing you so you won't jump on it.

Muse: I'm scared ... that's where I want 'em.

Sye: Are you saying that the Eisenhower board developed, or was named, because of the man who handled the lights at the theater?

Muse: I'm saying the Eisenhower board was made by the same man in the Federal Theater, when I got this other boy.... You see that picture over there. That's the set designer. His name is Nelson Bourmay [?]. He did the sets. I got a big mural in the room I'll show you later. Keep it on the wall. He's a young Frenchman who was born in Buffalo, New York. He came to me and told me he was trying ... and I accepted him to do the set and the water, which was the color scheme, based on the whole pattern ... like a quilt. The thing was a piece of beauty. And among them, they found this guy, Eisenhower, who was in the Federal Theater. And he came, and he's the guy that planted all these one hundred eighty lights and things in there. And when he had so much trouble.... It took three guys all month to get that lighting down ... to operate these things, to get them on cue. In his mind came the thought of why isn't there such a board that could do like this and make it happen. And he came up with it. The Eisenhower board. He invented it right after. It was accepted by the industry. And he became a very wealthy man. He's a very rich man today because of it.

Muse is talking about a lighting control system, referred to as a "piano board;" that has a control lever for every specific light. It has been replaced in modern times by a computerized board that coordinates both lights and sounds.

Ena: When you go to CBS studio ... and look at the lights for television and things ... It's a big console.

Muse: It's like playing the piano.

Ena: And you have a draft. The lighting man has a draft of all that he wants ... Well, you know that. So that he can touch this button and so on.

Muse: Terrific job, I done put on it. I told him, I don't care how he got it through there, but get it through there, baby. I'm sitting out front. We had a marble table where there was a scene the gal did, and I wanted to bring on the stage the technique of a close-up. And the gal says, "I'm going with him, with or without you." It [the technique achieved through lighting] stopped the show.... And the reason it stopped the show was that we had a marble table, and we had a hole drilled into the table. And I put a light, a little baby light in this hole. And when this line comes in, they're [performers] are leaning over the table – "I'm going with or without" – this light hit and you had a perfect close-up scene in the theater, which was an innovation at that time. And they rolled. This man Eisenhower was something, boy. You see we had a double set, you can see the yard, the backyard, and you could see the interior; and you could see the church in the wild wood back in the scene. It was a double set.... And it was the first double set, broken set ever, and that man created it.

Sye: But I was concerned primarily about the lights, you know. Because that's a very important thing.

Muse: You can't light well today and pay the bills if you don't have a board, because you'd have so darn many assistants ... [who charge a lot of money to work on the show]. That board cut that thing down.

Ena: And he's no relation to the late Eisenhower.

Sye: Is he black?

Muse: No, white. I - I-z-e. Izenhour. Not E. I- Ize. Got it now?

In his book on theatrical lighting, Albert F.C. Wehlberg explains that there is "thyrotron tube light board," that has a trade name, Izenhour, derived from its creator, "George Izenhour, of Yale University."[114]

Muse: Now all that ... See I like these questions you're asking because you know what you're getting? You're getting a construction of this thing we've talking about. This is really going around the inside. The inside is what makes a business. Not what happens on the outside. See....

CUT

The film Muse is discussing here is So Red the Rose *(1935). A Paramount film directed by King Vidor. Laurence Stallings, Maxwell Anderson, and Edwin Justin Mayer adapt the antebellum story from a novel by Stark Young. The narrative deals with the final days of the Civil War as Union troops ravage the South and the wife of a plantation owner struggles to maintain order at home while her husband is away in battle and the slaves want their freedom. The cast includes Margaret Sullavan, Walter Connolly, Randolph Scott, and Robert Cummings. Clarence Muse plays Cato, the slave who rises up against his owners. For more information on Muse and the film, see the King Vidor interview.*

Muse: [Cato] starts telling these folks, "This house is yours, burn it down, take it away, tear up the property...." Then the lady [Vallette Bedford, played by Margaret Sullavan] comes down with the white ribbon, stretches the tape, and walks up – this is the original script – [and] she smacks me on the face and the revolution is over. I said, "Oh, no." I held up the studio two days and a half. They couldn't stop because they had too ... money [already spent on the production], and I knew they couldn't stop. And finally we settled the situation.

When you see the picture, you're gonna enjoy it. The only way that they could stop the revolution at that moment, when they did burn up the joint, was to come up and ... smack somebody. So she smacked the mulatto. This was the deal. So we saved the black. So until today, I still say, "black is beautiful," and can a man keep going in life without a song.

[Muse begins singing]

Without a song
The day would never end.
Without a song
A man ain't got a friend.
When things go wrong
A man ain't got a friend.
Without a song
That field of corn would be deserted now.
That field of corn would never see a plow
When things go wrong.
A man ain't got a friend
Without a song.
I got my troubles and woes
But sure as I know
The Jordan will roll.
I'll get along
As long as a song
Is strong in my soul.
I'll never know
What makes the rain to fall.
I'll never know

What makes the grass so tall.
I only know
There ain't no love at all
Without a song.

CUT

Muse: King Vidor was the same guy who directed *Gone With the Wind*. Southern man. When I was telling you a minute ago, I forgot to bring in, when I was telling you about Louise Rainer's [debut] in ... *Cabin in the Cotton*. It was directed by a Viennese man named [Michael] Curtiz who didn't know nothing. I did all his legwork at the library, acquainting him with books and things about the sharecropping thing, and he did this successful, great picture of the sharecroppers. He ... thought he was a Texan.

Muse is confusing the Viennese actress Luise Rainer's success as a European film star with the Hungarian director Curtiz. She made her American debut in Escapade (1935).

Muse: So the moment comes when the star [Bette Davis] comes out, and [she is walking downstairs] and gets to the last step ... I [Muse is playing a butler] reach over, and I touch her by the arm, and help her down. He [Curtiz] called me, and he said, "Clarence," he said, "you know we got to take that out." "What's wrong with it?"[Muse asks]. "you just lost nine states in the south," [Curtiz replied]. He was acting as if he were in *Gone With the Wind*. He was so damned white. I couldn't face it.

Muse is referring to the practice in Hollywood during the studio era when producers considered any contact between the races to be an affront to Southern audiences. Thus, no scenes between whites and blacks touching ever were seen in the tight narrative of the film. If you did have a scene where the performers touched (such as in a dance routine), these scenes had to be unconnected to the important narrative development of the film. This allowed disgruntled exhibitors to edit the scene without affecting the logic of the film.[115]

Muse: That's not the fault of that studio, and that's not the fault – that's on the tape – that's not the fault of the director, and that's not the fault of the actor. It's the fault of the receiving end, which is the customers out there in the South, and whose managers ran the communities like they ran yours. And if he [the exhibitor or the censor] said they ain't gonna play the picture, even you, as a professor, can't make him play it. In your little town. That's the situation all through the South.

Manchel: What was the name of the picture with Luise Rainer? Do you remember?
Muse: *The Toy Wife* [1938].
Manchel: *The Toy Wife?*
Muse: Big thing. She got an academy award for it.
Manchel: She got an academy award for that?
Muse: I think so.

Muse is wrong on this point. Neither Ms. Rainer nor the film was nominated for an Oscar. The actress, however, did have two previous nominations: in 1936 for The Great Ziegfeld, *and in 1937 for* The Good Earth, *and she won both times. Interestingly, her career ended almost a year later, causing a number of people in the industry to refer to successive wins as the "Rainer Jinx."*

Sye: How did you handle it?
Muse: ... I didn't touch the woman. If the writer is on the ball.... I said, "Oh, well, I'm not going to break up the studio and ...". He ain't done nothing on another picture so, how far we talking back? Forty years. He ain't never done another picture....

I am not quite sure who Muse was talking about, the director or the writer. Whichever one, he is wrong. The director is Richard Thorpe, who is credited with helming over a hundred films. Best known as a reliable contract director for MGM, he began his screen career in the mid-1920s and retired in the mid-sixties. He died on May 1, 1991.[116]

Zoe Akins is the credited screenwriter on The Toy Wife. *A distinguished dramatist who won the 1935 Pulitzer Prize for her drama* The Old Maid, *she entered films in 1930 and is credited with more than a dozen movies, the last being* Desire Me *(1947). The playwright died in 1958.*

Muse: You don't win 'em that way. They control the wagon. I rode in the damn wagon and pulled the screws ... Frank Capra tells it in his book ... about me.

In his autobiography, The Name above the Title *(1971), Frank Capra states that he made four films with Muse. The first was a screen adaptation of the 1928 Broadway musical* Rain or Shine. *The 1930 screen adaptation had Muse playing a black organist. Their next encounter was on* Dirigible *(1931), where the actor was cast as a participant in planting a flag at the South Pole. In this section, Capra refers to Muse as his "pet actor" (128). Capra's third assignment for Muse was the 1934 film* Broadway Bill *(which was remade by the populist director in 1950 as* Riding High, *again with Muse).*

Of all the entries, this is the most interesting because of the racial issue associated with the film and its remake. In his book, Capra includes the character actor in his praise for a 1934 cast he considered "one of the greatest collections of time-saving, sure-fire entertainers ever assembled...."[117] However, he makes no mention of the racist controversy associated with the film. Only later, when talking about Riding High, does the director cite critic Manny Farber's attack on the way Capra depicts African-American images. The director defends himself by pointing to other reviewers who compliment Capra on the way he has Muse perform his role.

Joseph McBride, however, makes clear what the problem is with both film versions. In Broadway Bill, the central protagonist physically mistreats Whitey, the black stable hand – Muse's character. In the 1950 remake, Farber, aware of how much Capra had homogenized behavior by and toward Whitey, nevertheless felt compelled to attack Capra's stereotyping of the character as "a happy slave personality." McBride's assessment is that Capra seemed incapable of going beyond "his shy, sadly tentative relationship with Muse, whom he called 'a wonderful guy....'" At the same time, the critic praised Muse as "a fine actor ... who always managed to keep a measure of dignity no matter how demeaning the part...."[118]

Muse: Of course, he has a philosophy; he never hired an actor twice in his pictures. All his casts were all original [actors]. I did four pictures [with him].... He's a city boy, you know spiritually. And ... he wrote to me the other day.... He wouldn't write no letter to the average guy. So there's closeness there.

CUT

Muse: My name is Clarence Muse, M-U-S-E. I spell it because during a long career the ... [name] is spelled many, many different ways. So it's M-U-S-E. Muse. Like in music.

I was born in a little town in the east called Baltimore, Maryland. My parents [Alexander and Mary Muse] were from Virginia and North Carolina. My grandparents ... my grandfather was born in Martinique, one of the islands out there in the Caribbean, discovered by the French.

So much for the early thing of being born. At that time, I had no special reason other than to go to school. My mother was quite a stickler for education. And after finishing high school and making the preparation for college work and the regent's examinations, I went to Dickinson University [sic] in Carlisle, Pennsylvania, and received the Degree of Law [in 1911].

And then suddenly, being penniless, I began working in a hotel in Palm Beach, Florida, as one of the members of a quartet. In fact, I had been singing all during my school career ... to keep alive and keep the tuition paid up. And at the end of the season, in Palm Beach at the Breakers Hotel. It was an odd set-up; the help was brought down there from New York City on a special train. [They] had a special railroad right into the hotel. The swells and the [Thorpes] and all that gang were the type of people that came to the hotel.

In a 1977 interview, Muse talked about the famous Breakers Hotel, where millionaires congregated. He explained that he had gotten the job because of a friend he worked with in Philadelphia. The reference to the Thorpes is about the wealthy Harry K. Thorpe family. Muse made a good living at the resort, getting a monthly salary of $150, plus tips (ranging anywhere from $5 to $20). He fondly remembered being part of a quartet, where his special contribution was the singing of "Old Black Joe." Sounding defensive, he explained, "People say that's another of them Tom Songs, but it was a glorification of a Black man."[119]

Muse: ... The arrangement was that you would receive a salary, working as an entertainer, but you also had to have some other employment, so I became what they called a "water boy" for the hotel. People in those days didn't drink the water in Florida. They always wanted French Vichy or some fine water, some imported water, and that was my job during the meal hours. I wore a beautiful green suit with a silver circle around it saying, a big 'W' on it meaning "the water boy."

Well, at the end of the season.... The salary was very low; I think it was a couple hundred, two hundred fifty dollars to cover all three months. And the money came in one lump.

A guy by the name of Rube Foster, who carried the baseball teams down there to play for the guests, [he was] out of Chicago, had the concession at the quarters where they helped set up all the gambling. It was a little Las Vegas sort of set up.

Rube Foster, one of baseball's immortal pitchers, played a major role in the success of the Negro Baseball League.

Muse: And I got into the game, that last night, when we were packing up to go early in the morning. And I won something like eight thousand dollars in a poker game. Young guy out of school, lots of ambition, going to practice law or whatnot.

And I had what they call a money belt, and I strapped this money on it early in the morning about nine o'clock, to save me when I'm working at the desk and having this money. Because on the train, they used the baggage car to re-open the gambling club, and I felt if I ever got in there again, between there and New York which took about two days in those days, they'd have the money.

So when I got to Jacksonville, Florida and my bag was checked up front ... I didn't have much. Anyhow, I bought a brand new suit of clothes that they sold at the hotel there, and a new Stetson hat. I felt that I was quite sharp.... I stepped off the train, went into the station and hid out in the men's room, until the train pulled out.

There I was in Jacksonville, Florida, with this money round, raining pitchforks, scared to death. So I just took a few dollars ... fifteen to twenty dollars from the belt, and got on to a little surrey and went uptown, through the Colored section of the city, and found a hotel room.

And it wasn't long after that before I met a fellow who was quite big. Important personality around the town who later became famous in New York. His name was Broadway Jones. He introduced me around, and I had a few sheets of work, [as it was] known, of professional music, and they had never seen anything like that in the South. So I gave him that, a couple numbers, professional numbers from right off of Broadway. We became great buddies.

There was a little theater there called the Airdome. And this Airdome Theater, meaning theater without a roof, ran these stock companies. I finally got a job of singing in the Olio. The Olio means [an act performing] between curtains.

Muse is talking here about his early days as a minstrel performer. Robert C. Toll describes the Olio as originally being "the second part of the show, the variety section...."[120] *By the time performers like Muse began performing in the Olio manner, the original structure of the minstrel show had vanished. It now functioned as a specialty act. The history of white people in burnt cork and of African-Americans performing their own minstrel shows, however, has recently become a popular topic in academic circles, thanks to Eric Lott's* Love and Theft: Blackface Minstrelsy and the American Working Class. *More recently, Michael Rogin has drawn parallels between blackface minstrelsy and the American film industry in* Blackface, White Noise: Jewish Immigrants in the Hollywood Melting Pot.[121]

Muse: Funny thing is that up to that time, on the stage, all the Colored artists had adopted a peculiar thing.... [African-Americans used burnt cork to appear in sync with the "blackface tradition"]. Because in checking back on the history of the black-faced comedians, the blackface business started in Philadelphia, during the slavery time when Negroes used to entertain on the plantations. And then when the whites began to realize this was good kind of entertainment, they took a steal on it, and they blacked up.

Then it kept moving along. So in my time, when I come along, even the Colored artist thought he had to black up to be a successful artist.

The debate about the effects of "blackface" and minstrelsy on the public in general and the African-American community in particular, is far too complicated to discuss here. Suffice to say the cultural history of America in inundated with performers and critics who argue over its place in the development of vaudeville, the theatre, and motion pictures.[122]

Muse: I was kind of against this, so I went on the stage for the first time in Jacksonville, Florida, in a full-dress suit without makeup. Well, that was a tremendous point in my success. In those days, I was only singing bass songs like "Sleep in the Deep" and "When the Bells in the Lighthouse Ring, ding-dong." There was an old man named Masoola, played on his big bass ... and all that sort of things. I became quite a big hit.

Muse's 1912 Jacksonville season also included a turn at Frank Crowd's Globe Theater.

Muse: And there were a couple fellows who put me in a stock company.... One was named Freeman, and the young chap in short pants who was named [Leonard] Harper, who later became the very successful dance director for the Cotton Club in New York, in later years when he grew up. And before I knew it, they had wiggled me around to the point where I bought a third interest in the stock company.
[Muse's new partners] owed people in every county they had ever been in, and every sheriff in the South was looking for them. I got a great kick out of the fact that on the marquee my name went out "Freeman, Harper, and Muse." So that was big enough for me.
Funny thing is I met Broadway [Jones], and I told him that I'd make the jump from there to Atlanta, and that I'd meet him in New York in the next three or four weeks. He went down and hired himself out as a steward on a ship to get to New York. And seven years later [Laughter] I got there ... and Broadway Jones was a big success in New York.
Then I traveled all through the South with this stock company. Putting on these little short plays, after pieces, and singing and whatnot, and finally landed in New York City [in the late teens], got married at the time [to Willabelle Marshbanks, who was billed as Ophelia Muse].

I do not know when Muse's first marriage ended, but he married Irene Ena Kellman in 1953. She remained his companion for the next twenty-six years until his death on October 13, 1979.

Muse: Before I got to New York City, I was living in Kansas City for quite a while, long enough to become almost a citizen there. In fact, that's where I cast my first vote as a citizen of this country. I remember that I voted for Woodrow Wilson. And I was trained that this was a new day and a new way of thinking. It sort of caught on, and I sort of remained with the [Democratic] Party all these years.

And in Kansas City, my oldest son was born, now lives in Colorado Springs.

I went to New York, and I saw and met Broadway again. I was still sort of in the entertaining field in vaudeville. That included Keith and Proctor, Bill Robinson "Bojangles," and we're having quite a time in the vaudeville field. And in the summer months, we played the Shinnacock Casino, that was a millionaire spot where Caruso, and [Giuseppe] Amato ... and those guys used to come ... and we lived on tips.

We had a kind of very clever thing going, whenever these big writers and great novelists used to come there, come down in this boat, to the club. The chauffeur would pick them up early in the morning in his Rolls Royce; and he'd come by water and he'd go back home on land. And Caruso used to make quite a trick of going out in the boats on the lake, and you would hear him singing across these waters in the lobby of the hotel, with this Japanese lantern. It was sort of a musical impression I've never forgotten.

And then when we got back to New York, couple of years later, they organized in Harlem, what they call a stock company, on 135th Street known as the Lincoln Players.

It is worth remembering, as Jervis Anderson points out, that before World War I, "the theaters of Seventh Avenue and 125th Street were off limits to blacks. Their theaters were the Lincoln and the Crescent, on 135th Street between Lennox and Fifth Avenues. This was Harlem's 'Off Broadway.' Harlem's 'Broadway' was Seventh Avenue and 125th Street...."[123] I suspect that the Lincoln Players were also known as the "The Colored Dramatic Stock Company" and later "The Anita Bush Company," the forerunner of the famous Lafayette Players. The group first performed at the newly created Lincoln Theater in 1915. It is also worth noting that Ms. Bush was the first African-American actress to appear in all-black western, The Crimson Skull *(1921).*[124]

Muse: And they were doing these little plays like ... *Oliver Twist*. [It] was done in forty-five minutes. And they practically built it [the Lincoln Theater]; it was doing a terrific business. My wife was the star of one of the companies.

One week the villain of the play walked out on them, and they were stuck. So they come after me to see if I'd help them. And I went down to help them, and I became the villain. So that hung on to me. I became quite the successful villain in the stock company for two, three years; and then later they got very ambitious since this dramatic thing was catching on in Harlem.

The old Lafayette Theater had failed as a vaudeville house. Charles S. Gilpin, who did *The Emperor Jones*, had tried to revive it, but he couldn't make it go. So then, they [Anita Bush] took us over to where they'd organized another company called the Lafayette Players.

And they did one show, and we were still mounting our own on 135th Street. That was a time like the Westerns today. The villain always got killed at the end of the show. He had to do them spinning falls, you know. One time we got very polished, and I got killed at the end of the show, and then made one of those sensational falls. The curtain went down and no applause; nobody moved. So we had to do the scene over again and take one of those falls out.

Then the beginning of the Lafayette Players ... welcome to a new era of show business. It was brand new to Negroes.

Few sources agree on just when the Lafayette Players organized – 1914, 1915, or 1916. All agree, however, that it earned its reputation as "black Harlem's first legitimate-theater group." Since there were few black plays available, the idea was to do uptown what was being done downtown by white authors and actors. The Lafayette Players' productions changed every week, yet the pioneering company's many successes did not come without criticism from some African-American intellectuals who strongly objected to primarily white plays being presented to mainly black audiences. On the other hand, the majority of Harlem supported the idea of a professional company that provided black performers with acting opportunities not to be found anywhere else in America.[125] Among the distinguished performers associated with the Lafayette Players were Charles S. Gilpin, Evelyn Ellis, Frank Wilson, Evelyn Preer, Edna Thomas, and Clarence Muse.

Muse: They decided to do Broadway plays, successful Broadway plays. They got them from the play bureau. [They did the plays] completely. Things like *Lena Rivers, Dr. Jekyll and Mr. Hyde, The Mastermind, Thais*. Somehow, I ended up [staying with the Lafayette Players] seven years ... doing all of these different sorts of things.

I attribute this kind of experience in my background to learning what characterization is all about and how to be a real actor of the old school. So after putting a couple of hundred plays under my belt ... my biggest hit was *Dr. Jekyll and Mr. Hyde*.

Here Muse is being uncharacteristically humble about his success. According to Langston Hughes and Milton Meltzer, the now-very popular stage performer had first stunned Harlem audiences by appearing "completely white" in a melodrama called Within the Law. *In their words, the play "in Harlem became a S.R.O. Hit."*[126] *Thus, when Muse talks, in a moment, about his success in whiteface in Dr. Jekyll and Mr. Hyde, he is forgetting about his earlier triumph.*

Muse: Might I add here that another very interesting thing ... [about] the company that was formed, the Lafayette Players, [was that they] were handpicked; and they were all mulattos because they're playing Broadway shows, white shows, trying to play them as realistic as possible.

A photograph of the Lafayette Players in 1924 suggests the tradition continued almost to the end of the company's history.[127]

Muse: And I don't know, you can't see me on this thing [the tape], I'm not a mulatto. I'm one of the Ethiopians of the darker hue, and I developed quite an art to meet the competition of makeup. I'm considered the first and most successful [actor] in the art of making up as a white man.

The books I have consulted on the subject support Muse's first claim.

Muse: The opening performance of *Fine Feathers* in New York ... was my first play with the Lafayette Players. When the horn blew outside of the French window, all the gang from 135th Street was sitting up there waiting for me to come on out. I was quite a favorite. They heard my voice and they applauded. And when I entered the stage fully a white man, with these long opera pink gloves I used to wear, makeup flesh colored, it was five minutes before I could open my mouth. My blond wig and ... – whatever his name is, that very famous German wigmaker – I had him make my wigs for me. And it [whiteface] upset New York tremendously that this was possible. Pretty soon, it became a known fact that I was the man that played ... was successful in making a Negro into a white man with the Lafayette Players. This went on for seven years.
One day, out in Columbus, Ohio, I had left the Lafayette Players then, and I was putting on shows for a very ambitious man who built a new theater called the Ogdeon Theater. I had a swell job I thought, producing whatnot; I had sixteen beautiful girls that we had brought in from Chicago. And I was interrupted in my rehearsals by a [telephone] call from Hollywood.

Despite the importance of Muse's entrance into films, the events surrounding the telephone call remained confused. Even the date is uncertain. Most sources suggest the call came in 1928, since the film appeared early in 1929. Moreover, The Jazz Singer *premiered on October 6, 1928. However, we need to remember that Muse was replacing Gilpin, and production may have already begun on the film. My best guess is that Muse was probably hired in late 1928, because the film opened in late February, 1929. In addition, most sources claim that Muse was performing in Chicago, not Columbus. Seven months after the actor and I had talked, he insisted in another publication that he had received a telegram, not a phone call, from William Fox, the head of Fox Studio, the company that made* Hearts in Dixie. *He further claims that he did not want to abandon his theatrical career, but they made him an incredibly lucrative offer, which he could not turn down.*[128]

Thomas Cripps, however, rejects Muse's oft-repeated stories and insists that the character actor was already in Hollywood, anxious for work, and accidentally met producer Winfield Sheehan who had just decided to fire Gilpin, and was looking for a replacement.[129] *Cripps' position is similar to that taken by Glendon Allvine, who, in his biography of William Fox, discusses the problems the studio had finding an African-American actor with a good singing voice. He makes no mention of Gilpin. Instead, the biographer points out that Muse, struggling to break into films, was having a hard time getting the attention of even the casting directors. "Possibly because he had no agent," theorizes Allvine, "he [Muse] was getting nowhere.... Until one night, around six, as Sheehan was being driven out into Western Avenue, Muse fell against the car or the driver brushed against him, or something...."*[130] *After everyone made certain no injuries had been sustained, the two men agreed to a screen test and that is how Allvine asserts Muse got into* Hearts in Dixie.

The only part that definitely is true is that Muse had no agent. In a letter he wrote to me (March 20, 1972), he said, "Soon after I decided to stay in California after the making of ... Hearts in Dixie, *Haven McQuarrie signed me up in his Agency, and I think his first contract deal was with Frank Capra in the making of ...* Dirigible. *What makes Allvine's account suspicious is the absence of any reference to Gilpin.*

In essence, Muse insists on his position vis-à-vis Hearts in Dixie *and returns to it later in the interview.*

Muse: This time, what's-his-name had just made *The Jazz Singer*.... Al Jolson had just made *The Jazz Singer*, and people in the theater kept sitting and talking [about the "sound" revolution], it was kind of a joke. It was something that wasn't going to last anyhow, and it wasn't particularly [important]. And I came to the telephone; they wanted to know if I could come to Hollywood to take a lead, a character lead, in a picture called *Hearts in Dixie*, which was written around 1930 [sic].

Hearts in Dixie *(1929), directed by Paul Sloane, was a nostalgic story about the romanticized South, where an elderly ex-slave struggles stoically to maintain a living for his family. Clarence Muse plays Nappus, the noble tenant farmer, who sells his farm to insure his son's education and future. "Although he is slightly melodramatic during certain emotional scenes," writes Miles Kreuger, "Clarence Muse brings to the principal role an aura of wise, quiet strength, and dignity that often carries the story through passages which might otherwise seem condescending."*[131] *Interestingly, Mordant Hall's review of* Hearts in Dixie *indicates that the cast is almost entirely black, points out the thematic importance of African-Americans getting formal education, and praises the characterization and performance of Nappus. However, the* New York Times *critic never mentions Muse's name.*[132] *Freddie Schader, on the other hand, not only blasted the movie as "just a lot of jigs jigging," but also found many of Muse's scenes "overdrawn and overplayed."*[133] *In addition, Hollywood's second significant sound film began Stepin Fetchit's rise to stardom.*

Muse: Charles Gilpin had the part, but he became ill, and they were stuck, and somebody had recommended me for the part.

Well, I didn't know what to do, the manager sitting right there. I had this nice big fat contract. So I thought I'd ask a figure to work that I'd never heard of anybody getting. And everybody laughed about it. I asked him for $1250 a week. Three tickets round trip. I knew that would fix it, that I'd never hear from him again.

Next morning, a long yellow telegram come with "Okay" and all that, and I knew something's screwy. It's got to be wrong. And sure enough, they gave me the two weeks. I had to give notice to this man, and I went on to Chicago. On New Year's Day, we left Chicago on the Santa Fe Railroad. Very interesting thing was that when I went into the [station] office on this holiday, I thought I had made a mistake....

According to Muse, the Fox Corporation had not only sent the tickets, but also an advance on his salary.

Muse: It was all set up; they gave me a very long stream of tickets. They had tickets in those days that almost reached to California, the tickets. And they give me ... [an advance] of a week's salary.

The thing that interests me most was that he [Fox, Sheehan, or the station master?] said, "Now, I picked you a drawing room on the right-hand side going in because the view is much better, and you will ride much easier in the center of the car." He didn't know it, but I got a great kick out of it, because all those years I had been riding on these trains down through the South, riding the Jim Crow, I didn't know the right side or the left side.

Sye: Mr. Muse, you've brought us up to the time when you came to Hollywood pretty well, but you've covered an awful lot of territory. There must be some details in that career you'd like to point out to us.

Muse: You know, I got to throw in there ... I got a little touch of the nostalgia, and I forgot a lot of little things. You see the period that I'm talking about is really a period that covers twenty years of show business. Of course, the Hollywood pictures, which we will be talking about later, that ran thirty or thirty-one [years] or something like that. I think it's around fifty-two years that covers my entire career.

But in looking at some of these notes my wife just handed me, that I just checked up on. Some of them are rather amusing [Laughter].... For example, in Kansas City, around the time of the Woodrow Wilson period, there were a couple of gangsters there, I can't seem to pick up their names right now, but they had lots of money. They were the big boys in the city, and they liked what we were doing. I had as a partner Hattie McDaniel's brother. She had a brother named Otis, who was older than she did. In fact, he's responsible for bringing her into show business.

In Carlton Jackson's biography of the star, he explains that it was Ms. McDaniel's father, Henry, who decided to get out of construction work and earn a living for himself and his family by going into show business. In 1910, he created his own minstrel show, the Henry McDaniel Minstrel Show, and featured two of his three sons, Otis and Sam, as clog dancers. The middle son, James, seems to have chosen another profession. Otis, the oldest brother, received considerable credit for keeping his father's troupe working. Tragically, the talented son died six years later. Although the daughter wanted to be in the show – she had been performing in minstrel shows by the time she was thirteen – her mother forbid it, because of the extensive traveling. No mention is ever made in the biography of Otis being responsible for his sister's entrance into world of entertainment. Mention is made that Sam McDaniel, known as "Deacon McDaniel or The Doleful Deacon," was responsible for getting his sister into radio.[134]

Jill Watts, in her biography of Hattie McDaniel, tells a different story about the star's family and early years. The author does, however, give considerable credit to Otis for starting his sister's career.[135]

Muse: We put on a show down there together ... we wrote a show called *Trip to the Moon*. We were way ahead at that time in the game. *Trip to the Moon* ran in Woodrow Wilson's time.

Although no mention is made of their early collaboration together, Ms. McDaniel's biographers repeatedly talk about the two of them, along with Stepin Fetchit and Louise Beavers, being attacked for playing endless "Uncle Tom" screen roles that one critic described as "devoted, dog-like servant[s], lazy, good for nothing, meek and happy."[136] At the same time, Jackson strongly defends the two colleagues against the charges made by Walter White. In addition, Watts makes clear that "offscreen, Muse emerged as a forceful activist, one of the local [Hollywood] black community's most tireless and politically dynamic figures."[137] Still further, both biographers report that Muse was a pallbearer at Ms. McDaniel's funeral on November 1, 1952.

As for Muse's claims about his partnership with Otis McDaniel, it could only have occurred before 1914, when Muse came to Harlem. Between 1910 and 1914, Otis is credited as working frequently with the Henry McDaniel Minstrel Show. It is well documented, however, that Muse remained a composer-producer-writer-director throughout his career, starting from his earliest days on the vaudeville circuit.

Muse: These couple of gangsters gave us an opportunity to build our own theater, around there at 18th and Vine. We built a theater called the Criterion Theater. I was so impressed with this Airdome down in Jacksonville, Florida, that this thing was built without top. But we did it a little better than they did down in Florida. We did cover the stage; the stage had a roof to it. The one in Florida didn't have a stage cover.

So this was quite an advance in the theater company of the period. And it was called the Criterion Theater, where we rehearsed this great show, *Trip to the Moon*, by Otis McDaniel and myself. And the night the show was to open, it rained, by George; it never rained like it rained [that time]. Water filled up the orchestra pit; it became a swimming pool. We had to delay the opening three days.... And Hattie's other brother [Sam] was a dancer; he had a partner named Brown. And they were very, very, very successful, in this *Trip to the Moon*. And they were booked on the big time; they went out on the Pantages Circuit.

That was a part of this T.O.B.A. business. Now I didn't mention in the early part about the T.O.B.A., when we traveled through the South. You might have gotten the idea we just went from theater to theater not knowing where we were going. [We did not.] They had an organization called the Theater Owners Booking Association, and the actors had nicknamed it because some of the tough theaters we got, "Tough On Black Actors," T.O.B.A. And the man that was head of it was a man named Mr. [Sam E.] Reevin.

According to Black Magic, "The T.O.B.A was a busy Negro vaudeville circuit extending from the First World War from New York to Florida, Chicago to New Orleans."[138] They go on to point out that, "The decline and slow death of the T.O.B.A *during the depression was a real loss to colored performers." In* Blacks in Blackface, *Mr. Reevin is identified as the T.O.B.A.'s treasurer and general manager.*[139]

Muse: Mr. Reevin lived in Chattanooga, up on Lookout Mountain. He was an invalid. He had to stay up on the mountain on account of his health, but he operated this whole circuit that would take care of you for forty weeks in the South. But they were forty of the hardest weeks you would ever work.... And he had a fine hatchet man in St. Louis by the name of Charlie Turpin, who ran the Booker T. Washington Theater in St. Louis. They would hound these bookings so to make sure that the producers of the show, like myself, never get too much money, because if they got too much money they could ... [become too independent]. They kept you broke, kept you right on the edge.

In Blacks in Blackface, *the author provides the details of the contracts between producers and the T.O. B. A.*[140] *But Muse's references to the circuit's activities in Atlanta are not supported by Sampson's commentary on the standard route followed by the performers during their forty-week bookings through the South.*[141] *Chris Albertson, however, commented that Atlanta was part of the T.O.B.A. and that Bessie Smith got her first big break there and made the theater "her home base."*[142]

What is interesting is Muse's failure ever to discuss the problems of independent black filmmakers to get their films booked at the hundreds of African-American theaters across the country. Unlike the major studios, which had a complex distribution system to insure their films being seen by the public, the independents had to book their films, film by film. Not only was this costly, but it was also precarious.

Pearl Bowser makes the point that, during the early 1900s, a man like Oscar Micheaux, the Dean of Black Independent Filmmakers, "had films appearing at fifty different theaters across the country and the traditional black vaudeville circuit." What enabled a person like Micheaux to exist was the clever way he handled his productions: "He would make a picture and then travel to the theaters that he wanted to have the film shown at with the film and book the film and get advance money. In that way, he was able to make money for the next picture. He also played bonds and stocks and so on. He was a very shrewd businessman."[143]

This type of distribution practice explains, in part, why so many independent black films imitated the work done by the majors. It also explains why it was so difficult for African-American performers to develop their screen acting. Unlike white performers who found work regularly as they started out and thus could be groomed for stardom, the independent actor rarely found work and thus had very little time to develop a screen style or polish his skills.

Muse: But the getting out place was in Atlanta. They had a theater in Atlanta, on Decatur Street, called the "81." Big "81," that was the name of the theater.

A guy named [Charles] Bailey ran it. He would wear his vest and stand out in the front. Each button on his vest was a two-carat diamond. And he was the greatest short-change artist that I've ever seen in any of my career in business. They had a way of ... I don't care what kind of money you laid up there [at the box office] ... a nickel, a dime, or a quarter. [He] pushed it along [switched it without the customer knowing what was happening and give the wrong change], nobody said a word.... Bailey ran the town, ran that end of the city.

And there's a little connection there with Walter White, who later became the executive secretary of the National Association for the Advancement of Colored People. His father was killed on that particular street, during one of the racial issues of the period.

And Bailey always presented himself to the populace there as one of their main benefactors. He had ways and means of taking care of all their troubles. If they'd go to jail, he'd get 'em out. In fact, the faithful saw him as sort of a prince because.... the suits he wore, Broadway street wardrobe, came up to the top level, because he had ways and means of getting this stuff at very short cost. And if anybody wanted to be bothered to know just what was happening, Mr. Bailey took care of it. So our company got "dressed up," every time we went through Atlanta at the "81" Theater. And then business was excellent. That was a great show town in the South ... Atlanta, Georgia.

Now, during those days, one time, we had an engagement with "81" Theater and a big hassle came along. The famous comedian of the day was a guy known as "Stringbean." He was the greatest comedian of all the Southern artists of his day. He had a number he used to sing ... he had undulating movements in his hips, twenty years guaranteed, he was a sensation.

So another opposition theater across the street, somehow or another, offered Stringbean a big deal. And he took the deal with this theater across the street, whose name seems to slip me right now. But anyhow, when he came to town, Mr. Bailey at "81," down the other street, met him at the station with the patrol wagon. And locked him up. [The police] carried him up to the station house, and explained to him that he couldn't play the opposition theater, and he stayed at the "81" Theater. They brought him from jail in the patrol wagon. He made his performance on stage. He put a beat down and ... [Bailey] raised his salary and whatnot. This other fellow [was] screaming murder down the street, but he couldn't do a thing about it. And at Stringbean's closing performance, he said, "Well, friends, I've got to leave you now. I got to depart because my carriage waits without. And I'm going to my fine private edifice, the county jail."

Well, [Laughter] he got paid a whole week there ... got twice the salary [he expected]. In fact, this particular incident closed down the other theater, this guy went out of business. So this Bailey was a powerful character on Decatur Street in Atlanta back in those days.

Along this same time came another team that still is called "Butterbeans and Susie."

Jodie and Susie Edwards, one of the most popular husband-and-wife teams on the vaudeville circuit, billed themselves as "Butterbeans and Susie." Both entertainers died before this interview.[144]

Muse: They were a terrific hit throughout the South. Their kickoff spot was at the Monogram in Chicago. That little storefront theater that ran real narrow, way back to the end of the world. But if you made good at the Monogram in Chicago, you played all of Reevin's [circuit] down South with the Theater Booking Association.

Then came Tim Moore, that who later became the very famous Kingfish in the television version of The *Amos n' Andy Show*. I met him for the first time while I was doing the show at the Jacksonville Theater. In the Airdome. They brought him in as a special attraction. And he had an attraction he called the "vest-pocket edition of *Uncle Tom's Cabin*." He made up one side of his face white, and the other side was cork. And he did this version.... I remember one of the lines he said, when he was playing Simon Legree. He said, "Tom, ain't you mine, ain't you mine, Tom, body and soul?" Tim would turn the other side of his face, the black side around, and say, "Yes, Massa, I'se yours, with all my soul." He would say that "all my soul" with intonation that I could never characterize, and wrecked the audience. Now he came to the stage one week and he was there seven weeks, and they wouldn't let him change a line in the show.

So this man had great histrionic ability. His background and T.O.B.A. are responsible, in my thinking, for his big success as the best Kingfish that *The Amos n' Andy Show* ever had.

Then Peg Leg Bates ... I found him there in Birmingham during those days.

Clayton "Peg Leg" Bates, a famous vaudeville headliner who, at twelve years of age, lost his leg in a car crash, not only was loved for his extraordinary dancing with one wooden leg, but also for his remarkable courage.

Muse: He wanted to travel [on the vaudeville circuit]. I was carrying forty, forty-five people, and I smuggled him on the train without a ticket. We had a trick where we used to move the guys around so fast; [the conductor never knew who had a ticket]. You know we chartered our own [railroad] car; that's the only way I thought we could beat the Jim Crow. We would charter our own car, just coach. And the guys became experts on fixing those seats, making lower berths and upper berths out of the seats. And then when the conductor would come through to pick up the tickets, I always would have a lecture. I got the company going now, I'm flashing them; and we got three, four of them coming in and out of the men's room, the girl's room, or whatever. And the guy would say, "How many tickets," and I would say, "forty-one," and he took my word for it. Well, I always had forty-three or forty-five on, and that's how we brought great big Peg Leg Bates up to Philadelphia.

The Will Mastin Trio was joining us up there somewhere, I think around Chattanooga or somewhere, and Sammy Davis was a little, bitsy baby in the basket backstage.

The Will Mastin Trio consisted of Sammy Davis, Sr., Will Mastin, and Sammy Davis Jr. For many years, it was one of the most successful nightclub acts and recording teams in the entertainment world.

Sammy Davis Jr., born on December 8, 1925, began performing on the stage by the time he was two. One of the legendary stars of the twentieth century, he died on May 16, 1990. For more information, see his two autobiographies.

Muse: Everybody took turns going back and feeding him the bottle. I don't know ... somehow I think Sammy Davis, with all his tremendous success today, is still the same boy. He was a marvelous youngster. His uncle ... they all loved him. He just grew up in show business. His own marvelous success, Sammy Davis; he went to the college of education in show business. And learned it in a very practical way.

In Chicago ... [Muse booked many big acts]; I'm just checking back on the old days. They had a cabaret in Chicago called The Sunset [Cafe] at 35th Street and Grand. That was a very famous place.... That was the Mecca of Chicago's nightlife. In fact, in those days, the big nightlife in Chicago was on the south side. And also in those days, Chicago was known throughout the country as the best night club city in America.

Well, at The Sunset, I was putting on the shows there. I brought the artists from New York. [Chicago] never had these floorshows before. And one of my distinguished customers on opening nights was Al Capone. His gang would book the ringside seats. They all liked the sound, and when they got drunk, the waiters would beat them up and throw them out on the streets.

But those were some rugged days. A fellow named Fox ran the

nightclub. Somehow a great band recorded there, and that was the first place that I've met Satchmo.

Considered one of the leading trumpeters and jazz cornetists of the twentieth century, Daniel Louis "Satchmo" Armstrong was born on July 4, 1900 in New Orleans. His fame extended to radio, television, and the moving pictures. Most sources claim that he gained his early fame playing in King Oliver's "Creole Jazz Band" in Chicago in the early 1920s. His "scat" singing style made him unique among jazz musicians. He died on July 6, 1971. In addition to a number of books about him, the great musician penned one useful autobiography: My Life in New Orleans.

Muse: Satchmo was the ... third trumpeter. And when Satchmo would play, he was just laughing. Laughing trumpet player; he became a sensation. And Joe Glaser, who was a partner [Armstrong's manager] of ... many years decided [they should] go out on the road.... Today, he is a big agent in New York, but he began by taking Satchmo on the road. Louis Armstrong ... [traveled with] new orchestration under his arm, and whatever city they were in, they hired the boys to play with them. They [Armstrong and Glaser] traveled – the two of them – all over the nation. And made lots of dough.

And then Joe Glaser decided that he didn't feel [like doing this anymore and instead liked] being an agent in New York. He later became one of the biggest agents in America, handling Colored artists. He is the same man, Joe Glaser, that gave the money to save the properties uptown for Sugar Ray Robinson when he was having trouble in Harlem. Everybody loves Joe Glaser. Joe Glaser was quite a man in New York.

Joseph G. Glaser, a white show business personality, began by owning nightclubs and hiring musicians to play in his clubs. One of Billie Holiday's biographers confirms Muse's assertion that Glaser began his rise to success by booking Louis Armstrong. He also later booked Billie Holiday.[145]

Muse: He told me that the reason he hung out at my rehearsals, watching me rehearse, was because he was then thinking of beginning preliminary training to be a showman. He didn't begin life as a showman. He was quite a ladies' man in his earlier days....

CUT

Muse: There was days at the cafe, The Sunset [Café].... We had a man ... he used to come in each year, I think, from around Kansas City, or down in Oklahoma somewhere. He had a big ranch, and he sold all the cattle. And he would come and book the whole house, lock the front doors, have his own little party. And pay all the bills, and that was something great because it was a big band, with Louis Armstrong and some other big artist recording from New York. He went out and tied the whole thing up the whole night; and he'd insist on everybody drinking champagne. Waiters and everybody on champagne, while he'd dance.

And then he had another little stump, that thing sort of lingers in my mind, and that was a handful of money. He would have a fifty-dollar bill, ten-dollar bill, and five-dollar bill, what have you. He'd tear it in half and stick one in one person's pocket, or hide it in another person's waiter or whatnot. Anyhow, he would tear the money in half, and you'd never know where the other half was; and that would go on until daybreak. And by George, by daybreak, he'd combed up and start for home. Then ... [we] would be there three or four hours down on our hands and knees, all over the place trying to match this money. Say, "Have you got a hundred dollar bill with X6662?" "Yeah, that's me." And that means that you had fifty dollars apiece. What a riot he was.

The glamour in the success of The Sunset in Chicago, I think, is a very fine tradition in the theater of that period, because they did show business at its best. Quite like they're doing now in Las Vegas. This man was way ahead of them, Joe Glaser. Chicago had another nightclub called The Entertainers that was terrific....

And, of course, what was coming up on the horizon ... were my days with the Lafayette Players. We used to play Washington, D.C. I think I mentioned it when I was talking about the Lafayette Players, we didn't play just those shows in New York; we had seven cities we turned to. We went to Chicago, Pittsburgh, and Philadelphia. Baltimore, Richmond, Washington, what have you.

But in Washington D.C., we played what they called the Howard Theater there, and ... that was a big deal. And you know that's the home of the Howard University?

The Howard Theater was one of the most famous of all black-operated theaters in the first half of the twentieth century. Along with the North Pole Theater in Philadelphia, it housed separate companies of the Lafayette Players.[146] *When Muse talks about the audience, he is talking about an exclusively African-American audience.*

Muse: And the man, two brothers ran the thing, the Thomas brothers [Andrew and Sylvester] ran the theater, and they had an idea that they ran each day, I think around five o'clock called the Supper Show. The Supper

Show ... they showed whatever was the outstanding picture of the day. And all of the kids and the students whatnot made it their business to come to the Supper Show, which cost the great big sum of five cents. But the theater was packed. And the great Duke Ellington in those days was a piano player, and he used to play the piano in one of those lower boxes on the side. They'd throw the light on, and he's just playing the piano for these kids at the Supper Show.

In Washington, D.C. during our stay there with the Lafayette Players. At that particular time I'm thinking of now, this "makeup deal" comes up again. They had a [fancy-dress] ball going, and the leading lady Miss [Ida] Anderson and I were invited to come to this ball, big society ball, you know. Washington, D.C. in those days had quite a caste system going there among the Negro group. They were divided with the mulattos, the browns, and the deep blacks. And they all kind of broke them down in sections in Washington in those days. They had a club called the Mooselit Club [?].

Anyhow, we'd been invited to this dance; it was over in this ... hall. So the star asked me if I would go ahead on.... I'd been getting sharp for a week ... you know, the cane, the long stick cane, and the opera hat that flopped back in on, all the stuff, trimmings. And I went up there to this hall, and entered the hall, the cloak room was right in front; and I met these very beautiful "high yellows" as we called them [light-skinned African-Americans] in those days. And they were gonna check my wraps, but they sort of looked at me as if they were wondering as if I wasn't in the wrong place. You know, I'd taken off the make-up and they didn't know me off stage. So I didn't pay much attention to them. Since [Miss Anderson had] told me to wait for her, I just hung around on the outside. In fact, nobody paid any attention. It was really forgotten [that] I was there; you know, "What does that fellow want?" And they went on into the hall, everybody dancing and having a good time. Pretty soon, Ida Anderson's coming, she's a very beautiful mulatto herself. And she said, "Alright Clarence, I'm here." And by George, quick as you can say jackrabbit, I became a sensational important person. [That is,] when they found out I was one and the same that had been on the stage with this white makeup.

That's a little study of what goes on the inner side of the Negro side of social life. And it went through the years. They were well divided as to color for many, many years.

Ethel Waters used to tell a very interesting tale about going to a certain church, and they didn't know whether they were allowed to go in the church. [First, they'd] look at the door and [then they'd] put their hand against the building. If the color of the skin [on your hand] didn't match the color of the door, that wasn't your place, buddy. Your skin had to be good and yellow, and if it matched the yellow door, then that's your church.

It's quite true. It's kind of humorous today; we can laugh at it. However, some of the transitions people go through, through life and show business ... appear to go systematically....

During the days that I was in the New York picture, I learned about and saw the great comedian known years ago as Ernest Hogan. That was during my vaudeville days. I don't think it's good in passing not to mention Ernest Hogan, because when [Oscar] Hammerstein.... I don't mean the [Oscar] Hammerstein [II], the great songwriter ... that was his uncle. The man with the cigar ... the man who brought Caruso and all those great stars to this country was Oscar Hammerstein. He had a big nightclub ... what we would call nightclubs today, right there on the corner of 42nd and Broadway. And he featured Ernest Hogan, who was a great singer of "On That Emancipation Day." That was his big number.

Ernest Hogan, who graduated from minstrel shows to black musicals on Broadway, was one of the great show business personalities at the turn of the century. He died in 1909.

Muse: And he [Hammerstein] would insist on Ernest Hogan [being] dressed ... [in fine clothes]. In fact, all of those artists in those days, if you were going to be a great artist in show business, first thing ... [would be to] pick a good tailor. You had to dress or you were nobody.... So you put all your money into ... [fine clothes]. Ernest Hogan was magnificent. And Hammerstein insisted that he come to the front door so he could greet the customers as they go by. He'd shake hands with Mr. Carnegie and Mr. Thorpe and Mr. Whathaveyou, all the big boys of the day....

Now the thing that stands out so prominently and ought to be kept in ... [our memory] is that the [bill] board out front, in great big letters ... life-size, read, "Ernest Hogan, the Unbleached American." And this is over fifty-seven years ago. Boy, did they change the billing since that day! And they loved it, and he was an unbleached American. I thought that was a dignified way of presenting a Colored artist. That goes to the credit of Oscar Hammerstein.

Count Basie of the day has an interesting little touch in my passing. In Kansas City, he'd be playing the piano. He was a great pianist all his life. He was playing down in the basement, and they just called him, Mr. Basie. Some millionaire, I've forgotten his name, made it his business to collect some [music] from these great artists and put them on records ... Roy Meese [?], and he dubbed him and set him out and he put the title of "Count" Basie, and he certainly has worn that title well. Today, I think he is one of the greatest piano playing artists and orchestra [leaders] that we have on the boards. I saw him the other night in the Garland show, the Judy Garland show, and he was absolutely sensational, the setting, and what have you. And I thought of Mr. Basie, who has now become Count Basie from Kansas City.

Now we can go on and on in trying to master and collect everything that happened in that earlier twenty years of show business before coming to Hollywood. But I imagine that anybody that's pushed the little button and listened to this thing is saying, "Well, let's get on with that. We've come to the Hollywood museum to see and hear about Hollywood people and enough of what happened back east. It's sufficient to know that you was in show business before you got here." So we'll travel on and try to quicken your ears and carry into the great thirty years of making motion pictures.

My first picture when I came [was] for the ... William Fox Studio. In those days, [it] wasn't Twentieth Century business, it was the William Fox, and he was the big master of the studio, Mr. Fox. In fact, when you arrived, he was the first man you would see. And I did a picture there called *Hearts in Dixie*, and this was written by an ex-vaudeville man, who used to do a thing called "Old Judge from Virginia," named Walter Weems. He wrote the story, and it was a terrific tale.... He was originally from Virginia, and he knew his technique in that type of a story.

But there were some amusing things coming on before getting to *Hearts in Dixie*, and this arrival in this great place called Hollywood. I was just as far up in the air about Hollywood as the rest of them, because I didn't know what it was all about. On the train, when we got to Albuquerque, New Mexico, we got a telegram. Now it may be hard for you to picture, but in these days of my type of show business and traveling, I had never heard of anybody getting a telegram on the train. So when the man said, "You have a telegram," it took me five minutes to try to figure out how in the world did the telegram get to me on a railroad train. Well, they explained it to me, and the telegram was from the studio.

Now remember, I'd just got on the train kind of reluctantly in Chicago, didn't know what I was going into, but the salary of twelve hundred and fifty dollars a week sounded awful good to me. Now I'm on the way to get it, and it guaranteed twelve weeks. Boy, what a bankroll I'm gonna have to take back. So, the telegram said, "Be sure not to go on to Los Angeles, and get off the train." In those days, we didn't have a fine railroad station in Los Angeles, had nothing but a station down there at Fifth Street, Fifth and Central I think it was. But to get off the train in Pasadena. The reason being that a tremendous mob and crowd were gathered around the station, and they didn't want to have me all ruffled up with the crowd of greeters and fans. Boy, imagine my chest went up; I'm coming to a place I'd never heard of, yet people were waiting. A crowd got to the point where I need protection. So it went on to Pasadena.

When we get off the train in Pasadena, the director of the picture was, name was Paul Sloane, met Walter Weems, the writer and me. And they had two Cadillacs, not one, two.... They put my wife and my daughter in number two ... they had to ride in their separate Cadillac. And I rode with Mr. Weems and Mr. Sloane.

Now, soon as we get in the car and start her off, bam, they slam a script in front of me, and say this is it. They start telling me the story and so forth on the way over. But before that, Mr. Weems or Mr. Sloane said, "Oh my goodness, he's a young man." Well, you see I was going to Hollywood, I was going like the rest of them, I'd been down to the barbershop, I had a fine haircut, and I was as sharp as a whistle. It turns out ... He said, "Well, Clarence, the part you're play is a man, ninety years old." [Laughs] I thought there goes [the job] out the window. I said, I got nothing to worry about, I got my round-trip ticket. I hadn't got my twelve fifty. But he says, "I think we can overcome that with make-up." So then they took my hat off, started putting their finger round the top, and said, "Yeah we'll just shave him right off the top, and then he'll become bald, and then we put the age on and so on." Fine, don't worry about that. So then we get back to the studio after telling me all about the script and whatnot.

Now I had in my mind, I'm going to be walking around about two-three weeks learning what making pictures is all about. Where I was coming from, I was a man of the theater. And this new gag they had of talking pictures was quite a joke for people in the theater of those days.... "Oh no," they said. "You got to go right to work. The company's all waiting, and people standing by and that sort of thing. "

They rushed me right to the makeup man. That was another stumbling block. When they said, "Makeup man," I said, "What do you mean?" I never heard of such a thing, because in the theater every actor will do his business in his own makeup. So what'd they mean? I said, "Well, nobody have to make me up. I'm not an amateur; I'm an old hand in the theater."

Anyhow, we get to this man, I am still squawking about this fellow with the makeup, and he finally said to me one thing to convince me. He said, "Well, you know, I have to [put the makeup on actors]; this is the way I make my living, and I get a salary." "By George, go to it," I said. "Well, I can't stop you."

This is the funny thing. I actually got to sit down and somebody got to make me up. This was the lowest blow to actors. [Laughs] So finally, we get together. His name was Johnson; he was a fine fellow. And we made up, and he had these different pencils and whatnot.

And we go on the stage. The stage was on the ... what is now the Fox

Hills, and they just begin to build it out there, was mud and everything, the streets were not finished. Anyhow, we go on the streets there; and by George, they had about two thousand two hundred people on this big plantation set, and this little cabin where this girl is supposed to be sick.

And they had picked the toughest speech in the whole play that was my initial speech to make. And I had no concept of what mikes were like. I saw this long black thing laying down there in the grass, and I kept wondering what it was. So, finally, the assistant director told me that was the mike, but pay it no mind, don't let it bother me. And I had to lean against this little rail and recite this piece. All this big crowd is up there in the fields and were not worrying about the sick girl. So naturally being a man of the theater, I began to very legitimately project the number, and I read it just like you would in the theater. So the guy up in the top gallery would know what you're saying. But nobody told me they would say, "Cut."

And along about the seventh or eighth time I'm still doing it, and nobody told me that they didn't use that sort of technique for this mike, whatever it was, I'd never heard of one. Therefore, the little boy that's playing my son, who's now a terrific musician, Gene Jackson.... When he came back, this nine-year old kid said to me, "Mr. Muse, you know when you do that speech, you don't have to talk just like you're talking out to an audience in the theater." He said, "You know, [talk] just like you and I just stand here quietly talking." I said, "No kidding." He said, "Yes. See that thing got on the floor. They can make it big as they want, but if you make it too loud, it don't sound natural." This nine-year-old kid....

I said, well that's an idea. So I went in there and tried it down at the beginning, I remember the speech quite well, part of it. "Chinquapin [Jackson], ever since you were a little speck of sweetness, lying in your mammy's arms. I do love you. You hadn't grown very big before your mammy died and left you in my keeping. And now that you want to leave me and go way up north, get yourself the sort of education I ain't never had the chance, I want you to always remember your Pappi. And Chinquapin, don't worry 'bout me now. Don't worry 'bout me at all. I got a whole pack of hogs here I can take care of and you'll be back before I even know you're gone. But Chinquapin, when you go to bed at night, say your prayers, say them on your knees. And Chinquapin, when Saturday night comes, wash yourself all over."

Well, I get that speech through there, and that whole audience cheers. The director comes down, grabs me, and says, "Thank goodness we now have the man. This is the man that's gonna play the character of Nappus." Then they tell me. Then this same nine-year-old boy says, "I'm so happy because you're the nineteenth guy that's been tried out." [Laughs] And I thought they're gonna send me back home the next day.

So, that was my beginning into the great sphere and realm of motion pictures. I was being tried out and I didn't know it. Well, we did the picture, *Hearts in Dixie*. In my mind, it's one of the great things of the theater.

And there are certain things that I learned years later that in the production of the mike at that time, they had succeeded in recording voices, but the only voices that they had any great success with, fine recording and natural tones, were Negro voices. Both singing and speaking. I understand that's a matter of some kind of treatment with the wave lengths, what have you. And this picture was so beautifully done and sung and whatnot, they began to say around, "Well, this motion picture, talking pictures, are gonna be a special field for Negro actors and there's no hope for white actors. When they spoke, they say, 'Quack, quack, quack, quack.' They sounded terrible." Until the boys got smart enough to clean out some of them fine overtones that the Negroes had in their voices in favor of the white voices; and that's how the white boys got back in the talkies.

CUT

Muse: For a time being, [the coming of sound was a] pretty bad time for them.

Then after I started the picture, they [Fox Studio] asked me, because of the setbacks ... to help them to get [*Hearts in Dixie*] done quickly.... Why, I'd been a terrific study of lines, having had for several years had to stop and learn a bunch of lines quickly, like they had in pictures, this was a walkway for me. Anyhow, we finished the picture in less than six weeks.

Well, I thought all I had to do then was turn in my wardrobe and go up to the window where this guy gave me a big fat check for six weeks' money. Wasn't like that. I had to come each and every week of the other six weeks to get the money.

During that time, I began to say to myself, "What am I leaving this country for? This looks like a new world in Hollywood." I didn't know where the next job was coming from, but making money like this was something unusual.

One day, they asked me to bring back a few lemons from the grocery. Well, in Chicago in those days, that would have cost five, ten cents apiece, fifteen cents. I'd went in there, and I told the guy I wanted ten cents worth of lemons. He filled up the whole bag. The Japanese proprietor. I looked at him and said, "What?" He looked at me and said, "I'm very sorry; lemons very high, very high." And I gave him the dime, and I had a whole bagful of lemons. We got home, and I got called down, "What're you buying those lemons for?" I said, "This is ten cents worth of lemons." And on the basis of getting that many lemons for ten cents, we decided we'd better stay here in Hollywood. That was our mistake.

Now, going around town trying to find what to do next. Finally, I got fixed up with a guy named Bill Sharples. He had a radio program going on KNOX. It was a breakfast show.

And I'm a little ahead of my story, because I did do another thing out at RKO-Pathe. And it had a lot of circus stuff and choir business in it. In later years, I've learned that the man, who was my boss, I knew his name was Kennedy, but I learned in later years, this was Mr. Kennedy who was the President's father, who at that time owned the RKO-Pathe. He had bought it for a little bit of money and sold it for a whole lot of money. He told me he been trading that well all his life. He used to sit around and chat with us and was quite a person.

It is doubtful that Joseph Kennedy and Clarence Muse met in 1929, particularly since Muse's first known screen credit for an RKO film was Prestige *(1932). In this movie about white supremacists serving the French Foreign Legion in Asia, Muse played the loyal servant to Adolphe Menjou his embattled captain.*[147]

Muse: So then, while I was there, some guy was putting on a show for his daughter. He was a great comedian of his day. I am sorry, I can't remember that guy's name, but he was quite an artist. But his daughter wrote a show. Put it on ... over here on Pine Street, the Pine Street Theater was going up.... Where [they were going] to showcase a new star. And she put on the show, and he asked me to go down and do a part. I ... [played] a butler in the show, and it was called *Under the Virginia Moon*. That's where I later learned the name [of the actor being showcased]. So the great artist who was being introduced, [where this] was a showcase for him, was Randolph Scott. So they was trying to sell him as a big, possible star.

Muse may be confused about the theater. According to most sources, Randolph Scott spent two years developing his acting skills at the Pasadena Playhouse. His first role was a small part in The Far Call *(1929). The man generally acknowledged as advancing the actor's career was Howard Hughes, a friend of Scott's father.*

Muse: The director was not a bit happy with his awkward handling of the girl on the veranda scene, and he said to me, two days before the show opened, "Gee, Clarence, can you hum or sing something to pass that sort of, kind of cover that thing?" Right then was the era of what was coming into vogue called "theme song."

I had been trying to write some numbers here and there, and "Chloe" was a big hit at the time. So the moment he said something, I said, "How about me writing a special?" He said, "Oh, that'd be wonderful." On my way out of the theater, I asked him, "What was the name of the show?" And he said that they decided to call it, the girl decided to call it, *Under the Virginia Moon*. So he says, "I think they missed the boat." He says, "I heard a title there last night, among the group, and they certainly missed the boat by not using it." I said, "What was that?" He said, "When It's Sleepy Time Down South." I said, "Boy, that sounds like a hot one." That's it.

And when we went home, the two boys and I, the two [Renee] boys, got together and we'd eat our dinner there and we'd beat out, and we'd beat out what is now the very famous tune, "When It's Sleepy Time Down South." We go back the next day and sang it. The guy thought it was good, put it in the show, and on opening night, it took six encores....

Now we know we got a hit; we were so elated.... It took us two years from that day before anybody would publish it because when it said [singing]: "Da da da dada da da da da, da da da dadada dee dee dee," the great publisher, "Uh-uh, everybody's singing it too high, it's great for you." And two years later, Arthur Freed, who's now the big producer at MGM, went into the music business, and he finally decided he would like to publish [it], and that's how the number got published.

But we're not talking about "Sleepy Time Down South" in this episode so much now. We want to talk about what happened in connection ... [with] this thing called pictures. So "When It's Sleepy Time Down South" finally was born ... and ... when it became such a hit, this man named Bill Sharples, who had [the radio show] *The Breakfast Club* that ran every morning for two hours from seven to nine o'clock, heard the number, and I became a star on his program as a cook, and I stayed there seven years.

And *The Breakfast Club* radio broadcast brought me into the consciousness of the picture business. Then, because I was busy, which seems to be the technique here, everybody in the studio found some sort of part or something for me to get in. And I think my sum total of films is something around two hundred pictures in the run of my thirty years in pictures.

Now it seems to me that we're gonna have to go down and pick out some of the top ones, and roll along this thing to keep it within the keepings of the Hollywood medium.

Before I forget it, another very interesting thing about what happens in Hollywood was in the career of this very famous character known as Stepin Fetchit.

Muse is overstating the case about Fetchit's earlier screen work. Fox's first African-American star had arrived in 1927 and had been doing bit parts prior to Hearts in Dixie.

Muse: I met him when I arrived here. He'd already been a big success here with the Silents and whatever thing had been going on in Hollywood pictures, because he had two Cadillacs, each one had its own chauffeur. He loaned me one with the gas in the car and the chauffeur to take care of my needs.

And I was very much interested in the way he was being groomed to play this great character of Stepin Fetchit, being about the laziest man ever known in the picture field. Walter Weems, the writer of the story, had a big job on his hands, because Stepin Fetchit was one of the fastest dancers that was ever in the carnival game [circuses/fairs]. That's right, he'd been in the carnival two years, and he danced like lightning. Every move he made was swift and he was just a speedy guy; he could run, he was a fast runner. And Walter Weems told him that he was creating for him a new character, a character that would make him a universal success, which turned out to be the truth. And he would sit for hours and talk to Step and say, "Now, even if you picked up a grape in your hand, it would take you anywhere from one to the count of fifty before it could even get to your mouth. That's how slow you are, Step, that's how lazy this man is. And keep that concept, and when you move, you move slowly, you move your body slowly."

Step was one of those guys that took things very seriously. He used to have his chauffeurs bring him in eight, ten, fifteen bunches of grapes and raisins. He'd be eating raisins and grapes all day long, one grape after another, checking his speed. And then this laziness got into ... [his personality]. He even lived it off the stage. So much so that when he went out on location ....

CUT

Muse: ... Step would get in his Cadillac and come all the way to Los Angeles, go way downtown, to go to one special church for Mass. Now the lunch hour would be for one hour. Step could be anywhere from two, to three to four hours before he gets back from lunch....

One day, they had built this character and were getting well into the script now, and they had put glue on his head and put in a nappy head. He was supposed to have nappy type of hair. And they had shaved his head and put this nappy hair into his head. No, no, I got the story backwards. His hair was on the nappy side, and so when he went down to the Mass, for some reason, nobody ever knew he stopped at a barbershop and had his head shaved. When he came back to the studio, waiting for his next shot, here he is with his head shaved, clean as a ball. Well, [it cost the studio a lot of money before they figured out what to do]; it was terrible, but anyhow, they figured out. The makeup man got this fake hair, and took it piece by piece and matched his original picture. From then on, Stepin Fetchit kept his head bald and kept the makeup man busy two to three hours in the morning putting this hair on. He said the reason that he did that ... it helped him to rehearse how lazy he was....

Boy, he was a problem, but a tremendous success in pictures. One reason that we figured out later [was because] he had it on anybody else in pictures. He didn't care if they didn't write much in the picture for his scene. He had them licked because it take him all day to say, "Were you there, Joe?" It takes him five minutes [to say that line]; so, he got [laughs] five minutes of camera on him in a close-up. All that helped to make Stepin Fetchit an outstanding thing. I thought that was a good sidelight that passed in my life....

Now I think you'll be interested in some of the pictures, if I can remember a few of them. After *Hearts in Dixie*, I remember ... [going] down the line.... We had a picture called *A Royal Romance*.

Columbia Pictures film directed by Erle C. Kenton, A Royal Romance *dealt with a down-and-out American writer who travels overseas with his loyal butler (Muse) in hopes of getting money from his uncle living in Latvia. Interestingly, the 1930 film was not for Fox, reminding us that Muse had no extended contract.*

Muse: *Rain or Shine*, now that's a big deal. That was with the very famous director who became my buddy all through my career, Frank Capra.

Rain or Shine *(1930), another Columbia film, had Muse playing Nero, one of many people trying to help the protagonist make his father's circus solvent.*

Muse: Frank Capra is an outstanding man in the picture business, a real genius.... *Rain or Shine* was a marvelous story of a circus deal, and we began our long friendship.

No, it was not the beginning of our friendship, *Rain or Shine*. I did one before that. A picture called *Dirigible* [1931] with Frank Capra, ... down in New Jersey.

Muse is confused here. Rain or Shine *came before* Dirigible. *It was, however, another Muse picture for Columbia.*

Muse: That was a tremendous thing. The picture was all laid up in the Arctic. We wore furs and the Arctic caps and whatnot. To show how realistic he wanted the picture, you know how if you're up in cold country

... when you open your mouth on screen, you can see your breath. He had us all go to the dentist, and the dentist made up a gold cup that fit inside the mouth for protection. Then inside the cup, before you went on to do your scene, they put a little small piece of dry ice in so when you talk your breath was showing. All of making pictures was detail. One of the stars [Hobart Bosworth] got careless one day, and the piece of ice hit his tongue and he like lost his tongue. They finally saved him.

Then we had a picture called *Guilty*.

Guilty *(1930), a Columbia film directed by George B. Seitz, tells a melodramatic story about a politician's daughter who is ostracized after her father is sent to jail for bribery. Muse played Jefferson, the loyal retainer. The questions that interest me are why Fox did not put Muse to work, and how he got so many parts at Columbia. It could be because of his agent's deal, but why did not Fox offer to keep him on after* Hearts in Dixie?

Muse: Another great story was a picture called *The Last Parade*. That was a gangster thing with a London background.

The Last Parade *(1931), a Columbia Picture directed by Erle C. Kenton, dealt with crime in the big city. Muse played Alabam', whose bit-part prison characterization drew praise from the* New York Times' *reviewer: "... capital as a Negro whose musical soul is aroused by fear."*[148]

Muse: And *The Mind Reader*. Oh yeah, it was kind of a smart guy in the circus [picture].

The Mind Reader *(1933), a First National movie directed by Roy Del Ruth, is a screen adaptation of Vivian Cosby's play about a phony dentist who tries his luck at mental telepathy. Muse is cast as Sam, a chauffeur.*

Muse: *Cabin in the Cotton* [1932]. Now that was a big deal at Warner Brothers. In fact, *Cabin in the Cotton* is the first picture that this girl, this great girl, this big star ... uh ....

CUT

Muse: *Cabin in the Cotton* is the first time that Bette Davis had her break into pictures. She was in the scene in the bathroom and Curtiz, the director, did such a marvelous job with her that from that day on, Bette Davis became a name to be reckoned with.

And there was another one, *If I had a Million*. Boy, that was a Paramount picture, that was a terrific thing. Money in reverse. What would you do if you had a million? I guess you'll see all these on television, on the late hour.

If I had a Million *(1932), a Paramount Picture with eight episodes and just as many directors, tried to showcase the studio's important stars. From Muse's comments, it appears that he was in the W.C. Fields-Alison Skipworth episode.*

> Muse: And *From Hell to Heaven,*

From Hell to Heaven (1933), Muse's third Paramount film directed by Earle C. Kenton, was another ensemble film trying to benefit from the success of MGM's Grand Hotel. *Muse once again played an elevator operator named Sam.*

> Muse: Then a picture called *The Wrecker.*

The Wrecker *(1933), a Columbia film directed by Albert Rogell, followed the adventures of a construction man who enjoys destroying buildings. No credits are given for Muse. What is clear by now is that the character actor was shuttling back and forth between three studios – Columbia, Paramount, and Warner Bros. – First National – and being kept very busy, but given no long-term contract. Moreover, one can trace the development of his servant stereotype from one subordinate position to another one.*

> Muse: And then *Massacre.* Oh, boy, I played an Indian in that *Massacre.* Boy, I was the Indian chief. Now that's where I really had some fun in makeup. I was a pretty rough Indian, too, in *Massacre.*

Massacre *(1934), a First National film directed by Alan Crosland, featured Richard Barthlemess as a Sioux War Chief fighting corruption on The Spotted Eagle Reservation. Unbelievably, Muse portrays a Native American called Sam.*

> Muse: Down in Maryland, I think was *The Personality Kid.*

The Personality Kid *(1934), another Warner Film directed by Alan Crosland and using Muse, concerned a boxer trying to find success in the ring without losing his self-respect. Muse, named Clarence in the film, provided comic relief as a superstitious friend of the hero.*

> Muse: Then another picture with Frank Capra called *Broadway Bill* [1934]. Interesting thing about *Broadway Bill,* I did that one originally with Frank Capra. Then eighteen years later, he did the picture over again

under the title of *Riding High* [1950], and I played my same part. In fact, Mr. Capra said I looked younger in the second time around than I did in the first. But that's quite a story of a racehorse, a racehorse with a great heart ... Frank Capra.

In hindsight, as I listen to Muse talking, I'm struck by how much he tried to avoid any mention of the types of roles he played in the early days of sound, the problems for African-Americans in finding secure positions, and the controversies created by Hollywood's stereotyping of blacks in movies. Particularly interesting is his failure to refer to his playing the first Jim in director Norman Taurog's Huckleberry Finn *(1931) for Paramount Pictures.*

Muse: Then there was a picture, *Black Moon.*

Black Moon (1934), a Columbia production directed by Roy William Neill, appealed to audiences that believed in exotic stories about insane witch doctors practicing voodoo on remote islands. Fay Wray, one of the stars, only lists the film in her autobiography. Muse, called "Lunch" in the film, participated in the poorly reviewed mayhem.

Muse: Then there was ... *Harmony Lane. Harmony Lane* was the story of Stephen Foster. I had lots to do in that *Harmony Lane.* I think I had the chorus and what all, all the great numbers I did "My Lord Delivered Daniel".... It was quite a tale that *Harmony Lane.* Look for it on your late, late, late, late, late show.

Harmony Lane (1935), a Mascot production directed by Joseph Santly, served as a showcase for Foster's melodies. Muse served as the inspiration for the song, "Old Black Joe." Today, the film serves as an ideal example of how the blackface minstrel traditions appropriated African-American music and exploited the talents of slaves.

Muse: *O'Shaughnessy's Boy*, that was a circus picture done by the great Russian Boleslawski, who was the director. I think he passed on.

O'Shaughnessy's Boy (1935), an MGM film directed by Richard Boleslawski, was a star-studded production featuring Wallace Beery, Jackie Cooper, and a young Sparky McFarland. Somewhat of a spin-off of MGM's The Champ *(1931), where Beery and Cooper made film history, this tale switched the setting from a racetrack to a circus, where the hero falls apart when he loses his son. Muse plays Jeff, a stalwart friend. I suspect the reason why Muse praised the director so highly is that he was an impressive Polish stage director who had emigrated to Hollywood about the time that the actor did.*

Muse: *Daniel Boone*. I've been seeing that regularly. That's kind of a feature on one of these TV shows....

Daniel Boone *(1936), an RKO Radio Picture directed by David Howard, did an imaginative job of following the great trailblazer from North Carolina to Kentucky. Muse portrayed Pompey, the faithful servant. It is worth noting that while the names and the roles reveal the well-known stereotypes associated with in-house actors like Muse, the recognition accorded him in the credits and the reviews was unusual for the times.*

Muse: And there was *Laughing Irish Eyes*. That was done over here at – forgot the street –

Laughing Irish Eyes *(1936), a Republic Picture directed by Joseph Santley, mixed boxing and blarney, together with some favorite Irish songs. As Deacon, Muse got a chance to croon with Phil Regan.*

Muse: *Follow Your Heart*!

Follow Your Heart *(1936), a Republic Picture directed by Aubrey Scotto, was another musical outing for Muse, who played the choir leader, in a fanciful tale of a poverty-stricken singer who makes good. From what Muse is saying and the films that he is recalling, a picture emerges of an artist who is beginning to work less and less with the major studios by the mid-1930s.*

Muse: *ShowBoat* [1936]. Oh boy, Paul Robeson was here then. They brought him from London to do *ShowBoat*, and I had quite a part in that. I did a lot to help the great Paul Robeson break into what motion pictures was all about. He was kind of strange in the field. His wife [Eslanda] was so British at the time that she wouldn't be satisfied with any automobile. They brought an Oldsmobile from London that drove on the opposite side. But they [the studio] were very wonderful to Paul in *ShowBoat*. That was Carl Laemmle, Jr.'s, big picture, and a big deal.

This was Hollywood's second attempt at making the classical Broadway musical of Edna Ferber's novel; the first version had been the 1929 film by director Harry Pollard, with only a handful of singing and talking sequences. Stepin Fetchit had played the part of Joe. We can almost doubt everything that Muse says here about Paul Robeson. Not only had the distinguished actor been in four films before – most notably as the star of the Independent film The Emperor Jones *(1933)—, but also he had made known his considerable antagonism toward Hollywood's characterizations of African-Americans. If anyone deserves credit for bringing*

Robeson to the screen, it was, as Pearl Bowser points out, Oscar Micheaux, who directed the star's first film, Body and Soul *(1925).*[149]

In addition, it is well known that the part of Joe had been written with the baritone Robeson in mind, and he failed to enact the part on Broadway only because of prior commitments. He did, however, do the London production. In later years, the part became identified with him. His performance in the 1936 James Whale production only solidified that representation.

On the other hand, this production was the junior Laemmle's last attempt to make a hit film at the studio his father had built and turned over to him. By the time the production was released, Laemmle, Jr., had already been removed from power at Universal. Muse, as Sam the janitor, had a very small role in the movie.

Robeson himself remains one of the most memorable personalities of his era. Born on April 9, 1898, the remarkable scholar and athlete graduated Phi Beta Kappa and a football All-American from Rutgers University in 1919. Four years later he had earned his law degree from Columbia University. He abandoned the legal profession for the stage and soon earned an international reputation both for his acting and singing. In addition, Robeson spent much of his extraordinary life fighting against social injustice, leading in part, to his being blacklisted in the 1950s. This rare visionary on the American scene died on January 23, 1976.

An incident concerning Robeson stands out prominently in my mind from this period. In fall, 1973, after I had been working steadily on this project, I gave a talk, "The Afro-American in Hollywood Films," at a national theater Convention in New York City [Bulletin of Black Theater]. At some time during the convention, here my memory fails me, a special session was held to honor the memory of Paul Robeson. I cannot recall who the members of the panel were, but the last speaker stood up and stunned the more than five hundred people in the audience. He called them every derogatory name he knew, saying, and here I'm paraphrasing, they were low-lives because they were all here tonight honoring Robeson, but where were they during the years of blacklisting, when Robeson found himself all alone with not a friend to give him strength. Not a person stood to challenge the charge.

Muse: *Mysterious Crossing....*

Mysterious Crossing *(1936), a Universal Picture directed by Jefferson Parker, proved to be a routine whodunit featuring James Dunn as a roving journalist who ends up with the daughter of the murdered man. Muse played a minor character named Lincoln.*

Muse: And the *Jungle Menace.* Oh that was a tear down! They had a break-up scene in there; it would cost a million dollars to do it today. They really wrecked the whole town in that; they told the guys to wreck the set, and they did. They couldn't do that today; it would cost too much money.

Jungle Menace *(1937), a fifteen-episode serial for Columbia Pictures, may best be remembered for its series of "firsts": it was the first chapter drama for the studio and for the famous animal trainer, Frank Buck. According to film historian Alan G. Barbour, the filmmakers used very few fresh thrills, relying instead "on antique stock jungle footage from the Columbia vaults."*[150] *It also seems to be the only cliffhanger that Muse appeared in.*

Muse: Then there was a picture called *Spirit of Youth*. *Spirit of Youth* – I had a lot to do with the writing of it. It was the story of the life of our great champion, Joe Louis. And it was done by an Independent company, a tremendous number, and I think I had some six or seven musical numbers in that particular show.

Spirit of Youth *(1938), a Globe Pictures production directed by Harry Fraser, starred Joe Louis, then Heavyweight Champion of the World, but it was anything but his life story. The overly melodramatic plot had the champion playing a mixed-up-boxer who straightens out his life and wins the world championship and the woman of his dreams. The kindest thing is not referring to the reviews of the movie or of the boxer's acting skills. Muse not only wrote and sang a number of songs in the film, but he also had a featured role as Frankie Walburn, one of the boxer's closest friends.*

Muse: And ... [if you're] playing around [with the television channels], you'll see on the late show, *Secrets of Our Nurse*. It was quite a deal.

Secrets of Our Nurse *(1938), a Universal Picture directed by Arthur Lubin, had Muse in another mystery film about boxing, frame-ups, and shyster lawyers. Muse played Tiger, a hanger on.*

Muse: Then there was another big deal that tore life out of MGM. There was that great Hungarian artist. You remember her name? The girl who married the fellow who passed away a few weeks ago, the great screenwriter. I'll come back to that.

Although it is 1972 when we are talking, I suspect that Muse is trying to remember Luise Rainer, an Austrian émigré. She was married at the time to Clifford Odets, who died August 14, 1963. The film is MGM's The Toy Wife *(1938).*

Muse: *Prison Train*. One of the announcers on one of the stations, that's his big deal. Channel 5, I think, Dick Lane was in the *Prison Train* and was another one of your producers in the show. I only hear his name once in a while....

Prison Train *(1938), an Independent, low-budget film directed by Gordon Wiles, was a 'sleeper' about gangsters and adventures on a train heading west. I have not found any screen credits for the movie, except one that identifies Muse as part of the cast.*

Muse: *Way Down South*. I collaborated on the story in 1939! I collaborated on the story and the screenplay, and staged the ensemble, which appeared in *Way Down South*.

Way Down South *(1939), an RKO Radio Film directed by Bernard Vorhaus, followed the adventures of a young man who inherits his father's sugar plantation and then mistreats the slaves. Muse played Uncle Caton, the kindly old butler, who tutors the young man on humanitarian values. Historian Lerone Bennett, Jr. cites the screenwriters Clarence Muse and Langston Hughes with having created the first credited mainstream screenplay by African-Americans in the history of motion pictures.[151] Elsewhere, Muse recalled that Hughes and he finished the screenplay quickly because when they were working outside, a snake appeared and refused to go away: "'Twas too hot to go in, so we stayed there and worked and out sat 'im."[152] Muse returns to this film at the end of the interview.*

Muse: That was [producer] Sol Lesser's great masterpiece. That was a fine and very enjoyable set-up.... I wrote a book [*Way Down South*] about the T.O.B.A., and what he wanted to do was to use it as the title for his picture. He bought the title off my book and called it *Way Down South*. He didn't use any of the stuff that was on the inside. Then he paid me to do the ensemble, and I wrote the screenplay with Langston Hughes. It came out, and we had a ball.

Sol Lesser used to think he was the man at the head to preserve this great bit of nostalgia. This is very wonderful. [We had] many, many, many wonderful settings and readings, and we went to his home down in Palm Springs to relax. He just liked for you to make money and at the same time enjoy it. Sol Lesser.

We go on to another picture called *Broken Strings*, where we had a young, a really young, Colored boy who was a ... no, I was a violinist in that. That was quite a story. It appeared all around through the East and especially through the South. It was quite a hit. It's now finding its way on the late show.

Broken Strings *(1940)*, an L.C. Bordon Production with an all-black cast directed by Bernard B. Ray, dwelled on the problems faced by an unhappy musician who believes he will never play again and who has a son that rejects "serious" music. Once again, the actor wrote and starred in his own drama. Donald Bogle claims that Muse's performance as the injured classical violinist stands as the best of the actor's career.[153]

Muse: Then there was *Zanzibar*.

Zanzibar *(1940)*, a Universal Picture directed by Harold Schuster, put Muse (as Bino) back with whites fighting blacks in the jungle, this time because of a shipwreck.

Muse: *Sporting Blood* at MGM. Oh yeah!

Sporting Blood *(1940)*, an MGM film directed by S. Sylvan Simon, returned Muse to the South, champion horses, and romantic intrigue. Muse played Jeff, a racetrack type. What seems evident by 1940 is that the actor was still working regularly, but with lesser-known directors and in even more stereotyped roles. At the same time, Muse seems to be having more success with his own scripts and music. This decline in his roles helps explain why he resented so bitterly Walter White's crusading efforts in Hollywood.

Muse: *That Gang of Mine*.

That Gang of Mine *(1940)*, a Monogram film directed by Joseph H. Lewis, found Muse having fun with Leo Gorcey and the East Side Kids. Surprise, surprise ... the story took place at a racetrack.

Muse: *Murder over New York*. Oh boy, that was a big one. Twentieth Century-Fox! Fox had ceased being just Fox; now it was Twentieth Century-Fox.

Murder over New York *(1940)*, a Twentieth Century-Fox production directed by Harry Lachman, was the third outing for Earl Derr Biggers' novel of the same name. Curiously, the New York Times *reviewed none of the three screen adaptations. Screen aficionado Jon Tuska considers this version as one of the best Charlie Chan performances Sidney Toler ever gave.*[154] *I am not sure what Muse's role, as the Butler, had to do with the mysterious poisonous gas the detective was encountering. It should be noted that Toler's impersonation of the Chinese detective is problematic for modern-day audiences sensitive to what Joseph Won calls* "yellow face minstrelsy." This neologism, meant to call attention to the work on blackface minstrelsy developed by Lott, sensitizes us to the ways in which whites expropriate and ridicule what they perceive to be Asian and Asian-American cultural forms.

Muse: And I went on into *The Invisible Ghost*, with the Hungarian actor, [Bela] Lugosi. Oh boy, was he something in that.

The Invisible Ghost *(1940), a Monogram picture directed by Joseph Lewis, served as an excuse to have the famous horror star kill someone every ten minutes. Muse played Evans, the butler.*

Muse: Then *Gentlemen from Dixie* was another great big horse story.

Gentleman from Dixie *(1941), a Monogram film directed by Al Herman, followed an ex-con (Jack La Rue) making a successful readjustment to society. Muse, as Jupe, was singled out by* Variety *for offering much-needed "comic relief" and "singing well."*[155]

Muse: And, of course, we're going along so fast that I forgot there was a fellow named Tony Paton who met me on a plane going to New Orleans one time. We got to discussing great men of history. And the name of Dr. George Washington Carver [came up]. In fact, I was coming back from a conclave in New Orleans of the Phi Beta Sigma fraternity, which I'm a distinguished service chapter member. The name George Washington Carver rang a bell so deeply that this Tony Paton came back to Hollywood and found enough money, and we produced a picture of the life of George Washington Carver, in which I played George Washington Carver ... in color. And it was quite a sensational success through the colleges, especially through the South, and a good many in the North. And I think it was a great credit to Tony Paton to have taken the interest in the man as great as George Washington Carver was [and] to record him. I hope you'll find that picture and have it in the museum.

Muse has his dates confused here. He met Hollywood director Paton aboard a TWA flight in 1946. Within a year, the two had collaborated on producing The Peanut Man, *a forty-five minute movie about the famous African-American scientist.*[156]

Muse: *Jamaica Rum* was another picture in later years I did over at Paramount. That was quite a story, down in the islands.

Jamaica Rum *(1953), directed by Lewis R. Foster, is about salvaging lost treasure in the Caribbean.*

What is astounding is that in jumping from 1941 to 1953, Muse never mentioned many of the more interesting films of the era that he appeared in: e.g., The Black Swan *and* Tales of Manhattan *(both in 1942);* Shadow of a Doubt, Heaven Can Wait *and* Flesh and Fantasy *(all in 1943); and* My Forbidden Past *(1951). Moreover, he never returns to the film he just finished,* Buck and the Preacher *(1972).*

One needs to wonder if roles in these more famous films had anything to do with Muse's defense of the studio bosses against the charges made by Walter White. As noted, his screen appearances before 1942, when the NAACP leader arrived in Hollywood, had been in minor films.

Muse: And, of course, one of the last great masterpieces I got hung in was Sam Goldwyn's epic of *Porgy and Bess*. That was great as a picture. It was certainly great as a job. It was like some of the stuff we used to do with Frank Capra. Some of the Frank Capra jobs lasted seven months, eight months. I think *Dirigible* ran almost a year. That one picture, *Dirigible*, built my house. I paid cash; it was a nice day.

Porgy and Bess *(1959), a Goldwyn production directed by Otto Preminger, remains a very controversial adaptation from the George Gershwin opera based on the play and novel* Porgy *(1925) by DuBose Heyward. Sidney Poitier, who played the lead opposite Dorothy Dandridge, felt it was one of the major mistakes in his illustrious career. Muse had the role of Peter, the white-haired "honey-man." Other famous personalities in the cast included Pearl Bailey, Sammy Davis, Jr., Brock Peters, Diahann Carroll, and Ivan Dixon. In his scathing film review, James Baldwin observed that, "In short, the saddest and most infuriating thing about* Porgy and Bess *is that Mr. Otto Preminger has a great many gifted people in front of his camera and not the remotest notion of what to do with any of them."*[157]

Muse: Then when it got down here in the later days and got to Sam Goldwyn, I stayed on that one for a whole year. I didn't expect nothing like that to happen again. It happened. A whole year with Sam Goldwyn, on *Porgy and Bess*.

This is one of the rare moments when Muse reveals just how much it would have meant to have a seven-year contract.

Muse: Then was another great story preceding that, called *Night and Day*, the life of Cole Porter.

Night and Day *(1946)*, a Warner Bros. picture directed by Michael Curtiz, proved to be a poor vehicle for everything but Cole Porter's music. Although it was Cary Grant's first Technicolor film; he disliked the film experience so much that he lashed out at the director, saying, "Mike, now that the last foot of this film is shot, I want you to know that if I'm ever stupid enough to be caught working with you, you'll know I'm either broke or I've lost my mind."[158] Muse's name is not mentioned in the credits.

Muse: TV came in and [its] influence began taking over. Next thing you know, I found myself in *Playhouse 90*. That was a big TV sensation. Live that was. TV live is something. You run from one end to the other, and you jump up and down steps. Boy, that TV live is something. I don't blame most of the stars for dumping it. Most of them don't like it. They found it's too tough. *Hallmark Hall of Fame*. I played in it.

Although Muse played in a number of shows on television, his name only appears three times in the indices of major TV reference books: for playing Sam in Casablanca *(1955-56), for appearing in an episode called "Bourbon Street"(1954) in the anthology series,* Four Star Playhouse, *and for appearing in an ABC pilot film,* A Dream for Christmas *(1973).*

Muse: I played in the TV. Warner Bros. ... I did a complete series [on CBS] called *Casablanca*. That ran for thirty-nine weeks. That was a Warner Bros. [television production], where I was a pianist.

And, of course, I had a great time with the master, Walt Disney, in a thing called *The Swamp Fox*.

The Swamp Fox, *a television series that ran on ABC from October 23, 1959 to January 22, 1960, starred Leslie Nielsen (of* The Naked Gun *fame) as Francis Marion, the American commander known as "The Swamp Fox." Louise Beavers is listed as a regular on the show, but not Muse.*

Muse: That was late back in the revolutionary period, when Negroes had to learn to die ... [nobly]. They were all speaking good strict perfect English. They didn't get messed up until they got down around there in 1780s, and they brought a lot of the characters from Europe, whatnot, to mix with them. Then somewhere along the line, what is known as the Southern dialect was born. But it wasn't even in ... [use] during George Washington's time. [Look at] a man called Bannaeker and those ... Negroes who were working out of his [Washington's] home. They spoke as fine English as Mr. Washington.

George Bannaeker, a free African-American born in 1731 in America, gained fame as a writer of scientific almanacs. He died in 1806.

Muse: In fact, George Washington, whenever he had his clothes made —we had to learn all this in order to be sure about this picture we were doing, *The Swamp Fox*–, his butler, his chief butler, left on the boat with him, went to Paris, and every suit of clothes that Mr. Washington had made; the same was made for the butler. Because in those days, if you were a big man, you dressed well, and your servant was equally well dressed. Nobody should copy you.

Now I would be very interested in kind of winding up this thumbnail sketch of covering the theater, the stage and motion pictures and television, with your permission, [to relate] a brief experience I had in producing Hall Johnson's *Run, Little Chillun* [1938] at the Hill Street Theater in Los Angeles. It was done during the time they had the government theaters here, and I met a very famous artist by the name of Nelson Gourme, who is now one of the big designers for CBS. He did the sets for me. I directed the show, produced it, and he did the sets and the wardrobe. And the famous Izenhower, who made the big light board that they use on CBS, NBC, ABC, came out to do the lighting. He was the light man. And the show ran for two years, did top business, and Ed Sullivan wrote about it in a classic story, saying that this was the closest thing to the Moscow Art Theater. People in the profession who wanted to understand what real artistry was in the theater went to see *Run, Little Chillun* that had a cast of one hundred eighty-six people, and everybody was an outstanding actor.

This happened. One night when I went home, in my living room sat Mr. Sol Lesser. And I wondered why he was there; and he said, "I just left *Run, Little Chillun*, and I've come to talk to you about making a deal to help us produce *Way Down South*, our next picture. Because of the artistry we saw in *Run, Little Chillun*, we would like to capture it on the screen."

And I think in closing, if we would step back into the nostalgia of looking at a print of *Way Down South*, it would probably capture the dream that must have been in the mind of Sol Lesser when he thought about the Hollywood musical.

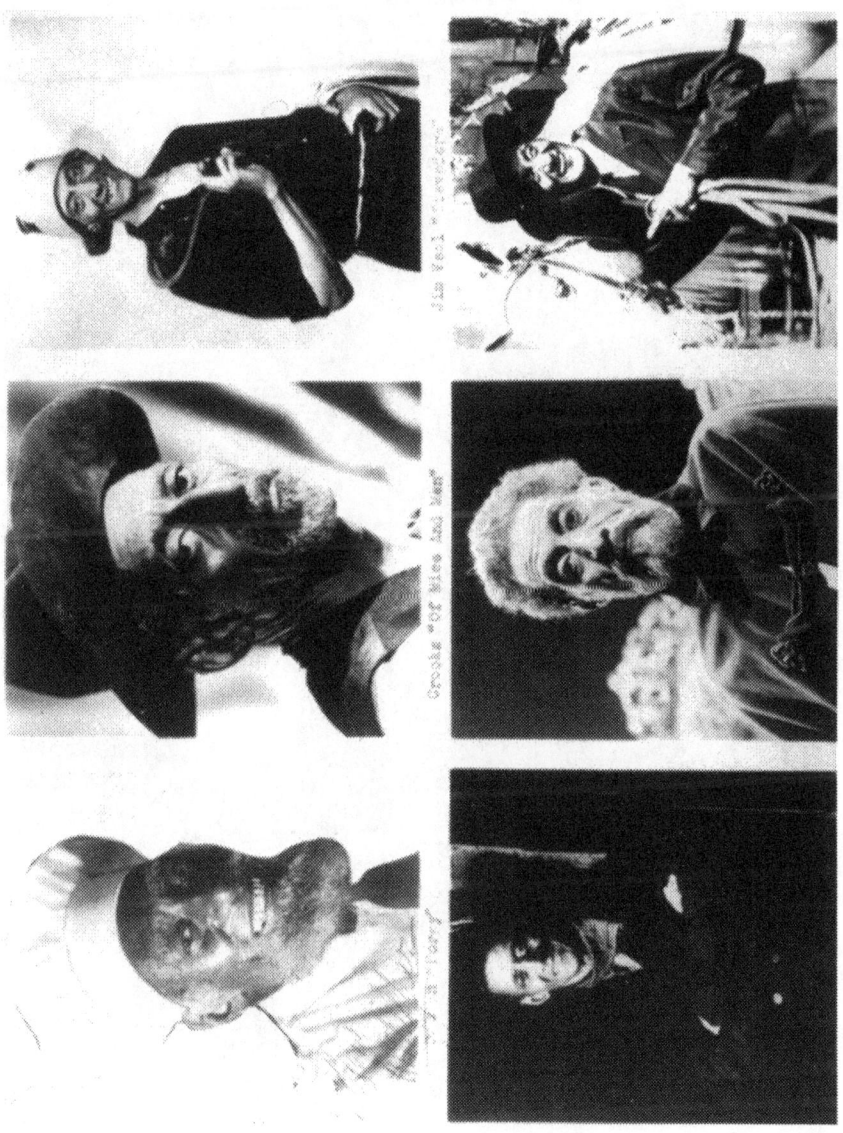

37. Leigh Whipper, one of film's memorable character actors, in various roles. Courtesy of The Manchel Collection, Burlington College.

38. From left to right, Dooley Wilson, Humphrey Bogart and Ingrid Bergman in *Casablanca* (1942). Courtesy of The Manchel Collection, University of Vermont.

39. Jack Johnson took pleasure in taunting his white challengers before his racist fight fans. Courtesy of The Manchel Collection, University of Vermont.

40. King Vidor's *So Red the Rose* (1935) rekindles the racial stereotypes begun at the birth of film history. Here is the myth of the happy slave (Daniel L. Haynes) serving his benevolent master (Walter Connolly) and mistress (Janet Beecher). Courtesy of The Manchel Collection, Burlington College.

41. The Civil War disrupts the serene plantation lives of the Bedford family. From left to right, Mrs. Bedford (Janet Beecher) and her faithful servant (Daniel L. Haynes) aid the Bedford's wounded son, Edward (Harry Ellerbe), while the courageous sister, Vallette (Margaret Sullavan), tries to save both the family and the plantation. Courtesy of The Manchel Collection, Burlington College.

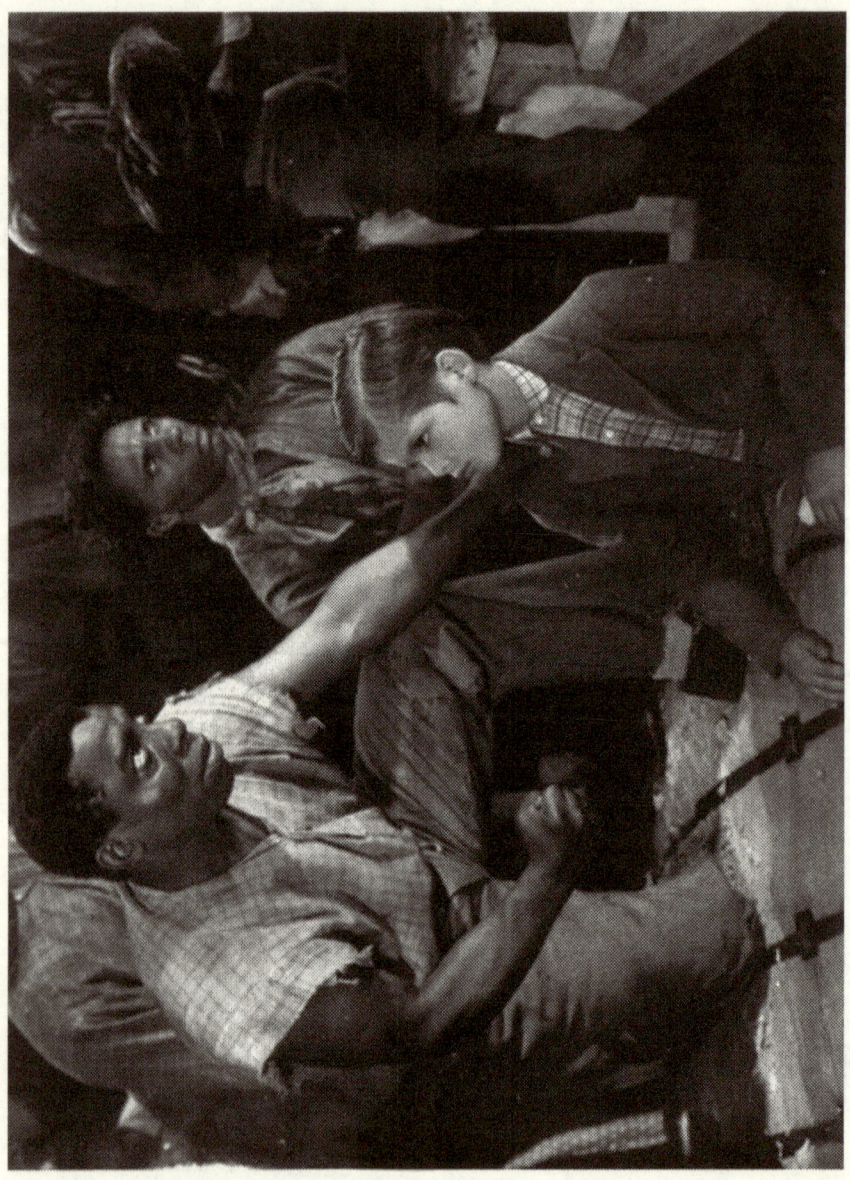

42. Cato (Clarence Muse), a "rebellious" slave, seeks to take advantage of the chaos caused by the war. The youngest Bedford son, Middleton (Dickie Moore), looks on in bewilderment. Courtesy of The Manchel Collection, Burlington College.

43. Cato seeks to stir up his fellow slaves. Courtesy of The Manchel Collection, Burlington College.

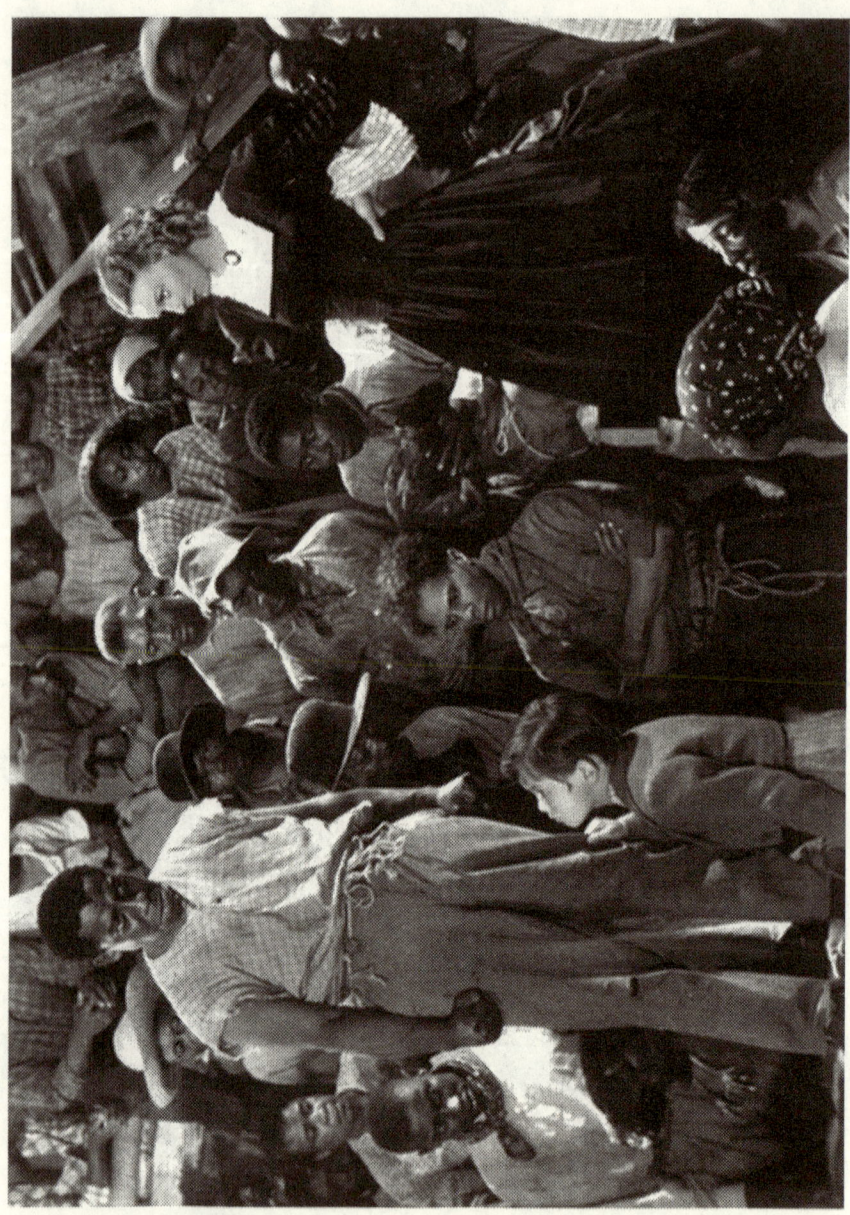

44. In this controversial scene, Cato (Muse) and Valette (Margaret Sullavan) face off to determine who will control the plantation. Courtesy of The Manchel Collection, Burlington College.

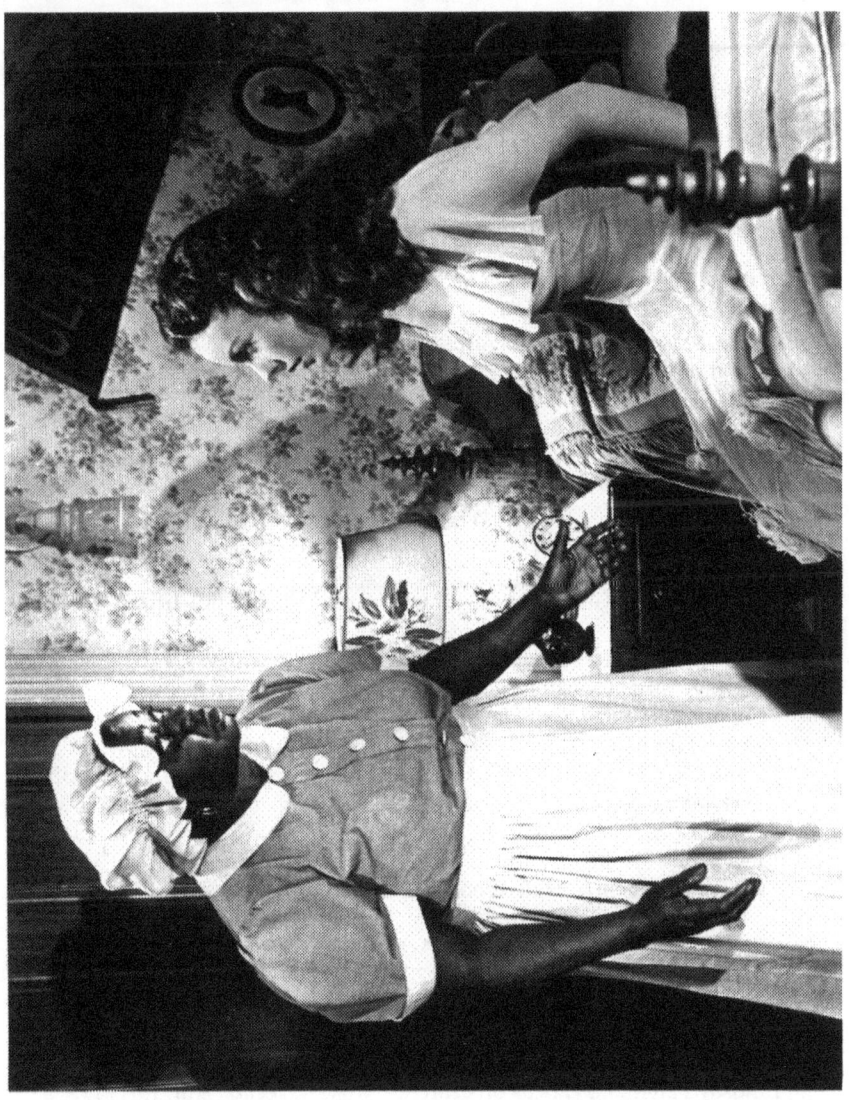

45. Hattie McDaniel became the first African-American actor to win an Academy Award. The year was 1939; the film *Gone With the Wind*. In this still, she plays opposite Jeanne Crain in Darryl F. Zanuck's 1946 film *Margie*. Courtesy of The Manchel Collection, University of Vermont.

Notes

[1] Bogle, *Toms, Coons, Mulattoes, Mammies, & Bucks: An Interpretive History of Blacks in American Films*, 56.

[2] Butters, *Black Manhood on the Silent Screen*, 202.

[3] Ibid.

[4] Buchanan, "A Study of the Attitudes of the Writers of the Negro Press toward the Depiction of the Negro in Plays and Films: 1930-1965," 234.

[5] Null, *Black Hollywood: The Negro in Motion Pictures*, 37.

[6] C. Gerald Fraser, "Clarence Muse, 89; Acted in 219 Films," *New York Times*, 17 Oct. 1979, 17.

[7] Lawrence F. LaMar, "Paper Faces Suit by Actor Clarence Muse," *Chicago Defender*, 23 Oct. 1943, 13.

[8] Bogle, *Toms, Coons, Mulattoes, Mammies, & Bucks: An Interpretive History of Blacks in American Films*, 53, 56.

[9] Donald Bogle, *Blacks in American Film and Television: An Encyclopedia* (New York: Garland, 1988), 431.

[10] Peter Noble, *The Negro in Films* (London: Skelton Robinson, 1948), 58.

[11] Barbara Lewis, "Spry Talk from Clarence Muse," *Encore American & Worldwide News*, 18 Apr. 1977, 33.

[12] Ruby Berkeley Goodwin, "A Lawyer Turns Vitaphone Artist," *Pittsburgh Courier*, 1929.

[13] Sister Mary Francesca Thompson, "The Lafayette Players: 1915-1932" (Dissertation, University of Michigan, 1972), 22-25.

[14] "Colored Nights in Film Houses," *Variety*, 13 Jan. 1926, 34.

[15] "Negro Filmusical Cycle," *Variety*, 6 Nov. 1935, 3.

[16] "Some 250 Cinemas in U.S. For Colored Fans," *Variety*, 24 Mar. 1937, 33.

[17] "Muse Stars in Film with Barthlemess," *Pittsburgh Courier*, 29 Nov. 1934.

[18] B. J. Mason, "The Grand Old Man of Good Hope Valley: Actor Clarence Muse Talks About His Work and His Life," *Ebony*, Sept 1972, 53.

[19] "What's Going on in Hollywood," *Chicago Defender*, 26 Sept. 1942, 19.

[20] Walter White, "A Letter from Walter White," *Close-Up* 5.2 (1929), 105.

[21] Clarence Muse, "Noted Screen Actor Thinks Performers Have Been Ignored," *Pittsburgh Courier*, 12 Sept. 1942, 20.

[22] Jill Watts, *Hattie McDaniel: Black Ambition, White Hollywood* (New York: Harper Collins, 2005), 213.

[23] Cripps, *Slow Fade to Black: The Negro in American Film, 1900-1942*, 4.

[24] Lindsay Patterson, "Focus on Clarence Muse," *Essence*, Apr. 1977, 17.

[25] Brooks, *Lulu in Hollywood*, 74.

[26] For a discussion of Sye's program during Negro History week, see "Black Cinema Expo '72: Black Cinema Library-Research," *Ebony*, May 1972.

[27] Charters, *Nobody: The Story of Bert Williams*, 64.

[28] Sampson, *Blacks in Blackface: A Source Book on Early Black Musical Shows*, 87. For more information see Charters, *Nobody: The Story of Bert Williams*.

[29] Langston Hughes and Milton Meltzer, *Black Magic: A Pictorial History of the Negro in American Entertainment* (Englewood Cliffs, NJ: Prentice Hall, 1967), 48.

[30] Leonard Courtney Archer, "The National Association for the Advancement of Colored People and the American Theatre: A Study of Relationships and Influences, Volume I" (Ohio State University, 1959), 29-33.

[31] Hughes and Meltzer, *Black Magic: A Pictorial History of the Negro in American Entertainment*, 54.

[32] For a description of the famous routine, see Archer, "The National Association for the Advancement of Colored People and the American Theatre: A Study of Relationships and Influences, Volume I," 118-119.

[33] Leab, *From Sambo to Superspade: The Black Experience in Motion Pictures*, 12-13. For more information, see Cripps, *Slow Fade to Black: The Negro in American Film, 1900-1942*.

[34] Quoted in Leab, *From Sambo to Superspade: The Black Experience in Motion Pictures*, 73.

[35] Noble, *The Negro in Films*, 31-32.

[36] Butters, *Black Manhood on the Silent Screen*, 174.

[37] Eileen Landay, *Black Film Stars* (New York: Drake, 1973), 18.

[38] Cripps, *Slow Fade to Black: The Negro in American Film, 1900-1942*, 159. For the best information on his career, see Sampson, *Blacks in Blackface: A Source Book on Early Black Musical Shows*.

[39] Sampson, *Blacks in Blackface: A Source Book on Early Black Musical Shows*, 14ff.

[40] For detailed information on both the play and the film, see Thomas Cripps and Marc Connelly, *The Green Pastures* (Madison: University of Wisconsin Press, 1979).

[41] Watts, *Hattie McDaniel: Black Ambition, White Hollywood*, 213.

[42] For more information, see Carlton Jackson, *Hattie: The Life of Hattie McDaniel* (Lanham, MD: Madison, 1989). and Watts, *Hattie McDaniel: Black Ambition, White Hollywood*.

[43] Joseph Sargent et al., *Bojangles* (United States: Showtime Entertainment, 2002), videorecording.

[44] James Haskins, *Mr. Bojangles: The Biography of Bill Robinson* (New York: W. Morrow, 1988), 28.

[45] Sargent et al., *Bojangles*.

[46] For some sympathetic anecdotes, see Haskins, *Mr. Bojangles: The Biography of Bill Robinson*.

[47] Gerald Jay Goldberg, "Hoofer's Progress," *New York*, June 26, 1988, 2b.

[48] "Review of West of the Pecos," *Variety*, 1 Jan. 1935, 18.

[49] "Review of the Arizonian," *Variety*, 31 July 1935, 19.

[50] Bogle, *Toms, Coons, Mulattoes, Mammies, & Bucks: An Interpretive History of Blacks in American Films*, 71-72.

[51] Buchanan, "A Study of the Attitudes of the Writers of the Negro Press toward the Depiction of the Negro in Plays and Films: 1930-1965," 230.

[52] Lewis, "Spry Talk from Clarence Muse," 33.

[53] Patterson, "Focus on Clarence Muse," 17.

[54] Joseph McBride, "Stepin Fetchit Talks Back," *Film Quarterly* 24.2 (1971), 20.

[55] "Stepin Fetchit Calls His Film Image Progressive," *New York Times*, 24 July 1968, 83.

⁵⁶ Lawrence F. LaMar, "Stepin Fetchit Sets New Fox Movietone Record: Assigned to Three Major Productions, 'Step' Is as Busy as the Proverbial Bee--Comic Will Be Seen in Novel Role," *Pittsburgh Courier*, 20 Jan. 1934, 6.

⁵⁷ Bernice Patton, "Writer Reviews Reactions to an Article on Step," *Pittsburgh Courier*, 18 May 1935, 8.

⁵⁸ Peter Noble, "The Coming of Sound," in *Anthology of the American Negro in the Theatre: A Critical Approach*, Ed. Lindsay Patterson (New York: Publishing House, 1970), 49.

⁵⁹ "Stepin Fetchit, Broke, Appeals to Mpls. Police," *Variety*, 26 Mar. 1941, 2.

⁶⁰ "Negro Actor Asks Public for Verdict," *Burlington Free Press [Vermont]*, 20 Sept. 1972, 2.

⁶¹ M.G., "Stepin Fetchit Did the Best He Could," *Oui*, Jan 1973, 30, 32.

⁶² Mordant Hall, "The Screen: Way Down Yonder," *New York Times*, 28 Feb. 1929, 30.

⁶³ Henry Dobbs, "Variations on the Same Theme," *Close-up*, Aug. 1929, 163-164.

⁶⁴ Alexander Walker, *The Shattered Silents: How the Talkies Came to Stay* (New York: W. Morrow, 1978), 188.

⁶⁵ Leab, *From Sambo to Superspade: The Black Experience in Motion Pictures*, 88.

⁶⁶ Patterson, "Focus on Clarence Muse," 103.

⁶⁷ Muse, "Noted Screen Actor Thinks Performers Have Been Ignored," 20.

⁶⁸ My only reservations about Cripps' analysis are available in Cripps, *Making Movies Black: The Hollywood Message Movies from World War II to the Civil Rights Era*, 345-347.

⁶⁹ The details of her life and career can be found in her autobiography, *Lena*. Other useful information can be found in Bogle, *Blacks in American Film and Television: An Encyclopedia*, Cripps, and Leab, *From Sambo to Superspade: The Black Experience in Motion Pictures*.

⁷⁰ For a more objective perspective on the NAACP leader, see Cripps, *Making Movies Black: The Hollywood Message Movies from World War II to the Civil Rights Era*.

⁷¹ Lena Horne and Richard Schickel, *Lena* (New York: Doubleday, 1965), 107.

⁷² For details on Ms. Horne's "passing," see *Lena*, 106ff and "Lena at 51," *Ebony*, Sept. 1968, 134.

⁷³ Gerald C. Fraser, "Ethel Waters Is Dead," *New York Times*, 2 Sept. 1977, A1.

⁷⁴ Ibid., 3.

⁷⁵ Ethel Waters, with Charles Samuels, "Mamba's Daughter," *Atlantic Monthly*, Mar. 1951, 31.

⁷⁶ William Gardner Smith, "Profile, Xxi: Ethel Waters," *Phylon* 11.1 (1950), 115.

⁷⁷ Susannah McCorkle, "The Mother of Us All: Ethel Waters," *American Heritage* 45.1 (1994), 73.

⁷⁸ "Eddie 'Rochester' Anderson Offered Seven-Year Contract," *Pittsburgh Courier*, 24 Oct. 1942, 20.

⁷⁹ Earl J. Morris, "Earl Morris Gives an Intimate Picture Showing Effect of Eddie Anderson's Work as 'Good-Will Ambassador," *Pittsburgh Courier* 31 Aug. 1940, 21.

[80] Jervis Anderson, *This Was Harlem: 1900-1950* (New York: Farrar, 1982), 156.
[81] "Heart Attack Fells Actor Rex Ingram," *Amsterdam News*, 29 Sept. 1969, 26.
[82] "Rex Ingram," *Variety*, 24 Sept. 1967, 71.
[83] Noble, "The Coming of Sound," 259.
[84] For more details, see Herb Bridges, *The Filming of 'Gone with the Wind'* (Macon, GA: Mercer University Press, 1984), Judy Cameron and Paul J. Christman, *The Art of 'Gone with the Wind': The Making of a Legend* (New York: Prentice Hall, 1989), Cameron and Christman, *The Art of 'Gone with the Wind': The Making of a Legend*, Roland Flamini, *Scarlet, Rhett, and a Cast of Thousands: The Filming of 'Gone with the Wind'* (New York: Macmillan, 1975), Richard Harwell, Ed., *'Gone with the Wind' as Book and Film* (Columbia, SC: University of South Carolina Press, 1983), Gavin Lambert, *GWTW: The Making of 'Gone with the Wind'* (Boston: Little, Brown, 1973), Cynthia M Molt, *Gone with the Wind on Film: A Complete Reference* (Jefferson: McFarland, 1989).
[85] For my comments on Griffith and the film, see Manchel, *Film Study: An Analytical Bibliography*, 1360-1391.
[86] "Review of Cabin in the Cotton," *Variety*, 4 Oct. 1932, 19.
[87] Noble, *The Negro in Films*, 159.
[88] James Baldwin, *The Devil Finds Work* (New York: Dial Press, 1976), 6-7.
[89] Larry Langman, *A Guide to American Screenwriters: The Sound Era, 1929-1982*. Vol. 1 (New York: Garland, 1984), 307.
[90] Denise J. Youngblood, *Soviet Cinema in the Silent Era, 1918-1935* (Austin: University of Texas Press, 1991).
[91] Bogle, *Bright Boulevards, Bold Dreams: The Story of Black Hollywood*, 237-238.
[92] "Butterfly McQueen: Who Knew Her Mind before 'Stereotype' Discussed," *New York Times*, 24 Nov. 1971, 6.
[93] Guy Flatley, "Butterfly's Back in Town," *New York Times*, 21 July 1968, 18.
[94] Charlayne Hunter, "Butterfly McQueen Has a Family Now," *Chicago Defender* 1970.
[95] "Canada Lee, Actor on Stage, Screen," *New York Times*, 10 May 1952, 21.
[96] "Canada Lee," *Current Biography*, 1944, 96.
[97] Mordant Hall, "Safe in Hell," *New York Times*, 19 Dec. 1931, 16.
[98] "Making of 'Reckless' " *Chicago Defender*, 26 Nov. 1935, 7.
[99] "Race Stars," *Chicago Defender*, 25 July 1936, 11.
[100] "Greatest 'Comeback' Title Goes to Nina Mae Mckinney," *Chicago Defender*, 10 June 1944, 11.
[101] Ethel Waters, with Charles Samuels, *His Eye Is on the Sparrow* (Garden City, NY: Doubleday, 1951), 76.
[102] Ibid., 124.
[103] Ibid., 176ff.
[104] For further information, see Maury Allen, *Jackie Robinson: A Life Remembered* (New York: F. Watts, 1987) and Jules Tygiel. Jackie Robinson, with and Alfred Docket, *I Never Had It Made* (New York: J. P. Putnam, 1972). Jules Tygiel, "Baseball's Greatest Experiment: Jackie Robinson and His Legacy" (1983). For a listing of African-Americans and Hispanics playing in the major leagues in 1970, see Harry A. Ploski and Ernest Eds. Kaiser, *The Negro Almanac* (New York: Bellweather, 1971), 614-616.
[105] For a listing of African-Americans and Hispanics playing in the National

Football league in 1970, see, Ploski and Kaiser, *The Negro Almanac*, 628-629.

[106] *"Buck and the Preacher," FilmFacts* 15.9 (1972), 195.

[107] "Movie Maker Belafonte," *Ebony*, July 1959, 94.

[108] Guy Flatley, "Be Thankful You're Not as Handsome as Harry," *New York Times*, 2 July 1972, D7.

[109] "Movie Maker Belafonte," 96.

[110] Flatley, "Be Thankful You're Not as Handsome as Harry," 7.

[111] Allen Woll, *Dictionary of the Black Theater: Broadway, Off-Broadway, and Selected Harlem Theater* (Westport, CN: Greenwood, 1983), 140-141.

[112] Alvin H. Marill, *The Films of Sidney Poitier* (Secaucus, NJ: Citadel, 1978), 47.

[113] Woll, *Dictionary of the Black Theater: Broadway, Off-Broadway, and Selected Harlem Theater*, 10.

[114] Albert F.C. Wehlburg, *Theater Lighting* (New York: Drama Book Specialists, 1975), 32.

[115] For more discussion of the practice, see Thomas Cripps, "The Myth of the Southern Box Office: A Factor in Racial Stereotyping in American Movies, 1920-1940," in *The Black Experience in America: Selected Essays*, Ed. James C. Curtis and Lewis L. Gould (Austin: University of Texas, 1970).

[116] "Richard Thorpe," in *Contemporary Theater, Film and Television* (Garden City, MD: Gale, 1993).

[117] Frank Capra, *The Name above the Title: An Autobiography* (New York: Macmillan, 1971), 406.

[118] Joseph McBride, *Frank Capra: The Catastrophe of Success* (New York: Simon and Schuster, 1992), 317.

[119] Lewis, "Spry Talk from Clarence Muse," 33.

[120] Robert C. Toll, *Blacking Up: The Minstrel Show in Nineteenth-Century America* (New York: Oxford University Press, 1974), 55.

[121] For my reactions, see my review of his book Frank Manchel, "Rogin on Race, Gender, and Identity," *Historical Journal of Film, Radio and Television* 17:1 (1997), 137-143.

[122] For a useful introduction to the subject, see Wallace, "Oscar Micheaux's *Within Our Gates*: The Possibilities for Alternative Visions," 56-66, 90-91.

[123] Anderson, *This Was Harlem: 1900-1950*, 110.

[124] For more information on the woman known as "The Mother of Negro Drama," see Sampson, *Blacks in Blackface*, 196-197. For useful information on the Lafayette Players, see Thompson, "The Lafayette Players: 1915-1932."

[125] Anderson, *This Was Harlem: 1900-1950*, 111-112.

[126] Hughes and Meltzer, *Black Magic: A Pictorial History of the Negro in American Entertainment*, 123.

[127] Thompson, "The Lafayette Players: 1915-1932," 20.

[128] Mason, "The Grand Old Man of Good Hope Valley: Actor Clarence Muse Talks About His Work and His Life," 53.

[129] Cripps, *Slow Fade to Black: The Negro in American Film, 1900-1942*, 237-238.

[130] Glendon Allvine, *The Greatest Fox of Them All* (New York: L. Stuart, 1969), 85.

[131] Miles Kreuger, "The Roots of the American Musical Film (1927-32)," *Museum of Modern Art Department of Film* (1971), 1.

[132] Hall, "The Screen: Way Down Yonder," 30.

¹³³ Freddie Schader, "Hearts in Dixie: Hot Jiggery Jig Jigs," *Motion Picture News*, 3 Mar. 1929, 711.
¹³⁴ Jackson, *Hattie: The Life of Hattie McDaniel*, 10-11, 21.
¹³⁵ Watts, *Hattie McDaniel: Black Ambition, White Hollywood*, 27-35.
¹³⁶ Jackson, *Hattie: The Life of Hattie McDaniel*, 31.
¹³⁷ Watts, *Hattie McDaniel: Black Ambition, White Hollywood*, 85.
¹³⁸ Hughes and Meltzer, *Black Magic: A Pictorial History of the Negro in American Entertainment*, 67.
¹³⁹ Sampson, *Blacks in Blackface: A Source Book on Early Black Musical Shows*, 16.
¹⁴⁰ Ibid., 16ff.
¹⁴¹ Ibid., 15.
¹⁴² Chris Albertson, *Bessie* (New York: Stein and Day, 1972), 28.
¹⁴³ Julius Prod. and host. Lester, "Black Films," in *Free Time* (Channel Thirteen, New York, 1972).
¹⁴⁴ Sampson, *Blacks in Blackface: A Source Book on Early Black Musical Shows*, 350-352.
¹⁴⁵ John Chilton, *Billie's Blues: The Billie Holiday Story 1933-1959* (New York: Da Capo, 1975), 33. For another, more detailed look at the relationship between Armstrong and Glaser, see Geoffrey C. Ward, *Jazz: A History of America's Music* (New York: Alfred A. Knopf, 2000), 214-216.
¹⁴⁶ Sampson, *Blacks in Blackface: A Source Book on Early Black Musical Shows*. 124.
¹⁴⁷ For a good source on Kennedy's association with RKO, see Betty Lasky, *RKO: The Biggest Little Major of Them All* (Englewood Cliffs, NJ: Prentice Hall, 1984).
¹⁴⁸ Mordant Hall, "Killing the Killer," *New York Times* 2 Mar. 1931, 19.
¹⁴⁹ Lester, "Black Films."
¹⁵⁰ Alan G. Barbour, *Days of Thrills and Adventure* (New York: Macmillan, 1970), 111.
¹⁵¹ Bennett, Lerone, Jr., "Black Firsts in Politics, Entertainment, Sports and Other Fields," *Ebony*, March 1982, 130.
¹⁵² Mason, "The Grand Old Man of Good Hope Valley: Actor Clarence Muse Talks About His Work and His Life," 53.
¹⁵³ Bogle, *Toms, Coons, Mulattoes, Mammies, & Bucks: An Interpretive History of Blacks in American Films*, 56.
¹⁵⁴ Jon Tuska, *The Detective in Hollywood* (New York: Doubleday, 1978), 145.
¹⁵⁵ "Review of Gentleman from Dixie," *Variety*, 12 Nov. 1941, 48-50.
¹⁵⁶ "The Peanut Man: New Film Indicts Hollywood Race Bias," *Ebony*, July 1947.
¹⁵⁷ James Baldwin, "On Catfish Row: Porgy and Bess in the Movies," *Commentary* Sept. 1959, 246.
¹⁵⁸ Jerry Vermmilye, *Cary Grant* (New York: Pyramid, 1973), 103.

46. King Vidor. Inscribed: "To Frank Manchel, With the friendship of King Vidor "Los Angeles, CA. 1972." Courtesy of The Manchel Collection, University of Vermont.

4
The Well-Intentioned Poet: King Vidor

> "If *Hallelujah is to be faulted*, it is for the *complete* exclusion of whites, even at the prison, and the subsequent imprecision about the family's relationship to the land they work."
>
> Raymond Durgnat and Scott Simmon[1]

Although King Vidor is one of the America's most noted directors, no one has ever had an easy time categorizing him. Eric Sherman, for example, claimed that few directors in film history were more personally involved in the stories they constructed than this distinctive artist. It may have been the reason, the critic explains, "why Vidor is more a director of great moments than of great films."[2] John Baxter was not quite sure. In one publication, he called him "an erratic" filmmaker;[3] while in another book, *The Master of the Cinema*, Clive Denton saw him as "a poet, of man and nature."[4] Richard Schickel, however, believed that the key to Vidor's art was in his silent films: "For though he made many fine sound pictures, the fact remains that he was the most sophisticated American-born master of the silent film."[5] Raymond Durgnat may have summed it up best when he wrote that the director was a man of "fragments." Depending on which of his more than fifty films you analyzed, he was a "radical maverick," a "contract man," a "humanist," "the propagator of 'hysteric' and 'delirious' sexual struggles," "a socially conscious realist," a "surrealist," and "a muscular poet of elemental vigor." That is, Durgnat quipped, "... we agree with them all – as far as they go."[6]

There is just as much controversy over Vidor's themes. Conventional wisdom suggests that Vidor used just three basic themes: war, wheat, and steel. But that does not satisfy Michael Selig, who thinks that at the heart of the director's great works "are the biblical resonances of a Christian Scientist, where Nature is ultimately independent from and disinterested in Man, who always remains subordinate in the struggle against its forces."[7] Echoing Selig's perspective is David Thomson's view that, "Nothing demonstrates Vidor's vitality more than the way his natural sense of the primitive has concentrated with the years."[8] However, Richard Combs insists, "For King Vidor ... the family and the group experience are ... central, and ... a model for the growth of America itself...."[9] The extremely influential director "worked through the fluctuating fortunes of the family – from optimistic affirmation and expression to neurotic withdrawal and disintegration – as a way of measuring shifting versions of the American dream."[10]

That "American dream," as recounted by white artists, like Vidor and Gish, presents a traditionalist's biases on white supremacy and American history. Throughout the twentieth century, these distortions became part of motion picture mythology, found frequently in Hollywood's all-black spectacles: e.g., *Hallelujah* and *Hearts in Dixie* (both in 1929), *Cabin in the Sky* (1943), and *The Color Purple* (1985). According to Ed Guerreno, these formula pictures "locate their narratives in the rural black South in a romantic, historical void that occurs somewhere between World Wars I and II." He adds, that such films "locate the black community in naïve or idyllic rural settings removed from the unrelenting containment and oppression of the surrounding, hostile white community. Further, all these productions construct black folk as simple country beings without the slightest inkling of political consciousness or recognition of their precarious historical situation."[11] Like Gish, Vidor offers his reasons for the "plantation" movies he made. The reader will have to decide whom to blame – historical circumstances or the individual himself.

Born on February 8, 1894, in Galveston, Texas, King Wallis Vidor transformed his childhood love of photography into documentary filmmaking by the time he was a teenager. His biographers also credit him with being a projectionist and a part-time ticket-taker at his hometown's first movie house, the Globe. During the early teens, he found himself not only making movies for the Mutual Film Corporation, but also getting married to an aspiring Texas actress, Florence Arto, in 1914. A year later, the couple migrated to Hollywood, where his wife secured a contract at Universal Pictures, and her husband settled for work as a studio extra and clerk. Over the next four years, Vidor wrote scripts, studied filmmaking first hand, and directed movies for a Christian Science company named the Brentwood Film Corporation. Next, he directed for an upcoming distribution organization, First National, before forming his own company, King W. Vidor Productions. Throughout, Florence Vidor became the essential attraction in all his films. However, his career stalled when the pair separated in 1922, and they were divorced two years later.

The year of Vidor's separation was also the year that he found employment as a contract director for Metro, run by Louis B. Mayer. In 1924, after the company merged with Goldwyn Studios and Loew's Inc. to become MGM, Irving Thalberg moved over from Universal and became the production head of the new studio. Meanwhile, the soft-spoken Texan had remarried, this time to actress Eleanor Boardman (they were divorced in 1932). Very quickly, the "experienced director" convinced Thalberg that he "was weary of making ephemeral films"[12] and got the boss' permission to make *The Big Parade* (1925), the first feature film to show war from the doughboy's point of view. Looking back years later, Vidor expressed disdain for the movie, but in 1925, no one questioned its impact. "It brought stardom to John Gilbert," explained one historian, "and turned Vidor from a contract drudge into a director of prestige and influence."[13]

Before Vidor retired from the screen at the end of the fifties, he worked at a number of studios, directing notable works such as *La Boheme* (1926), *The Crowd* (1928), *Hallelujah* (1929), *Street Scene* and *The Champ* (both in 1931), *Our Daily Bread* (1934), *Stella Dallas* (1937), *Northwest Passage* (1940), *Duel in the Sun* (1947), and *The Fountainhead* (1949). Among his other noteworthy achievements during these years was to help found the Screen Director's Guild in 1936, as well as do some uncredited directing on *The Wizard of Oz* and *Gone With the Wind* (both in 1939).

The retirement years were good to Vidor. In addition to many awards and testimonials (including an Honorary Oscar in 1978), he did some teaching and writing. On November 1, 1982, the distinguished director died of a heart attack.

Throughout his nearly forty-five years of filmmaking, Vidor often took great risks, daring to challenge Hollywood standards and formulas. His passionate, humanistic spirit, revealed often in his haunting and expressionistic visual style, inspired fellow artists and the public alike. Ironically, he dared to be different by relying on his unique use of "ethnic and social stereotypes."[14] His sophisticated approach to popular filmmaking frequently confused audiences and left him open, then and now, to patronizing judgments from both the left and the right on the intellectual merit of his films. It was not that anyone doubted his good intentions. It was that his good intentions often were perceived as producing negative results.

For our purposes, one Vidor film – *Hallelujah* (1929) – stands as a paradigm of the paradox. On the one hand, Scott Simmon praises Vidor's historic work as laying "claim to being the first masterpiece of the sound era."[15] Combs cites it as "the strongest of all Vidor pastoral idylls, his explorations of the roots of home and community" with "its fierce sense of internal contradictions; of the individual energies that may or may not find themselves grounded in such a community."[16] Herbert G. Luft declared, "In *Hallelujah*, labeled by Vidor 'an examination of the Negro community in America,' he achieved the impossible in his creative use of sound and visuals."[17] Richard Watts, Jr. was even more ecstatic, calling it "one of the most distinguished and exciting moving-pictures ever made" and placing it on a par with Sergi Eisenstein's *The Battleship Potemkin* (1925).[18] In addition, *The Crisis* urged everyone to see the film, calling it "as fine an evening's entertainment as I have had in many a day."[19]

On the other hand, protests against the film appeared almost as soon as it opened. For example, one outraged African-American wrote an angry letter to New York's *Herald Tribune*, denouncing Vidor by saying that, "The producer of ... [the film], who claims to be from the South, is evidently acquainted only with the shiftless type of Negro and has made little effort to find any other."[20] The *Pittsburgh Courier* announced that "the thinking Negro in Chicago ... does not like the picture."[21] Selig dismisses the film with the observation, "Although considered a politically-astute director for Hollywood, the film exposes Vidor's political shortcomings in its paternalistic attitude toward blacks."[22] Baxter seems the most perplexed. First, he praises Vidor's "Flaherty-type [style]," saying, "So convincing are the scenes of black life in the South, shot around Memphis, Tennessee, that footage of cotton-picking and the loading of a river boat from lines of bale-laden wagons have been mistaken for newsreel and used in compilation films."[23] Then he attacks the film, stating that "... inevitably it reflects, like Griffith's films, a now-disconcerting paternalism."[24] Finally, he concludes that Vidor's "vision of the black as a mindless hedonist singing the day away may be specious, but it is of its time."[25]

Because *Hallelujah* is central to the interview that follows, the reader may benefit from a reminder of its major credits and a summary of its narrative. The 1929 MGM production was scripted by Wanda Tuchock, but was based on an original screenplay by Vidor, with music by Irving Berlin. The plot involves a family of African-American cotton pickers in the Deep South: Parson, the father (Harry Gray); Mammy, his wife (Fannie Belle de Knight); Zeke, the oldest son (Daniel L. Haynes); Spunk, another son (Everett McGarrity); and three younger brothers (Milton Dickerson, Robert Couch, and Walter Tait). In addition, there is Missy Rose (Victoria Spivey), a friend of the family, who is in love with Zeke.

Early in the story, we learn that Zeke is a prodigal son; he scoffs at his father's spiritual values, lusts after Missy Rose, and is easily led astray. His emotional problems reach a crisis when he is entrusted with delivering the family's cotton harvest to market. Once in town, he falls under the spell of a sensuous and devious dancer, Chick (Nina Mae McKinney), who persuades him to try his luck in a crap game run by her boyfriend, Hot Shot (William Fountaine). When Zeke loses all his money and realizes that he has been swindled by Hot Shot, a fight breaks out. In the struggle, Zeke accidentally kills his younger brother, Spunk. Later, at the family wake, the distraught Zeke "finds" religion and turns to a life of preaching as atonement for his sins. When next we see him, the now noted preacher is traveling through the state in search of converts, one of whom turns out to be Chick. Despite their avowed commitment to spiritual values, neither Zeke nor Chick can control their passion for each other and eventually run away from the religious community. Months pass, and we see the ex-minister working hard in a sawmill. When his shift is over, Zeke returns home to Chick, who, unbeknownst to him, has again taken up with her ex-boyfriend. That night, as she seeks to flee with Hot Shot, the angry Zeke pursues them, causing their carriage to overturn and resulting in Chick's death. Zeke then proceeds to chase Hot Shot through the swamps and, when he catches him, strangles the frightened man to death. Sentenced to work on a chain gang, Zeke finally overcomes his passions and is eventually paroled, allowing him to return to his family and marry Missy Rose.

While Zeke's misfortunes, his flirtation with religion, and his eventual salvation, offer rich possibilities for examining Vidor's thematic values and his expressionistic style, that was not my interest when I met with the nearly seventy-eight-year-old Vidor. I wanted to talk about the treatment of African-Americans in Hollywood movies. After a decade of film study, I knew *Hallelujah,* but not *So Red the Rose* (1935). However, having met with Muse earlier (see the Clarence Muse Interview), I became interested in both films.

Although *So Red the Rose* is discussed in the Muse interview, perhaps some comment is helpful here about the characterizations in the film. In particular, Edward D.C. Campbell, Jr. comments that neither the head of the plantation (Walter Connolly) nor his future son-in-law (Randolph Scott) rushed to the South's defense in the Civil War; they joined the cause only later in the conflict. Such characterizations, the historian points out, ran contrary to the standard image of Southern white gentleman in Civil War films.[26] Campbell did, however, chide Vidor for his portrayal of the slave Cato (Muse), remarking that the image of a black person as "a disruptive force" was a depiction that had not been presented since *The Birth of a Nation* (1915).[27] Baxter agreed, feeling that the movie "fell back on the cliches of amiable, simpleton slaves and elegant gentry."[28] Even harsher were judgments reported by Jack Temple Kirby, who told of the film and the novel both being deemed "reactionary, culturally and politically," as well as the film's commercial failure being based on "poor filmmaking."[29]

In fairness, some reviews of the day praised the film. *Newsweek*, for example, found the film "beautifully acted."[30] Nowhere were the praises more lavish than in the South. The Montgomery *Advertiser* proclaimed it a "challenge to *The Birth of Nation*;" while the Atlanta *Constitution* told its readers that, "It is another great portrayal of romanticism and a splendid production of its director, King Vidor."[31]

Taken collectively, these perspectives remind us again how much Vidor's memory of the past and its transference to his films typecast him as Durgnat said: "An unrepentant – unreconstructed – Southern."[32] That being said, a close study of the director's depictions of "ethnic and social stereotypes" serves as an historical record of what influential Hollywood personnel felt about blacks, the American Civil War, and film representation. They also serve as lightning rods for the reactions of the studio heads, the public, and the black press to such depictions. Neither *Hallelujah* nor *So Red the Rose* was a trivial release. The distribution system insured that they would be shown widely in theaters around the nation; MGM's and Paramount's publicity departments guaranteed that the films would be extremely well publicized. That is not the same, however, as saying that the publicists understood what to communicate in the publicity. As recent as May 3, 2006, Donald Bogle questioned MGM's ability to successfully market the film in 1929.[33] Thus, the commercial and critical reception of the films tells us about the popularity of such stories, characters, and themes. They help measure the progress that African-Americans were making in Hollywood during the 1930s.

I first wrote to King Vidor, asking for an interview, on December 9, 1971. He responded two weeks later, saying that he would be available during the first week of January, 1972. The letter closed with a caveat: "About two weeks ago, I did the same chore with a young writer from New York, Don Bogle. He seemed pleased with the result. I hope your two books do not conflict."[34]

Contrary to Richard Schickel's comment that he found Vidor somewhat bitter in retirement,[35] I found the aging director extremely friendly and jovial. The one fascinating subject that did not get recorded was his asking me to work on a project about the unsolved February 2, 1922 murder of director William Desmond Taylor, the president of the Directors Association and the man in charge of Paramount's West Coast studios. To say that Vidor was passionate about the project is an understatement. After a prolonged discussion about the murder being related to Christian Science values, we agreed that he would send me some material to review, and I would get back to him with my reactions about whether it was a feasible project. Over the next three months, he sent me parts of what appeared to be an unfinished manuscript. Actually, there were dozens of boxes containing diaries, letters, newspaper articles, and other material that Vidor had been collecting over the years, all for solving the crime and making a movie about the case. I found the material Vidor sent me not only unconvincing, but also terribly disorganized. I, therefore, begged off the project. Nearly fifteen years later, Sidney J. Kilpatrick did a splendid job of organizing the manuscript and published a fascinating book, *A Cast of Killers*.

Interview with King Vidor
January 2, 1972

We began the interview by talking about Hallelujah. *Vidor is discussing an African-American that helped him work with other black members of the film. I suspect he is talking either about a local minister named Reverend Jackson, whom Vidor hired specifically to work with members of his congregation for the religious scenes (A Tree is a Tree, 1971) or Harold Garrison, an employee of MGM, who had the working title of "Assistant Director."[36] In addition, Bogle mentions a Charles Butler, who hired extras for the film.[37]*

Vidor: He was a ... he sort of handled all the black people in that picture ... he was some contact between us and.... But I don't know what happened to the fellow who played the lead in *Hallelujah* ... Daniel L. Haynes.

A thumbnail sketch of Haynes' career is provided in the Clarence Muse interview. It is interesting to note that the actor's original plan to become a minister is not mentioned by Vidor. Surely, it would have lent some credence to the director's choice. Vidor does say later that his decision to make Hallelujah *was based on his past; and that he landed the assignment on* So Red the Rose *because he was a Southerner.*

Manchel: I heard he was a difficult person to work with. That's what I got from Clarence Muse. And after *So Red the Rose*, he just gave up and went back east.

Vidor: Un huh! Probably so. He was fine in *Hallelujah*. I noticed that he seemed to be perhaps drinking a little more in *So Red the Rose*. I remember, certainly, he was more difficult than he was in *Hallelujah*. I don't think he was. I don't remember that he was difficult in *Hallelujah*. I heard that Nina Mae McKinney, who played the lead, I heard she died.

Manchel: I heard that too. Of dope.

Vidor: Of dope. Uh-huh, could be. Last report I heard of her, somebody said they were having dinner some place in New York. She came in as the maid, or the cook, or someone – fat, tremendously fat.

You know, when we finished the picture at MGM (*Hallelujah*), shortly afterwards some Maharajah came along and picked her up. I don't know whether that's in my book or not. And she wrote a letter back to this "Slick 'em." He got his name "Slick 'em" because he was the boot black on the studio lot.

In his autobiography, Vidor identifies the prop man simply as "Bert," a man whom he found to be "particularly efficient."[38]

Vidor: She wrote back to him, and I think that's in my book. I don't know exactly. [It was not recorded in the autobiography.] Well anyway, I'll tell it quickly. She said, "I was riding down the Champs-Elysee, standing up (or something) and was showing my pearl string, pearls, or diamond necklace (or something like that) and the other day with the Maharajah beside me." And she says, "You can tell all those MGM Niggers to go kiss my ass." [Laughter] And he took this letter around and showed it all over the place.

The Maharajah came along, picked her up and took her to Paris, or India. Wherever else, I don't know, but certainly Paris. And then I would hear from her occasionally. I mean somebody would tell me about her.

But, God, you know she's terribly attractive in that film. A wonderful girl. And if she'd taken charge of her self, she could have gone a long way. Either night clubs, or singing, or.... She was so damn beautiful and attractive, the eyes and everything. She could have had a career, an important career.

A thumbnail sketch of Nina Mae McKinney's life is provided in the Muse interview. Although the "dope allegations" were told to me by a handful of individuals interviewed during this project, no mainstream authors have yet validated it in their accounts of the struggles of African-American women in Hollywood. At the time of my interview, Peter Noble makes no mention of it in his pioneering 1947 book. He does point out, however, that she was still working at the time of his research.[39] *Later, other authors talked about her difficulty in finding roles in films or about her sad appearance. The general reasons given for her unemployment were her outspokenness and her unsuitability for Hollywood's stereotyped roles, never her personal problems.*

To put Vidor's comments about the actress, who became known in the U.S. as "the dusky Clara Bow" and in Europe as "the Black Garbo" in some perspective, it is useful to quote some major film historians about Miss McKinney. Summarizing the majority opinion is Donald Bogle, who continually credits her with being both the first black female movie star and the one individual most responsible for breaking down the barriers against African-American women in Hollywood. The last point is particularly important, because it has to do with the issue of skin-color and representation. As Bogle explains, African-American women were typed into two pigment categories: "Dark black women would be cast as dowdy, frumpy, overweight mammy figures. Those black women given a chance at leading parts would have to be close to the white ideal: straight hair, keen features, and light skin. They would become Hollywood's treasured mulattoes; women often doomed in their films seemingly because their blood was mixed. This tradition started with McKinney and continued with Fredi Washington, Lena Horne, and Dorothy Dandridge."[40] *Eileen Landay, who insists that Nina Mae McKinney became the prototype of the vulnerable and talented actresses like Washington and Dandridge, who were destroyed by the system, raises another essential point.*[41]

On the other hand, there are critics who maintain the roles created by stars like Miss McKinney in Hallelujah *reinforced, as Langston Hughes commented, "the cliche of the childish, irresistibly funny, laughing-dancing-singing Negro."*[42] *Twenty years later, in her last film, (1949), she was still playing objectionable parts in the eyes of Mark A. Reid: "Nina Mae McKinney, as a razor-toting primitive."*[43] *Equally disturbing, Thomas Cripps reports that black actresses in* Hallelujah *were publicized as "dusky belles," with Miss McKinney called a "jungle Lorelei."*[44]

Manchel: I remember from reading the book that you said that you found her in a chorus.

Vidor: Yes. It was a black.... Let's see now, the film was made in 1929 ... I guess. And I guess the show was called either, *The Blackbirds of 1928*, or '29 [Lew Leslie's *Blackbirds of 1928*]. And we were looking, looking, looking, and went to the show; and she was third from the right in the chorus, you know. And she was so outstanding that it didn't take much argument after that.

Actually, Vidor is not very precise here. Almost every study on Hallelujah *explains that the director had first wanted Ethel Waters for the part. In her autobiography, Miss Waters's states, "The talent man King Vidor sent east to wave gold bags at me was stalled on the job by colored theatrical people unfriendly to me. He reported that he was unable to find me."*[45] *Vidor then rented a hall in New York, where he tested hundreds of women from the choruses of popular Broadway shows. This was the period, after all, when the Harlem Renaissance made possible many opportunities for black female entertainers not only in swank Harlem night clubs, but also in black musicals, not the least of which were a series of musical revues like Lew Leslie's* Blackbirds of 1928. *Moreover, Daniel Leab records that the search for talent for the MGM production was done with "much fanfare and publicity" and "extensively reported in the black press."*[46]

According to a report in the New York Times, *Vidor narrowed his choice to two black singers: Nina Mae McKinney and Honey Brown. The latter was chosen, not the former. However, when the popular cabaret singer became ill during the production, Miss McKinney was hired.*[47] *According to Bogle, the sensuous youngster was only sixteen when she joined the cast of the film.*[48]

Manchel: Had you gone there with the idea of finding her? Had someone told you about her, or was it just luck that you saw her?

Vidor: No. We were casting the whole picture in New York, and so I was going to any play that had a lot of people in it, a lot of black people, they were all blacks, I guess. And we were interviewing and auditioning and all this sort of stuff. And the agent, who was one agent that was taking me around this show, was part of it. I don't remember whether he said, "There is a girl in the chorus." But there was this bunch of good-looking chorus girls, you know. You look over the whole chorus.

Manchel: How did you meet Daniel L. Haynes? How did you locate him?

Vidor: Well, he was understudy for [William] Warfield in *ShowBoat* (1928). *ShowBoat* was running at the time at the Ziegfeld theater. And he was the understudy there. And he was singing whenever he got a chance to go on. Wallace Warfield, I think it is.

Manchel: William.

Haynes was understudying Jules Bledsoe, not William Warfield, in ShowBoat *(1928). Vidor has the correct information in his autobiography.*[49] *The confusion occurred because Warfield played Joe in MGM's 1951 version of* ShowBoat.

Vidor: William Warfield, yeah. So, I guess we interviewed him because, probably auditioned his voice, and I think he got out of *ShowBoat* to play the part, as I remember it. I had in mind Paul Robeson, you know.... But I don't know, I'm not sure, and I wanted Paul Robeson, but I think he was in Russia at that time. I think that was the period. I know I had to give up the idea.

Bogle confirms that Vidor originally wanted Paul Robeson for the role of Zeke, but goes further, claiming that "the picture was written with him in mind."[50]

Manchel: But he was the one you wanted?

Vidor: Yes.

Manchel: How would you come to that? I remember you said in the book that you always wanted to do a picture on the Negro film, on Negroes in film, because of your background in east Texas. What had stopped you over the years? You had been in Hollywood for so long.

Vidor: Well, they just wouldn't go for it. They were afraid that ... I mean I say "they" – MGM. I was with MGM. And every time I proposed it, they turned me down. Every time! I kept notes, and I was able to talk what kind of a story it was going to be. It was so.... It happened, all the incidents happened that I observed. I knew all the incidents, and I just put them down. I could then talk it. So I kept getting turned down.

The basis of turning down was that they were afraid that the picture would attract a great amount of blacks to the theater, and they didn't want this done. They didn't want to attract a big bunch of blacks, you know.

The dilemma of African-American silent film audiences in the Deep South has been described in two valuable studies. Gregory Waller's report looks at conditions in Lexington, Kentucky; pointing out that a separate entrance was created so that black patrons going to the balcony would not be able to mingle with white customers. Robert C. Allen's research examined Durham, North Carolina, and confirmed similar practices.

Vidor: It may even go back to Chicago, to the separate section [in the theaters] that they had for the blacks. Could be that they might have had a separate section in the balcony. I think they did in some ticketed theaters in the South. They didn't want an overflow. They didn't want to attract them. That was the basis.

Vidor discusses this problem in his autobiography, blaming it first on Southern white exhibitors.[51] However, he then discusses the problems he had with Chicago exhibitors.[52] Because northern theaters are implicated in the potential boycott, it is an important point. Up until 1972, scholars like Thomas Cripps had indicated that the basis for the way African-Americans had been treated in films was due in large measure to the myth of the strong Southern box office. By the end of the seventies, Ian C. Jarvie was pointing out that the studio system was more interested in profits than in race. In other words, "Why risk making any [film] that could cause controversy?"[53] Here Vidor is indicating that it had to do with the fear of theaters across the country having to have blacks and whites intermingle on a large scale.

While NATO/SHOWEST '92's panel, discussed in the Introduction, did not get much attention either at the Las Vegas convention or in the media, it serves as an illustration of how the problems Vidor experienced in 1929 were still evolving in 1992.

Vidor: So, I think, I would say over a period of three years, I kept being refused. And I tell about that in the book.[54] I know that I was in Paris when I read *Variety*. That Hollywood was going one hundred percent sound, and going all out for sound. So I came home quicker, took an earlier boat.

And that story has been told. I was in New York. I probably got Irving Thalberg, or somebody on the phone; and they said, "Go see Nick Schenck," who was actually the president, the head of MGM. And I did, and I told him the idea. I was under contact to be paid a pretty good sum of money for each picture. And I said, "I'll put my salary in. I'll gamble my salary with the cost." And I wanted to make it for a low cost. I wanted to make the picture, no big salaries or anything. So when I got through telling it, he said, "Well...." (when I put the gambling thing in), he said, "Well, if you're gonna talk like that, I'll let you make a picture about whores."[55]

That was that story. So then, he gave the "Okay" when I came back to MGM.

Vidor fails to mention here, as Combs reminds us, that he also "promised to deliver 'river baptisms, prayer meetings accompanied by spirituals, Negro preaching, banjo playing, dancing, the blues.'"[56]

A History Channel Classroom *presentation illustrated just how timely Vidor's work was in 2006. Clips from* Hallelujah *liberally shown in the documentary* Black Preachers *served as reminders of what a "fire and brimstone," flamboyant preacher looked like in the antebellum South. It was one more reminder of the film's visual power. Equally significant, the documentary's narrator explained the importance of African-American preachers throughout the last two hundred years in the United States: "They are the prophets of the black community, the voice of hope and heartbreak, of solace and inspiration." He went on to point out "the complexity and contradictory nature of their calling," and concluded by explaining that "Black preachers have united their community, incited it, and propelled it forward. And above all, they raised their voices and lifted the hopes and dreams of a people.[57]*

Manchel: One of the arguments when I was talking with Clarence [was that] he claimed that there never was any kind of prejudice against black people in Hollywood from the day that he got here. When I talked to him about all the fights and arguments about black people not being able to get work, or their [objecting to] stereotypes, he said that any black man who wanted to work and had talent could work. And I'm just wondering, as I listen to you talk about MGM and about Schenck and them not wanting to do it ... whether this was just another aspect of the story – or whether you, too, feel that there was never any kind of segregation in the films.

Vidor: Well, when he says that, you have to define that a little more clearly. I mean, does he mean crews, or staffs? They were using black people for predominantly black roles. I mean, they were using them for Pullman porters, and butlers. I don't think there was any prejudice. But the thinking was just to keep them in those roles. People were not thinking beyond the fact that if you wanted, maybe a chauffeur, a porter, or a doorman, or a waiter, then you use black people. *No prejudice* [italics mine]. But the expansion into clerks and managers and radio announcers, you know, that hadn't happened yet. That was forced, not forced, but called attention to.

I was then on the Board of Directors of the Directors Guild when letters arrived. These discussions started about....

The Screen Directors Guild was recognized in January, 1936, with King Vidor as its first president.[58]

Vidor: I think it was from the NCAAP [NAACP]. But that started directors thinking in terms of expanding the use in more places. It was just like advertising in clothes catalogues; they [the models] were all whites, all the time. They didn't start to use blacks.... Well, the same thing with national, I mean pro football, and major league baseball.

Worth noting is that on September 1, 1971, baseball history was made when the Pittsburgh Pirates had a line-up consisting of all-Black and Latino ballplayers for the first time in Major League baseball.[59]

Vidor: So this has been a tremendous change. Practically, I'd say, that except for going to the Moon and jet travel, it's been to me one of the number one great changes in progresses in our thinking.

Manchel: I gathered from your book that you said that *Hallelujah* did not make money outside the large cities. That there was a kind of boycott by the box offices, or the distributors, for actually running the film. At one point, you even made a bet of a thousand dollars with a fellow in Florida or Louisiana?

Vidor only mentions in his book that the film was boycotted in the South.[60] *Leab offers a fine discussion about the "discriminatory policies of exhibitors," but offers no specific information on how successful the film was at the box office.*[61] *The best analysis of the reaction to* Hallelujah *is provided by Cripps, who not only describes the criticisms of the press and the public to the film, but also explains what paradoxical philosophical problems the film presented to intellectuals and filmmakers.*[62] *Although he offers no evidence, the historian labels the film (and* Hearts in Dixie*) successes that, unfortunately, the "conservative studios" never pursued.*[63]

Vidor: Well, you see, the way I sold Nick Schenck, I just said. Now I couldn't go around and sell every theater, every theater chain. MGM got me to go up to what was called then "The Publix Theatre," which was predominantly Paramount, or was controlled by Paramount, and talk to the head booker for that circuit ... big, huge circuit, three or four hundred theaters.

According to Douglas Gomery, The Publix Theatres Corporation, sometimes called the Paramount-Publix theatre circuit, was "at its apex in 1930 ... [the] most profitable theatre chain in cinema history."[64] *At the time Vidor is discussing,*

Gomery reports "... Publix controlled 1,200 theaters, dominating the southern United States, New England, and the States of Michigan, Illinois, Minnesota, Iowa, Nebraska, and the Dakotas."[65]

To appreciate the problem that Vidor is alluding to in 1929, it may be helpful to review how films were distributed and exhibited in 1930. By the end of the Silent Era, the big studios had taken almost complete control of exhibition through an intricate process that involved prescribed territories (the United States was divided into thirty-two key areas), clearances (a time designating how long a film ran at a theater in a specific territory), first runs (the initial opening of a movie in a specific territory), and second and later runs (the showing of a film after it completed its exclusive first run). In essence, the five major film companies – MGM, Fox, Paramount, Warner Bros., and RKO – decided not only what films would be seen by most of the public, but also which films had a chance of making money. The minor companies – those studios without theaters – like Columbia, Universal, and United Artists – had "Gentleman Agreements" with the big studios to get their films shown in all territories. For that matter, the Big Five also had such agreements, since no one studio had exclusive control in every territory.[66]

Vidor: And ... he [Schenck] said, "I don't know what the picture is all about." I don't think he'd seen it. He said, "I don't know what it's all about." He's just fighting the showing of it. And he called in the secretary and said, "You saw the picture. Do you know what it was all about?" And she said, "No, I don't," I said, "Well, you can attack it from some other direction, but you can't attack it from 'you don't know what it's all about;' it's right there in front of you." And there was a fellow sitting there, from Florida. And he said, "Well, we can't show this.... I mean, the Florida man didn't say it, the booking man said it. He said, "We can't show this picture in the South." And I said, "That's where you're wrong. The Southern people are really interested in this and the Negro." And that was the fellow from.... And he perked up his ears and got interested. And that's why I said, "I'll bet you a thousand dollars that ... I don't know what picture you're showing now, but if it doesn't do better than that one, then I'm out a thousand dollars." So he said, "Well, that's a great gamble." I had to really go to town, you know, to get it shown. So, I never heard from him, so I presume that it did better. I never had to pay the thousand.[67]

Manchel: Did you ever have any repercussions from the film? Were people saying, "Why are you making the film like that?"

Vidor: No. No. No. Well, when we showed it in 1929, we had the first preview one morning at the Grauman's Chinese [Theatre on Hollywood Boulevard in Los Angeles]. And [Samuel] Goldwyn came. They [MGM] had invited some people, ten or eleven o'clock in the morning. And he came out on the sidewalk, and I heard Goldwyn offer Thalberg or [Louis B.]

Mayer two million dollars for it. The picture was supposed to cost around $250,000, $300,000. And Thalberg kept the cast waiting around for four, five, six months and so it ran up to $550,000, $600,000.

No one should take this as unusual for Thalberg. As Bob Thomas explains, the studio executive oversaw fifty films a year. He had no time or interest in following the daily progress of production, once he had given permission to proceed for the film to be made. "He preferred," Thomas says, "to reserve his judgment until the film was completed and assembled." Then he would use the preview system, pre-screenings to unsuspecting audiences, to perfect the film. Whatever got a bad reaction was reshot, even if it meant reassembling the cast and crew and reconstructing the set. His motto was, "Movies aren't made; they're remade."[68]

Vidor: It still shows in Paris every year on the Left Bank. It still runs around colleges, of course.

Manchel: I teach it in my [film history] course [on the Talkies].

Vidor: You do huh?

Manchel: The students like it very much, really enjoy it. In fact, I'm going to show them *So Red the Rose* this year as well. I'm starting a course on "The Black Man in Film."

Vidor: What University?

Manchel: University of Vermont.

Vidor: Very good. Very good. I was just trying to.... Let's see.... Well, the other showing which may be in the book, is Chicago. They got me to go out there. And they wouldn't book it. The big circuit was called Balaban and Katz, big tremendous theaters.

Balaban & Katz was the biggest theater chain in America during the silent era. Headed by the Balaban brothers, Barney and Abe, and Sam Katz, it merged with Adolph Zukor's Paramount chain in 1925.[69]

If you listen to the NPR African-American Roundtable, *you would discover that nothing much seems to have changed. On April 28, 2006, for example, host Ed Gordon discussed with his informed panel the marketing of black films. "Often a complaint from the blacks in Hollywood," he observed, is that "movies aren't marketed in the right way, that tell the real story, that often they are 'ghettoized' in the trailer and in the advertising." Professor E.R. Shipp agreed. He cited Denzel Washington's* Antwone Fisher *as an illustration. While applauding Fox-Starlight's greenlighting of such films, he nevertheless complained that "... they didn't know what to do with them."*[70] *Other films highlighted on the broadcast included* Fat Girls, The Best Man, Waiting to Exhale, Brown Sugar, Rosewood, *and* The Five Heartbeats. *Joe Davidson, an editor for the* Washington Post, *concluded "... it is clear that we don't have nearly enough [positive films]."*

He also pointed out that, "There are far too many negative stereotypes in black films by black people and in white films about black people."[71]

Vidor: They wouldn't book it there because, same reason, afraid of attracting too many black people. So they had an idea at MGM public relations: advertising. I should invite all the critics, [show the film] in a small projection room, and get the reviews, [and then] put the reviews in the papers before booking, which was never done before. And we did that, and got great reviews.[72]

And then [there was] a fellow with a little theater ... we had no.... You see, we had no chain of art theaters as such, as we have today. So one fellow, with a small [independent] theater, needed films. He conceived the idea of a black tie opening. [This was] the beginnings of the art theater. He conceived that and had invitations printed, engraved invitations, and he had an opening. Everybody came and talked about it; and his theater was filled for a couple of weeks. And then Balaban and Katz, with the big Chicago theater, they booked it after that, which was first time ever that it could be called a second run. And that's the first time that they ever broke that precedent.[73]

Manchel: What was your method of working with the actors? Most of them had never been in films before. I guess you had the added problems of having sound films that had just come in.

Vidor: Yes. But, you see, the Negro has that quality that some other ethnic groups have ... also Italians, and children, and so forth.... They, I mean when they're able to let themselves go, when they can express themselves, they have an uninhibited way of performing. They're so natural with it, you know. And I wouldn't be fooling them, I'd be pretty stupid if I tried to have them copy me, or copy some other preconceived idea. So my entire directing was always to either tell them what I was trying to get and then let them express themselves, or [let them] do it in their own way. And they are inventive. And they felt this stuff. I wasn't forcing. I'd seen all this stuff, observed all this stuff, but it's okay where you get something that's sort of unreal to the Negro that you would have to force them to do it a certain way. But I had none of that. It was all stuff that they very, very much invented right on the ... improvised right on, during the scene in the picture.

Manchel: Dialogue too?

Vidor: Yes.

Although the assertion seems credible, the dialect and the grammar in which the dialogue is delivered raises strong doubts. Haynes, in particular, was an educated man, and certainly did not speak as if he were an ignorant field hand.

Manchel: You wrote almost no dialogue? You just told them the scene, and then they would improvise it?

Vidor: Yeah! The script was a silent picture script. They used to think in terms of titles in the script, and the basis was we were still in the thinking of writing in the form of titles. And there's a lot of it. I can see it. I can see it, I can see it. When I look at the picture today, a lot of it that was ad-libbed.

Manchel: What about the rehearsals? Were there many rehearsals before the film itself?

Vidor: No, we didn't rehearse at all before the shooting. We didn't.... That was [a technique] developed later. Oh, I did on *Street Scene* (1931), with the play; that was all on one set. But we didn't rehearse ahead of time.

Manchel: What would you do? You'd go out and say, "This is the scene we're going to shoot. And this is what you're supposed to be doing." And then you just take one take?

Vidor: No. I wouldn't say we'd took one take always, we'd take several takes. But the number one thing, I started near Memphis in a cotton field, first day's shooting in a cotton field. And they had no portable sound equipment.... Here they say, "Okay, go ahead, do a sound picture" with nothing for exteriors. Well, my whole concept of this thing was to utilize interesting and Southern, real Southern exteriors, real cotton fields, and rivers and swamps and so forth. So here we were without any sound equipment, and then how you do this? Never been done before. And how do you keep it in sync? And keep the camera steady? And then when it came to editing, there's no editing equipment. No synchronous editing equipment that you could put the sound track on one and the picture on the other, and get them together. There was no synchronous shooting. There was, if you shot inside of the stage and inside of a big ice box deal. But not mobility of a camera on location.

All of the major books on Vidor, including his autobiography, discuss the importance of this revolutionary sound technique. What I found incredible was an introduction to Hallelujah *given on the Turner Classics Movie Channel by Robert Osborne. Praising the movie as "bold" and "a landmark film," the enthusiastic host claimed that what made this motion picture so remarkable sixty-six years later [1994] was "its authenticity," that Vidor was "telling it like it was, back in the South in 1929."*

Vidor: So we just shot silent, and put the sound in afterwards, you see. We tried to make it match. I think that's in the book, too.[74] The film editors [Anson Stephenson and Hugh Wynn] went berserk, trying to get the damn things to match. Well, I liked it this way. It was a free way of shooting, because you're not recording anything. You can go ahead and sing and shout, or anything you want. And they [Laughter] can work it out afterwards. And it helped. There was a lot of talk about the walk through the swamp that was done with a free style. It wasn't confined, you know?

Manchel: Let me ask you one more question about *Hallelujah*. Was there any problem with the way in which the black [performers] had to live after shooting, or any problem on the set while you were down in the South making the film?

The film was shot in both Arkansas and Tennessee.

Vidor: Yes. Crossing the river. We went over by boat, by ferry, into Arkansas; and when you got off the boat, you went on a long, long wooden causeway over the swampy water. And the fellow that we had had white drivers. Now this ... there was problems about white drivers driving a load of blacks in the car....

Haynes told me that this fellow was driving recklessly over these roads, too fast; and they were very frightened. I said, "Regardless of"... I even tried objecting to the driver, and the driver got tough about it and so forth. So we got hold of the driver, and I said, "Forgetting the racial differences, I don't want anything to happen to any member of the cast. We can't afford to have dangerous drivers around." So we fired the guy; we dismissed him. And then we heard that there was a bunch of them ready to greet us when we got back that night and so forth. And I think we phoned ahead, or something, and checked that. Anyway, no open confrontation came. But there were objections to certain drivers.

Then we had to go through the thing of questioning them. "Listen" [we said], "we're making a movie, and we don't want anything brought in here. These people are brought from New York, and they know what they're doing. They're not just people we picked up off the streets around here. And we're paying them; and you're either going to do it cooperatively, or not." And then we got enough [cooperation] doing it that way; we got enough drivers who would cooperate and help.

[Other problems came] up in the Peabody Hotel. They wouldn't let the blacks up in the main elevators, so they had to come up [the] freight elevator. I had a room right next to a freight elevator in the back, and they [the black performers] would come up to show me clothes and everything in the freight elevator. We rented a hotel and had them in a separate hotel. After a couple of trips, it was embarrassing, them coming up the freight elevator, [a person like Haynes who had been the] understudy in *ShowBoat*. So I said, "Well, I'll go over to their hotel." So from then on, I went to their hotel instead of bringing them into the Peabody Hotel.

Manchel: It must have made them feel very good.

Vidor: Well, you know, I think it's sort of stupid racism and all that. I was ... even in Texas, where I lived, first time we ... [hired] a black chauffeur, my father did drive around in an automobile, why we had threats and everything. But we'd go along, take a gun and set it on the front seat or what have you, just to tell them that. Some of them said, "Your car be run into" and this sort of thing.

So then, I remember one day we were moving some cotton wagons, and Haynes was dressed like a cotton picker, rough looking. He's sitting over on the fence, and a bunch of fellows ... this wagon was in the mud, and everybody was pushing it, and one fellow says, "Come on, Nigger, grab hold of a wheel" or something. And here, you're talking to the guy who's playing the lead in a picture. He didn't move, but he just got all red, his eyes got red, and he started to shake sort of. He didn't move. So, I had a Southern assistant then, and I told the assistant, "Go tell the guy he better keep quiet, or get out of the way, leave the place. We didn't need him." And so forth.

We ran into trouble, I remember one day on the dock by the.... They had a Mississippi River steam boat and one of the women was called Madame [Fanny Belle] de Knight, her husband was called "Professor de Knight." So I called out on the loud speaker, "Where's Madame de Knight?" And a whole roar went up from all the people watching, [because] we were calling her, "Madame de Knight." Suddenly here it was, we looked around. "What's wrong?" [Someone said], "Oh yes, we're in Memphis, Tennessee."[75]

And the two kids, two of the kids were dancing in the lobby ... [kids] that played parts [in the film]. They were called Sears and Roebuck ... [Milton Dickerson and Robert Couch were the two oldest credited children in *Hallelujah*]. And they were dancing in the lobby for nickels and dimes and quarters in the lobby of the Peabody Hotel, and that's where we got them. I don't know how we got that far without having two of the ... [key parts cast]. Well, we got stuck in New York, or Chicago, and went all around the churches in Chicago and choirs and choruses and then.... But in taking them down there, I think we had to get a special car, or we had them served in the drawing room and compartments. They weren't allowed to go in the dining room.

Manchel: It was accepted. It was understood among them that there was to be no trouble. This was the way it was, if they were going to make the movie, and they just went along with it.

Vidor: Yes. That's right. Yes.

Manchel: No kind of militancy that you have today, or anything?

Vidor: No. No. No. We had no trouble with them at all. The head assistant I had was from Georgia, and he understood the situation. I was from Texas, and we just knew that we had to take hold of it and take it in hand.

Same thing happened [in my life]. I had a Colored woman in my family, and she went wherever we went. She went with us in a restaurant. She raised my sister, and she sat at the main table. We went on a trip, and in those days she had a berth and stayed [with us]. She wasn't pushed off into any segregated thing, you know.

It was just a question of ... we knew this. And this is the way we treated them. It was important, and we were making a picture, and you'd better accept it or else, you know? Once you take that stand, other people say, "Well, they must know what they're doing. " Something like that.

Listening now to Vidor talk about his personal recollections and how much they influenced his work suggests how difficult it is to generalize from one's experiences to movies about a specific time and place. Nevertheless, as Sherman points out, that is how Vidor made many of his films. Paraphrasing the director's philosophical perspective, he writes, "The world exists 'for me,' and I can know it only through being here and living through it. To abstract and generalize is useless, since I shape the whole thing in my image anyway."[76]

Manchel: Was there any trouble with the guilds or the unions, or anyone else refusing to work on that kind of film?
Vidor: No.
Manchel: None whatsoever?
Vidor: I don't know how strong the guilds, or unions were at that time?

Except for members of the International Alliance of Theatrical Stage Employees (IATSE), Hollywood had no serious union problems until 1933. At the time of Hallelujah, *the two-year-old Academy of Motion Picture Arts and Sciences (AMPAS) settled labor disputes.*[77] *However, Bogle insists racial lines were clearly drawn during the first fifty years of Hollywood's existence: "Not a single performer was blind to the town's racism."*[78]

Manchel: What about the screenplay? When you finished the screenplay, did it have to be submitted to anyone at MGM to check it out before?
Vidor: Oh, Thalberg was in charge. But he was making so many pictures; he didn't spend much time over any one picture like that. He'd wait and see the rushes and so forth. He was enthused, but he was out for anything a little different and new, something. I was turned down

three years until sound came in, until I gambled my salary. I think I'm still getting the salary back. [Laughter] I got a check about a year ago. They thought I had only a profit interest at first, and I tried to make it clear that [my contract called for] every dollar that came in, I had to get a percentage. I didn't have to wait for a profit, because my salary ... [arrangements gave me the power] to sue over the production costs.

Manchel: Were there ever any problems once the rushes came out, of certain things that had to be re-shot, or had to be thrown out because they were objectionable?

Vidor: No.

Manchel: No problems at all? The thing was clean once it got the go-ahead from Thalberg?

Vidor: Yes. Uh-huh.

Manchel: Alright. Let me ask you about....

Vidor: I think it [was] held up a little.... I was against the Irving Berlin songs. I wanted it more native all the way through, and I thought Irving Berlin was Tin Pan Alley. And I fought that a little bit. But it still gripes me a little today that we had to step out of the real basic Negro character.

Manchel: Did the cast ever suggest ... [that there were] certain things that they would like to see changed, or things that they thought might help the picture along? Because, I always understood in Hollywood that when a man was making a film, sometimes he would consult with the performers, and the changes would be made on the spot, or on location, because of certain things that would develop.

Vidor: Oh, there might be such things as bring along a fellow who had an interesting dance, he could dance a certain way and they'd show up with some people like this. And I hired a group called the Jesse Singers. And we would use them in little parts, and they were clowning and performing and putting on shows during lunch time, or while we were waiting and all that. They'd think up stuff which I'd use. After all, as far as I was concerned, it was right in the ethnic set-up. I didn't have to go very far to get really good, interesting stuff, you know.

Manchel: Were these people paid the same salaries that other people would have been paid for the similar roles?

Vidor: I think so, yes.

Manchel: There was no problem?

Vidor: No. They weren't big names. They weren't paid on the name basis.

Manchel: In this book, this is the book by Peter Noble [*The Negro in Film*], an Englishman.... It was the first one [that's] ever been done, 1949, about the black man in film. He's talking about *So Red the Rose*. He says that the Negro actor's salary is a great deal lower than the white actor's in the same category is.[79] Is there any truth to that statement?

Vidor: Well....

Manchel: This is in 1935.

Vidor: 1935. See, I never, I never dickered with them on the salary basis. Somebody else did that, an agent, a casting office. We had a casting office, a casting man, on each picture, and I don't know who made salary arrangements. But, I imagine that Haynes and Nina Mae McKinney got about, I would guess, they got around five hundred, six hundred dollars a week. Maybe she got three hundred fifty dollars, I don't know. And probably at that time, she probably got about one hundred fifty dollars in the chorus line, you know. So it seems probably she's getting a big advance. And maybe he would come along, and he would say, "I'm getting so and so for *ShowBoat*." And we'd probably say, "We'll pay you a one hundred fifty dollars on top of that."

In *Hallelujah*, I'll tell you, there was a black woman in my family who came when I was eight years old, my sister was born, and she was part of the family. And I had the idea of dedicating the film to her ... to her memory. Such a great woman; she was as much my mother as my real mother was. And my idea, I don't say I made the film entirely, I made the film because it was great film material: graphic, and certainly musically, and so forth. But I always had the idea to dedicate it. Then I didn't know whether the studio would go for that. I might have mentioned it.

Durgnat makes the same point about the dedication in his book.[80]

Vidor: I don't know exactly what that means, I must confess. As far as I was concerned, I've always thought of the Negro exactly like any one else. It's a question of individuals, and you have to look upon all of them as individuals. Just as there are good whites and bad whites, there are good blacks and bad blacks. And I certainly never had a thing in my make up at all, any place, about ever trying to picture laziness, or greed, or stereotype, whatever that means.

This is a fascinating comment by Vidor. In 1972, he was still smarting from a 1935 review of So Red the Rose *by Arthur Draper. The comment was, "The story is a libelous presentation of Southern Negroes of the Civil War period. It pictures their revolt from their owners as based upon laziness, greed and hysteria. In the picture, its leaders are opportunists, misleading a simple-minded people."*[81]

Manchel: Well, that's good. I want to just get that kind of statement so that when I write it, I have that. [Peter Noble] ... says also that the studio publicity [stated] "... King Vidor holds the opinion that the colored race is the most difficult of all people to handle as a group in the making of motion pictures. *Fundamentally living only for the joy they get out of life* [Noble's italics], they are inclined to laugh at serious things and this native comedy is sometimes difficult to overcome when sheer drama is necessary."[82] I gather what he's saying here is that it's difficult for them to act seriously when they're at work. Do you ever see that to be true at all?

Vidor: Not at all. I would say that my feelings are just the reverse of everything he says there. I said I think that there's acting, and there are performers. They are more natural performers than, if we're going to separate races, than most white people, most Americans anyway. English, because England produces great actors, so it's very hard....

But ... I wasn't confining my activity. I was going into churches and [on] street corners; I picked up the old man from the street corner. And I wasn't saying ... whereby with whites maybe I would be going to the experienced acting agencies, you know. I was willing to pick up blacks anyplace. A chorus is certainly no schooling for an actress; you know ... chorus lines. So, I just believed that they were great actors naturally, and [gave] great performances naturally, serious or not serious. I have serious scenes in *Hallelujah* certainly. I got a letter two days ago from a fellow, Herman Weinstein, a critic in New York. He says, "I never will forget the look on Missy Rose's face when Zeke comes back." There are many serious scenes in *Hallelujah*, and we certainly didn't have any problems, any trouble about them.

Manchel: That's the reason that I asked you those things, to get that reaction. There's one last ... [question] I want to ask you. Noble says that *So Red the Rose* "had a fair success due mainly to the performance of Margaret Sullavan, but was heavily criticized by the Negro press and by liberal organizations everywhere. Daniel L. Haynes was so hurt and disgusted when he finished the film that he returned to New York and refused to appear in movies again unless he had the right to approve his theme, and then only if the part gave him an opportunity to show his race in a sympathetic light. He bitterly regretted the contribution he had made to race hatred in this film, and to my knowledge, like Charles Gilpin, he never went back to Hollywood."[83] Did you ever hear that statement before?

Vidor: No, I never heard it before. And it can be true or not true. Because I never read the book, and I never heard it before.

Manchel: He [Haynes] never said anything to you during the filming? So there is no way you would have known about his feelings?

Vidor: No. No.

Manchel: Can I ask you about how you came to *So Red the Rose*? Do you remember at all how you got a script? Was it handed to you?

Vidor: Yes. It was bought by Paramount, and the producer's name was Douglas MacLean, who had been an actor, had been a star, a silent film star. And he was then a producer. I was taken in by my agent, Myron Selznick. He took me in, and being from the South, I was offered the job. I took [screenwriter] Laurence Stallings over [from MGM]. I guess they had an adaptation [of Stark Young's 1934 novel, *So Red the Rose*], probably they had a script before I got there. But Stallings worked on it; I worked on the script some, I don't remember how much. But it was bought by them. It was written by a fellow named Stark Young; I think I have a copy of it here still, of the book. My attitude, I think, was pretty much [to] follow the book. I might put in some treatment which I felt deeply about.... But I think we were motivated, in that case, pretty much, very much by the book, perhaps as [David O.] Selznick was by *Gone with the Wind* (1939).

For those unfamiliar with Hollywood history, David and Myron were brothers; and Vidor was one of the three directors on Gone with the Wind.

Manchel: Do you remember any stories at all about *So Red the Rose*? About the production? Or in the shooting? Or the characters – Randolph Scott was in the film; Margaret Sullavan; Robert Young, I think, too.

Vidor: Well.... Not Robert Young. It was Robert ... what's his name? Not Robert Young. I picked him up. That was his first part. Robert ... he became a pretty good star. What's his name? Not Armstrong. Not Montgomery. Cummings. Robert Cummings. That was his first part. My wife [Elizabeth Hall, his third wife, who died in 1973] said, "Come in the next room. There's a pretty good actor in there, reading." And I went in. He was supposed to be a Texan, I guess. And he gave a good reading. He said he was not a Texan, but because of the dialogue, he had adopted a dialect. And that was his first job.

I remember Margaret Sullavan flared up a couple of times. I remember she read an.... By then, we were doing some rehearsals. Sitting around a table. When I say "some," it probably added up to two one-half days. I remember she read a letter from one of the characters, and she read it so movingly that everybody had tears in their eyes, crying sitting around the table. And there was always a problem if [she could] do it as well [on film]. Could we capture that thing while shooting? I never felt that we did capture the exact ... [mood].

I used to feel that I could handle the movement of a lot of people in crowds. I remember my wife [Elizabeth Hall], who I think was the script girl on the film, said, "You certainly bring all these people into a group naturally, and they have some sort of rhythm." We'd work that out.

We had the Mansion now; I mean the front of it. It wasn't called Tara....

I don't know what it was called. [We shot] at Sherwood Forest, about one hour from town. We used to work out there. I stayed and lived near by.

I don't remember any incidents. I remember vaguely the one you mentioned about Clarence Muse objecting to something. I don't know quite how it was solved. But I remember that he objected. Certainly not for two-and-a-half days! [Laughter] Because we would have just.... You couldn't do that.

Manchel: The idea [in *So Red the Rose*] was that the slaves, I think, were going up to the house and the father [Walter Connolly] was dying, and the daughter [Sullavan] had to stop the revolution. What she did was to slap the ringleader [Muse] in the face. He objected to being slapped that way, so he ... [argued] that the way to resolve it was to have a mulatto slapped in the face. [You agreed and] then the picture went on. From what he tells me, the revolution was broken with that slap in the face.

Vidor: Yeah. Well, that could be. But I would say that we would have lost a half-hour. [Laughter] Tops! Not more.

Manchel: Can I ask you what you think about *Hallelujah* now, after all these years?

Vidor: I get a big kick out of it. I've seen it in Paris, I've seen it in two or three places in the last eight, ten years. I enjoy it. My big interest is always how do the blacks accept it today. I have a girl who works for me, occasionally, an assistant, a secretary and so forth. She reports whenever UCLA gives it a run, they're very enthusiastic. They'll be, you know, three or four [black] students or something in the audience, and she says they all like it.

I'm usually interested to see whether they object. There are a few little things there that, probably, if I did it today I would not include. About telling time. [A black] fellow can't tell time. But these are stories that I heard when I was a boy.

This scene occurs early in the film, when a man playing a banjo, shows the family his watch. The scene is played for comic relief, with the entire family unable to tell time.

Vidor: The Negro, as I said before, has certainly been.... This is of a period. This was made in a time and in a locale that had existed. I don't think there is anything that wasn't going on at the time. The place that we shot *[Hallelujah]* was sort of controlled ... [owned] almost by a dynasty. The white people who owned the plantation owned the town. I'm trying to think of their name. They owned the gambling house and the house of prostitution. They used to say they paid off all their [help] on Saturday night, and they had most of it back by Monday morning. [Laughter] And the black man who ran the gambling house – upstairs over the gambling house was the house of prostitution – he had a big tremendous diamond, a necktie. They used token money, you know; they paid them in token money. They got it all back mostly....

When the Albert E. Smith-Herbert Hoover election, I think it was, went on.... The fellow drove out ... the white fellow, the young son drove out, and said, "If any of you fellows want to vote the Democratic ticket, come on." I said, "Well, we're registered in California." He said, "That's all right. We'll take care of that." And we drove in and stood in line. I voted twice for Albert E. Smith on the Democratic ticket ... under two different names! [Laughter] And he won. He carried Arkansas very big! I didn't have to register or anything. Those people, who wanted to vote for Smith, they could come along. The others for Hoover, they could stay and wait. And they drove us into town. [Laughter]

It was an absolutely controlled dynasty, this town. They had a store, everything; they had a home there; they had black servants. They called it "black entertainment." We had dinner there once.... And it really was the remains of it [the antebellum period], with a landing place on the Mississippi, where the cotton was picked up. And they told stories about having to.... They'd say that blacks would work a few days and then they wouldn't come out. Then they'd have to go and roust them out of their beds and make them work.

It's the Deep South, you know. It's still going on. I don't know what's there today.

Manchel: Do you have any comments about black films being made today [1972]?

Vidor: No. I see *Shaft* [1971] is showing at the Guild. See, I live up in the country. I've seen a lot of films. I haven't seen the black films. I want to. I've heard of one made in Kansas. What's the name?

Manchel: *The Learning Tree* [1969] by Gordon Parks.

Gordon Parks, a distinguished photographer, cinematographer, author and musician, died on March 8, 2006. Among his many achievements, the legendary chronicler of racism and poverty for Life *magazine believed, according to the* Washington Post, *in, "Not allowing anyone to set boundaries, cutting loose the imagination, and then making new horizons."[84] The* Post *writer also eulogized Parks as a "revered elder and cultural icon."[85] In the* New York Times *obituary, Donald Faulkner, head of the New York Writers Institute, considered the artist "the Jackie Robinson of film," while both Spike Lee and John Singleton praised Parks because he did so much to "open doors for a lot of people...."[86]*

Vidor: Yeah. I'd like to see that. I'd like to see some of them. I don't know how *Shaft* is. I think I'll see that. It's showing at the Guild the next couple of days. I try to keep up with what they are doing.

Manchel: Thanks very much.

47. King Vidor (hand on bag) preparing *Hallelujah*'s opening scene in the cotton fields. Shot to the singing of "Old Folks at Home". Courtesy of The Manchel Collection, Burlington College.

48. Publicity shot of Mammy (Fanny Belle DeKnight), Pappy/Parson (Harry Gray), Chick (Nina Mae McKinney), Zeke (Daniel L. Haynes) and Vidor. Courtesy of The Manchel Collection, Burlington College.

49. After getting his pay for the cotton, Zeke sees and lusts for Chick. Standing next to him is Hot Shot (William Fountaine), the crooked gambler. (Publicity Shot). Courtesy of The Manchel Collection, Burlington College.

King Vidor 339

50. Zeke loses his money at a crooked crap game set-up by Hot Shot. Courtesy of The Manchel Collection, Burlington College.

340 THE WELL-INTENTIONED POET

51. Zeke discovers that Hot Shot cheated him, a fight breaks out, and Zeke's younger brother, Spunk, is killed in the mayhem that follows. Courtesy of The Manchel Collection, Burlington College.

52. The family prays for the soul of Spunk. (Publicity Shot). Courtesy of The Manchel Collection, Burlington College.

53. Zeke turns to religion after Spunk's death and becomes a traveling preacher. Courtesy of The Manchel Collection, Burlington College.

King Vidor 343

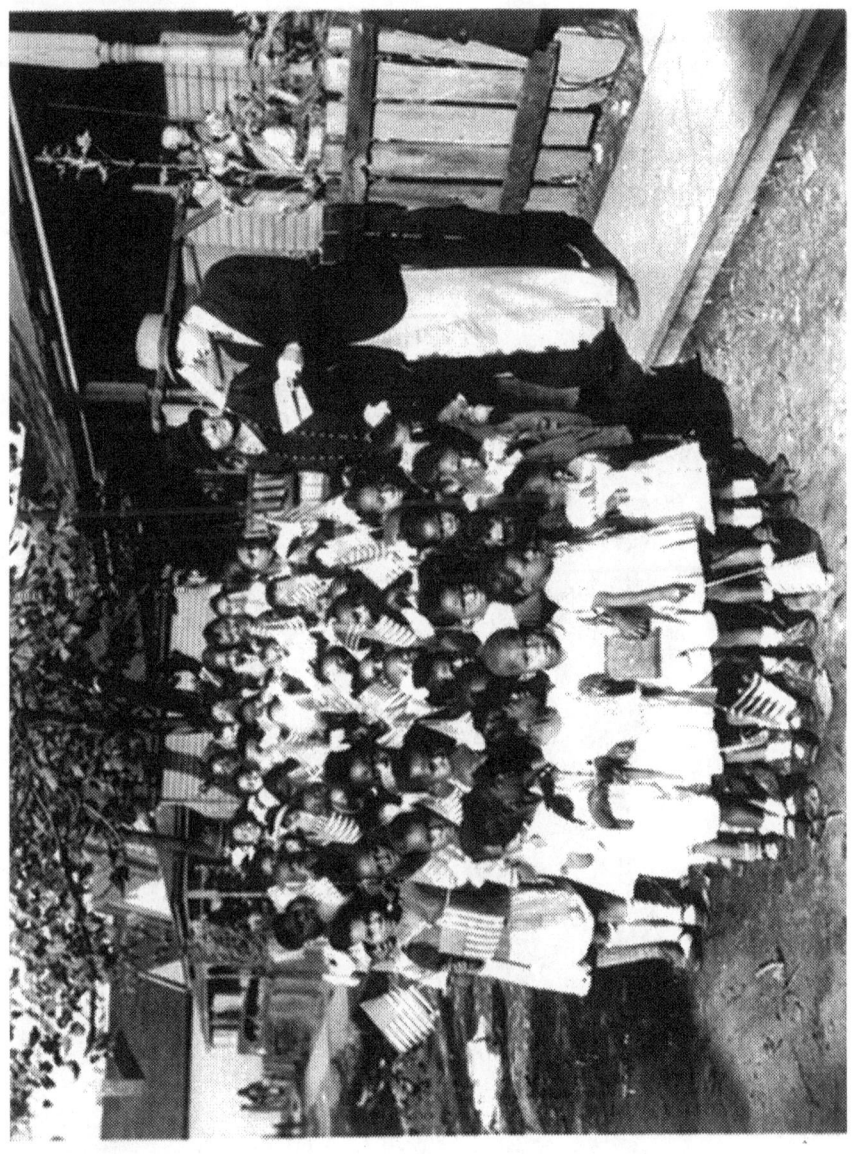

54. King Vidor preparing the children for the parade to welcome the famous preacher. Courtesy of The Manchel Collection, Burlington College.

55. Setting up for the mass baptismal. Courtesy of The Manchel Collection, Burlington College.

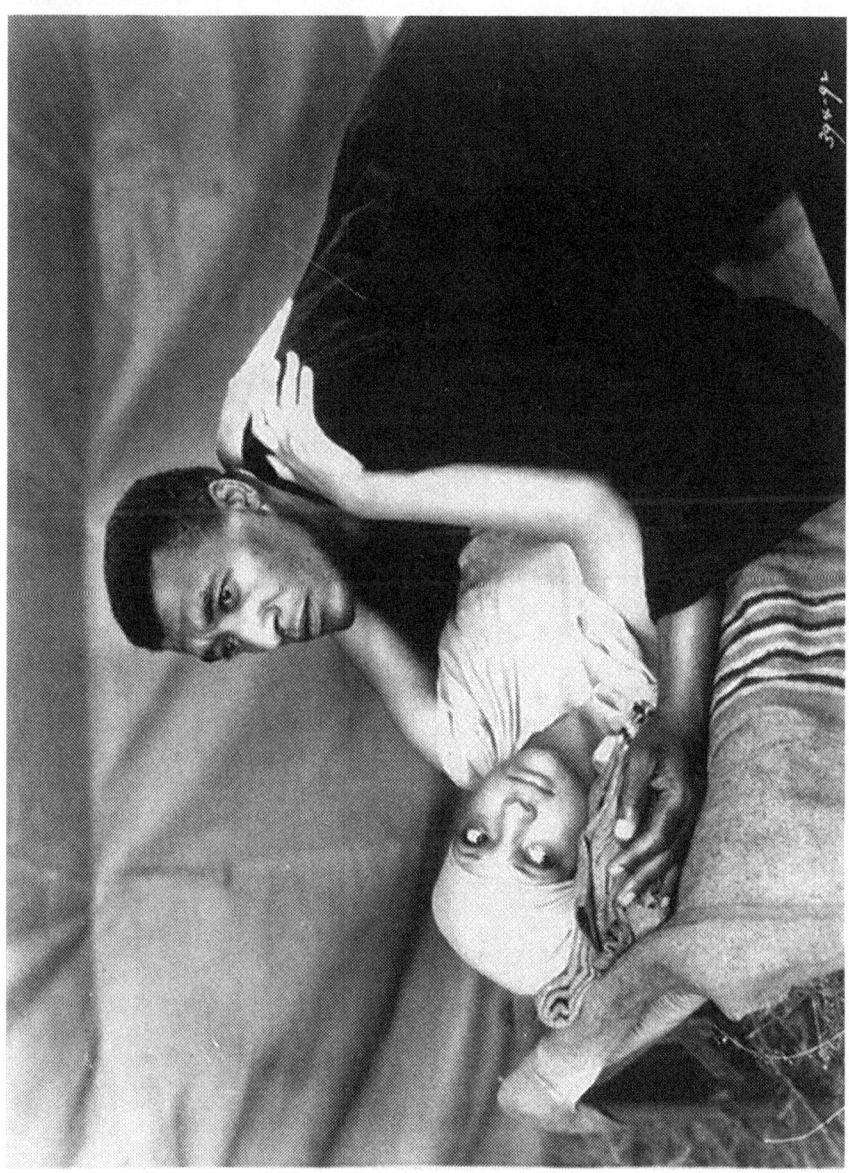

56. Zeke converts Chick, but his passion for her begins to shake his faith. Courtesy of The Manchel Collection, Burlington College.

346 THE WELL-INTENTIONED POET

57. An old-fashioned revival meeting revives Zeke's lust for Chick. Courtesy of The Manchel Collection, Burlington College.

58. Zeke gives up his ministry for Chick. (Publicity Shot). Courtesy of The Manchel Collection, Burlington College.

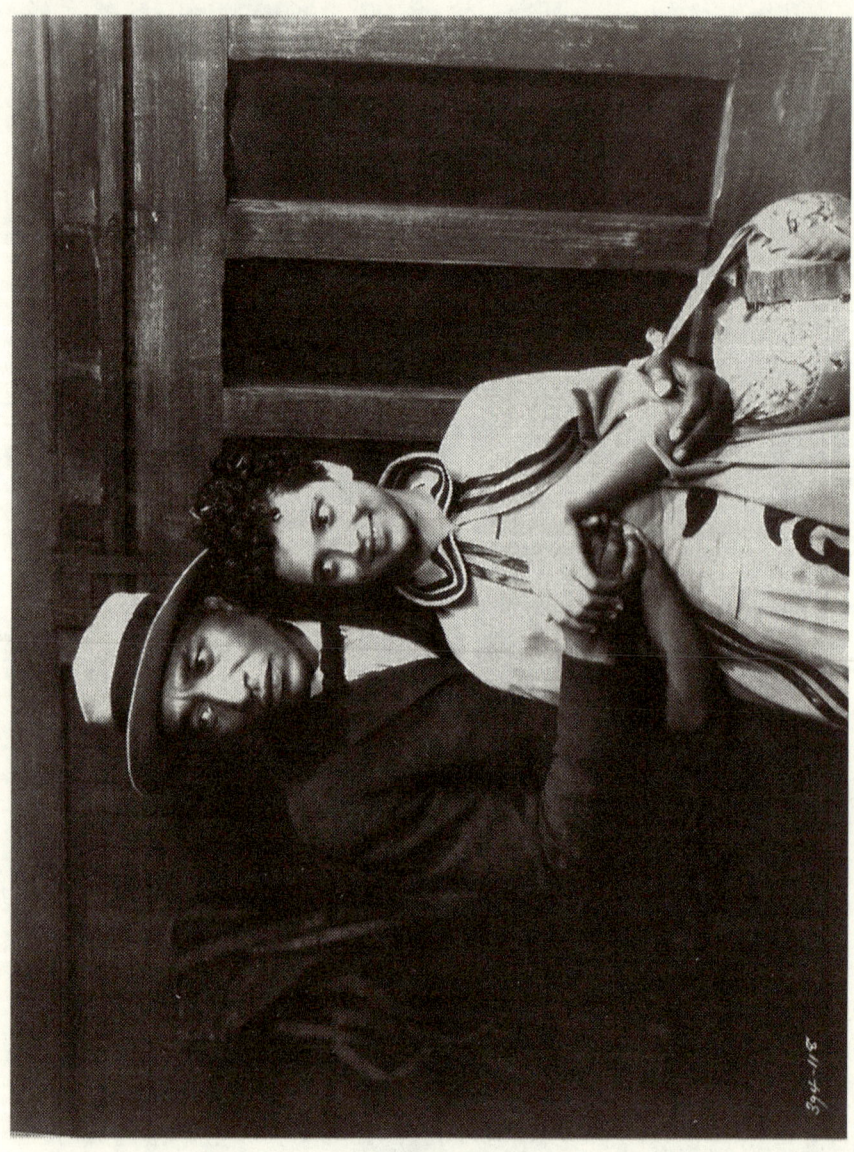

59. Zeke suspects that Chick is two-timing him with Hot Shot. Courtesy of The Manchel Collection, Burlington College.

60. Zeke is sent to prison for killing Hot Shot. Courtesy of The Manchel Collection, Burlington College.

61. Zeke is given probation. Near the film's end he sings the movie's theme song, "End of the Road." Vidor sets up the scene in this publicity shot. Courtesy of The Manchel Collection, Burlington College.

Notes

[1] Raymond Durgnat and Scott Simmon, *King Vidor, American* (Berkeley: University of California Press, 1988), 98.

[2] Eric Sherman, "King Vidor (1895-1982)," in *American Directors*, ed. with Pierre Sauvage Jean-Pierre Courson (New York: McGraw-Hill, 1983), 348.

[3] John Baxter, *Hollywood in the Thirties* (New York: A.S. Barnes and Company, 1968), 111.

[4] Clive Denton, "King Vidor: A Texas Poet," in *The Hollywood Professionals* (New York: A. S. Barnes, 1976), 6-55.

[5] Richard Schickel, *The Men Who Made the Movies* (New York Atheneum, 1975), 132.

[6] Durgnat and Simmon, *King Vidor, American*, 2.

[7] Michael Selig, "Vidor, King," in *The International Dictionary of Films and Filmmakers, Vol. 2: Directors/Filmmakers*, Ed. Christopher Lyon and Susan Doll (Chicago: St. James, 1984), 557.

[8] David Thomson, *A Biographical Dictionary of Film, 2nd Ed.* (New York: William Morrow, 1981), 628.

[9] Richard Combs, "King Vidor," in *Cinema: A Critical Dictionary--the Major Film-Makers*, Ed. Richard Roud (New York: Viking, 1980), 1026.

[10] Ibid., 1026-1027.

[11] Ed Guerrero, *Framing Blackness: The African American Image in Film* (Philadelphia: Temple University Press, 1993), 50-51.

[12] Combs, "King Vidor," 1031.

[13] "Vidor, King (Wallis)," in *World Film Directors. Vol. 1--1890-1945* (New York: H. W. Wilson, 1987), 1132.

[14] Combs, "King Vidor," 1028.

[15] Scott Simmon, "Hallelujah," in *The International Dictionary of Films and Filmmakers, Vol. 1: Film*, Ed. Christopher Lyon and Susan Doll (Chicago: St. James, 1984), 192.

[16] Combs, "King Vidor," 1030.

[17] Herbert G. Luft, "A Career That Spans Half a Century," *Film Journal* 1.2 (1971), 35.

[18] "Primitive Emotions Aflame in a Negro Film," *The Literary Digest*, 5 Oct. 1929, 42-43.

[19] "Hallelujah," *The Crisis*, Oct. 1929, 342.

[20] "Primitive Emotions Aflame in a Negro Film," 49.

[21] "Hallelujah," *Pittsburgh Courier*, 8 Feb. 1929, 16.

[22] Selig, "Vidor, King," 557.

[23] John Baxter, *King Vidor* (New York: Monarch, 1975), 41.

[24] Ibid., 43.

[25] Ibid.

[26] Campbell, *The Celluloid South: Hollywood and the Southern Myth*, 16.

[27] Ibid., 57.

[28] Baxter, *King Vidor*, 53.

[29] Jack Temple Kirby, *Media-Made Dixie* (Baton Rouge: Louisiana State University Press, 1978), 70.

[30] "Review 'So Red the Rose'," *Newsweek*, 30 Nov. 1935, 28.

[31] "Review of 'So Red the Rose'," *The Literary Digest*, 23 Nov. 1935, 26.

[32] Durgnat and Simmon, *King Vidor, American*, 177.

[33] Donald Bogle, "Introduction to Hallelujah," (Atlanta, GA: Turner Classic Movies, 2006).

[34] King Vidor, letter, 18 December 1971.

[35] Schickel, *The Men Who Made the Movies*, 132.

[36] Cripps, *Slow Fade to Black: The Negro in American Film, 1900-1942*, 243.

[37] Bogle, *Bright Boulevards, Bold Dreams: The Story of Black Hollywood*, 91.

[38] King Vidor, *Vidor, King. A Tree Is a Tree* (New York: Harcourt, Brace, 1952), 176.

[39] Noble, *The Negro in Films*, 187.

[40] Donald Bogle, *Brown Sugar: 80 Years of America's Black Female Superstars* (New York: Harmony, 1980), 55.

[41] Landry, "U.S. Films: Black, Red & Blue," 39.

[42] Hughes and Meltzer, *Black Magic: A Pictorial History of the Negro in American Entertainment*, 306.

[43] Reid, *Redefining Black Film*, 45.

[44] Cripps, *Slow Fade to Black: The Negro in American Film, 1900-1942*, 245.

[45] Waters, *His Eye Is on the Sparrow*, 198.

[46] Leab, *From Sambo to Superspade: The Black Experience in Motion Pictures*, 92.

[47] "Finding Screen Negroes," *New York Times*, 25 Aug. 1929, 61.

[48] Bogle, *Bright Boulevards, Bold Dreams: The Story of Black Hollywood*, 92.

[49] Vidor, *Vidor, King. A Tree Is a Tree*, 176.

[50] Bogle, *Toms, Coons, Mulattoes, Mammies, & Bucks: An Interpretive History of Blacks in American Films*, 31.

[51] Vidor, *Vidor, King. A Tree Is a Tree*, 170.

[52] Ibid., 185.

[53] I. C. Jarvie, *Movies as Social Criticism: Aspects of Their Social Psychology* (Metuchen, NJ: Scarecrow, 1978), 165.

[54] Vidor, *Vidor, King. A Tree Is a Tree*, 175.

[55] Ibid., 176.

[56] Combs, "King Vidor," 1030.

[57] "Black Preachers. Sam Pollard," (Two Dollars and a Dream, Inc., 2006).

[58] Durgnat and Simmon, *King Vidor, American*, 172.

[59] David Maraniss, *Clemente: The Passion and Grace of Baseball's Last Hero* (New York: Simon & Schuster, 2006), 252-253.

[60] Vidor, *Vidor, King. A Tree Is a Tree*, 187.

[61] Leab, *From Sambo to Superspade: The Black Experience in Motion Pictures*, 194-195.

[62] Cripps, *Slow Fade to Black: The Negro in American Film, 1900-1942*, 247-253.

[63] Ibid., 253.

[64] Douglas Gomery, "U.S. Film Exhibition: The Formation of a Big Business," in *The American Film Industry*, Ed. Tino Balio (Madison: University of Wisconsin Press, 1985), 226.

[65] Ibid., 225.

[66] For more discussion, see Manchel, *Film Study: An Analytical Bibliography*. Vol. 1, 620ff.

[67] Vidor, *Vidor, King. A Tree Is a Tree*, 186.
[68] Bob Thomas, *Thalberg: Life and Legend* (Garden City, NY: Doubleday, 1969), 139.
[69] For details, see Gomery, "U.S. Film Exhibition: The Formation of a Big Business," 220ff.
[70] Shipp, "Taking Control of Old Demons by Forcing Them into the Light," H13+.
[71] National Public Radio Podcast Series, "The Marketing of Black Movies," in *NPR African-American Roundtable* (April 28, 2006).
[72] For good summaries of the reviews, see Cripps, *Slow Fade to Black: The Negro in American Film, 1900-1942*, Leab, *From Sambo to Superspade: The Black Experience in Motion Pictures*.
[73] Vidor, *Vidor, King. A Tree Is a Tree*, 184-185.
[74] Ibid., 181-183.
[75] Ibid., 178-179.
[76] Sherman, "King Vidor (1895-1982)," 350.
[77] Manchel, *Film Study: An Analytical Bibliography*, 1067ff.
[78] Bogle, *Bright Boulevards, Bold Dreams: The Story of Black Hollywood*, xiv.
[79] Noble, *The Negro in Films*, 65.
[80] Durgnat and Simmon, *King Vidor, American*, 108.
[81] Arthur Draper, "Uncle Tom, Will You Never Die?," *New Theatre* (1936), 31.
[82] Noble, *The Negro in Films*, 65.
[83] Ibid., 67.
[84] Yvonne Shinhoster Lamb, "'Life' Photographer and 'Shaft' Director Broke Color Barriers," *The Washington Post*, 18 May 2006, A01.
[85] Ibid.
[86] Andy Grunberg, "Gordon Parks, Photojournalist Who Showed Dignity Amid Oppression, Dies at 93," *New York Times*, 8 March 2006, C:1.

62. Woody Strode. "To Frank Manchel; My Official Biographer; Woody Strode; 1972". Courtesy of The Manchel Collection, University of Vermont.

5
The Man Who Made the Stars Shine Brighter: Woody Strode

"Strode's *Sergeant Rutledge* is a phantom. His titular prominence makes up for the black male dignity Hollywood has withheld. It's meant to haunt decent moviegoers' consciousness (as such later postmodern black screen icons as John Coffey in *The Green Mile* and Rubin 'Hurricane' Carter in *The Hurricane* are also intended to do)."

Armond White[1]

"Why [is] it," asked Marcel Carne, "that [I am] always being honored and celebrated abroad, while in the country that is my own, in which I was born, I encounter only attacks, sarcasms, and even disdain from those who claim to love an Art to which I have devoted my life?"[2] It is a question many African-American performers in Hollywood film history routinely ask themselves. How can they justify their contributions performing in a racially distorted system to a skeptical world? On the one hand, having good motives is never an adequate alibi for helping perpetuate racist conventions and negative images of African-Americans. On the other hand, to follow a controversial path and still be true to your beliefs often leads to critical misinterpretations and public misperceptions. How should independent thinkers respond? Should they listen to their critics and alter their behavior? Why not go along with the crowd? After all, none of us is impervious to the damage done to our egos as day after day we meet with rejection and disappointment. Moreover, how can we be certain that our way is better than the collective wisdom? Still, there are those who cannot or will not fit into a pattern. They possess a vision denied to others. What keeps these nonconformists afloat in a sea of disfavor?

This transcription is about one such individualist. His name is Woody Strode, called by *Jet* magazine, "the Jackie Robinson of cinema."[3] For nearly two decades, he remained a pioneer against racism in the film and television industry. Although he made more than sixty movies, not many young people remember him now. In his last film, *The Quick and the Dead* (1995), even loyal fans had trouble recognizing him in his momentary appearance during the opening sequence. Fewer African-Americans view him as a role model for this generation. When he died on December 31, 1994, only a smattering of periodicals published his obituary.

What did he do that the present establishment discounted his achievements? These revisionists have almost erased him from our national memory. Yet, this famous athlete-turned-actor overcame the segregation hurdle in professional football when they signed him with the Los Angeles Rams in the National Football League in 1946. Not many sports historians report that fact. Nor in books about famous black athletes is there much space devoted to his breaking the color barrier in professional wrestling during the mid-1950s.

Woody Strode's place in film history is equally precarious. Although he worked with some of the movies' most impressive directors – e.g., Richard Brooks, Budd Boetticher, Francis Ford Coppola, Cecil B. DeMille, John Ford, Stanley Kubrick, Sergio Leone, Daniel Mann, and Lewis Milestone – commentators on the African-American experience generally dwell on the black film pioneer's superb physique and his sensational athletic feats, while ignoring his groundbreaking roles in film.

The problem may have been timing. He had made the transition from sports to films during a new era of ethnic pride in America. The Melting Pot theory had lost its appeal, and in its stead stood Cultural Pluralism. Assimilationists became unfashionable; champions of ethnic diversity were the vogue. While Strode's allegiance to a displaced aesthetic and cultural system made him popular with an older generation of filmmakers, it made him a pariah to the vanguard of a fresh age. In essence, what Ben Vereen said of Bojangles is true of Strode: He was "a black man caught in a white system, who tried to be an American."[4]

Honors like becoming the first black actor to be admitted into the Walk of Western Stars in 1993 are overshadowed by glaring omissions when it comes to honoring the memory of his screen achievements. A case in point is his link with the famous U.S. 9th and 10th Cavalry Regiments that served on the American frontier after the Civil War. Despite the fact that Woody Strode became the first African-American featured in a 1960s mainstream theatrical film about this distinguished corps, no one at the July 25th, 1992 ceremonies dedicating a monument to these heroic troopers, or the TV show about the event, thought to acknowledge the significance of *Sergeant Rutledge* (1960) in memorializing the Buffalo Soldiers.[5] The issue of adequate recognition for whom and what he was followed Woody Strode throughout his life.

"Born Woodrow Wilson Woolwine Strode in Los Angeles on July 28,

1914, the son of a brick mason, benefited from his family's migration from New Orleans to Los Angeles four years earlier. It momentarily provided a safe haven from the extremes of racial prejudice found in the South."

His untroubled childhood on the West Coast is described lovingly in his memoirs, *Gold Dust: An Autobiography*. He never felt threatened because of his heritage or his color. In Strode's mindset, a person was judged by what he achieved, not by who he was. The illusion of acceptance encouraged Strode to always brag about his "mixed" blood. His father was the son of Creek and Blackfoot Native Americans, while his mother was the daughter of a slave. The prejudice against "mixed breeds" (Strode's term, not mine) would become a major factor in his life, compounded when he married a Hawaiian woman in 1940. There was one positive side, as he explained in his autobiography, "... because of my mixed background I could play anyone from the third world."[6]

By the early thirties, when Strode first became sensitive to the subtle racism in California, the now 6'3, one hundred seventy-five-pound strapping youth, never a strong student but a superb athlete, had attracted the attention of college scouts. Although he graduated from high school in 1934, a member of the all-city football team, his poor academic background prevented colleges from offering him any scholarships. However, he was determined to succeed. Two-and-a-half years later, as the result of a self-designed study regimen (there were no remedial college preparatory programs in existence), he finally got the scholastic credentials to be accepted by UCLA. Most of his energy now was devoted to playing football and running track. So impressive was the muscular athlete at 6'4, two hundred ten pounds, the controversial German filmmaker, Leni Riefenstahl, during a good will tour in California, used him as a model for a painting commissioned by Hitler for the 1936 Olympics in Berlin. It was that same physical appearance and flair for action that shaped his screen image.

In their junior year at UCLA, teammates Woody Strode (who played end) and Kenny Washington (the star running back) were joined on the football field by a transfer from a junior college, whose name was Jackie Robinson (soon to become UCLA's best all-around athlete). By 1939, the trio gave UCLA its greatest football season up to that point, and the athletes gained national fame as "The Gold Dust Gang." Strode makes it quite clear, however, that his best friend Kenny and he were not buddies with Jackie Robinson, primarily because the latter had a more militant attitude toward racism in America than the two assimilated Los Angeles kids.[7] According to Robinson's daughter Sharon, the great athlete, a football All-American in his senior year at UCLA in 1941, was "called cocky and arrogant by some, the man to stop by rival coaches, and 'The Dusky Flash,' 'Midnight Express,' and 'The Dark Demon' by West Coast sportswriters."[8]

In 1940, Strode quit school, six months before graduation. Not only did he feel that he had learned all that he could from his studies, but also his chances for running track in the Olympics ended when the war in Europe forced the cancellation of the games. Not willing to abandon his athletic career, he and Kenny entered semi-pro ball for Paul Schissler's Hollywood Bears, since professional football was not a possibility for them. Eight years earlier, the National Football League, which had once hired black athletes, acquiesced to the complaints of white ballplayers who felt that blacks cut down job opportunities for Caucasians, and they had built a racial barrier. It was during this period that the easygoing black athlete also began his training as a wrestler and got his first film role in Henry Hathaway's *Sundown* (1941).

Another principal event in Strode's life was his marriage in 1940 to Hawaiian Princess Luuialuanna Kalaelola, affectionately called "Luana" by friends and "Mama" by her husband. Their courtship had lasted two years. As he recalled in an *Ebony* interview, "You'd have thought I was marrying Lana Turner, the way the whites in Hollywood acted."[9] The problems that their "mixed" marriage caused the couple are described in *Gold Dust*. Their forty-year union ended when Luana died at sixty-four of Parkinson's disease in 1980. Two years later, Woody married Tina, who survived him.

With America's entry into World War II on December 7, 1941, Woody Strode joined his coach and other members of the team in enlisting in the Army Air Corps. Some examples of the racial harassment that Strode experienced while serving in a segregated Army during the conflict are described in his autobiography. Nevertheless, the primary focus in this section of the book is on his three-year service as a member of an integrated football team, the March Field Fliers (so named because they played at March Field in Riverside, California). Orchestrated by General Hap Arnold and Paul Schissler, the team made money for the survivors of men killed in combat.

In 1944, Strode and his teammates were shipped overseas to the Pacific. There, more racist incidents occurred. He was at Guam on August 10, 1945, the day the Second World War officially ended. According to a 1971 radio interview he gave to Barry Farber [Third World Media News], Strode got sent home early because a general saw him playing football, found out that he might still be eligible for professional football (now a real possibility), and arranged both an honorable discharge and a ride back to Los Angeles on a C-47.

Strode's career from 1946 to the late 1980s is gingerly sketched in his autobiography. Anyone reading his memoirs learns about his bitter professional football career in the United States and Canada, his professional wrestling pursuits, and his successful transition to film and television in the 1950s. We discover delightful stories about his family and amusing tales about the people who helped him make his way in the difficult, competitive, and racist worlds of sports and entertainment.

Missing from this invaluable record is a candid account of what it meant to be a conservative African-American actor during the Civil Rights struggle of the sixties and seventies. A question always plaguing these unique performers, and not their white peers, was whether one had to be first a black actor and then an actor. For Woody Strode, the answer was that he was straightforward. He was a cowboy, not a white or a black actor. Having grown up in California and socialized by an integrationist ethic, Strode remained self-isolated from the revolutionary struggle against racism that had been fermenting in the nation.

Why is never fully explained. Nor is any satisfactory explanation offered for one of his public outbursts in 1972, explained in the following interview, that branded him as a reactionary for the rest of his life: "I'm tired of this black, black, black business," he is quoted as saying. "Me, I don't care. If the money is right, I'll play Mickey Mouse."[10] It was not that Strode was mercenary; rather, he believed that the way to break down prejudice was to demonstrate your ability and not depend upon someone's goodwill. Overlooked is the fact that *The Sporting News* (August 6, 1990) argued that, "Strode's career stands as a vivid testimony to the possibilities in multi-racial harmony." Moreover, the *Los Angeles Times* (March 26, 1991), in talking about breaking down Jim Crow barriers in professional sports, writes, "In many ways, Woody Strode was the best of them. He certainly was the first of them."

No doubt, the authors of *Gold Dust* had their reasons for oversimplifying the source of Strode's confusion, anger, and ostracism by a younger generation of black progressives. However, it is disappointing that there is no thoughtful analysis of the culture shock he experienced from the 1965-Watts riots in Los Angeles or his professional crisis during the changing racial scene in California. Ironically, the logic of why modern audiences dismiss his performances as wooden, his roles as demeaning, and his values as reactionary only reinforce Strode's place in film history as a symbol of Hollywood's racism and adds to his stature as a pioneer in the movie business.

I first met Woody Strode Monday, January 3, 1972. He had recently returned from Italy and was quite agitated about the direction the Human Rights movement was taking in the United States. In addition, his longtime comrade, Kenny Washington, had died the year before, and Strode felt badly about how his friend had not received enough credit for opening doors for blacks in sports. Moreover, his new film, Valerio Zurlini's

Black Jesus (1968), was not getting the support he had wished. To make matters worse, his cherished confidant, John Ford, was gravely ill (and died the following year).

Woody Strode was one of nearly a dozen celebrities I was interviewing for a history of black images in American films. Over the next several days, we spent many hours reminiscing about his life and the times we were going through. A week later, Monday, January 10, he took me to John Ford's home, where we talked for hours with the legendary director about his relationship with Strode. Although they had a father-son association, other members of the family did not always appreciate Strode. At times, the tension between Ford, his wife (who often shouted comments from another room), and Strode became apparent. Ford did not allow me to tape the extraordinary session, but I recorded notes on the meeting afterward. Months later, Strode sent me tapes of an interview that he had done on a New York radio station publicizing *Black Jesus*. Except for some brief correspondence, we never were in contact again.

The man I interviewed had tremendous pride in his ethnic heritage and in his personal achievements, but he had great difficulty in reconciling his deeply held assimilationist views with those of current black progressives. Eventually, his increasing isolation from the sixties generation drove him to a three-year self-exile in Europe (1969 to 1971) and nearly wrecked his film career at home.

Yet, he never deserted the pragmatic lessons he had learned during his formative days in film. To him, the movies were a vehicle to educate others about black talent and black history. His professional training stressed the business side of moving pictures and the necessity of gaining a foothold in the industry before you tried to change it. Paradoxically, the more the actor found favor with traditional directors, the more isolated he became from the unprecedented changes taking place in film and society. Not surprisingly, contemporary critics attacked his commitment to outdated conventions and goals.

After 1973, Woody Strode never again played a leading role in motion pictures. He finished his career doing bit parts. Yet, what makes him so valuable for us is that his career serves as a significant record of the price those African-American artists paid when the times and the standards changed.

Interview with Woody Strode
January 3, 1972

Manchel: First question. Tell me how you met John Ford.

Strode: Oh, I've known him for maybe like twenty-five years. I was in school with a couple of boys that he had adopted, Hawaiian kids. He was very hung up with the Hawaiian people, you know for years, and my wife went to school with his children.

But I never really got to meet Mr. Ford until I did a little picture called *Pork Chop Hill* [1959], and we're out [working] for Sy Bartlett.

Pork Chop Hill, *directed by Lewis Milestone, is an unjustly ignored film about an ironic 1953 incident showing the cost of propaganda struggles in the Korean War, with an outstanding cast that includes Gregory Peck, Harry Guardino, Rip Torn, James Edwards, Robert Blake, Harry Stanton, and Martin Landau. Woody Strode plays Franklin, a disillusioned black soldier who at first loses his courage and then performs heroically in battle.*

Strode: This is the first dramatic thing that I had done, and he [Ford] was on the same lot with me, and he sent his chauffeur over to find me. So I went over to see him, and he says, "I hear you're trying to be an actor." At that point, I was wrestling for a living, and I said, "Oh, I'm just making a little money." I didn't really go into detail. He said, "I'll tell you what, Woody. I got a little job for you, and I'll tell you about it when I get through with this picture that I'm doing." He was doing [*The*] *Horse Soldiers* [1959], with John Wayne and Bill Holden. In the meantime, I didn't pay any attention to that. I took off. I figured that I would go back into the ring. And my agency said, "Well, Woody, you might become an actor, blah, blah, blah. Why don't you stick around?" So I stayed in town for about three months and caught *Spartacus* [1960].

Spartacus, *directed by Stanley Kubrick, is an epic film about the slave rebellion against the strength of the Roman Empire during the first century B.C. The outstanding cast includes Kirk Douglas, Laurence Olivier, Jean Simmons, Peter Ustinov, and Charles Laughton. Woody Strode plays Draba, the heroic gladiator who sacrifices his life rather than kill a fellow slave.*

Strode: I didn't [think] that I was going to get me a motion picture career going until I worked there for fifteen weeks. Caught another picture called the [*The*] *Last Voyage* [1960], with Bob [Stack].

The Last Voyage, *written and directed by Andrew Stone, is a Hitchcock-like story about an explosion aboard a luxury liner at sea, featuring Robert Stack, Dorothy Malone, George Sanders, and Edmund O'Brien. Woody Strode plays Hank Lawson, a heroic seaman who bravely tries to rescue the heroine during the catastrophic fire aboard ship. He was billed fifth in the cast credits. It was released in mid-February, 1960, three months before* Sergeant Rutledge *[May] and eight months before* Spartacus *[October]. A reexamination of these three films will show that Strode was much more than the current conventional wisdom that all Strode did in his early films was to look imposing and perform meaningless tasks.*

Strode: Went to Japan. At the end of the picture, I got a wire from Mr. Ford, and he said [that] he's got a picture for me. It is called *Sergeant Rutledge* [1960]. And boy, I flew in, just got in time. And I went down to the horse ranch, sat up on a horse for a few days, and off we go to Monument Valley with all the Navajos.

Sergeant Rutledge, *directed by John Ford, reveals the director's continuing post-World War II efforts to revise his image of minorities in the old West, and features Jeffrey Hunter, Constance Towers, Billie Burke, and Juano Hernandez. Strode, billed third in the credits, plays Sgt. Braxton Rutledge, the heroic master sergeant of the U. S. Ninth Black Cavalry, unjustly facing a court-martial for the rape and murder of a white woman and her father. Ignored when it first appeared, the film has undergone a rebirth in the last few years. Typical of the revisionist thinking is Armond White's judgment, "What I once disdained as an icon of American traditionalism, white supremacy, and historical distortion was newly revealed to be of genuine interest. And in* The Sun Shines Bright *and* Judge Priest *– the films that explain how Ford got to* Sergeant Rutledge *– I saw an unexpected, authentic complexity about race and history and American social temperament."*[11]

Strode: So, in the meantime, it is very interesting about the job because the big studios wanted an actor like Sidney [Poitier] or [Harry] Belafonte. And this is not being facetious, but Mr. Ford defended me; and I don't know that this is going on. He said, "Well, they're not tough enough to do what I want *Sergeant Rutledge* to be."

So I get on this Navajo Reservation.... I'm sitting up on a horse ... I haven't been on a horse for about fifteen years. You know, we get educated and we got away from it. I was born out here where you rode all the time. And I'm sitting up on top of a mountain and the wrangler is up there with me, and John Ford is now going to put the needle to me. And he says, "You know, Woody, no black man has ever done this on the screen." He said, "I'd sure hate to double you." And now he turned me on. And so the cowboy is standing right beside me, and he says, "You know, Woody, when you ride along this edge, you just pull this horse up and when you get ready to start down that mountain, don't you try to guide him. Just let him go. He doesn't want to fall down."

All right, here comes the ride. *Sergeant Rutledge* is about to escape because he is up for rape and murder of two [sic] white women. And at this point, as I come along this ridge and there is about a twenty foot drop, I look across and I see the Indians about to trap the black cavalry and now I got to make a choice. And you'll see a moment on screen when I make a decision. And I turn and I start to go, down the mountain I go. Well, I let this horse pick his own way down, and I got to cross the Pecos River. So at that moment John Ford give me such a shot, so I got the whole race on my back, now and I'm going down that mountain, I got this nine-pound gun. Instead of holding it in front of me, I decided to give it a glory hallelujah ride; and I raised it up in the air and here across the river I start. And as the horse hit the river, he had to make a clearance, and he leaped. I'm still in the saddle. By the time he hit the river, it was so slippery out there, he's on a dead run and the nine-pound gun was just about to pull me out of the saddle. We'd just made it across, and I skidded in the horse. I looked at old Jeffrey Hunter, and they said, "Cut." Well, I've been on horseback ever since *Sergeant Rutledge*.

[It's] on account of this old man that I am really hung up in the West, you know. So the Ford thing is really something unique, and Monday I hope to have you talk with Papa Ford, because....

Interestingly, almost everyone in the John Ford Stock Company and Ford's biographers refer to Ford as "Pappy." It seems that only Strode called him "Papa." I adopted Strode's appellation ever since.

Manchel: Tell me about *Sergeant Rutledge*. What was it like with the script?

Strode: Well, Papa Ford, let me give you an idea why. He said, "Woody, we'd like to show what the black man did in American history that most of us don't know anything about." I knew my mother was born back in those days, but most of the people your age, even when it was made, they didn't know, not even the blacks knew. He said, "We would like to show that they helped build the American West also." And we were lost in the history because eighty-five years of our history was in the archives and nobody had printed it. So John Ford thought he would do something graceful. Way before anybody started to march or decided to do anything, he just did it on his own.

And they weren't even ready for *Sergeant Rutledge*. Because the unique thing about it ... and it's not a facetious thing I'm trying to say. I've got to say it's a trend of the times. To get star billing takes a lot of maneuvering to star in a picture. Other stars have their rights.

So I had the main title [role] ... in *Sergeant Rutledge*, but I [only] had feature billing. Do you understand? But I was the star of the picture; and Mr. Ford said, "Woody, it's not my fault." Well, I know the script rights that the stars have; and most of the public, they don't know anything about that.

This is just about how Hollywood, how it really was. For any white actor to star, he, like [Steve] McQueen, would have the say, whose name's going to be first, who's going to be next to me? It's got to be a guy comparable, Henry Fonda or somebody like that. It's very difficult for the new actor to come through.

Manchel: What about the script itself? Did you have a chance to react to the script? Or did you take it just as it was?

Strode: Oh no. I tell you the script was so well written. I have scenes like this. The scene on the stand where I've refused to talk, and they're hollering and screaming and says, "This Negro ... raped these two [sic] young blah, blah...." This hammered on me. Well, the old man started persecuting me, but he was playing me just like the harp because at this moment the sensitivity had to show.

Now, here's what happened on that morning. The line was, it made me cry. It's got to be well written and you have to able to take direction, but I had to get the real true emotion from me. Why did I come back? My answer to the prosecuting attorney was, "Because the Ninth Cavalry was my home, and my real freedom, and my self-respect. And the way I was running, I wasn't nothing but a swamp-running Nigger and I ain't that. I'm a man!" And I stood up, and the water started. And I got mad, because I was embarrassed; and I hit the seat and I broke the seat in the first scene. And John Ford said, "Woody, that's it. Now hold the tears back. Complete crying is a weakness." And that was in session five hours.

Now that's been twelve years. When I say them lines, I still feel it. Do you hear me? Because it was true. Because at that moment I had never been in the South in my whole life, but I had to become a Southern black, because I'm Western. No white man had kicked me that I couldn't punch back, but I had to become Sergeant Rutledge, and John Ford got it out of me. After *Sergeant Rutledge*, I was capable of going into anything where I knew that I had the confidence at all. I didn't realize what I really had. John Ford saw it in me.

Another scene in *[The Man Who Shot] Liberty Valance* [1962]....

The Man Who Shot Liberty Valance, *directed by John Ford, is one of the legendary filmmaker's classic tales. It focuses on a greenhorn lawyer from the East who unknowingly gets help from a rugged cowboy in taming the frontier. The splendid cast includes John Wayne, James Stewart, Lee Marvin, Vera Miles, Andy Devine, Lee Van Cleef, Strother Martin, and John Carradine. Woody Strode plays Pompey, Wayne's devoted sidekick.*

Strode: The old scene, hair, old man, John Wayne is dead. My eyes are down. Now I've got to get up and cry and say, "Oh Miss Halley." [She's] coming through the door. And I'm about to panic. I don't know how to act crying. I have to have the moment.

The old man [Ford] starts the organ going for me all for about four hours on the set ... got me in the room ... playing "Sweet Lalanne" and all this funeral music. At one o'clock in the afternoon he says, "Are you ready?" I'm kind of half-mad at him now; I says, "Yeah I'm ready." He's playing me again like a harp. He's ready to split my personality again. So I've got my head bowed down and he's sitting there looking at me like a rattlesnake. He said, "Are you ready?" I said, "Yeah." I'm getting mad at him now. He said, "Well, pull your head up." I said, "Can I start with my eyes down?" He said, "Keep them down then." And when he said, "Action." I said to myself, "You old son of a bitch." And he said, "Now stand up and look at the door." And I stood up and the tears started. And I'm ashamed, I shut my eyes. And he said, "Open your eyes." He said, "That's it."

Now, he done split my personality again, that son of a bitch. Do you hear me? I had the greatest direction from this guy. I don't know. He's played all my emotions. I had them all there. He just [led me] bing, bing, bing.

Manchel: He played with the greatest [stars] though.

Strode: Right. Now, I get away from him and I go off. And I do a picture, and I come back. And he does another one called *Two Rode Together* [1961], and he made me play Stone Calf.

Two Rode Together, *directed by John Ford, told the story of a misanthropic marshal paid by the army to rescue whites long held captive by the Comanches. Included in the distinguished cast are James Stewart, Richard Widmark, Shirley Jones, Andy Devine, James McIntire, Harry Carey, Jr., Olive Carey, and Mae Marsh.*

Strode: He had a big fight about that even. Because he said, "Woody, I can't make a star out of you, but I'm going to make you a character actor." That was the trend of the times. There was no black stars. But he said, "I'll make you a character actor and you will make money." Got feathers now ...

played a chief; he taught me the Navajo language at the moment.

I tell you what. [I finish] *Genghis Khan* [1965].

Genghis Khan, *directed by Henry Levin, is a second-rate film that mutilates the life of the fabled Mongolian hero. Among the important actors badly miscast are Omar Sharif, James Mason, Robert Morley, Stephen Boyd, Eli Wallach, and Telly Savalas. Woody Strode plays Sengal, the warlord's mute follower.*

Strode: I come back from overseas, [and Ford] stuck me in *Seven Women* [1966].

Seven Women, *the last feature film directed by John Ford, transports the conventions of the Western to Mongolia, where a group of innocent people are saved from an evil warlord by a heroic female doctor. The famous cast included Anne Bancroft, Sue Lyon, Margaret Leighton, Flora Robson, and Eddie Albert. Woody Strode plays Lean Warrior, who fights the warlord in a battle to the death.*

Strode: He put a hold on me. What a dignified thing he did. He closed my eyes.... I'm on a set with a bunch of Chinese kids. I'm a little embarrassed because I got the best role. The Chinese kids said, "Woody, you look more Chinese than we do. It's great." So it made me feel good.

John Ford had laid right on top of that [my image] "character actor," "character actor!" Because the black day hadn't arrived yet where you have instant stars. But I'm much happier now in this position like I told the *New York Times*. I don't have to represent. I have fans all over the world now.

Manchel: Woody, did you ever resent the fact that he said to you, "I'll make you a character actor?"

Strode: No! No! I knew, I knew that this is a white medium. The white audiences of the whole world was there. They hadn't found the black audience yet. That was the trend of the times, but I was able to skin the cat. The only time I ever got embarrassed.... I lost a job in *Major Dundee* [1965]. I might as well call the names because this is going to have to go down in history.

[Working with] Jerry Bressler, after I'd done Tarzan with Jock Mahoney, I played a Mongol.

Tarzan's Three Challenges *(1963), directed by Robert Day, is an underrated story about Tarzan's protection of a Tai prince threatened by his evil uncle. Woody Strode plays Tarzan's warrior antagonist. Gabe Essoe, in his significant study of films about Edgar Rice Burroughs's legendary hero,* **Tarzan of the Movies,** *states that it "was the most visually arresting of the entire series [by independent* *producer Sy Weintraub]."*[12] *It's worth noting that Woody had appeared in a couple of earlier Tarzan films, one of which, H. Bruce Humberstone's* Tarzan's Fight for Life *(1958), allegedly started his screen image as a bald-headed giant.*

Strode: My first Mongol movie with my mustache. I had a Southern Chinese boy, who is brown-skinned, play my son who looked like my son [Kali, his first born child; he also had a daughter, June]. And these are unique things on the world market. I come home, and they brought me in for the interview, for what reason I don't know. And Mr. Bressler was saying, "Woody, you're magnificent and blah, blah, blah, but we have a part with a blackie, and he is shining a fellow's shoes. And he's going to call him a Nigger. But when they look at the screen...." And he kept fumbling around with the words. And Sam Peckinpah was sitting over in the corner. And he says, "Woody, what he's trying to tell you, you're not a black, you're a Mongolian."

Well, now he done slap my face. Here I'd been slipped around, made a pretty good living, just playing anything but a white man. I'd done everything but be white! And if I'd kept fooling around, I'd got some contact lenses, put some blond hair on, cause we did that once when I was bald headed, I looked like a sun-tanned Viking. I said, "Well, I'm through!"

I went back to my little agent, and I said, "Well, Sid, what am I going to do?" I've never gone on these oriental interviews. The producers have just said, "We better get Woody, because he knows how to fight. He can ride and he can do this." I get a job. He backed me up against the wall and he said, "Are you a coward or you got the guts?" He gave me a real pep talk. I said, "What the hell am I going to do?" He said, "Just relax."

So the next month, here comes Columbia, like an apology. I go out there with my big speeches. "Why don't we make something like *Sergeant Rutledge*? Could you imagine *Sergeant Rutledge* with [Harry] Belafonte, Sidney Poitier, Sammy Davis?" I said, "I had to carry the whole thing alone." I don't know what it would have been if we had some muscle up there, in the same plot, but had the top black actors, together, sort of separated. He said, "Go down and see my man Jerry Airs [?]."

I went downstairs and started lecturing; and he's looking at me and he's casting. I got nothing wrong with a bunch of head skin. He said, "Irwin Allen is about to make a picture called *Genghis Khan*. He's probably cast it all. But I think I'm going to call him." He called him up. "Irwin?" "Yeah." "Woody." "Yeah." "Got upstairs." "Yeah. I got a part for Woody." "Is it the mute?" "No, Woody can talk." He said, "The mute goes all the way with Omar Sharif." He said, "I'll call his agent." "No," he said, "I'll call his agent." This is now apology time. I'm sorry. Do you understand? He told me I wasn't a Nigger.

Mrs. Strode: You had a chance with Papa again in *Cheyenne Autumn* [1964]. But they still thought they didn't want you.

Strode: They have always fought against my type of character. I don't know. Here's what they haven't gotten used to. I'm possibly the only black that has played Indians, Chinese.... I'm actually the only real character actor. I don't consider myself a glamorous star, but I have a lot of fans because I am an action character actor. If it calls for a Mongol, old Woody can shave his head. I'd stick the pigtail, and I can convince them that I am a Mongol. And so I think what they had to adjust to here in this industry, they all like Woody, but "Woody play the chief?" It was beyond their thinking; and you know, in Rome, the Italians just shoved me in the pictures because I had the abilities and I just about become an Italian. The color meant nothing there, but I think the Europeans' mind is much more open. We're too hung up emotionally with the blacks here.

So, everybody who liked me in the industry kept me working. But when it really got down to it, I'm the only one who can get up on that horse and convince somebody that I'm Crazy Horse. The rest of them can say the lines and talk, blah, blah, blah, but I can say the lines and start a war dance. And this is what I think convinces the audience.

I watched [Toshiro] Mifune with my son. I watched him ride horses. I've watched him fight. He handles that samurai sword like a gun fighter. Sergio Leone's *Fistful of Dollars* [1964], which Clint Eastwood made, was taken off of the samurai. I can't call it, my son called it off for me. Yes! *Yojimbo* [1961]. He come into the town like a gunman and he worked both sides. And when the shootout come ... swish, swish, swish with the sword, and it was beautiful. Now, when I saw this man, I told my son, "This is why he's on the world market."

Stanislavski, I've read his books. I've never gone to his theory, but Ted Post, the director, gave me a book, five years away. "Woody, I want to show you what you're doing. But don't let nobody teach you that." I read *An Actor Prepares* by Stanislavski. I found out that I was using my own emotions. Then they was playing me like a harp, that was when I got mad at all the directors, because they took advantage of me, of my sensitivity. When I got mad, I got mad. That's why the audience believes the scenes. When I suffered, I cried. I don't know how to act. I don't know how to do that. I have to cry, and I was capable of doing it and this was convincing. And an actor friend of mine, Jimmy Edwards, said, "Woody, if you're true, you do not have to act."

But here's where they're lost. Stanislavski had taught that [it was important] to take care of the body, not just the mind. Acting is coming to only the middle scene now. And then they cut to the double, and he walks and runs to the door. But I think [that's when] I've got the audience. They come in on me [for] the close-up, then the lion comes to the door, he jumps on Woody, and he got the camera there. And Woody has to get the sword, and he has to kill the lion. And that gives me fans because they believe it. Without being a star!

Manchel: Nobody doubts it.

Strode: Without being a star! They wouldn't believe me, and I got ... [credibility. She, the spectator, does say], "Oh, Woody Strode!"... only because she believes what I was doing. Because I didn't have the glamorous role, but I was [impressive] with those little moments I did, [I] was convincing. If I got killed, they say, "Jesus Christ, he come right through the door, poor guy, you know." This is the whole scene. I believe ... for me, I'm always playing cowboy and Indians. I'm playing cowboy now. My whole mind is cowboy. So, when I get the script I just get on the horse. I'm there. I'm right back in 1880. It ain't no big deal with me. You don't have to bring me, my mind out of.... As soon as I get on....

I told my director there, Danny Mann, who had some of the great classics, *The Rose Tattoo* [1955] and *Come Back Little Sheba* [1952]. This director who's had all these classics, and he looked at me and I said, "Well." He said, "Are you going to double?" I said, "No." I said, "All I got to do is just put on the guns." As the scene starts. Can you imagine that? It's magic. And he says, "Well, Woody." I said, "No, I don't have to rehearse. I don't want to rehearse. It will just wear me out." I said, "Just give me the lines. Let me just put the guns on. What do you want me to do?" Do you hear me? It starts the.... And I said, "If I'm true, the magic starts and you believe it."

And this is how it happened. I have the enthusiasm like if I was nineteen years old. Now, the well-studied actors, they know so much until ... just when it's ready for their scenes. And because of the blah, blah, blah, and then they go back to sleep. But my insecurity. I'm right here when she's talking and you're talking and that guy's talking and boom, now it's my turn. I'm going to stop and say "My god," and it's kept me alive in the goddam scene before I knew what I was doing.

And that's why the directors used to call my office. "I don't know how Woody is doing it." And I would be just working my ass off. "Woody, learn your lines. Learn your lines. Don't pay any attention to what they tell you about acting." It took me all these years and watch me go over there and try to say these new paragraphs that they had given me. Be having to scratch my eyes and don't be looking, I'd be looking up in the sky waiting for the words to be coming back to me. So all I needed was a good director, a writer, and an artistic writer to put the words in your mouth. That's all you need.

Manchel: What's the story on [*Major*] *Dundee* though?

Strode: *Major Dundee* [1965]? Ah! They had to have ... the image of the American black is not a mixture. Hollywood created an African image for us. And we don't have it. We're mixtures. We're different than any other group, black group, in the whole world. Most of us are some part of the white or of the Indian extraction. That's the American black. And so, there's no such thing as....

I'll tell you what, the actors now, I'd hate to call their names, but like Brock [Peters] and Sidney [Poitier]. Those guys come out of the Caribbean who are of African extraction. But they're not the American Negro. We could see the American Negro. He's all mixed up. He's just ... we got all kinds of colors. He says, "Well, what is he?" We got some of them like Chinamen. They got Chinese blood in them. We got Jewish blacks.

The man who is a manager for Ray Charles, father was a Jew, Joe Adams. Did you know that? Imagine the blacks have to hide and go and duck and hide. We used to look at him, and he had that nice brown skin and the Jewish boy had rosy cheeks. He is good looking; he and his brother, Joe Adams, father was a Jew; and as far as anybody says, he's just another Nigger. It's a funny thing about the black's blood. It seems to have negated everything that you might be mixed with. I used to tell this to Papa Ford. He said, "Woody, why didn't you ever say you had Indian blood?" I said, "Papa, after forty years being a Nigger, if you hadn't got on the screen and looked at me with my shaved head, my big old cheek bones, nobody would of thought nothing." Now, I'm a Sioux. They'll laugh. But I said, "You can say I'm Irish, Spanish, French-Indian. And nobody thinks nothing if it's a white man that says that."

But the black in this country is in an awkward position. Adam Clayton Powell is a white man. He's sitting on the [David] Susskind program, who's got kinky hair. This is ten, twelve years ago. Susskind is nailing him and says, "Well, Mr. Powell, how much black blood have you got?" Powell looked back at Susskind, and he says, "I think you got more in you than in me." Because his hair was kinky, and Powell looked like an Italian.

So, we're the most affluent black group in the whole world and we have poverty. I'm not going to ignore that. Of course, I'm baffled because I was born out in the West. I don't know what Southern poverty is. And I can't even talk in that area. But, all I know is that if you move over ... you've got to have a certain amount of drive to get up off the ground. I ain't no genius. And I've been able to go to Italy. And because I ride and I fight and I run up and down that mountain and I saw that rope and I shoot the bow, the Italian says, "Well, give this ditch digger a job."

If I'm able to do that in a foreign land, then in this affluent country, I should be able to steal the money. It's amazing here, that's all.

Manchel: Well, how about *Major Dundee*?

Strode: Well, I lost the job on *Major Dundee* because I wasn't black enough. What they wanted was a man that was black in color and they didn't know how to tell me. And all that [Sam] Peckinpah! I found out in later years, why he's so hung up; his mother was Indian. He resents it. Can you imagine that, Peckinpah? That's why he got that goddam name.

Manchel: What happened on the *Cheyenne Autumn* story?

Strode: Well, I read both books, Howard Fast's book and Mari Sandoz's book; and I said, "Papa, you'll have to use both books because Howard Fast wrote about the white officers. You cast them out of his book. Mari Sandoz's book wrote how the Indians fought and retreated, dug trenches. The first hundred pages made me cry, *Cheyenne Autumn*, and I was going to play Little Wolf because I could physically do everything; and he called Anthony Quinn to get him to play Dull Knife.

In the 1964 John Ford film, the part of Little Wolf is played by Ricardo Montalban; the part of Dull Knife is played by Gilbert Roland; and Howard Fast's name is not in the film's credits.

Strode: When it got out at Warners and the big people got involved, they decided against me. Another big fight. He [Ford] said to me, "Woody would you like to.... I'm fighting about you again...Would you like to play the medicine man?" I said, "No, Papa. You go ahead and do your picture."

So, before I went away on *Genghis Kahn*, he was shooting and I took off. But I wouldn't go on the set to see him because we were very dear friends, and I didn't want him to be embarrassed. Or I didn't want to be embarrassed with someone on the set saying, "Woody, when are you going to start working?" So, I went to Europe, finished *Genghis Kahn*, come home, and I stopped in London.

I had mixed emotions to go and see *Cheyenne Autumn*. My personal opinion, he didn't do it. He got mad. In addition, I do not know why ... [and] I will never know why, but he didn't do it. He disjointed it, and he was a big enough man to disjoint it because I was closer to *Cheyenne Autumn* than anybody, because I read both books for him a year away before they got prepared to even do the picture. And I sat in the show with mixed emotions.

I came home and I said, "Papa, you didn't do *Cheyenne Autumn*." He said, "It was good enough for them."

I witnessed the scene again when Woody and I were talking in Ford's bedroom, where the director was recovering from a hip operation. At one point in our conversation, Strode suddenly began listing various reasons why Cheyenne

Autumn *was not accurate. Ford, who treated Woody like a son, stared Strode down, saying, "It was good enough!"*

Strode: But Little Wolf's story is still there to be done. You see *Cheyenne Autumn* is so great; it was like the Greek's march to the sea. It was such a disgrace until they give the land back. Little Wolf and sixty warriors.

I get emotional when I talk about it because I'm close to it, see. That's why in the newspaper I told them, "They ain't going to ever stick me in a suit of clothes, because I've got something to tell." I got the fire. Very few of the actors got the fire left to really put it on the screen.

Manchel: Woody, let me ask you a question. It's always bothered me about you knowing Ford that well [and there being so much talk about his and John Wayne's alleged racist attitudes]. John Wayne recently did an interview for *Playboy* [1971]. It was one of the ugliest interviews I've seen.

Strode: Well, let me see. I think he's misquoted. You see, John Wayne is unfortunate because he is the right wing. I don't care if you was, whatever you believe in, you believed in the devil, as long as you didn't try to be a missionary and incorporate old Woody, we'd work together. But John is always standing up for, they call him a complete right wing this and right wing that. But they got him over the barrel, and they misquoted him. I believe they misquoted him because I don't believe he is stupid enough or facetious enough to just quote, "I don't like Jews, and I don't like them niggers, and I don't like them Indians." And he wipes us all out.

A valuable documentary about the relationship between Wayne and Ford, as well as their politics, is Sam Pollard's documentary show on American Masters: John Ford/John Wayne: The Filmmaker and the Legend *(2006). The relevant quote from the movie deals not only with the fourteen films the men made together, but the view that their association "showed all the contradictions and paradoxes of our country's power in the twentieth century: it's generosity and its racism, its pioneering spirit and its despair over our loss of innocence." Sydney Pollack, the narrator, goes on to say, "Together, these two men created a series of images that even a generation after their death defines in many ways both what this nation represents to the world and ultimately how we've come to think of ourselves."*

Manchel: Is he that kind of guy?

Strode: No! No! No! He's not like that. I don't believe that. All he did was.... He wouldn't dignify it by fighting back. So John Wayne will go down in history, whatever they say he is, who I wanted to be like when I first started.

Manchel: He's the greatest cowboy star.

Interestingly, when Strode and I were visiting with Ford, I raised the issue of how he would classify Woody as an actor: "The greatest black cowboy of them all?" Ford replied, "A great actor!" I repeated my question, "A great cowboy actor?" Moreover, he repeated his position, "A great actor."

Strode: Yeah. But they weren't just ready for me, that's all. They just weren't ready to see a man like me do this. Now, it will come a time when they will make a black cowboy. And I hope he just ain't phony, just for expediency.

Another Ford anecdote worth mentioning in this connection concerns our discussions about black celebrities Jesse Owens and Lincoln "Stepin Fetchit" Perry, who were both being attacked at the time as "Uncle Toms." Strode and Ford both insisted that these two men, along with Joe Louis, made the major breakthroughs for blacks in the 1930s. It was a point echoed by Jim Brown in my interview with him the next day, Tuesday, January 11, 1972. Woody elaborates his defense of Stepin Fetchit in Gold Dust.[13]

Manchel: Ford is through? Is he going to make any more movies, John Ford?

Strode: He's interested now in a project. That's why I'm going by the house now. I read his nephew's script, and I was explaining to him, you don't write it for a black man. Just write a good script, and then let's see what parts in there, and let's select one.

So they give me a script. I read the first twenty-eight pages, and I was a little panicky because I couldn't see anything to read myself into. It was pure Mexican. And all of a sudden here comes a white boy called Steve ... but a part showed up there on page thirty, of Steve, the man who would help the Mexicans take this machine and bring it back.

There's where he could have inserted me, a black, a Chinaman, Japanese, actor, or an Italian, or an Englishman, or anybody, and this is what I'm trying to get across. If you write for a black ... now since I've never.... I hadn't been born in the South.

Now, you see how my attitude is. You've been to [interview] most of the blacks. I'm pure Western. I've been with Mama, and it's rubbed off on me. So you can't say that I'm stereotyped. So all I am is an American. But we could get with certain groups of blacks where I wouldn't fit with because their attitudes are entirely different.

Manchel: Me, too, with whites.

Strode: Right. See, okay. Now when you go to writing for a black, then you get yourself hung up because now you have to almost say, well what type of black? Now they've got educated Southern blacks, but when a white man has to sit and write for a black, he's really in a bind. The best thing to do is to pick the period, write a good script, and there's not that much difference between you and I anyway.

Manchel: Oh yes there is!

Strode: I don't believe [it].

Manchel: There's the difference between a star and a guy.

Strode: No! No! Let's look at us now. If they had to photograph....

Mrs. Strode: [Referring to an invitation Strode has just received in the mail] Can you imagine Woody is invited to this thing? It's a sports vacation travel. The Indians want Woody to represent them. Now that's something!

Strode: Well, I'll be down there on the 14th signing autographs and going through the motions. But I don't know, I tell you I don't believe.... I told my agent when I first got home.... I said, "Jack, how are you going to write for me? I ain't black. I'm a cowboy, and I just happen to have a little dark skin, that's all." Now just go on and write it. I'm either rustling cattle.... I'm either going to be a goddam gunslinger; or they can make me a runaway slave, I'm running. Anything! Just write it! Somebody's broke away from a goddam farm, they're after him, and that's it. But I will meet some white friends out there who won't agree with that rigmarole. Do you understand?

Mrs. Strode: [Continues to talk about the sports vacation travel invitation to have Strode represent Native Americans. Among the celebrities she identifies as having signed on for an Indian Actors' Workshop are Glenn Ford, Jonathan Winters, and Jay Silverheels.]

Manchel: I've been reading the *New York Times*. They've [Native-Americans] got the same problem the blacks have had. They haven't been represented properly on the screen, either. He [Jay Silverheels] played the Lone Ranger's Tonto.

Woody, can I ask you some questions about the background as I go back to this? Woody, it says in one of the articles that you were denied a place in football because of color, and you mentioned something about the defensive line.

Strode: Oh! Because of Mama! Here's the thing that happened. The Rams moved to Los Angeles [in 1946]. (Of course, you can edit this you know. We don't want to start no race riot. I'll give you an idea what really happened.) And the white people out here said to the Rams at that particular time, would Kenny Washington get a tryout with your ball club? And they said, "Well, we don't have any blacks in the National League and blah, blah, blah." So the whites said, "Well, if Kenny Washington don't get a tryout, you cannot have the Coliseum."

So that must have ... give you an idea what the Western people were thinking. At that point, we've been doing this all our life. So, they went to

Kenny and said, "Who do you want as a partner?" He said, "Well, I want Woody Strode." They said, "Did you know that Woody Strode married out of his race?" (I married a Hawaiian.) That was their attitude. He said, "If I don't get Woody Strode, I don't want anybody." So they reluctantly took me.

Manchel: Whose attitude was that, that you married out of your race? The owners?

Strode: The owners of the club.

Manchel: Well, why would they be concerned? They were white people.

Strode: Well, those times.... Can you imagine the difference in the whites? You see what I'm trying to say? I had the best white men in the world. Out here in the West, they didn't care. I obeyed the law, and Mama wasn't a white woman. Still, they had that bigotry somewhere, and those white people out here didn't care.

So, when I got on the team, I was offensive and defensive. I only weighed two hundred pounds. They stuck me on defense. So I was ignorant enough and I could play well enough to survive that. I went through the whole year and I was.... I got released.

This is the excuse they use after that year. "Well, it's not your ability but we're going to start a young ball club." I was thirty-two years old. Imagine what shape I must have been in at thirty-two if I'm in this shape now. You can just imagine! All I knew how to do was to run and fight and run. I never knew nothing else. I was like a racehorse, in that generation, like your Dad.

Alright. I didn't get discouraged so I went back east.... The American League started and they [the New York Yankees of the All-American Football Conference] began to say, "Hey, Woody." But I was discouraged, and I'm begging to play football, and nobody liked me, so I don't want to play ball for them.

No! I'll tell you how I got cut. The owners were drunk at a hotel on Sunset Boulevard. And I was living on Hollywood Boulevard, and some bookies knocked on my door. This is embarrassing. "Woody? We want to talk to you." I said, "Wait a minute." I put on a robe and they says, "You know, you got cut off the club last night."

This is how I found out. Hoodlums! Gangsters! "We don't like the way they did it." I said, "What'd they do?" "They were falling down drunk. The owner and the coach by the name of Bob Snyder. Do you want to fight?" I said, "No." I said, "We've been out here all our life, met the Italians, met the Jews, met the Pollacks [sic], every goddam race in the world came out here in the West and no problem. We all lived together in peace." And I said, "No. We've been together all these years, and I'm not going to start the ball going." I said, "I'll lay down." He said to me, "I just want to know if you want to fight." "Forget it!"

Woody Strode describes the incident differently in his autobiography, claiming that he was fired in his second year with the Los Angeles Rams, and that he was first told of being let go by George Trafton, the line coach. He does, however, recount the visit by mobsters. The major differences here is that he claims they were sent by his teammate, Kenny Washington; and the team drunks who discussed his firing the previous evening are identified as Dan Reeves [owner] and Bob Snyder [coach].[14]

Manchel: The bookies were pulling?
Strode: Yes, the enemy. Goddam it, not the City Hall. This is what really shook me up. This is what rerouted my whole life. Now, another white scout approached me, American League. "No," I said, "I don't ever want to go through this again." In addition, he said, "Woody, it won't be like that." In addition, he begged me.
Six months away, I signed. I go back East, they bad-mouthed me because, half million at that period twenty years ago, man if you got cut you got cut because you didn't have blah, blah, blah. I got back there, and this man said to me, "I thought you were an old man, Woody." I was in the best shape of anyone in the camp. Well, the muscles started way back then.

In his Barry Farber interview, Strode talked about his bitter experiences with the New York Black Yankees, who played in a mixed league on the East Coast. One time, he recalled, the team was playing against the Point Pleasant Pelicans in Point Pleasant, New Jersey, and the Yankees couldn't get dressed in the locker room. They had to suit up at the home of a black family down the road. Another time, they had a game in Danbury, Connecticut, and the team went to have lunch in a nearby diner. The owner took one look at the Black Yankees and said, "I'm closed for the day." The team refused to move, and the sheriff came, and closed down the restaurant. It got so, Strode explained, that the team used to eat their meals in reverse. That is, the big, heavy meal came at breakfast, because the players never knew when they could get another meal during the day.

Strode: I didn't get to the scrimmages. So, when they cut me they said, "You know Woody, it's not your ability; it's just that we're going to build a fresh, blah, blah." They went through the whole rigmarole. By then, I was so mad I went to the Buffalo station to get a train to come back home.
Some Frenchman, the only mistake I made, a man by the name of Don Junet, owned the racetracks in Montreal. "Are you Mr. Woody Strode?" I said, "Yes." "I'd like you to come to Montreal." I said, "No thank you, I'm

never going to play football again." I got to fight and worry while playing the whole game of football.

I've never been to the South so, first pressure that I've ever had. I go back to other white people that I know, not these white people. So I stopped in Chicago, licked my wounds, and I got drunk for one week at my cousin's place.

I get a call from Canada, Alberta, Canada. The guy played tackle beside me, Les Lear [player-coach of the Calgary Stampeders]. I go home, and he said, "Woody, I'm coaching." He got cut the same as me. And he says, "I'll give you all the money I can get and pay all of your expenses."

So I'm not going to do anything else. I'm coming. I got my shoes and I go up there [to join The Calgary Stampeders]. He said, "I want you to look at this, like if you were on the Los Angeles Rams, Woody, because the fields are not like it is in the States. I don't want you to act any different." I said, "I won't." I walked on a hockey field. I had canvas pants to practice in.

We went ahead and in 1948 won the National championship, that cup you see me kissing. That was enough to heal all the wounds that they had done to me on this side.

Now, I had met another white group who loved me. Do you understand? All westerners, white people, but they were Canadians and in one year I become immortal up there. It took me all the years in that scrapbook to hang in down here.

So, we were sitting around the table, we had four Americans – Keith Spaith, threw me the passes – and another boy that couldn't get arrested, went to Ohio State, must have been a bad actor. He couldn't get a job. We had Johnny Aguirre from USC, and we're like the Daltons, we're outlaws. We had won a national championship because I picked up the ball and set the scene up for the forty-yard line for the goal, carried it forty yards down that field, was immortalized right there and every province in Canada, was saying, "Congratulations." It had become embarrassing for the American counsel. Finally, the *Times* had to send to the Daltons, "Congratulations." All Los Angeles boys. We were bandits. We were the misfits, but we'd gone into a foreign country and become the kings over football.

Well, I stayed there for three years and got a leg muscle up there in my shoulder, reconstructed the shoulder from playing football. They didn't have a down field block, and I was going both ways.

When I quit, I quit because I got my ribs over the heart busted, and I stayed in the wrestling until the motion picture scene. But I didn't watch football for five years; it always left a bad taste in my mouth.

And so when I got back East for *Black Jesus* [1968, 1971], I wouldn't go into my persecution scene, because I'd say if UPI wanted me to get right on the wire service, I'd say, "If I did this now, twenty-five years later," I'd say, " The young blacks...." Why they would burn down Randall Stadium. I came back here to advertise *Black Jesus*. I'm an actor. It's another ball game.

Black Jesus, an Italian-made film directed by Valerio Zurlini, gave Woody Strode his first star billing. The original screenplay focused on Maurice Lalubi [Strode], an incarcerated, persecuted, and executed African idealist who advocated nonviolence against a brutal white regime. In his interview with Barry Farber, Woody told how he worked four days a week, from seven a.m. to eleven p.m., to create his trance-like appearance. For him, the picture meant a chance for Americans to see on screen how blacks are willing to sacrifice their lives for a cause. While the film got almost universally bad notices, the star received high praise from the New York Times, saying that "The face of Mr. Strode is memorable."[15] *Woody provides a brief description of the film in his autobiography, listing it as* Seduto Alla Sua Black Jesus/Seated at His Right. *Interestingly, neither the movie nor Strode is mentioned in Kenneth M. Cammeron's* Africa on Film: Beyond Black and White *(1994).*

    Manchel: Woody, was there any other trouble about the interracial marriage ... in films at all?
    Strode: No. Only there, [in the football world] because out here, black and whites been slipping around with one another, they've been sleeping in beds....
    Mrs. Strode: Only once, when I tried to get Woody in my film.
    Strode: Mama was good in film. She was doing pictures and she wanted me to play her lover. But it wasn't Monogram Studio. I'm right there on the set. They said, "Luana, they ain't going to accept Woody." And I'm her husband. She had to play opposite a little white blond-headed kid. And I'm right there on the set and the producer was great, but I wondered where are we going to sell it? At that point, it wasn't here. It was how do they put it out there.
    Manchel: What was the film? Do you remember?
    Strode: *Sweet Hawaiian Dreams*, and I was going to be her lover.
    Manchel: When was this? What year?
    Mrs. Strode: l939! And then we made a picture together. We walked in....

The date is clearly wrong, since Strode did not marry Luana until 1940, and the next two films she made were in 1952 and 1953. In addition, there are no records of such a film. The project probably was in 1951.

Strode: We walked in Universal Studios, *Caribbean Gold* [released as *Caribbean* [1952]. And I told Mama, I said, "Mama, it's something that we are able to walk through the studio gates together...."

Caribbean, directed by Edward Ludwig, is a typical B-film about a swashbuckling hero warring against vicious pirates and the slave trade in the 18th century. The cast includes John Payne, Cedric Hardwicke, Arlene Dahl, and Francis L. Sullivan. Woody Strode played Esau, a captured slave.

Mrs. Strode: That wasn't *Caribbean Gold*. That was *City Beneath the Sea* [1953].

City Beneath the Sea, directed by Budd Boetticher, is another negligible B-film; this time about robust deep-sea divers searching for lost treasures in the West Indies. The cast includes Robert Ryan and Anthony Quinn. Woody Strode plays Djion, the first mate.

Strode: *The City Beneath the Sea*, and we walked through the gate together. And she worked; she was working in a picture the same time I was. So I personally don't believe Hollywood ever cared. It was just....
Manchel: The box-office?
Strode: No. They didn't know where the box-office really was. They catered to the Southern box-office.

During the heyday of Hollywood's studio system, the leaders of the American oligopoly believed that the powerful Southern film audience operated as a barometer on racial stereotypes. Hollywood filmmakers, therefore, shaped their images of minorities to fit those regional prejudices. Although the studio system was dismantled by the end of the fifties, many Hollywood insiders continued to believe that the Southern box-office remained paramount in determining the commercial success of a movie. In the Hollywood of the sixties, many groundbreaking productions struggled to disprove that long-held assumption.

Woody Strode's attitudes about that myth remind us of its lingering effect on the film industry. Professor Thomas Cripps, who has written the most relevant essay on how the myth influenced American filmmakers to falsify African-American values and behavior, argues that not only were "the tastes and prejudices of the American South ... at the core of ... [the major film companies'] decision-making processes ... [But also] it allowed them the luxury of creating the concomitant myth of their own innocence."[16] Ian Jarvie, however, disputes Cripps' position, insisting that at the core of racial stereotyping was the filmmakers' reluctance to make controversial movies that depleted potential profits.[17]

Manchel: I've heard that theory over and over again.

Strode: They didn't have the world market when you were a baby.

Manchel: Why the Southern box-office?

Strode: You know why? There was a lot of money in the South. There was a great market for them there. Can you imagine that?

Manchel: This is what I've heard over and over again.

Strode: No. But now they don't care, because they got the world market. See, what I quoted in the press, "We don't need the United States. You make a good picture, you and me, man. I don't care. We take it to Italy. We just make our money right there. I don't know when we are going to bring it in the States. We sent it to England and France and Germany." Bypass the States maybe two or three years. Until they said, "Well, we done got all the money and what can we do? Well, let's take it into the States and show it around theaters and kick it into TV and get some money." There's so many ways now.

Manchel: Has anyone picked it up on TV yet? *Black Jesus*?

Strode: Oh no. I tell you what. They're embarrassed. You see, what embarrasses the whole scene....

Manchel: They don't know what to do.

Strode: They don't know what to do *with me*! I've lasted long enough to get the fringe benefits. I didn't get my share of work....

Mrs. Strode: In Woody's picture that he made in Spain....

Strode: I got Marcello Mastroianni. My last picture in Rome, if they ever get that one. I'll tell you what I was doing. I am an actor. I'm not a Colored actor. Do you hear me? I'll tell you what I almost got. If I hadn't of come home, goddam it, I'd of made an Israeli western. Right. I had to come home and see my son.

I wish I could have made the Israeli western, and I would of wiped out the whole world. Do you understand me? Do you know what they were doing? They were contacting me because I was a cowboy. We'll make him the star because I can fight and do the thing.

And this is where I think I am embarrassed [when] I'm here [in America]. I think I am more like the prodigal son come home. And they thought that I was going to live in the promised land and never come back and we'd all be able to say, "Well, Woody was wonderful and we all love him and all that." And I don't fit the black scene. I don't fit the stereotype thing that they would want to produce.

Manchel: I think that that's changing, Woody. I think it is in the big cities, but I think in the small towns, I think it's different.

Strode: I hope so.

Manchel: Let me ask you another question. You made a statement in one of the papers that guns were only issued to blacks when there was fighting to be done during the war [World War II].

Strode: Oh. I was in an organization where the guns were locked up even overseas. I'll give you an example. There was a.... I was on Guam. I had a Jewish commanding officer. I didn't know he's Jewish, to show you how we really thought out in the West. What makes a Jew? How the hell do I know? Captain Green was all I know.

Saturday night we were laying in bed. Bam! I got up. We always slept naked with our shoes on. I got up and I said, "That was a shot." Looked over, the light was on at the headquarters. I go over, put a towel around me, and boom! Captain Green is saying to the blacks, "All right, you all go back to bed." He's taking over now.

I knew something happened. I got to know him. They were Southern blacks, I wasn't. I looked at him like he was a white man. I said, "I'm not going to bed until you tell me what happened." And he looked me dead in the eye, and he went right down to the floor. He says, "They aren't Jewish." I ain't never thought whatever he was. I don't think like that. He said, "They shot, the Marine next to us, shot this black boy." And the only thing he said, "He just felt like shooting a Nigger." He said, "They're not going to do anything about it." In addition, he says, "These are all the M-1s that we got locked up. If they was machine guns, I'd issue them." But he says, "I'm a Jew and I got a little boy and a wife that I want to see."

And I bowed my head down on the floor. Because he stopped me when he said he was a Jew. I just thought he was a white man. I know, he might as well be black. I said, "All right, I know, okay." And I got up and walked away. That cooled me off, right then, because we ain't got a chance. They weren't going to do nothing. This is in the archives. This is on record. This is recorded. I've seen it. To think....

Manchel: Do you object to my telling that story?

Strode: No! Tell it! Tell it! I don't care how you ... you might as well tell some goddam history! I ain't going to make no million dollars, and I'm not going to kiss nobody's ass. You might as well. Just go on and ... somebody's got to tell the goddam truth.

Leo Cantor, who's a Russian Jew.... And we never thought about that, and he's overseas in Honolulu. We've won through the service football. We did the whole rigmarole. We used to bootleg near March Field. Before we got overseas, we used to come into town and buy the whiskey and sell it to the officers.

Mrs. Strode: Woody did something. He had to. His life is dependent. He can sign up under contract to MGM like Lena Horne. She got signed. Woody can sign up because they were going to make a picture together. So, what can he do? When they picked up the numbers to be drafted, he was one of the first ones. So what did he do? He goes to his....

Strode: But, if we don't tell the truth now, it will never be told, because I'm not a Southern black, so I've got a whole new perspective.

You take General Hap Arnold [Commander-in-Chief of the Air Force in World War II] and Paul Schissler [coach and owner of the Hollywood Bears, a semi-pro football team in the Pacific Coast League]. I'm with the Southern ball club in March Field for three years, and they integrated me under the table in a white outfit and made me trail them from field to field until we got on that boat to be embarked to the Mariannas. It's a whole big facade.

I'm not mad because there's a bad white and there's a good one. You can't buck everybody, and my whole career has been earned because of hard work and some white looking in and saying, "Well, he knows how to do the job." Well, he's Colored.... Well, that doesn't matter. He can do the job. Bring him on in here. That was going on thirty years ago, whether we want to admit that or not. And all of a sudden this black day! But I don't believe anybody is ready for me because I haven't conformed to any church even.

Oh, but here's what I can say about Leo Cantor. He's laying in bed. I'm in the segregated army in Honolulu. They give me room and board with a black outfit, and I was assigned to this white group. And he was getting pressure because he had to lay in bed at night and hear them say "them goddam Jews." And they thought he was white, because he's more Russian.

We used to get in this big scene. What the hell is the joke? Because everybody else is either English, German, French, or something. You're crossed up and nobody can say there's one. In the west, we never did get involved with who was a Pollack [sic].

I tell you what threw me off there. In '46 when I went back east, everybody was sectioned off. I couldn't believe it, because there was more racial prejudices back there. If a Pollack [sic] crossed an Italian neighborhood, man he's in trouble. And if a black slid through there, the Jews were over here. And the Irish, I said, "Oh, my God. This was going on in '46." This was the first time that I had seen that.

But all of us out here were all mixed up together, and if you were white, we didn't know what you were. You just happened to be white, or maybe had dark hair, or he had blonde hair, and he had the blue eyes. But nobody says, "This one's an Irishman and this one's a Jewish one and this one's a...." We never even thought of that. We all became conscious of this during the Second World War. The war just scrambled [everything] up.

Manchel: But you had guns.

Strode: Oh, we had guns, but they were locked up. But I imagine they might of had mixed emotions, but most of the Southern blacks probably really had bones to pick. They didn't know where we were really at, I don't believe.

Manchel: I saw that when I was in the army [in Fort Jackson, South Carolina], too. And that was in 1957.

Strode: Oh, you saw it that close. See, they don't really know where the blacks are. But see, most of the blacks should realize that we hung here together with one another, and there's nothing we can do about it. Because four hundred years ago ... the whites today didn't have nothing to do with that. The blacks didn't either. We're just here. There ain't nowhere to go home now. The whites can't take up [settle in] these foreign countries unless you're just a first generation. But your family's been here three hundred years, man; you're stuck. There ain't nowhere to turn around and no place to go.

It shows up in Italy. The Italian-American, he tries to go over there. He thinks that he's an Italian until he gets there. He finds out that he's an American. I've seen it on....

Manchel: We're isolated [overseas]. We feel more what you are [there] than when you're in [your own] community.

Strode: We're Americans and we're going to have to accept that fact.

Manchel: Woody, let me ask you a question about.... Are there any interesting stories about *The Man Who Shot Liberty Valance* [1962] that you remember other than the one about...?

Strode: No. It was just fun. We had a lot of fun making it. Me and Lee Marvin become friends on that. There's never been any problem. The only problem thing that ever happened to me was with the Los Angeles Rams, and when we got segregated back East. We were in the airport, and they said that we couldn't live at the Stevenson Hotel, and I had already lived there during the track season. I asked Kenny, "What are they going to do? They are going to give us $400 a week?" I said, "Well man, we're going to get segregated." We've never been to Harlem in our life. We've never lived among our people. Kenny has lived among the Italians. He's more Italian than he was black.

Manchel: What happened to Kenny when you got let go?

Strode: They kept him. That was a token scene. For one year, then they retired him. And then it was such a bad sting until they shuttled in the blacks. They brought eight blacks in, and all of a sudden, "I love you." The love affair started.

Manchel: How about *The Last Rebel* [1971]?

The Last Rebel, directed by Denys McCoy, is an embarrassing B-film about a Confederate soldier who refuses to accept Lee's surrender and takes on mean-spirited citizens in Missouri after the Civil War. The cast includes Joe Namath, Jack

Elam, and Ty Hardin. Woody Strode plays Duncan, an ex-Union soldier almost lynched by a white mob.

   Strode: Fun. Fun, with old Joe Namath.
   Manchel: What kind of guy is he?
   Strode: Very nice. Nothing like the publicity.
   Manchel: That's what I mean.
   Strode: All propaganda. That boy. They say what they want to say about him.
   Mrs. Strode: A good clean-cut kid.
   Strode: That's right. He's a great ball player.
   Manchel: He's the best!
   Strode: May I have one of these [reviews of *Black Jesus*]?
   Manchel: Oh sure. Woody, the review. I haven't got it right in front of me, of *Black Jesus*. Do you think when the black newspapers are knocking it; it is more of a racial issue than an artistic one?
   Strode: Yeah. I think it is more of a racial [issue], because if you saw *Black Jesus*, the moments that I am on the screen are some of the most emotional moments that an actor could do. And when Wanda Hill quoted in her review that they didn't like the picture, that's all right, but they couldn't knock the performance. I think it was strictly because it was a militant era in the United States for a black. They couldn't understand a picture that was done four years ago [it was made in 1968, but didn't get to America until 1971] about an African leader and what had happened to him, that the Italian couldn't even afford to print. That it was [Patrice] Lumumba, because they would slap the government's face.

Patrice Emergy Lumumba, the first Prime Minister of the independent Democratic Republic of the Congo (now Zaire), was murdered during a separationist movement that he strongly opposed in 1961.

   Strode: So, they made a composite of all the African leaders and gave him a Christ-like figure because the good articles outweighed the bad articles ... and I think it was more political anyway.
   Manchel: I wanted to ask you about that. Next question that I wanted to get to. I want to get to the story that you told me in New York about the black/white relations.
   Strode: Well, here I am. I come out of Europe, and the main thing I have never said, was "black" and "white." I've either said, "Colored" or "Negro." And now I have a white producer, Sid Shore, who has to orientate me for "black," "black," "black." I have to remember to say "black."

While producer Sid Shore did not do well with Black Jesus, *his next film,* Superfly *[directed by Gordon Parks, Jr. in 1972], proved one of the most popular box-office hits of the seventies.*

Strode: Now, we have a press conference for one week with white writers, and in my conversation he's kicking me under the table because I'm forgetting to say "black." And I'm saying, "Colored," and I'm saying, "Negro." And that went on for one week. Then on the Saturday after from nine in the morning until midnight, he says, "Woody, did you know that you only said 'Negro' eight times all day?" I was so tired, you know, but I have to rehearse myself because I, we have went from the "Negro," "Colored," "Afro-American," and now we're in the "black" era, that I hadn't been adjusted to.

I found out that Sid Shore was blacker than me. A week away I'm ready now for the televisions. I'm almost professional. They're saying, "The blacks. They did this. And the whites did this." Three weeks away I'm like a man drowning because here in Europe, I've been completely free and relaxed and all of a sudden, I have to be conscious of color, black and white.

So the last couple of days, the last day in New York, I had some young white writers, and I had a couple of drinks and I told them just how I felt, after I had about three martinis. I said, "I'm going to tell you guys something." I said, "I'm so sick and tired of the black and white situation, that I am going to tell you just about how I feel." I said, "I want you to do me one favor. September 6, I'll be in Mexico, and then you print it." And this is how I left it.

Manchel: That's how the *New York Times* story (picturing you as a reactionary) came out?

Strode: Yeah. That's how the *Times* came out.

Manchel: Tell me the story again about Jock Mahoney and Tarzan.

Strode: We got down in Thailand, you know with Jock Mahoney, and he's a physical actor. He can do anything, he jumped in that Chao [Phraya], probably the most diseased river in the world, and he caught dengue fever and maybe dysentery and intestinal pneumonia. The last half-hour of the picture, he was sick. If we didn't get this, the whole pictures is ruined. We have to fight up on the twelve-foot net after falling in boiling oil and the whole bit. But we have to do a lot of running through the jungle, chases and all that stuff tied together, and Jock had lost forty pounds on a two hundred pound frame. So he was a real sick man. And after every sequence, they had to put Jock on oxygen. And they really didn't find out what was wrong with him until they got back in the United States.

Manchel: What was that?

Strode: He had dengue fever, maybe dysentery and intestinal pneumonia. He was a strong man. But it aged him about ten years. I was with him the other day at the City Hall. He's got his health back; he looks fine, but.... He gave me the clippings. He didn't realize that I had this *Times* article.

Manchel: Does he work now at all?

Strode: Yes. He's a dollar-a-year man. You know, if you shoot a motion picture.... He works with Howard Chappell, who's a former OSS. He captured Mussolini so he's really, he infiltrated the SS during the war. He spent the whole war.

Manchel: That was the war where they gave them a chance to kill themselves.

Strode: They gave these guys a chance to shoot themselves because they were Prussians. They had a moral code or something, you know.

Manchel: You told me a story earlier about *The Professionals* [1966], on Monday, about Richard Brooks.

The Professionals, *directed by Richard Brooks, is a classic western, set in 1917, that relates the action-packed adventures of four mercenaries hired by a manipulative tycoon to recover his kidnapped wife from a Mexican bandit. The star-studded cast includes Lee Marvin, Jack Palance, Burt Lancaster, Robert Ryan, Ralph Bellamy, and Claudia Cardinale. Woody Strode plays Jake Sharp, the tight-lipped soldier of fortune, America's best tracker, and an expert with a bow and arrow. Some accounts assert that Strode did not get star billing because of racial conventions, but in* Gold Dust, *he insists that it was the first time he received "on-screen billing ... ahead of Burt Lancaster's."*[18]

Mrs. Strode: Well, I can tell you that. That was with Woody and his instructor, that taught him how to shoot the bow. And they were in Las Vegas. There's a big sign that says, "Howdy Pardner." And across the way, there was a big gorilla. So what the instructor did, he shot the gorilla through the eyes. So Woody was trying to shoot, and he couldn't shoot the "Howdy Pardner." So they got him on the ledge. Well, the next day was a big headline in the Las Vegas newspaper, "Woody Strode Shot the Bow through the Naked Bust of the Watusi Dancers." At the Flamingo Club, they were dancers. They all got fired. They are not supposed to associate with any guest in the hotel.

Woody runs up to Lee Marvin's room and told him exactly what happened and to please hold the bows. He said, "Well, what did you do?" He said, "I shot Howdy Pardner." So he wanted to be in the act too, so he got his gun out, as he's a sharp shooter and shot the other half and all the lights went out. So that was the headline....

Manchel: Let me ask you. What was the publicity story that they released about Paul Robeson?

Strode: I don't know, because I was not here. He [Sid Shore] said, "He would like to have done that, for his next project."

Mrs. Strode: Sid Shore had received a story, a byline about the life of Paul Robeson, by a young Negro, a black Negro writer, and he would like to make it into a movie if Woody was willing to do it. That's the reason why the publicity was out. That he had a chance to portray the life of Paul Robeson. But we had other commitments, so he had to go to Mexico to do [producer] Martin Racklin's *The Revengers* [1972].

Manchel: Tell me about *The Revengers*.

The Revengers, *directed by Daniel Mann, is a controversial post-Civil War western about a rancher out to kill the gang that butchered his family. The cast features William Holden, Ernest Borgnine, Roger Hanin, and Susan Hayward (in her last screen role). Woody Strode, who receives third billing, plays Job, a former slave.*

Strode: Yes. The latest one is *The Revengers* with William Holden, [Ernest] Borgnine, and Susan Hayward, Roger Hanin, a French actor. We have a German by the name of [Rene] Koldehoff. And so we have an international cast, and we had a lot of fun on it because we brow beat the German all the way through it. We called him a Nazi and the whole thing. Finally, it ended up a love affair.

And Marty [Racklin] who is a very happy-go-lucky type of producer, you have a lot of fun on his pictures, they all got sick. He had a heart attack before the picture started. Well, that wasn't going to stop him. Van Heflin died on this, God rest his soul, and they replaced him with Borgnine, and then William Holden had African fever that we cursed.

So they postponed it for about three months. So we started around September, and I've just recently come back from there. And they were probably, they told me the other day that they have a rough cut that they'll have in another week or so. We'll probably get to see that, and they think we really got a good picture.

And that's all that's necessary in the world market. Some real knock down and drag out. This time we kill ... this time I have Mexican friends, and they said to me, "Woody, what ... are you going to kill Mexican friends again?" I said, "No! No! We're going to shoot down the Indians and gringos." So, it's all in a team. You cannot, you know.

Manchel: Woody, what about a picture called *Captain Buffalo*? Was that ever made?

Strode: *Captain Buffalo*? That was the name of *Sergeant Rutledge*. They had a big fight over the title. They didn't know which way to go. John Ford. There's a song in there ... "Captain Buffalo." That's what it is based on, but they decided to go with *Sergeant Rutledge*.

Manchel: How about *Shalako* [1968]?

Shalako, directed by Edward Dmytryk, is an intriguing western about pleasure-seeking European aristocrats hunting wild game and menaced by Apaches in New Mexico during the 1880s. The cast includes Sean Connery, Stephen Boyd, Brigitte Bardot, Jack Hawkins, Honor Blackman, and Alexander Knox. Woody Strode plays Chato, Cochise's son, who is trying to end bloodshed on the frontier.

Strode: *Shalako*. Sean Connery, Brigitte Bardot. I played an Apache chief. My Chickasaw friend, who is dead now, played my father, Red Wing, who could probably outdraw anybody in the world with a pistol. He taught most of the stars. And Elmer Smith, a full-blooded Sioux, taught me the Apache language. He knows several languages.

Manchel: I kept away from that film. I never saw it because of the publicity. It just seemed so crazy, Brigitte Bardot riding on a horse. I saw pictures of her riding sidesaddle.

Strode: Yeah. She was. They had her on a stallion. You see how they break the horses. They really break them. If you can sit your star on a stallion. It was a beautiful white stallion.

Manchel: And how was she in the film?

Strode: Very nice. Oh. Everybody. We had a lot of fun. We stayed down in Spain for four months.

Mrs. Strode: International cast.

Strode: International cast. Jack Hawkins! And we had another German actor who has passed away. We had French, English, Welsh, and we had real Indians, for the first time. Plus the gypsies.

Manchel: Was it a good film?

Strode: Well, it could have been better, but they didn't cut it properly. They wouldn't let the director, Eddie Dmytryk, cut it. Producers always get involved.

Manchel: I've heard a lot about that in Hollywood, where the producers take it away.

Strode: Yeah, that's terrible.

Mrs. Strode: After *Spartacus*. [There] was a young director, Stanley [Kubrick], and in my book I have a written letter from him. He's got a picture that he actually cut everything: *A Clockwork Orange* [1971].

Manchel: *2001* [1968] is a masterpiece.

Mrs. Strode: Yes. *Space Odyssey*. That is.

Manchel: What about *Once Upon a Time in the West* [1968]?

Once Upon a Time in the West, *directed by Sergio Leone, is a classic tongue-in-cheek Italian western, loosely based on* Johnny Guitar *(1954) that pits a vicious gang against a notorious gunslinger who plays a harmonica. The famous cast includes Charles Bronson, Henry Fonda, Claudia Cardinale, Jason Robards, Keenan Wynn, Jack Elam, and Lionel Stander. Woody Strode plays one of three vicious killers in dustcoats who die violently in a face-off against the mysterious stranger.*

Strode: Oh, Sergio Leone, I love him. You know, he's always been a friend of mine, and he was involved with Clint Eastwood, and then he was involved with Lee Van Cleef and with me. We had the same agency, me and Lee Van Cleef, but I was always sort of in the background.

He [Leone] always wanted to do something with me, but he got hung up with United Artists. So, he finally said, "I want to use Woody." So, he got me in an opening sequence. And he used Mama, played an Indian squaw, and she was sweeping out the buildings. Of course, we've never seen the picture.

Mrs. Strode: I did.

Strode: Mama, you saw it? And so he gives me a big highlight and they said, "For ten minutes, he got my face on the screen," and that's beautiful because we have a great relationship and after leaving Europe, I left Europe, I left there, and I had seen him before I left. I said I was going home to see my son. But we've sent all our friends over there like Sergio Leone, Christmas cards. *Once Upon a Time in America.* If they ever do it, I'll be in that one.

The film was made in 1984, and Strode did not appear in it.

Strode: It's a gangster film. It's not going to be the Italians this time. It's gonna be Irish, the Jews, and the Negroes. Before, the Mafia took us over and bam! You see the Mafia walk in and bam! They took the numbers, and they did this and that. But they're going to show the other side of the coin, and this will be probably the first picture, and then he'll do it in Chicago and New York, and in Kansas. Boy, they're going to really wrap it up.

Manchel: Woody, outside of John Ford, I assume he's the best one you've worked with, who have been your favorite directors?

Strode: I've enjoyed every one of them between John Ford. I wish I had Sergio Leone. But I think by them saying "spaghetti westerns," they insulted this man, because he loved the West. That's why I fell in love with him. He took a book, when I saw his *Fistful of Dollars* [1964] and *For a Few Dollars More* [1966], his saloon was a Rembrandt, the spittoons; the whole scene was a painting. And right then, I don't know this man, I hadn't got there yet, I said, "God, he loves us, to get this out of a book, to read it and not be born in it and be hung up with us."

Now Richard Brooks, a fine man. I've had the best directors in the world.

Mrs. Strode: He had the greatest, Cecil B. DeMille in *The Ten Commandments* [1956].

Strode: Cecil B. DeMille, if he had been alive, I wish he was alive today to see how far I've come. Because when I was wrestling, I had a slave job [in *The Ten Commandments*]. They brought me in to him, and they couldn't get anybody to look the old man in the eye. And I looked him in the eye, and he said, "You're the King of Egypt." I didn't want the job because it only lasted for four days. They're going to make a star out of me, and I'll be a slave for five weeks. Do you understand? We had a big argument about that, me and Chico Day, his assistant. He says, "Woody, don't worry, we'll fix something up for you."

Four days away, I'm finished, put me in a slave costume, got me all dressed up and carried me into Mr. DeMille, and they said, "Mr. DeMille, do you know who this is?" "No, who is it?" "Oh, that's Woody." "Oh yeah, he can play the other part too." Then Mr. DeMille told me, "Now, don't tell anybody that you're playing two parts, because you're the King of Ethiopia."

Mrs. Strode: And he said, "Whenever he makes a picture...."

Strode: Oh, yes, he told me; he said, "Woody, I know you wrestle." And he said, "Anywhere you are in the world, if you hear I'm going to make a picture, get on a plane and come in." [Regrettably for Woody, *The Ten Commandments* was DeMille's last film.] So we had a very fine relationship, and I'm just sorry that these people are not alive today, to see how far I've come.

Mrs. Strode: Woody had his first director that was Cecil B. DeMille, then he had John Ford, and then he had Richard Brooks, Budd Boetticher, and Stanley Kubrick.

Strode: You can go right down the line. Top directors. You know what they saw in me. They saw what I had, and they pulled it out of me.

Manchel: They never saw a "black" man?

Strode: No! They gave me the part because I was the man. I impressed them, and so what they saw in me they pulled out of me. To make John Ford feel like, "Well, let me see. Who can play this Mongol? He's got to be ... Woody!"

It wasn't a black thing. You had to have the ability to sit on the horse and not be doubled, do the little bit of fighting that I had to do in it, and get off the screen, and hold up the part. Make it believable. And every time they selected me, [it] was because I could make a part believable, whether

I star in it or not. This is the most important thing when your star is there, the character actor has gotta be believable. Otherwise, the whole picture is weakened.

Manchel: Let me ask you about *Che!* That was a disaster.

Strode: *Che!* [1969]? It was a disaster because they got in a political fight with a dear friend of mine, Sy Bartlett, who gave me my first chance in doing *Pork Chop Hill*. And he's from the Second World War. He was probably the first one to raid Berlin. Imagine that? Drop the bombs.

Che!, directed by Richard Fleischer, is an empty-headed movie about how Che Guevara, a young Argentine doctor and revolutionary, agrees to help Fidel Castro overthrow the Batista regime in Cuba and become a dictator. The miscast performers include Omar Sharif, Jack Palance, and Robert Loggia. Woody Strode plays Guillermo, a forgettable guerilla.

Strode: And they had a political fight. The left wing got involved, they had a little more muscle, they pulled a little more strings, and they destroyed *Che!* We should have shot *Che!* You see we were going to do the devil. We are going to show the devil. We're going to show Castro, and we're going to show that Che Guevara, a lot. We're going to put it on the screen. He's a guerilla, and let's let him rot. Let's do his life. If we're going to do Mao, if we're going to do Peking, let's do Peking. Let's don't slam it. Do you understand? And they tried to slam, and they ruined *Che! Che!* could have been a classic.

Manchel: The film seems to break right in half. One half seems to be all negative, and the other half is all positive. It's as if they were trying to appease both sides.

Strode: I wouldn't go in there, because it was a political ball. That's the only reason why I don't say anything more about. I've never seen *Che!*

Manchel: It was at a theatre in New York. It was open a week, and I went to see it because I wanted to find out about it. There were four people in the theatre.

Mrs. Strode: They ruined the picture. And not only that, Sy is such a wonderful writer, that when people take over his picture, they get the credit. They don't think that he's.... He did *The Big Country* [1958]. Now, when you see it, you don't see Sy Bartlett's name on it. You see William Wyler, and that's pitiful. Now, look at his *Twelve O'Clock High* [1949]; they took it away from him.

Strode: *Twelve O'Clock High*. It is Sy Bartlett's story. Sy Bartlett was probably one of the ballsiest guys. Now he's old now, and he was the first polo player that I knew. He played polo, and he does all this horse riding and all this physical stuff, see. He knew Mama when she was sixteen, or fifteen or sixteen years old, in Hawaii. And then we meet in Hawaii, and he's maintained this, but he's sort of like a father relationship with everybody. They take advantage of Sy Bartlett. He is a beautiful man. He has a picture now that he is trying to get off.... Probably one of the best-written things, and it's very difficult for him now to get the right production.

Mrs. Strode: ... and the *Face of Death*.

Strode: *Face of Death* is about Tad Brown, one of our greatest police chiefs. The only reason why they don't want to do his story is because they don't want to glorify a cop.

So, we're in a bad time now. We're in a bad moral period where when I said to you, "It's lucky that you teach what you teach." Could you see yourself teaching philosophy and semantics and all this rigmarole and have to take it now and pervert it? See, they can't pervert this, as they have to do this. See, everything has to be run by rule. You can't make motion pictures without some kind of rules. You can't make this thing run without the right rules.

But they have been able to juggle academic courses around, pervert history. You can corrupt history. The only thing you can't corrupt is math. You can't corrupt the math. All the positive things are like mathematics counting dollars and cents.

Arts? There's one way to get on is to learn the lines, do you understand? You gotta say them right or they ain't going to work. So they can't corrupt you, and you gotta put it on film, and you gotta get the right processing, and you got to keep it on tape and this period thing. It might get a little more elevated, more sophisticated, but it's going to be basic and you're safe in that area.

Now, politically, political science, my god. You would be insulted because you graduated from your, got your doctor's degree, and here comes some politician with a gun. He said, "Well, Frank, I'm sorry, but here's your new textbook." You open it up and it's trash. The people on the street don't know it.

Manchel: That's what they did in Germany.

Strode: Well, they're doing this here. Can you imagine that? Why are they corrupting here? I come home and they had signs, "legalize pot." They just got that store off the strip. Are they trying to pull a Germany over here.

Manchel: It can go either way.

Strode: I knew it. I knew it.

Mrs. Strode: They disgust me. Now, we lived in Rome for three years, and all our reading papers were from England or *Tribune Herald* from France. And especially in England, they say how it is. They don't....

Strode: The English press is more objective. They will say, "Woody

Strode chopped off Frank's head, plucked his eyes out, put him in the oven, and cooked him. Now, we will have cricket." That's British, baby. I love 'em. When you're overseas, BBC will tell it exactly like it is.

The whole African war, I knew about because you can't find out in our media. Well, I found out what was going on in Nigeria, South Africa, Rhodesia, and over here, it's not even mentioned. When I found out that we were dealing with Russia, we were buying chromium from Russia before we started buying it from Rhodesia, and we were with the enemy, I don't understand all this.

Mrs. Strode: I didn't like to go to theaters, especially on stage. The Cistina Theatre, you hear good music like Count Basie might be in town, or Duke Ellington. And here we have singers [but] when the[y become] preaching singers, the preaching talkers, I don't like. They have their own views, and it's mostly left wing. And they try to preach and tell their audience and all, "You brothers and sisters, you know the whites did this."

And when you look at your audiences, there's more mixed colors there, sitting. Here's a blonde; here's an African. I never see Negroes. It's all African students. So how can you tell whether they are black and white?

If they're from Africa, they speak good English. But they're an embarrassment when they preach. And it's our left wing. And she, Miriam Makaba, is a wonderful singer if she would sing and stick to her native singing. But don't preach, not because she's married to an American who is a left-winger too. But they forget that they are there.

One thing I can say about the Italians. There's no color line. They love the blues, they love everything American.

Strode: The Italians, is such, it says in the paper, they're natives. I saw it in one write up in the *Times*. I said, "They don't even act like white people." The Italian, the European Italian, is just like a goddamn native, just like any Polynesian. You know, one o'clock, they shut down all of Italy. And they go to have lunch and ... they drink the wine. They don't get drunk because they have been drinking the wine ever since they have been little babies, mixing a drop of water and a drop of wine. By the time you get to your age, you sit here, have lunch, and drink the whole bottle. You're not drunk. You just feel relaxed and you talk. At 4:30, they go back to work. I don't know how they can go back to work and work eight hours.

Manchel: I never could figure that out either. How you could drink and go back to work?

Strode: The Italian does it. Now, we are Americans and we cannot drink.

Manchel: We eat a light lunch if we are going to work eight hours, or we get sluggish.

Strode: Right! Right! And they're so beautiful. They lie to the women;

"I love you." It is great for the woman to visit Europe and to have an Italian fall in love. In addition, it feeds the woman's ego. It is beautiful.

Manchel: Is your part equal to all the others in *The Revengers*?

Strode: *Revengers*?

Manchel: Yes. Will you be getting star billing?

Strode: I have star billing for the first time in the United States.

Manchel: Why is that?

Strode: I don't know.

Manchel: You got enough muscle now where they can't....

Strode: Yes. I think because of *Black Jesus* [1968], when they put my name on the billboard, regardless of what they think of the picture, it did the job. Woody Strode is *Black Jesus*. That wiped me out. Imagine me on Broadway? I've never had that before. And all of a sudden, I walk up there; I was embarrassed at first.

Mrs. Strode: It was such a big....

Strode: Cinerama, Woody Strode is *Black Jesus*. I got into Los Angeles, and I refused to come to town. I refused to leave Mexico. I said, "Not in my home town." Pantages Theatre down the street, my name is across the billboard. I said, "No!" It's just pitiful. How do you overlook somebody? How do you like someone and overlook him? This is what happened to me. It wasn't hate or dislike. It was just....

Manchel: Just nobody thought about it.

Strode: Nobody thought about it. You're right, you're exactly right!

Manchel: I've heard it over and over again from people I've talked to, from white men who lived in the heyday of Hollywood when it started. And I asked them, "Why does it have to...?" And they said, "It just never occurred to us. That's just what the situation was.... We didn't hate anybody."

Strode: Nobody hated anybody. There was no hate. They'd just go out and get a picture together. At that time, you couldn't have nothing but chauffeurs and maids. And if you had a comedian or a band, or if Lena Horne was singing in a club or something like that; those were big steps for the men who invested their money.... I wonder if the whites are going to look at it?

Do you hear me? Because the Southern whites are.... How could they set a black down to the dinner table? So, it was a big hang-up, and we all went through this period, and we all out here [the West] didn't care. We all out here jumped into bed.... Everybody was sleeping together out here anyway.

So the screen was telling a lie. Can you imagine this scene? The maid and the cook in the picture were all getting drunk when the picture was made ... "yes, sir," "yes ma'am." They were in their Cadillacs and their suit of clothes. The only thing the whites were were the star of the picture. It's a funny double standard that was going on.

The Second World War proved to Hollywood ... that this was a propaganda instrument. They never knew it. We were interested in making money. We'd show all our badness. We'd show bad on the screen. Well, that's how the Americans are. Well, they're all gangsters. We didn't know what we were doing to ourselves.

Manchel: When I was in England last year, I talked at nine different schools. Two questions that ... [the students] asked me all the time, "Have I ever been with the cowboys?" They still think America is overrun with cowboys. And the other was, "Is there a killing every day in America?" Because they had seen the Kennedy brothers and Martin Luther King murdered, they thought that every day there was a murder in America.

Strode: You know what? We're the only country in the world that washes our linen right out in the open. We're really honest about that. "We're sons of bitches. I don't like them, and goddam it." Hang it up there and tell them. That's America. That's why I think that we're the most gracious group of all the people.

The European is a bigger bigot in this area because he has a caste system. "You poor whites, you ain't ever going to get up off the ground."

This white man over here, he thinks he's a bigot. "Well, them Negroes, Jews, Pollacks [sic]. Goddamn them Negroes and Jews. They don't stay in their goddamn areas. Yeah, I know that they got Cadillacs, but I don't have to live with them." That's all he is. He thinks he's a bigot. He's just got a little ego ball going round in him.

Now what the British hear, when you move into this neighborhood. "Well – what was his family? He was a butcher. What do you mean? And a white man? We'll run you out of the neighborhood." I've seen that in Europe.

So what do we care about this old [white American] bigot here? He ain't bullshit. We can bullshit him out of everything. You hear me! We can steal the goddamn country from him. And finally, he's a ... "Goddamn that Woody and Frank. I never did think I'd like a Nigger and a Jew. But I love them." In the South, they ain't that tough. They've been taught certain ways by their grandparents. And when they find out that their grandparents are liars. Now, he falls in love with us. And he becomes your biggest, strongest friend. In America, they do that. You can change them here. But you can't change them in Europe.

Manchel: Woody, there's an article in *Variety*, November 1970. They said that you were set for a lead in *Nigger Charley*. What was that about? Whatever happened to that?

Strode: They got carried away. We started out to do this. Mama gave this man a picture....

Mrs. Strode: Well, Larry Spangler was the producer of the picture, *The Last Rebel* [1971], with Joe Namath. Well, he told me that they were looking for a project for Woody. And I said, "I got a script that was given by [James] Warren Bellah's son." Warren Bellah was one of the writers that did Papa's pictures.

James Warren Bellah wrote three short stories that served as the basis for Ford films: "Massacre," was the source for Frank S. Nugent's screenplay for Fort Apace *(1948); "War Party," Frank Nugent's and Laurence Stallings' screenplay for* She Wore a Yellow Ribbon *(1949); and "Mission With No Record," James Kevin McGuinness' screenplay for* Rio Grande *(1950). He also was a co-screenwriter on two Ford films:* Sergeant Rutledge *(1960) and* The Man Who Shot Liberty Valance *(1962).*

Strode: He works for Mr. Ford, storywise about the West. So I gave *Nigger Charley* to Mr. Spangler hoping he, that Woody ... you know that was Woody's project. When they got the story, they changed it around and changed it for a young black. So they got this [Fred] Williamson, who portrays Nigger Charley.

The film, Legend of Nigger Charley, *was directed by Martin Goldman and released in 1972; a year later, a sequel,* The Soul of Nigger Charley, *appeared.*

Mrs. Strode: When we came back in January, the Indians, when it got out in the paper, the Indians, Jay Silverheels and their group, was fighting the Screen Guild because of Woody's not going to make the picture.

So Woody refused when they changed the complete story. Woody said he was willing to do it if they stuck to history, but they didn't. Now you explain the history of this.

Strode: *Nigger Charley* was a very unfortunate incident. The man that wrote this, his son came all the way to Rome to discuss it with me to try to get it off the ground. I showed it to my Italian producers, and they were not geared in black and white. And they said, "Woody, we don't want you to do anything like this, because it might hurt your image in Europe." And he was right, so we laid it on the shelf.

Here comes Larry Spangler. We'd just finished *The Last Rebel*. So he comes through, and he was doing some dubbing, and he said, "We are looking for a project." In the meantime, Mama said, "Well, we have a picture called *Nigger Charley*." Well, that just about wiped him out. The story is about a black, who's a slave, with a stepmother who's raised by a Baptist minister who died. On his death bed, he says, "I want you to be a good Nigger, Charlie, and I want you to be good and blah, blah. Now we get to a slave sale, and he sells me and my stepmother to a stranger, a real slaver. All right! There's a little black girl on the plantation that I fall in love with. So I am a Christian, so I wanted to ask this white slaver for her hand to marry. Well, in those years no slave ever married, and it was a joke as far as this white man is concerned. But it really was, this black girl was his girl. To show you what chattel slavery was, she thought nothing wrong with being in love with me and sleeping with him. So, he says to his brother, "I'll teach this Nigger." So, he sends for me. And as I come in, he's in bed with my black chick. I had to stand through that ordeal. That breaks me up. The next scene, we are on the plantation, and the girl's crossing the field. And she runs, "Oh, Charlie, I'm married, that's nothing what I was doing." Chattel slavery, that's what we would have shown. I slapped her face. She goes back and tells on me, and he says, "I'll teach Nigger Charlie." He gets his gun, gets on his horse, and comes to me. In the meantime, the thing that you cut wheat with, a scythe, I was sharpening this thing. I'm a blacksmith, I've been taught by the Christian, the Baptist. He starts to kill me and I cut him in half. He says, "Oh my God" and he dies. And his horse runs off with the slave. Now Nigger Charlie starts on the run. He crosses the United States. The Civil War is over, and the man's brother is going to search for Nigger Charlie. A white family picks me up, and they want me to go to the gold mine fields with them. I'm with the white family, and the man's brother approaches us, and he makes contact. He leaves the wife with my people, but they don't let him know that I'm Nigger Charley because there's a love affair between us. On our trip, we're crossing the river outside of San Burdue, and we're attacked by the Piautes. And I send the whites on, and Nigger Charley dies in the stream. And this is historical fact. And they found his bones in 1966. Now this is how I got involved with Nigger Charley.

63. Johnny Sheffield and Woody Strode in what may be *The Lion Hunters* (1951). Courtesy of The Manchel Collection, Burlington College.

64. A publicity shot from *The Buccaneer* (1958). Courtesy of The Manchel Collection, Burlington College.

65. A behind the scenes shot from *The Last Voyage* (1960). Courtesy of The Manchel Collection, Burlington College.

66. A publicity shot from *The Last Voyage*. Tammy Marihugh is the child. Courtesy of The Manchel Collection, Burlington College.

67. Woody Strode being mistreated by Gordon Scott in *Tarzan's Fight for Life* (1958).

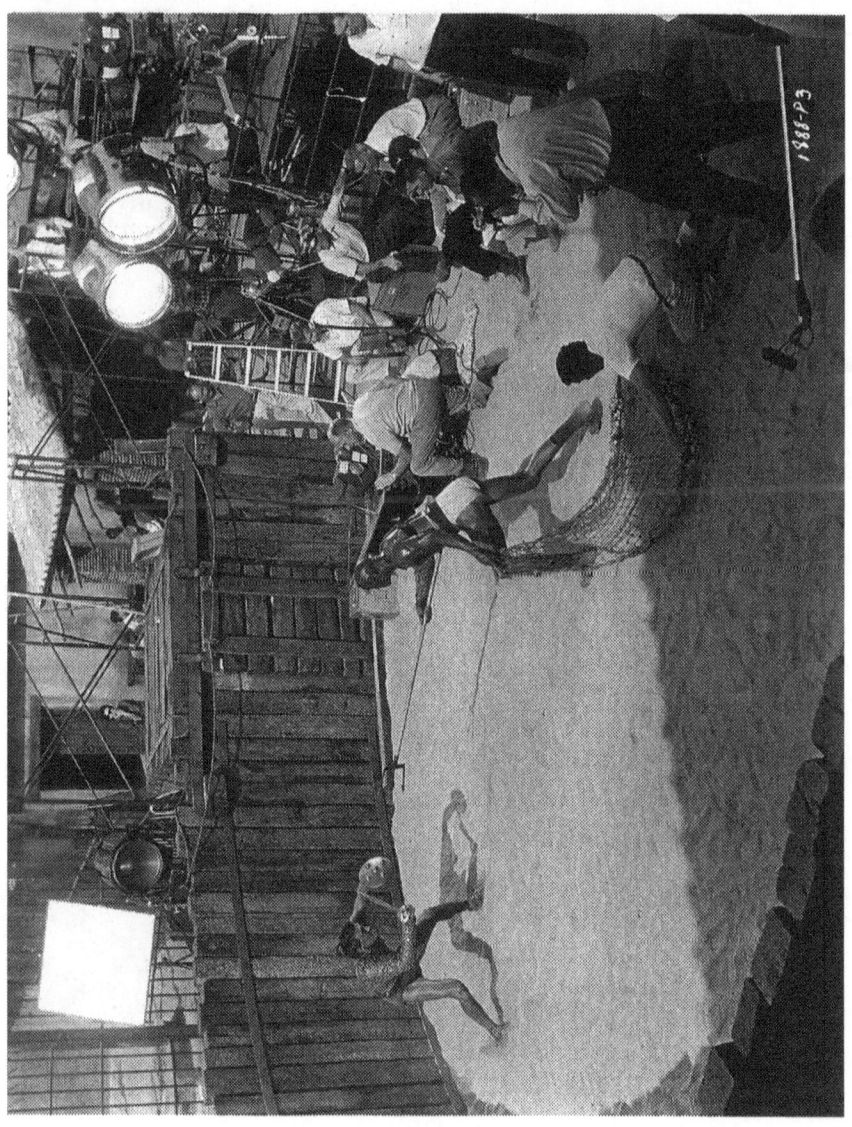

68. A behind the scenes shot from *Spartacus* (1960). Courtesy of The Manchel Collection, Burlington College.

69. The courtroom scene in *Sergeant Rutledge*. (1960). Woody Strode is in the upper right, seated. Just below him, seated, is Jeffrey Hunter, his defense attorney. To his left, Carleton Young, the prosecutor, staring. The presiding officer is Willis Bouchey, in white. Comforting the women is Hank Worden. Courtesy of The Manchel Collection, Burlington College.

70. John Ford. The director told Woody he could make a place for him in films, but never make it possible for the actor to be a star. Courtesy of The Manchel Collection, Burlington College.

71. Woody Strode being led by Jock Mahoney in *Tarzan's Three Challenges* (1963). Courtesy of The Manchel Collection, Burlington College.

72. A publicity shot from *Genghis Khan* (1965). Courtesy of The Manchel Collection, Burlington College.

73. Woody Strode in a publicity shot for *The Professionals* (1966). Courtesy of The Manchel Collection, Burlington College.

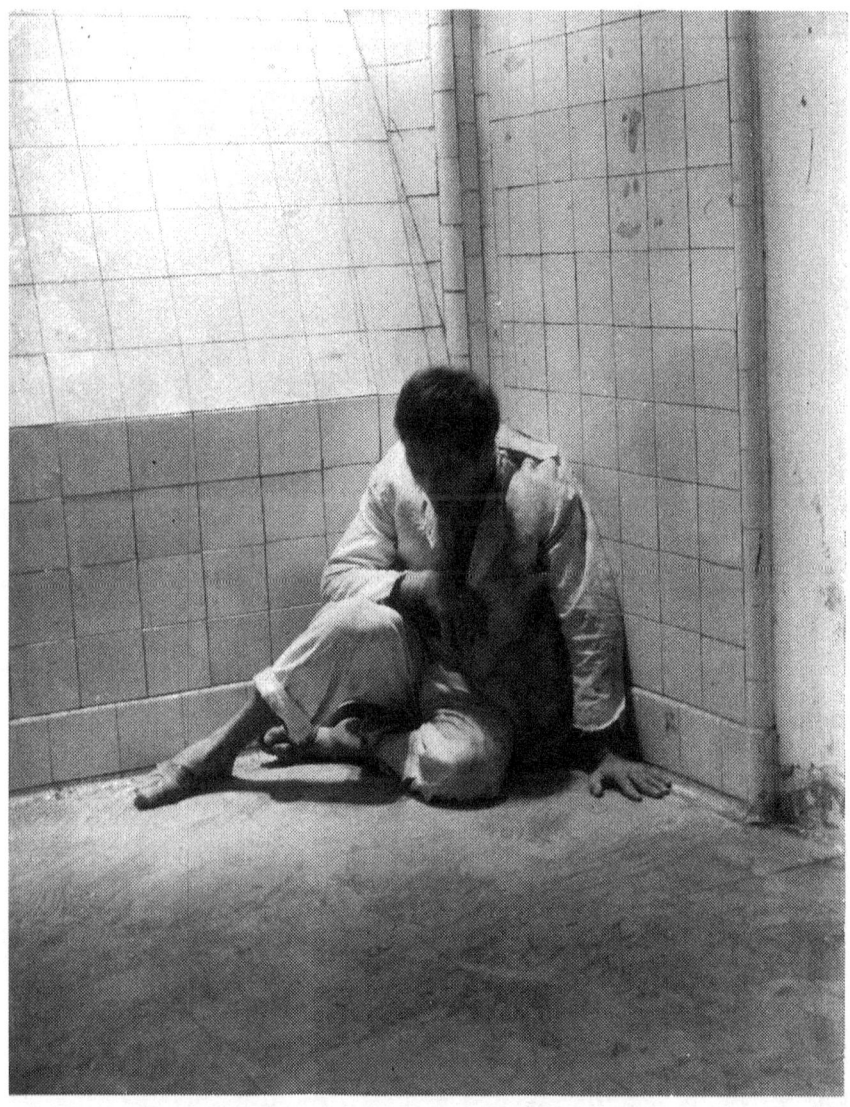

74. Woody Strode in *Black Jesus* (1968/1971). Courtesy of The Manchel Collection, Burlington College.

75. Joe Namath and Woody Strode in *The Last Rebel* (1971). Courtesy of The Manchel Collection, Burlington College.

Notes

[1] White, "Stepping Forward, Looking Back," 39.
[2] Edward Baron Turk, *Child of Paradise: Marcel Carne and the Golden Age of Cinema* (Cambridge: Harvard University Press, 1989), 11.
[3] "Cowboys Honored," *Jet*, 3 May 1993, 34.
[4] Michael Schlossman, "Bojangles: The Legacy," (Showtime, 2000).
[5] Frank Manchel, "Losing and Finding John Ford's Sergeant Rutledge (1960)," *Historical Journal of Film, Radio and Television* 17.2 (1997), 245-259.
[6] Woody Strode and Sam Young, *Gold Dust: An Autobiography* (Lanham, MD: Madison Books, 1990), 5.
[7] Ibid., 86-88.
[8] Sharon Robinson, *Stealing Home* (New York: Harper Collins, 1996), 9.
[9] Walter Rico Burrell, "Whatever Happened to Woody Strode?" *Ebony*, June 1982, 141.
[10] Ronald Bergan, "Black and Proud in the West. Obituary: Woody Strode," *The Gaurdian*, 14 Jan. 1995, 28.
[11] White, "Stepping Forward, Looking Back," 33. For a detailed discussions of *Sergeant Rutledge*, see Manchel, "Losing and Finding John Ford's Sergeant Rutledge (1960)."
[12] Gabe Essoe, *Tarzan of the Movies: A Pictorial History of More Than Fifty Years of Edgar Rice Burroughs' Legendary Hero* (New York: Citadel Press, 1968), 177.
[13] Strode and Young, *Gold Dust: An Autobiography*, 189.
[14] Ibid., 154-155.
[15] "Untitled," *New York Times*, 26 August, 1971.
[16] Cripps, "The Myth of the Southern Box Office: A Factor in Racial Stereotyping in American Movies, 1920-1940," 144.
[17] Jarvie, *Movies as Social Criticism: Aspects of Their Social Psychology*, 164-165.
[18] Strode and Young, *Gold Dust: An Autobiography*, 225.

76. The famous dramatist inscribed this picture: "To one of the Best Researchers goin.' fondly, Charles Gordone. Good luck Frank! on your book." Courtesy of The Manchel Collection, University of Vermont.

6
Somebody Who Refused to Be Nobody: Charles Edward Gordone

> "The cultural script of being a black man doesn't tell you what he has come to cherish or revile: but it gives you a good idea of the issues history has presented him with."
>
> Henry Louis Gates, Jr.[1]

Charles Edward Gordone, the first African-American playwright to win the Pulitzer Prize, committed himself to teaching, directing, and bettering the lot of black performers. His advice to African-American writers who focused on the black experience was "to include the humanity of all people, the will to survive and the will to live – of all people – and the strength of people against fantastic odds."[2]

He did not have many screen credits to his name, nor did he write more than one important drama. Yet, Gordone played a pivotal role not only in the development of black theater, but also in some of the most important movies about African-Americans in the sixties.

Because his acrobatic mother was touring with the Ringling Brothers Circus, Charles Edward Gordone was born on October 12, 1925, in Cleveland, Ohio. He grew up, however, in Elkhart, Indiana, when the family settled down because of her discovering Seventh-Day Adventism.[3]

Despite the Gordones being black, they lived in a white neighborhood. His mother's religious beliefs exerted a major influence on his life and that of his two sisters and two brothers. Gordone described her religion as "force-fed," and said that he grew up a "stoned Hoosier."[4] By his late teenage years, the precocious adolescent had had enough of pedantic religion and white neighborhoods. "I didn't know who I was," he once confessed to a reporter, "and I knew if I stayed in Elkhart, I'd never find out."[5]

So Gordone moved to California in 1944, and there enlisted in the Air Force Special Services. A year later, having his Honorable Discharge in hand, the ex-soldier met his first wife. Not much is known about the woman or their marriage, not even when it ended. By the end of 1945, however,

Gordone began finding work as a calypso singer, a policeman, and a bit actor in films. Most of his time was given to studying dramatics at Los Angeles City College, and later he graduated from Los Angeles State College of Applied Arts and Sciences in 1952.

Since acting was what he most wanted to do now, he moved that same year to New York City, where he struggled to get roles on the legitimate stage. Over the next seven years, he got small parts in some Broadway shows – Moss Hart's *The Climate of Eden* (1952) and Charles Sebree-Greer Johnston's *Mrs. Patterson* (1955) – but by the end of the decade, he turned his attention more and more to directing. Among his significant efforts were the Judson Poet's debut production of *Faust* (1959), as well as three important productions for the Equity Library Theater – *Moon of the Carabees*, *Hell Bent for Heaven*, and *Detective Story* – all in 1960. The fifties also found Gordone involved in the new medium of television. Although no evidence exists, the actor-director told me he worked often with Sam Peckinpah, a friend from his Hollywood days.

However, to support himself, Gordone took a job as a waiter at Johnny Romero's bar in Greenwich Village. It was his experiences there that formed the source for his first play, *No Place to Be Somebody*.

Before tackling playwriting full time, however, Gordone tried once more to establish himself as an actor. This time, things went better. For example, he had an essential role in Jean Genet's *The Blacks* (1961). "It changed my life," he stated in a *Newsweek* article. "Genet knows everything there is to know about niggers. The day he was born it got to him that he was a piece of s – –. He said, 'If that was what I was gonna be, I could be any kind I want to be.' For me that meant I could be any kind of nigger I wanted to be."[6] He won an Obie award for his Lennie in Luther James' all-black production *Of Mice and Men* (1963), and had the lead role in Nigerian dramatist Wole Soyinka's *The Trials of Brother Jericho* (1967).

By the mid-sixties, Gordone was also making his way back into films. In 1963, he was the casting director for *Black Like Me*, and the next year, the associate producer for *Nothing But A Man*. According to a press release from Springer/Warner Productions, the actor also appeared in a film *The Virgin Prince* [I can find no listing anywhere for this film], and received his first screenwriting credit for *From These Ashes* (1966). He also found occasional work on television, such as Luther James' *The Face in the Mirror* (1967) for WGBH, Boston.[7]

Gordone began writing *No Place to Be Somebody* in 1960, the same year that he married his second wife, Jeanne Warner. Seven years later, the race-conscious drama had two debut performances at New York City's Sheridan Square Playhouse in November. The following month, after some revisions, it opened in its final form at Richard Barr's Playwrights Unit.

Produced by Warner, the dark comedy focuses on a black bartender named Johnny Williams, a con artist who tries to inveigle his way of petty deceptions by taking on the white Mafia, as well as hassling regular customers like a mulatto actor, a gay ballet dancer, an African-American prostitute, a Jewish hooker, and a mentally unbalanced drummer. Eventually, Johnny's deceptions do him in, and he gets shot and loses everything.

Over the next two years, performances of the play occurred first at the New York Shakespeare Festival's Public Theatre and then at the American Negro Theater on Broadway, before settling in December, 1969, at the Promenade Theatre on 76th Street and Broadway.[8] Among those actors appearing in the drama were Ron O'Neal, later to gain screen notoriety as the star of the film, *Superfly* (1972), Nathan George, Julius Harris, Marge Eliot, and Gordone himself.

The *New York Times* drama critic, Walter Kerr, began his 1969 review of *No Place to Be Somebody*, "Let's be simple about this. Charles Gordone is the most astonishing new American playwright to come along since Edward Albee ... [and] he lurches at us not like the younger Albee or the one-act Albee, but like the already ripe and roaring Albee of *Who's Afraid of Virginia Woolf?*"[9] *Time* claimed that the play "owed as much to the saloon drama of O'Neill and Saroyan as it did to the black theater renaissance of the sixties."[10] And Lawrence Bommer observed, "Although its harrowing tale of survivors and non-survivors in a West Side bar hits melodramatic intensity in its final scenes, it is the quieter moments as blacks and whites cope with racism and self-hatred that make the longest-lasting impression. With the suppleness of jazz riffs and the exuberance of unvarnished street talk, Gordone's dialogue seems tailor-made to each vibrant character."[11]

Nevertheless, the play ran into trouble with African-American artists over the issue of color. As *Ebony* commented, Gordone's refusal to exclude whites from his work had made him "the prime target of black nationalists, who contend that all Broadway is 'sick,' as is most of off-Broadway, and that black theater must be relevant to the black masses as well as functional in terms of presenting positive black images and suggestions for a future course."[12]

Gordone refused to duck the issue. For example, he explained, "The Negro Ensemble Company turned down my play because brother Robert Hooks said, 'We're an all-black theater – no white actors allowed.' Well, I wrote white characters in my play because that is part of life, man!"[13] The most influential black critic at the time, Clayton Riley, attacked the play publicly, lamenting that "Brother Gordone is an eminently gifted and hard-working artist who has fallen prey to that lamentable inclination of Black men in America to trot down someone else's road – those paved boulevards of good intentions that lead inevitably to ... ah. Need we say?"[14]

Gordone had a different slant on African-American drama. For him, the black and white experiences were inseparable. They each affected the other. That was a concept that he felt his friend Riley did not grasp. In his words, Gordone commented that "... brother Clayton is uptight. He can't face it that the Man is helping one of his brothers."[15]

Moreover, the dramatist insisted that "in the last analysis, I do believe there never has been such a thing as 'black theater.' What is called black theater has, as it should, come out of the civil rights movement. Before that, it was simply called 'the Negro in the theater.' The commercial theater – the Broadway stage – in the past has depicted blacks in sensational and stereotypical ways. The Broadway stage has never really had an interest in the black experience."[16]

The forty-four-year-old dramatist won a victory of sorts when *No Place to Be Somebody* garnered the 1970 Drama Desk Award, the Critic's Circle Award, and the Pulitzer Prize. In his letter to Gordone awarding him the Pulitzer Prize, President Andrew W. Cordier of Columbia University congratulated him on a "distinguished and significant achievement."[17]

Despite the Pulitzer Prize, Gordone never again achieved national recognition. He would write only a few more plays, including *Gordone is a Muthah* (1973) and *The Last Chord* (1976).[18] In 1982, Kerr would query his readers, "Has anyone seen hide or hair of the Pulitzer-prize winning Charles Gordone, whose *No Place to Be Somebody* was once – once – so exciting?"[19] The remainder of the actor-director-dramatist's life was spent directing and lecturing in community theaters across America, penning a few dramas, taking bit parts in other people's plays, and teaching college courses.

Although he worked on and in dozens of films during the fifties and sixties, Gordone is only credited with three screen assignments: the previously mentioned Carl Lerner's *Black Like Me* and Michael Roemer's *Nothing But a Man*, as well as an actor in Ralph Bakshi's *Coonskin* (1975). The latter, a highly controversial movie about black life in the United States, mixes live action and animation. Donald Bogle remains one of the few critics defending the film, saying that its plot "is actually not too different from those countless black action films of the period, starring the likes of Jim Brown and Fred Williamson. And perhaps for that reason, the black audience (much of which was lured into seeing the film simply because of the controversy) did not view it with either shock or outrage."[20]

Gordone's activism, however, never diminished. In 1962, reported Warren Marr, II, the activist co-founded and co-chaired with Godfrey Cambridge the Congress of Racial Equality's Committee for the Employment of Negro Performers, whose primary goal consisted of getting black performers work in the legitimate theater.[21] "All we wanted to do," explained Gordone, "was to get black performers a chance to audition for jobs same as white actors."[22] In 1975, he worked with a group of inmates at the Bordertown, New Jersey, Youth Correctional Institution on Clifford Odets' play, *Golden Boy*. He also staged Cell Block Theatre in Yardville Prison, also in New Jersey, from 1977 to 1978. During the late 1980s, "He weighed in on the controversial concept of nontraditional casting, arguing that minority actors should be included in realistic American plays, but not without acknowledging their ethnicity or the play's historical context."[23]

Charles Edward Gordone died on November 17, 1995. He was seventy years old.

Four months before I met Gordone, Margaret Harford wrote in the *Los Angeles Times*, "A writer eruption has sparked the resurgence of black theater in America, and no one stands taller at the head of the black authorship brigade than Charles Gordone."[24] I knew little of this, although I had seen *No Place to be Somebody* the year before. Once I arrived in Los Angeles in January, 1972, Sylvia Silvano, a friend of Jason Robards, arranged a meeting with Gordone.

Our limited relationship began badly. Somehow, we had misunderstood when the meeting was to take place. On January 5, Sylvia called me, quite agitated. Gordone had canceled a rehearsal to meet with me that morning, and I had not shown up. I thought the meeting was set for the 10th. She asked me to call him and apologize. Therefore, I called, and a man speaking Spanish asked who was calling and what I wanted. When I explained how distressed I was, and how much I wanted to meet with Gordone, the actor-director acknowledged that he was the speaker, and we agreed to meet the morning of the 10th.

When I arrived, I believe I was at the lowest point in my feelings for the project. After meeting with a number of personalities since November – e.g., Lorenzo Tucker, King Vidor, Clarence Muse, Woody Strode, Cicely Tyson, Roscoe Lee Browne, Brock Peters, and John Ford – I felt terribly confused. Nothing seemed to make sense, and few celebrities were willing to give me direction. Gordone and I talked about this for over an hour, long before the taping began. Although the reader will get some idea of how Gordone tried to help me, the actual tape conversation is too brief to do justice to his kindness. The finest reminder for me is an autographed picture he later sent me, inscribed "To one of the best researchers going."

Gordone once described himself by drawing on William Wordsworth's observations, "What is a poet? He is a man speaking to men ... a man pleased with his own passions and volitions, and one who rejoices more than other men in the spirit of life that is in him."[25] That is the way I remember him thirty-four years later.

Charles Gordone Interview
January 10, 1972

Gordone: Well, first of all, my introduction to film.... See, I graduated from Los Angeles State College. I married out here. Had children out here. I went to Los Angeles City College. Then eventually graduated from Los Angeles State College. And then in 1952, I went to New York. But during the time I was out here, which was about thirteen ... fifteen years, I worked in some sixty films as an actor.

Manchel: I didn't know that.

Gordone: Well, a lot of people don't know that. Because you see.... What I mean by fifty, sixty films is that.... I'd just show up at central casting and just go out, because I could ride a horse or whatever. But that took some time, too. I was a black actor, but they didn't consider me as being a black actor because, you know, my type.... And they couldn't cast me in the films they were doing, these cha-cha movies.... You know, bullshit movies ... at the time. You know, Rouben Mamoulian.

The films Mamoulian made during this time period were Golden Boy *(1939),* The Mark of Zorro *(1940),* Blood and Sand *(1941),* Rings on Her Fingers *(1942),* Summer Holiday *(1947). According to biographer, Tom Milne, the director also worked on* Laura *(1944) and* Gone to Earth *(1950).*[26]

Gordone: People like Rouben Mamoulian, and Michael Curtiz, and Otto Preminger. And these people were principally working with black actors. In other words, they were white directors who had a reputation for being able to work with Negroes.

The noted black actors that worked with these directors in the period from 1939 to 1952 were individuals like Dooley Wilson in Curtiz's Casablanca *(1943), Clinton Rosemond in Mamoulian's* Golden Boy *(1939), and Stymie Beard in Preminger's* Fallen Angel *(1945). I suspect Gordone is confusing the directors' early works with later productions by Preminger like* Carmen Jones *(1954) – with an all-black cast, including Dorothy Dandridge, Harry Belafonte, and Pearl Bailey –* Porgy and Bess *(1959) – again featuring Dandridge and Bailey, along with Sidney Poitier and Sammy Davis, Jr. – and* Hurry Sundown *(1967) – with performers like Diahann Carroll, Beah Richards, and Rex Ingram. Interestingly, Mamoulian began as the director of* Porgy and Bess, *but was later replaced by Preminger.*[27]

Gordone: And as a kid, I worked in some of these films. You know, things with Esther Williams ... and Fernando Lamas. And all that jive, you know. And eventually ... I went to City College.... Ray Hamilton, who has been in films ever since he was a kid, runs the Citadel over here, a nightclub which he can't quite get together, so he sells Christmas trees. His brother is Chico Hamilton, the drummer.... You know Chico Hamilton, the drummer?

Manchel: No.

Gordone: The jazz drummer?

Manchel: Nope.

Gordone: A very famous jazz drummer. And Bernie Hamilton, you know, he did things on television, if you ever talk to him a little bit. He did things on television like *Body and Soul*.... He works on television a lot. But still doing small parts. He's a fellow about my age. You know, we were like kids together.... I've seen and I've studied not only blacks in theater, because that's where it all begins.... It begins there, and then they come out here [Hollywood]. People like Ivan Dixon.

Ivan Dixon was one of the individuals I interviewed while in Hollywood in January 1972. We met the day after my meeting with Gordone. Dixon's observations will appear in the next volume of interviews. According to Donald Bogle, both Dixon and Hamilton "ushered in a new style of black sexuality in the 1960s."[28] Among Dixon's credits up to 1972 were Richard Brooks' Something of Value *(1957), Otto Preminger's* Porgy and Bess *(1959), Michael Roemer's* Nothing But a Man *(1964), and Guy Green's* A Patch of Blue *(1965). The actor had also gained celebrity status as Corporal James Kinchloe in the hit TV sitcom,* Hogan's Heroes, *that ran from 1965 to 1971 on CBS. The year we talked, he had started directing. His first film was* Trouble Man *(1972). Later, he would take on* The Spook Who Sat By the Door *(1973).*

Gordone: I was associate producer on a movie called *Nothing But a Man*. I came out here to recruit Ivan for that. I went down to Florida to get Abbey Lincoln, you see, to do it. And then Julius Harris, you know, who played Sweets in my play [*No Place to Be Somebody*].

In addition to Nothing But a Man, *Julius Harris played character roles in some of the most popular black action films of the sixties and seventies: e.g., Herbert J. Biberman's* Slaves *(1969), Ivan Dixon's* Trouble Man, *Gordon Parks, Jr.'s* Superfly, *and* Shaft's Big Score *(all in 1972), Larry Cohen's* Black Caesar *(1973), and Joseph Sargent's* The Taking of Pelham One Two Three *(1974).*

Gordone: I had nothing to do with Ivan in the business, but I did have something to do with Julius and Abbey in the business, because Abbey had no inkling that she would begin to turn to acting. Because when I first called her.... I spoke to my wife [Jeanne Warner], and we were trying to think who would be the girl [in *Nothing But a Man*], and we went down the line – Diana Sands on down. Who could do it? We finally came up with the name Abbey Lincoln. So we called Max, Max Roach, who was her husband. They're since divorced. We called Max, and he said, "She's down there in Miami in a Playboy Club, singing. So give her a call." So we called her, and she was amenable to it, and she came up and we tested her. After that, she was cast in it.

Manchel: Incredible.

Abbey Lincoln made her screen debut in Nothing But a Man. *Although a delightful screen personality, she only appeared in two more films – Daniel Mann's* For Love of Ivy *(1968) and Frank Tashlin's* The Girl Can't Help It *(1956) – while always maintaining her popular singing career.*

Gordone: So I've had a very salutary experience with a lot of black actors. For instance, Godfrey Cambridge, you know, when he first came from Nova Scotia ... when he first came down from Canada to New York. At the time, I was directing... at that particular time, I was directing *Detective Story* [1960]. And I wanted to use a Mexican act with it, and not because I wanted to do that particular thing. I just wanted to have some Americana in there. I didn't know him at the time. I had seen him around a little bit. A couple of days I had seen him around. I saw he was a big fat black cat with a lot of spirit and a lot of laughs and everything. A big ego, you know, compensating for obeseness.

A very talented comedian, Godfrey Cambridge became one of the most visible black stars of this era. Although he made his screen debut in Daniel Mann's The Last Angry Man *(1959), his first big success was in the 1961 stage production of Jean Genet's* The Blacks, *when he played an African-American male turned into an aging white female, for which he won an Obie Award. By then, he began appearing in films stressing racial themes, such as Nicholas Webster's* Gone Are the Days *(1963) and Melvin van Peebles'* Watermelon Man *(1970). His biggest film success was in Ossie Davis'* Cotton Goes to Harlem *(1972), where he starred as the wisecracking Grave Digger Jones, the partner of Coffin Ed Johnson (Raymond St. Jacques). The spunky cops were such a hit that they appeared in a sequel, Mark Warren's* Come Back, Charleston Blue *(1972). Cambridge died at age 43, from a heart attack while on the set of the TV movie,* Victory at Entebbe, *on November 29, 1976.*

Gordone: He's walking down the street.... They recognized me right away, he and Hugh Hurd. I said, "I'm directing *Detective Story* over at

Equity Library Theatre." That's when the old Equity Library Theater was over there on 70th-something Street. East 76th Street or something like that. So they came over, and I didn't even read him. And Godfrey had just gotten in town. And he did Brody, the.... What's the name of the actor who did it [in the film], who did Brody?

Manchel: Kirk Douglas?

Gordone: No, no. Kirk Douglas played the detective. His sidekick was played by ... what's his name? He died ...

Manchel: What else had he done?

The actor was William Bendix. The 1951 screen adaptation of Sidney Kingsley's play was co-authored by Philip Yordan and Robert Wyler, with William Wyler directing.

Gordone: I can't think of his name. He was marvelous ... a big cat ... that played with Kirk Douglas in it, in the movie.... Oh, mamma mia. I'll think of his name....

When he [Cambridge] did Brody, his career [claps his hands] ... I mean immediately, his career began to zoom, and he went to nightclubs. And from nightclubs – he went to nightclubs as a standup operator – and then from nightclubs, he went into films, which he is into now.

So a lot of these actors – for instance, you mention Brock Peters. Well, Brock Peters, his name is not Brock Peters. His name is George Fisher.

Brock Peters was another performer I interviewed while in Hollywood in January, 1972. His observations will also appear in the next volume of interviews. Because of his powerful presence, Peters often specialized in playing menacing black figures on screen. Among his best-known films are Carmen Jones *(1954),* Porgy and Bess *(1959), Sydney Lumet's* The Pawnbroker *(1965), and Larry Peerce's* The Incident *(1967). Three of his finest performances, however, were in unique roles as the falsely accused rapist in Robert Mulligan's* To Kill a Mockingbird *(1962), the gay jazz musician in Bryan Forbes'* The L-Shaped Room *(1963), and the driven minister in Daniel Mann's* Lost in the Stars *(1973).*

Gordone: The first time I met George was in Harlem, when we were doing a play, a musical called *The Year Round* (1959). A lot of cats that worked in that musical, called *The Year Round*, are now, you know, doing very well.

So we come from a period, for instance, out of *The Blacks*, you know. You realize the people that come out of *The Blacks* [1961]. There's Cicely Tyson. There's James Earl Jones. There's Roscoe Lee Browne. There is Raymond St. Jacques. There's Maya Angelou Mackay up in Berkeley, who wrote the book.... Maya Angelou Mackay. And Lou Gossett.

Produced by Sidney Bernstein in the spring of 1961, Jean Genet's The Blacks *had one of the most extraordinary casts in the history of black drama. In addition to those performers mentioned by Gordone, the gritty play attacking whites also had during its New York Lower East Side run the following actors: Godfrey Cambridge, Charles Gordone, and Helen Martin.*[29] *Gordone himself wrote that the play "introduced a force of talented, competent black actors who went on to influence change in all of the entertainment media."*[30]

Gordone: All those people, that was a turning point at which those people from the stage came into film and are now moving with the film area. Well, because ... first of all, they had a good basis. They had a good basis for what is happening historically in films now. Historically, what I mean is, these people have the technique and have the acting know-how, instead of the old hat of where they went to nightclubs to get actors. Now they can go to the New York stage or the off-Broadway stage, and get actors who can do the job. Whereas before they went to nightclubs, you know. Lena Horne never studied a day in her life in terms of acting. Eartha Kitt....

I could name you any number of people who were basically performers, and there's a difference between performing and acting. And we don't even use the term "acting" anymore in the business. People who are really with it, we don't use the term "acting" anymore. We use the term "behaving." You behave that part, you don't act that part. You call yourself an actor, yes. And you act, yes. But these are only advisory terms. You use the term advisedly. When you are with your craft, you don't call it acting. You call it behaving. You behave the part.

Now, you have to understand the differences between ... because we are moving into.... In other words, you have the kind of actor, like you have Woody Strode; and you may have a Harry Belafonte or a Sidney Poitier. These people do not know the craft, you see. Because they are caught up in a time that you didn't have to know the craft. And the people that were moving them around, the white people that were moving them around, didn't require them to act. They said, "Just walk down the street, baby; and we'll take a picture of you and make you look groovy."

You know, but the actors today, the young ones coming up, the young ones coming up. These people are not interested in how they look, but what they do. They are interested in something substantive. You know. They are not interested in the fucking planet, because you see what happened here was that when they couldn't, we reached a point when we couldn't get an American actor to do the things that I'm speaking from the white business point of view, you know, the California banks. When we reached a point where we couldn't get ... I mean, the people really didn't want the cats who were studying and getting with it.

They didn't know about us coming up, so they went out and got, excuse the expression, "foreigners." They went and got Harry Belafonte who was not an American; he wasn't born here [sic].

They went and got Sidney Poitier, he wasn't born here. And had him do, you know, the things historically and sociologically which he had no.... Because his money is back in Nassau. And, you know, whenever he wants to spend any money, he's got a fifty, sixty thousand dollar home down there in Nassau. You know, he lives about mile and a half from me. I ain't ... I live in a shack like. I mean I don't give a shit. You know, I mean, I can work there and so forth, and I'm close to the ocean.... He has a big swimming pool, and everything. He's a big friend of ... the Prime Minister there. And he's groovy with the Nassau white group. And he don't put his money in the United States. The only money he puts in the United States, man, is whatever apartment he has. Other than that, man, he takes his money back down in the islands. You know, I know this for a fact.

Time would prove Gordone clearly wrong about Belafonte and Poitier's contributions to American cinema. For examples on how the latter helped train young blacks, see almost any biography on the actor. Since less is written on Belafonte, a good place to start is Marilyn Stasio's essay on the making of Jan Kadar's The Angel Levine *(1970).*[31]

Gordone: So, he's a victim, he's a victim of what that system is. And they don't fool me. That's why they don't dig being around me worth a shit. Because the minute I place my eyes on them, they know they've been looked at. And I know, you see now ... and I use the word again in quotes, they either get "foreigners," what they have done before, "foreigners," you know "black foreigners," or they get women, you know, that they can maneuver. Dorothy Dandridge was a perfect, a very good example of that.

Now you talk about Clarence Muse. He's a fucking Uncle Tom. He's not going to say anything against Hollywood. He still thinks he's going to try to pretty much make some kind of comeback.

Manchel: He is. He's in Sidney Poitier's *Buck and the Preacher* [1972].

Gordone: So, you see, they don't fool me one goddamned bit. But they are going to be usurped. Because us new Niggers is coming in, and we're going to like wipe them off the face of the earth. And they are going to be coming around and saying, "Oh, we lost it, didn't we? We got bread, we got money, but we lost it."

You take Roscoe [Lee Browne], you know, if Roscoe were here, I would tell him....

Roscoe Lee Browne, one of the movies' most overlooked character actors, was still another personality I interviewed in Hollywood that January. To my everlasting regret, however, the tape broke and could not be repaired. Over the years, I tried to get back with him, but circumstances never permitted it.

Manchel: Do you want me to turn off the tape recorder?

Gordone: No. Don't turn nothing off. You take Roscoe. Roscoe has had a fantastic life. He's one of my favorite people. Well, they are all my favorite people, you know. I mean, if I make a criticism of them, it's purely my personal opinion. You can quote me, or you may not quote me. I don't give a shit. You have my tacit consent, because I have no secrets. I have no secrets with my family. I have no secrets with them. Because they know, were they all sitting here, I would say the same goddamned thing.

Because as a former policeman, I learned that you have to be, you have to be as realistic and truthful from your own conceptualization as possible. That keeps you from being killed, man; and I worked in three types of police work. You know, and I've been shot at, stomped on, kicked on, you know. Sometimes when I think about my life, I wonder why I'm still alive. You know, my friends are all falling down dead, you know, with heart attacks; and they got all kinds of shit going on with them, and they fall down....

Afolabi Ajayi, a Nigerian actor, who was a very close friend of Wole Soyinka. Do you know who Wole Soyinka is? Well, he wrote *Kongi's Harvest* [1970]. He wrote *The Strong Breed* and [*The Trials of Brother Jero*]. He spent a lot of time in a South African prison. He was a big poet and a political cat in Africa. He spent a lot of time in jail and so forth. And sometimes somebody would say, "Well, you know, I'm just very sorry that he's dead."

Ossie Davis directed the screen adaptation of Kongi's Harvest, *the Nigerian drama about an insane tyrant who takes over a fictional African nation and fights an attempt by the deposed ruler to regain power. The play was first performed by the Negro Ensemble Company on April 14, 1968, in New York.*[32] *Soyinka's other two short plays were performed in November, 1967.*[33]

Gordone: Just like my man in the West Indies, out of Jamaica. He's a poet and everything. What the fuck's his name? Good friend of mine. Sometimes I get to thinking about all of this jive, and I can't remember. Because of the complexion of what has happened in the past, in the past ten, fifteen years. So much has happened in terms of the black artist, the black painter, the black sculptor, all the aspects of art. It has been so impressive. A ... [person] comes in and says, "Give us the message." "Give us the message." Well, it's just come on; it's just come upon on the scene. Now, everybody is looking to buy black, you know.

Ernest Tidyman included, you see. And look what happens. Ernest Tidyman, he wrote *Shaft*.

Tidyman wrote the screenplay for Gordon Parks' Shaft (1971), which starred Richard Roundtree, the most famous African-American detective in black film history. In a fine bit of nostalgia, the writer put a new spin on his updated script for director John Singleton's Shaft (2000). This time, the popular private eye (now played by Samuel L. Jackson) is the nephew of the legendary blaxploitation hero.

Gordone: Well, he wrote a few other things. He was a fucking hack writer. So he jumps on the black bandwagon, and he writes his first big number, *Shaft*. He don't come to the people who have been in the theater or whatever. He goes, and he gets somebody that he feels the world knows. A still photographer [Gordon Parks]! Now I know that the man has not necessarily worked in still photography. He has worked in 8 mm or 16 mm; or if he is more agile, he goes and buys himself some kind of 35 mm, and he starts experimenting with movement and everything. But what he don't realize is while he's doing that, he don't know a goddamned thing about acting. So we're going to put his name up there, saying, "Gordon Parks directed." And he don't know a goddamn thing about acting. He knows a lot about pictures. He knows how to do that, but he don't know how to direct the actors.

So the actors, they go, and they talk behind his back. They all say, "He don't know shit about acting." He can get a picture, but, you see, a photographer has to know what acting can do to complement the picture, and what the picture can do to complement the actor. You can't just have a series of ... [pictures]. You've seen that in Hollywood for years and years and years. You know people who should've ... [studied] pictures. How many westerns have you seen? How many actors come in ... [unprepared]?

Now you talked a while ago about the fact....

Manchel: Jumping on the bandwagon?

Gordone: Well, yeah! For instance, pictures like *Sweetback* and *Shaft* and so forth and so on, are like carbon copies, you know, of former white movies. If you are going to do that, I'm talking to a group of black chicks the other night. We were sitting around drinking and talking, and so somebody said, "How come we never see you with a black woman?"

Manchel: What the hell does that mean?

Gordone: Black women don't do that? That's part of the whole women's lib now. Black women, you know, are going to assert themselves. I've had this argument with Maya Angelou. She will have a lot to say to you about that. So they say, "How come I never see you getting personal with me?" I know why they are saying that. First of all, they are saying that because they got eyes for me. They got eyes for me. And they want to know why, since they are lovely and beautiful and groovy, why I don't hang out with them.

Manchel: You're not interested in them.

Gordone: No. It's not the fact that I'm not interested in them. Shit, that's not the reason. I mean a woman is a woman to me, if she's a woman. I don't give a damn be she blue, green, orange or yellow. But there is such a thing as the psychological and sociological ... concept or gap. In other words, you see, my background ... and I don't want to use the term "unique." I grew up in the section of the country, in many sections of the country, in which I didn't have to deal with race in a direct way.

Manchel: That's what Woody said. That's what Woody said. The same thing.

Gordone: Who?

Manchel: Woody Strode said the same thing. He grew up in the same context. He didn't know about racism.

Gordone: Well, that's bullshit! You see, you can't make that statement that directly. In other words, that's common. There was not a black, a person of Color; I don't give a damn if they are Chinese, Mexican, Puerto Ricans, or whatever. There is not a time that you don't walk down the street that you are not reminded that you are a person of Color. I think it's a fucking total lie for him to say that. He's saying what he would like you to believe.

Manchel: Okay.

Gordone: You know, I mean, the cat, he was a star. He was a high school star. He was a handsome movie cat. The chicks dug him. The white folks bowed down to him, because he was like somebody different. Because of what he did as a football player.

You know, Willie Mays don't have to suffer no racial bullshit. All he has to do is call up ... [the restaurant] and say, "Willie Mays is coming in." Everyone is going to say, "Oh, yes, Mr. Mays" or whatever.

Jim Brown is a total victim of that kind of system. He got so frustrated that he had to strike out. He had spent years being miserable, you know, and getting his way.

In an angry interview expressing his views on the Civil Rights Movement and the Vietnam War, Gordone concluded with a poem expressing his hopes for the sixties. One stanza read, "An' please, Lawd!! Lay yo' sweet evah loving foot/On Jimmie Brown the actor's ass/ So he don't blow his cool so much."[34]

Gordone: He wouldn't hit no black chick. He ain't hit a black chick yet. If he did, you wouldn't hear about it. The only women he hit were all white women. Because he's been plagued by them pretty much all his life. Now, he's trying to make a turn about, he's been talked to by the studios. He's trying to make a turn about and trying to create, as they say, a new image. He goes on the radio and talks about how he got to do this and that and the other thing.

Jim Brown was yet another personality I had interviewed that January. We met the day after my meeting with Gordone. Brown's observations will appear in the next volume. One of the key sources for me on the ex-football-star-turned-actor during that time was James Toback's Jim. *In 1971, Toback wrote, "It was Jim Brown who, during the decade from 1957 to 1965, had done more than any other man to originate what became a national obsession with the game [football].... More, he introduced a new dimension to the sport, as its first black hero.... When he shifted gears and became, in less than a year [1965], a movie star, the potential of his influence erased limitation."*[35] *Bogle, however, makes the important observation that despite what black audiences thought about the presumed African-American rebel they perceived on the screen, "Brown was a phenomenon simply because films had rarely featured black men of action.... [and he] was often incorporated into the system itself."*[36] *Sally Beauman took a very different tack. Arguing that the new black hero was quite different from Poitier's Virgil Tibbs in* The Heat of the Night *(1967), she emphasized that the current hero was "in essence an outlaw.... a loner, unsympathetic to the methods and the personalities of the white authorities." Beauman went on to add that actors like Brown in* Slaughter *(1972) "tend to be a womanizer, and extremely violent."*[37]

At the time we met, Jim Brown was under heavy attack in the media for allegedly beating up white women. The rumors abounded that the studios had blacklisted him, not only for his mistreatment of women, but also for having an affair with Raquel Welsh. Brown writes about his blackballing in his recent autobiography, Out of Bounds. *Of all the performers I met in January, 1972, none had starred in more films or had a more striking screen presence than Brown did. A brief look at some of the key films in his career during this period reveals just how isolated he became after 1972. His films include Steve Sekely's* Kenner *and Gordon Douglas'* Rio Conchos *(both in 1964), Robert Aldrich's* The Dirty Dozen *(1967), Buzz Kulik's* Riot, *Gordon Flemyng's* The Split, *Jack Cardiff's* Dark of the Sun, *and John Sturgess'* Ice Station Zebra *(all in 1968), Tom Gries'* 100 Rifles *(1969), Jerry Paris'* The Grasshopper, *Ralph Nelson's* Tick...Tick...Tick, *and John Guillermin's* El Condor *(all in 1970), Robert Hartford-Davis'* Black Gunn *and Jack Starrett's* Slaughter *(both in 1972), Gordon Parks, Jr.'s* Three the Hard Way *(1974), and James Toback's* Fingers *(1978). It would be five years before he made his next film, Fred Williamson's* One Down, Two to

Go *(1983)*. *His most recent films are Larry Cohen's* Original Gangstas *(1996), John Woo's* Face/Off *(1997), and Bruce Brown's* On Any Sunday *(2000). In addition, there is a fine documentary by Spike Lee on the actor,* Jim Brown: All-American.

Manchel: Let me ask you a question about Jim Brown. Everyone that I talk to in the black community seems to hate him so much. Because of the public ... [furor]. Yet everything I read about him ... [gives the impression] that he is the most wonderful guy you would ever want to meet. And he is. They say he is the most warm and wonderful guy. There is a guy running the black exposition here, a guy named Bob Sye. I don't know whether you've been in touch with him or not. He's putting together a program on the black cinema. And he said he once needed five thousand dollars, and Jimmy said, "Here, take it." And he never pressed him for the money. He never made a big deal about it. Nothing. He [Sye] said he was the nicest guy....

Gordone: Of course, he [Brown] is. But you see, he's pushy, he's pushy. Now he is a very gentle man. A chick will say, "Well, how come...?" You see, chicks are this way, like if they.... All of a sudden, if they're with you and you're like an idol, a sometime idol. They want to be with that idol. And they don't want you to have nothing to do with nobody else. You see, if they hear about you being out with somebody else, they gonna raise hell with you. So you just say, "Will you please shut up. Will you please be cool. I don't want to hear it, baby." Well, I mean, if you're a cat that's not too hip, you're going to say, "Well baby, you know, these chicks don't matter. You're the one." Well, the chick knows you're lying. "You're the one I love. Well, I've got to go out with this one, or I have to do that, because that's what the public demands and that's where I am." So the chick's just bitching at you, just bitching. And all of a sudden, you look at her, and you want to just throw the shit out of her. Well, a cat like that has no recourse. He'll go at it, man. He'll just pick her up and throw her ass down a flight of stairs. I know it. I know the feeling. And they want to identify with that. Well, maybe we're getting away from [our discussion of blacks]; or maybe we're not.

Manchel: No, no. You're teaching me how to understand, helping me to understand....

Gordone starts laughing, and the tape shuts off momentarily.

Manchel: You know, I lived all my life like a Jew in the ghetto. And I'm just trying to understand where I went wrong [in these interviews].
Gordone: You didn't have to tell me that. You weren't ready.

Manchel: I know. I had a guy [Leroy Bowser in the Tucker interviews] who gave me a real going over in New York. Who told me that I had to learn the seven something of blackness. "Did I know what the seven something of blackness were?" And I said, "No." And he said, "That's what explains everything."

So I said, "What are the seven something of blackness?"

Gordone: Who was that?

Manchel: A guy who was a teacher. A black teacher, who was really going wild about a liberation fight in New Jersey. How that was so great, and he was praising a film called *The Bus is Coming*. Not *The Bus is Coming; Sweetback*. The greatest film ever made.

Gordone: Bullshit.

Manchel: That's what I said. And he said to me, "You don't understand." And I said, "Well, teach me. I want to learn." And he said, "Nobody can teach you. You have to learn for yourself."

Gordone: It's a racist statement. It's a racist statement. In other words, you begin the premise with this. I ask my daughter, who was about eight, my young daughter. I have nine children. She was eight in October. We were born a week apart, like. And my wife tried to press her out for my birthday, because I was born on the 12th. And I asked my daughter, "What is the difference between a man and a woman?" And she couldn't tell me. I said, "Well what is the difference between your dog and you?" She says, "I am a clothespin." I say, "What, a clothespin?" She said, "Yes. Because I walk on split ends." I said, "Ooh, that's heavy. Walking on the split ends." I got a picture over here. I'll show you.

Manchel: Tell me what you see in black films. I told you what I see in black films.

Gordone: You spoke about something a while ago, about the fact of black films today following on the heels of the formulas of yesterday, being white. And that's a very good point. I feel that we should talk more now, in my ... [perspective] Leroy Jones, or some of the more militant ... Eldridge Cleaver or whatever, or with Malcolm X. I had the good fortune of knowing all of them. Not very well, but in varying degrees. I think we should begin to talk a little bit....

If we are going to do black films, we should do something more about their more personal lives, familial, the things they have to resort to, you know, internally, as opposed to always delivering invectives against the white man. You see the white man has been cussed out enough. He's been cussed out so much that he digs it.

Manchel: He makes money on it.

Gordone: As long as the white man hears Niggers, you know, cussing him out and telling him how rotten they are and so forth and so on, he digs it, man.

Manchel: He makes money on it.

Gordone: Yeah, but if blacks resort to ... came back and started talking about the beautiful families and the things that they do among themselves, and the kinds of stories that go on, you know, just among themselves, *sans* the white man ... Well, then we are going to get back on the right track. But if we keep, you know, cussing out the white man and talking about how much we hate him, and all that jive, I mean that gets old.

Manchel: It distracts you from what you're supposed to be doing.

Gordone: Right on. You see, Ibsen, Strindberg, Pirandello, Shaw, and going back to Shakespeare, clear on back, most of those stories were just about the problems that the families had. *Hamlet*, you know, is a beautiful story about the difficulty that he had with his own family, not about the world outside. Even though the world outside was there always and Shakespeare didn't let you forget it, you know. But we have to begin to talk about, if black is beautiful, then let's not ... black ain't beautiful if you are calling somebody a "mother fucker" all the time. You know, then you say, "Well fuck it man, you've heard that before. Is there anything new?" You know, this cat that told you, you know, do you know the seven this and the seven that. I mean, this cat, man, I would have just walked out on him.

Manchel: I can't. My job is as a beggar. I'm going out looking for information. I've got to take it in order to learn.

Gordone: Then get with the cats, man, who are amenable to what you are doing and don't have any particular malice toward you.

Manchel: But I can't get to them. They won't see me, Chuck. They're too busy. They're too big. I'm a nobody. I've been trying to get to [Godfrey] Cambridge. Thanks to Sylvia Silvano [Jason Robards' friend]. She got me to Gordon Parks, and she got me to Melvin van Peebles.

I actually contacted these people, but, unfortunately, the interviews never materialized.

Manchel: I can't get to Lena Horne, I can't get to Sammy Davis, Jr. I can't get to Sidney Poitier. I can't get to Harry Belafonte.

Gordone: I don't give a shit.

Manchel: But they're part of the story. Otherwise, what I am is just a bullshit artist.

Gordone: Well, then get it from somebody else.

Manchel: From whom? From whom?

Gordone: Well, I don't know. I've talked to you about these people. I mean, I don't give a shit whether I'm quoted or not. In other words, I'm just giving you my opinion. If they want to hire equal time, but it will be too late. It will be absolutely too late. I mean if they can't see you, well fuck 'em. That's part of that milieu, that's part of that area of which people don't want to rap to you.

Manchel: Now tell me about that.

Gordone: I just played Bangla Desh, I was playing Bangla Desh when you came in.

What Gordone is referring to is the recording of The Concert for Bangla Desh, *held at Madison Square Garden on August 1, 1971. Earlier that year, General Yahya Khan had set aside the democratically held elections in East Pakistan (Bangla Desh) and began oppressing millions of Pakistanis. By the summer, over a million people from Bangla Desh had been murdered, with ten million more fleeing the country. In an effort to offer relief from the mass tragedies, illnesses, and starvation, George Harrison and Ravi Shankar had contacted various people for a relief concert. Among those who participated beside Shankar, were Eric Clapton, Bob Dylan, Billy Preston, and Leon Russell. The album includes a booklet describing a brief history of the events, along with pictures of the concert.*

Gordone: Well, these are cats, man, these are the cats ... they move with the ... they're part of history. They are very closely tied with India. But also, they partake of what's going on over here. Because they borrow from the United States, and also they can borrow from India. Ravi Shankar, you know, they have helped Ravi Shankar tremendously. Also, the concert was given for Bangla Desh. You know, I mean, that's where it's at, man.

These people, man, they are way behind. They got money. They got money in the bank. What do they need with you?

Manchel: That's my problem.

Gordone: What do they need with you? I mean, I don't need you. I mean, why do I need you?

Manchel: No. But the point I'm.... What I'm trying to do is to write an honest book. Whether it's for me or anyone else. Trying to educate people.... I think the whole answer is in education.

Gordone: Well, they don't want.... You see, my opinion of that is that they don't want to give away no secrets. They want ... they are not honest people. First of all, they are not built for honesty. Harry Belafonte is not built on honesty. People like Sammy Davis, Jr. are not built on honesty. Otherwise, he never would have like, you know, called himself Jewish. I mean, he may be Jewish, he may have some Jewish background, somewhere, say you know if he looked it up and found out that perhaps he may have come out of Ethiopia or somewhere, which I doubt, you know.

I mean, for instance, in the press, you know, people quote me as saying that I am part Indian, part Irish, part Italian, and various other sundry things. And they ended up with maybe that I am a Nigger. You know what Niggers read in that is, "What the fuck is he doing there? What's he saying?" But it's true, it's documented. It's there, it's on my birth certificate. You know, my name is not Gordone for nothing. You know, some Niggers don't believe my name is Gordone, you know. I was a product of the First World War, you know. Well, I mean my name is not Williams, my name is not Johnson, my name is not Jones, and I'm certainly not going to change to no X's or Y's or Z's. So, you know, you have to spend time sorting yourself out from all these different social, political philosophies which are going on even amongst people of color. Not only that, but also with whites.

Manchel: But how a man with your background and your abilities.... Can you make a film you want to make, or you don't want to deal with that?

Gordone: Yeah, I mean it's inevitable. You see, I just finished a screenplay of *No Place to Be Somebody*.

According to a report at the time, Gordone had also finished a screenplay of Julius Horowitz's novel, The W.A.S.P.; *a new drama,* A Little More Light Around the Place; *and a musical based on Herb Leoro's* The Block. *None of the four works ever was shown, or if they were, they failed commercially.*

Manchel: Did you cast it?

Gordone: We don't know yet. You see, I just finished the screenplay. And we're looking forward to getting into production in April.

Manchel: Have you got a studio?

Gordone: Yeah.

Manchel: Who's going to handle it?

Gordone: I can't divulge that. We were just talking about that at USC the other night. I can't say.

Manchel: Are you going to shoot in New York? Do you know where you are going to shoot?

Gordone: Yeah. We're going to shoot in New York, San Francisco, and [do] the studio work out here.

Manchel: Is Equity going to be part of it?

Gordone: Not Equity, Screen Actors Guild.

Manchel: I'd love to be there. Do you think you have a walk-on part for me?

Gordone: There might be. [We both laugh.]

Manchel: Tell me about the problems you had with films in the sixties or the forties.

Gordone: I gotta tell you about that. I had a young wife, who at the time when I was here.... She was sixteen years old, and I was about twenty-one, twenty-two. And she was sixteen, moving into seventeen, pregnant.

And I was living over here in Risso Village, which is way east of Los Angeles, in a project house. Even today if you go over to Risso Village, you'll see a plaque with Franklin Delano Roosevelt's imprint on it. And I was getting about one hundred twenty-five dollars from the government as a veteran, and you know pay the rent, support my pregnant family. And going from there to Los Angeles City College and back, you know. Well, I had one hundred twenty-five dollars, just to do it. At that particular time, there were cats like Jim Coburn, Bob Vaughn.... Well, I mean, you know, there were some other people like ... who was Judy Garland's wardrobe cat, made costumes, still does. And there was Mark Hammond, who later married ... his name is Mark Harron now, at the time his name was Truman. And there were cats like Hugh O'Brien, you know; at that time, his name was Hugh Crampy. Yeah, Crampy. And he was going out with.... what's her name? Garner?

Manchel: James Garner?

Gordone: No, the girl?

Manchel: What was she in?

Gordone: Garner? Gardner? She played the little girl in the film, *A Tree Grows in Brooklyn* [1945].

Manchel: Margaret O'Brien?

Gordone: No, no. I'm so awful with names.... Something, something Garner.

Manchel: Peggy Ann Garner.

Gordone: Peggy Ann Garner. And he was like making out with her, you know, Hugh Crampy. We had people that came out in droves and went to Hollywood, and today are still making good. As a matter of fact, as a school for people who went into the Hollywood business, that school is very famous for that. They could boast all kinds of names, including a Pulitzer Prize winner.

Anyway, we were talking about....

Manchel: Segregation and the problems that made you famous.

Gordone: I have always had a tendency to... once you mention something, it puts me into something else. You asked me something, and I went into this....

77. Abbey Lincoln. Publicity shot from *Nothing But a Man*. Courtesy of The Manchel Collection, Burlington College.

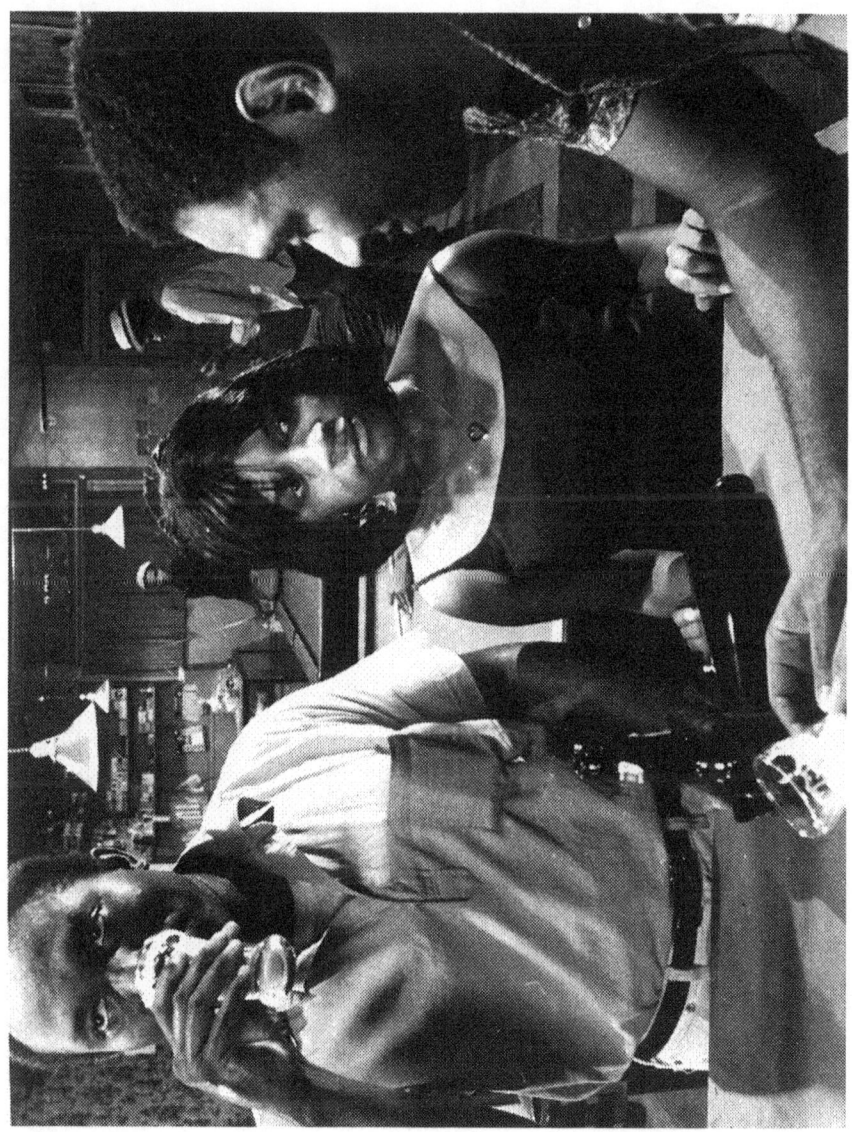

78. From left to right, Leonard Parker, Helene Andindell, and Ivan Dixon. *Nothing But a Man.* Courtesy of The Manchel Collection, Burlington College.

Notes

[1] Henry Lewis Gates, Jr., *Thirteen Ways of Looking at a Black Man* (New York: Random House, 1997), xvii.
[2] Charles Gordone, "A Quiet Talk with Myself," *Esquire*, January 1970, 326.
[3] "The Prize Winners," *Ebony*, July 1970, 36.
[4] Jack Kroll, "From the Muthah Lode," *Newsweek*, 25 May 1970, 95.
[5] Patricia Bosworth, "From Nowhere to 'No Place'," *New York Times*, 8 June 1969, 11.
[6] Kroll, "From the Muthah Lode," 95.
[7] "Charles Gordone Press Release," (Springer/Warner Productions, 1972).
[8] Gordone, "A Quiet Talk with Myself," 326.
[9] Walter Kerr, "Not since Edward Albee...." *New York Times*, 18 May 1969, 1.
[10] "Milestones," *Time*, 4 Dec. 1995, 29.
[11] Lawrence Bommer, "Stage Acting; Studio Rekindles Rage of '68," *Chicago Tribune*, 24 Feb. 1994, 11C.
[12] "The Prize Winners," 37.
[13] Quoted in Bosworth, "From Nowhere to 'No Place,'" 1.
[14] Clayton Riley, "O, Blacks, Are We Damned Forever?" *New York Times*, 18 May 1969, 22.
[15] Quoted in Bosworth, "From Nowhere to 'No Place,'" 11.
[16] Charles Gordone, "Yes, I Am a Black Playwright, But...." *New York Times*, 25 Jan. 1970, 1.
[17] Andrew W Cordier, "Letter to Charles Gordone," (1970).
[18] Woll, *Dictionary of the Black Theater: Broadway, Off-Broadway, and Selected Harlem Theater*, 210.
[19] Quoted in Robin Pogrebin, "Charles Gordone Is Dead at 70; Won a Pulitzer for His First Play," *New York Times*, 19 Nov. 1995, 51.
[20] Bogle, *Blacks in American Film and Television: An Encyclopedia*, 66.
[21] William Marr, II, "Black Pulitzer Prize Awardees," *The Crisis*, May 1970, 188.
[22] Quoted in Bosworth, "From Nowhere to 'No Place,'" 11.
[23] Pogrebin, "Charles Gordone Is Dead at 70; Won a Pulitzer for His First Play," 51.
[24] Margaret Harford, "Gordone Puts Spark in Black Theater," *Los Angeles Times*, 8 Sept. 1970, H1.
[25] Lawrence Christon, "Gordone: An Arresting Darkness," *Los Angeles Herald-Examiner*, 27 Sept. 1970, 7.
[26] Tom Milne, *Mamoulian* (Bloomington: Indiana University Press, 1969), 173.
[27] Ibid., 173-174.
[28] Bogle, *Blacks in American Film and Television: An Encyclopedia*, 204.
[29] Loften Mitchell, *Black Drama: The Story of the American Negro in the Theatre* (New York: Hawthorn Books, 1967), 186.
[30] Gordone, "Yes, I Am a Black Playwright, But...", 11.
[31] See also Gates, *Thirteen Ways of Looking at a Black Man*.
[32] Woll, *Dictionary of the Black Theater: Broadway, Off-Broadway, and Selected*

Harlem Theater, 95-96.

[33] Ibid., 158-159.

[34] Gordone, "A Quiet Talk with Myself," 331.

[35] James Toback, *Jim: The Author's Self-Centered Memoir on the Great Jim Brown* (Garden City, NY: Doubleday, 1971), 6-7.

[36] Bogle, *Blacks in American Film and Television: An Encyclopedia*, 363.

[37] Sally Beauman, "Goodbye, Mr. Tibbs: The Selling of Pseudo-Soul," *New York*, 4 Sept. 1972, 52.

79. Frederick Douglass O'Neal. Inscribed: "To Frank Manchel; with best wishes in his search for truth. Frederick Douglass O'Neal." Courtesy of The Manchel Collection, University of Vermont.

7
From Actor to Activist: Frederick Douglass O'Neal

> "By definition, black popular culture is a contradictory space. It is a sight of strategic contestation. But it can never be simplified or explained in terms of the simply binary opposition that are still habitually used to map it out: high versus low; resistance versus incorporation; authentic versus inauthentic; experiential versus formal; opposition versus homogenization. There are always positions to be won in popular culture, but no struggle can capture popular culture itself for our side or theirs."
>
> *Stuart Hall*[1]

In his last interview in 1991, Frederick Douglass O'Neal said, "I don't claim to be a champion. I simply believe in what I do and do what I believe. I'll let my record speak for me."[2] That record is clear. No African-American artist in the twentieth century was more involved in helping establish a black presence in the theater than Frederick Douglass O'Neal. He founded important theatrical troupes, became the first African-American to head Actors Equity Association (AEA), and was president of the Associated Actors and Artistes of America. Theodore Bikel, who succeeded the veteran actor in each of the presidential offices, stated, "He was a champion of actors' rights, of minorities' rights, and of the rights of all working men and women. He was a fine actor, but he subjugated his professional life to these causes. As a consequence, he served his profession better than it served him because he was always more ready to give than to receive."[3]

Not much useful material is available on this extraordinary individual. Although he granted many interviews and historians on the black theater credit him with considerable breakthroughs, film scholars have mostly ignored the treatment given O'Neal in the nearly ten films he made between 1949 and 1970. Fortunately, Renee A. Simmons' biography on his contributions to the American theater provides important information on his background and ideas.

Born in Mississippi on August 27, 1905, to Ransome James and Minnie Bell (Thompson) O'Neal, Frederick Douglass O'Neal was the sixth of eight children. He was named after Frederick Douglass, the famous nineteenth century black abolitionist, rhetorician, and correspondent. Sheila Rule points out that despite the fact that O'Neal and "his seven brothers and sisters were often painfully aware of segregation, they did not suffer economically."[4] It was during his childhood in his hometown of Brooksville, Mississippi, that O'Neal developed a love for the theater. Simmons dates his stage debut in an elementary school play in 1913.[5]

Two years after his father's death, when the boy was seventeen, the family moved to St. Louis, Missouri, where he graduated high school in 1921. Over the next decade, O'Neal took a number of jobs and experimented with a variety of professions. At the same time, he pursued courses in acting and occasionally performed with various community theater groups in different parts of the United States.

The turning point came in 1927, when he formed and headed the Aldridge Players, christened for Ira Aldridge, the first African-American actor to play Shakespeare's famous Moor. (For many years, the Players remained the second longest-running black stock company in America; the Gilpin Players were the first.) The community theater group grew out of the annual dramas staged by St. Louis' Urban League. Ever since 1921, O'Neal had played a part in the productions, and eventually persuaded several of his peers that they should do more than one play a year. The result was a mixture of traditional dramas and new productions. Because of his bulky size, O'Neal himself specialized in three character types: fathers, preachers, and villains. These roles eventually became the ones he performed in films.

An essential feature of the Aldrich Players was learning the basics of stage drama. As the interview will show, O'Neal always prided himself on not only his training, but also the training he provided for those who worked with him. In this instance, it helps to remember that for almost half of the twentieth century, African-Americans found few opportunities in the theater, film, and radio for serious work or meaningful roles.

Ten years with the Aldrich Players left the aspiring character actor hungry for Broadway. Thus in 1937, he left St. Louis and came to New York, where he tried to benefit from the Federal Theater program. By then, the activist theater was under attack from the recently formed House Un-American Activities Committee (HUAC) for its "leftist" activities. It would be closed permanently in 1939. (HUAC would blacklist him in the 1950s.) Consequently, O'Neal found it impossible to get a job on Broadway. Between 1937 and 1942, the struggling actor found it difficult to perform, so he divided his time with working as a laboratory assistant at a pharmaceutical company and taking drama classes in the evening at the New School. He also worked with experimental black stock companies like the Rose McClendon Players and the Richard Huey Players.

Now in his late twenties, O'Neal dreamed of creating a black theater modeled somewhat after Harlem's Lafayette Players, but on a national scale. The breakthrough came in 1939, when he met the dramatist, Abram Hill. The playwright, known for his pioneering work in the Federal Theatre and for creating the Negro Playwrights Company, worked with O'Neal and a handful of other African-American artists from the Rose McClendon Players to establish the American Negro Theater (ANT) in the summer of 1940. It was this group that helped train such famous performers as Ossie Davis, Ruby Dee, Earle Hyman, Harry Belafonte, and Sidney Poitier. Alternating between variety shows (to bring in money) and stage productions (to provide both experience and training for black actors), the group struggled for recognition. The first play they performed was Hill's comedy, *On Striver's Row,* in September, 1940. The next production was Theodore Brown's *Natural Man* in 1941. O'Neal describes those first steps in the interview that follows.

After serving in the army from late 1942 to the spring of 1943 [he was given an honorable discharge, but no reason has ever been given for his brief tour in the military], O'Neal returned to the ANT. Then came their memorable production of *Anna Lucasta* in 1944.

According to Loften Mitchell, the idea to turn Philip Yordan's play about a Polish home into a black family was initiated by Claire Leonard, who served as the agent for both Yordan and Hill. Yordan rewrote the work, then gave it to director Harry Wagstaff Gribble, and he cast the now famous budding performers: Hilda Simms, Earle Hyman, Frederick O'Neal, Alice Childress, and Herbert Henry. The revised work opened first in Harlem and then moved to Broadway. Having outlined its roots, Mitchell then states, "*Anna Lucasta,* for all its trail blazing, is a mediocre play that could never have 'made it' as a 'white play.'"[6]

Nevertheless, the longest-running black drama in American theatrical history provided many heretofore unavailable opportunities for African-American performers. O'Neal, who finally made his Broadway debut as Frank, the domineering brother-in law, received the Clarence Derwent Award for the being the best budding actor of Broadway's 1944-45 season, the New York Drama Critic's Award for Best Supporting Actor, and the Donaldson Award for his performance in that year's drama season. He would repeat the role not only in the 1945 Chicago production and the 1947 London performance, but also in director Arnold Laven's 1958 screen adaptation. It was during his time in England that O'Neal organized the British Negro Theater in London in 1948. These years constituted the first time that the actor could survive solely on the money he made as an entertainer.[7]

What was fascinating about O'Neal's career was that he rarely was treated the same in movies as he was on the stage. Usually he found himself in heavy roles in film. Among his better known films were John Ford/Elia Kazan's *Pinky* (1949), Joseph L. Mankiewicz's *No Way Out* (1950), Richard Brooks' *Something of Value* (1958), and Ossie Davis' *Cotton Comes to Harlem* (1970). In his TV stints, where O'Neal became one of the first black performers on TV, he often-played comic roles in sitcoms like *Car 54, Where Are You?* (where he played Officer Wallace for the 1962-63 season) and *Sergeant Bilko* (1957).

In 1964, the actor and civil rights leader became president of AEA (then a ninety-six percent white organization,[8] the first African-American to serve in that position, and remained in office for another nine years). According to Rule, the "soft-spoken, big-boned six-footer" was such a gentle man that "his gentleness sometimes irritated the more militant younger black members of Equity."[9] From 1970 to 1988, he served as the president of Associated Actors and Artistes. The 4A's, as it is known, functions as the clearinghouse for all performers' groups and the AFL-CIO. He also served as a vice-president with the AFL-CIO, as a member of its executive council from 1969 to 1988, and as a chairperson of its Civil Rights Committee.

Over his lifetime, the actor-activist received many honors. Loften Mitchell spoke for many people who bestowed such honors on O'Neal: "The only thing that one can say about Frederick O'Neal is that he is one of the great men of our time...."[10] The National Association for the Advancement of Colored People named him Man of the Year in 1979. A decade later, in 1990, the veteran American actor was singled out by the Black Film Makers' Hall of Fame.

Frederick Douglass O'Neal died on August 25, 1992. He was survived by his wife of fifty years, Charlotte Talbot Hainey.

I met the distinguished actor for the first and only time at his New York office on 46th Street. He was just as had been described in the press: a big, strapping, modest, soft-spoken, and gentle man. Simmons has accurately called him the "Gentle Giant."[11] Interestingly, he never spoke of his marriage [he had married Charlotte Talbot Hainey on April 18, 1942], nor of the difficulties he had encountered as a struggling black actor in the entertainment world. He never even alluded to the blacklisting troubles he had in the 1950s. One needs to read carefully, therefore, to sense his frustration and disillusionment with the progress of African-Americans in film history and the stage. It becomes clear, however, that this black pioneer had an important story to tell. Moreover, as the actor Robert Earl Jones observed, O'Neal's life "served as an example to black people not to use their color as an excuse for not working hard for achievements ... nothing will take the place of persistence."[12]

Frederick Douglass O'Neal Interview
August 8, 1972

Manchel: Let's start with your reactions to movies about African-Americans in general ... your reactions to them?

O'Neal: Well, I remember some of them. You know there are many people who think today that the blacks are just beginning to make films. This is not true at all. These films were made by Oscar Micheaux way back in the twenties. There were also the two Goldberg brothers who made films. And – I believe his name was Alexander – who made films, too. The Goldberg brothers [Jack, Bert, and Lou], of course, they were Jewish producers, but Micheaux was black. That was back in the twenties. He made a number of films. I don't know where they are now. It would be wonderful if we could locate them again. I had heard that certain people had saved maybe one or maybe two of them – I don't exactly know where they are.

Manchel: Some are at the Schomberg [Museum]. There's a woman – Pearl Bowser – who has one or two of them.

O'Neal: Is that so?

Manchel: We have one, I think, at the university.

O'Neal: You know, they were not very good films, but I think most of the white films of that time weren't very good either, for that matter. As compared with today's work. I remember some of those. I think they wrote them as they went along. I don't think there were any prepared scripts at that time when they went into production. They sort of wrote them as the cameras rolled. There is available one book ... Peter....

Manchel: Peter Noble.

O'Neal: Peter Noble's book [*The Negro in Films*]. And then there is another pamphlet....

Manchel: [V.J.] Jerome [*The Negro in Hollywood Films*].

O'Neal: Jerome. I have those two. I don't know of any others.

Manchel: There's one that just came out – Ed Mapp – called *Blacks in Films* [*Blacks in American Film: Today and Yesterday*], or something like that. It's a thesis he did at NYU, which deals with blacks mostly in the sixties. And there's Langston Hughes' book, *Black Magic*. [*Black Magic: A Pictorial History of the Negro in American Entertainment*].

O'Neal: Well, yes, it doesn't deal exclusively with films. It deals with a number of other things.

Manchel: Right.

O'Neal: There is another fellow that – Excuse me for just a second.

[Break in tape]

Manchel: Have you met with Lorenzo Tucker?

O'Neal: Yes, I know Lorenzo Tucker. He is a good friend of mine.... I never met Mr. Micheaux. I did meet with one or two of the Goldberg brothers. But there is another source on films.

Manchel: Tom Cripps?

O'Neal: Yes, Cripps. He's got a bit of information on it. And then there's another young man – I can't think of his name at the moment. I will think of it shortly. I'm pretty sure he is in this file here. Griffin, Charles Griffin. Let me give you his telephone number and address. He's been doing quite a bit of work on it.

Manchel: You started in show business, I gather, sometime in the twenties? Did you ever think of going into motion pictures? Or trying to get into motion pictures?

O'Neal: Well, at that particular time, I was more interested in the stage. I worked in St. Louis at that time. I was in St. Louis between 1920 and 1936. The Urban League of St. Louis, they would do a production every year. I would usually be in those productions. Then we sort of felt that we would like to work a little more often. So I organized the Aldridge Players in 1927. We produced several shows each year there, until 1936 when I left ... it was still active ... the group was still active. I left in 1936, and I came here. I began working as a laboratory assistant on Long Island – a pharmaceutical house – which was later bought by William Morrow Warner. But I was going to school at night at the New Theater School, which is no longer in existence.

Then about 1939, latter part of 1939, Abe [Abram] Hill and I got together, and we started to talk about setting up an American Negro Theater here in New York. Because I had come to New York at the suggestion – or the insistence – of Zora Neale Hurston who was an orphan, wrote several books, anthropologist, and a very good friend of Fanny Hurst. So I thought that if there was any place where we can really start such a group, it should be here where there's the greatest concentration of blacks in the country.

Abe and I talked about this idea, and we discussed it over a period of months. We decided to call in several others who might be interested in this sort of thing. In the meantime, I was working with what we called the Rose McClendon Players at that time, under the direction of Dick Campbell.

So in 1940 – early in 1940 – we called together six people – making eight now – and after discussing just how many thousands of dollars we were going to need, we decided to send out cards to others, and we collected six cents that night. I'll never forget it.

It wasn't that we didn't have a little more money than that – we had it – but that's all we had with us out of the eight people. Anyway, we got the cards out ... to around twenty or thirty people. There were about thirty people who showed up at that meeting that night, and we got organized – the American Negro Theater got organized in April, 1940. Our first production, of course, was....

Manchel: *On Striver's Row?*

O'Neal: No, the first production was a variety show. We had to sort of get off the ground, and get off the ground pretty quickly. So we set that up hoping that we could get enough money out of that show to do a major production. Unfortunately, we went deeper into debt.

So the next show we did was *On Striver's Row*, and we did collect money from the people and from the members themselves. They were very, very committed to the idea. Some of them pawned articles and so forth. One fellow pawned his grandmother's ring ... don't know if he ever got it out or not.

Anyway, we got the money together; we did *On Striver's Row*. That was quite a hit. We ran for several months. That was Abram Hill's play. Then we did one or two other productions. We did [Theodore Brown's] *Natural Man*, which was based on the legendary figure John Henry. This, I think, was one of the most significant plays we did during the period of our existence. That was done at a time when – during the war – the men were being called one after another – and we finally had to close. We were never able to reassemble it again after the war. But out of that group came people like [Harry] Belafonte and [Sidney] Poitier who started in the school – the American Negro Theater School. We had the agreement of the Board of Education, and they allowed us to use the school at night for classes. That was the high school at 111th Street or 112th Street – Whatley High.

Manchel: What kind of school was it? What did you do at night?

O'Neal: We trained young actors in voice, movement, make-up, and acting, of course. So forth. All the fundamentals.

Manchel: Who did the actual teaching?

O'Neal: We had a group of teachers under the management of [actor-director] Osceola Archer, who was formally at Howard and worked one or two other schools. We had professionals teaching. We also taught play writing. Play writing was taught by Agee, who was probably the best play writing teacher in the country. The design was taught by ... what's his name? I can't think of his name right now. Anyway, he was a top designer here in the city. One of the classes of acting was taught by one of my teachers at the old theater school, Nadya Ramanov. Various others. Very good staff of teachers. Then, also, the people like Earle Hyman, who came out of there; Hilda Simms, Ruby Dee, Alice Childress, Alvin Childress.

Actually, Earle Hyman, at that time, was only seventeen, and he played in *Anna Lucasta* [1944] for several years. And all the while, he had been studying the Norwegian language – he was sort of smitten by Ibsen. So some years ago he went to Norway, and he played there for two or three years at the Norwegian State Theater, in the Norwegian language. Matter of fact, one of those years, he won the award for the best artist in the country. This award is not just restricted to the performing arts. As a matter of fact, members of the performing arts have only won it twice in the history of the award. The only other winner in the performing arts is Charlie Chaplin. And there is a bust of Earle in the State Theater in Oslo. He came out of that group. He's here in New York now. He's on one of the soaps. I don't remember which one it is now.

Manchel: Did he ever do much work in motion pictures?

O'Neal: Earle? No. No. No, he didn't do that much in motion pictures.

Manchel: You have in this biography here[13] ... one of the reasons why you started the American Negro Theater was because you were tired of the clichés and the stereotypes that had been done in the theater up to 1940.

O'Neal: Yes.

Manchel: Were people really consciously involved with attacking those stereotypes in the twenties and thirties?

O'Neal: No. People were just looking for work. While we were all looking for work, some of them were totally dependent upon finding an occasional job, whereas all of us who had jobs outside, we did not have to depend on that for a living. If we had, we would not have made it.

So we worked the day, and we rehearsed at night. We felt there was a place for the Negro Theater, just as there was a place for the Jewish Theater, the place for the German Theater, and so forth and so on. It should be this kind of ethnic theater. All of these people should also be a part of the mainstream American Theater as well, but I think it adds to the overall culture of this society if there are those various ethnic theaters.

Manchel: Absolutely. How do you see these attacks that are being made today on people like Stepin Fetchit, Clarence Muse, Rochester, and Mantan?

O'Neal: I think it's unwarranted. I hate to see this kind of thing happen, because these people came along at a time when a lot of people weren't conscious of the effects of that kind of performance. I think that ... I have a great deal of respect for these actors. Today, of course, you wouldn't do that kind of thing. I don't think so. But I don't think that we should hold them up to any kind of derision. Because I think that we're taking them out of the time context, their own context, so to speak. I think it's wrong. But today, of course, we still have not reached the point in films – or theater, for that matter – that I feel that we are capable of.

When the American Negro Theater was in operation, we did a number of different types of plays. And we did it deliberately because we wanted to ... out of the sort of ... out of this kind of experience we hoped to develop our own particular acting style, and I think we did. As a matter of fact, several critics in England spoke about it. One critic even went so far as to say the English actors should take a lesson from the *Anna Lucasta* company because here was ensemble performance at its best. Of course, there was a reason for it, because we had been together for so long, so that even if there was a mistake, we could anticipate them almost.

Manchel: Did you get much support at all from the white actors, from the legitimate theater, when you were trying to build this? I mean, Orson Wells was involved in all those projects. Was there – when you were trying to build the theater ... or the teaching, or opportunities for the young people who were in the schools – did anyone come along to help, or open doors?

O'Neal: Well, yes. As a matter of fact, these teachers that we had, most of them paid their own expenses – that's about all they got out of it. Most of them were white. We had – this theater was not restricted to blacks – we had several white members in the acting company. One of them was Honey Wallman who owns a small off-Broadway theater, as you know. Another was Harry Hess; he's a very good photographer. Still another was the girl who played in – played one of the leads in *Fiddler on the Roof* – what's her name? I can't think of her name right now. She was the lead there for a while. We had quite a few others that played with us from time to time.

Manchel: Did you ever go into motion pictures – I know you did *Anna Lucasta* (Arnold Laven, 1958) with Eartha Kitt – but did you ever try to get into films and get rebuffed, or have any difficulties getting in? Or were you just never interested?

O'Neal: Oh, I was interested, but I never had any offers, until 1949. I had been to London for quite a while – played there for about a year and a half. When I came back in 1949, it was my first motion picture – that is, commercial motion picture – I had been in the army. But the first commercial motion picture was *Pinky*; that was in 1949. Then followed *No Way Out* (Joseph L. Mankiewicz, 1950), and then came some of the Tarzan films that I'd like to forget.

Simmons lists two Tarzan films in O'Neal's filmography: Tarzan's Peril *(Byron Haskin, 1951) and a 1967 episode on the NBC TV series* Tarzan, *starring Ron Ely. She describes O'Neal's role in the latter "as a stereotypical black beast image of an African chief."*[14] *[65]. Interestingly, neither Henry T. Sampson nor Phyllis Rauch Klotman's important filmographies on black films list movie credits for O'Neal.*

Manchel: Let me ask you a question about *Pinky*, because that's a film that's really beaten today. Deep down. They object very much to the fact that Jeannie Crain played the role – that a black ... [woman] couldn't play it. They object to the relationship between her and the ending. [That] is what Ralph Ellison came down on – given the choice between going North and being in the South, she stayed in the South.

Simply put, Pinky *deals with a black nurse, who has been working in the North, returning to her Southern home. Then, at her grandmother's insistence, she cares for a dying white woman. In gratitude, the woman leaves Pinky a mansion. Rather than continue to pass as white, the light-skinned woman stays in the South, forgoes her love affair with a white doctor, and uses the mansion as a school for black children. The noted cast included Ethel Waters and Ethel Barrymore, both of whom, along with Jeanne Crain, were nominated for Oscars. The latter for Best Actress; the former for Best Supporting Actress.*

O'Neal: There was quite a bit of controversy over that at the time. There were those who insisted Fredi Washington play the part – or some other actress – and this was not done. The excuse given was that they had to have some kind of assurance that the film was going to be a success at the box office, and they wanted to have someone who could draw some money into the box office. I don't know....

Part of the reaction to the film, not often acknowledged, was that the star, Jeanne Crain, was yet another white woman playing a black role. This resulted, in large measure, because of the Motion Picture Production Code insisting that there be no mixing between the races. Ralph Ellison had other objections, more serious. He wrote, "Pinky ... is the story of another suffering mulatto, and the suffering grows out of a confusion between race and love. If we attempt to reduce the heroine's problem to sentence form we'd get something like this: 'Should white-skinned Negro girls marry white men, or should they inherit plantations of old white aristocrats (provided they can find old white aristocrats to will them their plantations) or should they live in the South and open nursery schools for black Negroes?' It doesn't follow, but neither does the action."[15]

Ellison was not the only one upset by Pinky. For example, V.J. Jerome found the film to be "the modern 'streamlined' version of the 'Mammy' cliche. Hollywood reverses the old stereotype to create the New Stereotype.... a reformist, segregationist, paternalistic solution. It is a 'solution' which, as in all past Hollywood films, builds on the acceptance of the 'superiority' of the whites and ends in the endorsement of Jim Crow – in this case, 'liberal,' 'benevolent,' Social democrat Jim Crow."[16] *William Lee Burke, however, dismisses much of "the Communist writer" Jerome's reactions, and offers in place one of the film's strongest defenses. He argues that up to 1949, Pinky "goes the farthest in presenting a leading 'Negro' character in a highly individualized way."*[17]

O'Neal: You see, I wouldn't like to argue Ellison's point here ... but I think that – you – we always hear a great deal of politics mixed up in art, and I think when you start mixing the two, it is confusing – very confusing. It's like, you can say anything you want to say in the theater, but you've got to say it in terms of theater. If you're going to use the theater for a lecture hall, you might as well forget it, because there's nobody listening except you and the people who believe the same as you do. You're not making any progress. If you take, for instance, the play – Arthur Miller's play, *Death of a Salesman* (1949) – there's a great propaganda piece there. But everything he says there, he says in terms of theater. And he's got you from the time the curtain goes up until it goes down. This is something that the progressive playwrights seem to forget. They go in there, and they start pounding, you know.... and then it's just all shit.

Manchel: ... in retrospect, now.... What do you think of *Pinky*? As you see it now? Or as you think back on it now.

O'Neal: Well ... I think it's – I don't think it's forced in any way. I think it was a slice of life – of that period. In the making of the picture, I think that there are some things that I might change – here and there. But other than that, I don't see too much wrong with it.

Worth noting is Henry Louis Gates, Jr.'s reaction to the issue of skin color in the history of African-Americans. Talking to Ophrah Winfrey about her past, the Harvard scholar insisted, "Racism was about economics. That's what it was about. It wasn't about skin color. That was the metaphor for deeper economic relationships. It was always fundamentally about who was going to control the pie, who got the biggest share of the pie."[18]

Manchel: Do you remember anything interesting about the making of the picture? Any incidents, stories, or anecdotes?

O'Neal: Not necessarily anecdotes.... We started out with one director

– a very famous director – I can't think of his name now. He directed John Wayne and others....

Manchel: John Ford?

O'Neal: John Ford started out. So we worked about two or three weeks with him, and then he got bursitis, and we had a little hiatus for about a week or two; then they brought in Kazan. He picked up from there. He decided to do the whole thing all over again. There were certain scenes that we made changes in. There was – Ford liked things one way and Kazan liked another way. But no particular incidents. Ford, at times, he would just like to hear Ethel sing. We'd just sit around while he ... well, he was thinking about putting it in the film, but all that he was doing was just listening to Ethel sing.

O'Neal's recollections are fascinating here, given that some historians have questioned Ford's attitude toward Pinky, *or his alleged fights with Ethel Waters. Ford also had personal problems with producer Darryl F. Zanuck, head of Twentieth Century-Fox. According to Donald Bogle, Zanuck removed Ford from the production because the studio head believed the director turned "his black actors into Aunt Jemimas. They were caricatures."*[19]

Manchel: How about *No Way Out*? That was kind of a radical film.

Sidney Poitier made his screen debut in this drama about a black doctor taunted by an injured convict and his brother. Ossie Davis and Ruby Dee also made their screen debuts in this trail blazing film.

O'Neal: *No Way Out* ... yes. It was a kind of a film that to me – as far as my part is concerned – I couldn't get the thing right to save my life. It was at a time when my mother was very ill, and she died during that period. So I couldn't remember a line. It was the most frustrating thing that I'd ever had to do. I don't know, I think I was cut completely out of the film. I haven't seen it. It was awful. The day I finished was the day my mother died, and I couldn't concentrate on anything.

Then we did *Take a Giant Step* (Philip Leacock, 1959).

Based on Louis S. Peterson's drama, the screen adaptation focused on a black adolescent's frustrations in a white society.

O'Neal: Of course, we did *Anna Lucasta* before that. We had a lot of fun making that, *Anna Lucasta*.... One of the reasons was because we lived with it for so long, you know. Most of my lines, I wrote myself, as a matter of fact. Alice Childress did too. Most of the lines of *Anna [Lucasta]*. We had quite a bit of fun making that. Now here again, where it's not so much a matter of color – they brought in Eartha Kitt for this part [Anna, a Brooklyn prostitute] knowing full well, of course, that Hilda Simms had done it for years. But Hilda did not have the name that Eartha had, you see, so it was a matter of box office. They brought in Sammy Davis to do the part of Danny, and Danny was an entirely different character. He certainly wasn't the type that Davis is [Canada Lee had played the part of the ex-boy friend on Broadway]. But they wanted box office, you see.

Manchel: Poitier had done it as an understudy, hadn't he? On the road, at one point. But he was unobtainable, or didn't want to?

O'Neal: He didn't do Danny. He did the part of the country lad. That part was done by [Henry] Hank Scott, I think, who had done two or three films prior to that time.

Manchel: And after that – you went *Anna Lucasta*, and then *Take a Giant Step* and then what?

O'Neal: Then we did *Free, White and 21* (Singer Buchanan, 1968). I don't know if you saw that?

Thomas Cripps is extremely critical of this film, writing it off as one of a number of films exploiting racial themes. Moreover, he saw it as clearly demonstrating "the undercurrent of white proletarian reservations toward the assimilation of Negroes into American life."[20] Edward Mapp goes even further, describing it as "trite dialogue, uneasy situations, and a glaring absence of cinematic expertise destroy any latent merit to which the film might pretend."[21]

Manchel: No.

O'Neal: *Free, White and 21*, we did that in Dallas, Texas. It was based on an actual story. It was an actual happening. That fellow [Ernie Jones, played by O'Neal] was out of Chicago; he was not too well schooled. He was not too intelligent, but he knew how to make money. He owned the newspaper there in Dallas. He ran – every Sunday afternoon – those big band concerts with the orchestra – sold beer at this place – in the afternoon; then he came to this big place out at one of these country clubs there in Dallas – and he had a big band out there at night. He was really a hustler. He was in real estate.

But he was charged with rape. He was supposed to have raped a Swedish girl who was working with a Job Core – one of the civil rights organizations or something. He beat the rap. This was in Texas, which was very unusual. Whether he was guilty or not – as long as he's charged with it – he's going to be found guilty. Well, he beat it. I understand it cost him around thirty-five, forty thousand dollars. He was still operating.

As a matter of fact, when I went out to do the picture, I went out to meet him – they took me out to meet him. I met him in this hall – there was music going on, people were drinking beer all over the place. And the funny thing about it is he and I had on the same tie. Identical tie. When we met. Of course, the picture was later released by American International. Made quite a bit of money I suppose.

Then we made a television show that was later made into a motion picture, which was called *Pattern for Violence*. The television show was made into two parts – they were joined for the motion picture. Let's see, what else?

O'Neal may be thinking of Strategy of Terror *(1969).*

Manchel: When you were out there, did you have any problem at all, as far as working, or discrimination, or any kind of difficulty on the sets?

O'Neal: You see, I didn't live out there. I only went out to do a picture, and then I came back home.

Manchel: Was there any question of differences of wages that I've read about in the thirties and the forties? For the same scene, a black man would get less money than a white person would.

O'Neal: Well, he probably would except for the fact that all of this is done by agents. Agents do the negotiating with these people. The amount of money that you get depends upon your past record, and your ability to bring people into the box office.

Manchel: Did you have white agents or black agents? Were there black agents who had that kind of moxy or muscle who could negotiate?

O'Neal: We didn't have any black agents then. Except one, or two; I don't remember which agents we had here. I don't think there were any out on the West Coast. So they were all white agents.

Manchel: What about a guy like Poitier? And Belafonte? What were they like in the beginning, as young people coming into your group?

O'Neal: Well, when Poitier first came to us, he wanted to get into the school. He had spent, I think, some time in the army. He had a very thick West Indian accent – although he tells the story that I told him with that accent he'd never get anywhere. What I said to him was that if he was going to be in the theater, he had to get rid of that accent. Nothing against the accent itself, but if you're not able to get rid of it, then the only time you're going to be called is when they want an actor with a West Indian accent. You ought to be able to do all types of accents. At least more than just one. Well, he didn't particularly like it so well, but later Sidney bought a number of records. He sat and listened to them, and he listened to them, and he listened to them, and now if you hear him in a picture, you don't get that accent, except in a highly emotional scene, you might get it. It might come through, but otherwise you don't get it.

According to film critic, Charles Champlin, Poitier's version of the story was that he had only been to school for a year and a half and could not read very well. So when he went for the audition that he had read about in the Amsterdam News, *Poitier's thick West Indian accent and his low reading angered Frederick O'Neal who was conducting the try-outs.* "He came up on the stage, furious, and grabbed me by the scruff of my pants and my collar and marched me toward the door. Just before he threw me out, he said, 'Stop wasting people's time! Why don't you get yourself a job as a dishwasher.' He did go back to washing dishes, but also bought a radio and spent all his spare time listening to the announcers – 'trying to lighten the broad 'A' that characterizes West Indian speech patterns.'"[22]

Manchel: He was a hard worker?
O'Neal: Yes. He was a very hard worker. The same is true of Belafonte. Belafonte really wanted to be an actor. He didn't just want to be a singer – an entertainer. I think even today, he would like to be an actor; it would be his preference. But somehow....
Manchel: What about a woman like Hilda Simms, who was a real talent? I just saw her last week in a movie, *The Joe Louis Story* (Robert Gordon, 1953). Almost wasted in the film. She never seemed to go anyplace in movies at all.
O'Neal: No. I don't think that.... She was in one other picture that I remember. I can't think of the name of it now. I don't know. Of course, she was a splendid actress. A splendid actress. But she just never seemed to be able to catch hold.

Klotman lists Simms' other film as Black Widow *(Nunnally Johnson 1954). She played a black waitress being interrogated by Broadway producer, Van Hefflin, in his attempt to solve a murder mystery.*[23]

Manchel: Is she still alive?
O'Neal: Oh, yes.
Manchel: What about a person ... the one who was in *Hallelujah* [1929]? The beautiful....
O'Neal: Is that...?
Manchel: Nina? Not Nina?
O'Neal: Nina Mae McKinney is dead. I thought you meant Fredi Washington. Nina Mae is dead now.
Manchel: She had a very tough career.
O'Neal: Yes, she did.

Manchel: Tough life.

O'Neal: She was with us in *Pinky*, you know.

Manchel: Fredi Washington is alive and living in Connecticut, now. One of my students did an interview with her. I was tremendously impressed with her.

O'Neal: Oh yes. Yes. She was a very good actress, Fredi was. But here again, they just simply weren't employing black talent at that time. Now, I think that they're beginning to move ahead now. But at that time, people like Fredi and people like Hilda just weren't being hired. The only ones being employed were the people who wanted blacks to do maids, comedy – ridiculous types of comedy – these were the only ones being employed. Someone that you could laugh at.

Manchel: Or, women were used as sex symbols – had to either sing or look sexy. Almost all the women, I think, that I've traced in the history of films, have either come from the chorus or from nightclubs. Very few – I don't think any of them – have ever come from the [dramatic] stage.

O'Neal: Very few of them made it.

Manchel: What is your reaction to this current wave of black films? Films made by people like the *Shaft* movies and the *Sweetback* movies?

O'Neal: Well, actually, I don't particularly care for them. That's a rather personal reaction. Some of them are better than others. Some of the films ... for instance, the one that Gordon Parks made, *The Learning Tree* [1969], was very good.

Manchel: Oh, it was lovely, lovely.

O'Neal: We've got to go through this phase, I feel. It's a period that we must experience. Out of it is going to come something much more solid than we've seen so far.

Manchel: Where do you see – hope – that it will go? Let's say, for example, having an ethnic theater – a black or Jewish theater – do you foresee an ethnic movie theater?

O'Neal: Yes. Fairly so. I don't know that it won't be an all black thing. It may be one or two companies, or something like that. But I think that most of the companies are going to be commercially oriented. They're going to have to be, if they're going to survive, because even the white production companies are not able to survive without having that sort of commercial touch. Now that blacks are getting into the production end of it – the management end of it – I think that this is a very good indication that we're going to move ahead in this area.

Manchel: I think so, too. We talked about that yesterday at lunch. Do you have any favorite films over the years that you think students ought to see – ought to be part of study programs and colleges and high schools? Films that tremendously impressed you, with your background?

O'Neal: Yes, there are several. Now, they won't like all of them, but I think they ought to see them nevertheless. They ought to see [D.W. Griffith's] *The Birth of a Nation*. A film like that. I think they ought to see [King Vidor's] *Hallelujah*. There is also a film that was made with very little money in Hollywood – it's really an art film. I can't think of the title of it now. It's only about – it's a short – only about thirty minutes long. It's based on the Faust legend. The central figure's a trumpet player. As I say, it's done very economically, because all of the sets are sort of cardboard sets, you know. With the exception of one or two of them that are made in a nightclub.... Other than that, they are – it's beautifully done.

Manchel: Who's in it?

O'Neal: There were several people in it. Well, I think of several people who were in it. I'm trying to think of the central characters. I know that Isabelle Cooley was in it. Charles Swain.... It's called "Blue" something. We had it at film festival in Michigan a few years ago.

Manchel: Was this a film by Bessie Smith? There was a short that she made (*St. Louis Blues*, 1928).

The Dudley Murphy-Carl Van Vechten short remains one of the most admired movies about African-American nightlife made in the first thirty years of film history. In addition to Bessie Smith's performance and Murphy's direction, the film benefited from the dancing of Jimmy Mordecai and the music of W.C. Handy.[24]

O'Neal: No, this was made not too long ago – about ten years ago.

Manchel: This is the one made out in Michigan – the film festival out in Michigan?

O'Neal: It wasn't made out there. It was shown [there].

Manchel: I've got their program – I'll drop you a line and let you know.

O'Neal: Yes.

Manchel: Any other films that really strike your fancy? A film like *Nothing but a Man* (Michael Roemer 1964)?

O'Neal: Yes, very good. That's a very good film.

Manchel: Did you see a film called *Slaves* (Herbert J. Biberman, 1969)?

O'Neal: No.

This very notorious film focused on an outraged slave (Ossie Davis) taking on the white establishment. It remains one of the most controversial movies of the late 1960s, mainly because viewers had mixed feelings as to whether this was revisionist history or sexual exploitation.

I remember Cripps disliking this film. He did point out, however, that it was co-written by John O. Killiam, "one of our better black novelists...."[25] *The other two credited writers were Biberman and Alida Sherman.*[26]

Manchel: That's a fine film. People have just sort of gone by it. In a sense, it presents a very accurate picture of what slave conditions were like. The distinctions between the Virginian slaves and the deep South slaves, the different plantation owners, the effect it had on the women, the house Negro, the field Negro, the white women, the different kinds of planters. Very interesting. Ossie Davis was in that film.

Do you have any favorite personalities? Any people who you really think make a real contribution, as opposed to those who are just going to be on the market for a short time and disappear?

O'Neal: Well, I think that James Earl Jones is going to be around for quite awhile. And there are others, too; but I think he is going to be around for quite some time.

Manchel: I want to end the book with him. Keep him for the last chapter. Because I want to start it off with the business of the problems that blacks had in the beginning, starting with the minstrel tradition in the 1890s, when movies begin. He, in a sense, is the great white hope. He has a Shakespearean background; he overshadows all those who came before.

O'Neal: Then, of course, you know – I think some attention should be given to a person like Frank Silvera.

Singer Alfred Buchanan in his study of the attitudes of the Negro press to the treatment of black actors talks about three personalities – Frank Silvera, Juano Hernandez, and Canada Lee – who helped revolutionize the film and stage worlds with their non-racial roles in the 1950s.[27] *Of Silvera, Buchanan wrote, "Silvera is very light-skinned and has no conspicuous Negro features. It probably would have been possible for him to pass had he elected to do so. He played small bits first as a Negro, then as Latins, South Americans, and other dark-skinned races, and then roles unidentified by race."*[28] *At one point in the 1950s, the* Pittsburgh Courier *critic stated, "Frank Silvera is the actor nobody knows. But he is our most successful performer in movies."*[29] *The* Chicago Defender *asserted that he became "the first to portray a white role in a film (Camino Real, 1950) of contemporary life without using makeup for it."*[30] *Some of Silvera's best known films are* Viva Zapata *(Elia Kazan, 1952),* Mutiny on The Bounty *(Lewis Milestone, 1962),* Toys in the Attic *(George Roy Hill, 1963),* Hombre *(Martin Ritt, 1967),* Up Tight *(Jules Dassin, 1968), and* The Stalking Moon *(Robert Mulligan, 1969). His last film,* Valdez is Coming *(Edwin Sherin, 1971), was released posthumously, Silvera having died on June 11, 1970. Donald Bogle stated, "Throughout his distinguished career, Silvera was a champion not only for black playwrights,* but for the black actor, too. And his very career indicated, of course, the great range of roles and opportunities a black performer might have if indeed he could be considered for any part."[31]

O'Neal: Also, there was a person by the name of Noble Johnson.
Manchel: Yes, yes. George and Noble Johnson.
O'Neal: He was a black man, but he played as a white person in films.
Manchel: I didn't know that.
O'Neal: Yes. I don't think anybody knew it, but he was Colored. Frank's done quite a bit of work not as a black actor. I thought he did a marvelous job in *Viva Zapata*. As General Huerta. He also – he came from stage – Frank came from stage. His first Broadway performance was in *Anna Lucasta*. He was in *A Hatful of Rain*. He played the Italian father.... On Broadway.

Michael V. Gazzo's play about an ex-Korean War veteran's drug addiction opened on Broadway in November, 1955. Among the original cast were Ben Gazzara, Shelley Winters, and Anthony Franciosa.

Manchel: Is he still alive? Frank?
O'Neal: No, he's dead. There was an accident. He went in to fix an automatic garbage disposal thing and electrocuted himself. [Snaps fingers]
Manchel: Is there anyone else you think I ought to highlight in the book? People who have since not been recognized, who made important contributions?
O'Neal: Well, there is another one, too, that I thought was a marvelous actor....
Manchel: Canada Lee?
O'Neal: Well, yes, Canada too. You know, a funny thing. Not many people know this about Canada, but Canada had four different careers – he was a success in all four of them. He played the violin almost to the point of being a concert artist. He fought for the welterweight title. He was a prizefighter. And he was the last black jockey to ride at Jamaica, except for modern times. See there was a period when there were no black jockeys. Now, of course, there are two or three. But at that particular time, he was the last black jockey to ride at Jamaica.
Manchel: Black jockeys used to dominate the sport, I understand, at the turn of the century?
O'Neal: Yes. Then there was this period when there weren't any. So he really had four different careers.
Manchel: He and [Earle] Hyman and [Paul] Robeson, I guess in the

thirties, were the big people. Did you ever work with Robeson? Or talk with him? Or meet with him?

O'Neal: I talked with him from time to time. There was a story in the *Times* about him, did you see it? That was first run in a magazine. We have a committee on Robeson citations. We're going to give an award each year to the person, individual, or organization that best exemplifies the qualities that Robeson espoused. That is the universal brotherhood of mankind. We're trying to get a theater named for him in the Broadway area. I think we will. At which time, we will probably commission an artist to do a full-length portrait of him, which we'll have in the lobby of that theater.

Manchel: Was he supported much by black people in the thirties?

O'Neal: Oh, yes.

Manchel: Because he was a very controversial figure.

O'Neal: I know. He was. There were a lot of people, you know, who probably weren't, because of his ideas and so forth – a number of things I didn't agree with myself....

At this point, the tape ran out, and we had to turn it to side B. When we resumed, we were talking about O'Neal's work in films.

O'Neal: *Something of Value* [Richard Brooks, 1957].

A screen adaptation of Robert Ruark's novel, the screenplay focuses on the friendship between two men, one white (Rock Hudson) and one black (Sidney Poitier), and the problems presented by the Mau Mau revolution in Kenya. Buchanan describes it as a unique film for the period, in that it was a major Hollywood production set in Africa and presenting an African-American's perspective. The historian concluded that it could be considered "yet another film emphasizing the uncivilized aspect of the black man...."[32]

Manchel: That was with Poitier and Rock Hudson.

O'Neal: Yes. Sidney was in that, too. Sidney Poitier. And William Marshall was in that, too. I played the part of the hatchet man, more or less.

Manchel: Yes, yes, I remember.

O'Neal: They cut a lot of those scenes out that I was in because they said they were just too violent. You know, what's his name made that picture. Can't think of the director. But – oh, God, he was – I had one scene there where they brought this white fellow out, you know; and the two of them are holding him, and he propped his head, and I just took this knife and YANG! And just like saying, "Take a drink of water," he says, "Take the head with you," and walked off. [We start laughing at this point.] Even the property managers were like, "Jesus Christ!" Brooks. Brooks it was.

Manchel: Richard Brooks.

O'Neal: That scene was cut out. We had two or three others that – he was really something.

Manchel: Did you ever do much work with Clarence Muse, at all?

O'Neal: I never worked with Clarence. But I know him very well. I've talked with him, and I visited with him when I was in California several years ago. Clarence – here was a guy who I thought was really a master at make-up. I have seen him in *Dr. Jekyll and Mr. Hyde,* and he had on a white make-up – you know that Clarence is about as dark as my shoe – and you couldn't tell he wasn't white three rows away. He would not let anybody see him make-up. It would take him almost two hours to do this because he had to put on layer after layer after layer of make-up on.

Manchel: I correspond with him every two weeks. How about Rochester? Did you ever do much with him?

O'Neal: Yes.

Manchel: What sort of guy was he?

O'Neal: Yes. Very nice.

Manchel: I found that a lot of these people were brought in by white people in the thirties. Bob Hope brought in Willie Best. They say Will Rogers brought in Stepin Fetchit. There was always, in some sense, some white guy sponsoring. Is that the way it was done in those days?

O'Neal: I imagine so. I don't really know. I imagine it was. I imagine so.

Manchel: Do you think there's anything that I ought to stress in the book from your experience – or that you'd like to see stressed – your understanding of an era?

O'Neal: Well, I think that one of the things that I would like to see is some understanding of these people who – these old comedians, who were working in that area – in that era – some understanding of them, and why they did it. I don't think it's right to just denigrate them out of hand.

Henry Louis Gates, Jr., during an episode of African American Lives, *mused about the struggles of black people to deal with their past and their identity. His inspirational words are worth savoring at the end of this pilgrimage:* "We live in a world so different than the world inhabited by our parents and our grandparents. How can we begin to understand their lives? We begin by listening to their stories."[33]

Manchel: Great.

80. Publicity shot for John Ford/Elia Kazan's 1949 *Pinky*. Ethel Waters and Jeanne Crain. The former was nominated for an Oscar for Best Supporting Actress. The latter was nominated for an Oscar for Best Actress. Courtesy of The Manchel Collection, University of Vermont.

81. Jeanne Crain and Ethel Waters in John Ford/Elia Kazan's *Pinky* (1949). It was Waters' artistic battles with John Ford that allegedly removed him from the film and turned the directing chores over to Elia Kazan. Courtesy of The Manchel Collection, Burlington College.

Notes

[1] Stuart Hall, "What Is This 'Black' in Black Popular Culture?" in *Representing Blackness: Issues in Film and Video*, Ed. Valarie Smith (New Brunswick, NJ: Rutgers University Press, 1997), 128.

[2] Quoted in Simmons, *Frederick Douglass O' Neal: Pioneer of the Actor's Equity Association*, xi.

[3] "Frederick O'Neal 1905-1992," *Backstage*, 4 Sept. 1992, 1.

[4] Sheila Rule, "Frederick O'Neal, 86, Actor and Equity President," *New York Times*, 27 Aug. 1992, D20.

[5] Simmons, *Frederick Douglass O' Neal: Pioneer of the Actor's Equity Association*, xiv.

[6] Mitchell, *Black Drama: The Story of the American Negro in the Theatre*, 122.

[7] Simmons, *Frederick Douglass O' Neal: Pioneer of the Actor's Equity Association*, 41.

[8] Ibid., xiii.

[9] Rule, "Frederick O'Neal, 86, Actor and Equity President," D20.

[10] Loften Mitchell, *Voices of the Black Theatre* (Clifton, NJ: J. T. White, 1975), 167.

[11] Simmons, *Frederick Douglass O' Neal: Pioneer of the Actor's Equity Association*, xi.

[12] Quoted in Ibid., 43.

[13] "O'Neal, Frederick (Douglass)," in *Current Biography* (1946).

[14] Simmons, *Frederick Douglass O' Neal: Pioneer of the Actor's Equity Association*, 65.

[15] Ralph Ellison, "The Shadow and the Act," in *Shadow and Act* (New York: Random House, 1964), 279.

[16] V.J. Jerome, *The Negro in Hollywood Films* (New York: Masses & Mainstream, 1950), 28.

[17] William Lee Burke, "The Presentation of the American Negro in Hollywood Films, 1946-1961: An Analysis of a Selected Sample of Feature Films" (Dissertation, Northwestern University, 1965), 187.

[18] Jesse Sweet and Henry Louis Gates Jr., "Listening to Our Past," in *African American Lives* (Kunhardt Productions, 2005).

[19] Donald Bogle, "Introduction to *Pinky*," (Atlanta, GA: Turner Classic Movies, 2006).

[20] Thomas R. Cripps, "The Death of Rastus: Negroes in American Films since 1945," in *Black Films and Filmmakers: A Comprehensive Anthology from Stereotype to Superhero*, Ed. Lindsay Patterson (New York: Dodd, Mead, 1975), 62.

[21] Edward Mapp, *Blacks in American Films: Yesterday and Today* (Metuchen, NJ: Scarecrow, 1972), 72.

[22] Charles Champlin, "From Dishwasher to Star: Sidney Poitier to Be Honored by Film Institute," *The Houston Chronicle*, 8 Mar. 1992, 24.

[23] Phyllis Rauch Klotman, *Frame by Frame: A Black Filmography* (Bloomington: Indiana University Press, 1979), 63.

[24] Cripps, *Slow Fade to Black: The Negro in American Film, 1900-1942*, 204-206.

[25] Cripps, "The Death of Rastus: Negroes in American Films since 1945," 62.

[26] Langman, *A Guide to American Screenwriters: The Sound Era, 1929-1982. Vol. 1*, 337.

[27] Buchanan, "A Study of the Attitudes of the Writers of the Negro Press toward the Depiction of the Negro in Plays and Films: 1930-1965," 113.

[28] Ibid., 114.

[29] Ibid., 115.

[30] Ibid., 96.

[31] Bogle, *Blacks in American Film and Television: An Encyclopedia*, 465.

[32] Buchanan, "A Study of the Attitudes of the Writers of the Negro Press toward the Depiction of the Negro in Plays and Films: 1930-1965," 263.

[33] Sweet and Jr., "Listening to Our Past."

Works cited

Albertson, Chris. *Bessie*. New York: Stein and Day, 1972.
Albright, Alex. "Micheaux, Vaudeville & Black Cast Film." *Black Film Review* 7.4 (1993).
Allen, Maury. *Jackie Robinson: A Life Remembered*. New York: F. Watts, 1987.
Allvine, Glendon. *The Greatest Fox of Them All*. New York: L. Stuart, 1969.
Anderson, Jervis. *This Was Harlem: 1900-1950*. New York: Farrar, 1982.
Archer, Leonard Courtney. "The National Association for the Advancement of Colored People and the American Theatre: A Study of Relationships and Influences, Volume I." Ohio State University, 1959.
Baldwin, James. *The Devil Finds Work*. New York: Dial Press, 1976.
_____. *Notes of a Native Son*. New York: Dial, 1963.
_____. "On Catfish Row: Porgy and Bess in the Movies." *Commentary* Sept. 1959, 246-248.
Balio, Tino. *Grand Design: Hollywood as a Modern Business Enterprise, 1930-1939*. Berkeley: U of California Press, 1995.
Barbour, Alan G. *Days of Thrills and Adventure*. New York: Macmillan, 1970.
Baxter, John. *Hollywood in the Thirties*. New York: A.S. Barnes and Company, 1968.
_____. *King Vidor*. New York: Monarch, 1975.
Beauman, Sally. "Goodbye, Mr. Tibbs: The Selling of Pseudo-Soul." *New York*, 4 Sept. 1972, 52-53.
Bennett, Jr., Lerone. "Black Firsts in Politics, Entertainment, Sports and Other Fields." *Ebony*, March 1982, 128-131.
Bergan, Ronald. "Black and Proud in the West. Obituary: Woody Strode." *The Guardian*, 14 Jan. 1995, 28.
"Black Cinema Expo '72: Black Cinema Library-Research." *Ebony*, May 1972, 151-54, 58, 60.
"Black Movies: New Dynamite at the Box Office." *Movie Digest* (1972): 54-61.
"Black Preachers. Sam Pollard." Two Dollars and a Dream, Inc., 2006.
Blake, Richard A. "Lillian Gish Dies after 75 Years in Film." *America*, 20 Mar. 1993: 14.
Blau, Eleanor. "With Dignity: Films by Blacks for Blacks." *New York Times*, 22 Oct. 1990, C13+.
Bogle, Donald. *Blacks in American Film and Television: An Encyclopedia*. New York: Garland, 1988.

———. *Bright Boulevards, Bold Dreams: The Story of Black Hollywood*. New York: One World Ballantine books, 2005.
———. *Brown Sugar: 80 Years of America's Black Female Superstars*. New York: Harmony, 1980.
———. "Introduction to *Hallelujah*." Atlanta, GA: Turner Classic Movies, 2006.
———. "Introduction to *Pinky*." Atlanta, GA: Turner Classic Movies, 2006.
———. *Toms, Coons, Mulattoes, Mammies, & Bucks: An Interpretive History of Blacks in American Films*. 2nd ed. New York: Continuum, 1989.
Bommer, Lawrence. "Stage Acting; Studio Rekindles Rage of '68." *Chicago Tribune*, 24 Feb. 1994, 11C.
Bone, Robert A. *The Negro Novel in America*. rev. ed. New Haven: Yale University Press, 1965.
Bosworth, Patricia. "From Nowhere to 'No Place'." *New York Times*, 8 June 1969, 1+.
Bowser, Pearl. "Black Women in Cinema." In *Black Cinema Aesthetics: Issues in Independent Black Filmmaking*, edited by Gladstone L. Yearwood, 42-51. Athens: Ohio University, 1982.
———. "The Micheaux Legacy." *Black Film Review* 7.4 (1993): 10-14.
Bowser, Pearl, and Jane Gaines. "New Finds/Old Films: Black Gold." *Black Film Review* 7.4 (1993): 2-5.
Bowser, Pearl, and Louise Spence. "Identity and Betrayal: The Symbol of the Unconquered and Oscar Micheaux's 'Biographical Legend'." In *The Birth of Whiteness: Race and the Emergence of U.S. Cinema*, edited by Daniel Bernardi, 56-80. New Brunswick, NJ: Rutgers University Press, 1996.
Boyle, Mary. "All Black Cinema, All the Time." *Burlington Free Press [Vermont]*, 6 Feb. 1997, D15.
Bridges, Herb. *The Filming of Gone with the Wind*. Macon, GA: Mercer University Press, 1984.
Brodie, Fawn M. *Thaddeus Stevens: Scourge of the South*. New York: W.W. Norton, 1959.
Brooks, Louise. *Lulu in Hollywood*. New York: Knopf, 1982.
Brown, Wesley, Thulani Davis, Toni Cade Bambara, Imamu Amiri Baraka, Louis Massiah, Scribe Video Center., and California Newsreel (Firm). *W.E.B. Du Bois: A Biography in Four Voices*. San Francisco, CA: California Newsreel, 1997. videorecording.
Brownlow, Kevin. "Lillian Gish." *American Film* 9.5 (1984): 22-27.
Buchanan, Singer Alfred. "A Study of the Attitudes of the Writers of the Negro Press toward the Depiction of the Negro in Plays and Films: 1930-1965." Dissertation, University of Michigan, 1968.
"Buck and the Preacher." *FilmFacts* 15.9 (1972): 194-197.
Burke, William Lee. "The Presentation of the American Negro in Hollywood Films, 1946-1961: An Analysis of a Selected Sample of Feature Films." Dissertation, Northwestern University, 1965.
Burrell, Walter. "Beulah or Bitch? The Soul Sister as a Sex Symbol." *Soul Illustrated* 1971, 21-24.
Burrell, Walter Rico. "Whatever Happened to Woody Strode?" *Ebony*, June 1982, 141.
"Butterfly Mcqueen: Who Knew Her Mind before 'Stereotype' Discussed." *New York Times*, 24 Nov. 1971, 6.

Works cited

Butters, Gerald R. *Black Manhood on the Silent Screen, Culture America*. Lawrence: University Press of Kansas, 2002.
Cameron, Judy, and Paul J. Christman. *The Art of 'Gone with the Wind': The Making of a Legend*. New York: Prentice Hall, 1989.
Campbell, Edward D.C., Jr. *The Celluloid South: Hollywood and the Southern Myth*. Knoxville: University of Tennessee Press, 1981.
"Canada Lee." *Current Biography* 1944.
"Canada Lee, Actor on Stage, Screen." *New York Times*, 10 May 1952, 21.
Canby, Vincent. "Are Black Films Losing Their Blackness?" *New York Times*, 25 April 1976, D15.
Cannon, Reuben, Don Kurt, Reggie Rock Bythewood, Nicole Ari Parker, Isaiah Washington, Imalinda Williams, Bill Dill, Kevin Krasny, Joel Plotch, Camara Kambon, Sue Chen, HBO Films, WeeCan Films, StarRise Entertainment, and HBO Video (Firm). *Dancing in September*. United States: HBO Home Video, 2001. videorecording.
Capra, Frank. *The Name above the Title: An Autobiography*. New York: Macmillan, 1971.
Carbine, Mary. "'The Finest Outside the Loop': Motion Picture Exhibition in Chicago's Black Metropolis, 1905-1928." *Camera Obscura* 23 (1990): 8-41.
"Censors Lift Ban on 'the Exile'; to Play at Roosevelt Next Week." *Pittsburgh Courier*, 13 June 1931, 9.
Champlin, Charles. "From Dishwasher to Star: Sidney Poitier to Be Honored by Film Institute." *The Houston Chronicle*, 8 Mar. 1992, 24.
"Charles Gordone Press Release." Springer/Warner Productions, 1972.
Charters, Ann. *Nobody: The Story of Bert Williams*. New York: Macmillan, 1970.
Chilton, John. *Billie's Blues: The Billie Holiday Story 1933-1959*. New York: Da Capo, 1975.
Christon, Lawrence. "Gordone: An Arresting Darkness." *Los Angeles Herald-Examiner*, 27 Sept. 1970, 7.
"Colored Nights in Film Houses." *Variety*, 13 Jan. 1926, 34.
Combs, Richard. "King Vidor." In *Cinema: A Critical Dictionary--the Major Filmmakers*, edited by Richard Roud, 1026-35. New York: Viking, 1980.
Cook, Raymond A. *Fire from the Flint: The Amazing Careers of Thomas Dixon*. Winston-Salem, N.C.: John F. Blair, 1968.
Cordier, Andrew W. "Letter to Charles Gordone." 1970.
"Cowboys Honored." *Jet*, 3 May 1993, 34.
Cripps, Thomas. *Making Movies Black: The Hollywood Message Movies from World War II to the Civil Rights Era*. New York: Oxford University Press, 1993.
———. "The Myth of the Southern Box Office: A Factor in Racial Stereotyping in American Movies, 1920-1940." In *The Black Experience in America: Selected Essays*, edited by James C. Curtis and Lewis L. Gould, 116-144. Austin: University of Texas, 1970.
———. "New Black Cinema and Uses of the Past." In *Black Cinema Aesthetics: Issues in Independent Black Filmmaking*, edited by L. Gladstone, 19-26. Athens: Ohio University, 1982.
———. "'Race Movies' as Voices of the Black Bourgeoisie: The Scar of Shame" (1927).

———. "Reaction of the Negro to the Motion Picture the Birth of a Nation." *The Historian* 25.3 (1963): 344-362.

———. *Slow Fade to Black: The Negro in American Film, 1900-1942*. London; New York: Oxford University Press, 1977.

Cripps, Thomas, and Marc Connelly. *The Green Pastures*. Madison: University of Wisconsin Press, 1979.

Cripps, Thomas R. "The Death of Rastus: Negroes in American Films since 1945." In *Black Films and Filmmakers: A Comprehensive Anthology from Stereotype to Superhero*, edited by Lindsay Patterson, 53-64. New York: Dodd, Mead, 1975.

Davis, Thulani. "Local Hero: Workin' 40 Acres and a Mule in Brooklyn." *American Film* 14.9 July/August (1989): 26-27.

Denton, Clive. "King Vidor: A Texas Poet." In *The Hollywood Professionals*, 6-55. New York: A. S. Barnes, 1976.

Dixon, Thomas. "Southern Horizons: An Autobiography," Unfinished manuscript.

Dobbs, Henry. "Variations on the Same Theme." *Close-up*, Aug. 1929, 163-165.

Draper, Arthur. "Uncle Tom, Will You Never Die?" *New Theatre* (1936): 30-32.

Durgnat, Raymond, and Scott Simmon. *King Vidor, American*. Berkeley: University of California Press, 1988.

Dyer, Richard. *The Matter of Images: Essays on Representation*. New York: Routledge, 1993.

Dyson, Michael E. *Race Rules: Navigating the Color Line*. Reading, MA: Addison-Wesley, 1996.

Early, Gerald. "White Noise and White Knights: Some Thoughts on Race, Jazz, and the White Jazz Musicians." In *Jazz: A History of America's Music*, edited by Geoffrey C. Ward and Ken Burns. New York: Alfred A. Knopf, 2000.

Ed Gordon, host. "NPR African-American Round Table." In *Whistleblowers*, 2006.

"Eddie 'Rochester' Anderson Offered Seven-Year Contract." *Pittsburgh Courier*, 24 Oct. 1942, 20.

Ellison, Ralph. "The Shadow and the Act." In *Shadow and Act*. New York: Random House, 1964, 273-281.

Essoe, Gabe. *Tarzan of the Movies: A Pictorial History of More Than Fifty Years of Edgar Rice Burroughs' Legendary Hero*. New York: Citadel Press 1968.

Everson, William K. "David Wark Griffith." *Film Society Newsletter* 1 (1963): 26.

Fabrikant, Geraldine. "The Harder Struggle to Make and Market Black Films." *New York Times*, 11 Nov. 1996, D1+.

Fay, Stephen. "The Era of Dummies and Darkies." *Commonwealth* 92.1 (1970): 125-28.

"Festival of Black Films." *Variety*, 7 Apr. 1971, 7.

"Finding Screen Negroes." *New York Times*, 25 Aug. 1929, 6.

Flamini, Roland. *Scarlet, Rhett, and a Cast of Thousands: The Filming of 'Gone with the Wind'*. New York: Macmillan, 1975.

Flatley, Guy. "Be Thankful You're Not as Handsome as Harry." *New York Times*, 2 July 1972, D7+.

———. "Butterfly's Back in Town." *New York Times*, 21 July 1968, D18.

Folkart, Burt A. "Lorenzo Tucker: 'Black Valentino' Dies." *Los Angeles Times*, 21 Aug 1986, 28.

Fraser, C. Gerald. "Clarence Muse, 89; Acted in 219 Films." *New York Times*, 17 Oct. 1979, D17.
Fraser, Gerald C. "Ethel Waters Is Dead." *New York Times*, 2 Sept. 1977, A1.
"Frederick O'Neal 1905-1992." *Backstage*, 4 Sept. 1992, 1+.
Fristoe, Roger. "Spotlight on Speed Museum's 'Black Film Series'." *The Courier-Journal*, 2 Feb. 1992, 26+.
Frook, John Evan. "Bff Unwraps Plan to Boost Black Pix." *Variety*, no. 39 (1992).
Gaines, Jane. "Fire and Desire: Race, Melodrama, and Oscar Micheaux." In *Black American Cinema*, edited by Manthia Diaware, 49-70. New York: Routledge, 1993.
―――. "The Scar of Shame: Skin Color and Caste in Black Silent Melodrama." *Cinema Journal* 6.4 (1987): 3-21.
Gates, Henry Lewis, Jr. *Loose Canons: Notes on the Culture Wars*. New York: Oxford University Press, 1992.
―――. *Thirteen Ways of Looking at a Black Man*. New York: Random House, 1997.
Gish, Lillian, and Ann Pinchot. *The Movies, Mr. Griffith & Me*. Englewood Cliffs, NJ: Prentice-Hall, 1969.
Goldberg, Gerald Jay. "Hoofer's Progress." *New York*, 26 June, 26, 1988.
Goldberger, Paul. "Critic's Notebook: From Page to Stage—Race and the Theater." *New York Times*, 22 Jan. 1997, C11+.
Gomery, Douglas. *Shared Treasures: A History of Movie Presentation in the United States*. Madison: University of Wisconsin Press, 1992.
―――. "U.S. Film Exhibition: The Formation of a Big Business." In *The American Film Industry*, edited by Tino Balio, 218-228. Madison: University of Wisconsin Press, 1985.
Goodwin, Ruby Berkeley. "A Lawyer Turns Vitaphone Artist." *Pittsburgh Courier*, 1929.
Gordone, Charles. "A Quiet Talk with Myself." *Esquire*, January 1970, 326-331.
―――. "Yes, I Am a Black Playwright, But...." *New York Times*, 25 Jan. 1970, 1+.
Graham, Cooper C. et al. *D.W. Griffith and the Biograph Company*. Metuchen, NJ: Scarecros, 1985.
Grant, William R. *Post-Soul Black Cinema: Discontinuities, Innovations, and Breakpoints, 1970-1995, Studies in African American History and Culture*. New York: Routledge, 2004.
"Greatest 'Comeback' Title Goes to Nina Mae Mckinney." *Chicago Defender*, 10 June 1944, 11.
Green, Abel, and Joe Laurie, Jr. *Show Biz from Vaude to Video*. New York: Henry Holt, 1951.
Green, J. Ronald, and Horace Neal, Jr. "Oscar Micheaux and Racial Slur." Reply To "The Rediscovery of Oscar Micheaux, Black Film Pioneer," *Journal of Film and Video* 40.4 (1988): 66-71.
Green, J. Ronald. "'Twoness' in the Style of Oscar Micheaux." In *Black American Cinema*, edited by Manthia Diaware, 26-48. New York: Routledge, 1993.
Grunberg, Andy. "Gordon Parks, Photojournalist Who Showed Dignity Amid Oppression, Dies at 93." *New York Times*, 8 March 2006, C:1.
Grupenhoff, Richard. *The Black Valentino: The Stage and Screen Career of Lorenzo Tucker*. Metuchen, NJ: Scarecrow, 1988.

———. "The Rediscovery of Oscar Micheaux, Black Film Pioneer," *Journal of Film and Video* 40.1 (1988): 40-48.
Guerrero, Ed. *Framing Blackness: The African American Image in Film*. Philadelphia: Temple University Press, 1993.
Hall, Mordant. "Killing the Killer." *New York Times*, 2 Mar. 1931, 19.
———. "Safe in Hell." *New York Times*, 19 Dec. 1931, 16.
———. "The Screen: Way Down Yonder." *New York Times*, 28 Feb. 1929, 30+.
Hall, Stuart. "What Is This 'Black' in Black Popular Culture?" In *Representing Blackness: Issues in Film and Video*, edited by Valarie Smith. New Brunswick, NJ: Rutgers University Press, 1997, 123-133.
"Hallelujah." *The Crisis*, Oct. 1929, 342.
"Hallelujah." *Pittsburgh Courier*, 8 Feb. 1929, 16.
Harford, Margaret. "Gordone Puts Spark in Black Theater." *Los Angeles Times*, 8 Sept. 1970, H1.
Harwell, Richard, ed. *'Gone with the Wind' as Book and Film*. Columbia, SC: University of South Carolina Press, 1983.
Haskins, James. *Mr. Bojangles: The Biography of Bill Robinson*. New York: W. Morrow, 1988.
"Heart Attack Fells Actor Rex Ingram." *Amsterdam News*, 29 Sept. 1969, 26.
Hendrick, Kimmis. "Seeking What Black Film Audiences Wan." *Christian Science Monitor*, (1970), 4.
Hoberman, Jay. "American Fairy Tales." *Village Voice*, 29 May 1984, 58.
———. "Blankety-Blank." *Village Voice*, 12 June 1984, 48.
Holly, Ellen. "Where Are the Films About Real Black Men and Women?" *New York Times*, 2 June 1974, B11.
hooks, bell. *Black Looks: Race and Representation*. Boston: South End, 1992.
Horne, Lena, and Richard Schickel. *Lena*. New York: Doubleday, 1965.
Hughes, Langston, and Milton Meltzer. *Black Magic: A Pictorial History of the Negro in American Entertainment*. Englewood Cliffs, NJ: Prentice Hall, 1967.
Hunter, Charlayne. "Butterfly Mcqueen Has a Family Now." *Chicago Defender*, 1970.
Jackson, Carlton. *Hattie: The Life of Hattie McDaniel*. Lanham, MD: Madison, 1989.
Jarvie, I. C. *Movies as Social Criticism: Aspects of Their Social Psychology*. Metuchen, NJ: Scarecrow, 1978.
Jerome, V.J. *The Negro in Hollywood Films*. New York: Masses & Mainstream, 1950.
"Jewish Museum's Retrospective on Black Filmmaking, Back to 1916." *Variety Weekly*, 25 Mar. 1970, 1+.
Jones, G. Williams. *Black Cinema Treasures: Lost and Found*. Foreword by Ossie Davis ed. Denton, TX: University of North Texas Press, 1991.
Kael, Pauline. "The Current Cinema: Notes on Black Movies." *New Yorker* 43.41 (1972): 159-165.
Kagan, Norman. "Black American Cinema: A Primer." *Cinema* 6.2 (1970): 2-7.
Keaton, Buster, and Charles Samuels. *My Wonderful World of Slapstick*. New York: Doubleday, 1960.
Kernfeld, Barry. "Sanders, Pharoah." In *New Grove Dictionary of Jazz*, 413-414. New York: Macmillan, 1988.
Kerr, Walter. "Not since Edward Albee...." *New York Times*, 18 May 1969, 1.

Kimball, Robert, and William Bolcom. *Reminiscing with Sissle and Blake*. New York: Viking Press, 1973.
King, Martin Luther, and Coretta Scott King. *The Words of Martin Luther King, Jr.* New York: Newmarket Press, 1987.
Kirby, Jack Temple. *Media-Made Dixie*. Baton Rouge: Louisiana State University Press, 1978.
Klotman, Phyllis Rauch. *Frame by Frame: A Black Filmography*. Bloomington: Indiana University Press, 1979.
Kreuger, Miles. "The Roots of the American Musical Film (1927-32)." *Museum of Modern Art Department of Film* (1971): 1.
Kroll, Jack. "From the Muthah Lode." *Newsweek*, 25 May 1970, 95.
LaMar, Lawrence F. "Paper Faces Suit by Actor Clarence Muse." *Chicago Defender*, 23 Oct. 1943, 13.
LaMar, Lawrence F. ""Stepin Fetchit Sets New Fox Movietone Record: Assigned to Three Major Productions, 'Step' Is as Busy as the Proverbial Bee—Comic Will Be Seen in Novel Role." *Pittsburgh Courier*, 20 Jan. 1934, 6.
Lamb, Yvonne Shinhoster. "'Life' Photographer and 'Shaft' Director Broke Color Barriers." *The Washington Post*, 18 May 2006, A01.
Lambert, Gavin. *GWTW: The Making of 'Gone with the Wind'*. Boston: Little, Brown, 1973.
Landay, Eileen. *Black Film Stars*. New York: Drake, 1973.
Landry, Robert J. "U.S. Films: Black, Red & Blue." *Variety* (1973): 45.
Langman, Larry. *A Guide to American Screenwriters: The Sound Era, 1929-1982*. Vol. 1. New York: Garland, 1984.
Lasky, Betty. *RKO: The Biggest Little Major of Them All*. Englewood Cliffs, NJ: Prentice Hall, 1984.
Leab, Daniel J. *From Sambo to Superspade: The Black Experience in Motion Pictures*. Boston: Houghton Mifflin, 1975.
Leland, John, and Allison Samuels. "The New Generation Gap." *Newsweek*, 17 Mar. 1997, 53+.
"Lena at 51." *Ebony*, Sept. 1968, 125+.
Lester, Julius. Prod. and host. . "Black Films." In *Free Time*: Channel Thirteen, New York, 1972.
Lewis, Barbara. "Spry Talk from Clarence Muse." *Encore American & Worldwide News*, 18 Apr. 1977, 33+.
"Lillian Gish Dies after 75 Years in Film." *Hollywood Reporter*, 1 Mar. 1993, 29.
Lott, Eric. *Love and Theft: Blackface Minstrelsy and the American Working Class*. New York: Oxford University Press, 1995.
Luft, Herbert G. "A Career That Spans Half a Century." *Film Journal* 1.2 (1971): 27-44.
Lusitana, Donna E. "Indians and the Army." In *The Real West*: Arts & Entertainment Network, 1993.
M.G. "Stepin Fetchit Did the Best He Could." *Oui*, Jan 1973, 30+.
"Making of 'Reckless' "*Chicago Defender*, 26 Nov. 1935, 7.
Manchel, Frank. *Film Study: An Analytical Bibliography*. Vol. 4. Rutherford, NJ: Fairleigh Dickinson, 1990.
———. Interview with Fredi Washington. Conducted by Barbi Mortimer for Dr. Frank Manchel, 1972. Audiocasette.

———. "Losing and Finding John Ford's Sergeant Rutledge (1960)." *Historical Journal of Film, Radio and Television* 17.2 (1997): 245-259.

———. "The Man Who Made the Stars Shine Brighter: An Interview with Woody Strode." *Black Scholar* 25.2 (1995): 37-46.

———. "Rogin on Race, Gender, and Identity." *Historical Journal of Film, Radio and Television* 17:1 (1997): 157-163.

———. "Teaching *Nothing but a Man.*" *Media and Methods*, October (1967): 10-13.

———. *Yesterday's Clowns: The Rise of Film Comedy.* New York: Franklin Watts, 1973.

Mapp, Edward. *Blacks in American Films: Yesterday and Today.* Metuchen, NJ: Scarecrow, 1972.

Maraniss, David. *Clemente: The Passion and Grace of Baseball's Last Hero.* New York: Simon & Schuster, 2006.

Marill, Alvin H. *The Films of Sidney Poitier.* Secaucus, NJ: Citadel, 1978.

Marr, William, II. "Black Pulitzer Prize Awardees." *The Crisis*, May 1970, 186-188.

Mason, B. J. "The Grand Old Man of Good Hope Valley: Actor Clarence Muse Talks About His Work and His Life." *Ebony*, Sept 1972, 52+.

Massood, Paula J. *Black City Cinema: African American Urban Experiences in Film.* Philadelphia: Temple University Press, 2003.

McBride, Joseph. *Frank Capra: The Catastrophe of Success.* New York: Simon and Schuster, 1992.

———. "Stepin Fetchit Talks Back." *Film Quarterly* 24.2 (1971): 20-26.

McCorkle, Susannah. "The Mother of Us All: Ethel Waters." *American Heritage* 45.1 (1994): 60-73.

McMillan, Penelope. "Death Takes Screen Legend Gish and Dance Star Keeler; Lillian Gish Starred in Epic Silent Movies." *Los Angeles Times*, 1993, 1A+.

"Micheaux Film Corp.: All-Talking Pictures Will Be Produced on More Expansive Scale." *Pittsburgh Courier*, 8 Jan. 1931, 8.

"Milestones." *Time*, 4 Dec. 1995, 29.

Milne, Tom. *Mamoulian.* Bloomington: Indiana University Press, 1969.

Mitchell, Loften. *Black Drama: The Story of the American Negro in the Theatre.* New York: Hawthorn Books, 1967.

———. *Voices of the Black Theatre.* Clifton, NJ: J. T. White, 1975.

Molt, Cynthia M. *Gone with the Wind on Film: A Complete Reference.* Jefferson: McFarland, 1989.

Morris, Earl J. "Earl Morris Gives an Intimate Picture Showing Effect of Eddie Anderson's Work as 'Good-Will Ambassador.'" *Pittsburgh Courier*, 31 Aug. 1940, 21.

"Movie Maker Belafonte." *Ebony*, July 1959, 94-96.

Muse, Clarence. "Noted Screen Actor Thinks Performers Have Been Ignored." *Pittsburgh Courier*, 12 Sept. 1942, 20.

"Muse Stars in Film with Barthlemess." *Pittsburgh Courier*, 29 Nov. 1934.

"Negro Actor Asks Public for Verdict." *Burlington Free Press [Vermont]*, 20 Sept. 1972, 2.

"Negro Filmusical Cycle." *Variety*, 6 Nov. 1935, 3.

Noble, Peter. "The Coming of Sound." In *Anthology of the American Negro in the Theatre: A Critical Approach*, edited by Lindsay Patterson. New York: Publishing House, 1970, 247-266.

_____. *The Negro in Films*. London: Skelton Robinson, 1948.
Null, Gary. *Black Hollywood: The Negro in Motion Pictures*. Secaucus, NJ: Citadel, 1975.
Nyong'o, Tavia. "Racial Kitsch and Black Performance." *The Yale Journal of Criticism* 15:2 (2002): 371-391.
"O'Neal, Frederick (Douglass)." In *Current Biography*, 1946.
Parks, Gordon. "Black Movie Boom--Good or Bad?" *New York Times*, 17 Dec. 1972 1972, D3+.
Patterson, Lindsay. "Focus on Clarence Muse." *Essence*, Apr. 1977, 17+.
Patton, Bernice. "Writer Reviews Reactions to an Article on Step." *Pittsburgh Courier*, 18 May 1935, 8.
"Paul Robeson, Miss Russell Star in Micheaux's Latest Film, Body and Soul." *Pittsburgh Courier*, 14 Feb. 1925, 3.
"The Peanut Man: New Film Indicts Hollywood Race Bias." *Ebony*, July 1947, 48-50.
Ploski, Harry A., and Ernest eds. Kaiser. *The Negro Almanac*. New York: Bellweather, 1971.
Pogrebin, Robin. "Charles Gordone Is Dead at 70; Won a Pulitzer for His First Play." *New York Times*, 19 Nov. 1995, 51.
Porter, Kenneth W. " Micheaux, Oscar." In *Dictionary of American Negro Biography*. New York: Norton, 1982.
Potter, Lou. *Liberators: Fighting on Two Fronts*. New York: Harcourt Brace Jovanovich, 1992.
Pouissant, Alvin F. "Stimulus/Response: Blaxploitation Movies—Cheap Thrills That Degrade Blacks." *Psychology Today* 7.9 (1974): 22+.
"Primitive Emotions Aflame in a Negro Film." *The Literary Digest*, 5 Oct. 1929, 42+.
"The Prize Winners." *Ebony*, July 1970, 36-37.
Pryor, Thomas M. "The Betrayal." *New York Times*, 26 June 1948, IQ.
_____. "One Mile from Heaven." *New York Times*, 19 Aug. 1937, 23.
""Race Stars." *Chicago Defender*, 25 July 1936, 11.
"Re-Creating the Era of Black Vaudeville." *New York Times*, 28 June 1990, C13+.
Regester, Charlene. "From the Buzzard's Roost: Black Movie-Going in Durham and Other North Carolina Cities During the Early Period of American Cinema." *Film History* 17 (2005): 113-124.
Reid, Mark A. *Redefining Black Film*. Berkeley: University of California Press, 1993.
"Rev. Of the Exile (Negro Talker)." *Variety*, 27 May 1931, 57.
"Review 'So Red the Rose'." *Newsweek*, 30 Nov. 1935, 27-28.
"Review of 'So Red the Rose'." *The Literary Digest*, 23 Nov. 1935, 26.
"Review of Cabin in the Cotton." *Variety*, 4 Oct. 1932, 19.
"Review of Gentleman from Dixie." *Variety*, 12 Nov. 1941.
"Review of the Arizonian." *Variety*, 31 July 1935, 19.
"Review of West of the Pecos." *Variety*, 1 Jan. 1935, 18.
"Rex Ingram." *Variety*, 24 Sept. 1967, 71.
Rhines, Jesse A. *Black Film/White Money*. New Brunswick, NJ: Rutgers University Press, 1996.
"Richard Thorpe." In *Contemporary Theater, Film and Television*. Garden City, MD: Gale, 1993.

Riley, Clayton. "O, Blacks, Are We Damned Forever?" *New York Times*, 18 May 1969, 22D.
Robeson, Paul, Oscar Micheaux, and Facets Video. *Body and Soul*. Chicago, IL: Facets Video, 1994. videorecording.
Robinson, Jackie and Alfred Docket. *I Never Had It Made*. New York: J. P. Putnam, 1972.
Robinson, Sharon. *Stealing Home*. New York: Harper Collins, 1996.
Rule, Sheila. "Frederick O'Neal, 86, Actor and Equity President." *New York Times*, 27 Aug. 1992, D 20.
Sampson, Henry T. *Blacks in Black and White: A Source Book on Black Films*. Metuchen, NJ: Scarecrow, 1977.
_____. *Blacks in Blackface: A Source Book on Early Black Musical Shows*. Metuchen, NJ: Scarecrow, 1980.
Sargent, Joseph, Gregory Hines, Richard Wesley, Robert P. Johnson, Peter Riegert, Kimberly Elise, Maria Ricossa, Savion Glover, Donald M. Morgan, B. J. Sears, Terence Blanchard, N. R. Mitgang, James Haskins, Darric Productions, MGM-TV, and Showtime Entertainment. *Bojangles*. United States: Showtime Entertainment, 2002. videorecording.
Schader, Freddie. "Hearts in Dixie: Hot Jiggery Jig Jigs." *Motion Picture News*, 3 Mar. 1929, 711.
Schickel, Richard. *The Men Who Made the Movies*. New York Atheneum, 1975.
Schlosser, Anatol I. "Paul Robeson: His Career in the Theatre, in Motion Pictures, and on the Concert Stage." Dissertation, New York University, 1970.
Schlossman, Michael. "Bojangles: The Legacy." Showtime, 2000.
Selig, Michael. "Vidor, King." In *The International Dictionary of Films and Filmmakers. Vol. 2: Directors/Filmmakers*, edited by Christopher Lyon and Susan Doll, 555-557. Chicago: St. James, 1984.
Series, National Public Radio Podcast. "The Marketing of Black Movies." In *NPR African-American Roundtable*, April 28, 2006.
Sherman, Eric. "King Vidor (1895-1982)." In *American Directors*, edited by with Pierre Sauvage Jean-Pierre Courson, New York: McGraw-Hill, 1983, 347-350.
Shipp, E. R. "Taking Control of Old Demons by Forcing Them into the Light." *New York Times*, 16 Mar. 1997, H13+.
Simmon, Scott. "Hallelujah." In *The International Dictionary of Films and Filmmakers, Vol. 1: Film*, edited by Christopher Lyon and Susan Doll, Chicago: St. James, 1984, 192-193.
Simmons, Renee A. *Frederick Douglass O' Neal: Pioneer of the Actor's Equity Association*. New York: Garland, 1996.
Sinclair, Abiola. "Oscar Micheaux Film Festival July 10-11." *Amsterdam News*, 5 July 1986, 27.
Smith, Valarie, ed. *Representing Blackness: Issues in Film and Video*. New Brunswick, NJ: Rutgers University Press, 1997.
Smith, William Gardner. "Profile, XXI: Ethel Waters." *Phylon* 11.1 (1950): 114-120.
Snead, James. *White Screens/Black Images: Hollywood from the Dark Side*. New York: Routledge, 1994.
"Some 250 Cinemas in U.S. For Colored Fans." *Variety*, 24 Mar. 1937, 33.
"Stepin Fetchit Calls His Film Image Progressive." *New York Times*, 24 July 1968, 83.

"Stepin Fetchit, Broke, Appeals to Mpls. Police." *Variety*, 26 Mar. 1941, 2.
Stern, Seymour. "Griffith: 1--the Birth of a Nation." *Film Culture* 36 (1965).
Strode, Woody, and Sam Young. *Gold Dust: An Autobiography*. Lanham, MD: Madison Books, 1990.
Sweet, Jesse, and Henry Louis Gates Jr. "Listening to Our Past." In *African American Lives*, 30 mins.: Kunhardt Productions, 2005.
Sye, Robert J. "Black Cinema Expo '72: Black Cinema Library-Research." *Ebony*, May 1972 (1972): 151+.
Taylor, Clyde. "Black Silence and the Politics of Representation." In *Oscar Micheaux & His Circle: African-American Filmmaking and Race Cinema of the Silent Era*, edited by Pearl Bowser et al. Bloomington: Indiana University Press, 2001.
_____. "Crossed over and Can't Be Black: The Crisis of 1937-1939." *Black Film Review* 7.4 (1993): 22-27.
Thomas, Bob. *Thalberg: Life and Legend*. Garden City, NY: Doubleday, 1969.
Thompson, Sister Francesca. "From Shadows 'N Shufflin' to Spotlights and Cinema: The Lafayette Players, 1915-1932." In *Oscar Micheaux & His Circle: African-American Filmmaking and Race Cinema of the Silent Era*, edited by Pearl Bowser et al. Bloomington: Indiana University Press, 2001.
Thompson, Sister Mary Francesca. "The Lafayette Players: 1915-1932." Dissertation, University of Michigan, 1972.
Thomson, David. *A Biographical Dictionary of Film*. 2nd ed. New York: William Morrow, 1981.
_____. *The New Biographical Dictionary of Film. Expanded and Updated*. New York: Alfred A. Knopf, 2004.
Thorpe, Margaret F. *America at the Movies*. New Haven: Yale University Press, 1939.
Toback, James. *Jim: The Author's Self-Centered Memoir on the Great Jim Brown*. Garden City, NY: Doubleday, 1971.
Toddy, Ted. " *******." *Motion Picture Herald*, 12 Apr. 1947.
Toll, Robert C. *Blacking Up: The Minstrel Show in Nineteenth-Century America*. New York: Oxford University Press, 1974.
Turk, Edward Baron. *Child of Paradise: Marcel Carne and the Golden Age of Cinema*. Cambridge, MA: Harvard University Press, 1989.
"Turn Stereotypes into 'Study Course': Black Cinema Group Defuses Valuaties." *Variety*, 9 Feb. 1972, 5.
Tuska, Jon. *The Detective in Hollywood*. New York: Doubleday, 1978.
Tygiel, Jules. "Baseball's Greatest Experiment: Jackie Robinson and His Legacy." (1983).
"Untitled." *New York Times*, 26 August 1971.
"*Veiled Aristocrats* at Roosevelt." *Pittsburgh Courier*, 31 Jan. 1934, 6.
Vermmilye, Jerry. *Cary Grant*. New York: Pyramid, 1973.
Vidor, King. letter, 18 December 1971.
_____. *Vidor, King. A Tree Is a Tree*. New York: Harcourt, Brace, 1952.
"Vidor, King (Wallis)." In *World Film Directors. Vol. 1—1890-1945*, New York: H. W. Wilson, 1987, 1130-1136.
Wagenknecht, Edward, and Anthony Slide. *The Films of D.W. Griffith*. New York: Crown, 1975.

Walker, Alexander. *The Shattered Silents: How the Talkies Came to Stay*. New York: W. Morrow, 1978.

Wallace, Michelle. "Oscar Micheaux's within Our Gates: The Possibilities for Alternative Visions." In *Oscar Micheaux and His Circle: African -American Filmmaking and Race Cinema of the Silent Era*, edited by Pearl Bowser et. al., 53-66, 2001.

Waller, Gregory. "Another Audience: Black Moviegoing, 1907-16." *Cinema Journal* 31.2 (1992): 3-25.

Ward, Geoffrey C. *Jazz: A History of America's Music*. New York: Alfred A. Knopf, 2000.

Waters, Ethel, with Charles Samuels. *His Eye Is on the Sparrow*. Garden City, NY: Doubleday, 1951.

———. "Mamba's Daughter." *Atlantic Monthly*, Mar. 1951, 31-35.

Watts, Jill. *Hattie Mcdaniel: Black Ambition, White Hollywood*. New York: Harper Collins, 2005.

Wehlburg, Albert F.C. *Theater Lighting*. New York: Drama Book Specialists, 1975.

Weintraub, Bernard. " Stirring up Old Terrors Unforgotten." *New York Times*, 19 Feb. 1997, D1+.

"What's Going on in Hollywood." *Chicago Defender*, 26 Sept. 1942, 19.

White, Armond. "Stepping Forward, Looking Back." *Film Comment* (2000): 32-39.

White, Walter. "A Letter from Walter White." *Close-Up* 5.2 (1929): 105-106.

"William Greaves: Chronicler of the African-American Experience." The Brooklyn Museum, 1992.

Williams, Barbara M. "Filth Vs. Lucre: The Black Community's Tough Choice." *Psychology Today* 7.9 (1974): 98+.

Wolfe, Ralph Haven. "The Gish Film Theater and Gallery: The Ohio Roots of Dorothy and Lillian Gish." *Journal of Popular Film and Television* 22.2 (1994): 58-59.

Woll, Allen. *Dictionary of the Black Theater: Broadway, Off-Broadway, and Selected Harlem Theater*. Westport, CN: Greenwood, 1983.

Young, Joseph A. *Black Novelist as White Racist: The Myth of Black Inferiority in the Novels of Oscar Micheaux*. Westport, CN: Greenwood, 1989.

Young, Kevin. "Blame It on the Boogie." *SF Weekly*, 18 May (1994): 11-12.

Youngblood, Denise J. *Soviet Cinema in the Silent Era, 1918-1935*. Austin: University of Texas Press, 1991.

Index

A

Abyssinia (1906), 217, 219
Academy of Motion Picture Arts and Sciences, 173, 248, 328
Academy of Television Arts and Sciences, 210
Across the Border, 114
Actors Equity Association (AEA), 28, 65, 70, 71, 77, 78, 87, 113, 414, 421, 432, 439, 442
Adams, Joe, 370
African Diaspora Images/C.E.F.S., 64
Aitken, Harry, 188
Aitken, Roy, 188
Ajayi, Afolabi, 424
Akins, Zoe, 253
Albee, Edward, 415, 436
Albert, Edward, 366
Albertson, Chris, 265, 307
Albright, Alex, 24, 25, 43, 47, 141, 164, 166
Aldridge Players, 440, 444
Aldridge, Ira, 440
Alexander, Jane, 79, 197
Alice Adams (1935), 221
Allen, Maury, 305
Allen, Robert, 14, 319
Allvine, Glendon, 261, 306
American Masters, John Ford/John Wayne, The Filmmaker and the Legend (2006), 372
American Negro Theater (ANT), 415, 441, 444-447
American Society of Composers, Authors & Publishers, 71
Amos 'n' Andy Show, 94, 95, 267
An Officer and a Gentleman (1982), 221
An Unseen Enemy (1912), 170
Anderson Stock Company, *see* Ida Anderson Stock Company,
Anderson, Eddie 'Rochester', 220, 230, 304, 446, 459, 467, 471
Anderson, Ida, 62, 70, 85, 271
Anderson, Jervis, 258, 305, 306
Anderson, John Murray, 243
Anderson, Lindsay, 173
Anderson, Maxwell, 67, 247, 250
Andindell, Helene, 435
Andrews, Billy, 106
Angel Levine, The (1970), 244, 423
Angelou, Maya, 22, 421, 422, 426
Anita Bush Stock Company, 219
Anna Lucasta (1944), 51, 98, 106, 108, 109, 110, 113, 231, 441, 446, 447, 450, 451, 457
Antwone Fisher (2002), 323
Archer, Leonard Courtney, 303
Armstrong, Daniel Louis 'Satchmo', 6, 183, 206, 268, 269, 270
Armstrong-Jones, Anthony Charles Robert, 182
Arnold, General Hap, 358, 382
Arsenic and Old Lace, 173
Associated Actors and Artistes of America, 439
Astoria Studios, 76
Audelco Recognition Award, 51

Index

B

Baadasssss! (2003), 121
Bacall, Lauren, 183
Bachman, Ellie, 79
Bailey, Charles, 266
Bailey, Pearl, 220, 290, 418
Bakshi, Ralph, 416
Balaban, Abe, 323, 324
Balaban, Barney, 323, 324
Baldwin, James, 6, 20, 42, 92, 234, 290, 305, 307
Balio, Tino, 24, 43, 352
Ballad, Carroll, 210
Bamboozled (2000), 5, 75, 85
Bancroft, Anne, 366
Bandana Land (1907), 217
Bannaeker, George, 292
Baraka, Imamu Amiri, 22
Barbour, Alan G., 286, 307
Bardot, Brigitte, 388
Barr, Richard, 414
Barrymore, Ethel, 448
Barrymore, Lionel, 173
Barthlemess, Richard, 233, 282, 302
Bartlett, Sy, 361, 391, 392
Basie, William 'Count', 272, 273, 393
Bates, Clayton 'Peg Leg', 267, 268
Battle of the Bulge, The (1965), 82, 83
Battleship Potemkin, The (1925), 312
Baxter, John, 309, 312, 313, 351
Baxter, Warner, 145
Beard, Stymie, 418
Beauman, Sally, 427, 437
Beavers, Louise, 208, 227, 238, 263, 291
Because I am Black, 108
Beecher, Janet, 296, 297
Beery, Wallace, 283
Belafonte, Harrold 'Harry' George, Jr., 6, 92, 144, 196, 220, 242, 243, 244, 362, 367, 418, 422, 423, 430, 431, 441, 445, 452, 453
Bellah, James Warren, 396
Bellamy, Ralph, 386
Bendix, William, 421
Bennett, Constance, 187
Bennett, Lerone, Jr., 287, 307

Benny, Jack, 230
Bergan, Ronald, 411
Bergman, Ingrid, 294
Berlin, Irving, 223, 312, 329
Bernstein, Sidney, 422
Berry, Halle, 220
Best Man, The (1999), 323
Best, William, 220, 223, 224, 226, 459
Betrayal, The (1948), 54, 57, 162
Biberman, Herbert J., 419, 455, 456
Big Country, The (1958), 391
Big Parade, The (1925), 311
Biggers, Earl Derr, 288
Bikel, Theodore, 439
Birth of a Nation, The (1915), 5, 24, 26, 78, 79, 84, 137, 138, 140, 169, 170, 171, 174-189, 193, 194, 195, 198, 202, 226, 233, 313, 455
Birth of a Race, The (1918), 189
Bishop, Andrew S., 102, 104, 105, 157
Bishop, George. *See* Peters, Brock
Black Boy (1926), 78, 100
Black Caesar (1973), 419
Black Cinema Library-Research Center, 84, 162, 211, 302
Black Garbo. *See* McKinney, Nina Mae
Black Jesus (1968), 360, 377, 378, 380, 384, 385, 394, 409
Black King, The (1931), 29, 153
Black Like Me (1963), 16, 414, 416
Black Moon (1934), 283
Black Stallion, The (1979), 210
Black Swan, The (1942), 290
Black Valentino. *See* Tucker, Lorenzo
Black Widow (1954), 453
Blackbirds of 1928, The (1928), 317
Blackman, Honor, 388
Blacks, The (1961), 414
Blake, Eubie, 63, 65, 99, 163
Blake, Richard A., 169, 172, 201
Blau, Eleanor, 42, 43, 161
Bledsoe, Jules, 318
Blondie (1938), 224
Blood and Sand (1941), 418
Boardman, Eleanor, 311
Boardman, True, 210
Body and Soul (1924), 54, 56, 162, 285

Body and Soul (1947), 237
Boetticher, Budd, 356, 379, 390
Bogart, Humphrey, 235, 294
Bogdanovich, Peter, 42
Bogle, Donald, 19, 25, 42, 53, 99, 100, 162, 165, 166, 178, 195, 201, 202, 205, 206, 224, 288, 302-307, 314-318, 328, 352, 353, 416, 419, 427, 436, 437, 450, 456, 462, 463
Bojangles. *See* Robinson, Luther 'Bill'
Bojangles (2001), 94
Bolcom, William, 163
Boleslawski, Richard, 283
Bommer, Lawrence, 415, 436
Bone, Robert A., 14, 46, 161
Bonnie and Clyde (1967), 2
Bontempts, Arna, 115
Bordon, L. C., 288
Borgnine, Ernest, 387
Bosworth, Hobart, 281
Bosworth, Patricia, 436
Bouchey, Willis, 404
Bourmay, Nelson, 249
Bowman, Laura, 106, 154
Bowser, Eileen, 64, 186
Bowser, Leroy, 26, 107, 114–41, 148, 429
Bowser, Pearl, 7, 20, 26, 39, 42, 43, 52, 60, 64, 69, 107, 113, 114–41, 149, 161-166, 265, 285, 443
Boy! What a Girl (1946), 51
Boyd, Stephen, 366, 388
Boyle, Mary, 81, 164
Boyz 'n the Hood (1991), 22
Bradford, Harry, 130
Brennan, Walter, 187
Bressler, Jerry, 366, 367
Bridges, Herb, 305
Bright Road (1953), 243
Broadway Bill (1934), 253, 254, 282
Brodie, Fawn M., 201
Broken Blossoms (1919), 171, 193
Broken Strings (1940), 205, 209, 287, 288
Bronson, Charles, 389
Brooks, Clarence, 93
Brooks, Louise, 17, 42, 213
Brooks, Richard, 356, 386, 390, 419, 442, 458, 459

Brown Sugar (1937), 236
Brown Sugar (2002), 323
Brown, Bruce, 428
Brown, Honey, 317
Brown, Jim, 3, 16, 22, 224, 373, 416, 426, 427, 428
Brown, Mae, 72
Brown, Theodore, 441, 445
Brown, Wesley, 161
Browne, Roscoe Lee, 16, 196, 417, 421, 423, 424
Brownlow, Kevin, 169, 201
Brownskin Models, 112
Brunstein, Robert, 69
Brute, The (1920), 98
Buccaneer, The (1958), 399
Buchanan, Singer Alfred, 94, 165, 206, 224, 302, 303, 451, 456, 458, 463
Buck and the Preacher (1972), 210, 242, 244, 290, 423
Buck, Frank, 286
Burke, Billie, 362
Burke, Georgia, 106
Burke, William Lee, 449, 462
Burnett, Charles, 19
Burrell, Walter, 49, 68, 161, 163, 411
Burroughs, Edgar Rice, 366
Bush, Anita, 62, 258, 259
Butch Cassidy and the Sundance Kid (1969), 2
Butler, Charles, 195, 315
Butler, David, 221
Butters, Gerald R., Jr., 184, 202, 205, 219, 302, 303
By Right of Birth (1922), 93
Bynoe, Yvonne, 125
Bythewood, Reggie Rock, 75

C

Cabin in the Cotton (1932), 233, 234, 235, 252, 281
Cabin in the Sky (1943), 20, 210, 224, 227, 229, 230, 231, 232, 235, 240, 310
Callaway, Blanche, 131
Cambridge, Godfrey, 416, 420, 421, 422, 430

Cameron, Judy, 305
Camille (1932), 172
Camino Real (1950), 456
Cammeron, Kenneth M., 378
Campanella, Roy, 10, 11
Campbell, Dick, 444
Campbell, Edward D. C., Jr., 169, 201, 313, 351
Canby, Vincent, 69, 163
Canegata, Leonard Lionel Cornelius 'Canada Lee', 236, 237, 247, 451, 456, 457
Cannon, Reuben, 43
Cantor, Eddie, 218
Cantor, Leo, 381, 382
Capone, Al, 234, 268
Capra, Frank, 253, 261, 280, 282, 283, 290, 306
Car 54, Where Are You? (TV, 1961-63), 442
Car Wash (1976), 210
Carbine, Mary, 49, 161
Cardiff, Jack, 427
Cardinale, Claudia, 386, 389
Carey, Harry Jr., 365
Carey, Olive, 365
Caribbean (1952), 379
Carmen Jones (1954), 20, 220, 232, 243, 418, 421
Carne, Marcel, 355, 411
Carolina (1934), 225
Carousel (Stage, 1945), 129
Carr, Jack, 105
Carradine, John, 365
Carroll, Diahann, 3, 220, 290, 418
Caruso, 258, 272
Carver, George Washington, 289
Casablanca (1942), 235, 294, 418
Casablanca (TV, 1955-1956), 210, 235, 291
Casey, Bernie, 3
Cassidy, Bruce, 246
Cayton, Horace R., 115
Cayton, William, 79
Centennial Summer (1946), 187, 188
Chalk Garden, The (1956), 172
Champ, The (1931), 283, 311
Champlin, Charles, 453, 463
Chaney, James E., 14

Chaplin, Charles, 446
Charles, Ezzard, 10
Charles, Ray, 370
Charters, Ann, 166, 215, 302
Che! (1969), 391
Chenault, Lawrence E., 97, 98, 106
Cherry, Don, 120
Chester, Alfred 'Slick', 15, 26, 30, 62–107, 142, 181, 315
Cheyenne Autumn (1964), 368, 371, 372
Childress, Alice, 441, 446, 450
Childress, Alvin, 446
Chilton, John, 307
Christman, Paul J., 305
Christon, Lawrence, 436
City Beneath the Sea (1953), 379
Clansman, The (1906), 174, 176, 189, 190
Clapton, Eric, 431
Cleaver, Eldridge, 429
Cleef, Lee Van, 365, 389
Clifton, Elmer, 185
Clifton, Sweetwater, 10
Climate of Eden, The (1952), 414
Clockwork Orange (1971), 388
Clune's Auditorium, 190
Coburn, Jim, 433
Cochran, Gifford, 76
Cohen, Larry, 419, 428
Cohn, Harry, 198
Colbert, Claudette, 238
Color Purple, The (1985), 310
Colored Players Film Corporation, 219
Colored Theda Bara. *See* Freeman, Bee
Coltrane, John, 120
Columbia Circuit, 72
Columbia Pictures, 242, 280, 281, 282, 283, 286, 322, 367
Comathiere, A. B., 97, 98, 106
Combs, Richard, 310, 311, 320, 350, 351
Come Back Little Sheba (1952), 369
Come Back, Charleston Blue (1972), 21, 420
Comedians, The (1967), 173, 196
Commandos Strike at Dawn, The (1942), 173
Congress of Racial Equality, 416
Connelly, Marc, 220, 230, 303

Index

Connery, Sean, 388
Connolly, Walter, 251, 296, 313, 333
Conroy, Jack, 115
Consolidated National Film Exchange, 93
Cook, Mercer, 134
Cook, Raymond Allen, 188, 189, 202
Cook, Will Marion, 133, 217
Cooley, Isabelle, 455
Coonskin (1975), 416
Cooper, Gary, 95
Cooper, Jackie, 283
Cooper, Miriam, 178, 195
Cooper, Ralph, 92, 93, 105, 111, 112
Coppola, Francis Ford, 356
Cordier, Andrew W., 416, 436
Cotton Club, The, 229, 257
Cotton Goes to Harlem (1972), 420
Cotton, Joseph, 246
Couch, Robert, 312, 327
Crain, Jeanne, 35, 187, 301, 448, 460, 461
Crawford, Joan, 67
Crimson Skull, The (1921), 258
Cripps, Thomas, 12, 14, 21, 25, 42, 43, 49, 50, 79, 161, 175, 177, 178, 180, 188, 201, 209, 210, 219, 227, 261, 302, 303, 304, 306, 317, 319, 321, 351, 352, 379, 411, 444, 451, 456, 462, 463
Crosland, Alan, 282
Crouch, Stanley, 6
Crowd, Frank, 257
Crowd, The (1928), 311
Crowell, Josephine, 194
Crowell, Lucy, 196, 197
Cry, the Beloved Country (1951), 10, 67, 236, 237, 247
Cukor, George, 233
Cummings, Robert, 251, 332
Curtiz, Michael, 233, 252, 418

D

Dahl, Arlene, 379
Dalio, Marcel, 235
Dancer, Earl, 240
Dancing in September (2001), 75
Dandridge, Dorothy, 220, 290, 316, 317, 418, 423
Daniel Boone (1936), 284
Dark of the Sun (1968), 427
Darktown Follies (1919 and 1921), 96
Darktown Jubilee (1914), 215
Darnell, Linda, 187
Darwell, Jane, 145
Dash, Julie, 19
Dassin, Jules, 456
Daughter of the Congo, A (1930), 56, 57
Davidson, Joe, 323
Davis, Bette, 169, 173, 233, 234, 252, 281
Davis, George, 104
Davis, Ossie, 92, 420, 424, 441, 442, 450, 455, 456
Davis, Sammy, Jr., 268, 290, 367, 418, 430, 431, 451
Davis, Sammy, Sr., 268
Davis, Thulani, 42, 48
Day Lincoln Was Shot, The (TV, 1956), 173
Day, Robert, 366
Dazey, Frank, 100
Death of a Salesman (1949), 449
Deceit (1921), 98
Dee, Ruby, 16, 441, 446, 450
DeKnight, Fanny Belle, 327, 336
Delaney, Martin, 125
DeMille, Cecil B., 356, 390
Denton, Clive, 309, 351
Desire Me (1947), 253
Detective Story (1960), 414, 420
Devine, Andy, 365
Dickerson, Milton, 312, 327
Dillard, William, 47
Directors Association, 314
Dirigible (1931), 253, 261, 280, 290
Dirty Dozen, The (1967), 427
Dixie National Pictures, 93
Dixon, Ivan, 16, 38, 290, 419, 435
Dixon, Thomas, Jr., 174, 188, 189, 192, 202
Dmytryk, Edward, 388
Do the Right Thing (1989), 37
Dobbs, Henry, 225, 304
Dobson, Tamara, 3
Doby, Larry, 10
Dodson, Buck, 73

Index   481

Douglas, Kirk, 361, 421
Douglas, Melvyn, 173
Downey, Robert, Jr., 75
Dr. Jekyll and Mr. Hyde. (1929), 114, 259, 260, 459
Dr. Strangelove or, How I Learned to Stop Worrying and Love the Bomb (1963), 197
Drake, Henry, 71
Drake, St. Clair, 115
Draper, Arthur, 330
Dream for Christmas, A (1973), 291
Drums of the Jungle (1935), 99
DuBois, W.E.B., 4, 48, 49, 59, 74, 115, 129, 180
Duel in the Sun (1946), 173, 236, 311
Duke is Tops, The (1938), 227
Dunbar, Paul Laurence, 209
Duncan, Arthur, 77
Duncan, Todd, 247
Durgnat, Raymond, 309, 314, 330, 351, 352
Dyer, Richard, 12, 42, 172, 201
Dylan, Bob, 431
Dyson, Michael Eric, 57, 162

E

Early, Gerald, 120, 166
Eastwood, Clint, 221, 368, 389
Eddie Murphy Raw (1987), 22
Edison, Thomas, 63, 140
Edwards, James, 361
Edwards, Jodie and Susie 'Butterbeans and Susie', 267
Eisenhower board. See Izenhour, George
Eisenhower, Dwight David, 13, 250
Eisenstein, Sergi, 312
Ekberg, Anita, 235
El Condor (1970), 427
Elam, Jack, 384, 389
Elder, Lee, 248
Elder, Lonnie, III, 22
Eliot, Marge, 415
Elite Amusement Company. See Lafayette Players
Ellerbe, Harry, 297

Ellington, Edward Kennedy 'Duke', 223, 271, 393
Ellis, Evelyn, 259
Ellison, Ralph, 448, 462
Ely, Ron, 448
Emperor Jones, The (1933), 20, 51, 76, 100, 106, 209, 219, 221, 238, 259, 284
Epoch Producing Corporation, 188
Equity Library Theatre, 421
Errol, Leon, 218
Escapade (1935), 252
Essoe, Gabe, 366, 411
Evers, Medgar, 11
Everson, William K., 201
Exile, The (1931), 56, 57, 162
Eyck, Peter Van, 235

F

Fabrikant, Geraldine, 42
Face in the Mirror, The (1967), 414
Face of Death (1978), 392
Face/Off (1997), 428
Fairbanks, Douglas, Sr., 173, 187
Fallen Angel (1945), 418
Famous Artists, 96
Famous Players, 76
Far Call, The (1929), 277
Farber, Barry, 358, 376, 378
Farber, Manny, 254
Farr, Finis, 222
Fat Girls (2006), 323
Faulkner, Donald, 334
Faust (1959), 414
Fay, Stephen, 91, 164
Ferrer, Mel, 40
Fields, W. C., 282
Fingers (1978), 418, 428
First National, 237, 281, 282, 310
Fistful of Dollars (1964), 368, 389
Flamini, Roland, 305
Flatley, Guy, 243, 305, 306
Fleming, Victor, 233
Fleming, Walter, 106
Flemyng, Gordon, 427
Flesh and Fantasy (1943), 290
Fletcher, Tom, 215

482   Index

Folkart, Burt A., 162
Follow Your Heart (1936), 284
Fonda, Henry, 364, 389
For a Few Dollars More (1966), 389
For Love of Ivy (1968), 420
Forbes, Bryan, 421
Ford, Glenn, 374
Ford, John, 16, 27, 35, 221, 224, 356, 360-366, 370-373, 388, 389, 390, 405, 417, 442, 450, 460, 461
Forkins, Marty, 223
Forsdale, Louis, 14
Forster, Marc, 220
Forsythe, Ida, 157
Fort Apache (1948), 396
Foster, Lewis R., 290
Foster, Rube, 255
Foster, Stephen, 283
Fountaine, William, 312, 337
Fountainhead, The (1949), 311
Fox Movietone Follies of 1929 (1929), 224
Fox, William, 261, 273
Franciosa, Anthony, 457
Francis, Arlene, 183
Fraser, C. Gerald, 206, 229, 302, 304
Fraser, Harry, 286
Frasher, James, 170, 173, 186
Free, White and 21 (1968), 451
Freeman, Bee, 26, 98, 107–141, 158
Freeman, Carlotta, 102
Freeman, Kenneth, 26, 107, 108, 113, 107–141, 160
Freeman, Morgan, 221
French Connection, The (1971), 22
Fristoe, Roger, 163
From Hell to Heaven (1933), 282
From These Ashes (1966), 414
Frook, John Evan, 43
Fuqua, Antoine, 221

G

Gaines, Jane, 43, 49, 53, 54, 65, 79, 161-165, 169, 172, 180, 201, 202
Gance, Abel, 173
Garland, Judy, 433
Garner, Peggy Ann, 433

Garrison, Harold, 315
Garvey, Marcus, 48, 118, 125, 138
Gary, Mabel, 106
Gates, Henry Louis, Jr., 42, 56, 79, 244, 413, 436, 449, 459, 462
Gazzara, Ben, 457
Gazzo, Michael V, 457
Genet, Jean, 414, 420, 422
Genghis Khan (1965), 366, 367, 407
Gentleman from Dixie (1941), 289
George Washington Slept Here (1942), 221
George, Nathan, 415
Gershwin, George, 290
Ghost Busters, The (1940), 224
Ghost Talks, The (1929), 224
Gibbon, Cedric, 248
Gibson, Hoot, 85
Gibson, John T., 71
Gilbert, John, 106, 311
Gilford, Willie Lee, 106
Gilliam, Jim, 10
Gilpin Players, 440
Gilpin, Charles S., 102, 207, 219, 221, 231, 259, 261, 262, 331
Giovanni, Nikki, 121
Girl Can't Help It, The (1956), 420
Gish, Dorothy, 170, 171, 173, 186, 187, 198, 200, 220, 233
Gish, Lillian, 4, 5, 15, 26, 31, 107, 109, 168-202, 310
Gish, Mary, 170
Glaser, Joseph G., 269, 270
Glenn, Roy, 220
Glory (1989), 221
God's Stepchildren (1937), 98
Godfather, The (1972), 22
Godfrey, Katherine, 106
Gold Bug, The (1896), 216
Goldberg, Bert, 72, 73, 92, 93, 95, 443, 444
Goldberg, Gerald Jay, 303
Goldberg, Jack, 72, 73, 86, 92, 93, 95, 102, 443, 444
Goldberg, Lou, 72, 73, 92, 93, 95, 443, 444
Goldberger, Paul, 69, 163
Golden Boy (1939), 417, 418
Golden West, The (1932), 221
Goldport Productions, 73

Goldwyn, Samuel, 290
Gomery, Douglas, 24, 43, 74, 162, 163, 164, 321, 322, 352, 353
Gone Are the Days (1963), 2, 420
Gone to Earth (1950), 418
Gone With the Wind (1939), 220, 221, 232, 233, 235, 236, 252, 301, 311, 332
Good Earth, The (1937), 253
Goodman, Andrew, 14
Goodwin, Ruby Berkeley, 302
Gorcey, Leo, 288
Gordon, Ed, 125, 166, 323
Gordon, Robert, 453
Gordone is a Muthah (1973), 416
Gordone, Charles Edward, 5, 16, 19, 27, 412–437
Gossett, Lou, Jr., 221, 422
Gourme, Nelson, 292
Grant, William R., IV, 180
Grasshopper, The (1970), 427
Gray, Harry, 312, 336
Great White Hope, The (1968), 79, 80, 138, 197
Great Ziegfeld, The (1936), 253
Greaves, William, 103, 104, 108, 146, 160, 165
Green Pastures, The (1936), 20, 206, 220, 230, 231, 232, 303
Green, Abel, 71, 163
Green, J. Ronald, 49, 161, 162
Green, Paul, 234
Gribble, Harry Wagstaff, 441
Grier, Pam, 3
Gries, Tom, 427
Griffith, David Wark (D. W.), 27, 31, 54, 79, 169-202, 226, 233, 312, 455
Grunberg, Andy, 352
Grupenhoff, Richard, 47, 50, 51, 55, 59, 83, 161, 162, 163, 164, 166
Guardino, Harry, 361
Guerrero, Ed, 310, 350
Guess Who's Coming to Dinner (1967), 2
Guillermin, John, 427
Guilty (1930), 281
Gunar, Arnold S., 10
Gunn, Moses, 3, 427
Guy Green, 419

Guy, Barrington, 106
Guyse, Sheila, 101, 160

H

Hackford, Taylor, 221
Hainey, Charlotte Talbot (O'Neal), 442
Haizlip, Ellis B., 121
Hall, Elizabeth, 332
Hall, Mordant, 225, 262, 304, 305, 306, 307
Hall, Stuart, 2, 439, 462
Hallelujah (1929), 20, 27, 32, 231, 237, 238, 309-317, 320, 321, 325, 326, 327, 328, 330, 331, 333, 335, 351, 352, 453, 455
Hallmark Hall of Fame, 210, 291
Hamilton, Bernie, 419
Hamilton, Chico, 419
Hamilton, Ray, 419
Hamlet (1936), 172
Hammerstein, Oscar, II, 220, 232, 272
Handy, W. C., 120, 130, 455
Hanin, Roger, 387
HarBel Productions Inc., 243
Hardwicke, Cedric, 379
Harford, Margaret, 417, 436
Harlem After Midnight (1934), 88, 155
Harlem Globetrotters, 10
Harlem Globetrotters, The (1951), 10
Harmony Lane (1935), 283
Harper, Leonard, 257
Harris, Julie, 229
Harris, Julius, 415, 419
Harris, Richard, 247
Harrison, George, 431
Harron, Bobby, 178, 183, 184
Harron, Mark, 433
Hart, Moss, 414
Hart, William, 84, 85
Harvey (1951-52), 78
Harwell, Richard, 305
Haskin, Byron, 448
Haskins, James, 303
Hastings on the House (1929?), 135
Hathaway, Henry, 358
Hati (1938), 231

484 Index

Hawkins, Jack, 388
Hayden, Lennie, 227
Hayes, Helen, 240
Haynes, Daniel L., 32, 220, 231, 232, 238, 296, 297, 312, 315, 318, 324, 326, 327, 330, 331, 336
Hays, William Harrison, 193
Hayward, Susan, 387
Haywood, Don, 133
Hearts in Dixie (1929), 20, 27, 101, 205, 208, 209, 224, 225, 261, 262, 273, 276, 278, 280, 281, 310, 321
Hearts of the World (1919), 171, 183, 184
Heat of the Night, The (1967), 427
Heaven Can Wait (1943), 290
Hell Bent for Heaven (1960), 414
Hendrick, Kimmis, 42
Henry, Herbert, 441
Herald Pictures, 73
Herman, Al, 289
Hernandez, Juano, 362, 456
Herrick, Margaret, 248
Hess, Harry, 447
Heyward, DuBose, 76, 241
Higgins, Billy, 120
Hill, Abram, 441, 444, 445
Hill, Errol, 111
Hill, George Roy, 456
Hill, Maggie and Joe, 239
Hill, Wanda, 384
Hines, Gregory, 222
His Double Life (1933), 172
Hitchcock, Alfred, 171, 237
Hitler, Adolph, 76, 248, 357
Hoberman, Jay, 55, 56, 162
Hofmannsthal, Hugo von, 182
Hogan, Ernest, 272
Holden, William, 361, 387
Holiday, Billie, 269
Holly, Ellen, 22, 43
Holly, Marty, 114
Hollywood Museum, 226
Hombre (1967), 456
Home of the Brave (1949), 10, 20
Homesteader, The (1919), 53, 54
Hoodoo Ann (1916), 192
hooks, bell, 11, 42, 54, 59, 162, 163

Hooks, Robert, 415
Hoover, Herbert, 334
Hope, Bob, 459
Hope, Frederic, 248
Horne, Lena, 22, 67, 90, 174, 220, 221, 226, 227, 228, 246, 259, 304, 316, 381, 394, 422, 430
Horowitz, Julius, 432
Horse Soldiers, The (1959), 361
House Party (1990), 22
House Un-American Activities Committee (HUAC), 440
Howard Theater, 270
Howard, David, 221, 284
Howard, Garland, 72
Howe, Herb, 225
Huckleberry Finn (1931), 283
Hudson, Rock, 458
Hughes, Langston, 214, 259, 287, 302, 303, 306, 307, 317, 351, 443
Hunter, Charlayne, 305
Hunter, Jeffrey, 362, 363, 404
Hurry Sundown (1967), 418
Hurst, Fannie, 238
Hurston, Zora Neale, 444
Huston, Branch, 237
Hyman, Earle, 441, 446, 457

I

Ice Station Zebra (1968), 427
Ida Anderson Players, 62
Ida Anderson Stock Company, 70, 77, 85
If I had a Million (1932), 281, 282
Imitation of Life (1934), 20, 66, 67, 99, 100, 238
Imitation of Life (1959), 20, 238
In Dahomey (1902), 110, 111, 217
In the Heat of the Night (1967), 2
Ince, Thomas, 177
Incident, The (1967), 65, 113, 421
Ingraham, Lloyd, 192
Ingram, Rex, 220, 227, 230, 231, 236, 418
Innocents of Paris (1929), 224
International Alliance of Theatrical Stage Employees (IATSE), 328
Intolerance (1916), 171, 175, 176, 177, 195

Intruder in the Dust (1949), 10, 20
Invisible Ghost, The (1940), 289
Invisible Ray, The (1936), 232
Irvin, Monte, 10
Irvin, Nat, 125
Island in the Sun (1957), 20, 238, 243
Izenhour, George, 249, 250

J

Jack Johnson (1970), 79
Jackie Robinson Story, The (1950), 10
Jackson, Carlton, 264, 303, 307
Jackson, Chinquapin, 275
Jackson, J. A., 81
Jackson, Samuel L., 425
Jacobs, Ken, 56
Jamaica Rum (1953), 290
James, Luther, 414
Jarvie, Ian C., 319, 351, 379, 411
Jazz Singer, The (1927), 224, 261
Jefferson, Jack, see Johnson, Jack, 79
Jerome, V. J., 25, 443, 462
Jim Crow, 18, 28, 47, 69, 74, 262, 268, 359, 449
Joe Louis Story, The (1953), 453
Johnny Guitar (1954), 389
Johnson, George P., 93
Johnson, Hall, 245, 292
Johnson, John Arthur 'Jack', 36, 79, 80, 137, 138, 139, 140, 143, 221, 222, 295
Johnson, Lincoln, 93
Johnson, Noble, 93, 457
Johnson, Nunnally, 453
Johnson, Saul, 105
Johnston, Charles Sebree-Greer, 414
Jolson, Al, 224, 261
Jones, Broadway, 256, 257
Jones, G. William, 165
Jones, James Earl, 3, 16, 79, 196, 197, 222, 247, 421, 456
Jones, Shirley, 365
Jordan, Dorothy, 233
Jubilee Pictures, 73
Judge Priest (1934), 221, 362
Juice (1991), 22
Junet, Don, 376

Jungle Menace (1937), 285, 286
Just Around the Corner (1938), 222

K

Kadar, Jan, 423
Kael, Pauline, 21, 43, 80
Kagan, Norman, 24, 43, 55, 73, 93, 96, 162, 164, 165
Kansas City (1996), 244
Katz, Sam, 323
Kazan, Elia, 14, 35, 238, 442, 450, 456, 460, 461
Keaton, Buster, 197, 202
Keeler, Ruby, 98
Keighley, George, 221
Keighley, William, 230, 232
Keith-Albee Circuit, 71, 73, 75
Kemp, Jack, 108, 159, 160
Kennedy, Joseph, 277
Kenner (1964), 427
Kenton, Erle C., 280, 281, 282
Kern, Jerome, 187, 188
Kernfeld, Barry, 166
Kerr, Walter, 415, 416, 436
Ketchel, Stanley, 143
Kilik, Jon, 18
Killiam, John O., 456
Kilpatrick, Sidney J., 314
Kimball, Robert, 163
Kinemacolor Clansman Corporation, 188
King W. Vidor Productions, 310
King, Coretta Scott, 43
King, Dr. Martin Luther, Jr., 11, 28, 43, 68, 243, 395
King, Henry, 145, 187, 225
King, Rodney, 23
King, Walter Woolf, 145
Kingsley, Sidney, 421
Kirby, Jack Temple, 313, 350
Kitt, Eartha, 109, 422, 447, 451
Klotman, Phyllis Rauch, 448, 453, 463
Knox, Alexander, 388
Kohner, Susan, 238
Korda, Zoltan, 67, 230, 236, 247
Kotto, Yaphet, 3

486   Index

Kraft Television Playhouse (TV, 1953-55), 231
Kreuger, Miles, 262, 306
Krimsy, John, 76
Kroll, Harry Harrison, 234, 436
Ku Klux Klan, 13, 138, 178, 179, 194
Kubrick, Stanley, 34, 197, 356, 361, 388, 390
Kulik, Buzz, 427

L

La Boheme (1926), 171, 311
Lachman, Harry, 288
Laemmle, Carl, Jr., 284, 285
Lafayette Players, 51, 62, 70, 98, 102, 104, 106, 114, 165, 206-209, 216, 219, 258, 259, 260, 270, 271, 441
LaMar, Lawrence F., 225, 302, 304
Lamas, Fernando, 418
Lamb, Yvonne Shinhoster, 352
Lambert, Gavin, 305
Lancaster, Burt, 386
Landau, Martin, 361
Landay, Eileen, 303, 316
Landry, Robert J., 43, 351
Lane, Richard, 287
Langlois, Henri, 173
Langman, Larry, 234, 305, 463
Last Angry Man, The (1959), 420
Last Chord, The (1976), 416
Last Mile, The (1932), 231
Last Parade, The (1931), 281
Last Rebel, The (1971), 383, 396, 410
Last Train from Madrid, The (1937), 210
Last Voyage, The (1960), 361, 362, 400, 401
Laughing Irish Eyes (1936), 284
Laughton, Charles, 361
Laura (1944), 418
Laurie, Joe, Jr., 71, 163
Laven, Arnold, 441, 447
Leab, Daniel, 25, 164, 218, 303, 304, 317, 321, 352. 353
Lear, Les, 377
Learning Tree, The (1969), 2, 334, 454
Lee, Canada. *See* Canegata, Leonard
Lee, Ford Washington (Buck), 75

Lee, Jennie, 178, 194
Lee, Spike, 18, 19, 37, 75, 334, 428
Legend of Nigger Charley, The (1972), 11, 395, 396
Leighton, Margaret, 366
Leland, John, 127, 166
Lennon, John, 128
Leonard, Claire, 441
Leone, Sergio, 356, 368, 389
Lerner, Carl, 16, 416
Lesser, Sol, 287, 292
Lester, Julius, 307
Levin, Henry, 366
Lewis, Barbara, 302
Lewis, Jacqueline, 106
Lewis, Joseph H., 288
Liberators, Fighting on Two Fronts in World War II (1992), 83
Library of Congress, 64, 188
Lichman, A.E., 71
Life With Father (1939), 172
Lifeboat (1944), 236, 237
Lilies of the Field (1963), 221
Lincoln Motion Picture Company, 53, 93
Lincoln Players, 258
Lincoln Productions, 73
Lincoln, Abbey, 419, 420, 434
Lindsay Patterson, 210, 302, 304, 462
Lion Hunters, The (1951), 398
Little Colonel, The (1935), 221, 222
Little Miss Marker (1934), 223
Littlest Rebel, The (1936), 222, 224
Littlest Yank, The (1917), 186
Loggia, Robert, 391
London, Jack, 79
Long, Walter, 178, 195
Lopez, Vincent, 106
Lost Boundaries (1949), 10, 20, 40, 237
Lost in the Stars (1949), 67
Lost in the Stars (1973), 247, 421
Lott, Eric, 20, 42, 256
Louis, Joe, 10, 95, 286, 373, 453
Lowe, Charles, 196
L-Shaped Room, The (1963), 421
Lubin, Arthur, 286
Ludwig, Edward, 379
Luft, Herbert G., 311, 351

M

Lugosi, Bela, 289
Lumet, Sydney, 421
Lumumba, Patrice Emergy, 384
Lusitana, Donna E., 42
Lyon, Sue, 366

M

Maassood, Paula J., 189
Macbeth (1936), 100, 237
MacLean, Douglas, 331
Madame X (1918?), 102, 103
Mahon, Carl, 106
Mahoney, Jock, 366, 385, 406
Major Dundee (1965), 366, 370, 371
Makaba, Miriam, 393
Malcolm X, 429
Male Animal, The (1942), 221
Malone, Dorothy, 362
Mamba's Daughters (1939), 100, 240, 241
Mamoulian, Rouben, 247, 418
Man Who Shot Liberty Valance, The (1962), 365, 383, 396
Mankiewicz, Joseph L., 442, 447
Mann, Daniel, 67, 356, 369, 387, 420, 421
Mapp, Edward, 443, 451, 463
Maraniss, David, 352
Margie (1946), 301
Marihugh, Tammy, 401
Marill, Alvin H., 306
Mark of Zorro, The (1940), 418
Marks, Rupert, 114
Marr, Warren, 416
Marr, William, II, 436
Marsh, Mae, 185, 192, 365
Marshall, Tully, 233
Marshall, William, 16, 458
Martin and Seig's Mastodon Minstrels, 215
Martin Beck Circuit, 72
Martin, Helen, 422
Martin, Strother, 365
Marvin, Lee, 365, 383, 386
Mason, B. J., 302, 307
Mason, James, 366
Massacre (1934), 282, 396

Massiah, Louis, 20
Massood, Paula J., 202
Mastin, Will, 268
Mastroianni, Marcello, 380
Mayer, Edwin Justin, 250
Mayer, Gerald, 243
Mayer, Louis B., 310, 322, 323
Mays, Willie, 10, 426
McBride, Joseph, 224, 254, 303, 306
McCorkle, Susannah, 304
McCoy, Denys, 383
McDaniel, Hattie, 208, 209, 220, 221, 226, 227, 228, 246, 263, 264, 301
McDaniel, Henry, 263, 264
McDaniel, Otis, 263, 264
McDaniel, Sam, 263, 264
McFarland, Sparky, 283
McGarrity, Everett, 312
McGraw, Charles, 235
McGuinness, James Kevin, 396
McHenry, Doug, 22, 23
McIntire, James, 365
McKay, Claude, 118
McKinney, Nina Mae, 35, 237, 238, 312, 315, 316, 317, 330, 336, 453
McMillan, Penelope, 172, 201
McQuarrie, Haven, 261
McQueen, Thelma 'Butterfly', 51, 78, 235, 236
Meany, George, 176
Meese, Roy, 272
Meltzer, Milton, 259, 303, 306, 307, 352
Member of the Wedding, The (1952), 229
Menjou, Adolphe, 277
Mercer, Mae, 16
Merman, Ethel, 183
Metro-Goldwyn-Mayer (MGM), 21, 67, 87, 90, 105, 171, 186, 227, 228, 230, 253, 278, 282, 283, 286, 288, 311-322, 324, 328, 332, 381
Michael Powell, 230
Micheaux Pictures Corporation, 92
Micheaux, Oscar, 26, 42, 43, 50-69, 76, 79, 85, 87-98, 103, 104, 106, 108, 112, 114, 120, 134, 135, 136, 147, 149, 151-158, 162, 163, 164, 232, 265, 285, 443, 444

Mifune, Toshiro, 368
Miles, Vera, 365
Milestone, Lewis, 356, 361, 456
Miller, Arthur, 449
Miller, Irvin C., 112
Million Dollar Baby (2004), 221
Million Dollar Productions, 93
Milne, Tom, 418, 436
Mind Reader, The (1933), 281
Minnelli, Vincente, 229
Miracle in Harlem (1948), 30, 101, 108, 159, 160
Miss Bandanda (1927), 207
Mission to Moscow (1943), 65, 113
Mitchell, Loften, 436, 441, 442, 462
Mitchell, Margaret, 232
Mix, Tom, 85
Miyeni, Eric, 247
Molt, Cynthia M., 305
Monagas, Lionel, 76
Montalban, Ricardo, 371
Moon of the Carabees (1960), 414
Moore, Archie, 10
Moore, Dickie, 298
Moore, Juanita, 238
Moore, Mary Tyler, 246
Moore, Tim, 267
Mordecai, Jimmy, 455
Moreland, Mantan, 220, 446
Morley, Robert, 366
Morris, Earl J., 230, 304
Moses, Ethel, 98, 99, 105, 151, 156
Moses, Julia, 98
Moses, Lucia, 98
Mother and the Law, The (1915), 175, 195
Motion Picture Producers of America, 193
Motion Picture Production Code, 2
Mrs. Patterson (1955), 414
Mulligan, Robert, 421, 456
Mullkins, Don, 134
Murder over New York (1940), 288
Murphy, Dudley, 76, 238, 455
Murray, James P., 25
Muse, Clarence, 5, 16, 19, 27, 33, 80, 94, 95, 101, 107, 114, 197, 204–92, 300, 306, 313, 315, 316, 333, 417, 423, 446, 459

Muse, Irene Ena Kellman, 211, 213, 245, 247, 249, 250, 257
Muse, Willabelle Marshbanks 'Ophelia, 257
Museum of Modern Art (MOMA), 64, 134, 186, 306
Mutiny on The Bounty (1962), 456
Mutual Film Corporation, 310
My Forbidden Past (1951), 290
Mysterious Crossing (1936), 285

N

Namath, Joe, 383, 384, 396, 410
National Association for the Advancement of Colored People (NAACP), 109, 209, 226, 227, 228, 266, 290, 321
National Association of Theatre Owners (NATO), 22, 23, 319
Natural Born Gambler, A (1914), 215
Natural Man (1941), 441, 445
Nazarro, Nat, 96
Neal, Horace, Jr., 58, 59, 162
Negro Actors Guild, 63, 65, 100, 110, 113
Negro Drama Players, 51, 64
Negro Dramatic Guild, 78
Negro Ensemble Company, 415, 424
Negro Harlow. *See* Moses, Ethel
Negro Playwrights Company, 441
Neill, Roy William, 283
Nell Gwyn (1926), 186, 187
Nelson, Ralph, 221, 427
Neroni, Hilary, 21, 42
New Jack City (1991), 22, 23
New Lafayette Theater, 118
New York Shakespeare Festival, 415
Newcombe, Don, 10
Nielsen, Leslie, 291
Night and Day (1946), 291
Night of the Hunter, The (1955), 173
No Place to Be Somebody (1970), 414, 415, 416, 419, 432
No Way Out (1950), 10, 442, 447, 450
Noble, Lincoln, 93
Noble, Peter, 25, 67, 206, 219, 225, 234, 302, 303, 304, 305, 316, 329, 330, 331, 351, 352, 443

Index 489

Noisette, Katherine, 106
North Pole Theater, 270
Northwest Passage (1940), 311
Nothing But a Man (1964), 2, 14, 20, 38, 414, 416, 419, 420, 435, 455
Nothing Sacred (1937), 221
NPR's *African-American Roundtable* (2006), 125
Nugent, Elliott, 221
Nugent, Frank S., 396
Null, Gary, 25, 54, 61, 162, 163, 206, 302
Nyong'o, Tavia, 85, 164

O

O'Brien, Edmund, 362
O'Connor, John J., 83
O'Neal, Frederick Douglass, 5, 16, 19, 26, 27, 35, 129, 130, 438-463
O'Neal, Ron, 3, 66, 415
O'Neill, Eugene, 76, 209, 219, 238
Odds Against Tomorrow (1959), 243
Odets, Clifford, 286, 417
Of Mice and Men (1937), 65, 113
Of Mice and Men (1963), 414
Offley, Hilda, 101
Ol' Man Satan (1932), 231
Olden, Charlie, 97
Olivier, Laurence, 361
On Any Sunday (2000), 428
On Striver's Row (1940), 441, 445
Once Upon a Time in the West (1968), 388, 389
One Down, Two to Go (1983), 428
100 Rifles (1969), 427
One Mile from Heaven (1937), 99, 105, 165
One More Spring (1935), 145
One Potato, Two Potato (1964), 2
One Romantic Night (1930), 172
Ono, Yoko, 128
Original Gangstas (1996), 428
Orphans of the Storm (1921), 171, 194, 200
Osborne, Robert, 325
Our Daily Bread (1934), 311
Owens, Jesse, 373
Ox-Bow Incident, The (1943), 65, 113

P

Painted Hills, The (1951), 210
Palance, Jack, 386, 391
Panama Hattie (1942), 227
Pantages Circuit, 71, 73, 264
Paramount Pictures, 76, 83, 186, 187, 250, 281, 282, 283, 289, 314, 321, 322, 323, 331
Pardon My Sarong (1942), 210
Paris, Jerry, 427
Parker, Leonard, 38, 435
Parks, Gordon, Jr., 385, 419, 427
Parks, Gordon, Sr., 22, 43, 334, 353, 425, 430, 454
Pasadena Playhouse, 277
Patch of Blue, A (1965), 419
Paton, Alan, 237, 247
Paton, Tony, 289
Patterson, Floyd, 10
Patterson, Lindsay, 303, 304, 462
Patton (1970), 83
Patton, Bernice, 225, 304
Pawnbroker, The (1965), 421
Payne, John, 379
Peanut Man, The (1946), 289
Peck, Gregory, 14, 361
Peckinpah, Sam, 367, 371, 414
Peebles, Mario Van, 19, 121
Peebles, Melvin Van, 7, 15, 19, 120, 136, 137, 430
Peerce, Larry, 421
Perry, Lincoln Theodore Monroe Andrew 'Stepin Fetchit', 27, 94, 95, 101, 159, 160, 205, 208, 220, 221, 223, 224, 225, 226, 262, 263, 278, 279, 280, 284, 373, 446, 459
Personality Kid, The (1934), 282
Peters, Brock, 16, 220, 290, 370, 417, 421
Peterson, Louis S., 450
Piccaninny Days (1919), 141
Pickford, Mary, 170
Piece of the Action, A (1977), 244
Pinchot, Ann, 202
Pinky (1949), 10, 20, 35, 229, 238, 240, 442, 447, 448, 449, 450, 454, 460, 461

Plaines, Elaine, 223
Plantation Club, 229
Player, The (1992), 244
Playhouse 90, 231, 291
Playwrights Unit, 414
Poet, Judson, 414
Pogrebin, Robin, 436
Poitier, Sidney, 6, 92, 196, 210, 221, 242, 243, 244, 247, 290, 306, 362, 367, 370, 418, 422, 423, 427, 430, 441, 445, 450, 451, 452, 453, 458, 463
Policy Players, The (1899), 217
Polk, Oscar, 158, 232
Pollack, Sydney, 372, 382
Pollard, Budd, 153
Pollard, Harry, 284
Pollard, Sam, 372
Pope, Oscar, 220
Popkin, Harry, 227
Porgy and Bess (Show), 206, 207, 229, 231, 232, 244
Porgy and Bess (1959), 20, 76, 100, 210, 290, 418, 419, 421
Pork Chop Hill (1959), 361, 391
Porter, Cole, 223, 290, 291
Porter, Kenneth W., 161
Portrait of Jennie (1948), 173
Potter, Lou, 164
Pouissant, Alvin F., 22, 43
Powell, Adam Clayton, 370
Preer, Evelyn, 207, 208, 238, 259
Preminger, Otto, 187, 210, 220, 243, 290, 418, 419
Prestige (1932), 277
Preston, Billy, 431
Pret-a-Porter (1994), 244
Princess Margaret Rose, 182
Prison Train (1938), 287
Professionals, The (1966), 350, 386, 408
Promenade Theatre, 415
Pryor, Richard, 3
Pryor, Thomas M., 57, 105, 162, 165
Publix Theatres Corp., 321
Putney Swope (1969), 75

Q

Quick and the Dead, The (1995), 356
Quinn, Anthony, 371, 379

R

Racklin, Marty, 387
Radio-Keith-Orpheum Movie Company, RKO, 71, 74, 222, 277, 284, 287, 322
Rain or Shine (1930), 253, 280
Rainer, Luise, 252, 253, 286
Raisin in the Sun, A (1961), 2
Ray, Bernard B., 205, 288
Rebecca of Sunnybrook Farm (1938), 222
Reckless (1935), 238
Reet-Petite and Gone (1947), 51
Reeves, Dan, 376
Reevin, Sam E., 264, 265, 267
Regan, Phil, 284
Regester, Charlene, 74, 164
Reid, Mark A., 53, 56, 161, 162, 317, 352
Reinhardt, Max, 182
Remick, Lee, 183
Remodeling Her Husband (1920), 171, 186
Reol Productions, 209
Republic Pictures, 284
Revengers, The (1972), 387, 394
Rhines, Jesse A., 20, 59, 163
Richard Huey Players, 441
Richards, Beah, 418
Richardson, Emory, 40
Richardson, Walter, 26, 107, 114–141
Riding High (1950), 253, 254, 282
Riefenstahl, Leni, 248, 357
Right On (1971), 115
Riley, Clayton, 415, 436
Ringling Brothers Circus, 413
Rings on Her Fingers (1942), 418
Rio Conchos (1964), 427
Rio Grande (1950), 396
Ritt, Martin, 22, 79, 197, 456
Roach, Max, 124, 420
Robards, Jason Jr., 5, 16, 389, 417, 430
Robeson, Paul, 20, 51, 54, 76, 78, 100, 133, 207, 220, 247, 284, 285, 318, 387, 457, 458

Robinson, Frank, 10
Robinson, Fredi, 105
Robinson, Jackie, 10, 11, 223, 241, 305, 334, 355, 357
Robinson, Luther 'Bill' 'Bojangles', 73, 94, 105, 145, 220, 221, 222, 223, 226, 239, 258, 356
Robinson, Sharon, 83, 357, 411
Robinson, Sugar Ray, 10, 269
Robson, Flora, 366
Rochemont, Louis de, 40
Rodgers, Hilda, 157
Roemer, Michael, 14, 38, 416, 419, 455
Rogell, Albert, 282
Rogers, Alex, 217
Rogers, Hilda, 105
Rogers, Will, 459
Rogin, Michael, 256
Rohauer, Raymond, 57
Romola (1924), 171, 187
Roodt, Darrell James, 247
Rose McClendon Players, 441, 444
Rose Tattoo, The (1955), 369
Rosemond, Clinton, 418
Rosewood (1997), 117, 323
Ross, Diana, 3
Roundtree, Richard, 3, 425
Royal Romance, A (1930), 280
Ruark, Robert, 458
Rule, Sheila, 440, 462
Run, Little Chillun! (1935), 100, 209, 245, 292
Runnin' Wild (1923), 67, 98
Russell, Leon, 431
Ruth, Roy Del, 281
Ryan, Robert, 379, 386

S

Sackler, Howard, 79, 197
Safe in Hell (1931), 237
Sahara (1943), 230, 231
Sampson, Earl, 240
Sampson, Henry T., 163, 164, 165, 166, 302, 303, 307, 448
Samuel, Allison, 127, 166
Samuels, Charles, 202, 304, 305

Sanders of the River (1935), 238
Sanders, George, 362
Sanders, Pharoah, 120, 127
Sands, Diana, 3
Santley, Joseph, 284
Sargent, Joseph, 94, 303, 419
Savalas, Telly, 366
Scar of Shame (1927), 100, 114, 135
Scarlet Letter, The (1926), 171
Schader, Freddie, 262, 307
Scheerer, Robert, 210
Schenck, Nick, 319, 320, 321, 322
Schickel, Richard, 174, 304, 309, 314, 351, 352
Schiffman, Frank, 71
Schissler, Paul, 358, 382
Schlosser, Anatol I., 165
Schlossman, Michael, 411
Schubert Circuit, 72
Schultz, Michael, 210
Schuster, Harold, 288
Schwerner, Ann, 14
Schwerner, Michael 'Mickey' H., 14
Scott, Henry, 451
Scott, Randolph, 251, 277, 313, 332
Scotto, Aubrey, 284
Screen Actors Guild, 77, 78, 88, 209, 224, 432
Screen Directors Guild, 311, 320, 321
Secrets of Our Nurse (1938), 286
Seitz, George B., 281
Selig, Michael, 309, 312, 351
Selznick, David O., 233
Selznick, Myron, 332
Sennett, Mack, 176
Sepia Mae West. *See* Freeman, Bee
Sergeant Bilko (TV, 1957), 442
Sergeant Rutledge (1960), 27, 355, 356, 362, 363, 364, 367, 387, 388, 396, 404
Seven Women (1966), 366
Shadow of a Doubt (1943), 290
Shaft (1971), 21, 66, 334, 419, 425, 454
Shalako (1968), 388
Shankar, Ravi, 431
Sharif, Omar, 366, 367, 391
Sharples, Bill, 277, 278
Shaw, Arnold, 244

Shaw, George Bernard, 8
She Wore a Yellow Ribbon (1949), 396
Sheehan, Winfield, 261, 262
Sheffield, Johnny, 398
Sheridan Square Playhouse, 414
Sherin, Edwin, 456
Sherman, Alida, 456
Sherman, Eric, 309, 328, 351, 353
Shipp, E.R., 117, 323
Shipp, Jesse A., 217
Shore, Frances Rose 'Dinah', 245, 246
Shore, Sid, 384, 385, 387
Show Boat (1928), 224, 318
ShowBoat (1936), 221, 224, 284, 330
Shuffle Along (1921), 63, 67, 98, 99, 107, 108
Sidney, George, 90
Siegmann, George, 177, 179, 180, 183
Silvano, Sylvia, 16, 417, 430
Silvera, Frank, 456, 457
Silverheels, Jay, 374, 396
Simmon, Scott, 309, 311, 350, 351, 352
Simmons, Jean, 361, 462
Simmons, Renee A., 25, 43, 47, 439, 440, 442, 448, 462
Simms, Hilda, 441, 446, 451, 453, 454
Simon, S. Sylvan, 288
Sinclair, Abiola, 56, 162
Singin' the Blues (1931), 100
Singleton, John, 19, 117, 334, 425
Sirk, Douglas, 238
Sissle, Noble, 63, 65, 99
Skipworth, Alice, 282
Slaughter (1972), 11, 41, 427
Slaves (1969), 419
Slide, Anthony, 202
Sloane, Paul, 205, 261, 274
Smith, Albert E., 334
Smith, Bessie, 120, 130, 220, 223, 265, 455
Smith, Elmer, 388
Smith, Gladys. *See* Pickford, Mary
Smith, J. T., 93
Smith, James Edward, 195
Smith, Valerie, 46, 84, 161, 462
Smith, William Gardner, 304
Snappy Tunes (1923), 63

Snead, James, 45, 47, 54, 61, 161, 162, 163
Snyder, Bob, 375, 376
So Red the Rose (1935), 205, 232, 250, 296, 313, 314, 315, 323, 329-333
Something of Value (1957), 419, 442, 458
Son of the Sheik (1926), 51
Soul of Nigger Charley, The (1973), 396
Sound and the Fury, The (TV, 1955), 173
Sounder (1972), 21
Soyinka, Wole, 414, 424
Spaith, Keith, 377
Spangler, Larry, 396
Spartacus (1960), 34, 361, 362, 388, 403
Spence, Louis, 52, 60, 61, 69, 91, 163, 164, 165, 166
Spirit of Youth (1938), 286
Spivey, Victoria, 312
Split, The (1968), 427
Spook Who Sat By the Door, The (1973), 419
Sport of the Gods, The (1921), 209
Sporting Blood (1940), 288
St. Jacques, Raymond, 420, 421
Stack, Robert, 361, 362
Stahl, John M., 238
Stalking Moon, The (1969), 456
Stallings, Laurence, 250, 332, 396
Stander, Lionel, 389
Stanislavski, Konstantin, 368
Stanley, George, 248
Stanton, Harry, 361
Starette, Jack, 41
Stasio, Marilyn, 423
Stella Dallas (1937), 311
Stephenson, Anson, 325
Stepin Fetchit. *See* Perry, Lincoln
Stern, Seymour, 174, 175, 184, 185, 186, 188, 192, 201, 202
Stevens, George, 10, 221
Stewart, James, 365
Stockwell, Dean, 14
Stone, Andrew, 362
Stormy Weather (1943), 20, 210, 235
Story of a Three-Day Pass, The (1968), 137
Story of Little Black Sambo, The (1899), 85
Straight to Heaven (1937), 51

Index 493

Strategy of Terror (1969), 452
Street Scene (1931), 311, 325
Streetcar Named Desire, A (1948), 172
Strode, Luuialuanna Kalaelola, 358, 368, 374, 378-396
Strode, Tina, 358
Strode, Woodrow Wilson Woolwine 'Woody,' 5, 16, 19, 27, 34, 248, 354, 378, 355–410, 417, 422, 426
Strong Breed, The (1967), 424
Struttin' Along (1923), 230
Sturgess, John, 427
Sublet, John William (Bubbles), 75
Sullavan, Margaret, 251, 297, 300, 331, 332, 333
Sullivan, Francis L., 379
Sul-te-Wan, Madame, see Wan, Nellie
Summer Holiday (1947), 418
Sundown (1941), 358, 418
Superfly (1972), 21, 66, 385, 415, 419
Susskind, David, 370
Swain, Charles, 455
Swamp Fox, The (TV, 1959-1960), 210, 291, 292
Sweet Sweetback's Baadasssss Song (1971), 7, 15, 19, 120, 122, 137, 425, 429, 454
Sweet, Jesse, 462
Swing (1936), 57
Sye, Robert J., 57, 162, 211, 213, 240, 243, 246-250, 253, 262, 302, 428

T

T.O.B.A.. *See* Theatre Owners Booking Association
Tait, Walter, 312
Take a Giant Step (1959), 450, 451
Taking of Pelham One Two Three, The (1974), 419
Tales of Manhattan (1942), 290
Tashlin, Frank, 420
Taurog, Norman, 283
Taylor, Clyde, 93, 162, 164
Taylor, William Desmond, 314
Temple, Shirley, 94, 222, 313
Temptation (1936), 57, 98, 105, 156, 157
Ten Commandments, The (1956), 390

Ten Nights in a Barroom (1926), 100, 219
Thalberg, Irving, 311, 319, 322, 323, 328, 329
Thank Your Lucky Stars (1943), 246
That Gang of Mine (1940), 288
The Micheaux Film and Book Company, 54
The Name Above the Title (1971), 253
The Negro Players, 219
Theatre Owners Booking Association (T.O.B.A.), 71, 72, 220, 231, 245, 264, 265, 267, 287
Thief of Baghdad, The (1940), 230
Thomas, Bob, 323, 352
Thomas, Edna, 259
Thompson, Creighton, 101
Thompson, David, 306
Thompson, Edward, 207
Thompson, Sister Mary Francesca, 165, 207, 302, 306
Thorpe, Harry K., 255, 272
Thorpe, Margaret, 24, 43
Thorpe, Richard, 253, 306
Thousands Cheer (1943), 90, 227
Three the Hard Way (1974), 428
Tick...Tick...Tick (1970), 427
Tidyman, Ernest, 425
Till, Emmett, 11
Tillie's Punctured Romance (1914), 176
To Kill a Mockingbird (1962), 421
Toback, James, 427, 428, 437
Toddy Pictures, 93
Toddy, Ted, 81, 92, 93, 164
Toler, Sidney, 288
Toll, Robert C., 256, 306
Torn, Rip, 361
Towers, Constance, 362
Townsend, Robert, 1, 19
Toy Wife, The (1938), 252, 253, 286
Toys in the Attic (1963), 456
Trafton, George, 376
Training Day (2001), 221
Tree Grows in Brooklyn, A (1945), 433
Trial of Mary Dugan, The (1919?), 102, 103, 114
Trials of Brother Jericho, The (1967), 414
Trip to Bountiful, A (TV, 1953), 173

Trotter, William Monroe, 48
Trouble Man (1972), 419
Tuchock, Wanda, 312
Tucker, John and Virginia (Lee), 50
Tucker, Julia, 62–141
Tucker, Lorenzo, 5, 15, 19, 26, 29, 44, 45, 50, 55, 92, 107, 62–141, 151, 154, 159, 164, 166, 181, 417, 444
Tucker, Sophie, 239
Tully, Jim, 100
Turk, Edward Baron, 411
Turner, Lana, 238, 325, 358
Turpin, Charlie, 265
Tuska, Jon, 307
Twain, Mark, 8, 170
Twelve O'Clock High (1949), 391
Twentieth Century-Fox, 21, 76, 105, 208, 222, 226, 227, 228, 243, 261, 262, 274, 276, 278, 280, 281, 288, 450
Two Rode Together (1961), 365
Tyson, Cicely, 3, 16, 417, 421

U

Uncle Tom, 6, 21, 27, 59, 61, 95, 118, 206, 210, 222, 225, 255, 263, 373, 423
Uncle Tom's Cabin, 79, 85, 216, 219, 267
Uncle Tomisina, 236
Uncle Vanya (1930), 172
Under the Virginia Moon (1932), 277, 278
Underworld (1936), 98, 158, 232
Unforgiven, The (1959), 173
United Artists, 78, 322, 389
Universal Pictures, 100, 219, 285, 286, 288, 310, 311, 322, 379
Universal Theatre Inc, 150
Up Tight (1968), 2, 456
Uptown Saturday Night (1974), 244
Urban League, 78, 94, 440, 444
Ustinov, Peter, 361

V

Valdez is Coming (1971), 456
Valentino, Rudolph, 51, 84
Vaughn, Bob, 433
Vaull, William de, 195

Vechten, Carl Van, 455
Veiled Aristocrats (1932), 57, 106, 154, 166
Vereen, Ben, 356
Vermmilye, Jerry, 307
Victory at Entebbe (1976), 420
Vidor, Florence Arto, 310
Vidor, King Wallis, 4, 5, 16, 22, 23, 27, 28, 32, 94, 205, 231, 233, 236, 238, 250, 251, 252, 296, 308, 309-353, 417, 455
Viva Zapata (1952), 456, 457
Vodery, Will, 217
Vorhaus, Bernard, 206, 287

W

Wagenknecht, Edward, 202
Wages of Sin (1928), 55, 57, 90, 151, 152
Waiting to Exhale (1995), 323
Walcott, Jersey Joe, 10
Walker, Ada Overton, 218
Walker, Alexander, 225, 304
Walker, Ethel, 71
Walker, George, 215, 216, 217, 218
Wallace, George, 11
Wallace, Michelle, 53, 161
Wallach, Eli, 366
Waller, Gregory, 43, 319
Wallman, Honey, 447
Walt Disney, 21, 291
Walthall, Harry B., 180, 233
Wan, Nellie (Madame Sul-te-Wan), 177, 178, 193, 196
Ward, Geoffrey C., 307
Warfield, William, 318
Warner Brothers, 21, 220, 233, 234, 235, 281, 282, 290, 291, 322, 371, 415
Warner, Jeanne (Gordone), 414, 420
Warren, Mark, 420
Warwick, Dionne, 248
Warwick, Granville, see Griffith, D. W., 192
Washington, Booker T., 48, 52, 59, 60, 215
Washington, Denzel, 221, 323
Washington, Fredericka Carolyn 'Fredi', 66, 78, 98, 99, 100, 101, 105, 238, 245, 316, 448, 453, 454
Washington, George, 292

Washington, Kenny, 27, 357, 359, 374, 376
Watermelon Man (1970), 420
Waters, Ethel, 90, 133, 220, 221, 228, 229, 230, 239, 240, 241, 271, 304, 305, 317, 352, 448, 450, 460, 461
Watts, Jill, 221, 263, 302, 303, 307
Watts, Richard, Jr., 311
Way Down East (1920), 31, 171
Way Down South (1939), 206, 287, 292
Wayne, John, 84, 361, 365, 372, 450
Wayne, Perceval, 106
Webster, Nicholas, 420
Webster, Pauline, 106
Wedding, A (1978), 173
Weems, Walter, 225, 226, 273, 274, 279
Wehlberg, Albert F.C., 250, 306
Weill, Kurt, 67, 247
Weinstein, Herman, 331
Weintraub, Bernard, 117, 166
Weintraub, Sy, 367
Welk, Lawrence, 77
Welles, Orson, 42, 237, 247, 447
Wellman, William, 221, 237
West of the Pecos (1934), 224
West, Cornell, 49
Whale, James, 221, 285
Whales of August, The (1987), 169, 173
When Men Betray (1927), 90
Whipper, Leigh, 65, 113, 293
White Man's Burden (1995), 244
White Sister, The (1923), 171
White, Armond, 170, 201, 355, 362, 411
White, Clarence, 85, 92, 96
White, Walter, 209, 221, 226, 227, 228, 264, 266, 288, 290, 302
Whitmore, James, 16
Widmark, Richard, 365
Wilcox, Herbert, 186
Wild Bunch, The (1969), 2
Wiles, Gordon, 287
Wilkie, Wendell, 226, 228
Williams, Barbara Morrow, 22, 43
Williams, Billy Dee, 3
Williams, Egbert 'Bert' Austin, 73, 214, 215, 216, 217, 218
Williams, Esther, 418
Williams, Tennessee, 172

Williamson, Fred, 3, 416, 428
Wilson, Arthur 'Dooley', 51, 78, 102, 235, 294, 418
Wilson, August, 69
Wilson, Frank, 206, 259
Wilson, President Woodrow, 190, 258
Wilson, Tom, 195
Wind, The (1928), 172
Winfield, Paul, 3
Winfrey, Ophrah, 449
Winters, Jonathan, 374
Winters, Shelley, 457
Within Our Gates (1919), 56, 79
Wizard of Oz, The (1939), 311
Wolfe, Ralph Haven, 201
Woll, Allen, 306, 436
Woo, John, 428
Worden, Hank, 404
World, The Flesh, and The Devil, The (1959), 243
Wrecker, The (1933), 282
Wright, Richard, 237
Wyler, Robert, 421
Wyler, William, 391, 421
Wynn, Hugh, 325
Wynn, Keenan, 389

Y

Yojimbo (1961), 368
Yordan, Philip, 421, 441
Young, Carleton, 404
Young, Joseph A., 52, 161
Young, Kevin, 42
Young, Sam, 411
Young, Stark, 250, 332
Youngblood, Denise J., 235, 305

Z

Zanuck, Darryl F., 94, 227, 228, 301, 450
Zanzibar (1940), 288
Ziegfeld Follies, 75, 217, 218
Zinneman, Fred, 229
Zrobeson, Eslanda, 284
Zukor, Adolph, 198, 323
Zurlini, Valerio, 359, 378
Zwick, Edward, 221